Travels in the Americas

Travels

in the
Americas

EDITED BY JACK NEWCOMBE

WEIDENFELD & NICOLSON
New York

To the memory of Polly

Published by Weidenfeld & Nicolson, New York
A Division of Wheatland Corporation
841 Broadway
New York, New York 10003-4793

Published in Canada by General Publishing Company, Ltd.

Library of Congress Cataloging-in-Publication Data

Travels in the Americas.

   Includes index.
   1. America—Description and travel.   2. Authors,
American—Journeys—America.   3. Authors, English—
Journeys—America.   I. Newcombe, Jack.
E27.T73 1989   917.3'04   88-37884
ISBN 1-55584-330-1

Manufactured in the United States of America

This book is printed on acid-free paper

Designed by Irving Perkins Associates

Maps by Joseph P. Ascherl

First Edition

10 9 8 7 6 5 4 3 2 1

Contents

Contents

CANADA AND THE FAR NORTH

MEXICO, THE CARIBBEAN, SOUTH AMERICA

Contents

Introduction

*L*ONG after European and Mediterranean countries had been crisscrossed by tourists taking the Grand Tour, the Americas, North and South, were still open for exploration by the adventurous and settlement by the hardy. These travelers were following and expanding on the routes of the New World discoverers of the fifteenth and sixteenth centuries who had come in search of wealth and land for their sovereigns, and riches and perhaps power for themselves. The precedent had been set by Christopher Columbus, who in 1492 and 1493 had been granted by royal Spain a monopoly of exploration in the transatlantic territories and the title of viceroy and governor of the islands and mainland he discovered.

But if possibilities of wealth and power motivated traveler-explorers during the 1700s and early 1800s, so did the excitement of probing the vast and varied lands on the two great continents. The distances themselves—the transcontinental length of the Amazon, the stretch of the American midlands and the formidable peaks of the Continental Divide, the boundless arctic barrens to the Far North—were magnetic challenges to the single searchers and the immigrants who followed. The imposing geographic features raised both dangers and deceptions. On their long way west, Lewis and Clark had no anticipation of the enormous distance between the Pacific Ocean and the Rockies they had just struggled so hard to cross. In their quest for a piece of the "new land," the early pioneers eagerly set out on the unknown expanse beyond the starting line, the Mississippi River. Survival stories about near starvation and escape from raiding Indians became an essential part of frontier lore.

The exploratory passages through North and South America were, of course, changed by rapid developments in transportation—rail links across America, steam-propelled boats on the Amazon, the Mississippi, and other great waterways. Trading settlements were scattered across the upper Canadian wilderness and along the frozen edges of the northern Pacific Ocean. But the drive to "discover" went on, that need to reach the most remote corners of the American continents. And there were so many corners.

The long travel boom in the West, begun by explorers and carried on by adventurers, scientists, settlers, job-seekers, profiteers and, finally, plain tourists, enriched the travel narrative. The early rough diary entries of explorers, recording reactions and geographic data, gave rise to travelers' tales that found their way into the literature of the land. Until the modern "autofocus" camera became the ubiquitous recorder, most of us who traveled often and far kept our own written accounts that enabled us to retrace our journeys.

When I was fifteen I had my first experience at "travel writing" keeping a daily account of a train trip from Vermont across Canada to the California coast and back. There were many stops for me and many changes of coaches, their hard-buttoned upholstery and dusty smell still part of the long-held memory crowded with impressions of cities and landscapes I had only heard or read about. I kept a journal, just as Robert Louis Stevenson had done on his trek by donkey through the Cévennes in France in the 1870s. "We are all travelers in what John Bunyan called the wilderness of the world," Stevenson wrote, and I felt like one as I watched the real wooded wilderness of western Ontario slowly recede through a Canadian Pacific coach window and, later, the awesome approach of the Rockies.

My journal of encounters and reactions to changing geographic features remained remarkably evocative—even helpful—when I repeated my pioneer trip some forty years later. In a persuasive way it led to a more intense reading of the original journals and books of traveler-explorers of the past and the writings of wayfarers who go for the sake of going. It also led to a book based on travels of my own and to this collection of favorite narratives, old and new, about journeys taken in the Americas.

Like many of my friends who grew up in the pretelevision years close to books and buoyed by the fantasies they lavishly supplied, I traveled long distances from my hometown in Vermont by turning to the Fletcher Free Library or the family bookshelves or the stack of *National Geographic* magazines kept in neat order by my parents. Early on, I thought of *Gulliver's Travels* as no more than a wondrous adventure. I followed Marco Polo in my school text and read and reread a condensed, illustrated edition of the journals of Lewis and Clark. The Walter Noble Burns biography *The Saga of Billy the Kid* was not just a reckoning of the brief life of a famous western outlaw, it was an introduction to the alien and exciting land of distant New Mexico. In his storytelling, Jack London revealed the world of train-hopping hoboes, life aboard small sailing ships and mysteries of the Far North. The protagonist of Thomas Wolfe's huge novels was forever boarding or leaving trains or hearing their whistle wail late on restless nights. Ernest Hemingway took me to the great savannahs of Africa and to a small thinly-heated inn near a fine trout stream in the Spanish Pyrenees. Mark Twain made the Mississippi a powerful symbol of getting away and he also explained the harsh realities faced by those who used the river to reach distant ports. For boat captains and their crews, the Mississippi, as much as any major passageway, represented the derivation of "travel" from *travail*.

I journeyed and learned from my reading of novels and histories long before I became devoted to travel books. I was never much concerned about the definition of travel literature as compared with regional or natural history. They have this in common: They have taken me to exciting places I did not know.

Novelist Mary Lou Settle has her own definition: "Travel books are like those full-color catalogues that come to gardeners to provide hope on winter days. I have traveled all over the world now, but I have never traveled so far and so magically as when Richard Halliburton found his way not only to the Yucatán, but to the local library when I was growing up."

Whether it's the Yucatán of Halliburton or that of John L. Stephens, who turned an archaeologist's explorations into a wonderful odyssey, a foreign place can be made to seem comfortably familiar to the reader. Stephens's two volumes, *Incidents of Travel in the Yucatán,* have the additional appeal of providing enough detail on sites and native customs to serve as valuable travel guides for visitors a century and a half after their publication. Visit Grenada with Patrick Leigh Fermor on his extended tour of the Caribbean and discover an inviting island not far different from the one that recently became the unlikely target of an American invasion. Albert Camus on the lecture circuit in Brazil and Bruce Chatwin on his overland way to Tierra del Fuego somehow make the inhospitable seem almost romantic.

If adventure-travel has been overrun by rampant tourism and the swiftness of modern transportation, there is still space for the risk-taking wanderer. In "The Bus Plunge Highway," Tom Miller looks back with humor at his experience as a rider of rickety buses on the steep and hazardous roads of Ecuador. Both Joe McGinnis and John McPhee relate to the dangers of arctic weathers faced by those who live in isolation in the Far North.

Journeying by oneself may heighten the risk and burden of moving across unfamiliar terrain but it also raises the rewards. Reflexes quicken, impressions run deep, a sense of discovery rises high. After his long journey via hobo trains of Northern California, Clyde Rice wrote: "What is there about the jerk and sway of travel, the strange and ever-changing scene, that throttles the ego but still pulls the transient into a more whole being? Is it that the rub of new vistas burnishes certain elements of man that in static living are dulled with somnolence?"

Washington Irving apparently found the jerk and sway of travel by horseback inspiring as he encountered the wildlife and far-reaching panoramas of the western plains. His diary is that of a traveler whose sharpened reactions enabled him to make the most of his experiences. Irving had an escort of soldiers for much of the way, and like any good travel writer, he drew from their concerns, complaints, and occasional triumphs. Somehow he managed to keep up his reportorial enthusiasm on a trip that had its share of primitive discomforts.

To an even greater degree the delight in discovery of John Muir infuses the pages of *My First Summer in the Sierra* and one forgets that he is, after all, making the lengthy climb into the alpine wilderness with a herd of reluctant, unpredictable sheep. Muir's reverential feeling for nature, from the busy mountain squirrel to the branches of the tall tree it occupies, dominates his rhapsodic narrative. It has given generations of readers a better appreciation of how nature and travel writing are splendidly combined.

A collection of travel writings should, I think, offer some of the surprising extremes of the journeys we take. If the reflections of John Muir and Henry David Thoreau enhance the act of walking paths of nature, the account by Charles A. Siringo of his hard cowboy ride of more than 1,000 miles is a reminder of the occasional vicissitudes of trying to reach home. I found a certain nostalgia in the recollection of R. L. Duffus as he faced his first major away-from-home, a journey across the continent to attend college. Leaving or returning home are journeys all of us have made, and often the emotions involved get in the way of the travel itself. In following selections, Duffus, Joan Didion, V.S. Naipaul, Margaret Atwood, and Clyde Rice are among the homebound travelers who find different ways of dealing with their reactions.

Traveling to and from home, the universal experience, helped give the British a large leap forward in the art of travel and natural-history writing. A wide curiosity and useful restlessness sent them in all directions within the British Isles and across the seas that surrounded them. In the encouragement of travel reporting two centuries ago the Royal Society announced, "Let travelers always have a Table-Book at hand to set down everything worth remembering, and then at night methodically transcribe the Notes they have taken in the day. . . ." The distance between diary keeping and travel literature was well demonstrated by the essays of Boswell and Thackeray, the quests for knowledge of Samuel Coleridge and Anthony Trollope, and later the detached, humorously-tuned writings of Evelyn Waugh. In 1945, his casual and lengthy traveling behind him, Waugh wrote, "Never again, I suppose, shall we land on foreign soil with letter of credit and passport (itself the first faint shadow of the cloud that envelops us) and feel the world wide open before us."

The notion of adventure, of encountering the new and unexpected, has drawn the British to the Americas, North and South, to write of their experiences since the early times of Western discovery. They became masters at turning thoughtful travel writing into stories of high adventure. The Amazon, in particular, the most awesome of tropical rivers, had a magnetic pull on British explorers and such pioneer biologists as Charles Darwin, Alfred Russel Wallace, and Henry Walter Bates. Bates spent eleven years in Amazonia in the mid-1800s, returning with more than 14,000 species—insects, reptiles, mammals, fish, birds—and wrote the monumental *Naturalist on the River Amazons,* used as a text by a parade of followers. (For purposes of this collection, I chose Englishman H. M. Tomlinson, who found his Amazonia in 1909, and American Peter Matthiessen, who sailed up the river half a century later.)

William Bartram, a determined naturalist of the late eighteenth century, carried on the scientific explorations of his father, Royal Botanist to the king of England, by traveling throughout the American Southeast, enthusiastically recording his botanical findings and relating his adventures in lands dominated by Indian tribes. Bartram was in the traditional mold of far-ranging explorer-writers, setting a pace for others to follow.

The excitement of trail breaking is beyond the reach of most modern travelers, but there has been a trend toward retracing old routes of exploration and building on the images of the itinerant life gained from novels and history books. British author Jonathan Raban, a victim of compelling wanderlust, was drawn to the Mississippi of Mark Twain as a young reader, and he chose not just to view it and visit the tourist exhibits of Hannibal, Missouri, but to learn the river. As a challenging substitute for the pilot training of Samuel Clemens, he set off in a small boat, battling the river's erratic flow from Minneapolis to New Orleans. Iowa-born Dayton Duncan decided on an equally arduous overland course for himself: to follow as best he could the historic route taken by Lewis and Clark in their government mission to find a northwest passage. Lewis and Clark managed with exceeding difficulty to canoe rivers and penetrate mountain wilderness to reach the Pacific without finding the passage they hoped was there; Duncan made it to the Pacific by driving his van through the maze of highways and towns developed by modern civilization. Along his slow way he did discover what the people of small-town western America—whose only connection to the expedition heroes of 1804–6 was the historic marker down the road—were doing with their lives.

"Oh, how I wish I had the power to describe the wonderful country as I saw it then." The deeply affecting remark of a Texas Ranger known to writer and artist Tom Lea could be echoed by generations of professional travelers, plain wayfarers, migrants, and settlers. Fortunately, we have Tom Lea's own writings and sketches of the American Southwest and Mexico he loved to take us back closer to the ranger's "wonderful country."

The best of travel writing does make us yearn for the way it was when the going was often difficult but the skies were clear. Of course, it can provide vicarious adventure—some consider it the essence of the travel story—but one does not have to ride with Willa Cather's visiting bishops in the high, frontierless country of northern New Mexico to share the author's understanding of them and their mission. We develop some of E. M. Frimbo's nostalgia as he boards the Twentieth Century Limited, New York to Chicago, for the last time and appreciate the wonder of poet Rupert Brooke while he gazes at the Canadian Rockies for the first time. John Steinbeck, traveling across the country with his dog, succeeds well in arousing another basic yearning of ours—to get up and go in a free, wayfaring way.

Expressing his own lifelong urge to be somewhere else, Steinbeck commented, "A journey is a person in itself; no two are alike." And so a collection of stories about journeys to many places in many periods of time, from the early thrusts of exploration to the swift trips along sign-posted highways, should offer companionship as varied and provocative as the well-traveled authors themselves.

Jack Newcombe

The
United
States

Peter Rugg: An American Folktale

WILLIAM AUSTIN

The traveler who is unable to find his way home again surely has been a haunting as old as human travel itself. In New England folklore one Peter Rugg and his child forever rode the rural roads and turnpikes without ever reaching Boston.

*I*N the summer of 1820 I took the stagecoach from Providence to Boston, where I had business and, all other seats being taken, accepted the place next to the driver, a pleasant and civil fellow. We had proceeded some 10 miles when suddenly the horses laid their ears back on their necks, like hares, and the driver asked if I had an overcoat with me. "No," said I, "why do you ask?" "The horses see the storm breeder," he replied. "And we shall see him soon."

I looked at him curiously. There was not a cloud in the sky, much less any suggestion of a storm, and all I could see was a tiny speck far down the road.

"There comes the storm breeder," said the driver. "I suppose the poor fellow suffers much, indeed much more than is known to the world."

The speck became a carriage drawn by a black horse and carrying a little girl and a man who was driving very fast and who looked oddly at us as we passed. He seemed dejected, but he did not hail us. When he had gone by, the horses' ears rose up again and I inquired who the man was.

"Nobody knows," said the driver, "but I've met him and the child more than a hundred times. I've been asked the way to Boston so often by that man, even when he was traveling directly away from it as he was now, that I have finally refused any communication with him."

"Does he never stop anywhere?"

"No longer than to inquire the way to Boston. He always says he has to reach Boston by nightfall."

We had ascended a high hill near Walpole and I commented a little mischievously to the driver on how clear the heavens were. But when we topped yet another hill he pointed to the east and I saw a little black seed cloud no bigger than a hat. "You have to look in the direction whence the man came," he said. "The storm never meets him, it follows him. I hope we reach Polley's tavern before the weather reaches us."

Unbidden, the horses began to increase their pace, and the little cloud boiled up into a big black one. Presently, just as we reached Polley's, the rain poured down in torrents.

Soon after our arrival a gentleman who had been traveling behind us arrived and he was in turn followed by a pedlar. Some of my fellow passengers asked the newcomers if they had seen the man with the little girl. Both of them had. "He asked me the way to Boston," said the gentleman, "and the moment he went on a thunderclap broke over his head and his horse sprang forward. They seemed to travel as fast as the thundercloud."

"I've met that man in four different states in the past fortnight," the pedlar added. "Each time I met him a thundershower deluged me so badly I am thinking of taking out marine insurance. And do you know, my horse behaved in a very frightened way each time we met this man. I don't think he belongs to this world."

This was all I could learn at the time. When the weather improved we went on and I gradually forgot about it. That was three years ago. And then, not long ago, I was standing outside Bennett's hotel in Hartford and heard a man say, "There goes Peter Rugg and his child—farther from Boston than ever." And there driving past me, wet and weary with the same child and black horse, was the man I had seen three years before.

"And who is Peter Rugg?" I asked.

"That is more than anyone can tell exactly," said the other man. "He is a famous traveler held in light esteem by all innkeepers, for he never stops to eat, drink or sleep. I wonder why the government does not employ him to carry the mail."

"Ay, and how long would it take him to get a letter to Boston?" said a sarcastic bystander.

"But does he never stop anywhere?" I asked. "Pray, sir, give me some account of this man."

"Sir, those who know the most respecting this man say the least. I am rather inclined to pity than to judge. The last time Rugg inquired of me how far it was to Boston I told him 100 miles."

" 'Why,' said he, 'how can you deceive me so? It is cruel to mislead a traveler. Pray direct me the nearest way to Boston.'

"I repeated it was 100 miles.

" 'How can you say so?' he cried out. 'I was told last evening it was but 50 and I have been traveling all night.'

" 'But you are traveling *from* Boston. You must turn back.'

" 'Alas!' said he. 'It is all turn back! Boston shifts with the wind and the guideposts, too; they all point the wrong way. And it has been foul weather since I left home.'

" 'Stop, then, and refresh yourself.'

" 'No,' said he, 'I must reach home tonight if possible, though I think you must be mistaken in the distance to Boston.' A few days later I met him again a little this side of Claremont, again driving like fury.''

That was all he could tell me. But at this point horse, carriage, man and child returned down the street. They would have passed but I was resolved to speak myself to Peter Rugg, or whoever he might be. I stepped into the street and the man reined his horse. "Sir," said I. "May I be so bold as to inquire if you are not Mr. Rugg?''

"My name is Peter Rugg. I have unfortunately lost my way. I am wet and weary.''

"You live in Boston, do you? And in what street?''

"In Middle Street.''

"How did you and your child become so wet? It has not rained here today.''

"It has just rained a heavy shower up the river. Would you advise me to take the old road to Boston or the turnpike?''

"Why, the old road is 117 miles, and the turnpike is 97.''

"You impose on me. You know it is but 40 miles from Newburyport to Boston.''

"But this is not Newburyport. It is Hartford.''

"Do not deceive me, sir. Is not this town Newburyport, and the river the Merrimac?''

"No, sir; this is Hartford, and the river the Connecticut.''

He wrung his hands. "Have the rivers, too, changed their courses as the cities have changed places? Ah, that fatal oath!'' His impatient horse leaped off.

But I had discovered a clue to the history of Peter Rugg. When business next called me to Boston I collected the following particulars from a Mrs. Croft, an aged lady who has resided in Middle Street for the last 20 years. She said that the previous summer a stranger had stopped at the door of the late Mrs. Rugg. He was in an old carriage with a black horse and a small child and he asked for Mrs. Rugg. Betsey Croft told him Mrs. Rugg had not lived there for the last 19 years.

Said he, "Though the paint is rather faded, this looks like my house." And the little girl added, "Yes, that is the stone before the door that I used to sit on to eat my bread and milk."

"But," said the stranger, "it seems to be on the wrong side of the street. Indeed, everything seems misplaced. Has John Foy come home from sea?"

"Sir," said Mrs. Croft, "I never heard of John Foy. Where did he live?"

"In Orange Tree Lane just above here. Are the streets gone?"

"There is no such lane now."

The stranger seemed disconcerted. "Strange mistake! How much this looks like the town of Boston."

"Why, this *is* Boston. I know of no other Boston."

His horse began to chafe and strike the pavement with his forefeet. The stranger, bewildered, said vaguely, "No home tonight," and gave the reins to his horse.

Upon my request, Mrs. Croft directed me to an elderly neighbor named James Felt for further information, and upon finding him, I asked for more details. "It is true," said Mr. Felt, "sundry stories grew out of Rugg's affair—but stranger things have happened in my day, without even a newspaper notice."

"Sir," said I, "Peter Rugg is now living; I have lately seen him."

"My friend," said James Felt, "that Peter Rugg is now a living man, I will not deny. But that you have seen Peter Rugg and his child is impossible because Jenny Rugg, if living, is now about—let's see, the Boston Massacre was in 1770—is now more than 60 years of age. Peter himself would be about 90."

I concluded Mr. Felt was in his dotage. For if Peter Rugg had been traveling since the Boston Massacre, there is no reason why he should not travel to the end of time. That evening I related my Middle Street adventure, and one of the company said his grandfather had known the Peter Rugg story and believed it.

"Sir," said I, "let us compare your grandfather's story with my own."

He replied, "Peter Rugg, sir, if my grandfather was worthy of credit, once lived in Middle Street, a man in comfortable circumstances, and generally esteemed. But, unhappily, his temper at times was altogether ungovernable; and then his language was terrible. If a door stood in his way, he would kick its panels through. He would sometimes throw his heels over his head and come down on his feet, uttering oaths in a circle. Peter, at these moments of violent passion, would become so profane that his wig would arise from his head. He had no respect for heaven or earth. Except this infirmity, all agreed Rugg was a good sort of man.

"One morning in late autumn Rugg was returning in his chaise with his daughter from Concord, when a storm overtook them and at dark he stopped at Menotomy, now West Cambridge, at the home of a friend. The friend, a Mr. Cutter, urged him to tarry the night—'the tempest is increasing,' he said.

" 'Let the storm increase,' said Rugg with a fearful oath. 'I will see home tonight in spite of the last tempest, or may I never see home!'

"At these words he gave his whip to his high-spirited horse, and disappeared in a moment. But Peter Rugg did not reach home that night, or the next. He was never traced beyond Mr. Cutter's in Menotomy. But for a long time after on every dark and stormy night his wife and their neighbors heard the crack of his whip and the rattling of his carriage past their doors. The clatter shook the houses on both sides of the streets.

"There were rumors that he was seen in various places, but the more his friends inquired, the more they were baffled. If they heard of Rugg one day in Connecticut, the next day they heard of him winding around the hills in New Hampshire. In time, Peter Rugg came to be forgotten. But one chain of incidents kept the story alive. They occurred at Charlestown Bridge.

"There is a toll-gatherer there and he asserted that, about the time Rugg was first missing, on dark and stormy nights a horse and carriage would roar over the bridge, at midnight, loud as a troop in utter contempt of the toll that should have been paid. This occurred so frequently that the toll-gatherer resolved to attempt a discovery.

"Soon after, at an appropriate time, he saw the same horse and carriage approaching the bridge from Charlestown Square and took his stand near the middle of the bridge, with a large three-legged stool in his hand. As the horse and carriage rolled past, he hurled the stool at the horse. But nothing happened, except that the stool skittered across the bridge. The tollman said the stool went *through* the horse. Thereafter, he seemed anxious to waive the subject of Peter Rugg. And Rugg, his child, his horse and carriage remain a mystery to this day."

This is all that I could learn of Peter Rugg in Boston.

Memories of a Day's Walk

ANTHONY BAILEY

A veteran of hiking in his native England and of jaunts elsewhere in the world, Anthony Bailey set a short course for himself while visiting a Massachusetts town: to walk the Atlantic coastline of New Hampshire, all eighteen miles of it. Occasionally the irregular beach stroll put him in touch with his past.

WALKING, and especially walking on beaches, provides good exercise for one's memory. I passed a green notice board with the chalked information that high tide that day was 11:12 A.M., low tide 5:05 P.M. The water temperature was yet to be announced. Another notice told the public to "Contact Life Guard About Lost Children." I remember being lost on the beach at Sandown, Isle of Wight, when I was four or five—or rather (the truth doesn't turn up until one begins thinking about the occasion more intently), remember being found, being hugged and kissed, "Nothing to worry about, it's all right," and recall how vast that tiny beach had seemed with nearly the whole population of the known world on it and no sign of my parents or my bucket and spade. And possibly because the water of the English Channel in those prewar British summers didn't strike me as hospitably warm, forcing me to take adventurous excursions on foot, I didn't learn to swim until I reached America the first time—was "evacuated" for the duration of the war in Europe, and found myself, with great good fortune, living with an Ohio family who spent the summer of 1941 on Cape Cod. In Chatham, aged eight, on the splendid beach which encloses Pleasant Bay, I discovered that the withdrawing tide left pools of various depths, which were soon heated by the sun. So I proceeded from shallow pool to deep, from feet on the bottom to strenuous dog paddle, and on Labor Day was awarded the cup for the dog-paddle stakes in the end-of-season swim meet of the local beach club. The cup still sits in a glass-fronted corner cupboard in my parents' house, my sole contribution of prize silverware among the many pieces won at county athletic meets by my father, a middle-distance runner.

I was forced to stay on Route 1A for the next mile or so, behind Great Boars

Head and along North Beach. The beach, already narrow by natural circumstance, was made even more so by the rising tide. Rather than hop from rock to rock, I walked on the sidewalk, which was sheltered from the waves of storms by a four-foot-high green-painted steel seawall, a bit rusty in places. From this point, I could see the remainder of the New Hampshire coast stretching ahead—could see, in fact, across the mouth of the Piscataqua River, where the state ends, to Gerrish Island, Maine. From this angle, four of the Isles of Shoals were visible. At this point, too, it became palpable that my sailing sneakers weren't ideal road shoes, and at 10 A.M. I was happy to clamber down to the actual beach again. Here, at the north end of North Beach, groins had been built of large granite blocks to preserve the sand, and seemed to be doing their job. But the beach thus formed was zigzag, the seaward edge of the sand between each groin slanting outward toward the northeast. From dry sand on one side of a groin, one climbed over the granite barrier and was met with water on the other side. This forced one to scramble inland a little along the groin before arriving over dry beach again that one could jump down to. Inland, behind a single row of houses spaced out on the inshore side of 1A, marshy meadows ran for a mile or so westward; then there was a range of low green hills. Along the road itself, a procession of cars streamed north, faster here, perhaps, because under the seawall drivers had no view of the sea. Unlike cars that notoriously flood into cities on weekday mornings with a single occupant, these cars were generally full to bursting with children, dogs, sleeping bags, suitcases, and sometimes bikes on the back, carried like lifeboats in davits.

Here I began to wonder about 1A's potential for southbound hitchhikers. An unworthy thought at this time of the morning, no doubt. Would Scott have reached the South Pole if he'd worried about getting back? Ah, but Scott didn't get back. My hitchhiking life flashed before me. At one time or another, I had given plenty of rides to high-school students clearly stranded by later-than-usual school hours and no bus service, and to backpacking youngsters on the way from London to the cross-Channel ferries. But I'd also passed a lot of hitchhikers by in the years since I had last put myself out on that particular roadside limb, and I doubted if my standing was good in the record of whatever god or goddess (Mercury? Iris?) looked after hitchhikers' interests. Drivers, of course, think of the risks to them, but as I remember it, the peril for the rider should also be considered. One wet Good Friday, hitching from Dieppe to Paris, I was given a lift by a French angler, and drinker, who as the car went round the bends of a slippery *route nationale* at numerous kilometers an hour kept taking his hands off the steering wheel to demonstrate to me, in the back among his rods and baskets, the length of a fish he had caught or was going to catch (the tenses were hard to make out), often turning round to grin amiably at me as he gestured. Coming east from Wisconsin, armed with cardboard and crayon for making destination signs, I had an apprehensive ride across part of Indiana with a man whose business card, produced with a snap of the fingers from a point in midair up near the rearview mirror, proclaimed him a vice-president of the International Society of Magicians. (I expected rabbits to pop from the cigar lighter. I neglected to ask how the lady was sawn in half.) And from Chillicothe, Ohio, to Charleston, West Virginia, on the great-circle route I took to New York City, I rode with a truck driver whose reminiscences consisted largely of the number of times he had overturned his tractor-trailer rig, skidding great distances and skittling Burma-Shave signs.

At the north end of North Beach, a small, unnamed promontory gave a measure of shelter from the north and west to a dozen boats moored there, bobbing. Two lads were joyfully rowing a pair of brightly painted dories in the gentle surf. I made my way over the rocks that buttressed the headland, with its complement of unpretentious, well-built shingled summer houses. The rocks, interspersed with patches of mud and eel grass, ran out to an offshore ledge, and as I negotiated them, three small girls in swimsuits came by. One, also wearing purple bedroom slippers, said to her friends, "You guys going out on the rocks?" It was the sort of place where things are assembled by wind and tide. I saw a dead seagull; a single flip-flop; fragments of foam mattress; a crushed take-away coffee container; a plastic spoon; a frayed strand of polypropylene lobster-pot line. But very little driftwood. There were midges in the air, and a swooping band of swallows, presumably gobbling up midges. Friends had warned me of the possibility of "greenheads"—fearsome flies that torment beachgoers, at least in Massachusetts, forcing communities to set up expensive trap boxes to try to catch them. But so far no greenheads.

One difficulty with beach walking is that after a while you feel one leg is getting longer than the other. As I stepped out onto the sand again, I tried walking backward for a way to put things into balance. It may not have helped my muscles, but it certainly gave me more "visibility." Several people, turning their heads to look at me, said "Good morning," and an elderly man in sun hat, swimsuit, and sneakers called out, "How's it going there, young fella?" On the extensive porch of one beachfront house, a crowd of informally dressed people had gathered. I was wondering if it was a property owners' meeting, when I heard a boy call out to a woman coming down the steps from the porch, "Was he old?" Perhaps it was—albeit in bright Bermuda shorts and terry-towel wraps—a wake.

For a change, the parking lot at this North Hampton beach (just south of Little Boars Head) was free. However, one had to pay if one wanted to use the little shingled bathhouses—fifty cents for a quick change, $3.00 daily rate, according to a sign. I crossed 1A behind the beach at this point in order to reach the Sand Dollar Sandwich Shoppe for what back home we call elevenses. I'd had a boiled egg and an English muffin for breakfast much earlier that morning, and now felt the need of some small thing to get me through to lunchtime. I found a place at the crowded counter, next to a woman eating a blueberry muffin, which looked scrumptious. When approached by one of the pair of somewhat sullen-looking girls—who wore the nurse-like uniform of white dress and white shoes that is apparently *de rigueur* for summer help along this coast—I said I would like a cup of coffee and a blueberry muffin, please. "We're fresh out of blueberry muffins," she said. "How about an English?"

I'm usually a pushover for English muffins. I sometimes take a large box of Thomas's back to England, since the English muffin as known in America is just about unobtainable there (Sainsbury's, a supermarket chain, sells a muffin that isn't a patch on Thomas's) and I've gone off a former love, the crumpet. But one muffin a day keeps desire at bay. I made do with a coffee while I tried to read that morning's Manchester (N.H.) *Union Leader* (a single-seat space at coffee shops doesn't give much scope for page turning; I read what I could of the *Union Leader's* front page, folded up, on my lap). The paper goes in for blue headlines, a bouncy line in white stars on a blue band printed down the right-hand margin, and under the paper's name an epigraph from Daniel Webster: "There is nothing so powerful as truth." However, this particular edition seemed to support the belief that there is nothing as effective as tickling the reader's sense of *déjà vu*. I was carried back to the summer of 1953 and McCarthy country by the banner headline, SOVIETS GET U.S. WARNING, subheaded "Told to Keep 'Hands Off' of Portugal." Surely a redundant "of"? The front-page editorial began flatly and ungrammatically "The key to straightening out the mess that this country is to be found is in informing the people of the United States as to what is actually going on." The woman on my left, who had just finished the ultimate blueberry muffin, was saying to her female companion, "But if they're not living together anymore, why does she still get up at seven?"

Travels
with Billy Bartram

WILLIAM BARTRAM

When first published in 1791, the journals of botanist and naturalist William Bartram carried the comprehensive title Travels Through North and South Carolina, Georgia, East and West Florida, the Cherokee Country, the Extensive Territories of the Muscogulges, or Creek Confederacy, and the Country of the Chactaws. *He had earlier accompanied his father, John Bartram, Royal Botanist to King George III, on a plant-collecting tour through the American wilderness. His own enthusiastic findings and his belief in spiritual forces at work in the abundant land of America's Southeast inspired poets Samuel Coleridge and William Wordsworth and have appealed to readers centuries later.*

*A*PRIL 22, 1776, I sat off from Charleston for the Cherokee nation, and after riding this day about twenty-five miles, arrived in the evening at Jacksonsburg, a village on Ponpon river. The next day's journey was about the same distance, to a public house or inn on the road.

The next day, early in the morning, I sat off again, and about noon stopped at a public house to dine. After the meridian heats were abated, proceeding on till evening, I obtained good quarters at a private house, having rode this day about thirty miles. At this plantation I observed a large orchard of the European Mulberry tree (Morus alba) some of which were grafted on stocks of the native Mulberry (Morus rubra); these trees were cultivated for the purpose of feeding silk worms (phalaena bombyx). Having breakfasted, I sat forward again.

I soon entered a high forest, continuing the space of fifteen miles to the Three Sisters, a public ferry on Savanna river: the country generally very level; the soil a dark, loose, fertile mould, on a stratum of cinereous-coloured tenacious clay; the ground shaded with its native forests, consisting of the great Black Oak, Quercus tinctoria, Q. rubra, Q. phellos, Q. prinos, Q. hemispherica, Juglans nigra, J. rustica, J. exaltata, Magnolia grandiflora, Fraxinus excelsior, Acer rubrum, Liriodendron tulipifera, Populus heterophylla, Morus rubra, Nyssa sylvatica, Platanus occidentalis, Tilia, Ulmus campestris, U. subifer, Laurus sassafras, L. Borbonia, Ilex aquifolium, Fagus sylvatica, Cornus Florida, Halesia, Æsculus pavia, Sambucus, Callicarpa, and Stewartia malachodendron, with a variety of other trees and shrubs. This ancient sublime forest, frequently intersected with extensive avenues, vistas and green lawns, opening to extensive savannas and far distant Rice plantations, agreeably employs the imagination, and captivates the senses by scenes of magnificence and grandeur.

The gay mock-bird, vocal and joyous, mounts aloft on silvered wings, rolls over and over, then gently descends, and presides in the choir of the tuneful tribes.

Having dined at the ferry, I crossed the river into Georgia: on landing and ascending the bank, which was here a North prospect, I observed the Dirca palustris, growing six or seven feet high. I rode about twelve miles further through Pine Forests and savannas. In the evening I took up my quarters at a delightful habitation, though not a common tavern. Having ordered my horse a stable and provender, and refreshed my spirits with a draught of cooling liquor, I betook myself to contemplation in the groves and lawns. Directing my steps towards the river, I observed in a high Pine forest on the border of a savanna, a great number of cattle herded together, and on my nearer approach discovered it to be a cow pen: on my coming up I was kindly saluted by my host and his wife, who I found were superintending a number of slaves, women, boys and girls, that were milking the cows. Here were about forty milch cows and as many young calves; for in these Southern countries the calves run with the cows a whole year, the people milking them at the same time. The pen, including two or three acres of ground, more or less, according to the stock, adjoining a rivulet or run of water, is enclosed by a fence: in this enclosure the calves are kept while the cows are out at range: a small part of this pen is partitioned off to receive the cows, when they come up at evening: here are several stakes drove into the ground, and there is a gate in the partition fence for a communication between the two pens. When the milkmaid has taken her share of milk, she looses the calf, who strips the cow, which is next morning turned out again to range.

I found these people, contrary to what a traveller might think, perhaps, reasonably expect, from their occupation and remote situation from the capital or any commercial town, to be civil and courteous: and though educated as it were in the woods, no strangers to sensibility, and those moral virtues which grace and ornament the most approved and admired characters in civil society.

After the vessels were filled with milk, the daily and liberal supply of the friendly kine, and the good wife, with her maids and servants, were returning with it to the dairy; the gentleman was at leisure to attend to my enquiries and

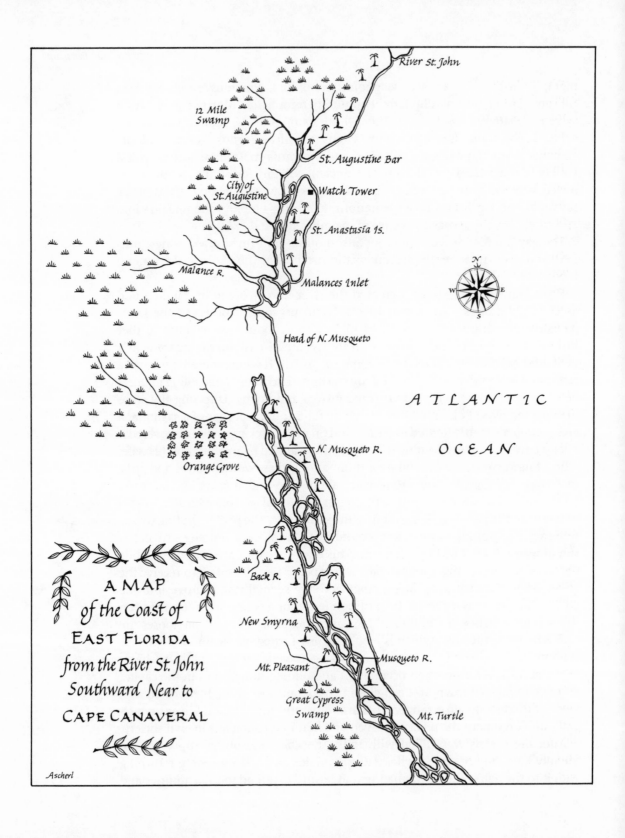

River St. John

12 Mile Swamp

St. Augustine Bar

City of St. Augustine

Watch Tower

St. Anastasia Is.

Malance R.

Malances Inlet

Head of N. Musqueto

ATLANTIC OCEAN

Orange Grove

N. Musqueto R.

Back R.

New Smyrna

Mt. Pleasant

Musqueto R.

Great Cypress Swamp

Mt. Turtle

A MAP of the Coast of EAST FLORIDA from the River St. John Southward Near to CAPE CANAVERAL

Ascherl

observations, which he did with complaisance, and apparent pleasure. On my observing to him that his stock of horned cattle must be very considerable to afford so many milch cows at one time, he answered, that he had about fifteen hundred head: "my stock is but young, having lately removed from some distance to this place; I found it convenient to part with most of my old stock and begin here anew; Heaven is pleased to bless my endeavours and industry with success even beyond my own expectations." Yet continuing my interrogatories on this subject: your stock I apprehend must be very profitable, being so convenient to the capital and sea port, in affording a vast quantity of beef, butter and cheese, for the market, and must thereby contribute greatly towards your emolument: "yes, I find my stock of cattle very profitable, and I constantly contribute towards supplying the markets with beef; but as to the articles of butter and cheese, I make no more than what is expended in my own household, and I have a considerable family of black people, who, though they are slaves, must be fed, and cared for: those I have, were either chosen for their good qualities, or born in the family, and I find from long experience and observation, that the better they are fed, clothed and treated, the more service and profit we may expect to derive from their labour: in short, I find my flock produces no more milk, or any article of food or nourishment, than what is expended to the best advantage amongst my family and slaves."

He added, come along with me towards the river bank, where I have some men at work squaring Pine and Cypress timber for the West India market; I will show you their day's work, when you will readily grant that I have reason to acknowledge myself sufficiently gratified for the little attention bestowed towards them. At yonder little new habitation near the bluff on the banks of the river, I have settled my eldest son; it is but a few days since he was married to a deserving young woman.

Having at length arrived near the high banks of the majestic Savanna, we stood at the timber landing: almost every object in our progress contributed to demonstrate this good man's system of economy to be not only practicable but eligible; and the slaves appeared on all sides as a crowd of witnesses to justify his industry, humanity, and liberal spirit.

The slaves comparatively of a gigantic stature, fat and muscular, were mounted on the massive timber logs; the regular heavy strokes of their gleaming axes re-echoed in the deep forests; at the same time, contented and joyful, the sooty sons of Africa forgetting their bondage, in chorus sung the virtues and beneficence of their master in songs of their own composition.

The log or timber landing is a capacious open area, the lofty pines having been felled and cleared away for a considerable distance round about, near an almost perpendicular bluff or steep bank of the river, rising up immediately from the water to the height of sixty or seventy feet. The logs being dragged by timber wheels to this yard, and landed as near the brink of this high bank as possible with safety, and laid by the side of each other, are rolled off, and precipitated down the bank into the river, where being formed into rafts, they are conducted by slaves down to Savanna, about fifty miles below this place.

Having contemplated these scenes of art and industry, my venerable host, in company with his son, conducted me to the neat habitation, which is situated in a spacious airy forest, a little distance from the river bank, commanding a comprehensive and varied prospect; an extensive reach of the river in front; on the right hand a spacious lawn or savanna; on the left the timber yard; the vast fertile low lands and forests on the river upwards; and the plantations adjoining. A cool evening arrived after a sultry day. As we approach the door, conducted by the young man, his lovely bride arrayed in native innocence and becoming modesty, with an air and smile of grace and benignity, meets and salutes us! what a Venus! what an Adonis! said I in silent transport; every action and feature seem to reveal the celestial endowments of the mind: though a native sprightliness and sensibility appear, yet virtue and discretion direct and rule. The dress of this beauteous sylvan queen was plain but clean, neat and elegant, all of cotton, and of her own spinning and weaving.

Next morning early I sat forward prosecuting my tour. I pursued the high road leading from Savanna to Augusta for the distance of one hundred miles or more, and then re-crossed the river at Silver Bluff, a pleasant villa, the property and seat of G. Golphin, esquire, a gentleman of very distinguished talents and great liberality, who possessed the most extensive trade, connections and influence, amongst the South and South-West Indian tribes, particularly with the Creeks and Chactaws; of whom I fortunately obtained letters of recommendation and credit to the principal traders residing in the Indian towns.

Silver Bluff is a very celebrated place. It is a considerable height upon the Carolina shore of the Savanna river, perhaps thirty feet higher than the low lands on the opposite shore, which are subject to be overflowed in the spring and fall. This steep bank rises perpendicularly out of the river, discovering various strata of earth; the surface for a considerable depth is a loose sandy loam, with a mixture of sea shells, especially ostreæ; the next stratum is clay, then sand, next marl, then clays again of various colours and qualities, which last insensibly mix or unite with a deep stratum of blackish or dark slate coloured saline and sulphureous earth, which seems to be of an aluminous or vitriolic quality, and lies in nearly horizontal lamina or strata of various thickness. We discovered bellemnites, pyrites, marcasites and sulphureous nodules, shining like brass, some single of various forms, and others conglomerated, lying in this black slaty-like micaceous earth; as also, sticks, limbs and trunks of trees, leaves, acorns, and their cups, all transmuted or changed black, hard and shining as charcoal: we also see animal substances, as if petrified, or what are called sharks' teeth, (dentes carchariæ); but these heterogeneous substances or petrifactions are the most abundant and conspicuous where there is a looser kind of earth, either immediately upon this vast stratum of black earth, or in the divisions of the laminæ. The surface of the ground upon this bluff, extends a mile and a half or two miles on the river, and is from an half mile to a mile in breadth, nearly level, and a good fertile soil; as is evident from the vast Oaks, Hickory, Mulberry, Black walnut and other trees and shrubs, which are left standing in the old fields which are spread abroad to a great distance; and discovers various monuments and vestiges of the residence of the ancients; as Indian conical mounts, terraces, areas, &c. as well as remains or traces of fortresses of regular formation, as if constructed after the modes of European military architects, which are supposed to be ancient camps of the Spaniards who formerly fixed themselves at this place in hopes of finding silver.

But perhaps Mr. Golphin's buildings and improvements will prove to be the foundation of monuments of infinitely greater celebrity and permanency than either of the preceding establishments.

The place which at this day is called fort Moore, is a stupendous bluff, or high perpendicular bank of earth, rising out of the river on the Carolina shore, perhaps ninety or one hundred feet above the common surface of the water; and exhibits a singular and pleasing spectacle to a stranger, especially from the opposite shore, or as we pass up or down the river, presenting a view of prodigious walls of party-coloured earths, chiefly clays and marl of various colours, as brown, red, yellow, blue, purple, white, &c. in horizontal strata, one over the other.

Waiting for the ferry boat to carry me over, I walked almost round the under side of the bluff, betwixt its steep wall and the water of the river, which glided rapidly under my feet. I came to the carcase of a calf, which the people told me had fallen down from the edge of the precipice above, being invited too far by grass and sweet herbs, which they say frequently happens at this place. In early times, the Carolinians had a fort, and kept a good garrison here as a frontier and Indian trading post; but Augusta superseding it, this place was dismantled: and since that time, which probably cannot exceed thirty years, the river hath so much encroached upon the Carolina shore, that its bed now lies where the site of the fort then was: indeed some told me that the opposite Georgia shore, where there is now a fine house and corn field, occupies the place.

The site of Augusta is perhaps the most delightful and eligible of any in Georgia for a city. An extensive level plain on the banks of a fine navigable river, which has its numerous sources in the Cherokee mountains, a fruitful and temperate region, whence, after roving and winding about those fertile heights, they meander through a fertile hilly country, and one after another combine in forming the Tugilo and Broad rivers, and then the famous Savanna river; thence they continue near an hundred miles more, following its meanders and falls over the cataracts at Augusta, which cross the river at the upper end of the town. These falls are four or five feet perpendicular height in the summer season when the river is low. From these cataracts upwards, this river with all its tributaries, as Broad river, Little river, Tugilo, &c. is one continued rapid, with some short intervals of still water, navigable for canoes. But from Augusta downwards to the ocean, a distance of near three hundred miles by water, the Savanna uninterruptedly flows with a gentle meandring course, and is navigable for vessels of twenty or thirty tons burthen to Savanna, where ships of three hundred tons lie in a capacious and secure harbour.

Augusta thus seated at the head of navigation, and just below the conflux of several of its most considerable branches, without a competitor, commands the trade and commerce of vast fruitful regions above it, and from every side to a great distance; and I do not hesitate to pronounce as my opinion, will very soon become the metropolis of Georgia.

I chose to take this route up Savanna river, in preference to the straight and shorter road from Charleston to the Cherokee country by fort Ninety Six, because by keeping near this great river, I had frequent opportunities of visiting its steep banks, vast swamps and low grounds; and had the advantage, without great delay, or deviating from the main high road, of observing the various soils and situations of the countries through which this famous river pursues its course, and of examining their various productions, mineral, vegetable and animal: whereas had I pursued the great trading path by Ninety-Six, I should have been led over a high, dry, sandy and gravelly ridge, and a great part of the distance an old settled or resorted part of the country, and consequently void of the varieties of original or novel productions of nature.

Before I leave Augusta, I shall recite a curious phenomenon, which may furnish ample matter for philosophical discussion to the curious naturalists. On the Georgia side of the river, about fifteen miles below Silver Bluff, the high road crosses a ridge of high swelling hills of uncommon elevation, and perhaps seventy feet higher than the surface of the river. These hills, from three feet below the common vegetative surface, to the depth of twenty or thirty feet, are composed entirely of fossil oyster shells, internally of the colour and consistency of clear white marble: the shells are of incredible magnitude, generally fifteen or twenty inches in length, from six to eight wide, and two to four in thickness, and their hollows sufficient to receive an ordinary man's foot: they appear all to have been opened before the period of petrifaction, a transmutation they seem evidently to have suffered; they are undoubtedly very ancient or perhaps antediluvian. The adjacent inhabitants burn them to lime for building, for which purpose they serve very well; and would undoubtedly afford an excellent manure when their lands require it, these hills being now remarkably fertile. The heaps of shells lie upon a stratum of a yellowish sandy mould, of several feet in depth, upon a foundation of soft white rocks, that has the outward appearance of freestone, but on strict examination is really a testaceous concrete or composition of sand and pulverised sea shells: in short, this testaceous rock approaches near in quality and appearance to the Bahama or Bermudian white rock.

These hills are shaded with glorious Magnolia grandiflora, Morus rubra, Tilia, Quercus, Ulmus, Juglans, &c. with aromatic groves of fragrant Callicanthus Floridus, Rhododendron ferrugineum, Laurus Indica, &c. Æsculus pavia, Cornus Florida, Azalea coccinea, Philadelphus inodorus and others; but who would have expected to see the Dirca palustris and Dodecatheon meadea grow in abundance in this hot climate! it is true they are seen in the rich and deep shaded vales, between the hills and North exposure; but they attain to a degree of magnitude and splendour never seen in Pennsylvania.

FROM

The History of Plymouth Plantation

WILLIAM BRADFORD

The man who served as governor of Plymouth from 1621 to 1657 recorded the story of the voyage aboard the Mayflower *and the early struggle to establish the colony in Massachusetts.*

Of their vioage, and how they passed the sea, and of their safe arrival at Cape Codd

SEPT[r]: 6. [1620] These troubls being blowne over, and now all being compacte togeather in one shipe, they put to sea againe with a prosperus winde, which continued diverce days togeather, which was some incouragmente unto them; yet according to the usuall maner many were afflicted with sea-sicknes. And I may not omite hear a spetiall worke of Gods providence. Ther was a proud and very profane yonge man, one of the sea-men, of a lustie, able body, which made him the more hauty; he would allway be contemning the poore people in their sicknes, and cursing them dayly with greevous execrations, and did not let to tell them, that he hoped to help to cast halfe of them over board before they came to their jurneys end, and to make mery with what they had; and if he were by any gently reproved, he would curse and swear most bitterly. But it plased God before they came halfe seas over, to smite this yong man with a greeveous disease, of which he dyed in a desperate maner, and so was him selfe the first that was throwne overbord. Thus his curses light on his owne head; and it was an astonishmente to all his fellows, for they noted it to be the just hand of God upon him.

After they had injoyed faire winds and weather for a season, they were incountred many times with crosse winds, and mette with many feirce stormes, with which the shipe was shroudly shaken, and her upper works made very leakie; and one of the maine beames in the midd ships was bowed and cracked, which put them in some fear that the shipe could not be able to performe the vioage. So some of the cheefe of the company, perceiveing the mariners to feare the suffisiencie of the ship, as appeared by their mutterings, they entred into serious consulltation with the m^r and other officers of the ship, to consider in time of the danger; and rather to returne then to cast them selves into a desperate and inevitable perill. And truly ther was great distraction and differ-ance of opinion amongst the mariners them selves; faine would they doe what could be done for their wages sake, (being now halfe the seas over,) and on the other hand they were loath to hazard their lives too desperately. But in examen-ing of all opinions, the m^r and others affirmed they knew the ship to be stronge and firme under water; and for the buckling of the maine beame, ther was a great iron scrue the passengers brought out of Holland, which would raise the beame into his place; the which being done, the carpenter and m^r affirmed that with a post put under it, set firme in the lower deck, and otherways bounde, he would make it sufficiente. And as for the decks and uper workes they would calke them as well as they could, and though with the workeing of the ship they would not longe keepe stanch, yet ther would otherwise be no great danger, if they did not overpress her with sails. So they commited them selves to the will of God, and resolved to proseede. In sundrie of these stormes the windes were so feirce, and the seas so high, as they could not beare a knote of saile, but were forced to hull, for diverce days togither. And in one of them, as they thus lay at hull, in a mighty storme, a lustie yonge man (called John Howland) coming upon some occasion above the grattings, was, with a seele of the shipe throwne into [the] sea; but it pleased God that he caught hould of the top-saile halliards, which hunge over board, and rane out at length; yet he held his hould (though he was sundrie fadomes under water) till he was hald up by the same rope to the brime of the water, and then with a boat hooke and other means got into the shipe againe, and his life saved; and though he was something ill with it, yet he lived many years after, and became a profitable member both in church and commone wealthe. In all this vioage ther died but one of the passengers, which was William Butten, a youth, servant to Samuell Fuller, when they drew near the coast. But to omite other things, (that I may be breefe,) after longe beating at sea they fell with that land which is called Cape Codd; the which being made and certainly knowne to be it, they were not a litle joyfull. After some delibera-tion had amongst them selves and with the m^r of the ship, they tacked aboute and resolved to stande for the southward (the wind and weather being faire) to finde some place aboute Hudsons river for their habitation. But after they had sailed that course aboute halfe the day, they fell amongst deangerous shoulds and roring breakers, and they were so farr intangled ther with as they conceived them selves in great danger; and the wind shrinking upon them withall, they resolved to bear up againe for the Cape, and thought them selves hapy to gett out of those dangers before night overtooke them, as by Gods providence they did. And the next day they gott into the Cape-harbor wher they ridd in saftie. A word or too by the way of this cape; it was thus first named by Capten Gosnole and his company, An°: 1602, and after by Capten Smith was caled Cape James; but it retains the former name amongst seamen. Also that pointe which first shewed those dangerous shoulds unto them, they called Pointe Care, and Tuckers Terrour; but the French and Dutch to this day call it Malabarr, by reason of those perilous shoulds, and the losses they have suffered their.

Being thus arived in good harbor and brought safe to land, they fell upon their knees and blessed the God of heaven, who had brought them over the vast and furious ocean, and delivered them from all the periles and miseries therof, againe to set their feete on the firme and stable earth, their proper elemente. And no marvell if they were thus joyefull, seeing wise Seneca was so affected with sailing a few miles on the coast of his owne Italy; as he affirmed, that he had rather remaine twentie years on his way by land, then pass by sea to any place in a short time; so tedious and dreadfull was the same unto him.

But hear I cannot but stay and make a pause, and stand half amased at this poore peoples presente condition; and so I thinke will the reader too, when he well considers the same. Being thus passed the vast ocean, and a sea of troubles before in their preparation (as may be remembred by that which wente before), they had now no freinds to wellcome them, nor inns to entertaine or refresh their weatherbeaten bodys, no houses or much less townes to repaire too, to seeke for succoure. It is recorded in scripture as a mercie to the apostle and his shipwraked company, that the barbarians shewed them no smale kindnes in refreshing them, but these savage barbarians, when they mette with them (as after will appeare) were readier to fill their sids full of arrows then otherwise. And for the season it was winter, and they that know the winters of that cuntrie know them to be sharp and violent, and subjecte to cruell and feirce stormes, deangerous to travill to known places, much more to serch an unknown coast. Besids, what could they see but a hidious and desolate wildernes, full of wild beasts and wild men? and what multituds ther might be of them they knew not. Nether could they, as it were, goe up to the tope of Pisgah, to vew from this wildernes a more goodly cuntrie to feed their hops; for which way soever they turnd their eys (save upward to the heavens) they could have litle solace or content in respecte of any outward objects. For summer being done, all things stand upon them with a wetherbeaten face; and the whole countrie, full of woods and thickets, represented a wild and savage heiw. If they looked behind them, ther was the mighty ocean which they had passed, and was now as a maine barr and goulfe to seperate them from all the civill parts of the world. If it be said they had a ship to sucour them, it is trew; but what heard they daly from the m^r and company? but that with speede they should looke out a place with their shallop, wher they would be at some near distance; for the season was shuch as he would not stirr from thence till a safe harbor was discovered by them wher they would be, and he might goe without danger; and that victells consumed apace, but he must and would keepe sufficient for them selves and their returne. Yea, it was muttered by some, that if they gott not a place in time, they would turne them and their goods ashore and leave them. Let it also be considred what weake hopes of supply and succoure they left behinde them, that might bear up their minds in this sade condition and trialls they were under; and they could not but be very smale. It is true, indeed, the affections and love of their brethren at Leyden was cordiall and entire towards them, but they had litle power to help them, or them selves; and how the case stode betweene them and the marchants at their coming away, hath allready been declared. What could now sustaine them but the spirite of God and his grace? May not and ought not the children of these fathers rightly say:

> Our faithers were Englishmen which came over this great ocean, and were ready to perish in this willdernes; but they cried unto the Lord, and he heard their voyce, and looked on their adversitie, etc. Let them therfore praise the Lord, because he is good, and his mercies endure for ever. Yea, let them which have been redeemed of the Lord, shew how he hath delivered them from the hand of the oppressour. When they wandered in the deserte willdernes out of the way, and found no citie to dwell in, both hungrie, and thirstie, their sowle was overwhelmed in them. Let them confess before the Lord his loving kindnes, and his wonderfull works before the sons of men. . . .

The remainder of An°: 1620

I shall a litle returne backe and begine with a combination made by them before they came ashore, being the first foundation of their govermente in this place; occasioned partly by the discontented and mutinous speeches that some of the strangers amongst them had let fall from them in the ship—That when they came a shore they would use their owne libertie; for none had power to command them, the patente they had being for Virginia, and not for Newengland, which belonged to an other Goverment, with which the Virginia Company had nothing to doe. And partly that shuch an acte by them done (this their condition considered) might be as firme as any patent, and in some respects more sure.

The forme was as followeth.

In the name of God, Amen. We whose names are under-writen, the loyall subjects of our dread soveraigne Lord, King James, by the grace of God, of Great

Britaine, France, and Ireland king, defender of the faith, etc., haveing under-taken, for the glorie of God, and advancemente of the Christian faith, and honour of our king and countrie, a voyage to plant the first colonie in the Northerne parts of Virginia, doe by these presents solemnly and mutualy in the presence of God, and one of another, covenant and combine our selves togeather into a civill body politick, for our better ordering and preservation and furtherance of the ends aforesaid; and by vertue hearof to enacte, constitute, and frame such just and equall lawes, ordinances, acts, constitutions, and offices, from time to time, as shall be thought most meete and convenient for the generall good of the Colonie, unto which we promise all due submission and obedience. In witnes wherof we have hereunder subscribed our names at Cape Codd the 11. of November, in the year of the raigne of our soveraigne lord, King James, of England, France, and Ireland the eighteenth, and of Scotland the fiftie fourth. An⁰: Dom. 1620.

After this they chose, or rather confirmed, Mr. John Carver (a man godly and well approved amongst them) their Governour for that year. And after they had provided a place for their goods, or comone store, (which were long in unlading for want of boats, foulnes of winter weather, and sicknes of diverce,) and begune some small cottages for their habitation, as time would admitte, they mette and consulted of lawes and orders, both for their civill and military Govermente, as the necessitie of their condition did require, still adding therunto as urgent occasion in severall times, and as cases did require.

In these hard and difficulte beginings they found some discontents and mur-murings arise amongst some, and mutinous speeches and carriags in other; but they were soone quelled and overcome by the wisdome, patience, and just and equall carrage of things by the Govr and better part, which clave faithfully togeather in the maine. But that which was most sadd and lamentable was, that in 2. or 3. moneths time halfe of their company dyed, espetialy in Jan: and February, being the depth of winter, and wanting houses and other comforts; being infected with the scurvie and other diseases, which this long vioage and their inacomodate condition had brought upon them; so as ther dyed some times 2. or 3. of a day, in the foresaid time; that of 100. and odd persons, scarce 50. remained. And of these in the time of most distres, ther was but 6. or 7. sound persons, who, to their great comendations be it spoken, spared no pains, night nor day, but with abundance of toyle and hazard of their owne health, fetched them woode, made them fires, drest them meat, made their beads, washed their lothsome cloaths, cloathed and uncloathed them; in a word, did all the homly and necessarie offices for them which dainty and quesie stomacks cannot endure to hear named; and all this willingly and cherfully, without any grudging in the least, shewing herein their true love unto their freinds and bretheren. A rare example and worthy to be remembred. Tow of these 7. were

Mr. William Brewster, ther reverend Elder, and Myles Standish, ther Captein and military comander, unto whom my selfe, and many others, were much beholden in our low and sicke condition. And yet the Lord so upheld these persons, as in this generall calamity they were not at all infected either with sicknes, or lamnes. And what I have said of these, I may say of many others who dyed in this generall vissitation, and others yet living, that whilst they had health, yea, or any strength continuing, they were not wanting to any that had need of them. And I doute not but their recompence is with the Lord. . . .

The Lonely Road to Mora

WILLA CATHER

In Death Comes for the Archbishop, *Father Latour and Father Vaillant make a missionary journey to a small village in the Sangre de Cristo mountains.*

*T*HE Bishop and his Vicar were riding through the rain in the Truchas mountains. The heavy, lead-coloured drops were driven slantingly through the air by an icy wind from the peak. These raindrops, Father Latour kept thinking, were the shape of tadpoles, and they broke against his nose and cheeks, exploding with a splash, as if they were hollow and full of air. The priests were riding across high mountain meadows, which in a few weeks would be green, though just now they were slate-coloured. On every side lay ridges covered with blue-green fir trees; above them rose the horny backbones of mountains. The sky was very low; purplish lead-coloured clouds let down curtains of mist into the valleys between the pine ridges. There was not a glimmer of white light in the dark vapours working overhead—rather, they took on the cold green of the evergreens. Even the white mules, their coats wet and matted into tufts, had turned a slaty hue, and the faces of the two priests were purple and spotted in that singular light.

Father Latour rode first, sitting straight upon his mule, with his chin lowered just enough to keep the drive of rain out of his eyes. Father Vaillant followed, unable to see much—in weather like this his glasses were of no use, and he had taken them off. He crouched down in the saddle, his shoulders well over Contento's neck. Father Joseph's sister, Philomène, who was Mother Superior of a convent in her native town in the Puy-de-Dôme, often tried to picture her brother and Bishop Latour on these long missionary journeys of which he wrote her; she imagined the scene and saw the two priests moving through it in their cassocks, bareheaded, like the pictures of St. Francis Xavier with which she was familiar. The reality was less picturesque—but for all that, no one could have mistaken these two men for hunters or traders. They wore clerical collars about their necks instead of neckerchiefs, and on the breast of his buckskin jacket the Bishop's silver cross hung by a silver chain.

They were on their way to Mora, the third day out, and they did not know just how far they had still to go. Since morning they had not met a traveller or seen a human habitation. They believed they were on the right trail, for they had seen no other. The first night of their journey they had spent at Santa Cruz, lying in the warm, wide valley of the Rio Grande, where the fields and gardens were already softly coloured with early spring. But since they had left the Española country behind them, they had contended first with wind and sand-storms, and now with cold. The Bishop was going to Mora to assist the Padre there in disposing of a crowd of refugees who filled his house. A new settlement in the Conejos valley had lately been raided by Indians; many of the inhabitants were killed, and the survivors, who were originally from Mora, had managed to get back there, utterly destitute.

Before the travellers had crossed the mountain meadows, the rain turned to sleet. Their wet buckskins quickly froze, and the rattle of icy flakes struck them and bounded off. The prospect of a night in the open was not cheering. It was too wet to kindle a fire, their blankets would become soaked on the ground. As they were descending the mountain on the Mora side, the grey daylight seemed already beginning to fail, though it was only four o'clock. Father Latour turned in his saddle and spoke over his shoulder.

"The mules are certainly very tired, Joseph. They ought to be fed."

"Push on," said Father Vaillant. "We will come to shelter of some kind before night sets in." The Vicar had been praying steadfastly while they crossed the meadows, and he felt confident that St. Joseph would not turn a deaf ear. Before the hour was done they did indeed come upon a wretched adobe house, so poor and mean that they might not have seen it had it not lain close beside the trail, on the edge of a steep ravine. The stable looked more habitable than the house, and the priests thought perhaps they could spend the night in it.

As they rode up to the door, a man came out, bareheaded, and they saw to their surprise that he was not a Mexican, but an American, of a very unprepossessing type. He spoke to them in some drawling dialect they could scarcely understand and asked if they wanted to stay the night. During the few words they exchanged with him Father Latour felt a growing reluctance to remain even for a few hours under the roof of this ugly, evil-looking fellow. He was tall, gaunt and ill-formed, with a snake-like neck, terminating in a small, bony head. Under his close-clipped hair this repellent head showed a number of thick ridges, as if the skull joinings were overgrown by layers of superfluous bone. With its small, rudimentary ears, this head had a positively malignant look. The man seemed not more than half human, but he was the only householder on the lonely road to Mora.

The priests dismounted and asked him whether he could put their mules under shelter and give them grain feed.

"As soon as I git my coat on I will. You kin come in."

They followed him into a room where a piñon fire blazed in the corner, and went toward it to warm their stiffened hands. Their host made an angry, snarling sound in the direction of the partition, and a woman came out of the next room. She was a Mexican.

Father Latour and Father Vaillant addressed her courteously in Spanish, greeting her in the name of the Holy Mother, as was customary. She did not open her lips, but stared at them blankly for a moment, then dropped her eyes and cowered as if she were terribly frightened. The priests looked at each other; it struck them both that this man had been abusing her in some way. Suddenly he turned on her.

"Clear off them cheers fur the strangers. They won't eat ye, if they air priests."

She began distractedly snatching rags and wet socks and dirty clothes from the chairs. Her hands were shaking so that she dropped things. She was not old, she might have been very young, but she was probably half-witted. There was nothing in her face but blankness and fear.

Her husband put on his coat and boots, went to the door, and stopped with his hand on the latch, throwing over his shoulder a crafty, hateful glance at the bewildered woman.

"Here, you! Come right along, I'll need ye!"

She took her black shawl from a peg and followed him. Just at the door she turned and caught the eyes of the visitors, who were looking after her in compassion and perplexity. Instantly that stupid face became intense, prophetic, full of awful meaning. With her finger she pointed them away, away!—two quick thrusts into the air. Then, with a look of horror beyond anything language could convey, she threw back her head and drew the edge of her palm quickly across her distended throat—and vanished. The doorway was empty; the two priests stood staring at it, speechless. That flash of electric passion had been so swift, the warning it communicated so vivid and definite, that they were struck dumb.

Father Joseph was the first to find his tongue. "There is no doubt of her meaning. Your pistol is loaded, Jean?"

"Yes, but I neglected to keep it dry. No matter."

They hurried out of the house. It was still light enough to see the stable through the grey drive of rain, and they went toward it.

"Señor American," the Bishop called, "will you be good enough to bring out our mules?"

The man came out of the stable. "What do you want?"

"Our mules. We have changed our mind. We will push on to Mora. And here is a dollar for your trouble."

The man took a threatening attitude. As he looked from one to the other his head played from side to side exactly like a snake's. "What's the matter? My house ain't good enough for ye?"

"No explanation is necessary. Go into the barn and get the mules, Father Joseph."

"You dare go into my stable, you—priest!"

The Bishop drew his pistol. "No profanity, Señor. We want nothing from you but to get away from your uncivil tongue. Stand where you are."

The man was unarmed. Father Joseph came out with the mules, which had not been unsaddled. The poor things were each munching a mouthful, but they needed no urging to be gone; they did not like this place. The moment they felt their riders on their backs they trotted quickly along the road, which dropped immediately into the arroyo. While they were descending, Father Joseph remarked that the man would certainly have a gun in the house, and that he had no wish to be shot in the back.

"Nor I. But it is growing too dark for that, unless he should follow us on horseback," said the Bishop. "Were there horses in the stable?"

"Only a burro." Father Vaillant was relying upon the protection of St. Joseph, whose office he had fervently said that morning. The warning given them by that poor woman, with such scant opportunity, seemed evidence that some protecting power was mindful of them.

By the time they had ascended the far side of the arroyo, night had closed down and the rain was pouring harder than ever.

"I am by no means sure that we can keep in the road," said the Bishop. "But at least I am sure we are not being followed. We must trust to these intelligent beasts. Poor woman! He will suspect her and abuse her, I am afraid." He kept seeing her in the darkness as he rode on, her face in the fire-light, and her terrible pantomime.

They reached the town of Mora a little after midnight. The Padre's house was full of refugees, and two of them were put out of a bed in order that the Bishop and his Vicar could get into it.

In the morning a boy came from the stable and reported that he had found a crazy woman lying in the straw, and that she begged to see the two Padres who owned the white mules. She was brought in, her clothing cut to rags, her legs and face and even her hair so plastered with mud that the priests could scarcely recognize the woman who had saved their lives the night before.

She said she had never gone back to the house at all. When the two priests rode away her husband had run to the house to get his gun, and she had plunged down a washout behind the stable into the arroyo, and had been on the way to Mora all night. She had supposed he would overtake her and kill her, but he had not. She reached the settlement before day-break, and crept into the stable to warm herself among the animals and wait until the household was awake.

Kneeling before the Bishop she began to relate such horrible things that he stopped her and turned to the native priest.

"This is a case for the civil authorities. Is there a magistrate here?"

There was no magistrate, but there was a retired fur trapper who acted as notary and could take evidence. He was sent for, and in the interval Father Latour instructed the refugee women from Conejos to bathe this poor creature and put decent clothes on her, and to care for the cuts and scratches on her legs.

An hour later the woman, whose name was Magdalena, calmed by food and kindness, was ready to tell her story. The notary had brought along his friend, St. Vrain, a Canadian trapper who understood Spanish better than he. The woman was known to St. Vrain, moreover, who confirmed her statement that she was born Magdalena Valdez, at Los Ranchos de Taos, and that she was twenty-four years old. Her husband, Buck Scales, had drifted into Taos with a party of hunters from somewhere in Wyoming. All white men knew him for a dog and a degenerate—but to Mexican girls, marriage with an American meant coming up in the world. She had married him six years ago, and had been living with him ever since in that wretched house on the Mora trail. During that time he had robbed and murdered four travellers who had stopped there for the night. They were all strangers, not known in the country. She had forgot their names, but one was a German boy who spoke very little Spanish and little English; a nice boy with blue eyes, and she had grieved for him more than for the others. They were all buried in the sandy soil behind the stable. She was always afraid their bodies might wash out in a storm. Their horses Buck had ridden off by night and sold to Indians somewhere in the north. Magdalena had borne three children since her marriage, and her husband had killed each of them a few days after birth, by ways so horrible that she could not relate it. After he killed the first baby, she ran away from him, back to her parents at Ranchos. He came after her and made her go home with him by threatening harm to the old people. She was afraid to go anywhere for help, but twice before she had managed to warn travellers away, when her husband happened to be out of the house. This time she had found courage because, when she looked into the faces of these two Padres, she knew they were good men, and she thought if she ran after them they could save her. She could not bear any more killing. She asked nothing better than to die herself, if only she could hide near a church and a priest for a while, to make her soul right with God.

St. Vrain and his friend got together a search-party at once. They rode out to Scales's place and found the remains of four men buried under the corral behind the stable, as the woman had said. Scales himself they captured on the road from Taos, where he had gone to look for his wife. They brought him back to Mora, but St. Vrain rode on to Taos to fetch a magistrate.

There was no *calabozo* in Mora, so Scales was put into an empty stable, under guard. This stable was soon surrounded by a crowd of people, who loitered to hear the blood-curdling threats the prisoner shouted against his wife. Magdalena was kept in the Padre's house, where she lay on a mat in the corner, begging Father Latour to take her back to Santa Fé, so that her husband could not get at her. Though Scales was bound, the Bishop felt alarmed for her safety. He and the American notary, who had a pistol of the new revolver model, sat in the *sala* and kept watch over her all night.

In the morning the magistrate and his party arrived from Taos. The notary told him the facts of the case in the plaza, where everyone could hear. The Bishop inquired whether there was any place for Magdalena in Taos, as she could not stay on here in such a state of terror.

A man dressed in buckskin hunting-clothes stepped out of the crowd and asked to see Magdalena. Father Latour conducted him into the room where she lay on her mat. The stranger went up to her, removing his hat. He bent down and put his hand on her shoulder. Though he was clearly an American, he spoke Spanish in the native manner.

"Magdalena, don't you remember me?"

She looked up at him as out of a dark well; something became alive in her deep, haunted eyes. She caught with both hands at his fringed buckskin knees.

"Christóbal!" she wailed. "Oh, Christóbal!"

"I'll take you home with me, Magdalena, and you can stay with my wife. You wouldn't be afraid in my house, would you?"

"No, no, Christóbal, I would not be afraid with you. I am not a wicked woman."

He smoothed her hair. "You're a good girl, Magdalena—always were. It will be all right. Just leave things to me."

Then he turned to the Bishop. "Señor Vicario, she can come to me. I live near Taos. My wife is a native woman, and she'll be good to her. That varmint won't come about my place, even if he breaks jail. He knows me. My name is Carson."

Father Latour had looked forward to meeting the scout. He had supposed him to be a very large man, of powerful body and commanding presence. This Carson was not so tall as the Bishop himself, was very slight in frame, modest in manner, and he spoke English with a soft Southern drawl. His face was both thoughtful and alert; anxiety had drawn a permanent ridge between his blue eyes. Under his blond moustache his mouth had a singular refinement. The lips were full and delicately modelled. There was something curiously unconscious about his mouth, reflective, a little melancholy—and something that suggested a capacity for tenderness. The Bishop felt a quick glow of pleasure in looking at the man. As he stood there in his buckskin clothes one felt in him standards, loyalties, a code which is not easily put into words but which is instantly felt when two men who live by it come together by chance. He took the scout's hand. "I have long wanted to meet Kit Carson," he said, "even before I came to New Mexico. I have been hoping you would pay me a visit at Santa Fé."

The other smiled. "I'm right shy, sir, and I'm always afraid of being disappointed. But I guess it will be all right from now on."

This was the beginning of a long friendship.

On their ride back to Carson's ranch, Magdalena was put in Father Vaillant's care, and the Bishop and the scout rode together. Carson said he had become a Catholic merely as a matter of form, as Americans usually did when they married a Mexican girl. His wife was a good woman and very devout; but religion had seemed to him pretty much a woman's affair until his last trip to California. He had been sick out there, and the Fathers at one of the missions took care of him. "I began to see things different, and thought I might some day be a Catholic in earnest. I was brought up to think priests were rascals, and that the nuns were bad women—all the stuff they talk back in Missouri. A good many of the native priests here bear out that story. Our Padre Martínez at Taos is an old scapegrace, if ever there was one; he's got children and grandchildren in almost every settlement around here. And Padre Lucero at Arroyo Hondo is a miser, takes everything a poor man's got to give him a Christian burial."

The Bishop discussed the needs of his people at length with Carson. He felt great confidence in his judgment. The two men were about the same age, both a little over forty, and both had been sobered and sharpened by wide experience. Carson had been guide in world-renowned explorations, but he was still almost as poor as in the days when he was a beaver trapper. He lived in a little adobe house with his Mexican wife. The great country of desert and mountain ranges between Santa Fé and the Pacific coast was not yet mapped or chartered; the most reliable map of it was in Kit Carson's brain. This Missourian, whose eye was so quick to read a landscape or a human face, could not read a printed page. He could at that time barely write his own name. Yet one felt in him a quick and discriminating intelligence. That he was illiterate was an accident; he had got ahead of books, gone where the printing-press could not follow him. Out of the hardships of his boyhood—from fourteen to twenty picking up a bare living as cook or mule-driver for wagon trains, often in the service of brutal and desperate characters—he had preserved a clean sense of honour and a compassionate heart. In talking to the Bishop of poor Magdalena he said sadly: "I used to see her in Taos when she was such a pretty girl. Ain't it a pity?"

The degenerate murderer, Buck Scales, was hanged after a short trial. Early in April the Bishop left Santa Fé on horseback and rode to St. Louis, on his way to attend the Provincial Council at Baltimore. When he returned in September, he brought back with him five courageous nuns, Sisters of Loretto, to found a school for girls in letterless Santa Fé. He sent at once for Magdalena and took her into the service of the Sisters. She became housekeeper and manager of the Sisters' kitchen. She was devoted to the nuns, and so happy in the service of the Church that when the Bishop visited the school he used to enter by the kitchen-garden in order to see her serene and handsome face. For she became beautiful, as Carson said she had been as a girl. After the blight of her horrible youth was over, she seemed to bloom again in the household of God.

Galveston, Texas, in 1895

STEPHEN CRANE

In his most famous Western short stories, ''The Bride Comes to Yellow Sky'' and ''The Blue Hotel,'' Stephen Crane brought the reality of his own experience to mythical, heroic settings. His journalistic view of fast-growing Galveston reflects a certain disappointment in the city's lack of a rugged frontier face.

*I*T is the fortune of travellers to take note of differences and publish them to their friends. It is the differences that are supposed to be valuable. The travellers seek them bravely, and cudgel their wits to find means to unearth them. But in this search they are confronted continually by the resemblances and the intrusion of commonplace and most obvious similarity into a field that is being ploughed in the romantic fashion is what causes an occasional resort to the imagination.

The winter found a cowboy in south-western Nebraska who had just ended a journey from Kansas City, and he swore bitterly as he remembered how little boys in Kansas City followed him about in order to contemplate his wide-brimmed hat. His vivid description of this incident would have been instructive to many Eastern readers. The fact that little boys in Kansas City could be profoundly interested in the sight of a wide-hatted cowboy would amaze a certain proportion of the populace. Where then can one expect cowboys if not in Kansas City? As a matter of truth, however, a steam boiler with four legs and a tail, galloping down the main street of the town, would create no more enthusiasm there than a real cow-puncher. For years the farmers have been driving the cattlemen back, back toward the mountains and into Kansas, and Nebraska has come to an almost universal condition of yellow trolly-cars with clanging gongs and whirring wheels, and conductors who don't give a curse for the public. And travellers tumbling over each other in their haste to trumpet the radical differences between Eastern and Western life have created a generally wrong opinion. No one has yet dared to declare that if a man drew three trays in Syracuse, N.Y., in many a Western city the man would be blessed with a full house. The declaration has no commercial value. There is a distinct fascination in being aware that in some parts of the world there are purple pigs, and children who are born with china mugs dangling where their ears should be. It is this fact which makes men sometimes grab tradition in wonder; color and attach contemporaneous datelines to it. It is this fact which has kept the sweeping march of the West from being chronicled in any particularly true manner.

In a word, it is the passion for differences which has prevented a general knowledge of the resemblances.

If a man comes to Galveston resolved to discover every curious thing possible, and to display every point where Galveston differed from other parts of the universe, he would have the usual difficulty in shutting his eyes to the similarities. Galveston is often original, full of distinctive characters. But it is not like a town in the moon. There are, of course, a thousand details of street color and life which are thoroughly typical of any American city. The square brick business blocks, the mazes of telegraph wires, the trolly-cars clamoring up and down the streets, the passing crowd, the slight fringe of reflective and reposeful men on the curb, all disappoint the traveller, and he goes out in the sand somewhere and digs in order to learn if all Galveston clams are not schooner-rigged.

Accounts of these variations are quaint and interesting reading, to be sure, but then, after all, there are the great and elemental facts of American life. The cities differ as peas—in complexion, in size, in temperature—but the fundamental part, the composition, remains.

There has been a wide education in distinctions. It might be furtively suggested that the American people did not thoroughly know their mighty kinship, their universal emotions, their identical view-points upon many matters about which little is said. Of course, when the foreign element is injected very strongly, a town becomes strange, unfathomable, wearing a sort of guilty air which puzzles the American eye. There begins then a great diversity, and peas become turnips, and the differences are profound. With them, however, this prelude has nothing to do. It is a mere attempt to impress a reader with the importance of remembering that an illustration of Galveston streets can easily be obtained in Maine. Also, that the Gulf of Mexico could be mistaken for the Atlantic Ocean, and that its name is not printed upon it in tall red letters, notwithstanding the legend which has been supported by the geographies.

There are but three lifts in the buildings of Galveston. This is not because the people are skilled climbers; it is because the buildings are for the most part not high.

A certain Colonel Menard bought this end of the island of Galveston from the Republic of Texas in 1838 for fifty thousand dollars. He had a premonition of the value of wide streets for the city of his dreams, and he established a minimum width of seventy feet. The widest of the avenues is one hundred and fifty feet.

The fact that this is not extraordinary for 1898 does not prevent it from being marvellous as municipal forethought in 1838.

In 1874 the United States Government decided to erect stone jetties at the entrance to the harbor of Galveston in order to deepen the water on the outer and inner bars, whose shallowness compelled deep-water ships to remain outside and use lighters to transfer their cargoes to the wharves of the city. Work on the jetties was in progress when I was in Galveston in 1895—in fact, two long, low black fingers of stone stretched into the Gulf. There are men still living who had confidence in the Governmental decision of 1874, and these men now point with pride to the jetties and say that the United States Government is nothing if not inevitable.

The soundings at mean low tide were thirteen feet on the inner bar and about twelve feet on the outer bar. At present there is twenty-three feet of water where once was the inner bar, and as the jetties have crept toward the sea they have achieved eighteen feet of water in the channel of the outer bar at mean low tide. The plan is to gain a depth of thirty feet. The cost is to be about seven million dollars.

Undoubtedly in 1874 the people of Galveston celebrated the decision of the Government with great applause, and prepared to welcome mammoth steamers at the wharves during the next spring. It was in 1889, however, that matters took conclusive form. In 1895 the prayer of Galveston materialised.

In 1889, Iowa, Nebraska, Missouri, Kansas, California, Arkansas, Texas, Wyoming, and New Mexico began a serious pursuit of Congress. Certain products of these States and Territories could not be exported with profit, owing to the high rate of transportation to Eastern ports. They demanded a harbor on the coast of Texas with a depth and area sufficient for great sea-crossing steamers. The board of army engineers which was appointed by Congress decided on Galveston as the point. The plan was to obtain by means of artificial constructions a volume and velocity of tidal flow that would maintain a navigable channel. The jetties are seven thousand feet apart, in order to allow ample room for the escape of the enormous flow of water from the inner bar.

Galveston has always been substantial and undeviating in its amount of business. Soon after the war it attained a commercial solidity, and its progress has been steady but quite slow. The citizens now, however, are lying in wait for a real Western boom. Those products of the West which have been walled in by the railroad transportation rates to Eastern ports are now expected to pass through Galveston. An air of hope pervades the countenance of each business man. The city, however, expected 1,500,000 bales of cotton last season, and the Chamber of Commerce has already celebrated the fact.

A train approaches the Island of Galveston by means of a long steel bridge across a bay, which glitters like burnished metal in the winter-time sunlight. The vast number of white two-storied frame houses in the outskirts remind one of New England, if it were not that the island is level as a floor. Later, in the commercial part of the town, appear the conventional business houses and the trolly-cars. Far up the cross-streets is the faint upheaval of the surf of the breeze-blown Gulf, and in the other direction the cotton steamers are arrayed with a fresco upon their black sides of dusky chuckling stevedores handling the huge bales amid a continual and foreign conversation, in which all the subtle and incomprehensible gossip of their social relations goes from mouth to mouth, the bales leaving little tufts of cotton all over their clothing.

Galveston has a rather extraordinary number of very wealthy people. Along the finely-paved drives their residences can be seen, modern for the most part and poor in architecture. Occasionally, however, one comes upon a typical Southern mansion, its galleries giving it a solemn shade and its whole air one of fine and enduring dignity. The palms standing in the grounds of these houses seem to pause at this time of year, and patiently abide the coming of the hot breath of summer. They still remain of a steadfast green and their color is a wine.

Underfoot the grass is of a yellow hue, here and there patched with a faint impending verdancy. The famous snowstorm here this winter played havoc with the color of the vegetation, and one can now observe the gradual recovery of the trees, the shrubbery, the grass. In this vivid sunlight their vitality becomes enormous.

This storm also had a great effect upon the minds of the citizens. They would not have been more astonished if it had rained suspender buttons. The writer read descriptions of this storm in the newspapers of the date. Since his arrival here he has listened to 574 accounts of it.

Galveston has the aspect of a seaport. New York is not a seaport; a seaport is, however, a certain detail of New York. But in Galveston the docks, the ships, the sailors, are a large element in the life of the town. Also, one can sometimes find here that marvellous type the American sailor. American seamen are not numerous enough to ever depreciate in value. A town that can produce a copy of the American sailor should encase him in bronze and unveil him on the Fourth of July. A veteran of the waves explained to the writer the reason that American youths do not go to sea. He said it was because saddles are too expensive. The writer congratulated the veteran of the waves upon his lucid explanation of this great question.

Galveston has its own summer resorts. In the heat of the season, life becomes sluggish in the streets. Men move about with an extraordinary caution as if they expected to be shot as they approached each corner.

At the beach, however, there is a large hotel which overflows with humanity, and in front is, perhaps, the most comfortable structure in the way of bath-houses known to the race. Many of the rooms are ranged about the foot of a large dome. A gallery connects them, but the principal floor to this structure is the sea itself, to which a flight of steps leads. Galveston's 35,000 people divide among themselves in summer a reliable wind from the Gulf.

There is a distinctly cosmopolitan character to Galveston's people. There are men from everywhere. The city does not represent Texas. It is unmistakably American, but in a general manner. Certain Texas differentiations are not observable in this city.

Withal, the people have the Southern frankness, the honesty which enables them to meet a stranger without deep suspicion, and they are the masters of a hospitality which is instructive to cynics.

FROM

The Provincial Lady in America

E. M. DELAFIELD

*A diary selection in which the Provincial Lady
goes to Boston and attends a football game at
Harvard*

WEATHER gets colder and colder as I approach Boston, and this rouses prejudice in me, together with repeated assurances from everybody I meet to the effect that Boston is the most English town in America, and I shall simply adore it. Feel quite unlike adoration as train takes me through snowy country, and affords glimpses of towns that appear to be entirely composed of Gasoline Stations and Motion-Picture Theatres. Towards nine o'clock in the morning, I have an excellent breakfast—food in America definitely a very bright spot—and return to railway-carriage where I see familiar figure, hat still worn at very dashing angle, and recognise Pete. Feel as if I had met my oldest friend, in the middle of a crowd of strangers, and we greet one another cordially. Pete tells me that I seem to be standing up to it pretty well—which I take to be a compliment to my powers of endurance—and unfolds terrific programme of the activities he has planned for me in Boston.

Assent to everything, but add that the thing I want to do most of all, is to visit the Alcott House at Concord, Mass. At this Pete looks astounded, and replies that this is, he supposes, merely a personal fancy, and so far as he knows no time for anything of that kind has been allowed in the schedule. Am obliged to agree that it probably hasn't, but repeat that I really want to do that more than anything else in America. (Much later on, compose eloquent and convincing speech, to the effect that I have worked very hard and done all that was required of me, and that I am fully entitled to gratify my own wishes for one afternoon at least. Am quite clear that if I had only said all this at the time, Pete would have been left without a leg to stand upon. Unfortunately, however, I do not do so.)

Boston is reached—step out of the train into the iciest cold that it has ever been my lot to encounter—and am immediately photographed by unknown man carrying camera and unpleasant little light-bulb which he flashes unexpectedly into my eyes. No one makes the slightest comment on this proceeding, and am convinced that he has mistaken me for somebody quite different.

Two young creatures from the *Boston Transcript* meet me, and enquire, more or less instantly, what I feel about the Problem of the American Woman, but Pete, with great good feeling, suggests that we should discuss it all in taxi on our way to Hotel, which we do. One of them then hands me a cable—(announcing death of Robin or Vicky?)—and says it arrived this morning.

Cable says, in effect, that I must at all costs get into touch with Caroline Concannon's dear friend and cousin Mona, who lives in Pinckney Street, would love to meet me, has been written to, everything all right at flat, love from Caroline.

Am quite prepared to get into touch with dear friend and cousin, but say nothing to Pete about it, for fear of similar disconcerting reaction to that produced by suggestion of visiting Alcott House.

Am conducted to nice little Hotel in Charles Street, and told once by Pete, and twice by each of the *Boston Transcript* young ladies, that I am within a stone's throw of the Common. Chief association with the Common is *An Old-Fashioned Girl*, in which heroine goes tobogganing, but do not refer to this, and merely reply that That is very nice. So it may be, but not at the moment when Common, besides being deep in snow, is quite evidently being searched from end to end by ice-laden north-east wind.

Pete, with firmness to which I am by now accustomed, says that he will leave me to unpack but come and fetch me again in an hour's time, to visit customary bookshops.

Telephone bell in sitting-room soon afterwards rings, and it appears that dear Rose—like Caroline Concannon—has a friend in Boston, and that the friend is downstairs and proposes to come up right away and see me. I say Yes, Yes, and I shall be delighted, and hastily shut suit-cases which I have this moment opened, and look at myself in the glass instead.

Results of this inspection are far from encouraging, but nothing can be done about it now, and can only concentrate on trying to remember everything that Rose has ever told me about her Boston friend, called, I believe, Fanny Mason. Sum total of my recollections is that the friend is very literary, and has written a good deal, and travelled all over the world, and is very critical.

Am rather inclined to become agitated by all this, but friend appears, and has the good feeling to keep these disquieting attributes well out of sight, and concentrate on welcoming me very kindly to Boston—(exactly like England and all English people always love it on that account)—and enquiring affectionately about Rose. (Am disgusted to learn from what she says that dear Rose has written to her far more recently, as well as at much greater length, than to myself. Shall have a good deal to say to Rose, when we meet again.)

Friend then announces that she has A Girl downstairs. The Girl has brought a car, and is going to show me Boston this morning, take me to lunch at a Women's Club, and to a tea later. This more than kind, but also definitely disconcerting in view of arrangements made by Pete, and I say O Miss Mason— and then stop, rather like heroine of a Victorian novel.

Miss M. at once returns that I must not dream of calling her anything but Fanny. She has heard of me for years and years, and we are already old friends. This naturally calls for thanks and acknowledgements on my part, and I then explain that publishers' representative is in Boston, and calling for me in an hour's time, which I'm afraid means that I cannot take advantage of kind offer.

Miss M.—Fanny—undefeated, and says it is Important that I should see Boston, no one who has not done so can be said to know anything whatever about America, and The Girl is waiting for me downstairs. Suggest—mostly in order to gain time—that The Girl should be invited to come up, and this is done by telephone.

She turns out to be very youthful and good-looking blonde, introduced to me as "Leslie"—(first names evidently the fashion in Boston)—and evidently prepared to take me anywhere in the world, more or less, at any moment.

Explain all over again about Pete and the booksellers. Fanny remains adamant, but Leslie says reasonably: What about tomorrow instead, and I advance cherished scheme for visiting Alcott House. This, it appears, is fraught with difficulties, as Alcott House is impenetrably shut at this time of year. Feel that if Pete comes to hear of this, my last hope is gone. Leslie looks rather sorry for me, and says perhaps something could be arranged, but anyway I had better come out now and see Boston. Fanny is also urgent on this point, and I foresee deadlock, when telephone rings and Pete is announced, and is told to come upstairs.

Brilliant idea then strikes me, I introduce everybody, and tell Pete that there has been rather a clash of arrangements, but that doubtless he and Miss Mason can easily settle it between themselves. Will they, in the meanwhile, excuse me, as I positively must see about my unpacking? Retreat firmly into the bedroom to do so, but spend some of the time with ear glued to the wall, trying to ascertain whether Pete and Miss M.—both evidently very strong personalities—are going to fly at one another's throats or not. Voices are certainly definitely raised, usually both at once, but nothing more formidable happens, and I hope that physical violence may be averted.

Decide that on the whole I am inclined to back Pete, as possessing rock-like quality of immovability once his mind is made up—doubtless very useful asset in dealing with authors, publishers, and so on.

Subsequent events prove that I am right, and Pete walks me to bookshop, with laconic announcement to Leslie and Miss M.—Fanny—that I shall be at their disposal by 12.30.

November 16th

Most extraordinary revolution in everybody's outlook—excepting my own—by communication from Mr. Alexander Woollcott. He has, it appears, read in a paper (*Boston Transcript?*) that my whole object in coming to America was to visit the Alcott House, and of this he approves to such an extent that he is prepared to Mention It in a Radio Talk, if I will immediately inform him of my reactions to the expedition.

Entire *volte-face* now takes place in attitude of Pete, Fanny, and everybody else. If Alexander Woollcott thinks I ought to visit Alcott House, it apparently becomes essential that I should do so and Heaven and earth must, if necessary, be moved in order to enable me to. Am much impressed by the remarkable difference between enterprise that I merely want to undertake for my own satisfaction, and the same thing when it is advocated by Mr. A.W.

Result of it all is that the members of the Alcott-Pratt family are approached, they respond with the greatest kindness, and offer to open the house especially for my benefit. Fanny says that Leslie will drive me out to Concord on Sunday afternoon, and she will herself accompany us, not in order to view Alcott House—she does not want to see it, which rather shocks me—but to visit a relation of her own living there. Pete does not associate himself personally with the expedition, as he will by that time have gone to New York, Charlestown, Oshkosh, or some other distant spot—but it evidently meets with his warmest approval, and his last word to me is an injunction to take paper and pencil with me and send account of my impressions red-hot to Mr. Alexander Woollcott.

November 18th

Go to see football game, Harvard *v.* Army. Am given to understand—and can readily believe—that this is a privilege for which Presidents, Crowned Heads, and Archbishops would one and all give ten years of life at the very least. It has only been obtained for me by the very greatest exertions on the part of everybody.

Fanny says that I shall be frozen—(can well believe it)—but that it will be worth it, and Leslie thinks I may find it rather difficult to follow—but it will be worth it—and they both agree that there is always a risk of pneumonia in this kind of weather. Wonder if they are going to add that it will still be worth it, because if so, shall disagree with them forcibly—but they heap coals of fire on my head for this unworthy thought by offering to lend me rugs, furs, mufflers, and overshoes. Escort has been provided for me in the person of an admirer of Fanny's—name unknown to me from first to last—and we set out together at one o'clock. Harvard stadium is enormous—no roof, which I think a mistake—and we sit in open air, and might be comfortable if temperature would only rise above zero. Fanny's admirer is extremely kind to me, and can only hope he isn't thinking all the time how much pleasanter it would be if he were only escorting Fanny instead.

(Reminiscence here of once-popular song: "I am dancing with tears in my eyes, 'Cos the girl in my arms isn't you." Have always felt this attitude rather hard on girl actually being danced with at the moment of singing.)

Ask questions that I hope sound fairly intelligent, and listen attentively to the answers. Escort in return then paralyses me by putting to me various technical points in regard to what he calls the English Game. Try frantically to recall everything that I can ever remember having heard from Robin, but am only able to recollect that he once said Soccer was absolutely lousy and that I rebuked him for it. Translate this painful reminiscence into civilised version to the effect that Rugger is more popular than Soccer with Our Schoolboys.

Presently a mule appears and is ridden round the field by a member of one team or the other—am not sure which—and I observe, idiotically, that It's like a Rodeo—and immediately perceive that it isn't in the least, and wish I hadn't spoken. Fortunately a number of young gentlemen in white suddenly emerge on to the ground, turn beautiful back somersaults in perfect unison, and cheer madly through a megaphone. Am deeply impressed, and assure Fanny's admirer that we have nothing in the least like that at Wembley, Twickenham, nor, so far as I know, anywhere else. He agrees, very solemnly, that the cheers are a Great Feature of the Game.

Soon afterwards we really get started, and I watch my first game of American football. Players all extensively padded and vast numbers of substitute-players wait about in order to rush in and replace them when necessary. Altogether phenomenal number of these exchanges takes place, but as no stretchers visible, conclude that most of the injuries received fall short of being mortal.

Fanny's admirer gives me explanations about what is taking place from time to time, but is apt to break off in the middle of a phrase when excitement overcomes him. Other interruptions are occasioned by organised yellings and roarings, conducted from the field, in which the spectators join.

At about four o'clock it is said to be obvious that Harvard hasn't got a chance, and soon afterwards the Army is declared to have won.

Escort and I look at each other and say Well, and Wasn't it marvellous, and then stand up and I discover that I am quite unable to feel my feet at all, and that all circulation in the rest of my body has apparently stopped altogether—probably frozen.

We totter as best we can through the crowd—escort evidently just as cold as I am, judging by the color of his face and hands—and over bridge, past buildings that I am told are all part of the College, and to flat with attractive view across the river. As I have not been warned by anybody that this is in store, I remain unaware throughout why I am being entertained there, or by whom. Hot tea, for once, is extraordinarily welcome, and so is superb log-fire; and I talk to unknown, but agreeable, American about President Roosevelt, the state of the dollar—we both take a gloomy view of this—and extreme beauty of American foliage in the woods of Maine—where I have never set foot, but about which I have heard a good deal.

Notes from a Native Daughter

JOAN DIDION

Sacramento, the author's hometown, is hardly the California of the popular images enhanced by fiction, TV, movies, and the tales told by Eastern visitors. But Didion says ''Sacramento is California, and California is a place in which a boom mentality and a sense of Chekhovian loss meet in uneasy suspension.''

*I*T is very easy to sit at the bar in, say, La Scala in Beverly Hills, or Ernie's in San Francisco, and to share in the pervasive delusion that California is only five hours from New York by air. The truth is that La Scala and Ernie's are only five hours from New York by air. California is somewhere else.

Many people in the East (or "back East," as they say in California, although not in La Scala or Ernie's) do not believe this. They have been to Los Angeles or to San Francisco, have driven through a giant redwood and have seen the Pacific glazed by the afternoon sun off Big Sur, and they naturally tend to believe that they have in fact been to California. They have not been, and they probably never will be, for it is a longer and in many ways a more difficult trip than they might want to undertake, one of those trips on which the destination flickers chimerically on the horizon, ever receding, ever diminishing. I happen to know about that trip because I come from California, come from a family, or a congeries of families, that has always been in the Sacramento Valley.

You might protest that no family has been in the Sacramento Valley for anything approaching "always." But it is characteristic of Californians to speak grandly of the past as if it had simultaneously begun, *tabula rasa,* and reached a happy ending on the day the wagons started west. *Eureka*—"I Have Found It"— as the state motto has it. Such a view of history casts a certain melancholia over those who participate in it; my own childhood was suffused with the conviction that we had long outlived our finest hour. In fact that is what I want to tell you about: what it is like to come from a place like Sacramento. If I could make you understand that, I could make you understand California and perhaps something else besides, for Sacramento *is* California, and California is a place in which a boom mentality and a sense of Chekhovian loss meet in uneasy suspension; in which the mind is troubled by some buried but ineradicable suspicion that things had better work here, because here, beneath that immense bleached sky, is where we run out of continent.

In 1847 Sacramento was no more than an adobe enclosure, Sutter's Fort, standing alone on the prairie; cut off from San Francisco and the sea by the Coast Range and from the rest of the continent by the Sierra Nevada, the Sacramento Valley was then a true sea of grass, grass so high a man riding into it could tie it across his saddle. A year later gold was discovered in the Sierra foothills, and abruptly Sacramento was a town, a town any moviegoer could map tonight in his dreams—a dusty collage of assay offices and wagonmakers and saloons. Call that Phase Two. Then the settlers came—the farmers, the people who for two hundred years had been moving west on the frontier, the peculiar flawed strain who had cleared Virginia, Kentucky, Missouri; they made Sacramento a farm town. Because the land was rich, Sacramento became eventually a rich farm town, which meant houses in town, Cadillac dealers, a country club. In that gentle sleep Sacramento dreamed until perhaps 1950, when something happened. What happened was that Sacramento woke to the fact that the outside world was moving in, fast and hard. At the moment of its waking Sacramento lost, for better or for worse, its character, and that is part of what I want to tell you about.

But the change is not what I remember first. First I remember running a boxer dog of my brother's over the same flat fields that our great-great-grandfather had found virgin and had planted; I remember swimming (albeit nervously, for I was a nervous child, afraid of sinkholes and afraid of snakes, and perhaps that was the beginning of my error) the same rivers we had swum for a century: the Sacramento, so rich with silt that we could barely see our hands a few inches beneath the surface; the American, running clean and fast with melted Sierra snow until July, when it would slow down, and rattlesnakes would sun themselves on its newly exposed rocks. The Sacramento, the American, sometimes the Consumnes, occasionally the Feather. Incautious children died every day in those rivers; we read about it in the paper, how they had miscalculated a current or stepped into a hole down where the American runs into the Sacramento, how the Berry Brothers had been called in from Yolo County to drag the river but how the bodies remained unrecovered. "They were from away," my grandmother would extrapolate from the newspaper stories. "Their parents had no *business* letting them in the river. They were visitors from Omaha." It was not a bad lesson, although a less than reliable one; children we knew died in the rivers too.

When summer ended—when the State Fair closed and the heat broke, when the last green hop vines had been torn down along the H Street road and the tule fog began rising off the low ground at night—we would go back to memorizing the Products of Our Latin American Neighbors and to visiting the great-aunts on Sunday, dozens of great-aunts, year after year of Sundays. When I think now of those winters I think of yellow elm leaves wadded in the gutters outside the Trinity Episcopal Pro-Cathedral on M Street. There are actually people in Sacramento now who call M Street Capitol Avenue, and Trinity has one of those featureless new buildings, but perhaps children still learn the same things there on Sunday mornings:

Q. In what way does the Holy Land resemble the Sacramento Valley?
A. In the type and diversity of its agricultural products.

And I think of the rivers rising, of listening to the radio to hear at what height they would crest and wondering if and when and where the levees would go. We did not have as many dams in those years. The bypasses would be full, and men would sandbag all night. Sometimes a levee would go in the night, somewhere upriver; in the morning the rumor would spread that the Army Engineers had dynamited it to relieve the pressure on the city.

After the rains came spring, for ten days or so; the drenched fields would dissolve into a brilliant ephemeral green (it would be yellow and dry as fire in two or three weeks) and the real-estate business would pick up. It was the time of year when people's grandmothers went to Carmel; it was the time of year when girls who could not even get into Stephens or Arizona or Oregon, let alone Stanford or Berkeley, would be sent to Honolulu, on the *Lurline*. I have no recollection of anyone going to New York, with the exception of a cousin who visited there (I cannot imagine why) and reported that the shoe salesmen at Lord & Taylor were "intolerably rude." What happened in New York and Washington and abroad seemed to impinge not at all upon the Sacramento mind. I remember being taken to call upon a very old woman, a rancher's widow, who was reminiscing (the favored conversational mode in Sacramento) about the son of some contemporaries of hers. "That Johnston boy never did amount to much," she said. Desultorily, my mother protested: Alva Johnston, she said, had won the Pulitzer Prize, when he was working for *The New York Times*. Our hostess looked at us impassively. "He never amounted to anything in Sacramento," she said.

Hers was the true Sacramento voice, and, although I did not realize it then, one not long to be heard, for the war was over and the boom was on and the voice of the aerospace engineer would be heard in the land. VETS NO DOWN! EXECUTIVE LIVING ON LOW FHA!

Later, when I was living in New York, I would make the trip back to Sacramento four and five times a year (the more comfortable the flight, the more obscurely miserable I would be, for it weighs heavily upon my kind that we could perhaps not make it by wagon), trying to prove that I had not meant to leave at all, because in at least one respect California—the California we are talking about—resembles Eden: it is assumed that those who absent themselves from its blessings have been banished, exiled by some perversity of heart. Did not the Donner-Reed Party, after all, eat its own dead to reach Sacramento?

I have said that the trip back is difficult, and it is—difficult in a way that magnifies the ordinary ambiguities of sentimental journeys. Going back to California is not like going back to Vermont, or Chicago; Vermont and Chicago are relative constants, against which one measures one's own change. All that is constant about the California of my childhood is the rate at which it disappears. An instance: on Saint Patrick's Day of 1948 I was taken to see the legislature "in action," a dismal experience; a handful of florid assemblymen, wearing green hats, were reading Pat-and-Mike jokes into the record. I still think of the legislators that way—wearing green hats, or sitting around on the veranda of the Senator Hotel fanning themselves and being entertained by Artie Samish's emissaries. (Samish was the lobbyist who said, "Earl Warren may be the governor of the state, but I'm the governor of the legislature.") In fact there is no longer a veranda at the Senator Hotel—it was turned into an airline ticket office, if you want to embroider the point—and in any case the legislature has largely deserted the Senator for the flashy motels north of town, where the tiki torches flame and the steam rises off the heated swimming pools in the cold Valley night.

It is hard to *find* California now, unsettling to wonder how much of it was merely imagined or improvised; melancholy to realize how much of anyone's memory is no true memory at all but only the traces of someone else's memory, stories handed down on the family network. I have an indelibly vivid "memory," for example, of how Prohibition affected the hop growers around Sacramento: the sister of a grower my family knew brought home a mink coat from San Francisco, and was told to take it back, and sat on the floor of the parlor cradling that coat and crying. Although I was not born until a year after Repeal, that scene is more "real" to me than many I have played myself.

I remember one trip home, when I sat alone on a night jet from New York and read over and over some lines from a W. S. Merwin poem I had come across in a magazine, a poem about a man who had been a long time in another country and knew that he must go home:

> . . . But it should be
> Soon. Already I defend hotly
> Certain of our indefensible faults,
> Resent being reminded; already in my mind
> Our language becomes freighted with a richness
> No common tongue could offer, while the mountains
> Are like nowhere on earth, and the wide rivers.

You see the point. I want to tell you the truth, and already I have told you about the wide rivers.

It should be clear by now that the truth about the place is elusive, and must be tracked with caution. You might go to Sacramento tomorrow and someone (although no one I know) might take you out to Aerojet-General, which has, in the Sacramento phrase, "something to do with rockets." Fifteen thousand people work for Aerojet, almost all of them imported; a Sacramento lawyer's wife told me, as evidence of how Sacramento was opening up, that she believed she had met one of them, at an open house two Decembers ago. ("Couldn't have been nicer, actually," she added enthusiastically. "I think he and his wife bought the house next *door* to Mary and Al, something like that, which of course was how *they* met him.") So you might go to Aerojet and stand in the big vendors' lobby where a couple of thousand components salesmen try every week to sell their wares and you might look up at the electrical wallboard that lists Aerojet personnel, their projects and their location at any given time, and you might wonder if I have been in Sacramento lately. MINUTEMAN, POLARIS, TITAN, the lights flash, and all the coffee tables are littered with airline schedules, very now, very much in touch.

But I could take you a few miles from there into towns where the banks still bear names like The Bank of Alex Brown, into towns where the one hotel still has an octagonal-tile floor in the dining room and dusty potted palms and big ceiling fans; into towns where everything—the seed business, the Harvester franchise, the hotel, the department store and the main street—carries a single name, the name of the man who built the town. A few Sundays ago I was in a town like that, a town smaller than that, really, no hotel, no Harvester franchise, the bank burned out, a river town. It was the golden anniversary of some of my relatives and it was 110° and the guests of honor sat on straight-backed chairs in front of a sheaf of gladioluses in the Rebekah Hall. I mentioned visiting Aerojet-General to a cousin I saw there, who listened to me with interested disbelief. Which is the true California? That is what we all wonder.

The Midnight Train

R. L. DUFFUS

*In 1906, years before he became a prominent
newspaper editor, R. L. Duffus left Waterbury,
Vermont, to begin his freshman year at
Stanford University. He not only faced the
doubts and concerns of going to college far from
home but was also making the journey only
months after the historic San Francisco
earthquake had spread havoc along the
Northern California coast.*

A FEW minutes after five o'clock on the morning of April 18, 1906, the city
of San Francisco was shaken by an earthquake and shortly afterwards half-
destroyed by fire.

This calamity would not belong in these recollections if the earthquake had
not also shaken Stanford University, thirty miles southeast of San Francisco,
toppled over some buildings and killed two men, one of them an undergraduate;
if, secondly, my brother William had not been a student at Stanford at that time;
and if, thirdly, I had not been planning to join him at the opening of the
September term.

The truth is that many of us, young and old, were longing in those days to
abandon the lovely environment and bracing climate of our native state. My
Aunt Alice had gone to California with her tuberculous husband a few years
before I was born. They had had difficult times, and he had come home to die,
yet she remembered some things that stirred my imagination. She and Uncle
Lucius had lived in the beautifully-named San Bernardino Mountains. Once the
burro she was riding had gathered its four feet together and come down hard on
a rattlesnake, which my aunt found surprising. She and Uncle Lucius had
roughed it, and in spite of the tragedy and apprehension had had some good
times.

Sun and warmth, new opportunities, better living in California's uncrowded
spaces (as they certainly were then), oranges, peaches, prunes, and plums in the
valley, grapes on the foothill slopes and snow on the distant mountains—this
was the kind of allure California offered.

50

But what I wanted was escape. Why did I want to escape? Why did any Vermont boy of that generation want to escape?

At this late date I do not suppose I shall be able to make anybody believe that a young man should yearn with an undying fire to get away from Vermont, though the population figures, in 1906 and later, prove that many young men not only wanted to get away but did.

Today I am glad Vermont is romantic, or seems to be so; but in 1906 I wanted to travel, I wanted to cross the country, I wanted to go to Stanford University, which charged practically no tuition fees and where snow was prohibited, I wanted to go somewhere far away from Waterbury.

I am being careful at this point not to stir up the psychiatrists, who know that wherever you go you carry yourself with you, and that there is no real escape. I don't argue with them. They are good and helpful men.

What was wrong with Vermont? It wasn't necessarily lack of opportunity, for people who wanted to remain at home did so and got along all right. Perhaps I should ask what was wrong then, what is wrong now, what will forever and ever be wrong, with adolescents? If I had not loved Vermont I should not now be remembering it with warm affection and a degree of repentance. If I had loved it a little more I should have remained there.

But I left, or planned to leave, with a sort of whoop. I think I felt hemmed-in. The mountains came too close into the too narrow valleys. There were mountains, also, of old memories, of dead generations, of what one was expected to be—and wasn't. And in one sense the impulse that made my ancestors on my mother's side travel up from Massachusetts, and that had also made my father leave his own native land, made me, as well as my brother, turn toward another land and another promise.

There were depths beyond depths. In California, as I dreamed, I might be a more successful adolescent than I had been in Vermont. I turned toward California, perhaps, as a youngster today may borrow the key of his father's car and scoot madly down the smooth-surfaced highways. In my early day we had no cars to speak of, and no smooth-surfaced highways, but the impulse to scoot was certainly there.

On countless nights when I lay half-sleeping in my grandmother's house I heard the midnight train go by. We were so close, in that narrow village, that it was right under my window. I heard the rush and roar, I lifted up to see the lights of the cars, I heard the engineer whistle for a crossing this side of the Winooski River bridge. How musical that whistle, how fantastic that passage of tumult and lights, what romance and joy went by on the midnight train!

As I had done during my childhood days in Williamstown, so now, at eighteen, I still envied the engineer, opening and closing his throttle, easing his engine to the curves, letting her out on the straight, dashing through Vermont in the middle of the night, tied to no locality, bound, maybe, for Montreal. I never thought of a locomotive engineer as sleeping, I pictured him always at the throttle, serene, strong, unconquerable, traveling down the night and into the far-away dawn.

As I thus lay sleeping, on many a night, I dreamed myself aboard the midnight train, all my troubles behind me, all my wealth of family affection and tradition riding along with me—for I did not then know the cost of departures and late arrivals—into an unknown and fabulous world. If there were young and beautiful women in this enchanted world I would approach them confidently, as I had never done in the real universe called Waterbury; they would wait for me with grave but friendly smiles, hand in hand we would venture further and further into wonders and enchantments—but I believe this is sufficient to suggest why I got sleepy.

The midnight train stopped at Essex Junction to leave passengers destined for Burlington, or to take the luckier passengers who were on their way to Canada and the West. Then, as I knew but for many years never experienced, the train flew on into the abysses of the night, faster than the birds of passage I had seen vaguely overhead in spring, toward Montreal; toward Montreal, where people spoke French as though it were a real language and not something made up to be taught in school; and soon past Montreal, or by some other train into which one would be conducted by implacable destiny, the passenger would penetrate the unimaginable distances, the interplanetary ranges, of the West and Far West.

For five years and more I saw the sunset light die out at Bolton Notch, and darkness come, and in due time the midnight train flash by.

There will never be for me another train like that, never a plane bound for the ends of the earth that will carry the same freight of glamour, never a ship, with the white water under her bows, that will be poetry as was, once, the midnight train.

But for a while after April 18, 1906, I feared I would never catch the midnight train, never ride with it into the night toward the inexpressibly alluring world that drew it onward.

I had been duly notified that I would be admitted to Stanford University, that, as the pictures showed, lay brown and red under the foothills above the Santa Clara Valley. But was there any Stanford University any more? For a week no news came through, not even the telegram my brother had sent as soon as he realized that he had been in a big earthquake and was still alive.

San Francisco was burning. One Stanford student, at least, was dead. That was all we knew. No radio, no television, no transcontinental telephone, not even the overloaded telegraph lines, no airplanes, brought us closer to the scene of the disaster. California was further away than any civilized portion of the earth now.

My brother's telegram came at last, one morning as we sat at breakfast in the big, sunny dining-room, with cheerful smells of coffee and griddle-cakes coming from the kitchen. My aunt answered the knock at the kitchen door with almost startling swiftness, tore open the yellow envelope and came in with laughter. "He's all right," she said. And then she broke down and cried.

"I thought he was," said my mother slowly. But she hadn't been sure. None of us had been.

My grandmother reflected for a little. "I used to think," she began, "that God wouldn't allow the very worst things to happen. I knew they did happen, though. I learned that when I was a very young mother, during the Civil War. Being good, and loving their relatives and friends wouldn't keep men from being hurt or killed. It got so I never wanted to see another telegram—it was always grief they told about. This one didn't, and that's a comfort, for once. I'm selfish, I know. I'm glad Will Duffus is alive and well. If I could raise my hand and let that boy at Stanford who died come alive again, and Will Duffus be dead, I wouldn't. I would not." Her eyes were wet. "I'm a wicked old woman," she concluded.

She wasn't then as old as I am now, nor was she at that time or any other time a wicked woman, but in her honor and in loving memory of her I record this speech.

Little by little the nightmare lifted, I was wide awake again, it was a real world but not an unendurable one. Not only was my brother all right and in good health, not only was my father all right, who had gone to California some months after my brother did in a sad search for better health. Besides this good news, we also learned that Stanford University, several of its buildings lying in ruins, its triumphal arch abbreviated and humbled, its church unsafe for use, its students scattered and unsure, had announced that it would open the same as usual in the late summer of 1906. That was Stanford for you, that was California for you.

This meant that Stanford University was going to have me, myself, a refugee from the beauty, glory, wonder, and melancholy of Vermont, as an entering student. This meant I could pack up and prepare to go. This meant I could say farewell, a fairly long farewell, to Harry Whitehill, Justin Moody, and the *Waterbury Record* and *Stowe Journal,* to all the customers to whom I had faithfully delivered the *Boston Globe,* the *Boston Herald,* and the *Boston Journal* (but no *Boston Transcript,* God forgive us), according to their tastes; to those adorable adolescent, darkly misunderstanding, superficially scornful girls of my own generation who troubled me so much because I could never talk as I wished to them; to Lilith, the comer and goer, the undying principle of femininity, the wrecker and maker of men's souls and bodies, who had come to me so often in the night and often even in the daytime; to the old houses, and to the river and the hills I loved so much without knowing how much I loved them.

My term of service was about over. I went through the rest of it with a lightened heart and also a sense of foreboding, knowing in advance that the Emancipation Proclamation was about to be signed and issued and made absolute.

Every night, as before, the midnight train blazed through, its wheels throwing sparks as it swung to the curve, its windows glaring where the doomed or happy passengers sat, its whistle blowing down the corridors of darkness, like the shriek of a beneficent banshee.

Some day soon, I mused, as I turned on my pillow and felt the gentle, urgent tug of what I considered to be destiny, I shall be on that train. Some day I shall be where I will not have to please Harry Whitehill or listen to Justin Moody. Some day soon I shall lay down my last stick of type, run my last job through the small press, stand for the last time on the shelf of the thundering flat-bed.

Some day soon. I shrank somewhat, deep inside. I wanted to escape. I was also afraid to escape. I was fitted to the clothing of my work, my town, my relatives, my friends; these were not, and never would be threadbare; would I ever fit any other place or set of people again? (The answer, in case anybody is curious, was no; no for almost everybody in the twentieth century that was just beginning to take hold of us all.)

But every night the midnight train went through, and every night I either waked and heard it, or slept and dreamt it; it could not pass my vigil unheard and unobserved. Beauty and glory and fear rode with it down the dark highways of the night toward an uncertain dawn, and in my bed on the second story of my grandmother's house I was still safe and uncommitted.

My brother wrote that he had rented a room in a house in Palo Alto, a mile away from Stanford University, that he and my father would meet me in San Jose, and that we would not have trouble in finding work enough to keep us going comfortably while we went to college.

The days moved forward. I would have liked to see them go more slowly. Now that the weight was off my shoulders and no longer oppressed my mind I was in no hurry. Let July take its time, let the first weeks of August not concern themselves with speed.

Yet I would have sunk into deep despair if I had been told that I must stay and work my fate out under the shadow of my native hills. I did not want to stay, but it was hard to go.

On one of those final days in Waterbury I went uptown on some errand, and returning, saw my grandmother, sitting in her bay window, and waved to her.

She did not speak to me then of what she had been thinking. She had sacrificed much for her daughter's children, myself just one of the three. My brother had already gone. My sister alone would remain, a delicate and pretty little girl, four years younger than myself, who had bravely conquered a spell of ill health but still had to eat nourishing food and get plenty of sleep; I know now what a blessed link with youth she was for my grandmother, mother, and aunt after my brother and I had left.

My aunt looked at me sadly as I came in. "Do you know what your grandmother said?" she asked. "She said, that is the last time I shall ever see Robert walking down that street."

It was true. That street was not for me any more, after that summer. It was shut off, more surely than the time, many years later, when I drove back to Waterbury and found North Main Street being tarred and the State Police—my Lord, the State Police, in Waterbury!—turning traffic away on a Maple Street detour.

I could argue with the State Police, who were most polite and understanding; I could and did; but I could not argue with the years and time, and I couldn't make what wasn't so, and ought to have been so, and hadn't ever been so, become so again.

The State Police let me go through, down the untarred side of Main Street, past the library, on the left, which had been the home of Dr. Henry Janes; past the house, on the right, which had been my grandmother's, and which now offered to passing tourists a lodging for the night. A lodging for the night: that had been my five years in Waterbury, a lodging and a going-on.

But I couldn't foresee all this in 1906. I was a fair-to-middling foreseer, but not that good. I never dreamed, in 1906, that I myself, little Robbie, servant of the *Record*'s presses, distributor of journalistic dreams from Boston and Burlington, would ever sit in the driver's seat of a real automobile, and make the thing go, and tell it where to. I never dreamed I would be that important. Or that one could ever do such a thing and not be considered important.

I was going away, in the summer of 1906. That was the reality, and not the dream. I was going a long time and a long way away.

I did not go on the midnight train after all, but go I did, and in the direction the midnight train traveled. For me it was a midnight train, to be sure, a train running into darkness and from darkness into light, a train I had long wanted to take and feared to take. It left Waterbury about sundown on a date I do not more precisely remember, in the third week of August, 1906.

I never knew, I still do not know, how to deal with decisive occasions. I read and reread the words of great men who have dealt with them, but there are no words for the rest of us, the great majority, who are also touched, each one of us, with destiny. Romeo said when told that Juliet was dead, "Is it e'en so?" And I suppose he spoke for everybody, in good or evil fortune.

Frank Carpenter, as on lesser days and shorter journeys, came to take my trunk to the depot. This was, as usual, long before train time. This drummer-boy of the Army of the Potomac, rich, as I conceived, with memories of Antietam and the Grand Review of 1865, was glad enough to take my trunk, and not be asked about the Grand Review or Antietam. If I had been his age in 1861, I conjectured, would I have had the courage to become a drummer-boy? He did not look like a hero.

I could nevertheless have wished, even then, at the last possible opportunity, to ask Frank Carpenter, did they make you march in front of the company beside the color guard, or did they let you do your drumming a little nearer home, and did the enemy fire on the color-sergeant and let the little drummer go unharmed?

But I couldn't ask Frank Carpenter questions like that. Frank Carpenter was a kindly and now elderly man, patient with adolescents, but the time for the asking of questions was past. I didn't know then that anybody would ever ask questions of myself, such as how was it, what was it like, how did you feel to be a boy of eighteen in Vermont in 1906; I didn't suspect that an older me would ever make such inquiries of a boy who no longer existed—and I do hope this is clear to readers, for it is not very clear to me; it just exists and bothers me.

Frank Carpenter might have replied, it was like being alive at whatever age I then was, under whatever circumstances, and that the being alive matters more than the circumstances.

The great miracle called Now was going on when Frank Carpenter first beat his drum for the edification of a portion of Meade's Second Army Corps. It was still going on, though nobody was being invited to step briskly up and get killed, when I boarded the train in Waterbury, in August, 1906.

There was an extra hour or so after Frank Carpenter had taken my trunk and before it was time, even by the traditional standards of our more than punctual family, to walk down to the station. I sat with my grandmother, who would truly never see me again, nor I her; we sat on the side porch and I wanted very much to tell her a number of things.

What I did was to read her some funny stories out of a magazine we happened to have on a near-by table. She laughed a little, but not as much as I thought she might have.

Then there was a silence. I wanted to say, Grandma, you have given me a home and a high-school education, you and my mother and my Aunt Alice— but especially you, because this is your house in which I have found a lodging; you encouraged me to go on studying when I thought I would have to stop; to you I owe a good part of any adequate work I will ever do, and no part whatever of bad work, or weakness or cowardice; these things I wanted to say, and did not; in Vermont we did not, and the Scottish blood did not compel us.

I felt like crying, but laughed instead; and so I said good bye to Mary Ann Davis, my mother's mother, with all her wisdom, all her humor, and all the richness she had made out of living and partly out of pain and sorrow. I was to see my mother again, after a long interval, and my Aunt Alice, but I was never again in this life to see Mary Ann Davis.

We got through the last formalities, at the house and at the depot, with fortitude. I was on the train now, I was alone for a while, just as I had been five years earlier when I left Williamstown for virtually the last time. But today it was different, I was going on a long journey, and, in spite of possible visits and returns, there was no real going back.

It was five years before I saw Waterbury again.

The train came in, extracted me nonchalantly from my Waterbury life, like an oyster from its shell, and carried me away; I saw Camel's Hump on the left after we had passed Bolton, then it was dark, and I did not know how to go to bed in a Pullman berth.

Next morning early was Canada and a new world, with red-coated Canadian Mounted Police coming aboard for a while, only without horses; and at night the transfer across Chicago, and then the wideness of the continent, the brown-bleached Sacramento Valley, and California, and the new life.

But I know now that the sunset train and the midnight train kept running through Waterbury, with some sad and fatal interruptions, and where I longed to go other young Vermonters also longed, and as I went so did they.

This is what makes room for those who stay home. And where the true romance is, whether in Vermont or somewhere else, I still do not know.

FROM

Out West

DAYTON DUNCAN

*For his "American Journey," Dayton Duncan
followed the historic trail used by explorers
Lewis and Clark during 1804–1806. At
Seaside, Oregon, he watched with mixed
emotions a Pacific sunset somewhere close to
the end of the Lewis and Clark expedition.*

*I*N the spring of 1843 nearly a thousand people gathered their covered wagons
in Independence and Westport, Missouri, waiting for good traveling weather.
The tier of states between the Mississippi and Missouri rivers was already filling
with settlers. Expansion into the Plains was out of the question: It was popularly
known as the American Desert on the maps, and besides, it was still reserved for
the Indians.

Oregon—far beyond the Missouri, far beyond the Rockies—was the new
escape valve and magnet for the restless nation. Reports to the East from Marcus
Whitman and other early visitors to the Columbia region had described fertile
soil and a mild climate with a long growing season, particularly along the
Willamette River. Narcissa Whitman and Eliza Spalding had already proved that
the West was not the exclusive domain of mountain men; women—white
women—could survive and raise families. The government was eager to settle
Oregon as a way of resolving the northwest boundary question with Britain in
the United States's favor. The promise of free land and new opportunity hung
redolent in the spring air as the wagons left Missouri. The Great Migration had
begun.

Nothing like this had been done before. Expeditions like Lewis and Clark's
had covered this distance, but they had been military-exploratory parties whose
purpose was to venture west and return. Mountain men and gangs of fur traders
had formed impromptu communities in the wilderness with their yearly rendezvous, but those were only as permanent as a campfire and the whites who
showed up were exclusively male. Smatterings of missionaries had gone west, a
few with wives and families in tow, but their numbers were minuscule. This
wagon train of 1843 was something new. It would traverse two thousand land
miles not for exploration but for emigration; its goal was not trapping or

proselytizing but settling permanently in a new land. It was comprised primarily of families. There were more milk cows than people, and many of the people were women and children.

When the wagon train arrived at what now is The Dalles, the prairie schooners had to be abandoned for real boats to reach Fort Vancouver by river. From there, the emigrants moved up the Willamette River to a point south of modern Portland and selected homesites. Their arrival doubled the American population in Oregon.

The mighty engine of Manifest Destiny was fueled by many sources as it jumped the nation's boundaries over the Rockies and to the far West before turning back to settle the open stretches of the Plains. Land fever drew the wagons along the Platte River and over South Pass into Oregon, which became a state in 1859, thirty years before Montana and the two Dakotas were admitted to the Union. California was grabbed from Mexico in the war of 1846; the Gold Rush of '49 turned the stream of westbound settlers into a flood, and what had been Mexican territory only four years earlier became the thirty-first state in 1850. Meanwhile, the Mormons were also heading west along the opposite shore of the Platte, seeking neither gold nor land for its own sake but as much distance as possible between them and the mob that had murdered their martyr, Joseph Smith, in Illinois. Zion was reestablished in the basin of the Great Salt Lake. Only after the mountains had been conquered and the western coast populated did settlers begin filling the vast portion of America first explored by Lewis and Clark. The frontier collapsed upon itself, and in 1890 the Census Bureau declared it officially closed.

Most of the migrations since that time have been from the land of the pioneers to the gleaming cities. Jefferson's dream of a nation of small farmers has become a country of service-industry employees clustered in suburbs. The descendants of people who crossed half the continent in an ox-drawn wagon for the chance at 640 acres of free land now define space in terms of front lawns or so many square feet in a condominium complex. Their favored outlet for restlessness is cheap airfare to a vacation spot on the Mexican coast, or maybe a trip to Yellowstone to watch the bears feed at the garbage dumps.

Sucked into the vortex of rush-hour traffic as I approach Portland (population 366,383) and the mouth of the river valley that was the Promised Land for the Great Migration, the *Discovery* becomes just one more small fish in the school of cascading metal and rubber. For the first time since Omaha and Kansas City the big-city tension grips my body. Which exit from the six-lane thruway should I take? Which lane should I be in? Am I the only traveler unfamiliar with this city, uncertain of his route, unfocused in this hurried race between work and home?

Never fond of metropolises to begin with, I find my preference for small towns

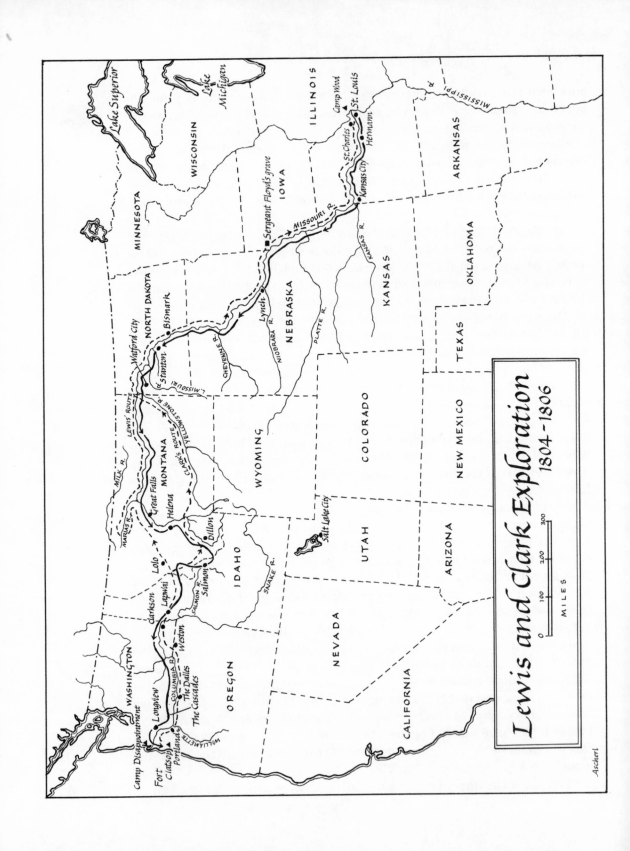

Lewis and Clark Exploration
1804-1806

MILES
0   100   200   300

Ascheri

and open spaces has only been reinforced by this trail. Towns like Hermann, Missouri; Lynch, Nebraska; Watford City, North Dakota; Dillon, Montana; Lapwai, Idaho; Stevenson, Washington; even all of Harrison County, Iowa— they could be lumped together and moved to a city and still not make a suburb big enough to warrant its own exit. But obviously I'm out of step. Most of those towns are, in fact, picking up and moving piecemeal from country to city. Within my own brief lifetime, nearly 80 percent of the 23 million Americans living on farms have moved, most of them to cities. Census Bureau statistics show that in the same thirty-five years, the percentage of Americans in non-metropolitan areas has declined from nearly a third to less than a quarter of the population.

Not that Portland is a bad place, as big cities go. It's cleaner than most, either because of civic pride or the heavy coastal rains or both. It feels both vibrant and laid back—a West Coast city with all the urban bustle but without the hard edge of, say, Los Angeles or any Eastern city you can name. (On the day of my visit, the major news is that city officials have become concerned about the growing population of hoboes and bums living in the freight yards under the interstate cloverleafs. But, in a spirit that Fry Pan Jack would appreciate, the city has decided to warn the transients in advance before dispatching the police to sweep the area; most of them will be offered temporary shelter by charities or the city government.) The city center has tree-lined boulevards and flowery parks; the big harbor is a working port, unmarked by the empty buildings or upscale boutiques that characterize the former commercial centers of too many other cities.

So many people: well-dressed professionals walking purposefully along the streets, the women wearing sneakers and bouncing as they stroll; teenagers displaying this year's fashion rebellion with their orange- and purple-tinted spikes of hair; hoboes on street benches, adjusting to the ambiance in the polite way they panhandle; and, proving that Jefferson's vision of the importance of interchange with the Orient has not been abandoned, a heavy mixture of Asian-Americans. (Just as every Missouri town from St. Louis to Weston claims to be the Gateway to the West, every town on the Columbia from Portland to the river's mouth calls itself the Gateway to the Pacific Rim.)

So many stores and shops: asking about a camera store to buy supplies, I am directed to three within a two-block area. I pass one cafe, bigger and busier than most I have eaten in for the last two months, that specializes just in cookies and coffee; on one street corner, enough newspaper boxes to provide papers for the entire population of a small town.

I find supper at a Thai restaurant, my first "non-American" meal since an ill-conceived visit to a Chinese restaurant in Bismarck; here, at least, the cuisine and personnel share the same heritage, and the meal is savory proof that the axiom "When in Rome, etc." has a lot of wisdom in it and should be remembered whenever you visit cities named after Prussian chancellors. Western hospitality isn't necessarily confined to small towns: one of the people I interview in Portland lets me sleep on a mattress in a spare room.

And so, despite my biases, I find myself liking Portland. Or at least not disliking Portland. One of the reasons I prefer smaller communities is brought back into focus on the day I leave and find myself again in the midst of the twice-daily, twentieth-century version of the Great Migration. One of the best local views of Mount Hood is from the interstate bridge crossing the Columbia River. When I turn for a final look at the volcano's cone, I inadvertently slow down to something approaching the legal speed limit and am nearly run over by the crush of vehicles intent on shaving four minutes off their three-mile trip.

> ROAD RULE 20: Prejudices are like heavy furniture in a Conestoga wagon on the Oregon Trail. In order to keep moving forward, sometimes you have to toss them out, even if they are family heirlooms.

More than fifty years ago, when Bob Lange was a young Boy Scout in Oregon, he went off to a summer camp named Camp Meriwether in honor of Captain Lewis. One of the camp activities was a mini-pageant in which the Corps of Discovery's historic journey was reenacted. The Scouts would walk forest trails, stop at small replicas of Mandan lodges, walk some more, stop at a miniature version of Fort Clatsop (the expedition's winter quarters on the Oregon coast), and learn about the explorers on the way. As he grew older and started traveling the state for an electrical-supplies distributor, Lange would stop at libraries and check out books about the expedition. At night, in a motel room, he began reading the first of the eight-volume edition of the journals. He hasn't stopped reading them since.

Retired now at age seventy, Lange spends about five hours every day in his study, literally surrounded by Lewis and Clark. As he sits at his desk, portraits of the captains are at his right shoulder. The rest of his study includes additional paintings and pictures of the expedition, framed maps, figurines and whiskey bottles commemorating individual expedition members, a rock from the site in northern Montana where Lewis fought and killed two Blackfeet Indians, loose-leaf notebooks systematically arranged with material about every aspect of the trail, and, of course, an edition of the journals that is his own, lined up on a rack within an arm's reach of his typewriter.

It is safe to say that, with the possible exception of professional historians who have studied it for a living, Bob Lange is the most knowledgeable living American on the topic of Lewis and Clark. He has visited every spot along the long trail not once, but several times. In addition to the captains' journals, he has read and reread those of Sergeants Patrick Gass and John Ordway and Private Joseph Whitehouse, and the abbreviated journal of Sergeant Charles Floyd, whose last entry was made shortly before he died near Sioux City. Lange's name crops up in the acknowledgments of most modern books written about the expedition, because he is as important a source as a library.

He is one of the leading lights of the Lewis and Clark Trail Heritage Foundation Inc., a nonprofit organization devoted to keeping the expedition's memory alive. The foundation has about a thousand members—schoolteachers, secretaries, business executives, farmers, lawyers, housewives—whose common interest is the Corps of Discovery. Lange served as president during its early years; his wife, Ruth, keeps the membership rolls.

Lange's labor of love is being editor of *We Proceeded On,* the group's quarterly magazine that takes its name from the most repeated phrase in the journals. In its pages, scholars and amateurs alike explore various aspects of the expedition, from sweeping topics such as the role of Clark's maps in American settlement of the West to the details of what happened to the plant specimens Lewis brought back to Jefferson; from Lewis and Clark as ethnologists to a description of how the air gun they used to impress the Indians actually worked. An edition devoted solely to Lewis's Newfoundland dog has gone into three printings.

He and I have lunch with Irving Anderson, whose specialty is the Charbonneau family: the French trapper-interpreter so often maligned in the journals, his infant son, Jean Baptiste, and of course Mrs. Charbonneau, the more-famous Sacagawea. If uniformity in the place names, statues, parks, and descriptions devoted to the Indian woman is ever achieved, it will be credited to Anderson's messianic mission to correct what he considers "false history."

A former documents specialist for the Bureau of Land Management, Anderson is a stickler for documentation. His persistence helped confirm the site near Danner, Oregon, where Jean Baptiste died in 1866. Anderson's self-imposed task of correcting the mistaken popular image of the Indian woman's name, her actual role in the expedition, and how and where her life ended is more daunting. Too many people have read the novels about her and accepted them as fact.

In any case, it is a pleasant afternoon with Lange and Anderson, swapping stories about the American epic as if we'd been along on it and had gotten together today in a reunion of the last three surviving members. We inspect the snowberry bush that grows outside the Lange home, a species Lewis discovered in the Bitterroots. It needs pruning, but Lange shakes his head. "You can't cut down Lewis's plant," he says. Ruth Lange serves a good meal and sits in on the conversation. Private George Shannon, the youngest member of the expedition, the one who seemed to have the habit of getting lost all the time, is her favorite, she says. Lange is one of the few Lewis and Clark buffs who doesn't have a favorite character or episode; he revels in it all.

At the urging of the Langes and Irving Anderson, I stop in Longview, Washington (population 30,950), to see Hazel Bain, a former president of the Lewis and Clark Trail Heritage Foundation. Her living room is a scaled-down version of Lange's study, filled with Lewis and Clark paintings, plates, bottles, placemats, postcards, and books. She takes me to the high, arched bridge that I need to cross to get back to U.S. 30 for the final drive to the coast. It used to be called the Longview Columbia River Bridge. In 1980, on the 175th anniversary of the explorers' passage, Hazel Bain was one of the dignitaries at the ceremony renaming it the Lewis and Clark Bridge. As testimony to her efforts in promoting the legislation necessary for the new name, among the memorabilia in Hazel's living room is the pen Washington's governor used to sign the bill.

Driving west toward the Coast Range you understand where all the "moisture" is that doesn't make it past the Cascades and Bitterroots and Rockies, and where all the trees grow that are missing from the Dakotas and Nebraska. The town names tell the story: Forest Grove, Woodland, Timber, Mist. The thick growth of conifers is one of the few examples of a true rain forest outside of the tropics. A lumber truck passes, fully loaded with just four trunk sections of a pine whose diameter is wider than the height of the burr oaks along the Missouri. The forests are so dense here that you wonder where the first tree is supposed to fall when a cutting operation begins; the air is so damp that an explorer without a razor would probably grow moss instead of a beard.

"Disagreeable" is the word that replaced "we proceeded on" as most used in the expedition's journal entries here. It rained constantly. On November 7, 1805, Clark reports "Great joy in camp we are in view of the Ocian, this great Pacific Ocian which we been so long anxious to See. and the roreing or noise made by the waves brakeing on the rockey Shores (as I suppose) may be heard disti[n]ctly." In truth, it was Gray's Bay near the broad mouth of the Columbia, not the Pacific itself, they were seeing and hearing. Wind, rain, and waves pinned the group on the lee side of Ellice's Point for five days until a break in the rough seas allowed them to round the point and make camp on the western side, where Clark decided this "would be the extent of our journey by water, as the waves were too high at any stage for our Canoes to proceed further down." Nine more "disagreeable" days were spent here in the rain while the men's buckskin clothing continued to rot on their soaked bodies. They were out of salt, flour, and meat, and survived on pounded salmon. Clark estimated that from the mouth of the Missouri to this "land's end," the Corps of Discovery had traveled 4,162 miles.

Small parties reconnoitered the area surrounding the promontory of Cape Disappointment (named such by Captain John Meares, who erroneously but understandably concluded in 1788 that the bay behind was not the mouth of the Great River of the West), hoping in vain to encounter a white trading vessel. Camping here for the winter was out of the question. Game was scarce, and the flea-infested Chinook tribes were bothersome. Told that elk were abundant on the southern, Oregon side of the river's mouth, the captains proposed moving across or returning to a site back up the Columbia. The issue was put to a vote, and in a ceremony that would predate the exercise of democracy in the United States by sixty-five and one hundred and fifteen years, respectively, York (a black slave) and Sacagawea (a woman and an Indian) were allowed to participate. The vote was overwhelming for wintering on the Oregon side if game could be found there. Elk was needed for food and for hides to replace the moldy clothing; the climate would be more moderate than farther upriver; salt would be available from the sea; and remaining near the coast was important because they still harbored the hope that a trading vessel would appear to replenish their supplies and take the journals and collected botanical specimens back to civilization. (The idea of returning the whole expedition by sea was apparently never contemplated.)

On November 26, 1805, a break in the weather allowed them to cross the fifteen-mile-wide river to a spot near modern-day Astoria. The weather was still miserable. "This is our present situation!" Clark notes, now using exclamation points more often in his entries, "Truly disagreeable." Lewis and a small group scouted the area. Before Lewis returned with the welcome news that a small rise several miles up what is now Lewis and Clark River would be a good spot for winter quarters, Clark, the inveterate graffiti artist, carved the following into the side of a spruce tree: "Capt William Clark December 3rd 1805. By land. U. States in 1804–1805." The expedition moved to Lewis's selected spot and began building a small fort on December 8. By the thirtieth, the finishing touches were made to Fort Clatsop, where they would remain for four wet, disagreeable months.

Chasing one more sunset, I spur the *Discovery* down U.S. 30 along the dense canyons of spruce and fir. There is no sky. A gray cloud cover rests on the treetops. Astoria, Oregon (population 10,000), appears on the hilly banks of the river mouth, the oldest town in the Pacific Northwest, founded in 1811 as part of John Jacob Astor's ill-fated attempt at a continental fur monopoly. Crossing the river on another toll bridge, I make a hurried visit to the Lewis and Clark Interpretative Center atop Cape Disappointment, an impressive display of the expedition's history on a site with an impressive view of the treacherous bar that had deceived and disappointed so many seagoing explorers until Gray sailed through to stake America's claim to the Columbia. The odometer on the *Discovery* says we've traveled 6,156 miles since we left Wood River, Illinois, a little shy of two months ago.

Back in Astoria, I stop for supplies. The Park Service has kindly agreed that tomorrow night, once the tourists leave, I can sleep in the reconstruction of Fort Clatsop. At a Scandinavian festival, I buy some Norwegian dark bread in honor of my grandmother's heritage. At a smokehouse, I purchase some salmon jerky, some smoked winter chinook salmon, and a bag of chocolate-covered huckleberries. No need to go overboard in trying to relive the expedition's experience. Like Clark, I'll take salmon over dog meat; but I'll also have bread where they didn't, and a dessert. (I've also got a bottle of Lewis and Clark bourbon from Montana, something the men would have killed for at this point.)

The chocolate-covered huckleberries and my inability to save them all for tomorrow night at Fort Clatsop almost bring my trip to a tragicomic end. Pulling up to a red light at the intersection of Highways 30 and 101, I pop a huckleberry in my mouth, chew it too quickly, and swallow in mid-breath. A big gob of chocolate and berry lodges in my windpipe. No air.

Lewis and Clark, I am pleased to report, were not the only explorers in American history who knew how to practice emergency folk medicine on the trail. In the time it takes to construct the headline *Failure to Find Passage Results in Corpse of Discovery* I am out the front door, put my doubled fists just below my rib cage, and run myself three times into the flat front of the camper. This is called a self-administered Heimlich Maneuver, a handy thing to know if you breathe through your mouth. The pressure on my diaphragm blows the ball of food up and out of the windpipe, and I can start rewriting the headline in the fresh, salt air. Climbing back into the front seat, I make a mental note to put the huckleberries in the cooler so the chocolate won't melt before tomorrow night. The light changes, and I proceed on. The guy in the car behind the *Discovery* is still sitting at the intersection with a stunned look on his face.

> ROAD RULE 21: Always carry a first-aid kit in your vehicle. Indians and non-Indians often require "medicine" in their travels.
>
> FIRST COROLLARY: Sometimes your vehicle itself is a first-aid tool. This is called "Big Medicine."

My last westbound sunset occurs in Seaside, Oregon (population 5,193), a honky-tonk resort community already bustling with summer tourists. For the first and only time on my journey, I have to stop at four motels before I can find one with a vacancy. The restaurant I visit for a supper of fresh razor clams is jammed with people, and there is a long wait for a table. History repeats itself:

prices for room and board are almost double what I have grown used to farther inland. At least there aren't any fleas.

During their winter at Fort Clatsop, a small contingent from the expedition established a camp here to boil seawater and make salt for the return trip. The salt cairn has been preserved, thanks primarily to Olin Wheeler, a historian who retraced the Lewis and Clark trail and wrote of the changes along the route on the centennial of the expedition. It rests in a small lot between two houses in the residential section of Seaside.

Farther south on the coast, Clark led an excursion in January to view a whale that the Indians reported had been washed ashore. Sacagawea pleaded to go along. "She observed that She had traveled a long way with us to See the great waters," Clark writes, "and that now that monstrous fish was also to be Seen, She thought it verry hard that She could not be permitted to See either (She had never yet been to the Ocian)." Indians had already picked the whale carcass clean by the time Clark's party, including Sacagawea, arrived. The captain bought three hundred pounds of blubbery meat and a few gallons of rendered oil, measured the 105-foot skeleton, and returned to the fort. At a campsite in what is now Ecola State Park, Clark "beheld the grandest and most pleasing prospect which my eyes ever surveyed, in my frount a boundless Ocian; to the N. and N.E. the coast as far as my sight could be extended, the Seas rageing with emence waves and breaking with great force." Cannon Beach, a more restrained and pleasant resort community than Seaside, sits along the sandy shore where the whale was beached; the waves still crash against Haystack Rock as spectacularly as they did when Clark and the astonished Indian woman surveyed the scene.

In Seaside, the main street, Broadway, runs due west past saltwater taffy shops, caramel stands, T-shirt emporiums, a bumpercar and video arcade, a one-hour photo business, more gift shops and cafes (one is named the Dog House, a place the expedition undoubtedly would have patronized), and a hotel before it reaches the Lewis and Clark Turnaround. A marker says that the Oregon legislature has declared this the official end of the Lewis and Clark trail and the westernmost point where the expedition camped. *Well* . . . Not quite on either count.

But it's as good a spot as any to sit and watch the sun sink into the water, a Farewell Sunset. The ocean, at low tide, hisses rather than roars. A thick mist clings to the hills to the south. Cloud banks out to sea look like yet another mountain range across a liquid plain. On Broadway, the traffic is heavy. Most of it is comprised of young kids, driving Jeeps and rumbling cars with their windows down and their tape decks blaring rock music. Westward they roll, one behind the other in an unending line, restless and impatient and exuberant in the summer of their youth. One by one the vehicles noisily, eagerly approach the "official end" of America's probe west. Each one sends a fragment of loud music, an insistent bass heartbeat of life pulsing out its window. Then they pass the marker and its flagpole, arc around the circle, catch one brief glimpse of the sun that can be pursued no farther, and head east down the same street.

The gold sun has touched the horizon now, distorting like a hot egg yolk dropped on water. It lingers for a moment, allowing one last look from the continent it has crossed in a day, and sinks from sight.

FROM

A Tour
on the Prairies

WASHINGTON IRVING

*The early popularity of Washington Irving's
"travel book," published in 1835, could be
attributed to the author's universally accepted
literary gifts. But his spontaneous joy in the
discovery of life and awesome landscapes
beyond the western frontier must have
rewarded readers then as it does today. Irving
accompanied a troop of U.S. Rangers on an
1832 mission that took them through the
Indian lands of what became Oklahoma. In
these journal entries he writes of a "beautiful
encampment," his education among the
Delawares, and the spectacle of prairie
thunderstorms.*

*H*AVING passed through the skirt of woodland bordering the river, we
ascended the hills, taking a westerly course through an undulating country of
"oak openings," where the eye stretched over wide tracts of hill and dale,
diversified by forests, groves, and clumps of trees. As we were proceeding at a
slow pace, those who were at the head of the line descried four deer grazing on a
grassy slope about half a mile distant. They apparently had not perceived our
approach, and continued to graze in perfect tranquillity. A young ranger obtained permission from the Captain to go in pursuit of them, and the troop
halted in lengthened line, watching him in silence. Walking his horse slowly and
cautiously, he made a circuit until a screen of wood intervened between him and
the deer. Dismounting then, he left his horse among the trees, and creeping
round a knoll, was hidden from our view. We now kept our eyes intently fixed
on the deer, which continued grazing, unconscious of their danger. Presently
there was the sharp report of a rifle; a fine buck made a convulsive bound and
fell to the earth; his companions scampered off. Immediately our whole line of
march was broken; there was a helter-skelter galloping of the youngsters of the

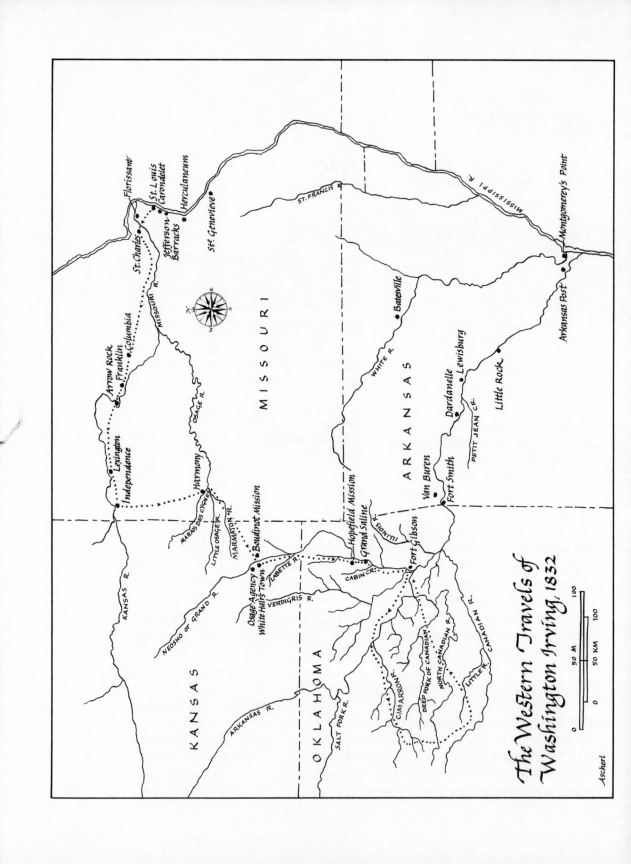

The Western Travels of Washington Irving, 1832

troop, eager to get a shot at the fugitives; and one of the most conspicuous personages in the chase was our little Frenchman, Tonish, on his silver-gray; having abandoned his pack-horses at the first sight of the deer. It was some time before our scattered forces could be recalled by the bugle, and our march resumed.

Two or three times in the course of the day we were interrupted by hurry-scurry scenes of the kind. The young men of the troop were full of excitement on entering an unexplored country abounding in game, and they were too little accustomed to discipline or restraint to be kept in order. No one, however, was more unmanageable than Tonish. Having an intense conceit of his skill as a hunter, and an irrepressible passion for display, he was continually sallying forth, like an ill-broken hound, whenever any game was started, and had as often to be whipped back.

At length his curiosity got a salutary check. A fat doe came bounding along in full view of the whole line. Tonish dismounted, levelled his rifle, and had a fair shot. The doe kept on. He sprang upon his horse, stood up on the saddle like a posture-master, and continued gazing after the animal as if certain to see it fall. The doe, however, kept on its way rejoicing; a laugh broke out along the line, the little Frenchman slipped quietly into his saddle, began to belabor and blaspheme the wandering pack-horses, as if they had been to blame, and for some time we were relieved from his vaunting and vaporing.

In one place of our march we came to the remains of an old Indian encampment, on the banks of a fine stream, with the moss-grown skulls of deer lying here and there about it. As we were in the Pawnee country, it was supposed, of course, to have been a camp of those formidable rovers; the Doctor, however, after considering the shape and disposition of the lodges, pronounced it the camp of some bold Delawares, who had probably made a brief dashing excursion into these dangerous hunting grounds.

Having proceeded some distance farther, we observed a couple of figures on horseback, slowly moving parallel to us along the edge of a naked hill about two miles distant; and apparently reconnoitering us. There was a halt, and much gazing and conjecturing. Were they Indians? If Indians, were they Pawnees? There is something exciting to the imagination and stirring to the feelings, while traversing these hostile plains, in seeing a horseman prowling along the horizon. It is like descrying a sail at sea in time of war, when it may be either a privateer or a pirate. Our conjectures were soon set at rest by reconnoitering the two horsemen through a small spyglass, when they proved to be two of the men we had left at the camp, who had set out to rejoin us, and had wandered from the track.

Our march this day was animating and delightful. We were in a region of adventure; breaking our way through a country hitherto untrodden by white men, except perchance by some solitary trapper. The weather was in its perfection, temperate, genial and enlivening; a deep blue sky with a few light feathery clouds, an atmosphere of perfect transparency, an air pure and bland, and a glorious country spreading out far and wide in the golden sunshine of an autumnal day; but all silent, lifeless, without a human habitation, and apparently without a human inhabitant! It was as if a ban hung over this fair but fated region. The very Indians dared not abide here, but made it a mere scene of perilous enterprise, to hunt for a few days, and then away.

After a march of about fifteen miles west we encamped in a beautiful peninsula, made by the windings and doublings of a deep, clear, and almost motionless brook, and covered by an open grove of lofty and magnificent trees. Several hunters immediately started forth in quest of game before the noise of the camp should frighten it from the vicinity. Our man, Beatte, also took his rifle and went forth alone, in a different course from the rest.

For my own part, I lay on the grass under the trees, and built castles in the clouds, and indulged in the very luxury of rural repose. Indeed I can scarcely conceive a kind of life more calculated to put both mind and body in a healthful tone. A morning's ride of several hours diversified by hunting incidents; an encampment in the afternoon under some noble grove on the borders of a stream; an evening banquet of venison, fresh killed, roasted, or broiled, on the coals; turkeys just from the thickets and wild honey from the trees; and all relished with an appetite unknown to the gourmets of the cities. And at night— such sweet sleeping in the open air, or waking and gazing at the moon and stars, shining between the trees!

On the present occasion, however, we had not much reason to boast of our larder. But one deer had been killed during the day, and none of that had reached our lodge. We were fain, therefore, to stay our keen appetites by some scraps of turkey brought from the last encampment, eked out with a slice or two of salt pork. This scarcity, however, did not continue long. Before dark a young hunter returned well laden with spoil. He had shot a deer, cut it up in an artist-like style, and, putting the meat in a kind of sack made of the hide, had slung it across his shoulder and trudged with it to camp.

Not long after, Beatte made his appearance with a fat doe across his horse. It was the first game he had brought in, and I was glad to see him with a trophy that might efface the memory of the polecat. He laid the carcass down by our fire without saying a word, and then turned to unsaddle his horse; nor could any questions from us about his hunting draw from him more than laconic replies. If Beatte, however, observed this Indian taciturnity about what he had done, Tonish made up for it by boasting of what he meant to do. Now that we were in a good hunting country he meant to take the field, and, if we would take his word for it, our lodge would henceforth be overwhelmed with game. Luckily his talking did not prevent his working, the doe was skilfully dissected, several fat ribs roasted before the fire, the coffee kettle replenished, and in a little while we were enabled to indemnify ourselves luxuriously for our late meagre repast.

The Captain did not return until late, and he returned empty handed. He had been in pursuit of his usual game, the deer, when he came upon the tracks of a gang of about sixty elk. Having never killed an animal of the kind, and the elk being at this moment an object of ambition among all the veteran hunters of the camp, he abandoned his pursuit of the deer, and followed the newly discovered track. After some time he came in sight of the elk, and had several fair chances of a shot, but was anxious to bring down a large buck, which kept in the advance. Finding at length there was danger of the whole gang escaping him, he fired at a doe. The shot took effect, but the animal had sufficient strength to keep on for a time with its companions. From the tracks of blood he felt confident it was mortally wounded, but evening came on, he could not keep the trail, and had to give up the search until morning.

Old Ryan and his little band had not yet rejoined us, neither had our young half-breed Antoine made his appearance. It was determined, therefore, to remain at our encampment for the following day, to give time for all stragglers to arrive.

The conversation this evening, among the old huntsmen, turned upon the Delaware tribe, one of whose encampments we had passed in the course of the day; and anecdotes were given of their prowess in war and dexterity in hunting. They used to be deadly foes of the Osages, who stood in great awe of their desperate valor, though they were apt to attribute it to a whimsical cause. "Look at the Delawares," would they say, "dey got short leg—no can run—must stand and fight a great heap." In fact the Delawares are rather short legged, while the Osages are remarkable for length of limb.

The expeditions of the Delawares, whether of war or hunting, are wide and fearless; a small band of them will penetrate far into these dangerous and hostile wilds, and will push their encampments even to the Rocky Mountains. This daring temper may be in some measure encouraged by one of the superstitions of their creed. They believe that a guardian spirit, in the form of a great eagle, watches over them, hovering in the sky, far out of sight. Sometimes, when well pleased with them, he wheels down into the lower regions, and may be seen circling with widespread wings against the white clouds; at such time the seasons are propitious, the corn grows finely, and they have great success in hunting. Sometimes, however, he is angry, and then he vents his rage in the thunder, which is his voice, and the lightning, which is the flashing of his eye, and strikes dead the object of his displeasure.

The Delawares make sacrifices to this spirit, who occasionally lets drop a feather from his wing in token of satisfaction. These feathers render the wearer invisible, and invulnerable. Indeed, the Indians generally consider the feathers of the eagle possessed of occult and sovereign virtues.

At one time a party of the Delawares, in the course of a bold excursion into the Pawnee hunting grounds, were surrounded on one of the great plains, and nearly destroyed. The remnant took refuge on the summit of one of those isolated and conical hills which rise almost like artificial mounds, from the midst of the prairies. Here the chief warrior, driven almost to despair, sacrificed his horse to the tutelar spirit. Suddenly an enormous eagle, rushing down from the sky, bore off the victim in his talons, and mounting into the air, dropped a quill feather from his wing. The chief caught it up with joy, bound it to his forehead, and, leading his followers down the hill, cut his way through the enemy with great slaughter, and without any one of his party receiving a wound.

Our march for a part of the day lay a little to the south of west, through straggling forests of the kind of low scrubbed trees already mentioned, called "post-oaks" and "black-jacks." The soil of these "oak barrens" is loose and unsound; being little better at times than a mere quicksand, in which, in rainy weather, the horse's hoof slips from side to side, and now and then sinks in a rotten, spongy turf, to the fetlock. Such was the case at present in consequence of successive thunder-showers, through which we draggled along in dogged silence. Several deer were roused by our approach, and scudded across the forest glades; but no one, as formerly, broke the line of march to pursue them. At one time, we passed the bones and horns of a buffalo, and at another time a buffalo track, not above three days old. These signs of the vicinity of this grand game of the prairies, had a reviving effect on the spirits of our huntsmen; but it was of transient duration.

In crossing a prairie of moderate extent, rendered little better than a slippery bog by the recent showers, we were overtaken by a violent thunder-gust. The rain came rattling upon us in torrents, and spattered up like steam along the ground; the whole landscape was suddenly wrapped in gloom that gave a vivid effect to the intense sheets of lightning, while the thunder seemed to burst over our very heads, and was reverberated by the groves and forests that checkered and skirted the prairie. Man and beast were so pelted, drenched, and confounded, that the line was thrown in complete confusion; some of the horses were so frightened as to be almost unmanageable, and our scattered cavalcade looked like a tempest-tossed fleet, driven hither and thither, at the mercy of wind and wave.

At length, at half past two o'clock, we came to a halt, and gathering together our forces, encamped in an open and lofty grove, with a prairie on one side and a stream on the other. The forest immediately rang with the sound of the axe, and the crash of falling trees. Huge fires were soon blazing; blankets were stretched before them, by way of tents; booths were hastily reared of bark and skins; every fire had its group drawn close round it, drying and warming themselves, or preparing a comforting meal. Some of the rangers were discharging and cleaning their rifles, which had been exposed to the rain; while the horses, relieved from their saddles and burdens, rolled in the wet grass.

The showers continued from time to time, until late in the evening. Before dark, our horses were gathered in and tethered about the skirts of the camp, within the outposts, through fear of Indian prowlers, who are apt to take advantage of stormy nights for their depredations and assaults. As the night thickened, the huge fires became more and more luminous; lighting up masses of the overhanging foliage, and leaving other parts of the grove in deep gloom. Every fire had its goblin group around it, while the tethered horses were dimly seen, like spectres, among the thickets; excepting that here and there a gray one stood out in bright relief.

The grove, thus fitfully lighted up by the ruddy glare of the fires, resembled a vast leafy dome, walled in by opaque darkness; but every now and then two or three quivering flashes of lightning in quick succession, would suddenly reveal a vast champaign country, where fields and forests, and running streams, would start, as it were, into existence for a few brief seconds, and, before the eye could ascertain them, vanish again into gloom.

A thunder-storm on a prairie, as upon the ocean, derives grandeur and sublimity from the wild and boundless waste over which it rages and bellows. It is not surprising that these awful phenomena of nature should be objects of superstitious reverence to the poor savages, and that they should consider the thunder the angry voice of the Great Spirit. As our half-breeds sat gossiping round the fire, I drew from them some of the notions entertained on the subject by their Indian friends. The latter declare that extinguished thunderbolts are sometimes picked up by hunters on the prairies, who use them for the heads of arrows and lances, and that any warrior thus armed is invincible. Should a thunder-storm occur, however, during battle, he is liable to be carried away by the thunder, and never heard of more.

A warrior of the Konza tribe, hunting on a prairie, was overtaken by a storm, and struck down senseless by the thunder. On recovering, he beheld the thunderbolt lying on the ground, and a horse standing beside it. Snatching up the bolt, he sprang upon the horse, but found, too late, that he was astride of the lightning. In an instant he was whisked away over prairies and forests, and streams and desert, until he was flung senseless at the foot of the Rocky Mountains; whence, on recovering, it took him several months to return to his own people.

This story reminded me of an Indian tradition, related by a traveller, of the fate of a warrior who saw the thunder lying upon the ground, with a beautifully wrought moccason on each side of it. Thinking he had found a prize, he put on the moccasons; but they bore him away to the land of spirits, whence he never returned.

These are simple and artless tales, but they had a wild and romantic interest heard from the lips of half-savage narrators, round a hunter's fire, on a stormy night, with a forest on one side, and a howling waste on the other; and where, peradventure, savage foes might be lurking in the outer darkness.

Our conversation was interrupted by a loud clap of thunder, followed immediately by the sound of a horse galloping off madly into the waste. Every one listened in mute silence. The hoofs resounded vigorously for a time, but grew fainter and fainter, until they died away in remote distance.

When the sound was no longer to be heard, the listeners turned to conjecture what could have caused this sudden scamper. Some thought the horse had been startled by the thunder; others, that some lurking Indian had galloped off with him. To this it was objected, that the usual mode with the Indians is to steal quietly upon the horse, take off his fetters, mount him gently, and walk him off as silently as possible, leading off others, without any unusual stir or noise to disturb the camp.

On the other hand, it was stated as a common practice with the Indians, to creep among a troop of horses when grazing at night, mount one quietly, and then start off suddenly at full speed. Nothing is so contagious among horses as a panic; one sudden break-away of this kind, will sometimes alarm the whole troop, and they will set off, helter-skelter, after the leader.

Every one who had a horse grazing on the skirts of the camp was uneasy, lest his should be the fugitive; but it was impossible to ascertain the fact until morning. Those who had tethered their horses felt more secure; though horses thus tied up, and limited to a short range at night, are apt to fall off in flesh and strength, during a long march; and many of the horses of the troop already gave signs of being way-worn.

After a gloomy and unruly night, the morning dawned bright and clear, and a glorious sunrise transformed the whole landscape, as if by magic. The late dreary wilderness brightened into a fine open country, with stately groves, and clumps of oaks of a gigantic size, some of which stood singly, as if planted for ornament and shade, in the midst of rich meadows; while our horses, scattered about, and grazing under them, gave to the whole the air of a noble park. It was difficult to realize the fact that we were so far in the wilds beyond the residence of man. Our encampment, alone, had a savage appearance, with its rude tents of skins and blankets, and its columns of blue smoke rising among the trees.

The first care in the morning [October 20], was to look after our horses. Some of them had wandered to a distance, but all were fortunately found; even the one whose clattering hoofs had caused such uneasiness in the night. He had come to a halt about a mile from the camp, and was found quietly grazing near a brook. The bugle sounded for departure about half past eight. As we were in greater risk of Indian molestation the farther we advanced, our line was formed with more precision than heretofore. Every one had his station assigned him, and was forbidden to leave it in pursuit of game, without special permission. The pack-horses were placed in the centre of the line, and a strong guard in the rear.

FROM

On the Road

JACK KEROUAC

*With about fifty dollars saved from veterans'
benefits, Jack Kerouac left New York City in
the summer of 1947 and hitchhiked to the
West Coast to see an old high school friend. It
was early in the young writer's restless search
for new, highly stimulated experiences, which
led to* On the Road *and his fame as the
spokesman for the beat generation.*

*T*HE greatest ride in my life was about to come up, a truck, with a flatboard at
the back, with about six or seven boys sprawled out on it, and the drivers, two
young blond farmers from Minnesota, were picking up every single soul they
found on that road—the most smiling, cheerful couple of handsome bumpkins
you could ever wish to see, both wearing cotton shirts and overalls, nothing else;
both thick-wristed and earnest, with broad howareyou smiles for anybody and
anything that came across their path. I ran up, said "Is there room?" They said,
"Sure, hop on, 'sroom for everybody."

I wasn't on the flatboard before the truck roared off; I lurched, a rider grabbed
me, and I sat down. Somebody passed a bottle of rotgut, the bottom of it. I took a
big swig in the wild, lyrical, drizzling air of Nebraska. "Whooee, here we go!"
yelled a kid in a baseball cap, and they gunned up the truck to seventy and
passed everybody on the road. "We been riding this sonofabitch since Des
Moines. These guys never stop. Every now and then you have to yell for pisscall,
otherwise you have to piss off the air, and hang on, brother, hang on."

I looked at the company. There were two young farmer boys from North
Dakota in red baseball caps, which is the standard North Dakota farmer-boy hat,
and they were headed for the harvests; their old men had given them leave to hit
the road for a summer. There were two young city boys from Columbus, Ohio,
high-school football players, chewing gum, winking, singing in the breeze, and
they said they were hitchhiking around the United States for the summer.
"We're going to LA!" they yelled.

"What are you going to do there?"

"Hell, we don't know. Who cares?"

Then there was a tall slim fellow who had a sneaky look. "Where you from?"

I asked. I was lying next to him on the platform; you couldn't sit without bouncing off, it had no rails. And he turned slowly to me, opened his mouth, and said, "Mon-ta-na."

Finally there were Mississippi Gene and his charge. Mississippi Gene was a little dark guy who rode freight trains around the country, a thirty-year-old hobo but with a youthful look so you couldn't tell exactly what age he was. And he sat on the boards crosslegged, looking out over the fields without saying anything for hundreds of miles, and finally at one point he turned to me and said, "Where *you* headed?"

I said Denver.

"I got a sister there but I ain't seed her for several couple years." His language was melodious and slow. He was patient. His charge was a sixteen-year-old tall blond kid, also in hobo rags; that is to say, they wore old clothes that had been turned black by the soot of railroads and the dirt of boxcars and sleeping on the ground. The blond kid was also quiet and he seemed to be running away from something, and it figured to be the law the way he looked straight ahead and wet his lips in worried thought. Montana Slim spoke to them occasionally with a sardonic and insinuating smile. They paid no attention to him. Slim was all insinuation. I was afraid of his long goofy grin that he opened up straight in your face and held there half-moronically.

"You got any money?" he said to me.

"Hell no, maybe enough for a pint of whisky till I get to Denver. What about you?"

"I know where I can get some."

"Where?"

"Anywhere. You can always folly a man down an alley, can't you?"

"Yeah, I guess you can."

"I ain't beyond doing it when I really need some dough. Headed up to Montana to see my father. I'll have to get off this rig at Cheyenne and move up some other way. These crazy boys are going to Los Angeles."

"Straight?"

"All the way—if you want to go to LA you got a ride."

I mulled this over; the thought of zooming all night across Nebraska, Wyoming, and the Utah desert in the morning, and then most likely the Nevada desert in the afternoon, and actually arriving in Los Angeles within a foreseeable space of time almost made me change my plans. But I had to go to Denver. I'd have to get off at Cheyenne too, and hitch south ninety miles to Denver.

I was glad when the two Minnesota farmboys who owned the truck decided to stop in North Platte and eat; I wanted to have a look at them. They came out of the cab and smiled at all of us. "Pisscall!" said one. "Time to eat!" said the other. But they were the only ones in the party who had money to buy food. We all shambled after them to a restaurant run by a bunch of women, and sat around over hamburgers and coffee while they wrapped away enormous meals just as if they were back in their mother's kitchen. They were brothers; they were transporting farm machinery from Los Angeles to Minnesota and making good money at it. So on their trip to the Coast empty they picked up everybody on the road. They'd done this about five times now; they were having a hell of a time. They liked everything. They never stopped smiling. I tried to talk to them—a kind of dumb attempt on my part to befriend the captains of our ship—and the only responses I got were two sunny smiles and large white corn-fed teeth.

Everybody had joined them in the restaurant except the two hobo kids, Gene and his boy. When we all got back they were still sitting in the truck, forlorn and disconsolate. Now the darkness was falling. The drivers had a smoke; I jumped at the chance to go buy a bottle of whisky to keep warm in the rushing cold air of night. They smiled when I told them. "Go ahead, hurry up."

"You can have a couple shots!" I reassured them.

"Oh no, we never drink, go ahead."

Montana Slim and the two high-school boys wandered the streets of North Platte with me till I found a whisky store. They chipped in some, and Slim some, and I bought a fifth. Tall, sullen men watched us go by from false-front buildings; the main street was lined with square box-houses. There were immense vistas of the plains beyond every sad street. I felt something different in the air in North Platte, I didn't know what it was. In five minutes I did. We got back on the truck and roared off. It got dark quickly. We all had a shot, and suddenly I looked, and the verdant farmfields of the Platte began to disappear and in their stead, so far you couldn't see to the end, appeared long flat wastelands of sand and sagebrush. I was astounded.

"What in the hell is this?" I cried out to Slim.

"This is the beginning of the rangelands, boy. Hand me another drink."

"Whoopee!" yelled the high-school boys. "Columbus, so long! What would Sparkie and the boys say if they was here. Yow!"

The drivers had switched up front; the fresh brother was gunning the truck to the limit. The road changed too: humpy in the middle, with soft shoulders and a ditch on both sides about four feet deep, so that the truck bounced and teetered from one side of the road to the other—miraculously only when there were no cars coming the opposite way—and I thought we'd all take a somersault. But they were tremendous drivers. How that truck disposed of the Nebraska nub—the nub that sticks out over Colorado! And soon I realized I was actually at last over Colorado, though not officially in it, but looking southwest toward Denver itself a few hundred miles away. I yelled for joy. We passed the bottle. The great blazing stars came out, the far-receding sand hills got dim. I felt like an arrow that could shoot out all the way.

And suddenly Mississippi Gene turned to me from his crosslegged, patient reverie, and opened his mouth, and leaned close, and said, "These plains put me in the mind of Texas."

"Are you from Texas?"

"No sir, I'm from Green-vell Muzz-sippy." And that was the way he said it.

"Where's that kid from?"

"He got into some kind of trouble back in Mississippi, so I offered to help him out. Boy's never been out on his own. I take care of him best as I can, he's only a child." Although Gene was white there was something of the wise and tired old Negro in him, and something very much like Elmer Hassel, the New York dope addict, in him, but a railroad Hassel, a traveling epic Hassel, crossing and recrossing the country every year, south in the winter and north in the summer, and only because he had no place he could stay in without getting tired of it and because there was nowhere to go but everywhere, keep rolling under the stars, generally the Western stars.

"I been to Og-den a couple times. If you want to ride on to Og-den I got some friends there we could hole up with."

"I'm going to Denver from Cheyenne."

"Hell, go right straight thu, you don't get a ride like this every day."

This too was a tempting offer. What was in Ogden? "What's Ogden?" I said.

"It's the place where most of the boys pass thu and always meet there; you're liable to see anybody there."

In my earlier days I'd been to sea with a tall rawboned fellow from Louisiana called Big Slim Hazard, William Holmes Hazard, who was hobo by choice. As a little boy he'd seen a hobo come up to ask his mother for a piece of pie, and she had given it to him, and when the hobo went off down the road the little boy had said, "Ma, what is that fellow?" "Why, that's a ho-bo." "Ma, I want to be a ho-bo someday." "Shet your mouth, that's not for the like of the Hazards." But he never forgot that day, and when he grew up, after a short spell playing football at LSU, he did become a hobo. Big Slim and I spent many nights telling stories and spitting tobacco juice in paper containers. There was something so indubitably reminiscent of Big Slim Hazard in Mississippi Gene's demeanor that I said, "Do you happen to have met a fellow called Big Slim Hazard somewhere?"

And he said, "You mean the tall fellow with the big laugh?"

"Well, that sounds like him. He came from Ruston, Louisiana."

"That's right. Louisiana Slim he's sometimes called. Yessir, I shore have met Big Slim."

"And he used to work in the East Texas oil fields?"

"East Texas is right. And now he's punching cows."

And that was exactly right; and still I couldn't believe Gene could have really known Slim, whom I'd been looking for, more or less, for years. "And he used to work in tugboats in New York?"

"Well now, I don't know about that."

"I guess you only knew him in the West."

"I reckon. I ain't never been to New York."

"Well, damn me, I'm amazed you know him. This is a big country. Yet I knew you must have known him."

"Yessir, I know Big Slim pretty well. Always generous with his money when he's got some. Mean, tough fellow, too; I seen him flatten a policeman in the yards at Cheyenne, one punch." That sounded like Big Slim; he was always practicing that one punch in the air; he looked like Jack Dempsey, but a young Jack Dempsey who drank.

"Damn!" I yelled into the wind, and I had another shot, and by now I was feeling pretty good. Every shot was wiped away by the rushing wind of the open truck, wiped away of its bad effects, and the good effect sank in my stomach. "Cheyenne, here I come!" I sang. "Denver, look out for your boy."

Montana Slim turned to me, pointed at my shoes, and commented, "You reckon if you put them things in the ground something'll grow up?"—without cracking a smile, of course, and the other boys heard him and laughed. And they were the silliest shoes in America; I brought them along specifically because I didn't want my feet to sweat in the hot road, and except for the rain in Bear Mountain they proved to be the best possible shoes for my journey. So I laughed with them. And the shoes were pretty ragged by now, the bits of colored leather sticking up like pieces of a fresh pineapple and my toes showing through. Well, we had another shot and laughed. As in a dream we zoomed through small crossroads towns smack out of the darkness, and passed long lines of lounging harvest hands and cowboys in the night. They watched us pass in one motion of the head, and we saw them slap their thighs from the continuing dark the other side of town—we were a funny-looking crew.

A lot of men were in this country at that time of the year; it was harvest time. The Dakota boys were fidgeting. "I think we'll get off at the next pisscall; seems like there's a lot of work around here."

"All you got to do is move north when it's over here," counseled Montana Slim, "and jes follow the harvest till you get to Canada." The boys nodded vaguely; they didn't take much stock in his advice.

Meanwhile the blond young fugitive sat the same way; every now and then Gene leaned out of his Buddhistic trance over the rushing dark plains and said something tenderly in the boy's ear. The boy nodded. Gene was taking care of him, of his moods and his fears. I wondered where the hell they would go and what they would do. They had no cigarettes. I squandered my pack on them, I loved them so. They were grateful and gracious. They never asked, I kept offering. Montana Slim had his own but never passed the pack. We zoomed through another crossroads town, passed another line of tall lanky men in jeans clustered in the dim light like moths on the desert, and returned to the tremendous darkness, and the stars overhead were pure and bright because of the increasingly thin air as we mounted the high hill of the western plateau, about a foot a mile, so they say, and no trees obstructing any low-leveled stars anywhere. And once I saw a moody whitefaced cow in the sage by the road as we flitted by. It was like riding a railroad train, just as steady and just as straight.

By and by we came to a town, slowed down, and Montana Slim said, "Ah, pisscall," but the Minnesotans didn't stop and went right on through. "Damn, I gotta go," said Slim.

"Go over the side," said somebody.

"Well, I *will*," he said, and slowly, as we all watched, he inched to the back of the platform on his haunch, holding on as best he could, till his legs dangled over. Somebody knocked on the window of the cab to bring this to the attention of the brothers. Their great smiles broke as they turned. And just as Slim was ready to proceed, precarious as it was already, they began zigzagging the truck at seventy miles an hour. He fell back a moment; we saw a whale's spout in the air; he struggled back to a sitting position. They swung the truck. Wham, over he went on his side, watering all over himself. In the roar we could hear him faintly cursing, like the whine of a man far across the hills. "Damn . . . damn . . ." He never knew we were doing this deliberately; he just struggled, as grim as Job. When he was finished, as such, he was wringing wet, and now he had to edge and shimmy his way back, and with a most woebegone look, and everybody laughing, except the sad blond boy, and the Minnesotans roaring in the cab. I handed him the bottle to make up for it.

"What the hail," he said, "was they doing that on purpose?"

"They sure were."

"Well, damn me, I didn't know that. I know I tried it back in Nebraska and didn't have half so much trouble."

We came suddenly into the town of Ogallala, and here the fellows in the cab called out, *"Pisscall!"* and with great good delight. Slim stood sullenly by the truck, ruing a lost opportunity. The two Dakota boys said good-by to everybody and figured they'd start harvesting here. We watched them disappear in the night toward the shacks at the end of town where lights were burning, where a watcher of the night in jeans said the employment men would be. I had to buy more cigarettes. Gene and the blond boy followed me to stretch their legs. I walked into the least likely place in the world, a kind of lonely Plains soda fountain for the local teenage girls and boys. They were dancing, a few of them, to the music on the jukebox. There was a lull when we came in. Gene and Blondey just stood there, looking at nobody; all they wanted was cigarettes. There were some pretty girls, too. And one of them made eyes at Blondey and he never saw it, and if he had he wouldn't have cared, he was so sad and gone.

I bought a pack each for them; they thanked me. The truck was ready to go. It was getting on midnight now, and cold. Gene, who'd been around the country more times than he could count on his fingers and toes, said the best thing to do now was for all of us to bundle up under the big tarpaulin or we'd freeze. In this manner, and with the rest of the bottle, we kept warm as the air grew ice-cold and pinged our ears. The stars seemed to get brighter the more we climbed the High Plains. We were in Wyoming now. Flat on my back, I stared straight up at the magnificent firmament, glorying in the time I was making, in how far I had come from sad Bear Mountain after all, and tingling with kicks at the thought of what lay ahead of me in Denver—whatever, whatever it would be. And Mississippi Gene began to sing a song. He sang it in a melodious, quiet voice, with a river accent, and it was simple, just "I got a purty little girl, she's sweet six-teen, she's the purti-est thing you ever seen," repeating it with other lines thrown in, all concerning how far he'd been and how he wished he could go back to her but he done lost her.

I said, "Gene, that's the prettiest song."

"It's the sweetest I know," he said with a smile.

"I hope you get where you're going, and be happy when you do."

"I always make out and move along one way or the other."

Montana Slim was asleep. He woke up and said to me, "Hey, Blackie, how about you and me investigatin' Cheyenne together tonight before you go to Denver?"

"Sure thing." I was drunk enough to go for anything.

As the truck reached the outskirts of Cheyenne, we saw the high red lights of the local radio station, and suddenly we were bucking through a great crowd of people that poured along both sidewalks. "Hell's bells, it's Wild West Week," said Slim. Big crowds of businessmen, fat businessmen in boots and ten-gallon hats, with their hefty wives in cowgirl attire, bustled and whooped on the wooden sidewalks of old Cheyenne; farther down were the long stringy boulevard lights of new downtown Cheyenne, but the celebration was focusing on Oldtown. Blank guns went off. The saloons were crowded to the sidewalk. I was amazed, and at the same time I felt it was ridiculous: in my first shot at the West I was seeing to what absurd devices it had fallen to keep its proud tradition. We had to jump off the truck and say good-by; the Minnesotans weren't interested in hanging around. It was sad to see them go, and I realized that I would never see any of them again, but that's the way it was. "You'll freeze your ass tonight," I warned. "Then you'll burn 'em in the desert tomorrow afternoon."

"That's all right with me long's as we get out of this cold night," said Gene. And the truck left, threading its way through the crowds, and nobody paying attention to the strangeness of the kids inside the tarpaulin, staring at the town like babes from a coverlet. I watched it disappear into the night.

FROM

The Wonderful Country

TOM LEA

"Oh, how I wish I had the power to describe the wonderful country as I saw it then" was the poignant remark of a Texas Ranger that Tom Lea used for the title of his novel set in the arid border lands of Texas and northern Mexico. In an early chapter three passengers share the disquieting experience of riding a buckboard on United States Mail Route 39094.

*A*N hour before daylight the wind came up and swept along the floor of the desert, moving the sand, changing the shapes of the hummocks under the dark mesquite. It blew across the bare mesas, over the summit stones of the mountains, down to a desert river flowing south through a pass where hills pitched steep to the edges of the narrowed water. Below the pass, the wind followed the stream into a valley where it found the houses of a lonely town sleeping by trees and plowed fields.

Hidden and small, four separate companies of travelers rode that morning before sunrise toward the lonely town. Unknown to each other, discovered only by the wind, they rode converging from the four compass points of the wide circling dark.

North, the wind struck a blow at the backs of three men hunched on the seats of an open buckboard headed south along the trees by the river. The wind bit at the hands of the driver holding the lines, of the man holding the rifle across his knees, of the man peering into the darkness by the mail sacks and the baggage.

West, on a long slope to the river, the wind puffed a sting of grit against the lips of six mounted cavalrymen and an officer escorting a mule-drawn ambulance headed east. The wind flapped at the fastenings on the wagon curtains; behind the canvas it brushed the face of a frightened woman alone on the jolting seat in the dark.

East, the wind stirred the dagger points of the stiff-rooted soapweed, clacking seeds in the pods dry on the brittle stalks. It blew powdery dust on an armed convoy of seven horsemen and two loaded frontier wagons headed west. The wind caught a tink of harness rings and a jingle of spur rowels in a multiple scuff of hooves, and lost them in the brush nearer the river.

South, in the twisting ruts of a road among hills and high mounded dunes, the wind cut against the moving shape of a massive high-wheeled Mexican cart. A driver with a pole walked beside the long double file of yoked oxen that brought the cart lumbering in the darkness. Two horsemen rode guarding the cart, headed north.

Half dozing under their hatbrims in the windy glare of early afternoon, it seemed to the three riders on Joe Wakefield's buckboard that they had been traveling the road by the river forever. Near now to the end of their journey, they saw the rutted tracks in the blowing dust twist and lose themselves southward where the gap of the pass loomed ahead.

After a night of driving hard, dreading Apaches from every bend of the road, and the tedious hours of jolting behind the trotting mules since daylight, the men on the wagon were shaky tired. Bitter coffee and greasy mush for breakfast at Cottonwood Station had done nothing to improve the taste of travel in their dry mouths, and they had no whiskey. Their eyes burned with the sand that since dawn had whirled in gusts timed and aimed at them with what seemed a personal, grit-edged malice whenever they looked out, or opened their mouths. With little to say to each other, and in no mood to shout it in the lashing wind, the three men rode tight-lipped, in the drifts of their separate minds.

Joe Wakefield's big fingers had sweated the lines damp as he drove. Employer of four mail riders and half a dozen rigs, he seldom carried the mail himself; this trip was special and it was a pain. He was so disgusted with the contract for United States Mail Route 39094 that he felt a wry satisfaction looking forward to the time when the railroad would run him out of business. He had been up to the north end of his route to claim three abandoned mail sacks, and to hunt for the rider, and a buckboard and a team, that last week had gone out of sight on the Stafford road. The rider had jumped the country. The buckboard and mules worth four hundred dollars had disappeared. The lost mail was a headache. Wakefield brooded over what he would do when he got his hands on the thieving brown bastard that skipped. He would fix his clock, permanently. He worked his jaw thinking about it and slapped at the mules.

Mr. Tedford Naylor, sitting stiffly upright on the seat by Wakefield, was having trouble with his bowels. All his thoughts now centered upon them. It was a humiliation to ask a man like Wakefield to stop the wagon so often, and Naylor considered himself very sensitive to humiliation of any sort. In his pockets he carried the names of twenty-odd new subscribers, and three more advertisements to run in the first issue of the Puerto *Eagle.* He had been hard put to find any but the papers upon which these were written, when he asked Wakefield to stop the wagon.

Naylor's editorial and canvassing trip up the river had been both profitable and pleasant until yesterday noon when the diarrhea had seized him. He had climbed on the buckboard at midnight in Charco shaken and uncertain. Thinking it over now, he was astonished. The expectation of attack by Indians, the tension of holding Wakefield's rifle and his own pistol ready for hours in cold threatening darkness, had been highly medicinal. Yet in the relaxation since daylight, his trouble had returned. He grimly awaited the comfort of a toilet in Puerto.

Chafing on the back seat with the dust-coated baggage and mail sacks, young Ludwig Sterner considered that a certain part of his anatomy was now almost leather; it must be as seamed as the back of Mr. Wakefield's neck. Across an ocean, a continent, Ludwig Sterner in four weeks had traveled from the banks of the Fulda to the Rio Grande. He could think back into what were surely cantos of this epic only dimly now, remembering pieces as in a dream, a dream of Ludwig Sterner on swaying, pitching seats that never stopped, never. The dear parents, Gimmeke, Minna, not one of them at home in Kassel could imagine it, what he had seen since S.S. *Klopstock* carried him from the gray mouth of the Elbe out upon the sea.

Holding his wool hat on his head, squinting against the blowing dust, he was proud of this immense journey. Yet he must admit to himself, if to no one else, that Uncle Sterner now appeared to live nearly at the end of the world. The last of creation. He was anxious to see the store; he wondered if it was built of mud. Frankly it was a wild place to learn a business.

Around the bend where the grainy, thorn-studded hills fell away from the river channel, the white pole of Fort Jefflin appeared, and the flag.

Seeing it again, Wakefield felt better. He cleared his throat, ready for talk, and glanced at his passengers. That wool hat on the Jakey boy reminded him of the lid on a coffeepot.

"How you making out back there, son?" Wakefield called over his shoulder.

"Ya, thank you!" Ludwig answered promptly. English was very difficult in the noise of the wind.

"I'm turning in to deliver the Jefflin sack," Wakefield told Naylor, who frowned. He felt very uneasy.

For an instant Ludwig Sterner frowned too. He glanced at the flag whipping out straight in the wind seven thousand miles from Prussians and conscription, then he stared at the sentry. The American soldier was perhaps one of the former slaves!

With the mules pulled up and stopped in front of the adjutant's, Wakefield climbed down from his seat and limbered his legs. His right foot was asleep and he stomped it.

"Would you mind watching those scoundrels for me, Mr. Naylor?" Wakefield spit toward the mules.

"And would you mind finding out for me when they expect the new commander?" Naylor answered. He worked for the Puerto *Eagle* even when he had to speak through clenched jaws. "Will you?"

The clerk was alone in the office, writing at a long table when Wakefield walked in with the mail sack.

"What's the news from over Stafford way?" the clerk asked.

"Not much." The mention of Stafford irritated Wakefield.

"Where'd you leave old Fuego?"

"Didn't see him, thank Christ—"

Tedford Naylor walked in the door. "Is there a toilet here?"

The clerk looked at him. "Toilet?"

"I said toilet!"

"There is a latrine fifty paces to the rear, Mister." He jerked his thumb over his shoulder, and raised his eyebrows at Wakefield as Naylor hurried out.

"One of my fares. Got a slipknot in the puckering string. Been stopping the wagon."

"Who is he? Lord Chesterfield?"

"He is a highly educated hired hand of Judge George Heffridge's. Name's Naylor. The judge set him up, with a newspaper."

"Looks like he needed a newspaper. Say, did you hear the news? Colton's here."

"Is that a fact?"

"Got here at noon. You must of ate his dust on the road."

"If that was all his, he can raise it, son."

"He's raising it." The clerk indicated the deserted office and the stacks of papers on his table. "I'll need a gallon of government ink to wet it down."

"Is he a pretty good man?"

"He's got those gold leaves on his straps."

"People around here don't know a gold leaf from a screwbean. He bring any new troops?"

"Nothing. A squad of escort and a wagon that goes back to Langman. He did bring his wife. Man, a good-looker!"

Wakefield was folding the mail receipt when he heard a faint rattle and shout in the wind outside. He remembered his mules.

Ludwig Sterner had taken Naylor's place on the front seat. He was alone, holding the lines as if he had live snakes by the tails. He was alternately calling for help and addressing the mules, in German, and in anguish. Wakefield got through the door just in time to see the wool hat go in the wind. He saw it sail high, and come down with a kind of wobbling magic perversity, squarely in front of the kicking mules. They spooked, breaking sideward from the hat, tilting the wagon crazy on two wheels, stinging dirt into Wakefield's face as he lunged.

"Pull them, goddammit, pull!" Wakefield yelled with his mouth full of sand. "Hold them, Buster!" He managed to catch on the skidding wagon and swing himself up clutching, climbing over, yanking the lines from Ludwig's hands.

"Ho goddamn you. Ho!" Wakefield bellowed, and bore down on the brake. The pulling tendons stood out like thongs in his thick wrists. "Ho you wall-eyed wild bog-spavined black rattle-brain sons of bitches, ho there, ho boys, whoa!"

When he had stopped them, their sides heaving, he spit sand from his mouth and looked at Ludwig. Wakefield felt sorry for him. Such a goddamned gourd-green jake of a Jew kid. The adjutant's clerk was whooping out the door; the commotion had brought troopers.

Ludwig's knuckles were white from his grip on the seat. He felt the eyes on him and did not know what to say or how to say it. Wakefield slapped him on the leg.

"You done all right, Buster," Wakefield said. He looked out at his audience and raised his voice. "None of these drillyard skinners around here ever monkeyed with mules in Dutch, did they? It rattled their hocks, didn't it? And that hat, by God, it brought fever in the south! It was a sight, son. Say, where is that hat?"

Ludwig looked and pointed ruefully out on the parade ground. The hat was still rolling.

"Well get it, boy! Run! Fore it crosses the river and somebody sews braid on it!"

He could see the white teeth showing in the black faces of the troopers. Wakefield was enjoying himself. The sight of Naylor easing around the windy corner of the adjutant's, his scissortail coat flapping, was nearly as rich as Jakey jumping for his hat.

And Naylor felt better, weak but so much better. "I told him to watch them, Wakefield! What happened?"

"They non speaken the Dootch! I got me a new star route mail rider if I can just find him some squareheaded mules! Come on, Buster!" Wakefield waved his arm. Ludwig was trying to dust the hat. "Climb this driving seat! Let's carry the Dutch mail—git up you long-eared bastards! Hear that, son? Talk mule to them!"

"Is long ear bastard," Ludwig said. "*Verdammter Maulesel.*" He held his hat on tight.

Beyond the far corner of the military fence, Wakefield and Naylor squinted at the water backed up behind the ragged dam built across the river bed. From it issued the *acequias* that irrigated the fields down the river; no one in that dry land passed without a look at the water.

Wakefield nudged Ludwig and pointed. "Son, you are seeing the sights. Right over that water you now gaze on the great repooblica of Mexico. And that dam there's what grows the beans your Uncle Ike trades in his store. No water, no beans. No beans, and we're in a hell of a fix."

Ludwig looked at the few thin streams that ran spilling over the jagged lip and sloped rock face of the downstream wall of the dam. He could not see much of Mexico because of the dust; the water was surely nothing for one who had seen the Niagara Falls, or even the dam in the Diemel above Karlshafen; he did not understand very well about the beans, either. But he nodded his head and smiled at Mr. Wakefield.

The road turned. The mules' hooves thumped across the cottonwood logs over the *acequia madre,* the mother ditch that came from just above the dam. Under them they smelled the water thick with mud flowing on its way to moisten spring planting somewhere beyond the brown trees. The buckboard followed the ditch along its weedy bank, made a climbing turn in a gale that blew the mules' tails sideward, and topped out of the river bottom jolting around a rise suddenly, into town.

Views of Society and Manners in America

LETTERS BY AN ENGLISH-WOMAN TO A FRIEND

From 1818 to 1820 an enthusiastic English visitor to America wrote a series of letters to a friend in London giving her impressions of the new country. The letters were later collected and published in New York. The anonymous correspondent's sharp insight and humor fill these letters about journeys to upstate New York and Vermont.

Canandaigua, August, 1819

*M*y dear friend,

What is there in life more pleasing than to set forward on a journey with a light heart, a fine sun in the heavens above you, and the earth breathing freshness and fragrance after summer rain? Let us take into the account the parting good wishes of friendship, recommending you to a kind fortune, and auguring pleasant roads, pleasant skies, and pleasant every thing. A preux Chevalier, in olden time, setting forth in a new suit of armour, buckled on by the hand of a princess, to seek adventure through the wide world, might be a more important personage than the peaceful traveller of these generations, who goes to seek waterfalls instead of giants, and to look at men instead of killing them; but I doubt if he was in any way happier, or felt one jot more exquisitely the pride and enjoyment of life, health, vigor, and liberty. These are the moments perhaps, which, in the evening of life, when seated in an easy arm-chair, we may rouse our drowsy senses by recurring to; and, like old veterans counting their honourable scratches, and all their "hair-breadth 'scapes in the imminent deadly breach," pour into the ears of some curly-pated urchin our marvellous adventures upon the back of a mule, or in the heart of a stage-wagon, with a summary of all the bruises and the broken bones, either received, or that might have been received, by riding in or tumbling out of it. Should I live to grow garrulous in this way, our journey hither may afford a tolerable account of bruises, though it is now a subject of congratulation with me, whatever it may be then, that there must remain a total deficit under the head of fractures.

If our journey was rough, it was at least very cheerful; the weather beautiful, and our companions good humoured, intelligent, and accommodating. I know not whether to recommend the stage-coach or wagon (for you are sometimes put into the one and sometimes into the other) as the best mode of travelling. This must depend upon the temper of the traveller. If he wants to see people as well as things—to hear intelligent remarks upon the country and its inhabitants, and to understand the rapid changes that each year brings forth, and if he be of an easy temper, not incommoded with trifles, nor caring to take, nor under-standing to give offence, liking the interchange of little civilities with strangers, and pleased to make an acquaintance, though it should be but one of an hour, with a kind-hearted fellow creature, and if too he can bear a few jolts—*not* a few, and can suffer to be driven sometimes too quickly over a rough road, and sometimes too slowly over a smooth one—then let him, by all means, fill a corner in the post-coach or stage-wagon according to the varying grade in civilization held by the American diligence. But if the traveller be a lounger, running away from time, or a landscape-painting tourist with a sketch-book and portable crayons, or any thing of a *soi-disant philosophe,* bringing with him a previous knowledge of the unseen country he is about to traverse, having *itemed* in his closet the character, with the sum of its population, and in his knowledge of how every thing ought to be, knowing exactly how every thing is—or, if he be of an unsociable humour, easily put out of his way, or as the phrase is, a *very particular gentleman*—then he will hire or purchase his own dearborn or light wagon, and travel *solus cum solo* with his own horse, or, as it may be, with some old associate who has no humours of his own, or whose humours are known by repeated experience to be of the exact same fashion with his companion's. In some countries you may, as it is called, *travel post,* but in these states it is seldom that you have this at your option, unless you travel with a phalanx capable of peopling a whole caravan; eight persons will be sufficient for this, the driver always making the ninth; seated three in a row.

In this journey, as I have often found before, the better half of our entertain-ment was afforded by the intelligence of our companions. It was our good fortune on leaving Albany to find ourselves seated immediately by a gentleman and his lady returning from Washington to this their residence. He was a native of Scotland, but came to this country in his early youth, followed the profession of the law, settled himself many years since in affluence on his farm (which seems rather to furnish his amusement than his business), married into a family that had emigrated from New-England, and settled down in the neighbourhood, and lives surrounded not only by all the comforts, but the luxuries of life. We were variously joined and abandoned by citizens of differing appearance and professions, country gentlemen, lawyers, members of congress, naval officers, farmers, mechanics, &c. There were two characteristics in which these our fellow travellers generally, more or less, resembled each other—good humour and intelligence. Wherever chance has as yet thrown me into a public conveyance in this country, I have met with more of these, the best articles of exchange that I am acquainted with, than I ever remember to have found elsewhere.

Our second day's journey was long and fatiguing, but withal very interesting; the weather delightful, and the scenery pleasing. The road bore every where heavy marks of the *flagellations* inflicted by the recent storms. It seemed often as if not only the rain but the lightning had torn up the ground, and scooped out the soil, now on this side, and now on that; into which holes, first the right wheel of our vehicle, and anon the left making a sudden plump, did all but spill us out on the highway. To do justice to ourselves, we bore the bruises that were in this manner most plentifully inflicted, with very tolerable stoicism and unbroken good humour.

Gaining the banks of the Mohawk, we traced its course for sixty miles, which, between the lower cataract of the Cohoez and the *upper falls,* flows placidly through a country finely varied, rich with cultivation, and sprinkled with neat and broad-roofed cottages and villas, shadowed with trees, and backed with an undulating line of hills, now advancing and narrowing the strath, and then receding and leaving vistas into opening glades, down which the tributaries of the Mohawk pour their waters. Massy woods every where crown and usually clothe these ridges; but indeed, as yet, there are few districts throughout this vast country where the forest, or some remnants of it, stand not within the horizon.

The valley of the Mohawk is chiefly peopled by old Dutch settlers; a primitive race, who retain for generations the character, customs, and often the language of their ancient country. Of all European emigrants, the Dutch and the German invariably thrive the best, *locate* themselves, as the phrase is here, with wonderful sagacity, and this being once done, is done for ever. Great must be the penury from which this harmless people fly, who are thus attached to the ways of their fathers, and who, once removed to a land yielding sustenance to the swart hand of industry, plant so peacefully their penates, and root themselves so fixedly in the soil. As a settler next best to the German, thrives the Scot; the Frenchman is given to turn hunter; the Irishman, drunkard, and the Englishman, speculator. Amusement rules the first, pleasure ruins the second, and self-sufficient obstinacy drives headlong the third. There are many exceptions, doubtless, to this rule; and the number of these increases daily—and for this reason it is a higher class that is at present emigrating. I speak now more particularly of England. It is men of substance, possessed in clear property of from five hundred to five thousand pounds, who now attempt the passage of the Atlantic. I know of thirteen families who lately arrived in these states from the Thames, not one of which is possessed of less than the former sum, and some of more than the latter. I fear that the policy of England's rulers is cutting away the sinews of the state. Why are her yeomen disappearing from the soil, dwindling into paupers, or flying as exiles? Tithes, taxes, and poor-rates—these things must be looked into, or her population will gradually approach to that of Spain, beggars and princes; the shaft of the fair column reft away.

Something less than twenty miles below Utica, the river makes a sharp angle, in the manner of the Hudson at West Point, running into a cleft or *gap*, forced in primeval times, with dreadful convulsion, through the ridge along the base of which it afterwards so peacefully winds. The Mohawk assumes here much the character of Loch Katrine at the Trosachs; the beetling crags, and rocks in ruin hurled, and shaggy wood, grooved in the dark crevices, and little coves, where the still clear water stirs not the leaf that has dropped upon its bosom. But there is no Ben-Venue and Ben-Ann to guard the magic pass; nor lady with her fairy skiff, nor is the fancy here entitled to image her; it may, however, if it be sportively inclined, picture out the wild Indian paddling his canoe, or springing from rock to rock, swift as the deer he pursues. It is evident that the water once occupied the whole breadth of the ravine, when it must have boiled and eddied with somewhat more tumultous passions than it shows at present. The huge misshapen blocks that now rise peacefully out of the flood, beetle over the head of the passenger, or, standing in the line of his rough path, force him variously to wheel to right or left, bear on their sides the marks of the ancient fury of the subdued element, which, now having sunk its channel, leaves room for the road to scramble an intricate way by its side. When about to issue from the chasm, you open upon the *Lesser Falls*, so called in contrast to the greater cataract at the mouth of the river. It is a wild scene, and helps the fancy to image out the uproar that must in former ages have raged in the depths of the pass below. How astounding it is to trace in the vast works of nature the operations of time; so mighty, and yet so slow, silent, and unseen! The whole known history of man reaches not back to the date of some crevice in a mountain; each fathom, worn by a river in his rocky bed, speaks of untold generations, swept from the earth, and lost from her records. How grand is the solemn march of nature still advancing without check, or stop, or threat of hindrance! Ages are to her as moments, and all the known course of time a span.

We reached Utica very tolerably fagged, and bruised as I could not wish an enemy. A day's rest well recruited us, however, and gave us time to examine this wonderful little town, scarce twenty years old. An innkeeper here, at whose door fifteen stages stop daily, carried, eighteen years since, the solitary and weekly mail in his coat pocket, from hence to Albany. This newborn Utica already aspires to be the capital of the state, and in a few years it probably will be so, though Albany is by no means willing to yield the honor, nor New-York the convenience, of having the seat of government in her neighbourhood; but the young western counties are such stout and imperious children that it will soon be found necessary to consult their interests.

Burlington, State of Vermont,
October, 1819.

My dear friend,

Ascending the waters of Lake Champlain, the shores assume a wilder and more mountainous character. The site of the flourishing town of Burlington is one of singular beauty; the neatness and elegance of the white houses ascending rapidly from the shore, interspersed with trees, and arranged with that symmetry which characterizes the young villages of these states, the sweet bay, and, beyond, the open waters of the lake, bounded by a range of mountains, behind which, when our eyes first rested on them, the sun was sinking in golden splendour;—it was a fairy scene, when his flaming disk, which might have dazzled eagles, dropt behind the purple screen, blazing on the still broad lake, on the windows and the white walls of the lovely village, and on the silver sails of the sloops and shipping, gliding noiselessly through the gleaming waters.

Not forty years since, and the ground now occupied by this beautiful town and a population of two thousand souls, was a desert, frequented only by bears and panthers. The American verb to *progress* (though some of my friends in this country deny that it is an Americanism) is certainly not without its apology; even a foreigner must acknowledge, that the new kind of advancement which greets his eye in this country, seems to demand a new word to portray it.

The young town of Burlington, is graced with a college, which was founded in the year 1791, and has lately received considerable additions. The state of Vermont, in which it stands, whose population may be somewhat less than 300,000, contrives to support two establishments of this description; and, perhaps, in no part of the Union is greater attention paid to the education of youth.

The territory passing under the name of Vermont is intersected, from north to south, by a range of mountains, covered with ever-green forests, from which the name of the country. This Alpine ridge, rising occasionally to three and four thousand feet, nearly fills up the breadth of the state; but is every where scooped into glens and valleys, plentifully intersected with streams and rivers, flowing, to the eastward, into the beautiful Connecticut, and, to the west, into the magnificent Champlain. The gigantic forests of white pine, spruce, cedar, and other evergreens, which clothe to the top the billowy sides of the mountains, mingle occasionally their deep verdure with the oak, elm, beech, maple, &c. that shadow the valleys. This world of forest is intersected by tracts of open pasture, while the luxuriant lands that border the water courses are fast exchanging their primeval woods for the treasures of agriculture. The most populous town in the state contains less than three thousand souls; the inhabitants, agricultural or grazing farmers, being scattered through the valleys and hills, or collected in small villages on the banks of the lakes and rivers.

In scrupulous regard to the education of her citizens, in the thorough democracy of her institutions, in her simple morals and hardy industry, Vermont is a characteristic daughter of New-England. She stands conspicuous, however, among her sister states for her patriotic spirit; her services have always been rendered to the nation unsparingly; nor could she ever be charged with separating her interests from those of the confederacy.

During the revolutionary struggle, her scanty population, thinly scattered along the borders of rivers and streams, in mountains and forests, were signally generous and disinterested. The short history of this spirited republic is not without a peculiar interest, and is very highly honourable to the character of her people.

During her colonial existence, she was engaged in a dispute with the neighbouring provinces, involving all those great principles which afterwards formed the basis of the quarrel between the colonies and the mother country. Under the administration of Great Britain, in consequence of various contradictory acts, passed at different periods, and under different reigns, the Vermont lands were claimed by the two adjoining provinces of New-Hampshire and New-York. Most of the early settlers held their possessions under the patent granted to the former, when the latter asserted a prior claim, and essayed to constrain the ejection of the proprietors. The proclamation of the royal Governor of New-York was answered by a proclamation of the royal Governor of New-Hampshire; the matter being referred to the home authority, a verdict was pronounced in favour of New-York against the wishes and claims of the Vermontese; but this imperial verdict was as little respected by the hardy mountaineers as had been the proclamation of the governor. "The gods of the valleys," cried the spirited Ethan Allen, "are not gods of the hills." An opposition was instantly organized, and the New-York claims and jurisdiction so set at defiance, that a civil war had very nearly ensued. The ground assumed by this infant colony was the right of a people to self-government, and accordingly she established her own in defiance of the threats of New-York and her governor. But a greater cause soon fixed the attention of this high-minded people. In the very heat of their contention with the New-York claimants and legislature, the quarrel broke out between the British government and the American people. From this quarrel the mountaineers of Vermont might easily have excused themselves. Far removed from the sea, without commerce, untaxed and ungoverned, the arbitrary measures of the English ministry clashed with no immediate interests of theirs, and, heated as they were in other disputes, might have been supposed little calculated to excite their opposition by wounding their pride; but, superior to all selfish considerations, their own quarrel was lost in that of the community. The news of the battle of Lexington had no sooner reached them, than we find Ethan Allen, at the head of a troop of Vermont mountaineers, surprising the important post of Ticonderoga. Summoning the surrender of the fort in the dead of night, *"In whose name?"* said the astonished and irritated commander. *"In the name of the great Jehovah and the continental congress,"* replied the patriot. This continental congress contained no representatives of the people of Vermont; it had not pronounced upon the justice or injustice of the claims preferred against them, nor acknowledged the independent jurisdiction which they had established; but it was an assembly gathered under the wings of freedom; it asserted for others those rights which the Vermontese had asserted for themselves;—without hesitation therefore, without waiting to be solicited, or essaying to make stipulations, voluntarily and unconditionally these champions of the rights of man forsook their ploughshares and their pruninghooks, recommended their women and children to the protection of heaven, and went forth to fight the battles of their brethren.

After the declaration of independence, the Vermontese appealed to the congress as to the supreme government, demanding to be admitted into the confederacy as an independent state. They grounded their plea upon the same great principles by which the other states had justified their resistance to Great Britain—the right of a people to institute their own government, and the invalidity of all contracts uncemented by a mutual agreement between the parties. New-York, on the other hand, could appeal only to royal grants and deeds legally rather than justly executed. The feelings of the congress were well disposed towards the Vermont cause; but New-York was too important an ally to be decided against rashly judgment therefore was deferred until the two states should come to agreement between themselves, or until more peaceful days should bring leisure to the congress to examine into all the bearings of the question. Thus thrown out of the pale of the Union, it was imagined by the enemy, that Vermont might easily be won from the common cause. She was now promised high privileges, and an individual existence as a royal province; but this generous republic was not to be so bought from honour: firm in her resistance to New-York, she was as true to the cause of America; her handful of freemen asserted their own rights, and sustained those of their brethren throughout that trying contest. At its close, and when the national independence was finally established, the dispute with her sister state was amicably adjusted; and she then voluntarily joined herself as a fourteenth state to the thirteen original confederated republics whose cause she had so zealously and magnanimously made her own.

In consequence of her resistance to the jurisdiction of New-York, Vermont had asserted and enjoyed an independent existence several years before the dismemberment of the colonial provinces from Great Britain; but the constitution, as it now stands, was not finally arranged until the year 1793.

The plan of government is among the most simple of any to be found in the Union. The legislative department is composed of one house, whose members are chosen by the whole male population of the state. In this mountainous district, peopled by a race of simple agriculturists, the science of legislation may be supposed to present few questions of difficulty; nor has it been found necessary to impede the process of law-making by forcing a projected statute to pass through two ordeals. You find in the constitution of Vermont another peculiarity which marks a people Argus-eyed to their liberties. In the other republics, the people have thought it sufficient to preserve to themselves the power of summoning a convention, to alter or amend their plan of government whenever they may judge it expedient; but the Vermontese, as if unwilling to trust to their own vigilance, have decreed the stated election of a Council of Censors, to be convened for one year at the end of every seven years, whose business it is to examine whether the constitution has been preserved inviolate; *"whether the legislative or executive branches of government have performed their duty as guardians of the people, or assumed to themselves, or exercised other or greater powers than they are entitled to by the constitution;"* to take in review, in short, every public act, with the whole course of administration pursued since the last meeting of the censors. If any acts appear to them to have been unconstitutional, their business is to refer them to the legislative assembly then sitting, stating the grounds of their objection, and recommending a revisal of the same. They are farther empowered to judge of the propriety of revising the existing constitution; and should any article appear defective, or not clearly defined, to promulgate the articles objected to, and the amendments proposed, which, being considered and approved by the people, other delegates are appointed to decree the same in convention, according to the instructions received from their constituents.

The assembly now meets in the little town of Montpelier, situated in a secluded valley in the centre of the state. Having gained the centre, the seat of government is now probably fixed. It is a strange novelty in the eyes of a European to find legislators assembled in a humble and lonely village to discuss affairs of state. How strangely has liberty been libelled! Behold her in the mountains of Vermont, animating a people, who, at the first sound of oppression, would rise like lions from their lair, but who, in the free exercise of undisputed rights, and, walking erect among their hills with a spirit untamed, and thought unshackled, live on a life of peace and industry, unharming and unharmed, proud as the noble in feudal seigniory, and peaceful as the flocks which graze upon their mountains!

The men of Vermont are familiarly known by the name of *Green-mountain boys;* a name which they themselves are proud of, and which, I have remarked, is spoken with much complacency, and not unfrequently with a tone of admiration or affection, by the citizens of the neighbouring states.

Before leaving Vermont, I would observe, that the Scotch emigrant would probably find it peculiarly suited to his habits and constitution. A healthy climate, a hilly country, affording either pasture or arable land—the frugal, hardy, and industrious Scotch farmer might here find himself at home, or rather in a home somewhat improved. There are many valuable tracts unreclaimed in the lower valleys, and much land of moderate value on the sides of the mountains. Our sons of the mist might here see their Grampians and Cheviots swelling out of a better soil, and smiling under a purer heaven. They would find too a race, of industry and intelligence equal or superior to their own, and animated with a spirit of independence that they might imbibe with advantage.

European emigrants are, perhaps, given to roam too far into the interior of this continent. The older states have still sufficient of vacant lands to settle down multitudes, and, as I have before remarked, men have usually many things to learn when they arrive in this country. The American enters the western wilderness skilled to vanquish all difficulties; and understanding to train his children in the love of their country, founded upon a knowledge of its history, and an appreciation of its institutions, he is fitted to form the advanced guard of civilization; the foreigner, in general, will be better placed in the main body, where he may himself receive instructions, and imbibe feelings suited to his newly assumed character as a citizen of a republic.

FROM

The Valley of the Moon

JACK LONDON

In this autobiographical odyssey Jack London put Billy and Saxon Roberts on the road in Northern California in search of the idyllic rural retreat in "the Valley of the Moon" above Sonoma. London himself left behind his wide-ranging travels, which resulted in such popular books as The Sea-Wolf *and* The Call of the Wild, *to develop what became the fourteen-hundred-acre Beauty Ranch beneath Sonoma Mountain. London died on his ranch in 1916. The site is now a California State Historic Park.*

*S*OUTH they held along the coast, hunting, fishing, swimming, and horse-buying. Billy shipped his purchases on the coasting steamers. Through Del Norte and Humboldt counties they went, and through Mendocino into Sonoma—counties larger than Eastern states—threading the giant woods, whipping innumerable trout-streams, and crossing countless rich valleys. Ever Saxon sought the valley of the moon. Sometimes, when all seemed fair, the lack was a railroad, sometimes madroño and manzanita trees, and, usually, there was too much fog.

"We do want a sun-cocktail once in a while," she told Billy.

"Yep," was his answer. "Too much fog might make us soggy. What we're after is betwixt an' between, an' we'll have to get back from the coast a ways to find it."

This was in the fall of the year, and they turned their backs on the Pacific at old Fort Ross and entered the Russian River Valley, far below Ukiah, by way of Cazadero and Guerneville. At Santa Rosa Billy was delayed with the shipping of several horses, so that it was not until afternoon that he drove south and east for Sonoma Valley.

"I guess we'll no more than make Sonoma Valley when it'll be time to camp," he said, measuring the sun with his eye. "This is called Bennett Valley. You cross a divide from it and come out at Glen Ellen. Now this is a mighty pretty valley, if anybody should ask you. An' that's some nifty mountain over there.''

"The mountain is all right," Saxon adjudged. "But all the rest of the hills are too bare. And I don't see any big trees. It takes rich soil to make big trees.''

"Oh, I ain't sayin' it's the valley of the moon by a long ways. All the same, Saxon, that's some mountain. Look at the timber on it. I bet they's deer there.''

"I wonder where we'll spend this winter," Saxon remarked.

"D'ye know, I've just ben thinkin' the same thing. Let's winter at Carmel. Mark Hall's back, an' so is Jim Hazard. What d'ye say?''

Saxon nodded.

"Only you won't be the odd-job man this time.''

"Nope. We can make trips in good weather horse-buyin'," Billy confirmed, his face beaming with self-satisfaction. "An' if that walkin' poet of the Marble House is around, I'll sure get the gloves on with 'm just in memory of the time he walked me off my legs—"

"Oh! Oh!" Saxon cried. "Look, Billy! Look!''

Around a bend in the road came a man in a sulky, driving a heavy stallion. The animal was a bright chestnut-sorrel, with cream-colored mane and tail. The tail almost swept the ground, while the mane was so thick that it crested out of the neck and flowed down, long and wavy. He scented the mares and stopped short, head flung up and armfuls of creamy mane tossing in the breeze. He bent his head until flaring nostrils brushed impatient knees, and between the fine-pointed ears could be seen a mighty and incredible curve of neck. Again he tossed his head, fretting against the bit as the driver turned widely aside for safety in passing. They could see the blue glaze like a sheen on the surface of the horse's bright, wild eyes, and Billy closed a wary thumb on his reins and himself turned widely. He held up his hand in signal, and the driver of the stallion stopped when well past, and over his shoulder talked draught-horses with Billy.

Among other things, Billy learned that the stallion's name was Barbarossa, that the driver was the owner, and that Santa Rosa was his headquarters.

"There are two ways to Sonoma Valley from here," the man directed. "When you come to the crossroads the turn to the left will take you to Glen Ellen by Bennett Peak—that's it there.''

Rising from rolling stubble fields, Bennett Peak towered hot in the sun, a row of bastion hills leaning against its base. But hills and mountains on that side showed bare and heated, though beautiful with the sunburnt tawniness of California.

"The turn to the right will take you to Glen Ellen, too, only it's longer and steeper grades. But your mares don't look as though it'd bother them.''

"Which is the prettiest way?" Saxon asked.

"Oh, the right hand road, by all means," said the man. "That's Sonoma

Mountain there, and the road skirts it pretty well up, and goes through Cooper's Grove."

Billy did not start immediately after they had said good-by, and he and Saxon, heads over shoulders, watched the roused Barbarossa plunging mutinously on toward Santa Rosa.

"Gee!" Billy said. "I'd like to be up here next spring."

At the crossroads Billy hesitated and looked at Saxon.

"What if it is longer?" she said. "Look how beautiful it is—all covered with green woods; and I just know those are redwoods in the canyons. You never can tell. The valley of the moon might be right up there somewhere. And it would never do to miss it just in order to save half an hour."

They took the turn to the right and began crossing a series of steep foothills. As they approached the mountain there were signs of a greater abundance of water. They drove beside a running stream, and, though the vineyards on the hills were summer-dry, the farmhouses in the hollows and on the levels were grouped about with splendid trees.

"Maybe it sounds funny," Saxon observed; "but I'm beginning to love that mountain already. It almost seems as if I'd seen it before, somehow, it's so all-around satisfying—oh!"

Crossing a bridge and rounding a sharp turn, they were suddenly enveloped in a mysterious coolness and gloom. All about them arose stately trunks of redwood. The forest floor was a rosy carpet of autumn fronds. Occasional shafts of sunlight, penetrating the deep shade, warmed the somberness of the grove. Alluring paths led off among the trees and into cozy nooks made by circles of red columns growing around the dust of vanished ancestors—witnessing the titanic dimensions of those ancestors by the girth of the circles in which they stood.

Out of the grove they pulled to the steep divide, which was no more than a buttress of Sonoma Mountain. The way led on through rolling uplands and across small dips and canyons, all well wooded and a-drip with water. In places the road was muddy from wayside springs.

"The mountain's a sponge," said Billy. "Here it is, the tail-end of dry summer, an' the ground's just leakin' everywhere."

"I know I've never been here before," Saxon communed aloud. "But it's all so familiar! So I must have dreamed it. —And there's madroños!—a whole grove! And manzanita! Why, I feel just as if I was coming home. . . . Oh, Billy, if it should turn out to be our valley."

"Plastered against the side of a mountain?" he queried, with a skeptical laugh.

"No; I don't mean that. I mean on the way to our valley. Because the way—all ways—to our valley must be beautiful. And this; I've seen it all before, dreamed it."

"It's great," he said sympathetically. "I wouldn't trade a square mile of this kind of country for the whole Sacramento Valley, with the river islands thrown in and Middle River for good measure. If they ain't deer up there, I miss my guess. An' where they's springs they's streams, an' streams means trout."

They passed a large and comfortable farmhouse, surrounded by wandering barns and cow-sheds, went on under forest arches, and emerged beside a field with which Saxon was instantly enchanted. It flowed in a gentle concave from the road up the mountain, its farther boundary an unbroken line of timber. The field glowed like rough gold in the approaching sunset, and near the middle of it stood a solitary great redwood, with blasted top suggesting a nesting eyrie for eagles. The timber beyond clothed the mountain in solid green to what they took to be the top. But, as they drove on, Saxon, looking back upon what she called *her* field, saw the real summit of Sonoma towering beyond, the mountain behind her field a mere spur upon the side of the larger mass.

Ahead and toward the right, across sheer ridges of the mountains, separated by deep green canyons and broadening lower down into rolling orchards and vineyards, they caught their first sight of Sonoma Valley and the wild mountains that rimmed its eastern side. To the left they gazed across a golden land of small hills and valleys. Beyond, to the north, they glimpsed another portion of the valley, and, still beyond, the opposing wall of the valley—a range of mountains, the highest of which reared its red and battered ancient crater against a rosy and mellowing sky. From north to southeast, the mountain rim curved in the brightness of the sun, while Saxon and Billy were already in the shadow of evening. He looked at Saxon, noted the ravished ecstasy of her face, and stopped the horses. All the eastern sky was blushing to rose, which descended upon the mountains, touching them with wine and ruby. Sonoma Valley began to fill with a purple flood, laving the mountain bases, rising, inundating, drowning them in its purple. Saxon pointed in silence, indicating that the purple flood was the sunset shadow of Sonoma Mountain. Billy nodded, then chirruped to the mares, and the descent began through a warm and colorful twilight.

On the elevated sections of the road they felt the cool, delicious breeze from the Pacific forty miles away; while from each little dip and hollow came warm breaths of autumn earth, spicy with sunburnt grass and fallen leaves and passing flowers.

They came to the rim of a deep canyon that seemed to penetrate to the heart of Sonoma Mountain. Again, with no word spoken, merely from watching Saxon, Billy stopped the wagon. The canyon was wildly beautiful. Tall redwoods lined its entire length. On its farther rim stood three rugged knolls covered with dense woods of spruce and oak. From between the knolls, a feeder to the main canyon and likewise fringed with redwoods, emerged a smaller canyon. Billy pointed to a stubble field that lay at the feet of the knolls.

"It's in fields like that I've seen my mares a-pasturing," he said.

They dropped down into the canyon, the road following a stream that sang under maples and alders. The sunset fires, refracted from the cloud-driftage of the autumn sky, bathed the canyon with crimson, in which ruddy-limbed madroños and wine-wooded manzanitas burned and smoldered. The air was aromatic with laurel. Wild grape vines bridged the stream from tree to tree. Oaks of many sorts were veiled in lacy Spanish moss. Ferns and brakes grew lush beside the stream. From somewhere came the plaint of a mourning dove. Fifty feet above the ground, almost over their heads, a Douglas squirrel crossed the road—a flash of gray between two trees; and they marked the continuance of its aerial passage by the bending of the boughs.

"I've got a hunch," said Billy.

"Let me say it first," Saxon begged.

He waited, his eyes on her face as she gazed about her in rapture.

"We've found our valley," she whispered. "Was that it?"

He nodded, but checked speech at sight of a small boy driving a cow up the road, a preposterously big shotgun in one hand, in the other as preposterously big a jackrabbit.

"How far to Glen Ellen?" Billy asked.

"Mile an' a half," was the answer.

"What creek is this?" inquired Saxon.

"Wild Water. It empties into Sonoma Creek half a mile down."

"Trout?"—this from Billy.

"If you know how to catch 'em," grinned the boy.

"Deer up the mountain?"

"It ain't open season," the boy evaded.

"I guess you never shot a deer," Billy slyly baited, and was rewarded with:

"I got the horns to show."

"Deer shed their horns," Billy teased on. "Anybody can find 'em."

"I got the meat on mine. It ain't dry yet—"

The boy broke off, gazing with shocked eyes into the pit Billy had dug for him.

"It's all right, sonny," Billy laughed, as he drove on. "I ain't the game warden. I'm buyin' horses."

More leaping tree squirrels, more ruddy madroños and majestic oaks, more fairy circles of redwoods, and, still beside the singing stream, they passed a gate by the roadside. Before it stood a rural mail box, on which was lettered "Edmund Hale." Standing under the rustic arch, leaning upon the gate, a man and woman composed a picture so arresting and beautiful that Saxon caught her breath. They were side by side, the delicate hand of the woman curled in the hand of the man, which looked as if made to confer benedictions. His face bore out this impression—a beautiful-browed countenance, with large, benevolent gray eyes under a wealth of white hair that shone like spun glass. He was fair and large; the little woman beside him was daintily wrought. She was saffron-brown, as a woman of the white race can well be, with smiling eyes of bluest blue. In quaint sage-green draperies, she seemed a flower, with her small vivid face irresistibly reminding Saxon of a springtime wake-robin.

Perhaps the picture made by Saxon and Billy was equally arresting and beautiful, as they drove down through the golden end of day. The two couples had eyes only for each other. The little woman beamed joyously. The man's face glowed into the benediction that had trembled there. To Saxon, like the field up the mountain, like the mountain itself, it seemed that she had always known this adorable pair. She knew that she loved them.

"How d'ye do," said Billy.

"You blessed children," said the man. "I wonder if you know how dear you look sitting there."

That was all. The wagon had passed by, rustling down the road, which was carpeted with fallen leaves of maple, oak, and alder. Then they came to the meeting of the two creeks.

"Oh, what a place for a home," Saxon cried, pointing across Wild Water. "See, Billy, on that bench there above the meadow."

"It's a rich bottom, Saxon; and so is the bench rich. Look at the big trees on it. An' they's sure to be springs."

"Drive over," she said.

Forsaking the main road, they crossed Wild Water on a narrow bridge and continued along an ancient, rutted road that ran beside an equally ancient worm-fence of split redwood rails. They came to a gate, open and off its hinges, through which the road led out on the bench.

"This is it—I know it," Saxon said with conviction. "Drive in, Billy."

A small, whitewashed farmhouse with broken windows showed through the trees.

"Talk about your madroños—"

Billy pointed to the father of all madroños, six feet in diameter at its base, sturdy and sound, which stood before the house.

They spoke in low tones as they passed around the house under great oak trees and came to a stop before a small barn. They did not wait to unharness. Tying the horses, they started to explore. The pitch from the bench to the meadow was steep yet thickly wooded with oaks and manzanita. As they crashed through the underbrush they startled a score of quail into flight.

"How about game?" Saxon queried.

Billy grinned, and fell to examining a spring which bubbled a clear stream into the meadow. Here the ground was sunbaked and wide open in a multitude of cracks.

Disappointment leaped into Saxon's face, but Billy, crumbling a clod between his fingers, had not made up his mind.

"It's rich," he pronounced; "—the cream of the soil that's ben washin' down from the hills for ten thousan' years. But—"

He broke off, stared all about, studying the configuration of the meadow, crossed it to the redwood trees beyond, then came back.

"It's no good as it is," he said. "But it's the best ever if it's handled right. All it needs is a little common sense an' a lot of drainage. This meadow's a natural basin not yet filled level. They's a sharp slope through the redwoods to the creek. Come on, I'll show you."

They went through the redwoods and came out on Sonoma Creek. At this spot was no singing. The stream poured into a quiet pool. The willows on their side brushed the water. The opposite side was a steep bank. Billy measured the height of the bank with his eye, the depth of the water with a driftwood pole.

"Fifteen feet," he announced. "That allows all kinds of high-divin' from the bank. An' it's a hundred yards of a swim up an' down."

They followed down the pool. It emptied in a riffle, across exposed bedrock, into another pool. As they looked, a trout flashed into the air and back, leaving a widening ripple on the quiet surface.

"I guess we won't winter in Carmel," Billy said. "This place was specially manufactured for us. In the morning I'll find out who owns it."

Half an hour later, feeding the horses, he called Saxon's attention to a locomotive whistle.

"You've got your railroad," he said. "That's a train pulling into Glen Ellen, an' it's only a mile from here."

Saxon was dozing off to sleep under the blankets when Billy aroused her.

"Suppose the guy that owns it won't sell?"

"There isn't the slightest doubt," Saxon answered with unruffled certainty. "This is our place. I know it."

My First Summer in the Sierra

JOHN MUIR

A student of botany and geology, an admirer of tall trees and massive cloud formations, John Muir recorded his joys in the discovery of nature in journals that eventually became classic studies on America's wilderness. In the summer of 1869 Muir helped move a herd of sheep to alpine pastures near the headwaters of the Tuolumne and Merced rivers by Yosemite—mountain country he called the Range of Light. In these journal entries he writes of firs and pines and the Douglas squirrel, "peppery, pungent autocrat of the woods."

July 8

NOW away we go toward the topmost mountains. Many still, small voices, as well as the noon thunder, are calling, "Come higher." Farewell, blessed dell, woods, gardens, streams, birds, squirrels, lizards, and a thousand others. Farewell. Farewell.

Up through the woods the hoofed locusts streamed beneath a cloud of brown dust. Scarcely were they driven a hundred yards from the old corral ere they seemed to know that at last they were going to new pastures, and rushed wildly ahead, crowding through gaps in the brush, jumping, tumbling like exulting hurrahing flood-waters escaping through a broken dam. A man on each flank kept shouting advice to the leaders, who in their famishing condition were behaving like Gadarene swine; two other drivers were busy with stragglers, helping them out of brush tangles; the Indian, calm, alert, silently watched for wanderers likely to be overlooked; the two dogs ran here and there, at a loss to know what was best to be done, while the Don, soon far in the rear, was trying to keep in sight of his troublesome wealth.

As soon as the boundary of the old eaten-out range was passed the hungry horde suddenly became calm, like a mountain stream in a meadow. Thenceforward they were allowed to eat their way as slowly as they wished, care being taken only to keep them headed toward the summit of the Merced and Tuolumne divide. Soon the two thousand flattened paunches were bulged out with sweetpea vines and grass, and the gaunt, desperate creatures, more like wolves than sheep, became bland and governable, while the howling drivers changed to gentle shepherds, and sauntered in peace.

Toward sundown we reached Hazel Green, a charming spot on the summit of the dividing ridge between the basins of the Merced and Tuolumne, where there is a small brook flowing through hazel and dogwood thickets beneath magnificent silver firs and pines. Here, we are camped for the night, our big fire, heaped high with rosiny logs and branches, is blazing like a sunrise, gladly giving back the light slowly sifted from the sunbeams of centuries of summers; and in the glow of that old sunlight how impressively surrounding objects are brought forward in relief against the outer darkness! Grasses, larkspurs, columbines, lilies, hazel bushes, and the great trees form a circle around the fire like thoughtful spectators, gazing and listening with human-like enthusiasm. The night breeze is cool, for all day we have been climbing into the upper sky, the home of the cloud mountains we so long have admired. How sweet and keen the air! Every breath a blessing. Here the sugar pine reaches its fullest development in size and beauty and number of individuals, filling every swell and hollow and down-plunging ravine almost to the exclusion of other species. A few yellow pines are still to be found as companions, and in the coolest places silver firs; but noble as these are, the sugar pine is king, and spreads long protecting arms above them while they rock and wave in sign of recognition.

We have now reached a height of six thousand feet. In the forenoon we passed along a flat part of the dividing ridge that is planted with manzanita (*Arctostaphylos*), some specimens the largest I have seen. I measured one, the bole of which is four feet in diameter and only eighteen inches high from the ground, where it dissolves into many wide-spreading branches forming a broad round head about ten or twelve feet high, covered with clusters of small narrow-throated pink bells. The leaves are pale green, glandular, and set on edge by a twist of the petiole. The branches seem naked; for the chocolate-colored bark is very smooth and thin, and is shed off in flakes that curl when dry. The wood is red, close-grained, hard, and heavy. I wonder how old these curious tree-bushes are, probably as old as the great pines. Indians and bears and birds and fat grubs feast on the berries, which look like small apples, often rosy on one side, green on the other. The Indians are said to make a kind of beer or cider out of them. There are many species. This one, *Arctostaphylos pungens,* is common hereabouts. No need have they to fear the wind, so low they are and steadfastly rooted. Even the fires that sweep the woods seldom destroy them utterly, for they rise again from the root, and some of the dry ridges they grow on are seldom touched by fire. I must try to know them better.

I miss my river songs to-night. Here Hazel Creek at its topmost springs has a voice like a bird. The wind-tones in the great trees overhead are strangely impressive, all the more because not a leaf stirs below them. But it grows late, and I must to bed. The camp is silent; everybody asleep. It seems extravagant to spend hours so precious in sleep. "He giveth his beloved sleep." Pity the poor beloved needs it, weak, weary, forspent; oh, the pity of it, to sleep in the midst of eternal, beautiful motion instead of gazing forever, like the stars.

July 9

Exhilarated with the mountain air, I feel like shouting this morning with excess of wild animal joy. The Indian lay down away from the fire last night, without blankets, having nothing on, by way of clothing, but a pair of blue overalls and a calico shirt wet with sweat. The night air is chilly at this elevation, and we gave him some horse-blankets, but he didn't seem to care for them. A fine thing to be independent of clothing where it is so hard to carry. When food is scarce, he can live on whatever comes in his way—a few berries, roots, bird eggs, grasshoppers, black ants, fat wasp or bumblebee larvæ, without feeling that he is doing anything worth mention, so I have been told.

Our course to-day was along the broad top of the main ridge to a hollow beyond Crane Flat. It is scarce at all rocky, and is covered with the noblest pines and spruces I have yet seen. Sugar pines from six to eight feet in diameter are not uncommon, with a height of two hundred feet or even more. The silver firs (*Abies concolor* and *A. magnifica*) are exceedingly beautiful, especially the *magnifica*, which becomes more abundant the higher we go. It is of great size, one of the most notable in every way of the giant conifers of the Sierra. I saw specimens that measured seven feet in diameter and over two hundred feet in height, while the average size for what might be called full-grown mature trees can hardly be less than one hundred and eighty or two hundred feet high and five or six feet in diameter; and with these noble dimensions there is a symmetry and perfection of finish not to be seen in any other tree, hereabout at least. The branches are whorled in fives mostly, and stand out from the tall, straight, exquisitely tapered bole in level collars, each branch regularly pinnated like the fronds of ferns, and densely clad with leaves all around the branchlets, thus giving them a singularly rich and sumptuous appearance. The extreme top of the tree is a thick blunt shoot pointing straight to the zenith like an admonishing finger. The cones stand erect like casks on the upper branches. They are about six inches long, three in diameter, blunt, velvety, and cylindrical in form, and very rich and precious looking. The seeds are about three quarters of an inch long, dark reddish brown with brilliant iridescent purple wings, and when ripe, the cone falls to pieces, and the seeds thus set free at a height of one hundred and fifty or two hundred feet have a good send off and may fly considerable distances in a good breeze; and it is when a good breeze is blowing that most of them are shaken free to fly.

The other species, *Abies concolor,* attains nearly as great a height and thickness as the *magnifica,* but the branches do not form such regular whorls, nor are they so exactly pinnated or richly leaf-clad. Instead of growing all around the branch-lets, the leaves are mostly arranged in two flat horizontal rows. The cones and seeds are like those of the *magnifica* in form but less than half as large. The bark of the *magnifica* is reddish purple and closely furrowed, that of the *concolor* gray and widely furrowed. A noble pair.

At Crane Flat we climbed a thousand feet or more in a distance of about two miles, the forest growing more dense and the silvery *magnifica* fir forming a still greater portion of the whole. Crane Flat is a meadow with a wide sandy border lying on the top of the divide. It is often visited by blue cranes to rest and feed on their long journeys, hence the name. It is about half a mile long, draining into the Merced, sedgy in the middle, with a margin bright with lilies, columbines, larkspurs, lupines, castilleia, then an outer zone of dry, gently sloping ground starred with a multitude of small flowers—eunanus, mimulus, gilia, with ro-settes of spraguea, and tufts of several species of eriogonum and the brilliant zauschneria. The noble forest wall about it is made up of the two silver firs and the yellow and sugar pines, which here seem to reach their highest pitch of beauty and grandeur; for the elevation, six thousand feet or a little more, is not too great for the sugar and yellow pines or too low for the *magnifica* fir, while the *concolor* seems to find this elevation the best possible. About a mile from the north end of the flat there is a grove of *Sequoia gigantea,* the king of all the conifers. Furthermore, the Douglas spruce (*Pseudotsuga Douglasii*) and *Libocedrus decurrens,* and a few two-leaved pines, occur here and there, forming a small part of the forest. Three pines, two silver firs, one Douglas spruce, one sequoia—all of them, except the two-leaved pine, colossal trees—are found here together, an assemblage of conifers unrivaled on the globe.

We passed a number of charming garden-like meadows lying on top of the divide or hanging like ribbons down its sides, imbedded in the glorious forest. Some are taken up chiefly with the tall white-flowered *Veratrum Californicum,* with boat-shaped leaves about a foot long, eight or ten inches wide, and veined like those of cypripedium—a robust, hearty, liliaceous plant, fond of water and determined to be seen. Columbine and larkspur grow on the dryer edges of the meadows, with a tall handsome lupine standing waist-deep in long grasses and sedges. Castilleias, too, of several species make a bright show with beds of violets at their feet. But the glory of these forest meadows is a lily (*L. parvum*). The tallest are from seven to eight feet high with magnificent racemes of ten to twenty or more small orange-colored flowers; they stand out free in open ground, with just enough grass and other companion plants about them to fringe their feet, and show them off to best advantage. This is a grand addition to my lily acquaintances—a true mountaineer, reaching prime vigor and beauty at a height of seven thousand feet or thereabouts. It varies, I find, very much in size even in the same meadow, not only with the soil, but with age. I saw a specimen that had only one flower, and another within a stone's throw had twenty-five. And to think that the sheep should be allowed in these lily meadows! after how many centuries of Nature's care planting and watering them, tucking the bulbs in snugly below winter frost, shading the tender shoots with clouds drawn above them like curtains, pouring refreshing rain, making them perfect in beauty, and keeping them safe by a thousand miracles; yet, strange to say, allowing the trampling of devastating sheep. One might reasonably look for a wall of fire to fence such gardens. So extravagant is Nature with her choicest treasures, spending plant beauty as she spends sunshine, pouring it forth into land and sea, garden and desert. And so the beauty of lilies falls on angels and men, bears and squirrels, wolves and sheep, birds and bees, but as far as I have seen, man alone, and the animals he tames, destroy these gardens. Awkward, lumbering bears, the Don tells me, love to wallow in them in hot weather, and deer with their sharp feet cross them again and again, sauntering and feeding, yet never a lily have I seen spoiled by them. Rather, like gardeners, they seem to cultivate them, pressing and dibbling as required. Anyhow not a leaf or petal seems misplaced.

The trees round about them seem as perfect in beauty and form as the lilies, their boughs whorled like lily leaves in exact order. This evening, as usual, the glow of our campfire is working enchantment on everything within reach of its rays. Lying beneath the firs, it is glorious to see them dipping their spires in the starry sky, the sky like one vast lily meadow in bloom! How can I close my eyes on so precious a night?

July 10

A Douglas squirrel, peppery, pungent autocrat of the woods, is barking overhead this morning, and the small forest birds, so seldom seen when one travels noisily, are out on sunny branches along the edge of the meadow getting warm, taking a sun bath and dew bath—a fine sight. How charming the sprightly confident looks and ways of these little feathered people of the trees! They seem sure of dainty, wholesome breakfasts, and where are so many breakfasts to come from? How helpless should we find ourselves should we try to set a table for them of such buds, seeds, insects, etc., as would keep them in the pure wild health they enjoy! Not a headache or any other ache amongst them, I guess. As for the irrepressible Douglas squirrels, one never thinks of their breakfasts or the possibility of hunger, sickness or death; rather they seem like stars above chance or change, even though we may see them at times busy gathering burrs, working hard for a living.

On through the forest ever higher we go, a cloud of dust dimming the way, thousands of feet trampling leaves and flowers, but in this mighty wilderness they seem but a feeble band, and a thousand gardens will escape their blighting touch. They cannot hurt the trees, though some of the seedlings suffer, and should the woolly locusts be greatly multiplied, as on account of dollar value they are likely to be, then the forests, too, may in time be destroyed. Only the sky will then be safe, though hid from view by dust and smoke, incense of a bad sacrifice. Poor, helpless, hungry sheep, in great part misbegotten, without good right to be, semi-manufactured, made less by God than man, born out of time and place, yet their voices are strangely human and call out one's pity.

Our way is still along the Merced and Tuolumne divide, the streams on our right going to swell the songful Yosemite River, those on our left to the songful Tuolumne, slipping through sunny carex and lily meadows, and breaking into song down a thousand ravines almost as soon as they are born. A more tuneful set of streams surely nowhere exists, or more sparkling crystal pure, now gliding with tinkling whisper, now with merry dimpling rush, in and out through sunshine and shade, shimmering in pools, uniting their currents, bouncing, dancing from form to form over cliffs and inclines, ever more beautiful the farther they go until they pour into the main glacial rivers.

All day I have been gazing in growing admiration at the noble groups of the magnificent silver fir which more and more is taking the ground to itself. The woods above Crane Flat still continue comparatively open, letting in the sunshine on the brown needle-strewn ground. Not only are the individual trees admirable in symmetry and superb in foliage and port, but half a dozen or more often form temple groves in which the trees are so nicely graded in size and position as to seem one. Here, indeed, is the tree-lover's paradise. The dullest eye in the world must surely be quickened by such trees as these.

Fortunately the sheep need little attention, as they are driven slowly and allowed to nip and nibble as they like. Since leaving Hazel Green we have been following the Yosemite trail; visitors to the famous valley coming by way of Coulterville and Chinese Camp pass this way—the two trails uniting at Crane Flat—and enter the valley on the north side. Another trail enters on the south side by way of Mariposa. The tourists we saw were in parties of from three or four to fifteen or twenty, mounted on mules or small mustang ponies. A strange show they made, winding single file through the solemn woods in gaudy attire, scaring the wild creatures, and one might fancy that even the great pines would be disturbed and groan aghast. But what may we say of ourselves and the flock?

We are now camped at Tamarack Flat, within four or five miles of the lower end of Yosemite. Here is another fine meadow embosomed in the woods, with a deep, clear stream gliding through it, its banks rounded and beveled with a thatch of dipping sedges. The flat is named after the two-leaved pine (*Pinus contorta*, var. *Murrayana*), common here, especially around the cool margin of the meadow. On rocky ground it is a rough, thickset tree, about forty to sixty feet high and one to three feet in diameter, bark thin and gummy, branches rather naked, tassels, leaves, and cones small. But in damp, rich soil it grows close and slender, and reaches a height at times of nearly a hundred feet. Specimens only six inches in diameter at the ground are often fifty or sixty feet in height, as slender and sharp in outline as arrows, like the true tamarack (larch) of the Eastern States; hence the name, though it is a pine.

July 11

The Don has gone ahead on one of the pack animals to spy out the land to the north of Yosemite in search of the best point for a central camp. Much higher than this we cannot now go, for the upper pastures, said to be better than any hereabouts, are still buried in heavy winter snow. Glad I am that camp is to be fixed in the Yosemite region, for many a glorious ramble I'll have along the top of the walls, and then what landscapes I shall find with their new mountains and cañons, forests and gardens, lakes and streams and falls.

We are now about seven thousand feet above the sea, and the nights are so cool we have to pile coats and extra clothing on top of our blankets. Tamarack Creek is icy cold, delicious, exhilarating champagne water. It is flowing bank-full in the meadow with silent speed, but only a few hundred yards below our camp the ground is bare gray granite strewn with boulders, large spaces being without a single tree or only a small one here and there anchored in narrow seams and cracks. The boulders, many of them very large, are not in piles or scattered like rubbish among loose crumbling débris as if weathered out of the solid as boulders of disintegration; they mostly occur singly, and are lying on a clean pavement on which the sunshine falls in a glare that contrasts with the shimmer of light and shade we have been accustomed to in the leafy woods. And, strange to say, these boulders lying so still and deserted, with no moving force near them, no boulder carrier anywhere in sight, were nevertheless brought from a distance, as difference in color and composition shows, quarried and carried and laid down here each in its place; nor have they stirred, most of them, through calm and storm since first they arrived. They look lonely here, strangers in a strange land—huge blocks, angular mountain chips, the largest twenty or thirty feet in diameter, the chips that Nature has made in modeling her landscapes, fashioning the forms of her mountains and valleys. And with what tool were they quarried and carried? On the pavement we find its marks. The most resisting unweathered portion of the surface is scored and striated in a rigidly parallel way, indicating that the region has been overswept by a glacier from the northeastward, grinding down the general mass of the mountains, scoring and polishing, producing a strange, raw, wiped appearance, and dropping whatever boulders it chanced to be carrying at the time it was melted at the close of the Glacial Period. A fine discovery this. As for the forests we have been passing through, they are probably growing on deposits of soil most of which has been laid down by this same ice agent in the form of moraines of different sorts, now in great part disintegrated and outspread by post-glacial weathering.

Out of the grassy meadow and down over this ice-planed granite runs the glad young Tamarack Creek, rejoicing, exulting, chanting, dancing in white, glowing, irised falls and cascades on its way to the Merced Cañon, a few miles below Yosemite, falling more than three thousand feet in a distance of about two miles.

All the Merced streams are wonderful singers, and Yosemite is the centre where the main tributaries meet. From a point about half a mile from our camp we can see into the lower end of the famous valley, with its wonderful cliffs and groves, a grand page of mountain manuscript that I would gladly give my life to be able to read. How vast it seems, how short human life when we happen to think of it, and how little we may learn, however hard we try! Yet why bewail our poor inevitable ignorance? Some of the external beauty is always in sight, enough to keep every fibre of us tingling, and this we are able to gloriously enjoy though the methods of its creation may lie beyond our ken. Sing on, brave Tamarack Creek, fresh from your snowy fountains, plash and swirl and dance to your fate in the sea; bathing, cheering every living thing along your way.

Have greatly enjoyed all this huge day, sauntering and seeing, steeping in the mountain influences, sketching, noting, pressing flowers, drinking ozone and Tamarack water. Found the white fragrant Washington lily, the finest of all the Sierra lilies. Its bulbs are buried in shaggy chaparral tangles, I suppose for safety from pawing bears; and its magnificent panicles sway and rock over the top of the rough snow-pressed bushes, while big, bold, blunt-nosed bees drone and mumble in its polleny bells. A lovely flower, worth going hungry and footsore endless miles to see. The whole world seems richer now that I have found this plant in so noble a landscape.

A log house serves to mark a claim to the Tamarack meadow, which may become valuable as a station in case travel to Yosemite should greatly increase. Belated parties occasionally stop here. A white man with an Indian woman is holding possession of the place.

Sauntered up the meadow about sundown, out of sight of camp and sheep and all human mark, into the deep peace of the solemn old woods, everything glowing with Heaven's unquenchable enthusiasm.

FROM

The Winter Beach

CHARLTON OGBURN, JR.

The author served with Merrill's Marauders in the China-Burma Theater in World War II and wrote a memorable account of that experience in The Marauders. *His Thoreaulike concern for nature has since been the theme of several works, including* The Winter Beach, *a study of the Atlantic coastline from Maine to North Carolina's Outer Banks.*

*J*UST as any visitor to Washington with a love of country should first pay homage to its father by a trip to Mount Vernon, so any partisan of the land itself who visits Cape Cod should go directly to a place that plays a stellar role in two classics of American nature-writing: Nauset Marsh. Thoreau, though he did not write of it, must have had a glimpse of the marsh as he walked along through Eastham with his companion. (One has a vivid picture of the two figures as they passed: "We walked with our umbrellas behind us since it blowed hard as well as rained, with driving mists, as the day before, and the wind helped us over the sand at a rapid rate. Everything indicated that we had reached a strange shore. The road was a mere lane, winding over bare swells of bleak and barren-looking land.") For a more panoramic view than the one Thoreau had from the road, which is now U.S. 6, you may turn onto a secondary road a mile before Eastham—which New Englanders, I found, pronounce *East-ham*, giving the second "a" full value.

From the elevation to which the road leads—a protuberance of the moraine half encircled by water—you look far out over the marsh as over a great brown buckwheat cake. Gaping with water-holes, the cake is in greater part surrounded by open tidal channels and fissured by them as well. On the other side of it is Nauset Beach, a long, narrow spit crested with dunes beyond which the surf can be seen like a border of frosting. At the extreme left, a background to the marsh in the north, is the high land that ends at the old Nauset Coast Guard

Station. Across the marsh directly in front of you, just inside the dunes, is the site of "The Outermost House," in which Henry Beston spent a round of seasons forty years ago to write eloquently and poetically of what he had observed of the changing natural scene with an inexhaustible, scrupulous and ardent attention and what may only be called empathy. Solitude is to the powers of perception what the thorn was to the nightingale which pressed its breast upon the point to provoke its most moving song, and *The Outermost House*, which compels our absorbed interest by the depth of its veracity, could have been the work only of a man who had lived alone with what he wrote of. (While the house has been moved away, one is glad to know that it still exists.)

From the field running down to the channel bordering the marsh, meadowlarks put up on their seemingly inadequate, triangular wings. One can hear in the mind their clear songs of four or five high, aspiring whistles, cutting the air like a knife, as Dr. Wyman Richardson used to hear them on an icy morning and be shamed into throwing off the warm covers. . . . There, in that robust individual, was a true New Englander, a leading Boston physician who yet never ceased to be a boy on the Cape, in fiber no less sensitive than tough, one would judge, who knew as home and studied with affection the marsh, river and woodland for which his gusto never flagged. The Old Farmhouse—*The House on Nauset Marsh*—lies just over the ridge on the left, and if no one is around you may go up to it as I did, a burning feeling in my throat from thinking of the death, only a few years before, of the man whose home this was and who had become so real to me from what he had written. I could not remember whether he had ever remarked on the junipers around his house which were sprinkled with fruit like bayberries but of a most strikingly bright pale blue, creating an effect, as some Christmas trees do, of a frosty, starlit northern night.

As Dr. Richardson demonstrated, the way to see Nauset Marsh (or any other) is by boat. I did the best I could by walking out in it from the parking area by the National Park amphitheater. Mussels grew in the salt meadow grass and so did a noted plant of the tidal flats, glasswort, which made me think of an earthworm that has stood up and branched out in the process of becoming a herb. Two months earlier the whole marsh would have been astir with flocks of shorebirds pausing on their way south. Even now there was a late-lingering flock of "peeps"—the collective term applied by desperate ornithophiles to the three species of small, brown-streaked sandpipers that are difficult to tell apart. These, by the look of their comparatively large, droop-tipped bills, were Western sandpipers—which would mean that the little creatures had flown here all the way from the far side of Alaska. There were several hundred, all hurriedly probing the mud, as anxious as travelers at a lunch-counter in a railroad station with the train on the point of departure. And indeed the analogy is probably valid; if something startled the flock every bird in it would be instantly and irresistibly snatched away even if a succulent worm were between its mandibles. As I drew nearer I could hear their continuous cheeping, sounding as if fingers of the wind were plucking the highest strings of a harp.

On Nauset Beach a day or two later a light snow was blowing like sand. Two groups of gannets came by well out beyond the breakers. Sailing along the green front of the waves, as white as the whitecaps, then beating with an easy, shallow stroke of their long, narrow, black-tipped wings, they made a grand sight. Larger, more aerial birds, they overtook the gulls without effort. "Sophisticated" would be the word today for the gannet's rakish design. Slim, tapered, with setback wings, the gannet reminds you of a bow and arrow, and like an arrow it dives from on high—like a judgment hurled earthward from Jove's down-flung arm. . . . Some of the female eiders I had missed in Maine were here. Two were close in among the breakers off the end of the moraine, a most unusual situation for ducks to let themselves get into. But clearly they knew what they were about. I watched enchanted as they would let a wave lift them up its front, then, just before it crashed upon them, would dive with a mighty kick under the toppling crest to shoot up on the other side as sleek and serene as mannequins. It was difficult to believe that the exercise had any other object than sport.

There were extraordinary things on Nauset Beach. I kept stopping as I walked to gaze down with what must have seemed a drunkenness of astonishment at the piles of washed-up seaweed with which the beach was fringed, of the kind I thought of as fried-bacon kelp; every pile of it was a mass of foam bubbles, large and small, seemingly blown out of gems, of magic purples, blues and greens, and some of true, unbelievable gold. At night there was an even more miraculous phenomenon. At every step I took pinpoints of white light shone and expired in the sand around my feet. I took it to be, like the firefly's illumination, a case of bioluminescence, as scientists call it, the product of some minute organism's agitation. But I felt like a god striding across the firmament and creating ephemeral constellations with every pace.

The perennial problem of where I was going to put up at night had presented itself at the start, of course. It was not going to be on any of the three large tracts (in addition to the small one by Nauset Marsh) so far incorporated in the National Seashore; that was made clear in official accents mild but brooking no discussion: "There is no provision for camping in any of these areas." Ah, but there was the Massachusetts Audubon Society's Sanctuary, which I knew did include a campground, not to mention guest cottages! The Sanctuary was on Cape Cod Bay, at the mouth of the subsidiary bay called Wellfleet Harbor, which is where the forearm muscle being displayed by the Cape would be had it not been—to judge by appearances—eaten away. I repaired to it.

There was a well-lived-in old house on high ground and a nature trail descending from it. The trail made a highly worthwhile circuit of marsh, shore and hillside and by means of numbered markers referring to a mimeographed booklet on sale at the headquarters gave you an introduction to the flora of the Cape such as would take you days to equal by working with books alone. The superintendent proved to be no less helpful than the book, and patient too. But the campground, he said, was closed for the winter. "Member Audubon Society Central Atlantic States," I had managed to insert mumblingly into the conversation. And: "Traveling alone, small self-contained bus." But it was no go. The campground was closed. *Fermé. Geschlossen.*

The liquor dealer in the big shopping center at Orleans was quite willing to let me park overnight in the alley beside his store. The arrangement was not quite the kind I had in mind in setting off for winter's wild littoral but I thought it would have to do until I could make some other. However, when I called at the police station for official sanction (what a pass of complexity we have reached when the State has to be squared before we can spend a night outside our own or someone else's four walls!) I raised the question of whether I could not stay in Nickerson Park, closed for the season though it was. The man in uniform at the desk, grey-haired but of unlined countenance, turned out to be an understanding and considerate gentleman. He undertook to intercede with the manager of the park and put in call after call on the telephone until he ran him down. The required permission being forthcoming, I was quartered like a landowner on his estates that night and subsequent nights. The park was entirely mine and I felt it so from my roost in the woods above Cliff Pond.

Wherever I happened to be at six o'clock in the evening I had dinner. Twice it was at Wellfleet, a small port in a deep recess of Wellfleet Harbor called The Cove. From the waterside, the picture of the town's casually clustered little white houses, brooded over like so many chicks in a brush-growth of trees by a solid white hen of a church with steeple alertly erect, must be fixed in the mind of every devotee of the Cape. Eight or ten boats lay side by side at the municipal wharf where I ate; the fishing fleet that reputedly was once second only to Gloucester's has not entirely melted away. About 35 feet over-all, I guessed, the boats had stout wooden hulls, heavy winches, cordage bestrewing masts, derricks and deck, and an eclectic assortment of names: *Huckleberry Finn, Navigator, Lilian C., Magellan, Hero, Old Glory, Squid.* Two hardy-looking Yankees in plaid jackets were working on *Florence and John* in the cold white light of the garish wharf-lamps. While I had no compunction about eavesdropping on their talk, which had a pleasantly didactic Cape Cod accent, I was over my depth. They were discussing the idiosyncrasies of an ammeter, if I got it right. "You mean to say the poles are reversed? Well, how will you know which is which?"

On occasion before returning to the park I walked around the streets of Orleans, past the big lighted houses, beneath the tall elms, which seemed a world's distance from the moorland, sea and barren sands I had quitted at the darker end of that hour known as "twixt dog and wolf." It was always black night when I rolled up to the campsite. Yet much of the evening remained. With the shades drawn to deny any chance wayfarer the advantage of me, I would sit sunk in comfort with a book beside the old-fashioned gas-mantle lamp which— incomparably superior to the up-to-date anemic electric lantern—emitted a brilliant, bus-filling light, a very welcome warmth and a steady, companionable hissing.

In a drizzle there was a penalty for camping in the woods; the trees caught and amalgamated the droplets and let fall great dollops on the aluminum roof. Lying sleepless beneath it you could believe that solid pellets were being bounced on it. However, grey though the skies habitually were, it was usually not raining. One morning it was even clear. Since the air had been aswirl with a light snow when I had turned in, the two stars I glimpsed when I pulled the shade aside were a joyful sight. With the first light I heard the clangor of a passing flock of geese. The lake, behind the black bars of the pines' trunks, was a mirror of the yellow light that presently filled the eastern sky. . . . There was, after all, much to be said for a Polar Canadian air-mass if it moved in without much wind, even if it dropped the temperature to the low twenties. While the color began to flood back into a landscape which for days had largely lacked it, so that one had almost forgotten what it was, I thought: here I sit, answerable to nobody, having ahead of me more of this new world to discover, with this fresh, unlived day before me and these warm boiled eggs, this hot coffee and toasty honey sandwich! I knew I was as happily disposed, even, as I should recognize myself in retrospect to have been.

All told, I spent many hours tramping the Great Beach. The cliff that rears up behind it is of even-textured, coarse sand the color of a lion, sparsely embedded with stones, and rises to remarkable heights—175 feet in one place. It appears very steep. On the strength of the impression it leaves, one might well guess, looking back on it, that the angle of its face is as much as 70 degrees. Studying it at the time, I guessed 45. But 35 is what it is, the Park Service tells us. All the same, it towers overawingly, and because its angle of declination is constant, it has, if very faintly, an air of the deliberately constructed, as if it were a breast-work erected by giants or a monument built by contemporaries of the Pharaohs to outstare Time from beneath its slightly overhanging brow of sod. The illusion is possible only because the bowlike bend of the beach, though slight, prevents your seeing more than a short stretch of the cliff at any one place.

I had the benefit of a full initiation on my first go at the Great Beach, heading into a driving northeaster which was armed with needles of rain. The wind sent the billows rolling massively in to break in a curl of plunging water the color of deep aquamarine or of dilute lime juice and with the sound of a great throaty rumble. Amid the roar on roar you felt yourself in the presence of enormous goings on. A few herring gulls rode along the edge of the cliff on the updraft caused by the slope's deflection of the wind. Six or eight others, evidently attracted by something in the water, held a position for a long time low over the sea, beating hard to hold their own in the teeth of the punishing wind, dropping to the surface and rising again to keep from being buried beneath a breaker. Not another soul was to be glimpsed from start to finish, even where cottages crowned the cliff. It was a monotone vista, harsh and unrelenting, with nothing in it to suggest that there was any ingredient of the universe to indulge the softer side of human nature. It did not matter. I felt tireless, as if, like the gulls borne on the upshot current of the wind, I tapped the forces of the boisterous elements, as if the very thunder of the surf were transmuted into an intoxicant in my veins.

From the Little Colorado to the Foot of the Grand Canyon

JOHN WESLEY POWELL

A classic in the library of American discovery, John Wesley Powell's Exploration of the Colorado River of the West and Its Tributaries *was published in 1875, six years after his hazardous expedition on the Green and Colorado rivers. It remains a fascinating guide and companion for those who raft safely on the great waterways today.*

August 13

WE are now ready to start on our way down the Great Unknown. Our boats, tied to a common stake, chafe each other as they are tossed by the fretful river. They ride high and buoyant, for their loads are lighter than we could desire. We have but a month's rations remaining. The flour has been resifted through the mosquito-net sieve; the spoiled bacon has been dried and the worst of it boiled; the few pounds of dried apples have been spread in the sun and reshrunken to their normal bulk. The sugar has all melted and gone on its way down the river. But we have a large sack of coffee. The lightening of the boats has this advantage: they will ride the waves better and we shall have but little to carry when we make a portage.

We are three quarters of a mile in the depths of the earth, and the great river shrinks into insignificance as it dashes its angry waves against the walls and cliffs that rise to the world above; the waves are but puny ripples, and we but pigmies, running up and down the sands or lost among the boulders.

We have an unknown distance yet to run, an unknown river to explore. What falls there are, we know not; what rocks beset the channel, we know not; what walls rise over the river, we know not. Ah, well! we may conjecture many things. The men talk as cheerfully as ever; jests are bandied about freely this morning; but to me the cheer is somber and the jests are ghastly.

With some eagerness and some anxiety and some misgiving we enter the canyon below and are carried along by the swift water through walls which rise from its very edge. They have the same structure that we noticed yesterday— tiers of irregular shelves below, and, above these, steep slopes to the foot of marble cliffs. We run six miles in a little more than half an hour and emerge into a more open portion of the canyon, where high hills and ledges of rock intervene between the river and the distant walls. Just at the head of this open place the river runs across a dike; that is, a fissure in the rocks, open to depths below, was filled with eruptive matter, and this on cooling was harder than the rocks through which the crevice was made, and when these were washed away the harder volcanic matter remained as a wall, and the river has cut a gateway through it several hundred feet high and as many wide. As it crosses the wall, there is a fall below and a bad rapid, filled with boulders of trap; so we stop to make a portage. Then on we go, gliding by hills and ledges, with distant walls in view; sweeping past sharp angles of rock; stopping at a few points to examine rapids, which we find can be run, until we have made another five miles, when we land for dinner.

Then we let down with lines over a long rapid and start again. Once more the walls close in, and we find ourselves in a narrow gorge, the water again filling the channel and being very swift. With great care and constant watchfulness we proceed, making about four miles this afternoon, and camp in a cave.

August 14

At daybreak we walk down the bank of the river, on a little sandy beach, to take a view of a new feature in the canyon. Heretofore hard rocks have given us bad river; soft rocks, smooth water; and a series of rocks harder than any we have experienced sets in. The river enters the gneiss! We can see but a little way into the granite gorge, but it looks threatening.

After breakfast we enter on the waves. At the very introduction it inspires awe. The canyon is narrower than we have ever before seen it; the water is swifter; there are but few broken rocks in the channel; but the walls are set, on either side, with pinnacles and crags; and sharp, angular buttresses, bristling with wind- and wave-polished spires, extend far out into the river.

Ledges of rock jut into the stream, their tops sometimes just below the surface, sometimes rising a few or many feet above; and island ledges and island pinnacles and island towers break the swift course of the stream into chutes and eddies and whirlpools. We soon reach a place where a creek comes in from the left, and, just below, the channel is choked with boulders, which have washed down this lateral canyon and formed a dam, over which there is a fall of 30 or 40 feet; but on the boulders foothold can be had, and we make a portage. Three more

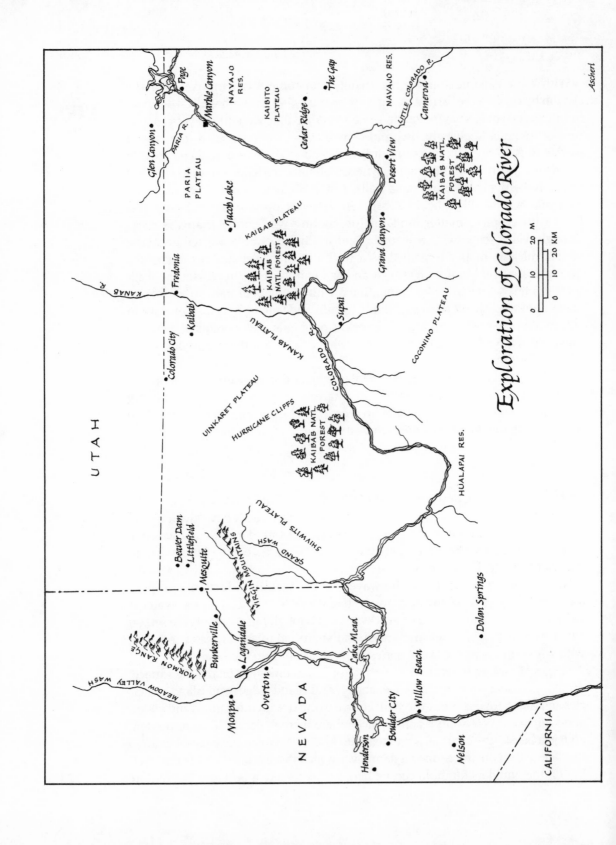

Exploration of Colorado River

such dams are found. Over one we make a portage; at the other two are chutes through which we can run.

As we proceed the granite rises higher, until nearly a thousand feet of the lower part of the walls are composed of this rock.

About eleven o'clock we hear a great roar ahead, and approach it very cautiously. The sound grows louder and louder as we run, and at last we find ourselves above a long, broken fall, with ledges and pinnacles of rock obstructing the river. There is a descent of perhaps 75 or 80 feet in a third of a mile, and the rushing waters break into great waves on the rocks, and lash themselves into a mad, white foam. We can land just above, but there is no foothold on either side by which we can make a portage. It is nearly a thousand feet to the top of the granite; so it will be impossible to carry our boats around, though we can climb to the summit up a side gulch and, passing along a mile or two, descend to the river. This we find on examination; but such a portage would be impracticable for us, and we must run the rapid or abandon the river. There is no hesitation. We step into our boats, push off, and away we go, first on smooth but swift water, then we strike a glassy wave and ride to its top, down again into the trough, up again on a higher wave, and down and up on waves higher and still higher until we strike one just as it curls back, and a breaker rolls over our little boat. Still on we speed, shooting past projecting rocks, till the little boat is caught in a whirlpool and spun round several times. At last we pull out again into the stream. And now the other boats have passed us. The open compartment of the *Emma Dean* is filled with water and every breaker rolls over us. Hurled back from a rock, now on this side, now on that, we are carried into an eddy, in which we struggle for a few minutes, and are then out again, the breakers still rolling over us. Our boat is unmanageable, but she cannot sink, and we drift down another hundred yards through breakers—how, we scarcely know. We find the other boats have turned into an eddy at the foot of the fall and are waiting to catch us as we come, for the men have seen that our boat is swamped. They push out as we come near and pull us in against the wall. Our boat bailed, on we go again.

The walls now are more than a mile in height—a vertical distance difficult to appreciate. Stand on the south steps of the Treasury building in Washington and look down Pennsylvania Avenue to the Capitol; measure this distance overhead, and imagine cliffs to extend to that altitude, and you will understand what is meant; or stand at Canal Street in New York and look up Broadway to Grace Church, and you have about the distance; or stand at Lake Street bridge in Chicago and look down to the Central Depot, and you have it again.

A thousand feet of this is up through granite crags; then steep slopes and perpendicular cliffs rise one above another to the summit. The gorge is black and narrow below, red and gray and flaring above, with crags and angular projections on the walls, which, cut in many places by side canyons, seem to be a vast wilderness of rocks. Down in these grand, gloomy depths we glide, ever listening, for the mad waters keep up their roar; ever watching, ever peering ahead, for the narrow canyon is winding and the river is closed in so that we can see but a few hundred yards, and what there may be below we know not; so we listen for falls and watch for rocks, stopping now and then in the bay of a recess to admire the gigantic scenery; and ever as we go there is some new pinnacle or tower, some crag or peak, some distant view of the upper plateau, some strangely shaped rock, or some deep, narrow side canyon.

Then we come to another broken fall, which appears more difficult than the one we ran this morning. A small creek comes in on the right, and the first fall of the water is over boulders, which have been carried down by this lateral stream. We land at its mouth and stop for an hour or two to examine the fall. It seems possible to let down with lines, at least a part of the way, from point to point, along the right-hand wall. So we make a portage over the first rocks and find footing on some boulders below. Then we let down one of the boats to the end of her line, when she reaches a corner of the projecting rock, to which one of the men clings and steadies her while I examine an eddy below. I think we can pass the other boats down by us and catch them in the eddy. This is soon done, and the men in the boats in the eddy pull us to their side. On the shore of this little eddy there is about two feet of gravel beach above the water. Standing on this beach, some of the men take the line of the little boat and let it drift down against another projecting angle. Here is a little shelf, on which a man from my boat climbs, and a shorter line is passed to him, and he fastens the boat to the side of the cliff; then the second one is let down, bringing the line of the third. When the second boat is tied up, the two men standing on the beach above spring into the last boat, which is pulled up alongside of ours; then we let down the boats for 25 or 30 yards by walking along the shelf, landing them again in the mouth of a side canyon. Just below this there is another pile of boulders, over which we make another portage. From the foot of these rocks we can climb to another shelf, 40 or 50 feet above the water.

On this bench we camp for the night. It is raining hard, and we have no shelter, but find a few sticks which have lodged in the rocks, and kindle a fire and have supper. We sit on the rocks all night, wrapped in our ponchos, getting what sleep we can.

August 15

This morning we find we can let down for 300 or 400 yards, and it is managed in this way: we pass along the wall by climbing from projecting point to point, sometimes near the water's edge, at other places 50 or 60 feet above, and hold the boat with a line while two men remain aboard and prevent her from being dashed against the rocks and keep the line from getting caught on the wall. In two hours we have brought them all down, as far as it is possible, in this way. A few yards below, the river strikes with great violence against a projecting rock and our boats are pulled up in a little bay above. We must now manage to pull out of this and clear the point below. The little boat is held by the bow obliquely up the stream. We jump in and pull out only a few strokes, and sweep clear of the dangerous rock. The other boats follow in the same manner and the rapid is passed.

It is not easy to describe the labor of such navigation. We must prevent the waves from dashing the boats against the cliffs. Sometimes, where the river is swift, we must put a bight of rope about a rock, to prevent the boat from being snatched from us by a wave; but where the plunge is too great or the chute too swift, we must let her leap and catch her below or the undertow will drag her under the falling water and sink her. Where we wish to run her out a little way from shore through a channel between rocks, we first throw in little sticks of driftwood and watch their course, to see where we must steer so that she will pass the channel in safety. And so we hold, and let go, and pull, and lift, and ward—among rocks, around rocks, and over rocks.

And now we go on through this solemn, mysterious way. The river is very deep, the canyon very narrow, and still obstructed, so that there is no steady flow of the stream; but the waters reel and roll and boil, and we are scarcely able to determine where we can go. Now the boat is carried to the right, perhaps close to the wall; again, she is shot into the stream, and perhaps is dragged over to the other side, where, caught in a whirlpool, she spins about. We can neither land nor run as we please. The boats are entirely unmanageable; no order in their running can be preserved; now one, now another, is ahead, each crew laboring for its own preservation. In such a place we come to another rapid. Two of the boats run it perforce. One succeeds in landing, but there is no foothold by which to make a portage and she is pushed out again into the stream. The next minute a great reflex wave fills the open compartment; she is water-logged, and drifts unmanageable. Breaker after breaker rolls over her and one capsizes her. The men are thrown out; but they cling to the boat, and she drifts down some distance alongside of us and we are able to catch her. She is soon bailed out and the men are aboard once more; but the oars are lost, and so a pair from the *Emma Dean* is spared. Then for two miles we find smooth water.

Clouds are playing in the canyon to-day. Sometimes they roll down in great masses, filling the gorge with gloom; sometimes they hang aloft from wall to wall and cover the canyon with a roof of impending storm, and we can peer long distances up and down this canyon corridor, with its cloud-roof overhead, its walls of black granite, and its river bright with the sheen of broken waters. Then a gust of wind sweeps down a side gulch and, making a rift in the clouds, reveals the blue heavens, and a stream of sunlight pours in. Then the clouds drift away into the distance, and hang around crags and peaks and pinnacles and towers and walls, and cover them with a mantle that lifts from time to time and sets them all in sharp relief. Then baby clouds creep out of side canyons, glide around points, and creep back again into more distant gorges. Then clouds arrange in strata across the canyon, with intervening vista views to cliffs and rocks beyond. The clouds are children of the heavens, and when they play among the rocks they lift them to the region above.

It rains! Rapidly little rills are formed above, and these soon grow into brooks, and the brooks grow into creeks and tumble over the walls in innumerable cascades, adding their wild music to the roar of the river. When the rain ceases the rills, brooks, and creeks run dry. The waters that fall during a rain on these steep rocks are gathered at once into the river; they could scarcely be poured in more suddenly if some vast spout ran from the clouds to the stream itself. When a storm bursts over the canyon a side gulch is dangerous, for a sudden flood may come, and the inpouring waters will raise the river so as to hide the rocks.

Early in the afternoon we discover a stream entering from the north—a clear, beautiful creek, coming down through a gorgeous red canyon. We land and camp on a sand beach above its mouth, under a great, overspreading tree with willow-shaped leaves.

August 16

We must dry our rations again to-day and make oars.

The Colorado is never a clear stream, but for the past three or four days it has been raining much of the time, and the floods poured over the walls have brought down great quantities of mud, making it exceedingly turbid now. The little affluent which we have discovered here is a clear, beautiful creek, or river, as it would be termed in this western country, where streams are not abundant. We have named one stream, away above, in honor of the great chief of the "Bad Angels," and as this is in beautiful contrast to that, we conclude to name it "Bright Angel."

Early in the morning the whole party starts up to explore the Bright Angel River, with the special purpose of seeking timber from which to make oars. A couple of miles above we find a large pine log, which has been floated down from the plateau, probably from an altitude of more than 6,000 feet, but not many miles back. On its way it must have passed over many cataracts and falls, for it bears scars in evidence of the rough usage which it has received. The men roll it on skids, and the work of sawing oars is commenced.

This stream heads away back under a line of abrupt cliffs that terminates the plateau, and tumbles down more than 4,000 feet in the first mile or two of its course; then runs through a deep, narrow canyon until it reaches the river.

Late in the afternoon I return and go up a little gulch just above this creek, about 200 yards from camp, and discover the ruins of two or three old houses, which were originally of stone laid in mortar. Only the foundations are left, but irregular blocks, of which the houses were constructed, lie scattered about. In one room I find an old mealing-stone, deeply worn, as if it had been much used. A great deal of pottery is strewn around, and old trails, which in some places are deeply worn into the rocks, are seen.

It is ever a source of wonder to us why these ancient people sought such inaccessible places for their homes. They were, doubtless, an agricultural race, but there are no lands here of any considerable extent that they could have cultivated. To the west of Oraibi, one of the towns in the Province of Tusayan, in northern Arizona, the inhabitants have actually built little terraces along the face of the cliff where a spring gushes out, and thus made their sites for gardens. It is possible that the ancient inhabitants of this place made their agricultural lands in the same way. But why should they seek such spots? Surely the country was not so crowded with people as to demand the utilization of so barren a region. The only solution suggested of the problem is this: We know that for a century or two after the settlement of Mexico many expeditions were sent into the country now comprising Arizona and New Mexico, for the purpose of bringing the town-building people under the dominion of the Spanish government. Many of their villages were destroyed, and the inhabitants fled to regions at that time unknown; and there are traditions among the people who inhabit the pueblos that still remain that the canyons were these unknown lands. It may be these buildings were erected at that time; sure it is that they have a much more modern appearance than the ruins scattered over Nevada, Utah, Colorado, Arizona, and New Mexico. Those old Spanish conquerors had a monstrous greed for gold and a wonderful lust for saving souls. Treasures they must have, if not on earth, why, then, in heaven; and when they failed to find heathen temples bedecked with silver, they propitiated Heaven by seizing the heathen themselves. There is yet extant a copy of a record made by a heathen artist to express his conception of the demands of the conquerors. In one part of the picture we have a lake, and near by stands a priest pouring water on the head of a native. On the other side, a poor Indian has a cord about his throat. Lines run from these two groups to a central figure, a man with beard and full Spanish panoply. The interpretation of the picture-writing is this: "Be baptized as this saved heathen, or be hanged as that damned heathen." Doubtless, some of these people preferred another alternative, and rather than be baptized or hanged they chose to imprison themselves within these canyon walls.

August 17

Our rations are still spoiling; the bacon is so badly injured that we are compelled to throw it away. By an accident, this morning, the saleratus was lost overboard. We have now only musty flour sufficient for ten days and a few dried apples, but plenty of coffee. We must make all haste possible. If we meet with difficulties such as we have encountered in the canyon above, we may be compelled to give up the expedition and try to reach the Mormon settlements to the north. Our hopes are that the worst places are passed, but our barometers are all so much injured as to be useless, and so we have lost our reckoning in altitude, and know not how much descent the river has yet to make.

The stream is still wild and rapid and rolls through a narrow channel. We make but slow progress, often landing against a wall and climbing around some point to see the river below. Although very anxious to advance, we are determined to run with great caution, lest by another accident we lose our remaining supplies. How precious that little flour has become! We divide it among the boats and carefully store it away, so that it can be lost only by the loss of the boat itself.

We make ten miles and a half, and camp among the rocks on the right. We have had rain from time to time all day, and have been thoroughly drenched and chilled; but between showers the sun shines with great power and the mercury in our thermometers stands at 115°, so that we have rapid changes from great extremes, which are very disagreeable. It is especially cold in the rain to-night. The little canvas we have is rotten and useless; the rubber ponchos with which we started from Green River City have all been lost; more than half the party are without hats, not one of us has an entire suit of clothes, and we have not a blanket apiece. So we gather driftwood and build a fire; but after supper the rain, coming down in torrents, extinguishes it, and we sit up all night on the rocks, shivering, and are more exhausted by the night's discomfort than by the day's toil.

August 18

The day is employed in making portages and we advance but two miles on our journey. Still it rains.

While the men are at work making portages I climb up the granite to its summit and go away back over the rust-colored sandstones and greenish-yellow shales to the foot of the marble wall. I climb so high that the men and boats are lost in the black depths below and the dashing river is a rippling brook, and still there is more canyon above than below. All about me are interesting geologic records. The book is open and I can read as I run. All about me are grand views, too, for the clouds are playing again in the gorges. But somehow I think of the nine days' rations and the bad river, and the lesson of the rocks and the glory of the scene are but half conceived.

I push on to an angle, where I hope to get a view of the country beyond, to see if possible what the prospect may be of our soon running through this plateau, or at least of meeting with some geologic change that will let us out of the granite; but, arriving at the point, I can see below only a labyrinth of black gorges.

August 19

Rain again this morning. We are in our granite prison still, and the time until noon is occupied in making a long, bad portage.

After dinner, in running a rapid the pioneer boat is upset by a wave. We are some distance in advance of the larger boats. The river is rough and swift and we are unable to land, but cling to the boat and are carried down stream over another rapid. The men in the boats above see our trouble, but they are caught in whirlpools and are spinning about in eddies, and it seems a long time before they come to our relief. At last they do come; our boat is turned right side up and bailed out; the oars, which fortunately have floated along in company with us, are gathered up, and on we go, without even landing. The clouds break away and we have sunshine again.

Soon we find a little beach with just room enough to land. Here we camp, but there is no wood. Across the river and a little way above, we see some driftwood lodged in the rocks. So we bring two boat loads over, build a huge fire, and spread everything to dry. It is the first cheerful night we have had for a week—a warm, drying fire in the midst of the camp, and a few bright stars in our patch of heavens overhead.

August 20

The characteristics of the canyon change this morning. The river is broader, the walls more sloping, and composed of black slates that stand on edge. These nearly vertical slates are washed out in places—that is, the softer beds are washed out between the harder, which are left standing. In this way curious little alcoves are formed, in which are quiet bays of water, but on a much smaller scale than the great bays and buttresses of Marble Canyon.

The river is still rapid and we stop to let down with lines several times, but make greater progress, as we run ten miles. We camp on the right bank. Here, on a terrace of trap, we discover another group of ruins. There was evidently quite a village on this rock. Again we find mealing-stones and much broken pottery, and up on a little natural shelf in the rock back of the ruins we find a globular basket that would hold perhaps a third of a bushel. It is badly broken, and as I attempt to take it up it falls to pieces. There are many beautiful flint chips, also, as if this had been the home of an old arrow-maker.

August 21

We start early this morning, cheered by the prospect of a fine day and encouraged also by the good run made yesterday. A quarter of a mile below camp the river turns abruptly to the left, and between camp and that point is very swift, running down in a long, broken chute and piling up against the foot of the cliff, where it turns to the left. We try to pull across, so as to go down on the other side, but the waters are swift and it seems impossible for us to escape the rock below; but, in pulling across, the bow of the boat is turned to the farther shore, so that we are swept broadside down and are prevented by the rebounding waters from striking against the wall. We toss about for a few seconds in these billows and are then carried past the danger. Below, the river turns again to the right, the canyon is very narrow, and we see in advance but a short distance. The water, too, is very swift, and there is no landing-place. From around this curve there comes a mad roar, and down we are carried with a dizzying velocity to the head of another rapid. On either side high over our heads there are overhanging granite walls, and the sharp bends cut off our view, so that a few minutes will carry us into unknown waters. Away we go on one long, winding chute. I stand on deck, supporting myself with a strap fastened on either side of the gunwale. The boat glides rapidly where the water is smooth, then, striking a wave, she leaps and bounds like a thing of life, and we have a wild, exhilarating ride for ten miles, which we make in less than an hour. The excitement is so great that we forget the danger until we hear the roar of a great fall below; then we back on our oars and are carried slowly toward its head and succeed in landing just above and find that we have to make another portage. At this we are engaged until some time after dinner.

Just here we run out of the granite. Ten miles in less than half a day, and limestone walls below. Good cheer returns; we forget the storms and the gloom and the cloud-covered canyons and the black granite and the raging river, and push our boats from shore in great glee.

Though we are out of the granite, the river is still swift, and we wheel about a point again to the right, and turn, so as to head back in the direction from which we came; this brings the granite in sight again, with its narrow gorge and black crags; but we meet with no more great falls or rapids. Still, we run cautiously and stop from time to time to examine some places which look bad. Yet we make ten miles this afternoon; twenty miles in all to-day.

August 22

We come to rapids again this morning and are occupied several hours in passing them, letting the boats down from rock to rock with lines for nearly half a mile, and then have to make a long portage. While the men are engaged in this I climb the wall on the northeast to a height of about 2,500 feet, where I can obtain a good view of a long stretch of canyon below. Its course is to the southwest. The walls seem to rise very abruptly for 2,500 or 3,000 feet, and then there is a gently sloping terrace on each side for two or three miles, when we again find cliffs, 1,500 or 2,000 feet high. From the brink of these the plateau stretches back to the north and south for a long distance. Away down the canyon on the right wall I can see a group of mountains, some of which appear to stand on the brink of the canyon. The effect of the terrace is to give the appearance of a narrow winding valley with high walls on either side and a deep, dark, meandering gorge down its middle. It is impossible from this point of view to determine whether or not we have granite at the bottom; but from geologic considerations, I conclude that we shall have marble walls below.

After my return to the boats we run another mile and camp for the night. We have made but little over seven miles to-day, and a part of our flour has been soaked in the river again.

August 23

Our way to-day is again through marble walls. Now and then we pass for a short distance through patches of granite, like hills thrust up into the limestone. At one of these places we have to make another portage, and, taking advantage of the delay, I go up a little stream to the north, wading it all the way, sometimes having to plunge in to my neck, in other places being compelled to swim across little basins that have been excavated at the foot of the falls. Along its course are many cascades and springs, gushing out from the rocks on either side. Sometimes a cottonwood tree grows over the water. I come to one beautiful fall, of more than 150 feet, and climb around it to the right on the broken rocks. Still going up, the canyon is found to narrow very much, being but 15 or 20 feet wide; yet the walls rise on either side many hundreds of feet, perhaps thousands; I can hardly tell.

In some places the stream has not excavated its channel down vertically through the rocks, but has cut obliquely, so that one wall overhangs the other. In other places it is cut vertically above and obliquely below, or obliquely above and vertically below, so that it is impossible to see out overhead. But I can go no farther; the time which I estimated it would take to make the portage has almost expired, and I start back on a round trot, wading in the creek where I must and

133

plunging through basins. The men are waiting for me, and away we go on the river.

Just after dinner we pass a stream on the right, which leaps into the Colorado by a direct fall of more than 100 feet, forming a beautiful cascade. There is a bed of very hard rock above, 30 or 40 feet in thickness, and there are much softer beds below. The hard beds above project many yards beyond the softer, which are washed out, forming a deep cave behind the fall, and the stream pours through a narrow crevice above into a deep pool below. Around on the rocks in the cavelike chamber are set beautiful ferns, with delicate fronds and enameled stalks. The frondlets have their points turned down to form spore cases. It has very much the appearance of the maidenhair fern, but is much larger. This delicate foliage covers the rocks all about the fountain, and gives the chamber great beauty. But we have little time to spend in admiration; so on we go.

We make fine progress this afternoon, carried along by a swift river, shooting over the rapids and finding no serious obstructions. The canyon walls for 2,500 or 3,000 feet are very regular, rising almost perpendicularly, but here and there set with narrow steps, and occasionally we can see away above the broad terrace to distant cliffs.

We camp to-night in a marble cave, and find on looking at our reckoning that we have run 22 miles.

August 24

The canyon is wider to-day. The walls rise to a vertical height of nearly 3,000 feet. In many places the river runs under a cliff in great curves, forming amphitheaters half-dome shaped.

Though the river is rapid, we meet with no serious obstructions and run 20 miles. How anxious we are to make up our reckoning every time we stop, now that our diet is confined to plenty of coffee, a very little spoiled flour, and very few dried apples! It has come to be a race for a dinner. Still, we make such fine progress that all hands are in good cheer, but not a moment of daylight is lost.

August 25

We make 12 miles this morning, when we come to monuments of lava standing in the river—low rocks mostly, but some of them shafts more than a hundred feet high. Going on down three or four miles, we find them increasing in number. Great quantities of cooled lava and many cinder cones are seen on either side; and then we come to an abrupt cataract. Just over the fall on the right wall a cinder cone, or extinct volcano, with a well-defined crater, stands on the very brink of the canyon. This, doubtless, is the one we saw two or three days ago. From this volcano vast floods of lava have been poured down into the river, and a stream of molten rock has run up the canyon three or four miles and down we know not how far. Just where it poured over the canyon wall is the fall. The whole north side as far as we can see is lined with the black basalt, and high up on the opposite wall are patches of the same material, resting on the benches and filling old alcoves and caves, giving the wall a spotted appearance.

The rocks are broken in two along a line which here crosses the river, and the beds we have seen while coming down the canyon for the last 30 miles have dropped 800 feet on the lower side of the line, forming what geologists call a "fault." The volcanic cone stands directly over the fissure thus formed. On the left side of the river, opposite, mammoth springs burst out of this crevice, 100 or 200 feet above the river, pouring in a stream quite equal in volume to the Colorado Chiquito.

This stream seems to be loaded with carbonate of lime, and the water, evaporating, leaves an incrustation on the rocks; and this process has been continued for a long time, for extensive deposits are noticed in which are basins with bubbling springs. The water is salty.

We have to make a portage here, which is completed in about three hours; then on we go.

We have no difficulty as we float along, and I am able to observe the wonderful phenomena connected with this flood of lava. The canyon was doubtless filled to a height of 1,200 or 1,500 feet, perhaps by more than one flood. This would dam the water back; and in cutting through this great lava bed, a new channel has been formed, sometimes on one side, sometimes on the other. The cooled lava, being of firmer texture than the rocks of which the walls are composed, remains in some places; in others a narrow channel has been cut, leaving a line of basalt on either side. It is possible that the lava cooled faster on the sides against the walls and that the center ran out; but of this we can only conjecture. There are other places where almost the whole of the lava is gone, only patches of it being seen where it has caught on the walls. As we float down we can see that it ran out into side canyons. In some places this basalt has a fine, columnar structure, often in concentric prisms, and masses of these concentric columns have coalesced. In some places, when the flow occurred the canyon was probably about the same depth that it is now, for we can see where the basalt has rolled out on the sands, and—what seems curious to me—the sands are not melted or metamorphosed to any appreciable extent. In places the bed of the river is of sandstone or limestone, in other places of lava, showing that it has all been cut out again where the sandstones and limestones appear; but there is a little yet left where the bed is of lava.

What a conflict of water and fire there must have been here! Just imagine a river of molten rock running down into a river of melted snow. What a seething and boiling of the waters; what clouds of steam rolled into the heavens!

Thirty-five miles to-day. Hurrah!

August 26

The canyon walls are steadily becoming higher as we advance. They are still bold and nearly vertical up to the terrace. We still see evidence of the eruption discovered yesterday, but the thickness of the basalt is decreasing as we go down stream; yet it has been reinforced at points by streams that have come down from volcanoes standing on the terrace above, but which we cannot see from the river below.

Since we left the Colorado Chiquito we have seen no evidences that the tribe of Indians inhabiting the plateaus on either side ever come down to the river; but about eleven o'clock to-day we discover an Indian garden at the foot of the wall on the right, just where a little stream with a narrow flood plain comes down through a side canyon. Along the valley the Indians have planted corn, using for irrigation the water which bursts out in springs at the foot of the cliff. The corn is looking quite well, but it is not sufficiently advanced to give us roasting ears; but there are some nice green squashes. We carry ten or a dozen of these on board our boats and hurriedly leave, not willing to be caught in the robbery, yet excusing ourselves by pleading our great want. We run down a short distance to where we feel certain no Indian can follow, and what a kettle of squash sauce we make! True, we have no salt with which to season it, but it makes a fine addition to our unleavened bread and coffee. Never was fruit so sweet as these stolen squashes.

After dinner we push on again and make fine time, finding many rapids, but none so bad that we cannot run them with safety; and when we stop, just at dusk, and foot up our reckoning, we find we have run 35 miles again. A few days like this, and we are out of prison.

We have a royal supper—unleavened bread, green squash sauce, and strong coffee. We have been for a few days on half rations, but now have no stint of roast squash.

Nevada
Old and New

ERNIE PYLE

*Long before he became America's most famous
World War II correspondent, Ernie Pyle
reported graphically on the long car journeys
he and his wife made throughout the United
States during the 1930s.*

*J*OSIE PEARL lived thirty-five miles from the town of Winnemucca, Nevada.
Lived all alone in a little tar-paper cabin, surrounded by nothing but desert.
From a mile away you could hardly see the cabin amidst the knee-high sagebrush. But when you got there it seemed almost like a community—it was such
a contrast in a place filled with only white sun and empty distance.

There really wasn't any road to Josie Pearl's cabin—merely a trail across
space. Your creeping car was the center of an appalling cloud of dust, and the
sage scratched long streaks on the fenders.

Josie Pearl was a woman of the West. She was robust, medium-sized, happy-
looking, and much younger than her years, which were sixty-some; there was
no gray in her hair. Her dress was calico, with an apron over it; on her head was
a farmer's straw hat, on her feet a mismated pair of men's shoes, and on her left
hand and wrist—six thousand dollars' worth of diamonds! That was Josie—
contradiction all over, and a sort of Tugboat Annie of the desert. Her whole life
had been spent in that weirdest of all professions, hunting for gold in the ground.
She was a prospector. She had been at it since she was nine, playing a man's part
in a man's game.

She was what I like to think of as the Old West—one day worth one hundred
thousand dollars, and the next day flat broke, cooking in a mining camp at thirty
dollars a month. She had packed grub on her back through twenty-below
Nevada blizzards, and had spent years as the only woman among men in mining
camps, yet there was nothing rough about her—she didn't drink, smoke, or
swear, and her personality was that of a Middle-western farm woman.

She had been broke as much as she'd been rich; but she could walk into any
bank in that part of the country and borrow five thousand dollars on five
minutes' notice. She had run mining-camp boardinghouses all over the West.

She had made as much as thirty-five thousand dollars in the boardinghouse business and put every cent of it into some hole in the ground. She had been married twice, but both husbands were dead now. She never depended on men, anyhow.

She had lived as long as nine years at a stretch at one of her lonely mines. She had found her first mine when she was thirteen and sold it for five thousand dollars. She had recently sold her latest mine and was well off again, but she was staying on in the desert.

Her cabin was the wildest hodgepodge of riches and rubbish I'd ever seen. The walls were thick with pinned-up letters from friends, assay receipts on ore, receipts from Montgomery Ward. Letters and boxes and clothing and pans were just thrown—everywhere. And in the middle of it all sat an expensive wardrobe trunk, with a seven-hundred-dollar sealskin coat inside.

She slept with a 30-30 rifle beside her bed, and she knew how to use it. In the next room were a pump gun and a double-barreled shotgun. And a dog. But Josie Pearl was no desert hermit, and she was not an eccentric. Far from it. She had a Ford pickup truck and when she got lonesome she would go and see somebody. She had a big Buick in town, but didn't drive it much because it made her look rich. She would put on her good clothes and take frequent trips to Reno and San Francisco. She knew the cities well and was no rube when she got there.

She talked constantly, and liked people to like her. Her favorite word was "elegant." She would say, "I have elegant friends all over the West." And, "I may tear down this cabin and build an elegant house here." Nobody could deny that Josie Pearl was elegant toward the human race. She had educated three girls and grubstaked scores of boys and found them jobs. She had nursed half the sick people in northern Nevada. She was known all over the western mining country.

She said gold brought you nothing but trouble and yet you couldn't stop looking for it. The minute you had gold, somebody started cheating you, or suing you, or cutting your throat. She couldn't even count the lawsuits she'd been in. She had lost fifteen thousand dollars, and sixty thousand, and eight thousand, and ten thousand, and I don't know how much more. "But what's eight thousand dollars?" she said. "Why, eight thousand doesn't amount to a hill of beans. What's eight thousand?" Scornfully.

People had been doing her dirt for forty years. But here's a strange thing: every person who had ever done Josie Pearl dirt had died within a couple of years. She wasn't dramatic or spooky about it when she told you, but she thought she had put the hex on them. She had been trimmed out of fortune after fortune by crooked lawyers, greedy partners, and drunken helpers. Yet she still trusted everybody. Anybody was her friend, till proved otherwise. On one hour's acquaintance she said to me, "You get your girl friend and come out and stay with me two days and I'll take you to a place where you can pick nuggets up in your hand. I'll make you rich.''

Which I consider exceedingly elegant of Josie Pearl. But if I got rich I'd have lawsuits, and even one lawsuit would put me in my grave, so I started back to town—goldless and untroubled. But on the way, a stinging little flame of yellow-metal fever started burning in my head. Me? Rich? Maybe just one little old lawsuit wouldn't kill anybody.

All the people you saw on the streets in Reno were obviously there to get divorces. You could tell by the look in their eyes. You felt like stopping each one and asking, ''Why couldn't you get along with him?'' And yet, when you checked up, you found that was just the way they looked.

There was a fairly constant year-round population of around three hundred people putting in their six weeks' residence. Many of these stayed at dude ranches outside of town, so there were maybe no more than two hundred actually living in Reno at a given time. Reno's population was twenty thousand. That would make only one divorce seeker for every hundred inhabitants.

Our hotel in Reno had paper-thin walls, and you could hear everything in the next room. One evening some new customers checked into the adjoining room and I could tell from their conversation that they were an elderly couple on a vacation trip. They retired early. I was trying to write, and the typewriter went bang-bang-bang like a little cannon, there in the stillness of the room. I knew it must bother them, and I got self-conscious about it, so I quit early and went to bed.

But next morning I was up early, as were also the old couple, and I started writing again about 7:30 A.M. Up to that time they had made no remarks about the noise in my room. But as I started pecking away the man's voice came plainly through the wall—not annoyed, but just making conversation with his wife. He said, ''There goes Charles Dickens again!''

You can read that Nevada is the most sparsely settled state in the Union, but it takes an example to make you really feel it. There was just one telephone book for the whole state! Every phone in Nevada was listed in it, plus four counties of adjoining California. And the whole thing made a thin little volume that you could stick in your topcoat pocket.

* * *

I asked a dealer in a Reno gambling house how many times he had seen the same number hit in succession on the roulette wheel. I had seen a number hit twice on several occasions, and a fellow told me he once saw one hit three times. But this dealer said he had seen the same number hit five times in a row.

I don't know what the odds are against such a thing's happening, but it must be in the millions. I know that if you played a dollar on the number the first time, and kept all your winnings on that number clear through, you would theoretically come out with better than fifty-two million dollars on the fifth whirl—but the house would have closed its doors on the third whirl—when you made forty-two thousand dollars—and the owner would have gone home in a barrel.

Virginia City, Nevada, sits right on top of the famous Comstock Lode, the richest vein of ore ever found in America. By the late 1930s, the Comstock had produced more than seven hundred million dollars in silver and gold. It was so rich it was ridiculous. It had ore running as high as five thousand dollars a ton—while all over the West they were mining five-dollar ore at a profit.

The Comstock was discovered in 1859, when Nevada was merely a territory and there were no more than a few dozen people in it. Within a couple of eyewinks Virginia City had a population of thirty thousand. It went wild; it splattered money in its Civil War type of splendor; the great actors of the world came to perform; there was a man for breakfast every morning, as the saying goes, and in the first seventy-two murders there were but two convictions; it was in Virginia City that a Samuel Clemens started reporting on a newspaper, and assumed the pen name of Mark Twain.

For nearly twenty years Virginia City was the hottest thing between Chicago and San Francisco. And then exhaustion came to the Comstock Lode; it had given its all and could give no more, they thought. The tycoons moved out in '78.

Virginia City didn't show until we came around the last bend on the twenty-mile drive from Reno and looked straight upon it. There it clung, six thousand feet high, plastered to the side of a steep hill—a little old town surrounded and impregnated with countless old shaft houses and long gray piles of dirt and rocks from the tunnel depths. An old town set amid rolling hills and deserts.

I wanted to be impressed and excited when I came round the bend and saw this sight of my grandfather's day. But I couldn't even have that privilege. The skeleton was there, but progress had slipped inside the bones and made a mundane stirring. There was life in Virginia City again—not the old riotous life of bonanza times, but twentieth-century life, flowing just as it flowed in countless hundreds of other American towns.

Virginia City could not truthfully be called a ghost town. True, it had withered and dwindled. Where it used to sprawl for blocks up the mountainside and spill over the divide for more blocks and blocks into Gold Hill, now the slope was bare and the houses stretched a mere two blocks from "C" street. But the houses were full. You couldn't rent a house in Virginia City. The mines were working again, since Roosevelt had raised the price of gold.

Why, I wonder, can't an old place really die? Why can't it lie down amid its old drama and pose there, ghostlike, for the trembling contemplation of us late-comers?

There was an old whitish house on a sort of ledge in the hillside on the upper edge of Virginia City. There was a white fence around it, and a gate with an old-fashioned latch. An oldish man, small, a little stooped, and wearing overalls, came out and shook hands. This was Jimmy Stoddard, the Comstock's only living bridge between the distant past and the present. He had been on the Comstock for seventy-five years.

"I guess you go back further than anybody else in Virginia City, don't you?" I asked. People had told me that.

"I think you called the turn on that one, son," he said. "I think you called that one right. I guess I'm the oldest, all right."

Jimmy Stoddard arrived in Virginia City with his parents from New York in 1864. He went to work in the bowels of the Comstock when he was thirteen, and there he worked until he was seventy-one—fifty-eight years in the mines, right beneath Virginia City. Jimmy Stoddard was eighty-four, but he was still going out into the hills and prospecting around.

He was a truthful man, and admitted he didn't remember awfully much about the early days. He didn't recall that he ever saw Mark Twain; he did remember seeing many a man hanging from the beams of the shaft houses in the old days; he said he ran the cage that brought General U. S. Grant up from the mines on his visit there in '78; he said that in the boom days miners on their way to work would slip an order for stock under the bank door, and when they came out of the earth that evening they'd be five hundred dollars richer, just by speculation; and then they'd go to San Francisco and spend it all. He was one of them. His memory was clear but not spectacular. Seventy-five years is a long time to recall details and keep things straight in your head.

Not all the old-timers remembered as unspectacularly as Jimmy Stoddard. The most remarkable remembering was done by those who would tell you all about Mark Twain. It was truly amazing how sharp their recollections were. One old fellow told me that although Twain came to be known as a humorist nobody around Virginia City ever saw him smile. This old man remembered him well, even referred to him as "Sam."

He said Twain used to stand all the time in the doorway of the *Enterprise* building and spit tobacco juice onto the steps of the adjoining doctor's office, *141* which happened to belong to this old man's uncle. So this old man—just a boy then, of course—called his uncle's attention to it, and the uncle put up a sign not to spit there. After that Twain stood in the doorway and instead of spitting on the steps he spit on the new sign.

I thought that was a grand little story, and I had a sort of thrill from talking with a man who had actually known Mark Twain in those far days when they called him "Sam." Before parting, I asked the old man his age, and he told me. When I got home I figured back on the dates, and discovered that this old man wasn't even born till a year after Mark Twain left Virginia City forever. That's the kind of memory I admire.

Not a single descendant of the Comstock's great bonanza kings had any financial holdings in the remnants of the Comstock. Some of the first-generation descendants were still interested in Virginia City, sentimentally. Some of them would make occasional visits, to talk and look over old spots. Clarence Mackay, of Postal Telegraph, whose father was the king of kings of the Comstock, used to come back every few years. He would always go into the Catholic church and say a prayer in memory of his parents.

But the second generation, people said, had no interest in Virginia City. In fact, some of them were quite, quite ashamed of the roughness of their grandfathers. One day the grandson of one of the bonanza kings showed up with his bride. A pleased old-timer volunteered to show them around. He steered the couple out past the edge of town, up a little gulch a hundred yards or so, and then he stopped and said, with an emotion that was filling him, "Right there is the spot where your grandfather staked his first claim."

And the rich grandson said, "Isn't the view gorgeous from here?"

The old-timer thought he hadn't been heard. So he said again, "There, right in front of you, is the very ground where your grandfather made his great strike."

And the rich grandson said, "Aren't the clouds over there magnificent?"

And the old-timer replied, with what seems to me exactly the proper answer: "Well, you can go straight to hell."

And he turned and went back down the gulch, leaving them there.

F R O M

Old Glory, an American Voyage

J O N A T H A N   R A B A N

A trip in 1979 down the Mississippi, from Minneapolis to New Orleans, was Jonathan Raban's fulfillment of a dream that had haunted him since he was seven and first read Huckleberry Finn *in his home in England. Raban's journey thirty years later was made in a sixteen-foot boat and took him three months with many stops—he met river characters Huck Finn could hardly have imagined. In the following stretch of his journey, approaching Memphis, he learned that an invitingly placid Mississippi can play a ''neat and nasty confidence trick.''*

*T*HE river had settled into a smooth, loping stride. Just south of Caruthersville, Missouri dissolved into Arkansas somewhere behind the levee on my right. Around the wide curve of Barfield Bend I saw two tow fleets coming upstream in convoy. There was plenty of room for all of us; the Mississippi was more than a mile across here, and although the channel stuck close in to the Arkansas shore, there was a broad reach of open water on the Tennessee side. I had wanted to stop and look at Tomato, Arkansas; the first town in my eighth state was named so enjoyably that I thought it couldn't help holding other pleasures too. Seeing the tows push up toward Tomato Landing, I decided to skip it and cut away to the far side of the river.

It was easy water. I could fill a pipe and let the boat take care of itself, idling along a few hundred yards out from the edge of the forest. I had gone a mile or so when I saw a line of long, crookbacked breakers with an edge of white peeling from their tops. For a tow's wake they seemed to have traveled an unusual distance across the river, but then, both tow fleets were big, and perhaps their wakes had married. Running the engine as fast as it would go, I turned the boat around and headed upstream toward the shore.

At least, that was what I had meant to do. I couldn't work out what was wrong. I seemed to be going faster than I'd ever been before, with the entire surface of the river pouring by in a glassy race of logs, twigs, cola cans and orange crates. The whole world was going past, a stream of pure motion. Yet I was making no wake at all. The river behind me was as unruffled as the river in front, although I could feel the propellor churning hard against the torrential movement of the water. I had quite lost my sense of place and dimension. I looked across to the trees on the bank. They were moving too: wavering slightly, then slipping back, as if they were being tugged up against the grain of the current. So if I was moving at all, I must be going backward downstream, when it felt as if I were traveling up it at an improbable speed.

There was no question of running in to the shore. The forest grew right out into the river, and the trees were knee-deep in water, with no space to slip a boat between them. I tried to get my bearings by switching my eyes from the boat to the streaming current, to the willows and to the sky. We were all out of sync with each other: all in motion, but in different directions and at different speeds. The line of breakers was now only a hundred yards behind me. I spun the boat around and went with the flow of things. For a few minutes, there was a lot of jolting and splashing, and then the long calm of the main channel again.

It was as near as I had come to meeting the river face to face. The Mississippi had behaved perfectly in character. It had been a neat and nasty confidence trick. That invitingly placid water must have been racing at fourteen or fifteen miles an hour over a shallow ledge of sand. Its speed had made it look deep when in reality there was probably only three or four feet between the surface and the bottom. I was still enough of a greenhorn to have been completely gulled.

Yet there was a queer, scary elation in feeling myself poised so fragilely on that sweep of river, watching the forest and sky tremble and start to run. I had touched the deep stillness of the Mississippi; it was as if the world moved around the river and not the river through the world. For a few moments, I had been the pivot, the dead point in the flux; and if the sky had swiveled above my head and raised a sudden shower of stars over Tennessee, I wouldn't have been especially surprised.

When I pulled up a wooded side channel into the town of Osceola, Arkansas, I felt like a sleepwalker. I was too full of the river to take in anything else. There was a motel room, but all I could see was water; gliding, streaming, spinning in on itself, sweeping up in jets from the river bottom. I sat in a café and saw more water. There were eddies on the streets. In a bar-and-poolroom I tried to steady my hand and thoughts by playing a game of pool. I lost, prematurely, as I sent the eight ball on a twisty, meandering course into the far pocket.

*   *   *

Since my entry into the lower river, I had been following my passage against the notes and maps in Zadok Cramer's *The Navigator*. After 165 years they were still impressively accurate. It was true that many of Cramer's islands had gone off to lodge a few miles upstate, where they were scratching out a landlubberly agricultural existence. When Cramer said that the channel went to the right of an island it now usually went to the left, and vice versa. Nevertheless, the portrait of the river held good in all its essentials. There wasn't a reach on it that was not recognizable from Cramer's descriptions.

Over breakfast the next morning, I was studying Cramer against the charts. My first big landmark of the day would be Chickasaw Bluff No. 2, where the Mississippi ran south into a cliff and made a sharp turn to the west. This was Cramer:

SECOND CHICKASAW BLUFF, THREE MILES BELOW NO. 34

Here you see on the left hand a bluff bank of from 150 to 200 feet in height, singularly shaped, and variegated with different colours of the earth, of which the yellow is the most conspicuous. The river bearing hard against the bluff subjects it to an almost constant caving down, hence the face of the bluff is kept fresh in its appearance. This bluff extends about two miles down.

The river here turns short to the right, and is very narrow. Close in to the bluff is an eddy, you may keep as near the outer edge of it as you please, and the channel is safe and good though very rapid.

Island 34, along with another substantial chunk of Tennessee, had been pushed over into Arkansas by a five-mile chute which had halved the distance of the reach from what it had been in 1814. From there on, though, Cramer was as good as new.

I could see the ragged overhang of the bluff ahead, its sods of tousled grass falling away from its face and the raw streaks of blue and yellow clay. At the point of the turn, the marker buoys directed me straight into a thicket of rough water. The waves were coming up like tongues of flame, pointed and vertical. They knocked and jostled at the boat as I elbowed my way through them. This was what Cramer meant by "safe and good though very rapid." It was rocky going, but I had to stick with the waves to avoid Cramer's eddy. That was there, just to the left of the breakers: a deep concave circle of smooth black water. I kept as near to the outer edge of it as I pleased—which was rather farther, I imagine, than Cramer would have dared to go himself.

For several days now, the river had been rising. It had come up over the top of the dikes, which showed as long ridges of turbulence and rags of scud. It had drowned many of the trees on the shores and sandbars and turned them into "sawyers," the oddest-looking of all the snags on the river. The current would get into the branches of the tree and slowly drag it down until it was completely underwater. Then the elasticity of the trunk would catapult it up again. The trees at the edge of the channel kept on sinking and arching their backs in a ritual rhythm; waving and drowning, waving and drowning. Eventually the river uprooted them, and one could see them spinning in the eddies—full-grown willows and cypresses, their bare roots and branches rolling over and over.

I hadn't seen a tow all morning. It was a lonely business this, riding the swollen river with the sky bleary and the wind just high enough to raise whitecaps on the chutes and make the boat's hull lurch and clank. The nearest towns were miles inland. I couldn't make a landing on either shore, because there was no shore: just a swamp forest which stopped along an arbitrary line where the trees had got the better of the water. A bare sandbar gave me a brief stopping place, where I ate a handful of P. T. Ferry's pecans and watched the movement of a big boil out in the stream. It was a grotesque, animated flower, spilling enormous petals of water from its center. It was bringing up horrible things from the bottom: rotten stumps, branches gone feathery and white with mold, chunks of black peaty stuff—all the garbage of the riverbed was being scoured out and scattered on the surface. I was certain that if I watched it long enough it would start to spew out bodies, boats, skulls.

Memphis had timed its arrival on the current at a perfect moment. On Brandywine Chute I was depressed and frightened by the Mississippi in a way I hadn't been before. I feared its emptiness and loathed its enormous cargo of dead matter, the jungly shore, the purulent, inflamed water. Then, five miles off, in faint outline through a haze of windy humidity, there was the Hernando De Soto highway bridge. I ached for the comfort of a new big city. For a spell, I wanted to stop being a snow goose.

Other People's Houses

ALASTAIR REID

The author comes from a long line of Scottish travelers and writes of his heritage and wanderings in Whereabouts: Notes on Being a Foreigner.

*H*AVING been, for many years, an itinerant, living in an alarming number of countries and places, I am no stranger to other people's houses. I am aware of a certain disreputable cast to this admission; I can almost feel my wizened little ancestors shaking their heads and wringing their hands, for in Scotland, people tend to go from the stark stone house where they first see the light to another such fortress, where they sink roots and prepare dutifully for death, their possessions encrusted around them like barnacles. Anyone who did not seem to be following the stone script was looked on as somewhat raffish, rather like the tinkers and travelling people who sometimes passed through the village where I grew up. I would watch them leave, on foot, over the horizon, pulling their worldly belongings behind them in a handcart; and one of my earliest fantasies was to run away with them, for I felt oppressed by permanence and rootedness, and my childhood eyes strayed always to the same horizon, which promised other ways of being, a life less stony and predictable.

My errant nature was confirmed by a long time I spent at sea during the Second World War, on a series of small, cramped ships, wandering all over the Indian Ocean. Then I learned that the greatest advantage was to have as little as possible, for anything extra usually got lost or stolen, and we frequently had to shoulder our worldly goods, from ship to ship. The habit stuck—today I have next to no possessions, and I have closed the door on more houses and apartments than I can remember, leaving behind what I did not immediately need. If I had a family crest, it should read *omnia mea mecum porto* (all that is mine I carry with me); but it would get left behind.

Innocent in themselves, houses can be given quite different auras, depending on the dispositions of their occupants—they can be seen as monuments to permanence, or as temporary shelters. In Scotland, you find abundant examples of the first on the fringes of small towns, standing in well-groomed gardens, their

148

brasses gleaming, their blinds half-drawn like lowered eyelids, domestic museums served by near-invisible slaves. When I first came to the United States, I felt it to be immediately liberating, in its fluidity, its readiness to change. Few people lived in the place they were born, moving held no terrors, and renting was the norm. Yet people inhabited their temporary shelters as though they might live there forever; and paradoxically, I felt at home. When I began to spend a part of each year in Spain, my other adopted country, I rented a series of sturdy peasant houses devoid of decoration, with whitewashed walls and tile floors, and no furnishings beyond the essentials of beds, tables, cross, and chairs. It was a time when a number of unanchored people came to rest in Spain— painters for the light, writers for the silence—setting up working outposts in the sun, whose constant presence does simplify existence. Within these anonymous white walls, one re-created one's own world—essential books and pictures, whatever other transforming elements lay to hand.

In Spain, I grew very aware of houses as presences—perhaps the residual aura of those who had lived lifetimes in them, perhaps a peculiarity of the space they enclosed. I recall visiting a house in Mallorca in the company of Robert Graves, and hearing him, after only a few minutes in the house, making peremptory excuses to leave. "Didn't you feel the bad luck in that house?" he said to me once we were out of earshot. With time, I came to feel what he meant, not in terms of good or bad luck, but of feeling welcome or unwelcome in the houses themselves, apart from the inhabitants.

Of all writers, Vladimir Nabokov read the interiors of other people's houses much as psychics read palms or tarot cards: with a wicked accuracy, he would decipher absent owners from the contents of rooms, from shelves, pictures, and paraphernalia. When he lectured at Cornell University, it was his practice, instead of having a house of his own, to rent the houses of others absent on sabbatical; and behind him already was a wandering life of exile in England, Germany, and France, in rented premises. Summers he spent in pursuit of butterflies, in motels across the United States; and when, with recognition, he came to rest, it was in a hotel apartment in Montreux, Switzerland. These various houses and interiors inhabit his books as vividly as living characters—he is always making precise connections between people and the places they choose to live in, between objects and their owners. His *Look at the Harlequins!* is a positive hymn to other people's houses.

I know just what he means. The act of inhabiting and humanizing a house, of changing it from impersonal space to private landscape, is an extremely complex one, a series of careful and cumulative choices; and, in living in other people's houses, one lives among their decisions, some inspired, others hardly thought through. I make for the bookshelves with a crow of expectation, for the books, however miscellaneous or specialized they may be, always yield up at least a handful I have never read, or even heard of, and travelling has deprived me of the possibility of keeping a library, beyond a shelf of essential or immediate reading. Kitchens are a less calculable adventure. Some of them are like shrines, where cooking has been raised to a level of high art, and invite culinary adventure; others, incomprehensibly, are as bare as hospital labs in plague-prone countries, their refrigerators bearing no more than a few viruses flourishing in jars, two or three bottles of what can only be assumed to be an antidote.

At one point in our lives, my son and I lived in London, on a houseboat we actually owned, though temporarily, moored at Cheyne Walk, in Chelsea. We had three special friends, families that lived in other parts of London; and we came to an arrangement with them to exchange houses from time to time, for appropriate weekends. We had a loose agreement—we left behind clean sheets and towels, a "reasonable amount" of food and drink, and, for the curious, some correspondence that could be read. We all relished these unlikely vacations, since we left one another elaborately written guidebooks, and we could take in another part of London—markets, greengrocers, pubs, restaurants. I often wonder why people never think of doing that oftener, except at the wrong times.

In our travels, my son and I occupied rented houses and apartments from Barcelona to Buenos Aires. He can remember every one of them in detail, down to its sounds—the creak and shudder of the houseboat as it rose off the Thames mud on the incoming tide, a house in Chile with a center patio cooled by the cooing of doves, a cottage in Scotland in a wood of its own, guarded by a cranky tribe of crows, and the small mountain house in Spain that was our headquarters. Moving was like putting on different lives, different clothes, and we changed easily, falling in with the ways of each country, eating late in Spain, wearing raincoats in Scotland, carrying little from one place to another except the few objects that had become talismans, observing the different domestic rites—of garden and kitchen, mail and garbage.

Since the fifties, I have lived off and on in many different parts of New York, but very intermittently, since I came and went from Spain and from Scotland, never settling decisively in any one of the three. This fall, I returned from a summer spent in Scotland with no apartment—I had given one up before I left, and was expecting another in the spring; but a friend of mine, a dancer, was to be away for a month, and offered me her place in the East Village. I moved in, and took stock.

The apartment itself immediately felt lucky to me, the kind of apartment you want to stay *in* in, with high windows looking out over St. Mark's churchyard, and light filtered in through leaves to a white, high-ceilinged room, with about a third of the books new to me, and a long Indian file of records. I fell in happily with the place, explored the neighborhood, and found its Meccas—a Ukrainian butcher shop, pawnshops fat with the appliances of yesteryear, small Indian restaurants that looked as though they might fold themselves up after dinner and silently steal away. I made half-hearted attempts to find a more lasting sublet—buying the *Village Voice* early on Wednesdays, marking up the *Times* real-estate section on Sunday and then losing it—but that place made me immune to urgency, although St. Mark's chimed the hours in my ear.

One evening, I was having dinner with a friend of mine, a camerawoman, who lives in a loft in SoHo. She moves fast and often, and always seems to be attached to the ends of five or six active wires, so when we have dinner, we have a lot of ground to cover. Over dessert, she suddenly sat up straight. "By the way, I have to shoot in Arizona most of October. Do you know anyone who would stay in my loft and look after my cats?" We made a deal there and then; and, in a flash, I could see the shape of fall changing. Looking out reflectively on the churchyard the following morning, I realized that I was ideally equipped to be an itinerant. I have an office at the *New Yorker* magazine, where I keep books and papers, get my mail, and do my writing, when the time is upon me. What furniture remained to me now graced my son's apartment, and I was portable, to the tune of two small bags. I was in touch with other itinerants, some of whom would likely be going somewhere; and I was myself leaving for South America after Christmas, until the spring. So I dropped the *Voice,* and went back to reading Michel Tournier's *Friday and Robinson: Life on Esperanza Island,* my latest bookshelf discovery.

I had never lived in SoHo, and my translation there in October opened it up to me. I had to have a small course of initiation, in the hand elevator, in the fistful of keys, in the cats, and then I saw my friend off in a welter of camera gear—a less portable profession, hers, compared to writing. But then, I have always given thanks that I did not play the harp. The cats. Alvin, the boss-cat was called, a massive, broad-shouldered animal who looked as if he might lift weights in secret. Sadie, his sidekick, was smaller and dumber, but she simpered and purred, which Alvin never did.

Every morning, I fed them first thing, grinding up liver, cleaning their dishes; and when I came back in the evening, they would collar me and drive me toward their empty bowls. The first Saturday, Alvin got through plastic, paper, and close to a pound of sole when I wasn't looking, about an hour after his ample breakfast. But cats are unpunishable by nature, and we came to terms, which meant that I fed them just enough to keep them from breaking into those nerve-rending cries of simulated starvation. Cats in SoHo have the best life going, I concluded, in a loft that must have seemed like an Olympic complex to them, with me to do the shopping. Sometimes I wished they would go out jogging. But I found I could take a brisk walk without leaving the loft, and there was cable television, which kept me up the first couple of nights. Out in the street I learned to stroll all over again, and I connected up SoHo with the rest of Manhattan. I even took to working there, learning how Alvin and Sadie spent their day.

By then, I had come to count on what John Osborne once called "the blessed alchemy of word of mouth," that most human of networks, and it put me in touch with a poet-friend, who was to be away giving readings for a spell in November. Could I stay and look after their plants? Unlike Alvin and Sadie, the plants fed slowly, in a slow seep; and I grew attached to one small fern that required drowning every day, and that rewarded me with new green. Their apartment was in the West Village, the part of New York I have lived in most. The stores were familiar, the kitchen a pleasure to cook in, the books unsurpassable, almost all of them good to read or reread. You can count on poets. Eerily enough, I had stayed in the same apartment once before, on a quick visit from Spain in the sixties, when other friends occupied it. Now it was dressed altogether differently; but every so often, I caught a whiff of its old self and experienced a time-warp, with the kind of involuntary start that often becomes a poem in the end.

As my days there were beginning to be countable, another friend called me, a woman who writes often on Latin America. She was going to Honduras quite soon, and she had two questions: Did I know anyone in Tegucigalpa? Did I know anyone who wanted to rent her apartment for December, while she was gone? Yes to both questions; and, a couple of weeks later, I gave her two addresses in exchange for her keys.

There was, however, a spell in November, between cats, plants, and travels, and also between apartments, when I was saved from the streets by being able to find a room on the Upper East Side. I was finishing a piece on writing at the time, working a long day; but even so I never became a familiar of the Upper East Side, never have. It is hardly itinerants' territory. People don't stroll much there— they seem more purposive, and you have to know where the stores are. You don't stumble on them. It was getting difficult, too, with the subways—I had to think, really *think*, where I was living, Uptown or Downtown, not to go hurtling on the subway in a wrong though familiar direction.

My last resting place lay on the Upper West Side, also a new territory to me, since I have always thought of Forty-fifth Street as the Northern Frontier. It was, however, a revelation. There were oases of movie theaters, comforting even though I never went inside, plenty of odd stores to stumble on, and the neighborhood, to my delight, was Spanish-speaking, even rich in Dominicans, the pleasantest people in Christendom. Moreover, a number of people I had always thought of as out of range turned out to live around the corner. I had had a hasty airport call from my Honduras-bound landlady that morning. "Just pile the papers so you can walk around," she told me tersely. Indeed, her apartment looked as though the negotiations over the Panama Canal had just been hastily concluded in it.

I cleared a camping space first, and then I put the place in order. I have a stern morality about occupying other people's houses: I feel they have to be left in better shape than I find them, and this may mean fixing faucets or supplying anything missing, from light bulbs to balloons. What her apartment needed was restoring to its original order, now only skeletally visible. Anyone who tries to keep up with Central America these days acquires a weekly layer of new information, and her layers went back a few months. When I had the papers rounded up and corralled, the books and records in their shelves and sleeves, the cups and glasses steeping, the place began to emerge and welcome me, and I found, under the sofa, an Anne Tyler novel I had not read. One thing did puzzle me: as I cleaned, I came everywhere on scatters of pennies, on the floor, on chairs, on desk and table, by the bed. I could not account for their ubiquity, but I gathered them in a jar, about enough to buy a good dinner. Christmas was coming to the Upper West Side, with great good cheer; but so was the cold weather, so I went one morning, and booked my air ticket.

Before I left the city, I retraced my wanderings of the fall, going home again and again. If you have lived in somebody's house, after all, you have acquired a lot in common with them, a lot to talk about, from the eccentricities of their pipes to the behavior of their furniture. The tree house by St. Mark's looked properly seasonal, with a fire burning. I find I can still occupy it in my head, with pleasure. I went by the West Village, sat talking for hours in the kitchen, and then walked down to SoHo, where I called on Alvin and Sadie, who looked keenly to see if I had brought fish before withdrawing to rest up. I dropped off a winter coat with my son, and made for the airport and the warm weather with my two bags, leaving behind not one city but several, I felt, shedding a cluster of distinct lives. I just had time to call my friend, newly back from Tegucigalpa. Her time had been good, yes, she had talked at length with my friends, the apartment was great, thanks for fixing the closet door, I had turned up things she thought she'd lost, she felt maybe she had caught a bug in Honduras. I asked her about the pennies. "Oh, yes, thanks for picking them up," she laughed. "It's just that I throw the *I Ching* a lot. Have a good trip."

Night Freight

CLYDE RICE

*During the Great Depression the author made
a winless effort to pan for gold in the High
Sierras of Northern California. He returned
home the only way he could afford, riding
freight trains with veteran hoboes and others
like himself who had run out of provisions and
their luck.*

*T*HE tracks and wheels hit up a wild rhythm after we topped a rise and soon
we were rolling at a great rate, but the lumber we'd piled around in the rescue
was on the move around us so that we began to fear it and anyhow the
professional bum told so many lumbercar horrors that we were glad to get shut
of it when the old man said that, considering the broken seal and all, we'd better
get out.

At Alder Point most of the bums left the train figuring to go down the track a
ways and build a big fire so they could dry out before they holed up in a barn the
true hobo had spotted.

"How about you?" the old man asked. "You gonna knuckle to the weather?"

"No," I answered, "once I get going in a direction, the going just takes over. I
don't think I could hole up now even if I wanted to."

"Probably because you're going toward a woman," he muttered bleakly.

"Well, yes and no," I answered. "Works as good when I'm going away from
her 'cept that she's there, and real."

"Makes no difference," he answered. "I know about the other."

"Your wife," I asked, "she alive?"

"Dead," he answered after a moment of thoughtful stillness. "Nine years."

I murmured that I was sorry, feeling cheap for my prying.

"So am I," he said, "so am I." Then he forced himself from the past and
looked about him. "Where's Glen?" he asked, grabbing manfully at the present.

Glen was sitting on his box almost under our feet in the deep shadows of the
station. "Right here," he said.

"Are you gonna stay here for the night or go on?" the old man asked.

"I'll keep going," Glen answered, "Pop said not to tarry by the way."

I had a brief vision of their home, the walls of its clean rooms cluttered with framed, decorated mottoes. I could see the room so clearly that I could even see the pictures of Glen's grandparents taken in the old country. The grandmother appeared to be consumptive and frightened while grandpa's fierce mustaches were matched by his eyes for sharpness. He was in military uniform and stood poised to defend country and honor.

Then I did one of those thoughtless, impelled things: "What did your grandfather on your father's side do in his military service?" I asked Glen.

"Why, he played the flute in the band," Glen answered. "Gosh!" he said and then smiled. "Why?"

"I don't know," I answered. "Just one of those things."

The old man came closer to me and as we stood in the dim lights around the station I saw him peering at me. "By God, you're a strange one," he said, and then he shifted his thoughts. "What we've got to do is find a better spot to ride."

"Why'n't you stay here for the night?" I asked him.

"Could," he said, "I easy could. Still, following the will-o'-the-wisp is a tangled business. Seems you can dally all you want in your ease, but stop in the rough spots—why, it's hanging through the rough spots that keeps your dues paid in this union. No, what we got to do is find a better spot and now is the time to look for it. Where's Max?"

"In the station by the stove," Glen said.

We found him with a crowd of footloose characters around the station stove. The clock on the station wall said eleven-thirty more or less. I went over to Max and asked him to come outside.

"Sure," he said. "Ya know, I like you. You ain't afraid to bust in a car if that's what you want to do. You and me could get along fine."

He followed me out to the old man. "Give me my bottle," he said as soon as he saw him.

"Uh, uh," the old man grunted. "I stalled you from jumping a couple of times tonight and you're paying in brandy, even having a nip of it from time to time yourself. Look, Max, you gonna hole up here tonight?"

"Nah," he answered and stood for a moment reeling solemnly in front of us. "Got no use for this whole redwood country. I'm going straight through Frisco and then down to L.A."

"Come on then," the old man said, "we're gonna find a better place to ride."

"Gimme a drink?"

"I'll do that when we're out of town. Now come on!"

We poked along the freight in the dark, our only light being from the station and town. Our luck was dim as well. All the tie cars were worse than the one we'd been on and it was still raining. Then I found a car of ties with a hollow space in the center that opened clear across the car. We wouldn't be able to sit upright in it, but there was plenty of leg room and we'd be sheltered from the wind and rain. I climbed up and felt around and found why the ties had been piled around it. In the decking of the car was a big hole: over a third of the decking was gone. I showed it to the old man.

"Look here," he said almost at once, "here's our chance. Now you three scrounge around for boards to cover it and shove what you get up in there. She may pull out early. I'll meet you here 'fore she does."

He hurried away into the darkness.

We spread out, kicking, feeling around in what we thought were likely places. I couldn't seem to find anything that was even wooden till I came upon a little sawmill below the tracks. I fell off of a narrow walk in it but landed in a sawdust pile. From there I saw a square shape, tumbled at one end and silhouetted in the light from town. Being in the sawdust I wondered if I was under the saw and if I might, in raising up, split my head open on the sharp teeth. Then I saw it quite close to me and I reached over the sawdust remover chute and felt one of its sharp teeth. Overhead the roof of the opensided mill loomed black in the dark sky and the sawdust was dry under my feet. Ever since I've always felt that sawmills are somehow cozy. I reached over and rapped the big disc of steel with my knuckles and it rang like a temple gong. Then I remembered what I came for and searched some more, but everything that was wooden was nailed down. I was heading back when I saw that the dark shape before me was a stack of long slabwood. I ran to find Glen and together we made four trips from stack to car before Max and the old man came through the gloom. Max had a piece of tarpaper torn from a shed and the old man had two immense cardboard boxes. Wordlessly, he slit the boxes at the corners and laid them flat over the hole. Then we laid the slabs side by side, flat side down, over that, and Max turned his paper, dry side up, for us to sit on. Glen helped the old man up and we crawled up after, thankful that the trainman had been too busy on the other side of the freight to see our activity.

In Alder Point you couldn't tell the storm existed: the place was walled away in a deep hole in the redwoods where mist and moss clung to everything, including quite probably the folks. The train didn't start, and Glen and I got out and relieved ourselves and did setting up exercises to get our blood circulating and then crawled up into our tunnel where I again tackled the bindings on my pack and soon had my floored lean-to miner's tent loose. We worked around till we were sitting in it side by side, riding backwards again. The tent sidewalls covered each outside man from the slip stream of the train, and its top swept up our backs from its sewn-in floor and went over our heads and out to our feet before us.

"We better not smoke or light matches," I said. "I waterproofed this tent with linseed oil, beeswax and paraffin." Right away I was hungry for a smoke.

"Rigged out like we planned it," said the old man.

Glen laughed. "Little different than back there on the ties. I began to think I'd never make Salt Lake."

"Why Salt Lake?"

"I figgered and figgered," said the boy, "and read in lots of books, and I chose Salt Lake for where I'd start."

"That's a long pull," I said, "over the Sierras in the winter. Too bad you haven't got enough dough to ride over the hump in a passenger coach—say a matter of four bucks." Ruefully I thought of my seven cents.

"Yeah," the boy rejoined, "but Papa said, 'Make your own way, Carl'—he never would call me Glen—'Make your own way but never buy it. Only way is to earn.' He had that framed in the shop."

I smiled—to myself, I thought—at how closely the boy's description matched my picture of it, but my smugness must have shown.

"You'll do," the old man said to me.

"How do you know?"

"I don't savvy why," he said, "but I feel that as an anticipator you've caught something. Now you're feeling pleased with yourself," he said. "Remember, anticipators are a dime a dozen."

The locomotive up the track hooted and wailed through the night. I felt the redwoods took it to their brittle, stately cores. And the river too, I felt, didn't deflect those sounds from its gliding bosom, but roiled them in with its currents and—along with everything else, even gold—bore some of it to the sea. Why to the sea, why not away? I asked myself. *You sound like an arty bastard—"some of it to the sea"—ya-a-ah.* Well, how about the black sands on these coasts? They've got gold in them that was brought down by rivers like this one. *Maybe it was washed up from under the sea.* Uh, uh, you can't wash gold uphill—it's heavy. It filters down, never up.

With a jerk that came crashing down the line of cars we began to move. The flat wheels made their sound slowly, softly. Like the Queen's carriage over the cobbles of London Town, we rolled to the tie noises. Presently the rhythm lost stateliness: the flat wheels began to tap out the increased speed of their revolutions and the cars to rack and groan as they coursed poorly-laid rails. We were under way. Far ahead the engine cast its wail deep into the forest once more and, as it did so, turned a curve so that the last of it was muted as if begging no echo.

"We're rolling now, Grandpa," said Max from his side of the car. "Pony up that drink."

"The way to make it last," said the old man, "is to wait until the next station and then one more."

"With you guys hogging in on it? That's a laugh! Come on, pony up!"

The old man stirred around and finally handed him the bottle. "Act cute with it and I'll break your arm."

"You're gonna have to prove that right now," Max snarled.

"It's your arm." The old man's voice was inflexible.

"I half believe you would."

"You know it."

The bottle came meekly back. I took a little snort.

"Still feel the same?" I asked Glen.

"Ain't tempted now," he laughed. "I feel better."

I handed the bottle back to the old man.

"We'll take your share, boy," he said. "What's in your kit?"

"Shoemaking tools," answered the boy. "I make shoes by hand same as Papa."

"Where'd your old man learn the trade?"

"Why, Switzerland, of course. The best comes from there."

"Sure," agreed the old man jovially, "best watches and milk goats, now you add shoes."

Glen, I imagined, was a young man without guile or humor. I realized he'd stick to his last because his temperament wouldn't urge him beyond it. Don't sneer, I said to myself—he'll be a superb craftsman, come much closer to real art with his nose to the grindstone than you ever will at your far-flung verse.

Strange, I thought, one of us chasing madly after things not truly seen or known; the other setting out sturdily, secure in improving his rather simple task—carving, curving, shaping until the boot has grace, true grace, the thing you seek everywhere and find so fleeting. But I knew definitely down deep that I was right for me. Pay it to the wind, I told myself, for goods received. He'll never breach those summits for a glance of where we've wantoned for hours. Yes, I meant we—the accumulate, the composite, the husband, searcher, fool and, deep in the silliness of us, a student of the anatomy of enigma. Mystic, even— one of those words that puts my back hair up, describing a type of person I despise—Mr. Sludge, the medium! Let it go, the calm part of me said, let it slide.

No wind came through our floor and the rain and sleet that rattled in from time to time were things to be observed, not felt. The heat of our bodies and of our breath filled the strange haven and slighted under the edge that covered our feet, so that the air was neither stagnant nor humid. After Max on the other side of the old man begged another snort and, downing it, curled up against him and began to snore, I too fell asleep sitting up. It was one of those sleeps where the resting and recuperating usual in eight hours are completed in one or two. I believe I slept an hour and a half at most and awoke lying on my back.

I was aware that Glen and the old man sitting on either side of me were awake in the dark. We banged and lurched, but this car was better than most. It glided over the rails with its heavy burden of green ties while we, though still wet and worn, took our ease. Some mist we were passing through laid the engine smoke low along the river and strands of it ravelled under our tent and came to our nostrils with the primal smell of steamships and locomotives, the exhalation of big travel. Under way, I thought, going somewhere, going home! The locomotive up ahead sent its cry out before it as a challenge that drifted back over us. The old man was talking to Glen, calling him "son" without the least condescension, giving it warmth. Son, said out of patriarch's beard in the dark, can be a rich thing when he who says it has his own teeth, and judging from the way he handled his consonants the old man had his.

"Son," he said, "how about these shoes?"

Well, the boy didn't say much for awhile but finally he began talking about them, about the lasts and about good leather. He seemed to like the word supple: supple leather, supple hands, and the supple insteps of the people who wore the handmade shoes. Though when he spoke of the arch of the foot it was high, keystoned rigidly with metatarsals. I relished his two incompatible views of one thing. He seemed to feel that he had to go out amongst us Americans and show us as his father had what wonderful people the Swiss are. Don't know how they got that into him at home, but he had it, though it was all wound up with shoes and religion.

It's funny how frail fellows like Glen, these almost translucent-bodied people with their narrow chests and ways can show a determination utterly masculine that hardier men seldom possess. It's something of the psyche or the soul of the man certainly, because there wasn't bone nor meat nor mind enough within the boy to house such a feeling. He was telling us how he helped his father soak the leather before they made a shoe and of the wooden lasts his father made in the shape of individual feet, of the wood he carved them from and how he boiled them in linseed oil so they wouldn't swell or crack. Glen thought it was dangerous to do it in the house.

"It catches on fire sometimes," he said. "You have to watch it in a little shop like that. Often we worked in the kitchen. It was warm there and we saved on fuel. We didn't get a great deal for our shoes, not as much as we should, but we were kind of proud of that. Us Schweitzers were giving them more than they paid for."

"So now you're taking your little kit and heading for the big city to get a job with some custom shoe outfit," said the old man.

"I'd like to start out," Glen said, "in a big wide city that was clean. They say Salt Lake City is clean. I don't know about the Mormons. Still, they're kinda Christly, I guess, though not enough to be saved. The straight way is really narrow, but they aim at the Way. They're trying to be part of His flock. From how I hear they laid out their city, I'd like to make shoes for them. They say—at least in the geographies at school—that the streets are broad and shaded with trees—lindens, maybe, like Ma talks about being in Europe—and maybe they wouldn't rush around there the way we do in Eureka. With that nippy wind coming in from the sea you got to keep moving most of the time. I'd like to make shoes for people to wear as they sauntered down broad, shaded walks, not spiked logging shoes or leather dairy boots, but shoes worn when folks took their ease and came down off of their porches for a warm, easy walk and felt the shoes on their feet was just right for it. I'd use wood pegs in the heels so they didn't make too much noise. Can't stand rubber heels myself—it kinda takes something out of the shoe, the something that Papa was putting in—but I don't like the nails sounding in the shoes either. But with the maple pegs—why, I can almost hear the sound, and people could get used to me making their shoes. I could make a lot of them, get a shop started, hire all Swiss. No, not all Swiss either—there's other people. My father says some Swedes make good shoes. I'd like him to come there too, after we got the trade started buying those supple fine-grained shoes up there."

I lay listening, knowing that a kaleidoscope of linden shade, finely shod feet, and a general air of rustic refinement was brushing by the backs of Glen's eyes, and as I further tried to imagine what he saw, he spoke again wistfully. "I'd certainly like to get started in Salt Lake City."

The old man was silent and Glen didn't say anything more. I felt he was staring into the darkness, still intent on his objectives. But after a time he slowly slumped, folding into sleep. The old man told him to hunker down and snooze easy while he could. When Glen laid down I sat up and tried to find something in my pack to put over him, but the down sleeping bag and all clothing were completely sodden. When we rounded a sharp turn and the rails squealed under the stubborn, unturning trucks, he trembled and muttered what sounded like a fragment of a prayer.

Cheyenne Autumn

MARI SANDOZ

*The desperate, fifteen-hundred-mile flight of
the Northern Cheyennes in 1878 from alien
government reservation land back to their
native Yellowstone country is an epic segment
of American Indian history. In her famous
narrative Mari Sandoz describes the dwindling
band of Cheyennes, pursued by as many as ten
thousand U.S. troops, near the end of their
effort to reach home.*

WHEN the scouts signaled that all the soldiers were gone beyond the
Niobrara, worn out and tired, and not chasing anybody around here for a while,
Little Wolf's Cheyennes began to come out of their scattered hidings, cautiously,
almost afraid to be seen by the sun. Silently they moved through the broken,
choppy sandhills west of the head of Snake River, one from here, another there,
toward the place of meeting. Then suddenly, in a little well-sodded pocket
already shadowing with the lowered sun, they were together, the first time since
north of the Platte.

Suddenly their chief was there too, on his spotted horse on a golden
bunchgrass slope. Quietly Little Wolf looked down over them, seeking out any
missing, counting them all. Then he lifted his hand and started away, his people
following around a hill and down into Lost Chokecherry, a valley so small and
sheltered it seemed held within the cupping of two warm palms. Yet there was a
lake clouded with fall ducks; muskrat houses rose from the evening water and
many sweet rushes. In the northwest end of the valley, a steep hill lifted itself
against the winds to come, with a scattering of box elders standing in their fallen
leaves on the steep slope. Lower hills made a wall all around, rising well-grassed
from the bottoms. At the south a wide strip of brush lay brown and russet along
the slope, with hackberry trees, some almost naked cottonwoods, and higher
up, the dark green of a few little cedars.

The Cheyennes trailed into the valley in a weary, bedraggled line behind their
chief, the women still led by Buffalo Calf Road, the small children balanced in
the hide sacks swung from the saddles, the larger ones riding behind the women

161

and clinging tight to their gaunted waists, even some grown people riding double, for there must be no betraying track of moccasin anywhere.

Gratefully the Indians dropped their bundles, the women making it as for another fast stop, looking back uneasily over their shoulders, always looking back. But there was only the shadowing western hill that seemed close and comforting as the folds of a blanket. Some looked around in the other directions too, watching, no longer hoping, not noticing one among them who wavered in her saddle, clutched at a bundle, and then slipped down under the horse that did not move, head sagging in weariness. There was a cry and Spotted Deer ran to pull his grandmother away from the hoofs. The medicine man came and spoke quietly to her, "My sister—"

"Let me die," Old Grandmother moaned softly. "I am played out—" as a chill of the southern fever shook her again.

But Spotted Deer built a little fire and accepted the blanket that Feather on Head brought, one of the few left whole. Gently he wrapped the old woman in it, stroking her thin gray braids, but his eyes strayed to the young Yellow Bead hurrying to the lake with a waterskin for the grandmother. It was fine to have the girl help, even for a moment.

Slowly the other women had returned to their work, trying to move faster now, clumsily hastening, for it would soon be night. Only one long streak of yellow was left. It cut across the sky to a hill rising over the crowding ridges far to the east and the lone pine tree on top, very small in the distance. The Cheyennes knew a scout was there, watching the white man's trail that cut deep as the Overland roads along the Platte. But this one went into their old country, into the Black Hills after more of the gold that made the whites run so crazy.

There were some, like Thin Elk and Black Coyote, who thought it was foolish to camp so close to the trail where two columns of soldiers had just passed and where bull trains and faster travel could be seen every day.

"It is the best place," Little Wolf said, and they let it be done, doubtfully, yet remembering that he got them away from the soldiers who rode so close from the Beaver clear across the Platte. Now for the half of a moon they spent coming through the sandhills most of the people here had seen no more of the soldiers than if none lived. Here the smell of their small fires could be from campers drawn off the worn trail for grass, their horse tracks from the wild herds or from meat hunters chasing deer and antelope or shooting the big gray wolves.

As the valley shadowed, a cold wind seemed to rise from the water and the sky turned gray and dark. But almost no one had time to think about the storm that was coming in perhaps a day or two. There were fires to build, small against the hill and shielded by sod or piled brush so the red light could not travel to an enemy. The water was close, and the meat put on to roast as soon as the hunters came in with arrow-shot deer and antelope across the horses. As the Indians ate at the little fires, licking fat from their fingers, they looked uneasily away into the darkness, although they knew that Little Wolf was out riding among the closer watchers. No camp in charge of him and his Elk soldiers had ever been surprised, and none would ever be, if he could help it. The people were worn out, barely stopping to draw the fire spots over the ground to heat the sleeping places. Here and there one smiled a little to another as the love flute of Young Eagle started up on the hillside, softly now, and for the first time since the Lewis fight. It was good to hear his sentimental pipings for still another girl, the third since Blue Fringe in the south. It was good that some could still be young and flighty in love.

When Little Wolf returned and Quiet One went to take his horse, he found Thin Elk at his fireside, bragging about the hunts and his war deeds around here as a young man. Across the fire sat Feather on Head and Pretty Walker, the women listening a little, as they rested and warmed themselves, and smiling to this big talk.

At the next fire Spotted Deer fed broth to his old grandmother who had been so homesick for the north that his southern parents sent him to take her there. He was doing it well, a very good thing in a young man of sixteen. When the old woman slept, snoring a little in her weariness, he went softly away toward the fire where Yellow Bead crouched beside her aunt. He knew the girl had heard his step and felt him standing at the edge of the shadows, his blanket around him as he would have stood waiting at her home lodge. But she gave no sign and he returned to his own fire, wondering if her thoughts were following Little Hump, away with his father Dull Knife, as her eyes had followed him all the way north.

So the Cheyennes settled to their first night of sleep in the place where Little Wolf thought they might stay a while, if everyone was careful. He had 40 men here, including the boys like Spotted Deer, 47 women, 39 children—126 people. There would be one less when Thin Elk took the two good horses Little Wolf offered him for his return to Fort Keogh on the Yellowstone. Tomorrow, perhaps, or the next day, before the swift hard storms of a Cheyenne autumn.

A Cowboy's Eleven-Hundred-Mile Ride Home

CHARLES A. SIRINGO

Many years after it was published in 1885, Charles A. Siringo's A Texas Cow Boy, or Fifteen Years on the Hurricane Deck of a Spanish Pony *became a classic among first-person narratives of the Old West. Siringo worked as a cowpuncher and later as a trail boss on the huge cattle drives across the plains. In the following chapter he tells of a much-detoured trip home, from West Texas to the Gulf Coast peninsula of Matagorda.*

*A*FTER laying around the ranch a couple of weeks, Mr. Moore put me in charge of a scouting outfit and sent me out on the South Plains to drift about all winter, watching for cattle thieves, etc.; also to turn back any cattle that might slip by the "sign riders" and drift across the plains.

During that winter we, that is, my crowd, went to church several times. A little Colony of Christians headed by the Rev. Cahart, had settled on the head of Salt Fork, a tributary of Red River, and built a church house in which the little crowd, numbering less than fifty souls, would congregate every Sunday and pray.

That same little church house now ornaments the thriving little city of Clarendon, county seat of Donley County. The old inhabitants point to it with pride when telling of how it once stood solitary and alone out on the great buffalo range two hundred miles from nowhere.

The Colony had come from Illinois and drifted away out there beyond the outskirts of civilization to get loose from that demon whisky. And early that coming spring a lot of ruffians started a saloon in their midst. A meeting was called in the little church house and resolutions passed to drive them out, if in no other way, with powder and lead. They pulled their freight and I am proud to state that I had a hand in making them pull it; for the simple reason that they had no business encroaching upon those good people's rights.

When spring opened Mr. Moore called me in from the plains and put me in charge of a rounding up outfit, which consisted of twelve riders and a cook.

To begin rounding up, we went over to Canyon Paladuro, where Chas. Goodnight had a ranch, and where a great many of the river cattle had drifted during the winter. There was about a hundred men and seven or eight wagons in the outfit that went over. We stopped over Sunday in the little Christian Colony and went to church. The Rev. Cahart preached about the wild and woolly Cow Boy of the west; how the eastern people had him pictured off as a kind of animal with horns, etc. While to him, looking down from his dry goods box pulpit into the manly faces of nearly a hundred of them, they looked just like human beings, minus the standing collar, etc.

About the first of July, Moore sent me to Nickerson, Kansas, with a herd of eight hundred shipping steers. My outfit consisted of five men, a chuck wagon, etc. Our route lay over a wild strip of country where there was no trails nor scarcely any ranches—that is, until reaching the southern line of Kansas.

We arrived at Nickerson after being on the road two months. "Deacon" Bates, Mr. Beals's partner, was there waiting for us. He had come through with several herds that had left the ranch a month ahead of us. He was still holding some of the poorest ones, south of town, where he had a camp established.

After loading my wagon with a fresh supply of grub, Mr. Bates, or the "Deacon" as he was more commonly called, sent me back over the trail he and his outfits had come, to gather lost steers—some they had lost coming through.

I was gone about a month and came back with eighteen head. We had a soft trip of it, as most of our hard work was such as buying butter, eggs, etc., from the scattering grangers along the Kansas border. We never missed a meal on the trip, and always had the best the country afforded, regardless of cost. Deacon Bates was always bragging on some of his bosses, how cheap they could live, etc. I just thought I would try him this time, being in a country where luxuries were plentiful, and see if he wouldn't blow on me as being a person with good horse sense. An animal of course, as we all know, will eat the choicest grub he can get; and why not man, when he is credited with having more sense than the horse, one of the most intellectual animals that exists?

On our return to Nickerson, I concluded to quit and spend the winter with Mother, whom I received letters from every now and then begging me to come home. As I wasn't certain of coming back, I thought it best to go overland and take Whisky-peet along, for I couldn't even bear the *thought* of parting with him; and to hire a car to take him around by rail would be too costly.

I got all ready to start and then went to Deacon Bates for a settlement. He took my account book and, after looking it over, said: "Why, Dum-it to h—l, I can't pay no such bills as those! Why, Dum-it all, old Jay Gould would groan under the weight of these bills!" He then went on to read some of the items aloud. They ran as follows: Cod-fish $10; eggs $40; butter $70; milk $5; bacon $150; flour $200; canned fruits $400; sundries $600, etc., etc. Suffice it to say, the old gent told me in plain Yankee English that I would have to go to Chicago and settle with Mr. Beals. I hated the idea of going to Chicago, for I knew my failings—I was afraid I wouldn't have money enough left when I got back to pay my expenses home.

That same evening a letter came from Mr. Beals stating that he had just received a letter from Moore, at the ranch, in which he informed him that there were two more herds on the trail for Nickerson, and, as it was getting so near winter, for Joe Hargraves, better known as "Jinglebob Joe," and I to go and turn them to Dodge City, the nearest shipping point.

After putting Whisky-peet and my "Missouri" mare, one I had bought to use as a pack-horse going home, in care of an old granger to be fed and taken good care of until my return, Joe and I struck out with only one horse apiece—just the ones we were riding.

On our arrival in Dodge I pulled out for Chicago, to get a settlement, with the first trainload we shipped. I took my saddle, bridle, spurs, etc. along and left them in Atchison, Mo., the first point we stopped to feed at, until my return.

Arriving in Chicago, I told Mr. Beals that I was going home to spend the winter, and therefore wanted to settle up.

He set 'em up to a fine Havana and then proceeded. Every time he came to one of those big bills, which caused the Deacon's eyes to bulge out, he would grunt and crack about a forty-cent smile, but never kicked.

When he had finished there was a few hundred dollars to my credit. He then asked me if I could think of anything else that I had forgotten to charge the "company" with? Of course I couldn't, because I didn't have time; his question was put to me too sudden. If I could have had a few hours to myself, to figure the thing up just right, I think I could have satisfied the old gent.

I remained in the city three days taking in the sights and feeding the hungry little boot blacks. When leaving, Mr. Beals informed me that he was going to buy a lot of southern Texas cattle, to put on his Panhandle ranch, the coming spring, and if I wanted a job, to hold myself in readiness to boss one of the herds up the trail for him. Of course that just suited me, providing I couldn't make up my mind to remain at home.

Landing in Nickerson, I hired a horse and went out to the old granger's ranch where I had left my two ponies. They were both fat and feeling good.

Before starting out on my little journey of only eleven hundred miles, I bought a pack-saddle and cooking outfit—that is, just a frying pan, small coffee pot, etc. I used the mare for a pack animal and rode Whisky-peet. I had just six dollars left when I rode out of Nickerson.

I went through Fort Reno and Fort Sill, Indian territory and crossed Red River into Texas on the old military road, opposite Henrietta.

When within ten miles of Denton, Texas, on Pecan Creek, Whisky-peet became lame—so much so that he could scarcely walk. I was stopping overnight with a Mr. Cobb, and next morning I first noticed his lameness.

I lacked about twenty-five cents of having enough to pay Mr. Cobb for my night's lodging that morning. I had sold my watch for five dollars a short while before and now that was spent.

Whisky-peet being too lame to travel, I left him with Mr. Cobb while I rode into Denton to try and make a raise of some money.

I tried to swap my mare off for a smaller animal and get some boot, but everyone seemed to think that she had been stolen; I being so anxious to swap.

I rode back to Mr. Cobb's that night in the same fix, financially, as when I left that morning.

The next day I made a raise of some money. Mr. Cobb and I made a saddle swap, he giving me twenty dollars to boot. He and I also swapped bridles, I getting four dollars and a half to boot. One of his little boys then gave me his saddle and one dollar and a half for my pack-saddle, which had cost me ten dollars in Nickerson. I then had lots of money.

Whisky-peet soon got over his lameness, having just stuck a little snag into the frog of his foot, which I succeeded in finding and pulling out before it had time to do serious damage, and I started on my journey again.

On arriving in Denton that time, a Negro struck me for a horse swap right away. I got a three-year-old pony and six dollars in money for my mare; the pony suited just as well for a pack animal as the mare.

The next day after leaving Denton, I stopped in a Negro settlement and won a

167

fifty-dollar horse, running Whisky-peet against a sleepy-looking gray. I had up twenty dollars in money and my Winchester, a fine silver mounted gun. I won the race by at least ten open feet, but the Negroes tried to swindle me out of it.

While riding along that evening three Negroes rode up and claimed the horse I had won. They claimed that the parties who bet him off had no right to him, as they just had borrowed him from one of them to ride to the Settlement that morning. I finally let them have him for twenty dollars.

I went through the following towns after leaving Denton: Ft. Worth, Clenborn, Hillsborough, Waco, Herrene, Bryant, Brenham and Columbus; besides scores of smaller places.

I rode up to Mother's little shanty on Cashe's Creek after being on the road just a month and twelve days.

To say that Mother was glad to see me would only half express it. She bounced me the first thing about not coming back the next fall after leaving, as I had promised. I had been gone nearly four years.

FROM

Travels with Charley

JOHN STEINBECK

*When John Steinbeck drove away from the
eastern tip of Long Island "in search of
America," he was accompanied only by his
French poodle Charles le Chien. The buoyant
story of his transcontinental adventures
eventually enabled many thousands of
America's armchair travelers to ride along
with him in Rociante, his custom-made camper
named after Don Quixote's horse.*

*I*LLINOIS did a fair autumn day for us, crisp and clean. We moved quickly
northward, heading for Wisconsin through a noble land of good fields and
magnificent trees, a gentleman's countryside, neat and white-fenced and I
would guess subsidized by outside income. It did not seem to me to have the
thrust of land that supports itself and its owner. Rather it was like a beautiful
woman who requires the support and help of many faceless ones just to keep
going. But this fact does not make her less lovely—if you can afford her.

It is possible, even probable, to be told a truth about a place, to accept it, to
know it and at the same time not to know anything about it. I had never been to
Wisconsin, but all my life I had heard about it, had eaten its cheeses, some of
them as good as any in the world. And I must have seen pictures. Everyone must
have. Why then was I unprepared for the beauty of this region, for its variety of
field and hill, forest, lake? I think now I must have considered it one big level
cow pasture because of the state's enormous yield of milk products. I never saw
a country that changed so rapidly, and because I had not expected it everything I
saw brought a delight. I don't know how it is in other seasons, the summers may
reek and rock with heat, the winters may groan with dismal cold, but when I
saw it for the first and only time in early October, the air was rich with butter-
colored sunlight, not fuzzy but crisp and clear so that every frost-gay tree was set
off, the rising hills were not compounded, but alone and separate. There was a
penetration of the light into solid substance so that I seemed to see into things,

169

deep in, and I've seen that kind of light elsewhere only in Greece. I remembered now that I had been told Wisconsin is a lovely state, but the telling had not prepared me. It was a magic day. The land dripped with richness, the fat cows and pigs gleaming against green, and, in the smaller holdings, corn standing in little tents as corn should, and pumpkins all about.

I don't know whether or not Wisconsin has a cheese-tasting festival, but I who am a lover of cheese believe it should. Cheese was everywhere, cheese centers, cheese cooperatives, cheese stores and stands, perhaps even cheese ice cream. I can believe anything, since I saw a score of signs advertising Swiss Cheese Candy. It is sad that I didn't stop to sample Swiss Cheese Candy. Now I can't persuade anyone that it exists, that I did not make it up.

Beside the road I saw a very large establishment, the greatest distributor of sea shells in the world—and this in Wisconsin, which hasn't known a sea since pre-Cambrian times. But Wisconsin is loaded with surprises. I had heard of the Wisconsin Dells but was not prepared for the weird country sculptured by the Ice Age, a strange, gleaming country of water and carved rock, black and green. To awaken here might make one believe it a dream of some other planet, for it has a non-earthly quality, or else the engraved record of a time when the world was much younger and much different. Clinging to the sides of the dreamlike waterways was the litter of our times, the motels, the hot-dog stands, the merchants of the cheap and mediocre and tawdry so loved by summer tourists, but these incrustations were closed and boarded against the winter and, even open, I doubt that they could dispel the enchantment of the Wisconsin Dells.

I stopped that night on a hilltop that was a truckers' place but of a special kind. Here the gigantic cattle trucks rested and scraped out the residue left by their recent cargoes. There were mountains of manure and over them mushroom clouds of flies. Charley moved about smiling and sniffing ecstatically like an American woman in a French perfume shop. I can't bring myself to criticize his taste. Some people like one thing and some another. The odors were rich and earthy, but not disgusting.

As the evening deepened, I walked with Charley among his mountains of delight to the brow of the hill and looked down on the little valley below. It was a disturbing sight. I thought too much driving had distorted my vision or addled my judgment, for the dark earth below seemed to move and pulse and breathe. It was not water but it rippled like a black liquid. I walked quickly down the hill to iron out the distortion. The valley floor was carpeted with turkeys, it seemed like millions of them, so densely packed that they covered the earth. It was a great relief. Of course, this was a reservoir for Thanksgiving.

To mill so close together is in the nature of turkeys in the evening. I remembered how on the ranch in my youth the turkeys gathered and roosted in clots in the cypress trees, out of reach of wildcats and coyotes, the only indication I know of that turkeys have any intelligence at all. To know them is not to admire them, for they are vain and hysterical. They gather in vulnerable groups and then panic at rumors. They are subject to all the sicknesses of other fowl, together with some they have invented. Turkeys seem to be manic-depressive types, gobbling with blushing wattles, spread tails, and scraping wings in amorous bravado at one moment and huddled in craven cowardice the next. It is hard to see how they can be related to their wild, clever, suspicious cousins. But here in their thousands they carpeted the earth waiting to lie on their backs on the platters of America.

I know it is a shame that I had never seen the noble twin cities of St. Paul and Minneapolis, but how much greater a disgrace that I still haven't, although I went through them. As I approached, a great surf of traffic engulfed me, waves of station wagons, rip tides of roaring trucks. I wonder why it is that when I plan a route too carefully it goes to pieces, whereas if I blunder along in blissful ignorance aimed in a fancied direction I get through with no trouble. In the early morning I had studied maps, drawn a careful line along the way I wished to go. I still have that arrogant plan—into St. Paul on Highway 10, then gently across the Mississippi. The S-curve in the Mississippi here would give me three crossings of the river. After this pleasant jaunt I meant to go through Golden Valley, drawn by its name. That seems simple enough, and perhaps it can be done, but not by me.

First the traffic struck me like a tidal wave and carried me along, a bit of shiny flotsam bounded in front by a gasoline truck half a block long. Behind me was an enormous cement mixer on wheels, its big howitzer revolving as it proceeded. On my right was what I judged to be an atomic cannon. As usual I panicked and got lost. Like a weakening swimmer I edged to the right into a pleasant street only to be stopped by a policeman, who informed me that trucks and such vermin were not permitted there. He thrust me back into the ravening stream.

I drove for hours, never able to take my eyes from the surrounding mammoths. I must have crossed the river but I couldn't see it. I never did see it. I never saw St. Paul or Minneapolis. All I saw was a river of trucks; all I heard was a roar of motors. The air saturated with Diesel fumes burned in my lungs. Charley got a coughing fit and I couldn't take time to pat him on the back. At a red light I saw that I was on an Evacuation Route. It took some time for that to penetrate. My head was spinning. I had lost all sense of direction. But the signs—"Evacuation Route"—continued. Of course, it is the planned escape route from the bomb that hasn't been dropped. Here in the middle of the Middle West an escape route, a road designed by fear. In my mind I could see it because I have seen people running away—the roads clogged to a standstill and the stampede over the cliff of our own designing. And suddenly I thought of that valley of the turkeys and wondered how I could have the gall to think turkeys stupid. Indeed, they have an advantage over us. They're good to eat.

It took me nearly four hours to get through the Twin Cities. I've heard that some parts of them are beautiful. And I never found Golden Valley. Charley was no help. He wasn't involved with a race that could build a thing it had to escape from. He didn't want to go to the moon just to get the hell away from it all. Confronted with our stupidities, Charley accepts them for what they are— stupidities.

Sometime in these bedlam hours I must have crossed the river again because I had got back on U.S. 10 and was moving north on the east side of the Mississippi. The country opened out and I stopped at a roadside restaurant, exhausted. It was a German restaurant complete with sausages, sauerkraut, and beer steins hanging in rows over the bar, shining but unused. I was the only customer at that time of day. The waitress was no Brunhild but a lean, dark-faced little thing, either a young and troubled girl or a very spry old woman, I couldn't tell which. I ordered bratwurst and sauerkraut and distinctly saw the cook unwrap a sausage from a cellophane slip cover and drop it in boiling water. The beer came in a can. The bratwurst was terrible and the kraut an insulting watery mess.

"I wonder if you can help me?" I asked the young-ancient waitress.

"What's your trouble?"

"I guess I'm a little lost."

"How do you mean lost?" she said.

The cook leaned through his window and rested bare elbows on the serving counter.

"I want to go to Sauk Centre and I don't seem to be getting there."

"Where'd you come from?"

"Minneapolis."

"Then what you doing this side of the river?"

"Well, I seem to have got lost in Minneapolis, too."

She looked at the cook. "He got lost in Minneapolis," she said.

"Nobody can get lost in Minneapolis," the cook said. "I was born there and I know."

The waitress said, "I come from St. Cloud and I can't get lost in Minneapolis."

"I guess I brought some new talent to it. But I want to go to Sauk Centre."

The cook said, "If he can stay on a road he can't get lost. You're on Fifty-two. Cross over at St. Cloud and stay on Fifty-two."

"Is Sauk Centre on Fifty-two?"

"Ain't no place else. You must be a stranger around here, getting lost in Minneapolis. I couldn't get lost blindfolded."

I said a little snappishly, "Could you get lost in Albany or San Francisco?"

"I never been there but I bet I wouldn't get lost."

"I been to Duluth," the waitress said. "And Christmas I'm going to Sioux Falls. I got a aunt there."

"Ain't you got relatives in Sauk Centre?" the cook asked.

"Sure, but that's not so far away—like he says San Francisco. My brother's in the Navy. He's in San Diego. You got relations in Sauk Centre?"

"No, I just want to see it. Sinclair Lewis came from there."

"Oh! Yeah. They got a sign up. I guess quite a few folks come to see it. It does the town some good."

"He's the first man who told me about this part of the country."

"Who is?"

"Sinclair Lewis."

"Oh! Yeah. You know him?"

"No, I just read him."

I'm sure she was going to say "Who?" but I stopped her. "You say I cross at St. Cloud and stay on Fifty-two?"

The cook said, "I don't think what's-his-name is there any more."

"I know. He's dead."

"You don't say."

The Silverado Squatters

ROBERT LOUIS STEVENSON

In 1880 the author of Treasure Island,
Kidnapped, The Strange Case of Dr. Jekyll
and Mr. Hyde *spent an idyllic honeymoon
living in the bunkhouse of an abandoned silver
mine on the side of a Northern California
mountain. His American wife, Fanny
Osbourne, shared his enthusiasms—
and the daily inconveniences—during their
extended stay in airy, economical quarters.*

*T*HERE were four of us squatters—myself and my wife, the king and queen of Silverado; Sam, the crown prince; and Chuchu, the grand duke. Chuchu, a setter crossed with spaniel, was the most unsuited for a rough life. He had been nurtured tenderly in the society of ladies; his heart was large and soft; he regarded the sofa-cushion as a bedrock necessary of existence. Though about the size of a sheep, he loved to sit in ladies' laps; he never said a bad word in all his blameless days; and if he'd been a flute, I am sure he could have played upon it by nature. It may seem hard to say it of a dog, but Chuchu was a tame cat.

The king and queen, the grand duke, and a basket of cold provender for immediate use, set forth from Cailstoga in a double buggy; the crown prince, on horseback, led the way like an outrider. Bags and boxes and a second-hand stove were to follow close upon our heels by Hanson's team.

It was a beautiful still day; the sky was one field of azure. Not a leaf moved, not a speck appeared in heaven. Only from the summit of the mountain one little snowy wisp of cloud after another kept detaching itself, like smoke from a volcano, and blowing southward in some high stream of air: Mount Saint Helena still at her interminable task, making the weather, like a Lapland witch.

By noon we had come in sight of the mill: a great brown building, half-way up the hill, big as a factory, two stories high, and with tanks and ladders along the roof; which, as a pendicle of Silverado mine, we held to be an outlying province of our own. Thither, then, we went, crossing the valley by a grassy trail; and there we lunched out of the basket, sitting in a kind of portico, and wondering, while we ate, at this great bulk of useless building. Through a chink we could look far down into the interior and see sunbeams floating in the dust and striking on tier after tier of silent, rusty machinery. It cost six thousand dollars, twelve hundred English sovereigns; and now, here it stands deserted, like the temple of a forgotten religion, the busy millers toiling somewhere else. All the time we were there, mill and mill town showed no sign of life; that part of the mountain-side, which is very open and green, was tenanted by no living creature but ourselves and the insects; and nothing stirred but the cloud manufactory upon the mountain summit. It was odd to compare this with the former days, when the engine was in full blast, the mill palpitating to its strokes, and the carts came rattling down from Silverado, charged with ore.

By two we had been landed at the mine, the buggy was gone again, and we were left to our own reflections, and the basket of cold provender, until Hanson should arrive. Hot as it was by the sun, there was something chill in such a homecoming, in that world of wreck and rust, splinter and rolling gravel, where for so many years no fire had smoked.

Silverado platform filled the whole width of the canon. Above, as I have said, this was a wild, red, stony gully in the mountains; but below it was a wooded dingle. And through this, I was told, there had gone a path between the mine and the Toll House—our natural northwest passage to civilisation. I found and followed it, clearing my way as I went through fallen branches and dead trees. It went straight down that steep canon, till it brought you out abruptly over the roofs of the hotel. There was nowhere any break in the descent. It almost seemed as if, were you to drop a stone down the old iron chute at our platform, it would never rest until it hopped upon the Toll House shingles. Signs were not wanting of the ancient greatness of Silverado. The footpath was well marked, and had been well trodden in the old days by thirsty miners. And far down, buried in foliage, deep out of sight of Silverado, I came upon a last outpost of the mine—a mound of gravel, some wreck of wooden aqueduct, and the mouth of a tunnel, like a treasure grotto in a fairy story. A stream of water, fed by the invisible leakage from our shaft, and dyed red with cinnabar or iron, ran trippingly forth out of the bowels of the cave; and, looking far under the arch, I could see something like an iron lantern fastened on the rocky wall. It was a promising spot for the imagination. No boy could have left it unexplored.

The stream thenceforward stole along the bottom of the dingle, and made, for that dry land, a pleasant warbling in the leaves. Once, I suppose, it ran splashing down the whole length of the canon, but now its head waters had been tapped by the shaft at Silverado, and for a great part of its course it wandered sunless among the joints of the mountain. No wonder that it should better its pace when it sees, far before it, daylight whitening in the arch, or that it should come trotting forth into the sunlight with a song.

The two stages had gone by when I got down, and the Toll House stood, dozing in sun and dust and silence, like a place enchanted. My mission was after hay for bedding, and that I was readily promised. But when I mentioned that we were waiting for Rufe, the people shook their heads. Rufe was not a regular man anyway, it seemed; and if he got playing poker—Well, poker was too many for Rufe. I had not yet heard them bracketed together; but it seemed a natural conjunction, and commended itself swiftly to my fears; and as soon as I returned to Silverado and had told my story, we practically gave Hanson up, and set ourselves to do what we could find do-able in our desert-island state.

The lower room had been the assayer's office. The floor was thick with *debris*—part human, from the former occupants; part natural, sifted in by mountain winds. In a sea of red dust there swam or floated sticks, boards, hay, straw, stones, and paper; ancient newspapers, above all—for the newspaper, especially when torn, soon becomes an antiquity—and bills of the Silverado boarding house, some dated Silverado, some Calistoga Mine. Here is one, verbatim; and if any one can calculate the scale of charges, he has my envious admiration.

Calistoga Mine, May 3rd, 1875.

John Stanley
   To S. Chapman, Cr.

To board from April 1st to April 30	$25 75
″ ″ ″ May 1st to 3rd	2 00
	———
	27 75

Where is John Stanley mining now? Where is S. Chapman, within whose hospitable walls we were to lodge? The date was but five years old, but in that time the world had changed for Silverado; like Palmyra in the desert, it had outlived its people and its purpose; we camped, like Layard, amid ruins, and these names spoke to us of prehistoric time. A boot-jack, a pair of boots, a dog-hutch, and these bills of Mr. Chapman's were the only speaking relics that we disinterred from all that vast Silverado rubbish-heap; but what would I not have given to unearth a letter, a pocketbook, a diary, only a ledger, or a roll of names, to take me back, in a more personal manner, to the past? It pleases me, besides, to fancy that Stanley or Chapman, or one of their companions, may light upon this chronicle, and be struck by the name, and read some news of their anterior home, coming, as it were, out of a subsequent epoch of history in that quarter of the world.

As we were tumbling the mingled rubbish on the floor, kicking it with our feet, and groping for these written evidences of the past, Sam, with a somewhat whitened face, produced a paper bag. "What's this?" said he. It contained a granulated powder, something the colour of Gregory's Mixture, but rosier; and as there were several of the bags, and each more or less broken, the powder was spread widely on the floor. Had any of us ever seen giant powder? No, nobody had; and instantly there grew up in my mind a shadowy belief, verging with every moment nearer to certitude, that I had somewhere heard somebody describe it as just such a powder as the one around us. I have learned since that it is a substance not unlike tallow, and is made up in rolls for all the world like tallow candles.

Fanny, to add to our happiness, told us a story of a gentleman who camped one night, like ourselves, by a deserted mine. He was a handy, thrifty fellow, looked right and left for plunder, but all he could lay his hands on was a can of oil. After dark he had to see to the horses with a lantern; and not to miss an opportunity, filled up his lamp from the oil can. Thus equipped, he set forth into the forest. A little while after, his friends heard a loud explosion; the mountain echoes bellowed, and then all was still. On examination, the can proved to contain oil, with the trifling addition of nitro-glycerine; but no research disclosed a trace of either man or lantern.

It was a pretty sight, after this anecdote, to see us sweeping out the giant powder. It never seemed to be far enough away. And, after all, it was only some rock pounded for assay.

So much for the lower room. We scraped some of the rougher dirt off the floor, and left it. That was our sitting-room and kitchen, though there was nothing to sit upon but the table, and no provision for a fire except a hole in the roof of the room above, which had once contained the chimney of a stove.

To that upper room we now proceeded. There were the eighteen bunks in a double tier, nine on either hand, where from eighteen to thirty-six miners had once snored together all night long, John Stanley, perhaps, snoring loudest. There was the roof, with a hole in it through which the sun now shot an arrow. There was the floor, in much the same state as the one below, though, perhaps, there was more hay, and certainly there was the added ingredient of broken glass, the man who stole the window-frames having apparently made a miscarriage with this one. Without hay or bedding, without a broom, we could but look about us with the beginning of despair. The one bright arrow of day, in that gaunt and shattered barrack, made the rest look dirtier and darker, and the sight drove us at last into the open.

Here, also, the handiwork of man lay ruined: but the plants were all alive and thriving; the view below was fresh with the colours of nature; and we had exchanged a dim, human garret for a corner, even although it were untidy, of the blue hall of heaven. Not a bird, not a beast, not a reptile. There was no noise in that part of the world, save when we passed beside the staging, and heard the water musically falling in the shaft.

We wandered to and fro. We searched among that drift of lumber—wood and iron, nails and rails, and sleepers and the wheels of trucks. We gazed up the cleft into the bosom of the mountain. We sat by the margin of the dump and saw, far below us, the green treetops standing still in the clear air. Beautiful perfumes, breaths of bay, resin, and nutmeg, came to us more often and grew sweeter and sharper as the afternoon declined. But still there was no word of Hanson.

I set to with pick and shovel, and deepened the pool behind the shaft, till we were sure of sufficient water for the morning; and by the time I had finished, the sun had begun to go down behind the mountain shoulder, the platform was plunged in quiet shadow, and a chill descended from the sky. Night began early in our cleft. Before us, over the margin of the dump, we could see the sun still striking aslant into the wooded nick below, and on the battlemented, pine-bescattered ridges on the farther side.

There was no stove, of course, and no hearth in our lodging, so we betook ourselves to the blacksmith's forge across the platform. If the platform be taken as a stage, and the out-curving margin of the dump to represent the line of the footlights, then our house would be the first wing on the actor's left, and this blacksmith's forge, though no match for it in size, the foremost on the right. It was a low, brown cottage, planted close against the hill, and overhung by the foliage and peeling boughs of a madrona thicket. Within it was full of dead leaves and mountain dust, and rubbish from the mine. But we soon had a good fire brightly blazing, and sat close about it on impromptu seats. Chuchu, the slave of sofa-cushions, whimpered for a softer bed; but the rest of us were greatly revived and comforted by that good creature—fire, which gives us warmth and light and companionable sounds, and colours up the emptiest building with better than frescoes. For awhile it was even pleasant in the forge, with the blaze in the midst, and a look over our shoulders on the woods and mountains where the day was dying like a dolphin.

It was between seven and eight before Hanson arrived, with a waggonful of our effects and two of his wife's relatives to lend him a hand. The elder showed surprising strength. He would pick up a huge packing-case, full of books of all things, swing it on his shoulder, and away up the two crazy ladders and the breakneck spout of rolling mineral, familiarly termed a path, that led from the car-track to our house. Even for a man unburthened, the ascent was toilsome and precarious; but Irvine scaled it with a light foot, carrying box after box, as the hero whisks the stage child up the practicable footway beside the waterfall of the fifth act. With so strong a helper, the business was speedily transacted. Soon the assayer's office was thronged with our belongings, piled higgledy-piggledy, and upside down, about the floor. There were our boxes, indeed, but my wife had left her keys in Calistoga. There was the stove, but, alas! our carriers had forgot the chimney, and lost one of the plates along the road. The Silverado problem was scarce solved.

Rufe himself was grave and good-natured over his share of the blame; he even, if I remember right, expressed regret. But his crew, to my astonishment and anger, grinned from ear to ear and laughed aloud at our distress. They thought it "real funny" about the stove-pipe they had forgotten; "real funny" that they should have lost a plate. As for hay, the whole party refused to bring us any till they should have supped. See how late they were! Never had there been such a job as coming up that grade! Nor often, I suspect, such a game of poker as that before they started. But about nine, as a particular favour, we should have some hay.

So they took their departure, leaving me still staring, and we resigned ourselves to wait for their return. The fire in the forge had been suffered to go out, and we were one and all too weary to kindle another. We dined, or, not to take that word in vain, we ate after a fashion, in the nightmare disorder of the assayer's office, perched among boxes. A single candle lighted us. It could scarce be called a house-warming; for there was, of course, no fire, and with the two open doors and the open window gaping on the night, like breaches in a fortress, it began to grow rapidly chill. Talk ceased; nobody moved but the unhappy Chuchu, still in quest of sofa-cushions, who tumbled complainingly among the trunks. It required a certain happiness of disposition to look forward hopefully, from so dismal a beginning, across the brief hours of night, to the warm shining of to-morrow's sun.

But the hay arrived at last, and we turned, with our last spark of courage, to the bedroom. We had improved the entrance, but it was still a kind of rope-walking; and it would have been droll to see us mounting, one after another, by candlelight, under the open stars.

The western door, that which looked up the canon and through which we entered by our bridge of flying plank, was still entire, a handsome, panelled door, the most finished piece of carpentry in Silverado. And the two lowest bunks next to this we roughly filled with hay for that night's use. Through the opposite, or eastern-looking gable, with its open door and window, a faint, diffused starshine came into the room like mist; and when we were once in bed, we lay, awaiting sleep, in a haunted, incomplete obscurity. At first the silence of the night was utter. Then a high wind began in the distance among the treetops, and for hours continued to grow higher. It seemed to me much such a wind as we had found on our visit; yet here in our open chamber we were fanned only by gentle and refreshing draughts, so deep was the canon, so close our house was planted under the overhanging rock.

179

Walking

HENRY DAVID THOREAU

*This essay on the art of walking, or
sauntering, was based on Thoreau's* Journals
of 1850–51.

I WISH to speak a word for Nature, for absolute freedom and wildness, as
contrasted with a freedom and culture merely civil—to regard man as an
inhabitant, or a part and parcel of Nature, rather than a member of society. I
wish to make an extreme statement, if so I may make an emphatic one, for there
are enough champions of civilization: the minister and the school-committee
and every one of you will take care of that.

I have met with but one or two persons in the course of my life who understood the art of Walking, that is, of taking walks—who had a genius, so to speak,
for *sauntering*: which word is beautifully derived "from idle people who roved
about the country, in the Middle Ages, and asked charity, under pretense of
going *à la Sainte Terre,*" to the Holy Land, till the children exclaimed, "There
goes a *Sainte-Terrer,*" a Saunterer, a Holy-Lander. They who never go to the
Holy Land in their walks, as they pretend, are indeed mere idlers and vaga-
bonds; but they who do go there are saunterers in the good sense, such as I
mean. Some, however, would derive the word from *sans terre*, without land or
home, which, therefore, in the good sense, will mean, having no particular
home, but equally at home everywhere. For this is the secret of successful
sauntering. He who sits still in a house all the time may be the greatest vagrant of
all; but the saunterer, in the good sense, is no more vagrant than the meandering
river, which is all the while sedulously seeking the shortest course to the sea. But
I prefer the first, which, indeed, is the most probable derivation. For every walk
is a sort of crusade, preached by some Peter the Hermit in us, to go forth and
reconquer this Holy Land from the hands of the Infidels.

It is true, we are but faint-hearted crusaders, even the walkers, nowadays,
who undertake no persevering, neverending enterprises. Our expeditions are
but tours, and come round again at evening to the old hearth-side from which
we set out. Half the walk is but retracing our steps. We should go forth on the
shortest walk, perchance, in the spirit of undying adventure, never to return—
prepared to send back our embalmed hearts only as relics to our desolate
kingdoms. If you are ready to leave father and mother, and brother and sister,
and wife and child and friends, and never see them again—if you have paid your

debts, and made your will, and settled all your affairs, and are a free man, then you are ready for a walk.

To come down to my own experience, my companion and I, for I sometimes have a companion, take pleasure in fancying ourselves knights of a new, or rather an old, order—not Equestrians or Chevaliers, not Ritters or Riders, but Walkers, a still more ancient and honorable class, I trust. The chivalric and heroic spirit which once belonged to the Rider seems now to reside in, or perchance to have subsided into, the Walker—not the Knight, but Walker, Errant. He is a sort of fourth estate, outside of Church and State and People.

We have felt that we almost alone hereabouts practised this noble art; though, to tell the truth, at least, if their own assertions are to be received, most of my townsmen would fain walk sometimes, as I do, but they cannot. No wealth can buy the requisite leisure, freedom, and independence which are the capital in this profession. It comes only by the grace of God. It requires a direct dispensation from Heaven to become a walker. You must be born into the family of the Walkers. *Ambulator nascitur, non fit.* Some of my townsmen, it is true, can remember and have described to me some walks which they took ten years ago, in which they were so blessed as to lose themselves for half an hour in the woods; but I know very well that they have confined themselves to the highway ever since, whatever pretensions they may make to belong to this select class. No doubt they were elevated for a moment as by the reminiscence of a previous state of existence, when even they were foresters and outlaws.

> When he came to grene wode,
> In a mery mornynge,
> There he herde the notes small
> Of byrdes mery syngynge.
>
> It is ferre gone, sayd Robyn,
> That I was last here;
> Me lyste a lytell for to shote
> At the donne dere.

I think that I cannot preserve my health and spirits, unless I spend four hours a day at least—and it is commonly more than that—sauntering through the woods and over the hills and fields, absolutely free from all worldly engagements. You may safely say, A penny for your thoughts, or a thousand pounds. When sometimes I am reminded that the mechanics and shopkeepers stay in their shops not only all the forenoon, but all the afternoon too, sitting with crossed legs, so many of them—as if the legs were made to sit upon, and not to stand or walk upon—I think that they deserve some credit for not having all committed suicide long ago.

I, who cannot stay in my chamber for a single day without acquiring some rust, and when sometimes I have stolen forth for a walk at the eleventh hour or four o'clock in the afternoon, too late to redeem the day, when the shades of night were already beginning to be mingled with the daylight, have felt as if I had committed some sin to be atoned for—I confess that I am astonished at the power of endurance, to say nothing of the moral insensibility, of my neighbors who confine themselves to shops and offices the whole day for weeks and months, aye, and years almost together. I know not what manner of stuff they are of—sitting there now at three o'clock in the afternoon, as if it were three o'clock in the morning. Bonaparte may talk of the three o'clock-in-the-morning courage, but it is nothing to the courage which can sit down cheerfully at this hour in the afternoon over against one's self whom you have known all the morning, to starve out a garrison to whom you are bound by such strong ties of sympathy. I wonder that about this time, or say between four and five o'clock in the afternoon, too late for the morning papers and too early for the evening ones, there is not a general explosion heard up and down the street, scattering a legion of antiquated and house-bred notions and whims to the four winds for an airing—and so the evil cure itself.

How womankind, who are confined to the house still more than men, stand it I do not know; but I have ground to suspect that most of them do not *stand* it at all. When, early in a summer afternoon, we have been shaking the dust of the village from the skirts of our garments, making haste past those houses with purely Doric or Gothic fronts, which have such an air of repose about them, my companion whispers that probably about these times their occupants are all gone to bed. Then it is that I appreciate the beauty and the glory of architecture, which itself never turns in, but forever stands out and erect, keeping watch over the slumberers.

No doubt temperament, and, above all, age, have a good deal to do with it. As a man grows older, his ability to sit still and follow indoor occupations increases. He grows vespertinal in his habits as the evening of life approaches, till at last he comes forth only just before sundown, and gets all the walk that he requires in half an hour.

But the walking of which I speak has nothing in it akin to taking exercise, as it is called, as the sick take medicine at stated hours—as the swinging of dumb-bells or chairs; but is itself the enterprise and adventure of the day. If you would get exercise, go in search of the springs of life. Think of a man's swinging dumb-bells for his health, when those springs are bubbling up in far-off pastures unsought by him!

Moreover, you must walk like a camel, which is said to be the only beast which ruminates when walking. When a traveler asked Wordsworth's servant to show him her master's study, she answered, "Here is his library, but his study is out of doors."

Living much out of doors, in the sun and wind, will no doubt produce a certain roughness of character—will cause a thicker cuticle to grow over some of the finer qualities of our nature, as on the face and hands, or as severe manual labor robs the hands of some of their delicacy of touch. So staying in the house, on the other hand, may produce a softness and smoothness, not to say thinness of skin, accompanied by an increased sensibility to certain impressions. Perhaps we should be more susceptible to some influences important to our intellectual and moral growth, if the sun had shone and the wind blown on us a little less; and no doubt it is a nice matter to proportion rightly the thick and thin skin. But methinks that is a scurf that will fall off fast enough—that the natural remedy is to be found in the proportion which the night bears to the day, the winter to the summer, thought to experience. There will be so much the more air and sunshine in our thoughts. The callous palms of the laborer are conversant with finer tissues of self-respect and heroism, whose touch thrills the heart, than the languid fingers of idleness. That is mere sentimentality that lies abed by day and thinks itself white, far from the tan and callus of experience.

When we walk, we naturally go to the fields and woods: what would become of us, if we walked only in a garden or a mall? Even some sects of philosophers have felt the necessity of importing the woods to themselves, since they did not go to the woods. "They planted groves and walks of Platanes," where they took *subdiales ambulationes* in porticos open to the air. Of course it is of no use to direct our steps to the woods, if they do not carry us thither. I am alarmed when it happens that I have walked a mile into the woods bodily, without getting there in spirit. In my afternoon walk I would fain forget all my morning occupations and my obligations to society. But it sometimes happens that I cannot easily shake off the village. The thought of some work will run in my head and I am not where my body is—I am out of my senses. In my walks I would fain return to my senses. What business have I in the woods, if I am thinking of something out of the woods? I suspect myself, and cannot help a shudder, when I find myself so implicated even in what are called good works—for this may sometimes happen.

My vicinity affords many good walks; and though for so many years I have walked almost every day, and sometimes for several days together, I have not yet exhausted them. An absolutely new prospect is a great happiness, and I can still get this any afternoon. Two or three hours' walking will carry me to as strange a country as I expect ever to see. A single farm-house which I had not seen before is sometimes as good as the dominions of the King of Dahomey. There is in fact a sort of harmony discoverable between the capabilities of the landscape within a circle of ten miles' radius, or the limits of an afternoon walk, and the threescore years and ten of human life. It will never become quite familiar to you.

Nowadays almost all man's improvements, so called, as the building of houses, and the cutting down of the forest and of all large trees, simply deform the landscape, and make it more and more tame and cheap. A people who would begin by burning the fences and let the forest stand! I saw the fences half consumed, their ends lost in the middle of the prairie, and some worldly miser with a surveyor looking after his bounds, while heaven had taken place around him, and he did not see the angels going to and fro, but was looking for an old post-hole in the midst of paradise. I looked again, and saw him standing in the middle of a boggy stygian fen, surrounded by devils, and he had found his bounds without a doubt, three little stones, where a stake had been driven, and looking nearer, I saw that the Prince of Darkness was his surveyor.

I can easily walk ten, fifteen, twenty, any number of miles, commencing at my own door, without going by any house, without crossing a road except where the fox and the mink do: first along by the river, and then the brook, and then the meadow and the woodside. There are square miles in my vicinity which have no inhabitant. From many a hill I can see civilization and the abodes of man afar. The farmers and their works are scarcely more obvious than wood-chucks and their burrows. Man and his affairs, church and state and school, trade and commerce, and manufactures and agriculture, even politics, the most alarming of them all—I am pleased to see how little space they occupy in the landscape. Politics is but a narrow field, and that still narrower highway yonder leads to it. I sometimes direct the traveler thither. If you would go to the political world, follow the great road—follow that market-man, keep his dust in your eyes, and it will lead you straight to it; for it, too, has its place merely, and does not occupy all space. I pass from it as from a bean-field into the forest, and it is forgotten. In one half-hour I can walk off to some portion of the earth's surface where a man does not stand from one year's end to another, and there, consequently, politics are not, for they are but as the cigar-smoke of a man.

The village is the place to which the roads tend, a sort of expansion of the highway, as a lake of a river. It is the body of which roads are the arms and legs—a trivial or quadrivial place, the thoroughfare and ordinary of travelers. The word is from the Latin *villa*, which together with *via*, a way, or more anciently *ved* and *vella*, Varro derives from *veho*, to carry, because the villa is the place to and from which things are carried. They who got their living by teaming were said *vellaturam facere*. Hence, too, the Latin word *vilis* and our vile; also *villain*. This suggests what kind of degeneracy villagers are liable to. They are wayworn by the travel that goes by and over them, without traveling themselves.

Some do not walk at all; others walk in the highways; a few walk across lots. Roads are made for horses and men of business. I do not travel in them much, comparatively, because I am not in a hurry to get to any tavern or grocery or livery-stable or depot to which they lead. I am a good horse to travel, but not from choice a roadster. The landscape-painter uses the figures of men to mark a road. He would not make that use of my figure. I walk out into a Nature such as the old prophets and poets, Menu, Moses, Homer, Chaucer, walked in. You may name it America, but it is not America; neither Americus Vespucius, nor Columbus, nor the rest were the discoverers of it. There is a truer account of it in mythology than in any history of America, so called, that I have seen.

However, there are a few old roads that may be trodden with profit, as if they led somewhere now that they are nearly discontinued. There is the Old Marlborough Road, which does not go to Marlborough now, methinks, unless that is Marlborough where it carries me. I am the bolder to speak of it here, because I presume that there are one or two such roads in every town. . . .

At present, in this vicinity, the best part of the land is not private property; the landscape is not owned, and the walker enjoys comparative freedom. But possibly the day will come when it will be partitioned off into so-called pleasure-grounds, in which a few will take a narrow and exclusive pleasure only—when fences shall be multiplied, and man-traps and other engines invented to confine men to the *public* road, and walking over the surface of God's earth shall be construed to mean trespassing on some gentleman's grounds. To enjoy a thing exclusively is commonly to exclude yourself from the true enjoyment of it. Let us improve our opportunities, then, before the evil days come.

American Hotels

ANTHONY TROLLOPE

Britain's highly respected and prolific author—more than forty novels, short story collections, travel books, an autobiography, and other works—held a civil service job with the General Post Office throughout much of his writing career. His travels for the Post Office sent him to America during the Civil War and resulted in a two-volume assessment of the war, the government in Washington, and the Constitution. Like any traveler, then and now, Trollope acquired some strong opinions on hotels and innkeepers in the United States.

I FIND it impossible to resist the subject of inns. As I have gone on with my journey, I have gone on with my book, and have spoken here and there of American hotels as I have encountered them. But in the States the hotels are so large an institution, having so much closer and wider a bearing on social life than they do in any other country, that I feel myself bound to treat them in a separate chapter as a great national feature in themselves. They are quite as much thought of in the nation as the legislature, or judicature, or literature of the country; and any falling off in them, or any improvement in the accommodation given, would strike the community as forcibly as a change in the constitution, or an alteration in the franchise.

Moreover I consider myself as qualified to write a chapter on hotels—not only on the hotels of America but on hotels generally. I have myself been much too frequently a sojourner at hotels. I think I know what an hotel should be, and what it should not be; and am almost inclined to believe, in my pride, that I could myself fill the position of a landlord with some chance of social success, though probably with none of satisfactory pecuniary results.

Of all hotels known to me I pronounce without hesitation the Swiss to be the best. The things wanted at an hotel are, I fancy, mainly as follows: a clean bedroom with a good and clean bed—and with it also plenty of water. Good food, well dressed and served at convenient hours, which hours should on occasions be allowed to stretch themselves. Wines that shall be drinkable. Quick attendance. Bills that shall not be absolutely extortionate, smiling faces, and an absence of foul smells. There are many who desire more than this—who expect

exquisite cookery, choice wines, subservient domestics, distinguished consid-
eration, and the strictest economy. But they are uneducated travellers who are
going through the apprenticeship of their hotel lives—who may probably never
become free of the travellers' guild, or learn to distinguish that which they may
fairly hope to attain from that which they can never accomplish.

Taking them as a whole I think that the Swiss hotels are the best. They are
perhaps a little close in the matter of cold water, but even as to this, they
generally give way to pressure. The pressure, however, must not be violent, but
gentle rather, and well continued. Their bedrooms are excellent. Their cookery
is good, and to the outward senses is cleanly. The people are civil. The whole
work of the house is carried on upon fixed rules which tend to the comfort of the
establishment. They are not cheap, and not always quite honest. But the exorbi-
tance or dishonesty of their charges rarely exceeds a certain reasonable scale,
and hardly ever demands the bitter misery of a remonstrance.

The inns of the Tyrol are the cheapest I have known, affording the traveller
what he requires for half the price, or less than half, that demanded in Switzerland. But the other half is taken out in stench and nastiness. As tourists scatter
themselves more profusely, the prices of the Tyrol will no doubt rise. Let us hope
that increased prices will bring with them besoms, scrubbing-brushes, and other
much needed articles of cleanliness.

The inns of the north of Italy are very good, and indeed, the Italian inns
throughout, as far as I know them, are much better than the name they bear. The
Italians are a civil, kindly people, and do for you, at any rate, the best they can.
Perhaps the unwary traveller may be cheated. Ignorant of the language, he may
be called on to pay more than the man who speaks it, and who can bargain in
the Italian fashion as to price. It has often been my lot, I doubt not, to be so
cheated. But then I have been cheated with a grace that has been worth all the
money. The ordinary prices of Italian inns are by no means high.

I have seldom thoroughly liked the inns of Germany which I have known.
They are not clean, and water is very scarce. Smiles too are generally wanting,
and I have usually fancied myself to be regarded as a piece of goods out of which
so much profit was to be made.

The dearest hotels I know are the French—and certainly not the best. In the
provinces they are by no means so cleanly as those of Italy. Their wines are
generally abominable, and their cookery often disgusting. In Paris grand dinners
may no doubt be had, and luxuries of every description—except the luxury of
comfort. Cotton-velvet sofas and ormolu clocks stand in the place of convenient
furniture, and logs of wood at a franc a log fail to impart to you the heat which
the freezing cold of a Paris winter demands. They used to make good coffee in
Paris, but even that is a thing of the past. I fancy that they import their brandy
from England, and manufacture their own cigars. French wines you may get

good at a Paris hotel; but you would drink them as good and much cheaper if you bought them in London and took them with you.

The worst hotels I know are in the Havana. Of course I do not speak here of chance mountain huts, or small far-off roadside hostels in which the traveller may find himself from time to time. All such are to be counted apart, and must be judged on their merits, by the circumstances which surround them. But with reference to places of wide resort, nothing can beat the hotels of the Havana in filth, discomfort, habits of abomination, and absence of everything which the traveller desires. All the world does not go to the Havana, and the subject is not, therefore, one of general interest. But in speaking of hotels at large, so much I find myself bound to say.

In all the countries to which I have alluded the guests of the house are expected to sit down together at one table. Conversation is at any rate possible, and there is the show if not the reality of society.

And now one word as to English inns. I do not think that we Englishmen have any great right to be proud of them. The worst about them is that they deteriorate from year to year instead of becoming better. We used to hear much of the comfort of the old English wayside inn, but the old English wayside inn has gone. The railway hotel has taken its place, and the railway hotel is too frequently gloomy, desolate, comfortless, and almost suicidal. In England too, since the old days are gone, there are wanting the landlord's bow, and the kindly smile of his stout wife. Who now knows the landlord of an inn, or cares to inquire whether or no there be a landlady? The old welcome is wanting, and the cheery warm air which used to atone for the bad port and tough beef has passed away—while the port is still bad and the beef too often tough.

In England, and only in England, as I believe, is maintained in hotel life the theory of solitary existence. The sojourner at an English inn—unless he be a commercial traveller, and, as such, a member of a universal, peripatetic, tradesman's club—lives alone. He has his breakfast alone, his dinner alone, his pint of wine alone, and his cup of tea alone. It is not considered practicable that two strangers should sit at the same table, or cut from the same dish. Consequently his dinner is cooked for him separately, and the hotel keeper can hardly afford to give him a good dinner. He has two modes of life from which to choose. He either lives in a public room, called a coffee-room, and there occupies during his comfortless meal a separate small table too frequently removed from fire and light, though generally exposed to draughts; or else he indulges in the luxury of a private sitting-room, and endeavours to find solace on an old horse-hair sofa, at the cost of seven shillings a day. His bedroom is not so arranged that he can use it as a sitting-room. Under either phase of life he can rarely find himself comfortable, and therefore he lives as little at an hotel as the circumstances of his business or of his pleasure will allow. I do not think that any of the requisites of a good inn are habitually to be found in perfection at our Kings' Heads and White Horses, though the falling-off is not so lamentably distressing as it sometimes is in other countries. The bedrooms are dingy rather than dirty. Extra payment to servants will generally produce a tub of cold water. The food is never good, but it is usually eatable, and you may have it when you please. The wines are almost always bad, but the traveller can fall back upon beer. The attendance is good, provided always that the payment for it is liberal. The cost is generally too high, and unfortunately grows larger and larger from year to year. Smiling faces are out of the question unless specially paid for; and as to that matter of foul smells there is often room for improvement. An English inn to a solitary traveller without employment is an embodiment of dreary desolation. The excuse to be made for this is that English men and women do not live much at inns in their own country.

The American inn differs from all those of which I have made mention, and is altogether an institution apart, and a thing of itself. Hotels in America are very much larger and more numerous than in other countries. They are to be found in all towns, and I may almost say in all villages. In England and on the Continent we find them on the recognized routes of travel and in towns of commercial or social importance. On unfrequented roads and in villages there is usually some small house of public entertainment in which the unexpected traveller may obtain food and shelter, and in which the expected boon companions of the neighbourhood smoke their nightly pipes, and drink their nightly tipple. But in the States of America the first sign of an incipient settlement is an hotel five stories high, with an office, a bar, a cloak-room, three gentlemen's parlours, two ladies' parlours, a ladies' entrance, and two hundred bedrooms.

These, of course, are all built with a view to profit, and it may be presumed that in each case the originators of the speculation enter into some calculation as to their expected guests. Whence are to come the sleepers in those two hundred bedrooms, and who is to pay for the gaudy sofas and numerous lounging chairs of the ladies' parlours? In all other countries the expectation would extend itself simply to travellers—to travellers or to strangers sojourning in the land. But this is by no means the case as to these speculations in America. When the new hotel rises up in the wilderness, it is presumed that people will come there with the express object of inhabiting it. The hotel itself will create a population—as the railways do. With us railways run to the towns; but in the States the towns run to the railways. It is the same thing with the hotels.

Housekeeping is not popular with young married people in America, and there are various reasons why this should be so. Men there are not fixed in their employment as they are with us. If a young Benedict cannot get along as a lawyer at Salem, perhaps he may thrive as a shoemaker at Thermopylæ. Jefferson B. Johnson fails in the lumber line at Eleutheria, but hearing of an opening for a Baptist preacher at Big Mud Creek moves himself off with his wife and three children at a week's notice. Aminadab Wiggs takes an engagement as a clerk at a steam-boat office on the Pongawonga river, but he goes to his employment with an inward conviction that six months will see him earning his bread elsewhere. Under such circumstances even a large wardrobe is a nuisance, and a collection of furniture would be as appropriate as a drove of elephants. Then, again, young men and women marry without any means already collected on which to commence their life. They are content to look forward and to hope that such means will come. In so doing they are guilty of no imprudence. It is the way of the country; and, if the man be useful for anything, employment will certainly come to him. But he must live on the fruits of that employment, and can only pay his way from week to week and from day to day. And as a third reason I may allege that the mode of life found in these hotels is liked by the people who frequent them. It is to their taste. They are happy, or at any rate contented at these hotels, and do not wish for household cares. As to the two first reasons which I have given I can agree as to the necessity of the case, and quite concur as to the expediency of marriage under such circumstances. But as to that matter of taste, I cannot concur at all. Anything more forlorn than a young married woman at an American hotel, it is impossible to conceive.

Such are the guests expected for those two hundred bedrooms. The chance travellers are but chance additions to these, and are not generally the main stay of the house. As a matter of course the accommodation for travellers which these hotels afford increases and creates travelling. Men come because they know they will be fed and bedded at a moderate cost, and in an easy way, suited to their tastes. With us, and throughout Europe, inquiry is made before an unaccustomed journey is commenced, on that serious question of wayside food and shelter. But in the States no such question is needed. A big hotel is a matter of course, and therefore men travel. Everybody travels in the States. The railways and the hotels have between them so churned up the people that an untravelled man or woman is a rare animal. We are apt to suppose that travellers make roads, and that guests create hotels; but the cause and effect run exactly in the other way. I am almost disposed to think that we should become cannibals if gentlemen's legs and ladies' arms were hung up for sale in purveyors' shops.

After this fashion and with these intentions hotels are built. Size and an imposing exterior are the first requisitions. Everything about them must be on a large scale. A commanding exterior, and a certain interior dignity of demeanour is more essential than comfort or civility. Whatever an hotel may be it must not be "mean." In the American vernacular the word "mean" is very significant. A mean white in the South is a man who owns no slaves. Men are often mean, but actions are seldom so called. A man feels mean when the bluster is taken out of him. A mean hotel, conducted in a quiet unostentatious manner, in which the only endeavour made had reference to the comfort of a few guests, would find no favour in the States. These hotels are not called by the name of any sign, as with us in our provinces. There are no "Presidents' Heads" or "General Scotts." Nor by the name of the landlord, or of some former landlord, as with us in London, and in many cities of the Continent. Nor are they called from some country or city which may have been presumed at some time to have had special patronage for the establishment. In the nomenclature of American hotels the speciality of American hero-worship is shown, as in the nomenclature of their children. Every inn is a house, and these houses are generally named after some hero, little known probably in the world at large, but highly estimated in that locality at the moment of the christening.

They are always built on a plan which to a European seems to be most unnecessarily extravagant in space. It is not unfrequently the case that the greater portion of the ground-floor is occupied by rooms and halls which make no return to the house whatever. The visitor enters a great hall by the front door, and almost invariably finds it full of men who are idling about, sitting round on stationary seats, talking in a listless manner, and getting through their time as though the place were a public lounging room. And so it is. The chances are that not half the crowd are guests at the hotel. I will now follow the visitor as he makes his way up to the office. Every hotel has an office. To call this place the bar, as I have done too frequently, is a lamentable error. The bar is held in a separate room appropriated solely to drinking. To the office, which is in fact a long open counter, the guest walks up, and there inscribes his name in a book. This inscription was to me a moment of misery which I could never go through with equanimity. As the name is written, and as the request for accommodation is made, half a dozen loungers look over your name and listen to what you say. They listen attentively, and spell your name carefully, but the great man behind the bar does not seem to listen or to heed you. Your destiny is never imparted to you on the instant. If your wife or any other woman be with you (the word "lady" is made so absolutely distasteful in American hotels that I cannot bring myself to use it in writing of them), she has been carried off to a lady's waiting room, and there remains in august wretchedness till the great man at the bar shall have decided on her fate. I have never been quite able to fathom the mystery of these delays. I think they must have originated in the necessity of waiting to see what might be the influx of travellers at the moment, and then have become exaggerated and brought to their present normal state by the gratified feeling of almost divine power with which for the time it invests that despotic arbiter. I have found it always the same, though arriving with no crowd, by a conveyance of my own, when no other expectant guests were following me. The great man has listened to my request in silence, with an imperturbable face, and has usually continued his conversation with some loafing friend, who at the time is probably scrutinizing my name in the book. I have often suffered in patience; but patience is not specially the badge of my tribe, and I have sometimes spoken out rather freely. If I may presume to give advice to my travelling countrymen how to act under such circumstances I should recommend to them freedom of speech rather than patience. The great man when freely addressed generally opens his eyes, and selects the key of your room without further delay. I can assure the traveller that the selection will not be made in any way to his detriment by reason of that freedom of speech. The lady in the ballad who spoke out her own mind to Lord Bateman was sent to her home honourably in a coach and three. Had she held her tongue we are justified in presuming that she would have been returned on a pillion behind a servant.

I have been greatly annoyed by that silence on the part of the hotel clerk. I have repeatedly asked for room, and received no syllable in return. I have persisted in my request, and the clerk has nodded his head at me. Until a traveller is known, these gentlemen are singularly sparing of speech—especially in the West. The same economy of words runs down from the great man at the office all through the servants of the establishment. It arises, I believe, entirely from that want of courtesy which democratic institutions create. The man whom you address, has to make a battle against the state of subservience, presumed to be indicated by his position, and he does so by declaring his indifference to the person on whose wants he is paid to attend. I have been honoured on one or two occasions by the subsequent intimacy of these great men at the hotel offices, and have then found them ready enough at conversation.

That necessity of making your request for rooms before a public audience, is not in itself agreeable, and sometimes entails a conversation which might be more comfortably made in private. ''What do you mean by a dressing-room, and why do you want one?'' Now that is a question which an Englishman feels awkward at answering before five-and-twenty Americans, with open mouths and eager eyes; but it has to be answered. When I left England, I was assured that I should not find any need for a separate sitting-room, seeing that drawing-rooms more or less sumptuous were prepared for the accommodation of ''ladies.'' At first we attempted to follow the advice given to us, but we broke down. A man and his wife travelling from town to town, and making no sojourn on his way, may eat and sleep at an hotel without a private parlour. But an Englishwoman cannot live in comfort for a week, or even, in comfort, for a day, at any of these houses, without a sitting-room for herself. The ladies' drawing-room is a desolate wilderness. The American women themselves do not use it. It is generally empty, or occupied by some forlorn spinster, eliciting harsh sounds from the wretched piano which it contains.

The price at these hotels throughout the Union is nearly always the same, viz., two and a half dollars a day, for which a bedroom is given, and as many meals as the guest can contrive to eat. This is the price for chance guests. The cost to monthly boarders is, I believe, not more than the half of this. Ten shillings a day, therefore, covers everything that is absolutely necessary, servants included. And this must be said in praise of these inns: that the traveller can compute his expenses accurately, and can absolutely bring them within that daily sum of ten shillings. This includes a great deal of eating, a great deal of attendance, the use of reading-rooms and smoking-rooms—which, however, always seem to be open to the public as well as to the guests—and a bedroom with accommodation which is at any rate as good as the average accommodation of hotels in Europe. In the large Eastern towns baths are attached to many of the rooms. I always carry my own, and have never failed in getting water. It must be acknowledged that the price is very low. It is so low that I believe it affords, as a rule, no profit whatsoever. The profit is made upon extra charges, and they are higher than in any other country that I have visited. They are so high that I consider travelling in America, for an Englishman with his wife or family, to be more expensive than travelling in any part of Europe. First in the list of extras comes that matter of the sitting-room, and by that for a man and his wife the whole first expense is at once doubled. The ordinary charge is five dollars, or one pound a day! A guest intending to stay for two or three weeks at an hotel, or perhaps for one week, may, by agreement, have this charge reduced. At one inn I stayed a fortnight, and having made no such agreement was charged the full sum. I felt myself stirred up to complain, and did in that case remonstrate. I was asked how much I wished to have returned—for the bill had been paid—and the sum I suggested was at once handed to me. But even with such reduction the price is very high, and at once makes the American hotel expensive. Wine also at these houses is very costly, and very bad. The usual price is two dollars, or eight shillings, a bottle. The people of the country rarely drink wine at dinner in the hotels. When they do so, they drink champagne; but their normal drinking is done separately, at the bar, chiefly before dinner, and at a cheap rate. "A drink," let it be what it may, invariably costs a dime, or fivepence. But if you must have a glass of sherry with your dinner, it costs two dollars; for sherry does not grow into pint bottles in the States. But the guest who remains for two days can have his wine kept for him. Washing also is an expensive luxury. The price of this is invariable, being always fourpence for everything washed. A cambric handkerchief or muslin dress all come out at the same price. For those who are cunning in the matter this may do very well; but for men and women whose cuffs and collars are numerous it becomes expensive. The craft of those who are cunning is shown, I think, in little internal washings, by which the cambric handkerchiefs are kept out of the list, while the muslin dresses are placed upon it. I am led to this surmise by the energetic measures taken by the hotel keepers to prevent such domestic washings, and by the denunciations which in every hotel are pasted up in every room against the practice. I could not at first understand why I was always warned against washing my own clothes in my own bedroom, and told that no foreign laundress could on any account be admitted into the house. The injunctions given on this head are almost frantic in their energy, and therefore I conceive that hotel keepers find themselves exposed to much suffering in the matter. At these hotels they wash with great rapidity, sending you back your clothes in four or five hours if you desire it.

Another very stringent order is placed before the face of all visitors at American hotels, desiring them on no account to leave valuable property in their rooms. I presume that there must have been some difficulty in this matter in bygone years, for in every State a law has been passed declaring that hotel keepers shall not be held responsible for money or jewels stolen out of rooms in their houses, provided that they are furnished with safes for keeping such money, and give due caution to their guests on the subject. The due caution is always given, but I have seldom myself taken any notice of it. I have always left my portmanteau open, and have kept my money usually in a travelling desk in my room. But I never to my knowledge lost anything. The world, I think, gives itself credit for more thieves than it possesses. As to the female servants at American inns, they are generally all that is disagreeable. They are uncivil, impudent, dirty, slow—provoking to a degree. But I believe that they keep their hands from picking and stealing.

I never yet made a single comfortable meal at an American hotel, or rose from my breakfast or dinner with that feeling of satisfaction which should, I think, be felt at such moments in a civilized land in which cookery prevails as an art. I have had enough, and have been healthy and am thankful. But that thankfulness is altogether a matter apart, and does not bear upon the question. If need be I can eat food that is disagreeable to my palate, and make no complaint. But I hold it to be compatible with the principles of an advanced Christianity to prefer food that is palatable. I never could get any of that kind at an American hotel. All meal-times at such houses were to me periods of disagreeable duty; and at this moment, as I write these lines at the hotel in which I am still staying, I pine for an English leg of mutton. But I do not wish it to be supposed that the fault of which I complain—for it is a grievous fault—is incidental to America as a nation. I have stayed in private houses, and have daily sat down to dinners quite as good as any my own kitchen could afford me. Their dinner parties are generally well done, and as a people they are by no means indifferent to the nature of their comestibles. It is of the hotels that I speak, and of them I again say that eating in them is a disagreeable task—a painful labour. It is as a schoolboy's lesson, or the six hours' confinement of a clerk at his desk.

The mode of eating is as follows. Certain feeding hours are named, which generally include nearly all the day. Breakfast from six till ten. Dinner from one till five. Tea from six till nine. Supper from nine till twelve. When the guest presents himself at any of these hours he is marshalled to a seat, and a bill is put into his hand containing the names of all the eatables then offered for his choice. The list is incredibly and most unnecessarily long. Then it is that you will see care written on the face of the American hotel liver, as he studies the programme of the coming performance. With men this passes off unnoticed, but with young girls the appearance of the thing is not attractive. The anxious study, the elaborate reading of the daily book, and then the choice proclaimed with clear articulation. ''Boiled mutton and caper sauce, roast duck, hashed venison, mashed potatoes, poached eggs and spinach, stewed tomatoes. Yes; and waiter, some squash.'' There is no false delicacy in the voice by which this order is given, no desire for a gentle whisper. The dinner is ordered with the firm determination of an American heroine, and in some five minutes' time all the little dishes appear at once, and the lady is surrounded by her banquet.

How I did learn to hate those little dishes and their greasy contents! At a London eating-house things are often not very nice, but your meat is put on a plate and comes before you in an edible shape. At these hotels it is brought to you in horrid little oval dishes, and swims in grease. Gravy is not an institution at American hotels, but grease has taken its place. It is palpable, undisguised grease, floating in rivers—not grease caused by accidental bad cookery, but grease on purpose. A beef-steak is not a beef-steak unless a quarter of a pound of butter be added to it. Those horrid little dishes! If one thinks of it how could they have been made to contain Christian food? Every article in that long list is liable to the call of any number of guests for four hours. Under such circumstances how can food be made eatable? Your roast mutton is brought to you raw—if you object to that you are supplied with meat that has been four times brought before the public. At hotels on the continent of Europe different dinners are cooked at different hours, but here the same dinner is kept always going. The house breakfast is maintained on a similar footing. Huge boilers of tea and coffee are stewed down and kept hot. To me those meals were odious. It is of course open to any one to have separate dinners and separate breakfasts in his own room; but by this little is gained and much is lost. He or she who is so exclusive pays twice over for such meals—as they are charged as extras on the bill; and, after all, receives the advantage of no exclusive cooking. Particles from the public dinners are brought to the private room, and the same odious little dishes make their appearance.

But the most striking peculiarity of the American hotels is in their public rooms. Of the ladies' drawing-room I have spoken. There are two and sometimes three in one hotel, and they are generally furnished, at any rate expensively. It seems to me that the space and the furniture are almost thrown away.

At watering places, and sea-side summer hotels they are, I presume, used; but at ordinary hotels they are empty deserts. The intention is good, for they are established with the view of giving to ladies at hotels the comforts of ordinary domestic life; but they fail in their effect. Ladies will not make themselves happy in any room, or with ever so much gilded furniture, unless some means of happiness be provided for them. Into these rooms no book is ever brought, no needlework is introduced; from them no clatter of many tongues is ever heard. On a marble table in the middle of the room always stands a large pitcher of iced water, and from this a cold, damp, uninviting air is spread through the atmosphere of the ladies' drawing-room.

Below, on the ground floor, there is, in the first place, the huge entrance hall, at the back of which, behind a bar, the great man of the place keeps the keys and holds his court. There are generally seats around it, in which smokers sit—or men not smoking but ruminating. Opening off from this are reading rooms, smoking rooms, shaving rooms, drinking rooms, parlours for gentlemen in which smoking is prohibited, and which are generally as desolate as the ladies' sitting-rooms above. In those other more congenial chambers is always gathered together a crowd, apparently belonging in no way to the hotel. It would seem that a great portion of an American inn is as open to the public as an Exchange, or as the wayside of the street. In the West, during the months of this war, the traveller would always see many soldiers among the crowd—not only officers, but privates. They sit in public seats, silent but apparently contented, sometimes for an hour together. All Americans are given to gatherings such as these. It is the much-loved institution to which the name of "loafing" has been given.

I do not like the mode of life which prevails in the American hotels. I have come across exceptions, and know one or two that are comfortable—always excepting that matter of eating and drinking. But taking them as a whole I do not like their mode of life. I feel, however, bound to add that the hotels of Canada, which are kept almost always after the same fashion, are infinitely worse than those of the United States. I do not like the American hotels; but I must say in their favour that they afford an immense amount of accommodation. The traveller is rarely told that an hotel is full, so that travelling in America is without one of those great perils to which it is subject in Europe. It must also be acknowledged that for the ordinary purposes of a traveller they are very cheap.

Old Times on the Mississippi

MARK TWAIN

The Mississippi River flows unforgettably through the pages of Mark Twain's most famous books, The Adventures of Tom Sawyer *and* The Adventures of Huckleberry Finn, *just as it had been a dominant part of his growing years in Hannibal, Missouri. "When I was a boy there was but one permanent ambition among my comrades in our village on the west bank of the Mississippi River. That was to be a steamboatman." He later wrote of his apprenticeship as a pilot for* Atlantic *magazine.*

THE pilot-house was full of pilots, going down to "look at the river." What is called the "upper river" (the two hundred miles between St. Louis and Cairo, where the Ohio comes in) was low; and the Mississippi changes its channel so constantly that the pilots used to always find it necessary to run down to Cairo to take a fresh look, when their boats were to lie in port a week; that is, when the water was at a low stage. A deal of this "looking at the river" was done by poor fellows who seldom had a berth, and whose only hope of getting one lay in their being always freshly posted and therefore ready to drop into the shoes of some reputable pilot, for a single trip, on account of such pilot's sudden illness, or some other necessity. And a good many of them constantly ran up and down inspecting the river, not because they ever really hoped to get a berth, but because (they being guests of the boat) it was cheaper to "look at the river" than stay ashore and pay board. In time these fellows grew dainty in their tastes, and only infested boats that had an established reputation for setting good tables. All visiting pilots were useful, for they were always ready and willing, winter or summer, night or day, to go out in the yawl and help buoy the channel or assist the boat's pilots in any way they could. They were likewise welcomed because all pilots are tireless talkers, when gathered together, and as they talk only about the river they are always understood and are always interesting. Your true pilot cares nothing about anything on earth but the river, and his pride in his occupation surpasses the pride of kings.

We had a fine company of these river inspectors along this trip. There were eight or ten, and there was abundance of room for them in our great pilot-house. Two or three of them wore polished silk hats, elaborate shirt-fronts, diamond breastpins, kid gloves, and patent-leather boots. They were choice in their English, and bore themselves with a dignity proper to men of solid means and prodigious reputation as pilots. The others were more or less loosely clad, and wore upon their heads tall felt cones that were suggestive of the days of the Commonwealth.

I was a cipher in this august company, and felt subdued, not to say torpid. I was not even of sufficient consequence to assist at the wheel when it was necessary to put the tiller hard down in a hurry; the guest that stood nearest did that when occasion required—and this was pretty much all the time, because of the crookedness of the channel and the scant water. I stood in a corner; and the talk I listened to took the hope all out of me. One visitor said to another:

"Jim, how did you run Plum Point, coming up?"

"It was in the night, there, and I ran it the way one of the boys on the *Diana* told me; started out about fifty yards above the wood-pile on the false point, and held on the cabin under Plum Point till I raised the reef—quarter less twain— then straightened up for the middle bar till I got well abreast the old one-limbed cottonwood in the bend, then got my stern on the cottonwood, and head on the low place above the point, and came through a-booming—nine and a half."

"Pretty square crossing, an't it?"

"Yes, but the upper bar's working down fast."

Another pilot spoke up and said:

"I had better water than that, and ran it lower down; started out from the false point—mark twain—raised the second reef abreast the big snag in the bend, and had quarter less twain."

One of the gorgeous ones remarked:

"I don't want to find fault with your leadsmen, but that's a good deal of water for Plum Point, it seems to me."

There was an approving nod all around as this quiet snub dropped on the boaster and "settled" him. And so they went on talk-talk-talking. Meantime, the thing that was running in my mind was, "Now, if my ears hear aright, I have not only to get the names of all the towns and islands and bends, and so on, by heart, but I must even get up a warm personal acquaintanceship with every old snag and one-limbed cottonwood and obscure wood-pile that ornaments the banks of this river for twelve hundred miles; and more than that, I must actually know where these things are in the dark, unless these guests are gifted with eyes that can pierce through two miles of solid blackness. I wish the piloting business was in Jericho and I had never thought of it."

At dusk Mr. Bixby tapped the big bell three times (the signal to land), and the captain emerged from his drawing-room in the forward end of the "texas," and looked up inquiringly. Mr. Bixby said:

"We will lay up here all night, captain."

"Very well, sir."

That was all. The boat came to shore and was tied up for the night. It seemed to me a fine thing that the pilot could do as he pleased, without asking so grand a captain's permission. I took my supper and went immediately to bed, discouraged by my day's observations and experiences. My late voyage's note-booking was but a confusion of meaningless names. It had tangled me all up in a knot every time I had looked at it in the daytime. I now hoped for respite in sleep; but no, it reveled all through my head till sunrise again, a frantic and tireless nightmare.

Next morning I felt pretty rusty and low-spirited. We went booming along, taking a good many chances, for we were anxious to "get out of the river" (as getting out to Cairo was called) before night should overtake us. But Mr. Bixby's partner, the other pilot, presently grounded the boat, and we lost so much time getting her off that it was plain the darkness would overtake us a good long way above the mouth. This was a great misfortune, especially to certain of our visiting pilots, whose boats would have to wait for their return, no matter how long that might be. It sobered the pilot-house talk a good deal. Coming up-stream, pilots did not mind low water or any kind of darkness; nothing stopped them but fog. But down-stream work was different; a boat was too nearly helpless, with a stiff current pushing behind her; so it was not customary to run down-stream at night in low water.

There seemed to be one small hope, however: if we could get through the intricate and dangerous Hat Island crossing before night, we could venture the rest, for we would have plainer sailing and better water. But it would be insanity to attempt Hat Island at night. So there was a deal of looking at watches all the rest of the day, and a constant ciphering upon the speed we were making; Hat Island was the eternal subject, sometimes hope was high and sometimes we were delayed in a bad crossing, and down it went again. For hours all hands lay under the burden of this suppressed excitement; it was even communicated to me, and I got to feeling so solicitous about Hat Island, and under such an awful pressure of responsibility, that I wished I might have five minutes on shore to draw a good, full, relieving breath, and start over again. We were standing no regular watches. Each of our pilots ran such portions of the river as he had run when coming up-stream, because of his greater familiarity with it; but both remained in the pilot-house constantly.

An hour before sunset Mr. Bixby took the wheel, and Mr. W. stepped aside. For the next thirty minutes every man held his watch in his hand and was restless, silent, and uneasy. At last somebody said, with a doomful sigh:

"Well, yonder's Hat Island—and we can't make it."

All the watches closed with a snap, everybody sighed and muttered something about its being "too bad, too bad—ah, if we could *only* have got here half an hour sooner!" and the place was thick with the atmosphere of disappointment. Some started to go out, but loitered, hearing no bell-tap to land. The sun dipped behind the horizon, the boat went on. Inquiring looks passed from one guest to another; and one who had his hand on the door-knob and had turned it, waited, then presently took away his hand and let the knob turn back again. We bore steadily down the bend. More looks were exchanged, and nods of surprised admiration—but no words. Insensibly the men drew together behind Mr. Bixby, as the sky darkened and one or two dim stars came out. The dead silence and sense of waiting became oppressive. Mr. Bixby pulled the cord, and two deep, mellow notes from the big bell floated off on the night. Then a pause, and one more note was struck. The watchman's voice followed, from the hurricane-deck:

"Labboard lead, there! Stabboard lead!"

The cries of the leadsmen began to rise out of the distance, and were gruffly repeated by the word-passers on the hurricane-deck.

"M-a-r-k three! M-a-r-k three! Quarter-less-three! Half twain! Quarter twain! M-a-r-k twain! Quarter-less—"

Mr. Bixby pulled two bell-ropes, and was answered by faint jinglings far below in the engine-room, and our speed slackened. The steam began to whistle through the gauge-cocks. The cries of the leadsmen went on—and it is a weird sound, always, in the night. Every pilot in the lot was watching now, with fixed eyes, and talking under his breath. Nobody was calm and easy but Mr. Bixby. He would put his wheel down and stand on a spoke, and as the steamer swung into her (to me) utterly invisible marks—for we seemed to be in the midst of a wide and gloomy sea—he would meet and fasten her there. Out of the murmur of half-audible talk, one caught a coherent sentence now and then—such as:

"There; she's over the first reef all right!"

After a pause, another subdued voice:

"Her stern's coming down just *exactly* right, by *George*!"

"Now she's in the marks; over she goes!"

Somebody else muttered:

"Oh, it was done beautiful—*beautiful*!"

Now the engines were stopped altogether, and we drifted with the current. Not that I could see the boat drift, for I could not, the stars being all gone by this time. This drifting was the dismalest work; it held one's heart still. Presently I discovered a blacker gloom than that which surrounded us. It was the head of the island. We were closing right down upon it. We entered its deeper shadow, and so imminent seemed the peril that I was likely to suffocate; and I had the strongest impulse to do *something*, anything, to save the vessel. But still Mr. Bixby stood by his wheel, silent, intent as a cat, and all the pilots stood shoulder to shoulder at his back.

"She'll not make it!" somebody whispered.

The water grew shoaler and shoaler, by the leadsman's cries, till it was down to:

"Eight-and-a-half! E-i-g-h-t feet! E-i-g-h-t feet! Seven-and—"

Mr. Bixby said warningly through his speaking-tube to the engineer:

"Stand by, now!"

"Ay, ay, sir!"

"Seven-and-a-half! Seven feet! *Six*-and—"

We touched bottom! Instantly Mr. Bixby set a lot of bells ringing, shouted through the tube, "*Now*, let her have it—every ounce you've got!" then to his partner, "Put her hard down! snatch her! snatch her!" The boat rasped and ground her way through the sand, hung upon the apex of disaster a single tremendous instant, and then over she went! And such a shout as went up at Mr. Bixby's back never loosened the roof of a pilot-house before!

There was no more trouble after that. Mr. Bixby was a hero that night; and it was some little time, too, before his exploit ceased to be talked about by river-men.

Fully to realize the marvelous precision required in laying the great steamer in her marks in that murky waste of water, one should know that not only must she pick her intricate way through snags and blind reefs, and then shave the head of the island so closely as to brush the overhanging foliage with her stern, but at one place she must pass almost within arm's reach of a sunken and invisible wreck that would snatch the hull timbers from under her if she should strike it, and destroy a quarter of a million dollars' worth of steamboat and cargo in five minutes, and maybe a hundred and fifty human lives into the bargain.

The last remark I heard that night was a compliment to Mr. Bixby, uttered in soliloquy and with unction by one of our guests. He said:

"By the Shadow of Death, but he's a lightning pilot!"

I promptly put such a strain on my memory that by and by even the shoal water and the countless crossing-marks began to stay with me. But the result was just the same. I never could more than get one knotty thing learned before another presented itself. Now I had often seen pilots gazing at the water and pretending to read it as if it were a book; but it was a book that told me nothing. A time came at last, however, when Mr. Bixby seemed to think me far enough advanced to bear a lesson on water-reading. So he began:

"Do you see that long, slanting line on the face of the water? Now, that's a reef. Moreover, it's a bluff reef. There is a solid sand-bar under it that is nearly as straight up and down as the side of a house. There is plenty of water close up to it, but mighty little on top of it. If you were to hit it you would knock the boat's brains out. Do you see where the line fringes out at the upper end and begins to fade away?"

"Yes, sir."

"Well, that is a low place; that is the head of the reef. You can climb over there, and not hurt anything. Cross over, now, and follow along close under the reef—easy water there—not much current."

I followed the reef along till I approached the fringed end. Then Mr. Bixby said:

"Now get ready. Wait till I give the word. She won't want to mount the reef; a boat hates shoal water. Stand by—wait—*wait*—keep her well in hand. *Now* cramp her down! Snatch her! snatch her!"

He seized the other side of the wheel and helped to spin it around until it was hard down, and then we held it so. The boat resisted, and refused to answer for a while, and next she came surging to starboard, mounted the reef, and sent a long, angry ridge of water foaming away from her bows.

"Now watch her; watch her like a cat, or she'll get away from you. When she fights strong and the tiller slips a little, in a jerky, greasy sort of way, let up on her a trifle; it is the way she tells you at night that the water is too shoal; but keep edging her up, on the bar now; there is a bar under every point, because the water that comes down around it forms an eddy and allows the sediment to sink. Do you see those fine lines on the face of the water that branch out like the ribs of a fan? Well, those are little reefs; you want to just miss the ends of them, but run them pretty close. Now look out—look out! Don't you crowd that slick, greasy-looking place; there ain't nine feet there; she won't stand it. She begins to smell it; look sharp, I tell you! Oh, blazes, there you go! Stop the starboard wheel! Quick! Ship up to back! Set her back!"

The engine bells jingled and the engines answered promptly, shooting white columns of steam far aloft out of the 'scape-pipes, but it was too late. The boat had "smelt" the bar in good earnest; the foamy ridges that radiated from her bows suddenly disappeared, a great dead swell came rolling forward, and swept ahead of her, she careened far over to larboard, and went tearing away toward the shore as if she were about scared to death. We were a good mile from where we ought to have been when we finally got the upper hand of her again.

During the afternoon watch the next day, Mr. Bixby asked me if I knew how to run the next few miles. I said:

"Go inside the first snag above the point, outside the next one, start out from the lower end of Higgins's woodyard, make a square crossing, and—"

"That's all right. I'll be back before you close up on the next point."

But he wasn't. He was still below when I rounded it and entered upon a piece of the river which I had some misgivings about. I did not know that he was hiding behind a chimney to see how I would perform. I went gaily along, getting prouder and prouder, for he had never left the boat in my sole charge such a length of time before. I even got to "setting" her and letting the wheel go entirely, while I vaingloriously turned my back and inspected the stern marks and hummed a tune, a sort of easy indifference which I had prodigiously admired in Bixby and other great pilots. Once I inspected rather long, and when I faced to the front again my heart flew into my mouth so suddenly that if I hadn't clapped my teeth together I should have lost it. One of those frightful bluff reefs was stretching its deadly length right across our bows! My head was gone in a moment; I did not know which end I stood on; I gasped and could not get my breath; I spun the wheel down with such rapidity that it wove itself together like a spider's web; the boat answered and turned square away from the reef, but the reef followed her! I fled, but still it followed, still it kept—right across my bows! I never looked to see where I was going, I only fled. The awful crash was imminent. Why didn't that villain come? If I committed the crime of ringing a bell I might get thrown overboard. But better that than kill the boat. So in blind desperation, I started such a rattling "shivaree" down below as never had astounded an engineer in this world before, I fancy. Amidst the frenzy of the bells the engines began to back and fill in a curious way, and my reason forsook its throne—we were about to crash into the woods on the other side of the river. Just then Mr. Bixby stepped calmly into view on the hurricane-deck. My soul went out to him in gratitude. My distress vanished; I would have felt safe on the brink of Niagara with Mr. Bixby on the hurricane-deck. He blandly and sweetly took his toothpick out of his mouth between his fingers, as if it were a cigar—we were just in the act of climbing an overhanging big tree, and the passengers were scudding astern like rats—and lifted up these commands to me ever so gently:

"Stop the starboard! Stop the larboard! Set her back on both!"

The boat hesitated, halted, pressed her nose among the boughs a critical instant, then reluctantly began to back away.

"Stop the larboard! Come ahead on it! Stop the starboard! Come ahead on it! Point her for the bar!"

I sailed away as serenely as a summer's morning. Mr. Bixby came in and said, with mock simplicity:

"When you have a hail, my boy, you ought to tap the big bell three times before you land, so that the engineers can get ready."

I blushed under the sarcasm, and said I hadn't had any hail.

"Ah! Then it was for wood, I suppose. The officer of the watch will tell you when he wants to wood up."

I went on consuming, and said I wasn't after wood.

"Indeed? Why, what could you want over here in the bend, then? Did you ever know of a boat following a bend up-stream at this stage of the river?"

"No, sir—and I wasn't trying to follow it. I was getting away from a bluff reef."

"No, it wasn't a bluff reef; there isn't one within three miles of where you were."

"But I saw it. It was as bluff as that one yonder."

"Just about. Run over it!"

"Do you give it as an order?"

"Yes. Run over it!"

"If I don't, I wish I may die."

"All right; I am taking the responsibility."

I was just as anxious to kill the boat, now, as I had been to save it before. I impressed my orders upon my memory, to be used at the inquest, and made a straight break for the reef. As it disappeared under our bows I held my breath; but we slid over it like oil.

"Now, don't you see the difference? It wasn't anything but a *wind* reef. The wind does that."

"So I see. But it is exactly like a bluff reef. How am I ever going to tell them apart?"

"I can't tell you. It is an instinct. By and by you will just naturally *know* one from the other, but you never will be able to explain why or how you know them apart."

It turned out to be true. The face of the water, in time, became a wonderful book—a book that was a dead language to the uneducated passenger, but which told its mind to me without reserve, delivering its most cherished secrets as clearly as if it uttered them with a voice. And it was not a book to be read once and thrown aside, for it had a new story to tell every day. Throughout the long twelve hundred miles there was never a page that was void of interest, never one that you could leave unread without loss, never one that you would want to skip, thinking you could find higher enjoyment in some other thing. There never was so wonderful a book written by man; never one whose interest was so absorbing, so unflagging, so sparklingly renewed with every reperusal. The passenger who could not read it was charmed with a peculiar sort of faint dimple on its surface (on the rare occasions when he did not overlook it altogether); but to the pilot that was an *italicized* passage; indeed, it was more than that, it was a legend of the largest capitals, with a string of shouting exclamation-points at the end of it, for it meant that a wreck or a rock was buried there that could tear the life out of the strongest vessel that ever floated. It is the faintest and simplest expression the water ever makes, and the most hideous to a pilot's eye. In truth, the passenger who could not read this book saw nothing but all manner of pretty pictures in it, painted by the sun and shaded by the clouds, whereas to the trained eye these were not pictures at all, but the grimmest and most dead-earnest of reading-matter.

Now when I had mastered the language of this water, and had come to know every trifling feature that bordered the great river as familiarly as I knew the letters of the alphabet, I had made a valuable acquisition. But I had lost something, too. I had lost something which could never be restored to me while I lived. All the grace, the beauty, the poetry, had gone out of the majestic river! I still kept in mind a certain wonderful sunset which I witnessed when steamboating was new to me. A broad expanse of the river was turned to blood; in the middle distance the red hue brightened into gold, through which a solitary log came floating, black and conspicuous; in one place a long, slanting mark lay sparkling upon the water; in another the surface was broken by boiling, tumbling rings, that were as many-tinted as an opal; where the ruddy flush was faintest, was a smooth spot that was covered with graceful circles and radiating lines, ever so delicately traced; the shore on our left was densely wooded, and the somber shadow that fell from this forest was broken in one place by a long, ruffled trail that shone like silver; and high above the forest wall a clean-stemmed dead tree waved a single leafy bough that glowed like a flame in the unobstructed splendor that was flowing from the sun. There were graceful curves, reflected images, woody heights, soft distances; and over the whole scene, far and near, the dissolving lights drifted steadily, enriching it every passing moment with new marvels of coloring.

I stood like one bewitched. I drank it in, in a speechless rapture. The world was new to me, and I had never seen anything like this at home. But as I have said, a day came when I began to cease from noting the glories and the charms which the moon and the sun and the twilight wrought upon the river's face; another day came when I ceased altogether to note them. Then, if that sunset scene had been repeated, I should have looked upon it without rapture, and should have commented upon it, inwardly, after this fashion: "This sun means that we are going to have wind to-morrow; that floating log means that the river is rising, small thanks to it; that slanting mark on the water refers to a bluff reef which is going to kill somebody's steamboat one of these nights, if it keeps on stretching out like that; those tumbling 'boils' show a dissolving bar and a changing channel there; the lines and circles in the slick water over yonder are a warning that that troublesome place is shoaling up dangerously; that silver streak in the shadow of the forest is the 'break' from a new snag, and he has located himself in the very best place he could have found to fish for steamboats;

that tall dead tree, with a single living branch, is not going to last long, and then how is a body ever going to get through this blind place at night without the friendly old landmark?''

No, the romance and beauty were all gone from the river. All the value any feature of it had for me now was the amount of usefulness it could furnish toward compassing the safe piloting of a steamboat. Since those days, I have pitied doctors from my heart. What does the lovely flush in a beauty's cheek mean to a doctor but a ''break'' that ripples above some deadly disease? Are not all her visible charms sown thick with what are to him the signs and symbols of hidden decay? Does he ever see her beauty at all, or doesn't he simply view her professionally, and comment upon her unwholesome condition all to himself? And doesn't he sometimes wonder whether he has gained most or lost most by learning his trade?

Last Run

ROGERS E. M. WHITAKER
AND ANTHONY HISS

The end of the line in 1967 for the Twentieth Century Limited, *the famous New York to Chicago train, was duly recorded by E. M. Frimbo, "World's Greatest Railroad Buff."*

ON Saturday, December 2, 1967, the *Twentieth Century Limited*, one of the most famous trains in the world, made its final run from New York to Chicago. We were aboard. We wouldn't have been if we hadn't received an agitated phone call the previous day from Ernest M. Frimbo. "Nobody knows it," Frimbo told us over the telephone, "but the *Century* is coming to an end tomorrow night." We said something, and he said, "Yes, yes, very funny. I am talking trains, not apocalyptics. I am telling you this because nobody is supposed to know. The New York Central is too embarrassed to admit that it's yanking the train. And it should be embarrassed. I find it impossible to speak about that railroad calmly. But I want to tell you that if you're quick about it, you can get a bedroom on that last run. You're bound to be the only members of the press making the trip, because your colleagues have been hoodwinked by Central flapdoodle."

We said that we had been hoping for some time to find an excuse to take the *Century*.

Frimbo went on, "It isn't what it was, you know, but I must have ridden on the *Century* maybe fifty times over the years, and it's still better than what will replace it. Wish I could be with you on that run, but I've got an unbreakable date with a train in Arizona. Don't forget—the *Century* leaves at six on Track 34. Make a note for me of what a railroad man would call its consist—the number and variety and order of its cars. Oh, yes. Lucius Beebe wrote a book about the *Century*, which you had better take along. It's fascinating and somewhat unreliable. Full steam ahead!"

Our friend rang off, and we steamed over to Grand Central Terminal, where we booked Bedroom B in Car 253 for the following night from a pleasant ticket agent, who said, "You're just in time—that's the last run. I guess a lot of people will be very sorry," and then looked abashed.

The next afternoon, just after five-thirty, we made our way back to Grand

Central, baggage and the Beebe in hand. A small crowd of rail fans and reporters and news photographers had gathered around the check-in counters at Track 34. The rail fans, standing on the famous red carpet that said "20TH CENTURY LIMITED," were taking pictures of the observation car at the end of the *Century*, and the newsmen were taking pictures of the rail fans taking pictures, and talking with the passengers checking in. The passengers all said, in effect, that they had had no idea that this was the last run of the *Twentieth Century Limited*, and wasn't it a shame?

We had our tickets taken and our pictures taken, and climbed aboard. Car 253 proved to be the second car from the observation car, and named *Missouri Valley*. We started making notes for Frimbo. The observation car was *Wingate Brook*, and the sleeping car between it and us was *Port Clinton*. Ahead of us were another sleeping car (*Peach Valley*), a dining car, a car that was half club car and half galley for the diner, a day coach that displayed reproductions of two paintings by Cézanne, a sleeper coach, a dormitory car (which is used by the dining-car staff and has triple-decker bunks), and an electric engine. Our bedroom was a comfortable room that showed signs of wear. It had metal walls painted gray, a large brown armchair with an antimacassar, a smaller brown armchair without an antimacassar, a red rug with a faded floral design, a small separate bathroom, an even smaller closet, and a picture window, which needed washing. On the seat of the large armchair was a brochure informing us that we would receive complimentary champagne with our dinner and complimentary newspapers and boutonnieres with our breakfast, that we could have our shoes shined and our suits pressed, and that, if we wanted them, a typewriter and an electric shaver were available.

At six o'clock precisely, the *Century* pulled out. We decided that Frimbo would expect us to settle down in the observation car, so we made our way back to *Wingate Brook*, carrying the Beebe with us. At the end of our sleeping car, two *Century* porters were saying good-by to two Grand Central redcaps, who were leaning on their pushcarts. The redcaps waved, and one of them looked as though he thought he ought to make a few appropriate remarks, but then he just grinned and waved again and said, "Well, see you, boys."

We liked the lounge in the observation car. It was outfitted with sofas, armchairs, a table and a lamp or two, three bunches of fresh yellow and white chrysanthemums, including a grand branch in the rear window. The lounge wasn't very full, so we chose chairs near the window with the chrysanthemums, and opened up the Beebe. Outside, there were flashes of light as the rail fans took their final pictures, and we waved to them. Mr. Beebe told us that he had unearthed a New York Central publicity release about the consist of the first run of the *Twentieth Century Limited*, on June 15, 1902:

> The trains [he quoted] will be composed of buffet, smoking, and library composite cars *Decius, Cyrus,* observation cars *Alroy* and *Sappho,* 12 section drawing-room state-room cars *Petruchio, Philario, Gonzalo* and *Benvolio....* The exterior of the car is painted Pullman standard color, the ornamentation in gold being simple, but very artistic.

Mr. Beebe said that the interiors of the cars were particularly noticeable for, in the railroad's words, an "absence of all heavy carvings, ornate grilles and metal work, stuffy hangings, etc."

After we had been reading for a while, the car filled up, and we fell into conversation with the man who had been standing in front of us in the check-in line and with a well-dressed young man who was carrying a camera. The man from the check-in line said that he was a dermatologist. "Heading for a convention at the Palmer House," he told the young man and us. "Held there every year at this time. I always start my Christmas shopping at that convention. Don't know why. Live in New York but always start my shopping in Chicago. Have a drink."

The young man said that he was a railroad buff, and that he would love a drink as soon as he had taken a picture of the observation-car porter. "I have over five hundred pictures of this train," he said. "I have been taking one a week since nineteen-fifty-nine. At home, I have over twenty-two thousand railroad pictures."

The porter brought us all a drink, and said, "Would you gentlemens like some hors d'oeuvres?"

The dermatologist said, "Just 'cause you asked me to."

The porter looked pleased. "I didn't have to twist *your* arm," he said.

The young man said he had heard that the New Haven Railroad had bought the observation car from the New York Central.

The porter grinned. "I wonder whatever *they'll* do with it," he said.

We asked the young man if, by any chance, he had ever met Ernest Frimbo.

He said, "I certainly have. He is the foremost rail fan there is. I'm a Frimbo disciple. In the days when the *Century* had a barbershop on board, he and his friends would get on and ride as far as Albany just to get a shave and a haircut."

Our two new friends went off to dinner, and the conductor of the *Century* came around checking tickets. He noticed a boy with long, fair hair, who had been sitting quietly in the observation car for some time, and went over to talk with him. The boy said that he hoped the conductor remembered him—that he was the person who had come down to the station to see a friend off, and then had decided he just had to take the final run of the *Century*. He said that the conductor had said he would accept a check.

The conductor looked very solemn, then said, "Well, it *is* the last run. You give me your check and I'll give you a receipt." The boy wrote out a check, and the conductor took a receipt form out of his pocket and punched it with his ticket punch. "That's my punch mark," he said as he handed the receipt to the boy. "Everybody in the country knows that punch mark."

After the conductor had left, we walked over to the boy and asked if we might see the conductor's punch mark. It was shaped like a tiny map of the United States and had a slightly exaggerated bulge in the region of Texas.

Around about Albany, we headed for the diner. The steward, a good-humored man in a dinner jacket and gold-rimmed spectacles, handed us a menu printed in gold and black. The menu said:

WELCOME TO

THE CENTURY ROOM

offering the ultimate in

dining car cuisine and service

We both ordered Spiced Apple Rings, Queen Olives, Rosetted Radishes, Stuffed Celery N.Y.C., Carrot Sticks, Bisque of New Asparagus, Roast Prime Ribs of Beef au Jus, with Baked Hubbard Squash and Camille Potatoes, Orange-Pecan Sticks and Dinner Rolls, Hearts of Lettuce with Thousand Island Dressing, Old-Fashioned Strawberry Shortcake with Whipped Cream, and Coffee. We drank our complimentary champagne with the roast beef, and the whole meal was fine. The steward told us that he would give us some after-dinner mints when we had finished our coffee, and an apple and an orange that we could take to our bedroom.

The *Century* stopped in Buffalo to pick up some cars from the *New England States*, a train that originated in Boston, and to change some of its crew. There was a delay. The *New England States* had had a fire in one of its sleepers and was running behind time. We climbed down onto the platform. Our new conductor, who was going as far as Toledo, was standing a few feet away from us, carrying a black dispatch box and talking with an elderly rail fan. The rail fan was carrying a copy of Beebe's book, and he asked the conductor to autograph it. The conductor looked as though he were about to say no. Instead, he said, "Well, it *is* the last run," and reached for the book. The rail fan said, "I came all the way from Niagara Falls to see the *Century* for the last time. That's about twenty-five miles. It used to be a great train."

The conductor agreed. "This was a train," he said. "Why, I've carried Jim Farley, Joe Louis, a lot of famous people on this train." He reached down and opened his dispatch box and took out two postcards. One showed a train with an old steam engine and was printed in brown ink on a gold background. "That was a long time ago," he said. He turned the card over. "See? It's even got that old green George Washington penny stamp on it." He held up the other card. The other card showed a train with a more modern steam engine. The train was thundering through hills that were orange because it was autumn, under a pale-blue sky with some fleecy white clouds in it. A great deal of gray smoke was pouring out of the engine's stack.

The rail fan referred to the *Century* by its official name, Train Number 25, and said he supposed the *Century* would lose that number as soon as it reached Chicago.

The conductor said it would lose the number sooner than that, because the new schedule went into effect at four o'clock in the morning. Officially, the *Century* would expire somewhere near Ashtabula. "We're Twenty-Five until four," he said. "Then we become Twenty-Seven, and that's the end of the *Century.*" He put his postcards back in his dispatch box and closed it.

We returned to our bedroom, which was now made up, with two beds where the large armchair had been, and decided to sleep for a couple of hours but to be awake at four, if we could manage it. We woke up sometime later. The train was standing still. We looked out the window and couldn't see anything. We checked our watches, and they said five minutes to four. It seemed like a good idea to go back to sleep, but we decided that Frimbo would have got up and investigated, so we put overcoats on over our pajamas and walked up the train, looking for the conductor. We found him sitting in the dining car working on some papers. He heard us coming and looked at his watch. It was now a few minutes after four. "Well, she's dead," he said. "But we're sitting here in Harbor Creek, Pennsylvania, only because an express train has been derailed up ahead. Looks like we'll have to detour around it over the Norfolk & Western tracks. I guess we may be late enough so that you'll get a free breakfast." He picked up his papers, and said, "There's a little good in every bad."

When we woke up again, our watches said twelve-forty-five, and the sky outside our window was bright gray, above flat brown fields. The train was moving. It had been due in Chicago at nine-forty. We had slept through the free morning papers and the free boutonnieres, and we were afraid we might have slept right through Chicago. We put on overcoats again. Outside the bedroom we found the conductor in conference with our porter. The porter said to us, "We're not into Cleveland yet," and the conductor said, "She sure is dying hard, isn't she? I'm afraid we'll be almost nine hours late into Chicago, and that will make the last run of the *Century* six hours longer than the first run. We got caught behind a slow freight on the Norfolk & Western tracks and did sixty miles in seven hours. When we finally got back on the Central track, at Madison, Ohio, we were still almost fifty miles east of Cleveland. I didn't get to church this morning."

The porter said, "Soon as we get to Cleveland, the dining car will take on some water, and they can serve lunch."

We went back to bed and ate the apple and the orange, and took another pull at the Beebe:

> In times of crisis [Mr. Beebe said] . . . the entire collective will power of the New York Central System seemed to focus on getting *The Century* through with the least possible delay. High priority freight might freeze to the tracks at Buffalo and other ranking trains go into the hole all the way from Cleveland to Elkhart, but extra gangs and flangers, wedge plows and helper engines diverted from other runs combined to get the line's crack varnish over the road with the least possible damage to its schedule.

Lunch, after Cleveland, was a quiet meal. The steward was cheerful, and said, "Want to sit down? Here's a seat right here. Things aren't so bad." The passengers were glum. We had some more asparagus soup and a mushroom omelette. There was no liquor, because there are laws in Ohio and Indiana about Sunday drinking. Afterward, we went back to the observation car, along with a number of other people, to look at Ohio, and by and by everyone cheered up. Four sailors sat down with a pack of cards and started to play poker. The sun came out. A woman who told us she was from Milwaukee said, "When we were stopped in those fields in the middle of the night, I felt just like that Dr. Zhivago." And a woman wearing a mink hat said, "Everyone seems placid, and I'm glad. I guess maybe it's because it's the last run there will ever be of the *Twentieth Century Limited*."

We reached Chicago that night, at a quarter to seven, Central time.

The Railroad

E. B. WHITE

"A link to the past" is what the railroad, particularly the trains of Maine, meant to the author and famous essayist for The New Yorker. *He lived long enough to see the link suddenly broken, the passenger cars halted, and the station houses abandoned.*

Allen Cove
January 28, 1960

What's the railroad to me?
I never go to see
Where it ends.
It fills a few hollows,
And makes banks for the swallows,
It sets the sand a-blowing,
And the blackberries a-growing.

*H*ENRY THOREAU, who wrote those lines, was a student of railroading. He was a devotee, though seldom a passenger. He lived, of course, in the morningtime of America's railroads. He was less concerned with where the railroad ended than with what the railroad meant, and his remarks on the Fitchburg seem fadeproof in the strong light of this century, their liturgical quality still intact.

And what's the railroad to me? I have to admit that it means a great deal to me. It fills more than a few hollows. It is the link with my past, for one thing, and with the city, for another—two connections I would not like to see broken. The railroads of Maine are eager to break these connections, having found them to be unprofitable, and are already at work on the problem. They hope to discontinue all passenger service within the state, and although they failed in their first try, in 1959, they may do better in the year ahead.

Bangor is the second-oldest railroad town in New England; a steam train pulled out of Bangor, bound upriver for Old Town, on November 6, 1836. The running time for the twelve-mile trip was two and a half hours, the conductor's name was Sawyer, passengers were aboard, and the fare was thirty-seven and a half cents. That was the first steam train to roll in Maine, the second to roll in New England. Soon Bangor may set another mark in rail history; it may watch the departure of the last train, and as this sad hulk moves off down the track (if it ever does), Maine will become the first state in the Union, except for Hawaii, to have no rail passenger service between its major cities.

What's the railroad to me? It is a lingering pain in the heart, an old friend who has tired of me and my antics. Unlike Thoreau, whose rail adventures were largely intellectual, I do go to see where the railroad ends. On some occasions— as on next Monday, for instance—I have no choice but to go; I will pay the tariff cheerfully and stare at the bare blackberry vines with affection. But the sleeper I had planned to take, the sleeper out of Bangor, has been pulled off, and I will have to find another one, a hundred and forty miles to the westward. (The distance to the depot gets longer and longer.) I live in the twilight of railroading, the going down of its sun. For the past few months I've been well aware that I am the Unwanted Passenger, one of the last survivors of a vanishing and ugly breed. Indeed, if I am to believe the statements I see in the papers, I am all that stands between the Maine railroads and a bright future of hauling fast freight at a profit. It makes me feel like a spoilsport.

But I have other sensations, too. I bought this house almost thirty years ago, confident that whatever else happened to me, the railroad would always pick me up and carry me here and there, to and fro. This morning our village lies under several thicknesses of snow. Snow has fallen almost without interruption for a week, beginning with a northeast storm, tapering off to dull weather in which the low clouds spat snow day and night, and today another storm from the northeast. The highway is a ready cake mix of snow, ice, sand, salt, and trouble. Within the fortnight there has been the greatest rash of air disasters in my memory. And on top of everything the railroad, which is my old love, is sick of me and the likes of me, and I feel that my connections have been broken, as sharply as by the man in coveralls who crawls between the cars and knocks apart the steam line with his hammer. My thoughts, as they sometimes do on sad occasions, revert to Concord and another railroad in another century.

"On this morning of the Great Snow, perchance," wrote Thoreau, "which is still raging and chilling men's blood, I hear the muffled tone of their engine bell from out the fog bank of their chilled breath, which announces that the cars *are coming*, without long delay, notwithstanding the veto of a New England northeast snowstorm. . . ." How different my village from his village, my century from his century! The only bell that is audible to me in this snowstorm is the one that rings inside my head, which announces that the cars *are going*—soon, perhaps, to be gone for good. For although the passengers' dilemma here in Maine is still unresolved, there is a strong suspicion that we are living on borrowed time; the railroads would like to chop my head off instanter and be done, but the Public

Utilities Commission, after looking at all sides of the matter, has given me a stay of execution, on good behavior. It stipulates that I must travel more often and that I must not go first class.

Maine has two railroads—the Bangor & Aroostook and the Maine Central. One serves the north country, hauling potatoes and newsprint from field and forest; the other serves the midsection, hauling mail and packages of bonbons between Portland and Bangor, with an occasional sortie to Vanceboro. Both roads carry passengers when any show up. A third road, the Boston & Maine, dips into the state as far as Portland. A fourth, the Canadian Pacific, comes in briefly across the border.

Several months ago, the two principal railroads petitioned the commission to be allowed to quit carrying passengers and thus free their talents for the exciting and rewarding task of moving freight and mail. Public hearings were held; for the most part they were poorly attended. While the commissioners listened, the railroad men told grim tales of ruin and utter desolation. At one hearing in Portland, a lawyer for the Maine Central summed up the disjointed times when he said, "We are right now engaged in the diagnosis of a very sick patient." At another hearing, a man speaking for a cat-food factory in Lubec—makers of Puss 'n Boots cat food—rose to say that unless the Maine Central could wriggle free from the stifling grip of its passengers, Puss 'n Boots might have to move on to a happier and more progressive territory. The future of America's cats seemed suddenly at stake.

All in all, the year 1959 was a schizophrenic time for Maine's railroads. On Monday you would open your morning paper and find a display ad seeking your patronage and describing the rapturous experience of riding the rails. On Tuesday you would open the same paper and get a tongue-lashing from an impatient spokesman for the line, pointing out that the railroad would be bringing prosperity right this minute if only you, the passenger, would stand to one side and allow the freights to roll. "I am refreshed and expanded when the freight train rattles past me," wrote Thoreau. So, without any question, is E. Spencer Miller, president of the Maine Central. And so, for that matter, are all of us refreshed, though for a different reason, when, after a long wait in a motionless car on a silent siding, we hear a freight train at last rattle past us, hauling its cartons of food to faraway cats and releasing us hungry passengers for the continuance of our journey.

To the lay passenger, or to the traveling layman, the bookkeeping of railroads is as mysterious as the backing up of a train in the night. Even to a public-utilities commission the account books of railroads are something less than perfectly transparent. The Maine railroads' books were, of course, opened to the commission, and some of the figures got into the papers. Every railroad, I gather, keeps two sets of books, one on its freight operation, the other on its passenger operation; and every once in a while the books themselves manage to draw close together and a sort of seepage takes place from one set to the other, so that to the unpracticed eye, it is hard to tell how deeply a profitable sack of potatoes is being eaten into by those rats, the passengers. But there is no question that we passengers, of late years, have *been* gnawing away at the potatoes. Some of us do it in desperation, because we are starving to death between station stops. No food is carried on the train that brings me up the Kennebec, and a passenger must live by his wits off the land. At Waterville, on the eastbound run of the State of Maine, there is a midmorning pause, and while mail sacks are being tossed about in the genial and relaxed way that has characterized the handling of mail since the beginning of time, the engineer and the passengers (all six of us) gather at the snack counter in the depot, where we huddle over coffee and doughnuts, some of us passengers breaking a thirteen-hour fast that began 456.6 miles to the westward in the cornucopia civilization of Grand Central. These late breakfasts in Waterville come to an end as ritualistically as does the President's press conference in Washington when one of the reporters rises and says "Thank you, Mr. President." In Waterville, it is the engine driver himself who breaks up the party. He simply steps down from his stool, adjusts his cap, and walks away, which is the signal for us passengers to climb back into our places behind him in the train.

I suppose the very quality in railroads that has endeared them to me all my life, their traditionalism, has helped bring them (and me) to our present plight. England is about the most traditional institution I know of, but American railroads run a close second. "What has always been shall always be" is their motto. For almost a hundred years the Iron Horse was America's mount; the continent was his range, and the sound his hoofs made in the land was the sound of stability, majesty, punctuality, and success. "Far through unfrequented woods on the confines of towns, where once only the hunter penetrated by day, in the darkest night dart these bright saloons without the knowledge of their inhabitants; this moment stopping at some brilliant station-house in town or city, where a social crowd is gathered, the next in the Dismal Swamp, scaring the owl and fox. The startings and arrivals of the cars are now the epochs in the village day. They go and come with such regularity and precision, and their whistle can be heard so far, that the farmers set their clocks by them, and thus one well-conducted institution regulates a whole country." It was all true. And gradually the railroads fell in love with the sound of their own whistle, with the brightness of the saloons and the brilliance of the station houses, and even after the whistle dwindled to little more than a faint pooping in the hills and the saloons were withdrawn from service and the lights in the station houses went out, the railroads stubbornly stuck to their accustomed ways and the ways of the horse. Some of the station houses were so solidly built they still stand, monuments to darkness and decay. The depot in Bangor, built in 1907, is a notable example of a railroad's addiction to the glorious past. Give it bars at the windows and it could as well be a federal penitentiary. Give it a moat with a drawbridge and it could be the castle where the baron lives. (On wet days it actually acquires a sort of moat, through which we surviving passengers wade and plunge with our luggage to gain the platform.) Reduce it to miniature size and it could be a model-railroad station built out of beautiful tiny blocks by yesterday's child. It is, in short, everything except what it ought to be—a serviceable shelter for arriving and departing passengers—and any railroad that hopes to attract customers and survive as a profitable carrier would certainly have to raze it as a first step toward the new day. Come to think of it, the depot at Bangor, although fit for a baron, was at one time the property of a hustling railroad called the European & North American, whose dream was to bring Europe closer by rushing people by rail to St. John, where an ocean liner would speed them on their way. The property in Bangor on which the present station stands fell into the hands of the Maine Central in 1882, when that railroad leased the European & North American. The lease was to run for nine hundred and ninety-nine years, and although the European was dissolved a while back, there seems a good likelihood that the depot will still be standing in the year 2881, its men's room still well patronized and its freight office ablaze with lights.

I made my first rail journey into Maine in the summer of 1905, and have been riding to and fro on the cars ever since. On that first trip, when I was led by the hand into the green sanctuary of a Pullman drawing room and saw spread out for my pleasure its undreamed-of facilities and its opulence and the porter holding the pillow in his mouth while he drew the clean white pillowcase up around it and the ladder to the upper and the three-speed electric fan awaiting my caprice at the control switch and the little hammock slung so cunningly to receive my clothes and the adjoining splendor of the toilet room with its silvery appointments and gushing privacy, I was fairly bowled over with childish admiration and glee, and I fell in love with railroading then and there and have not been the same boy since that night.

We were a family of eight, and I was the youngest member. My father was a thrifty man, and come the first of August every summer, he felt that he was in a position to take his large family on a month's vacation. His design, conceived in 1905 and carried out joyously for many summers, was a simple one: for a small sum he rented a rough camp on one of the Belgrade lakes, then turned over the rest of his savings to the railroad and the Pullman Company in return for eight first-class round-trip tickets and plenty of space on the sleeper—a magnificent sum, a magnificent gesture. When it came to travel, there was not a second-class bone in my father's body, and although he spent thousands of hours of his life sitting bolt upright in dusty day coaches, commuting between Mount Vernon and Grand Central, once a year he put all dusty things aside and lay down, with his entire family, in Pullman perfection, his wife fully dressed against the possibility of derailment, to awake next morning in the winy air of a spruce-clad land and to debouch, surrounded by his eager children and full of the solemnity of trunk checks, onto the platform of the Belgrade depot, just across the tracks from Messalonskee's wild, alluring swamp. As the express train pulled away from us in Belgrade on that August morning of 1905, I got my first glimpse of this benign bog, which did not seem dismal to me at all. It was an inseparable part of the first intoxication of railroading, and, of all natural habitats, a swamp has ever since been to me the most beautiful and most seductive.

Tour of
Northern California

From THE WPA GUIDE
TO CALIFORNIA

*The Federal Writers' Project Guide to 1930s
California remains an impressive volume of
history and travel information. Although
prepared and written more than fifty years
ago, this description of coastal Route 1, from
Westport south to Tomales Bay, is a most
useful tour companion today.*

WESTPORT—Fort Bragg—Point Arena—San Francisco—Santa Cruz—
Monterey—Carmel—San Simeon—Morro Bay—San Luis Obispo—Las
Cruces; 554.5 *m.* State 1.

> Roadbed paved except for stretches between Pismo Beach and Las Cruces,
> winding continuously, with frequent sharp turns; occasional slides during
> rainy season.
> Southern Pacific Lines parallel route between Davenport and Pacific Grove.
> Accommodations limited except in larger towns.

State 1 skirts closely the waters of the Pacific. It swings outward around
headlands and inland past sandy-edged coves in a succession of hairpin curves;
it climbs barren slopes and dips into brush-choked ravines. At times it edges
along sheer bluffs high above the surf. Eastward, wind-swept hills, wooded only
in patches, rise to the timbered crests of the Coast Range. After the first rains
these hills are briefly green; at other times their slopes are brown with dried
grass, close-cropped by grazing sheep.

Walled off by mountains, the narrow coastal shelf is sparsely settled except
around San Francisco and Monterey Bays. The half-primitive ways of the seventies and eighties, when lumbering, fishing, and sheep raising flourished, linger
on in the isolated villages and farms. The region now affords only a meager
living to its hard-working inhabitants. Along the northern section, where redwoods grow down to the sea in forest-choked ravines, the lumber towns at the

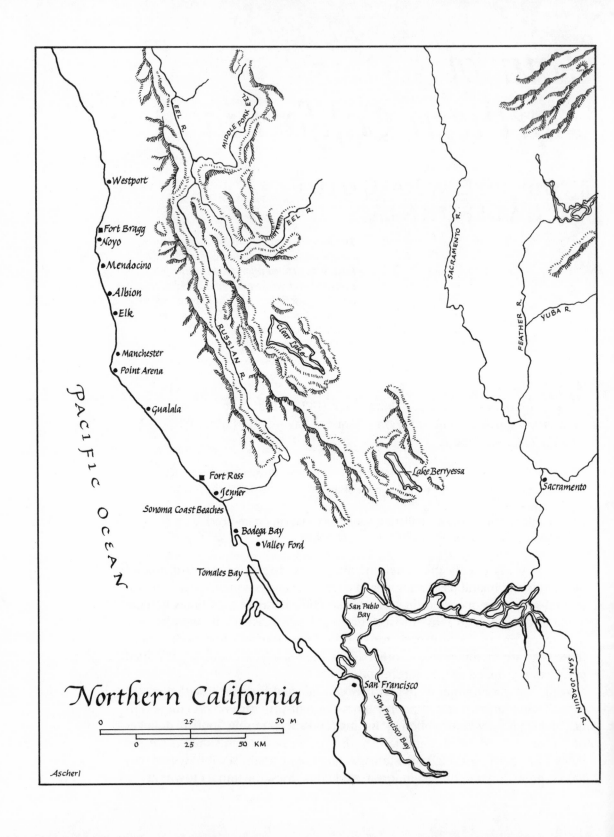

Northern California

Ascherl

mouths of rivers, once shipping points for logs hauled by narrow-gage railways from the forested hinterland, are sinking into decay beside abandoned mills.

Fishing is still a gainful pursuit at such points as Noyo, Tomales Bay, Monterey, and Half Moon Bay. Flocks of sheep roam over the hills up and down the coast and great herds of dairy cattle over the knolls and hollows around Tomales Bay. Berries and peas are grown around Fort Bragg; brussels sprouts and artichokes, in the foggy strip near Half Moon Bay; and apples in the Pajaro Valley; but most of the country is too rough, too bleak for farming. The occasional weather-beaten farm buildings huddle behind ragged, protective files of wind-battered cypress or eucalyptus trees.

The coastal strip between the mouth of the Russian River and Big Sur attracts increasing numbers of vacationers every year. It is a picturesque stretch, indented with rocky, islet-studded coves where crescent-shaped beaches of white sand lie between bold promontories. Along the highway in this area are a succession of resort towns and camps that offer bathing and fishing in the surf, clam and abalone hunting along the shore, and riding and hiking in the forested hinterland.

Section a. WESTPORT to SAN FRANCISCO; 205.4 m.

On the maps the northern end of State 1 is extended to a junction with US 101 not far south of Eureka, with feeders from US 101 north of Westport; but these connections are barely passable even in good weather.

WESTPORT, 0 *m.* (50 alt., 200 pop.), a rambling settlement of frame houses with rickety picket fences, perched on bare bluffs. First named Beal's Landing for Lloyd Beal, who arrived in 1864, the town was renamed Westport at the instigation of James T. Rogers, a native of Eastport, Maine. After construction of two wharves in 1878, it became for a while an important lumber-shipping point.

> North from Westport on a poor road (the sketchy continuation of State 1), past ROCKPORT, 11.5 *m.*, a small lumber camp with bleak, weatherbeaten shacks, to the junction with a narrow, ungraded dirt road, 14.5 *m.* Right here, up a long, steep forested grade to a summit, 25.5 *m.*, then downward to a junction with US 101, 30.1 *m.* (*see TOUR 2a*).

South of Westport State 1 winds over close-cropped pasture lands sloping to the sea. Crossing the marshy bottoms of sluggish Ten Mile River, 7.8 *m.*, it strikes through an eerie wilderness of storm-blasted pine and cypress groves, edged at intervals by sand dunes. Patches of farm land and orchard, crisscrossed by files of cypress windbreaks, hedge the road.

FORT BRAGG, 16.2 *m.* (60 alt., 3,022 pop.), spreads over a sloping coastal shelf to the edge of a wild and rocky coast line. A settlement of wooden buildings—false-front stores, steepled churches, and gabled frame houses in fenced yards—it has a weather-worn, settled air. Fort Bragg's chief stock in trade is lumber, but it also ships farm and truck-garden crops (especially berries), poultry and dairy products, and fish. Its racial make-up is mixed: Finns and Swedes predominate; after them, Germans and Italians.

In June 1857 Lt. Horatio Gates Gibson was ordered to establish a military post within the boundaries of the Mendocino Indian Reservation. The fort he set up here and named for Gen. Braxton Bragg of Mexican War fame covered a 10-acre clearing. The land was thrown open for purchase in 1867, when the reservation was abandoned, and a lumber town grew up. It was damaged by the earthquake of April 18, 1906, but rebuilt at once.

The heart of the town's industrial life is the UNION LUMBER COMPANY PLANT, a large redwood sawmill with a capacity of 350,000 to 400,000 board feet a day. Its red-painted mill buildings, lumberyards, and log pond lie along the railroad yards at the edge of the rocky bluffs. The UNION LUMBER COMPANY REFORESTATION AND ORNAMENTAL NURSERY (*open workdays 8-5*), on Main Street (R) near the southern outskirts, established in 1922, raises redwood and other seedlings for systematic reforestation of cutover lands.

NOYO (*boats for ocean fishing rented*), 17.9 *m.* (sea level, 93 pop.), lies at the mouth of placid, winding Noyo River, crowded with small fishing craft tied up alongside tumble-down warehouses. Noyo was the name given by Northern Pomo Indians to their village at the river's mouth. The village escaped the fate of most former lumber towns along the Mendocino coast by turning to fishing for a living. Settled largely by Italian fishermen, it is now the center of the area's commercial fishing industry. It has fish-canning and drying plants and a deep-water harbor protected by a breakwater.

CASPAR, 22.3 *m.* (52 alt., 250 pop.), on the edge of high bluffs at the mouth of Caspar Creek, is a collection of old frame houses amid weed-grown vacant spaces, dirt paths, and picket fences. The lumber mill beside the log pond and chute, occasionally operated, was built in 1861.

At 25.2 *m.* is the junction with a dirt road.

Right on this road 0.3 *m.* to RUSSIAN GULCH STATE PARK HEADQUAR-TERS (camping 50¢ per car a day, picnicking 25¢ per car a day). The park contains more than 1,000 acres of second-growth redwood. Along the fern-banked canyon bottom, deep among redwoods, alders, and Douglas fir, are scattered camp sites and picnic grounds.

MENDOCINO, 27.3 *m.* (41 alt., 500 pop.), ranges over the northern shore of a half-moon-shaped bay at the mouth of Big River—a jumble of weathered, gabled wooden buildings fronting dirt streets, edged by the gloomy pine woods of encircling hills. It was named for Cape Mendocino, which Juan Rodríguez Cabrillo discovered in 1542 and named for Don Antonio de Mendoza, first viceroy of New Spain (Mexico).

Intermittent lumbering provides Mendocino's main support. A party sent out from Bodega in 1851 to salvage tea and silk from a vessel wrecked nearby carried back information of the country's rich timber resources to Alderman Harry Meiggs of San Francisco, lumberman and mill owner. On July 19, 1852, the brig *Ontario,* chartered by Meiggs, arrived with sawmill machinery imported from the East. Meiggs, finding that one William Kasten had staked out a claim to the water-front, purchased the claim with the first lumber from his sawmill— the first on the Mendocino coast—as part payment.

The architecture of Mendocino's well-preserved buildings (there has been only one serious fire) reflects the New England origin of most of its early settlers. Notable remnant of a bygone era is the MASONIC HALL (R), on Main Street. A buff-colored, gable-roofed structure, the hall bears on its cupola a piece of sculpture carved from a single block of redwood. It represents the Masonic emblem and the symbolic figures of Masonic lore: the broken pillar, the maiden beside it with a sprig in her hand, and Father Time dallying with her wavy locks.

At 30.1 *m.* is the junction with a graveled road.

> Right on this road 0.3 *m.* to VAN DAMME BEACH STATE PARK HEAD-QUARTERS (*camping and picnicking fees as at Russian Gulch*). This 1,800-acre tract fronting a lagoon with a sloping bathing beach stretches 4 miles up the forested canyon of the Little River. The chief attraction for visitors is the fishing: trout are caught in the Little River; red, blue, and China cod in the surf; leaf cod and salmon in the bay.

ALBION, 34.3 *m.* (37 alt., 75 pop.), a village of brightly painted, shingle-roofed cottages, overlooks the cove at the mouth of the Albion River, where an abandoned lumber mill decays amid half-ruined company shacks. A sawmill was erected here in 1852–53 and operated until 1928. Today the inhabitants subsist chiefly by fishing and berry picking.

At 38.6 *m.,* in a deep valley where the broad Navarro River winds over marshy bottoms and through a sand bar into the sea, is the junction with paved State 28.

> Left on State 28, which runs along the riverbank, shadowed by a forest of second-growth redwood, 8.4 *m.* to DIMMICK MEMORIAL PARK (*picnick-

ing), a 12-acre reserve. The Navarro River offers fine swimming, and is one of the best trout and bass streams in the State.

On State 28 at 14.8 *m.* is NAVARRO. Many of its gray, weathered houses stand empty, reminders of its lively past as a lumber town.

The road enters Anderson Valley, a fertile basin given over to apple growing, and reaches BOONVILLE, 30.2 *m.* (pop. 315). Named in 1868 for an early settler, W. W. Boon, the settlement today furnishes supplies to ranchers and travelers. It celebrates an annual County Fair and Apple Show in October.

Southwest of Boonville the highway climbs over a succession of hills, winds past rolling sheep pasturage, and joins US 101 (*see TOUR 2a*) at 57.5 *m.*

ELK, 44.6 *m.* (200 pop.), also known as Greenwood, lying along the highway skirting the very edge of steep bluffs—is a string of frame store buildings, most of them left to sag and gather cobwebs since lumbering operations stopped in 1931. In its heyday, when two or three boats anchored offshore every week to load lumber brought from inland by railroad, Elk had nearly a dozen saloons and half as many hotels. The loading trestle remains, flung from the edge of the bluffs to a jagged islet in the surf. In the debris-littered gravel bottoms just south of town lie the remains of the mill, rusted and rotting.

State 1 winds between fences over sheep ranges and strips of farm land that roll upward from the narrow coastal shelf to forest-fringed hills. A vast sweep of surf-scalloped shore line appears at intervals, curving off in the long promontory of Point Arena (*see below*). A far stretch of rolling country sweeps to timbered hills (L) as the highway strikes inland from the shore.

MANCHESTER, 58.8 *m.* (300 pop.), a handful of buildings widely scattered among farms and pastures, lies in a farming, dairying, and sheep- and cattle-raising region, one of the few sections along the northern coast level enough to permit extensive farming.

At 62.6 *m.* is the junction with a paved road.

> Right on this road 2.5 *m.* to POINT ARENA LIGHT STATION (*visitors 1-3 Mon., Wed., Fri.*), where gray, red-roofed frame houses cluster around the tall cylindrical white light tower. On November 10, 1792, Capt. George Vancouver spent the night off this promontory in his ship *Discovery,* en route from Nootka to San Francisco. He named it Punta Barro de Arena (Sp., point sand bar). A brick light station erected here in 1870 was replaced, after its destruction in the 1906 earthquake, by the present 115-foot tower, which has a light of 380,000 candle power.

POINT ARENA, 64.5 *m.* (39 alt., 385 pop.), has scattered cottages in cypress-sheltered gardens and trim, stuccoed business buildings, churches, and schools.

It traces its history to the opening of a store here in 1859. Although it was said to be the most thriving town between San Francisco and Eureka at the height of lumbering operations, it was not incorporated until 1908. Today it is a trading center for a dairying region.

South of Point Arena State 1 again skirts the coast, running through dense patches of dwarf-pines and dipping into gulches choked with undergrowth.

GUALALA, 79.6 *m.* (sea level, 15 pop.), is on a curving beach at the mouth of the broad, forest-bordered Gualala River. Its name (pron. Wah-lá-la), is probably the Spanish spelling of the Pomo Indians' "wala'li" or "wa'lali," meaning a meeting place of waters. Gualala had its lumbering boom in the 1860's and 1870's—although its sawmill, abandoned now at the river's mouth, was operated until 1920. Its life centers today around the two-story, white frame GUA-LALA HOTEL (1903), with veranda and balcony. The fishing season attracts many visitors.

STEWART'S POINT, 91.3 *m.* (20 alt., 30 pop.), named for a pioneer lumberman and settler, is a handful of frame houses around a general store. On the rocky point at the edge of the cove, hidden by trees, are the abandoned sheds and trestle from which lumber was once shipped.

As State 1 winds southward, through rolling stretches thickly wooded with dwarf pines and littered with boulders, the coast becomes more and more rugged—saw-toothed with jutting promontories and rocky inlets where the surf crashes on kelp-strewn crags. The route makes a short swing inland through the KRUSE RHODODENDRON RESERVE, 99.3 *m.*, maintained in its natural state, where the rhododendrons, growing 20 to 30 feet high, blossom in late May and early June.

FORT ROSS, 107 *m.* (100 alt.), once chief outpost of Russian civilization in California, stands on a high shelf sloping from wooded hills to the edge of the cove. At this place, in the spring of 1812, the Russian-American Fur Company's vessel, the *Chirikov,* deposited a party of fur traders and Aleut hunters under command of Ivan Alexander Kuskof. Since 1806, when the Tsar's chamberlain, Nikolai Rezanof, had visited the San Francisco Presidio (*see SAN FRANCISCO*) in quest of food for the starving Russian settlement at Sitka, Alaska, the Russian-American Company had planned to establish settlements in California as sources of food supply for its fur-trading posts in the north. On May 15, 1812, Kuskof's party began building a fortress; three months later, on August 30, they dedicated it with ceremony, naming it Rossiya (Russia).

The settlement, laid out in a rectangle, was enclosed by a 14-foot stockade of hewn timbers and guarded by two-story blockhouses with portholes for cannon at the north and south corners. There were 59 buildings. Inside the enclosure were the chapel, the commandant's house, barracks, two warehouses, blacksmith and other shops, and a jail. Outside clustered the redwood huts of the Aleut hunters, a windmill, several farm buildings, and a tannery. At the foot of the steep bluffs were a small wharf, a workshop for shipbuilding, a blacksmith shop, a bathhouse, and sheds for the bidarkas (skin boats) of the Aleuts and for storing lumber.

Despite the efforts of apprehensive Spanish officials to check the growth of La Fuerte de los Rusos (the fort of the Russians), the colonists began a thriving trade with the San Francisco Presidio and mission, exchanging tobacco, sugar, kitchen utensils, iron, cloth, and wax candles for grain, peas, meat, tallow, flour, and hides. When Missions San Rafael and San Francisco Solano (*see TOUR 2a*) were founded to halt Russian expansion southward the Russians extended their trade to the missions themselves.

The Russian settlement began to face economic difficulties, however, when the revenue from sea-otter hunting diminished with the rapid extermination of the otter along the coast. Unable to make a living from farming, the colonists turned to shipbuilding; they used the green timber of oak to construct four vessels, two of 160 and two of 200 tons, between 1819 and 1824; but the timber decayed so rapidly that this activity was abandoned. The settlement was in the end a failure. Restrained from expanding southward by the Spanish, Russia agreed in 1824 to limit its future settlements to Alaska.

The man into whose hands Fort Ross finally passed, when in 1841 the Tsar ordered withdrawal of his subjects, was Johann August Sutter, founder of New Helvetia (Sacramento). The price agreed on for the entire property—buildings, chattels, livestock, and even the 20-ton schooner *Constantine*—was $30,000; of this Sutter agreed to pay $2,000 in cash and the rest in yearly installments of produce, chiefly wheat. Sutter dismantled fort and buildings and shipped everything he could carry on his schooner to New Helvetia. The transferred property included 1,700 head of cattle, 940 horses and mules, 9,000 sheep, agricultural implements and industrial machinery, and an arsenal, including brass pieces, cannon, and muskets—all French weapons picked up in 1813 in the path of Napoleon's retreat through the snow from Moscow. Even a 20-foot-square conservatory, with glass windows and doors, was removed in sections to Sacramento; Madame Rotchev, the Russian governor's wife, had begged Sutter (he wrote) "not to destroy the garden house which she had built and in which she had spent so many happy hours. . . . However . . . my men . . . could not put it together because they did not understand the workmanship of the Russian carpenters. . . ."

The few remaining buildings were neglected until in 1906, after damage by the earthquake, the State began restoration. The only part of the original stockade left is a heap of rotting redwood logs—the remains of the heptagonal blockhouse that stood at the north corner. At the eastern corner is the partly restored GREEK ORTHODOX CHAPEL (*open 8–5 except Tues.*), a crude structure 20 feet wide and 25 long, with a squat, dull yellow belfry and dome on its weather-worn red-gabled roof. Exhibited in its two rough-boarded rooms are Russian, Spanish, and Indian relics. The RUSSIAN COMMANDANT'S HOUSE, a spacious edifice with a shingled roof sloping over a wide veranda, preserves remnants of the original structure—including the fireplace and the log finish between the doors and windows of the facade—reinforced by later additions.

South of Fort Ross State 1 winds tortuously around brush-grown, rocky hillsides and through twisting ravines, on a narrow ledge overhanging the boiling surf. At 118.8 *m.* it swings up the broad valley of the Russian River (*see TOUR 2a*), which finds its way to the ocean through a narrow strait in the great sand bar that holds back its waters in a wide, placid lagoon.

JENNER-BY-THE-SEA, 119.7 *m.* (0 alt., 160 pop.), is a resort with peak-roofed white and green cottages hugging the steep slopes above the river.

At 120.8 *m.*, where State 1 crosses Russian River on a giant concrete and steel bridge, is the junction with paved State 12 (*see TOUR 2a*).

At 121.7 *m.* is the junction with a dirt road.

> Right on this road 0.2 *m.* to BODEGA-SONOMA COAST STATE PARK, which stretches along 5 miles of picturesque ocean shore from the mouth of the Russian River to Bodega Bay. The shore waters abound with shellfish and abalones and the surf with fish that can be caught by line from the rocks or by net in the breakers.

At 122.9 *m.* on State 1 is the junction with an oiled road.

> Right on this road 0.2 *m.* to SHELL BEACH in Bodega-Sonoma Coast State Park.

WRIGHT'S BEACH is at 124.3 *m.* and **ARCH ROCK BEACH** at 127 *m.* Both are wide sandy strands sheltered in rocky coves in the State park.

SALMON CREEK BEACH, 128.5 *m.*, rimmed by great sand dunes, lies at the mouth of Salmon Creek, where a sand bar impounds a lagoon below scattered cottages.

BAY, 130.4 *m.*, a string of frame houses sheltered by a lane of eucalyptus trees overlooking a row of small wharves where fishing smacks are moored, lies along the curving shore of BODEGA BAY.

Bodega Bay is now a shallow, sand-choked inlet, rimmed by mud flats at low tide; its egress to the sea on the south is blocked, except for a narrow strait, by a sandspit stretching from the mainland on the east to Bodega Head at the tip of the long promontory on the west. The bay was named for its discoverer, Lieut. Juan Francisco de la Bodéga y Cuadra, who anchored his schooner, the *Sonora,* off Bodega Head October 3, 1775. In 1809 the Russian-American Fur Company's agent, Ivan Kuskof, landed with a party from Sitka. They sowed wheat, and in August, with the harvested grain and a catch of 2,000 sea-otter skins, returned to Alaska. In 1811 the Russians returned to found the settlements of Port Roumiantzoff on the bay and Bodega (*see below*) and Kuskof in the hinterland. They cultivated land toward the tip of the Bodega peninsula and erected two warehouses.

First Yankee settlers at Bodega Bay were three sailors. In 1835 Gen. Mariano G. Vallejo gave them large land grants on condition that they settle at the border of the Russian claims to check Russian expansion. In 1843 Capt. Stephen Smith was granted the land formerly occupied by the Russians. Five years later he erected a small warehouse and in 1852 a hotel. By 1860 the port was alive with people and business, its harbor crowded with sails. The warehouses lining the shore overflowed with potatoes—a variety known as Bodega Reds for the bright maroon coat beneath their rough skins—raised on great ranches roundabout. Regular freight and passenger boats from San Francisco anchored in the open roadstead outside the sandspit, where they were loaded from small lighters. In the 1870's the bay began to fill with sand. In time, potato raising was supplanted by dairying, the chief industry of the region ever since. Vessels no longer call here—nor have they for a generation past.

State 1 winds inland over rolling farm lands where cattle graze in fenced pastures, bordered by lanes of eucalyptus trees and patches of orchards.

BODEGA, 136.4 *m.* (40 alt., 100 pop.), clusters amid cypress patches around a red-roofed schoolhouse and two white-spired churches.

Beside the road (R) at 138.4 *m.* stands the WATSON DISTRICT SCHOOL, built in 1856, a white clapboarded building with a bell tower jutting from its peaked red roof. It was named for James Watson, an immigrant of 1853, who acquired so many thousand acres of land from the yield of bumper crops of the high-priced Bodega Reds that he became a land baron, entertaining the whole countryside with horse racing at his private course.

VALLEY FORD, 142.3 *m.* (45 alt., 200 pop.), with old brick and frame stores, is among gently rolling pasture lands dotted with gracious white farmhouses, roomy barns, and corrals. It lies at the head of tidewater on the Estero Americano (American Creek), which empties into Bodega Bay; it was named for the "valley ford," where an ancient Indian and Spanish trail crossed the Estero. This is a dairying town: when the bank was organized in 1893, it was called The Dairymans Bank.

TOMALES, 149.3 *m.* (75 alt., 450 pop.), a trim looking town, rambles over the slopes of a hollow. The countryside is noted for its butter, cheese, and milk. Tomales' first house was built in 1850 by John Keyes, who operated a small schooner between Bodega Bay and San Francisco and opened a trading post here in the spring of 1854.

State 1 winds through the shallow gully of San Antonio Creek to its mouth in a delta of mud flats at TOMALES BAY, 151.9 *m.,* and then runs for 13 miles along the shore. (Tomales is a Spanish corruption of the Coast Miwok Indian word *tamal,* bay.) The bay is a long, narrow, fingerlike inlet, resembling a firth in the Scottish Highlands. On the east bare brown hills slope down to the shore; on the west, low, tumbled peaks densely forested with green. In the shallow water offshore, oyster beds are fenced in by a long file of slender stakes.

At **NICK'S COVE** (*boats for hire*), 153.2 *m.,* cottages cluster around the store and the wharf, where small dories bob up and down with the lapping tide.

The lower end of Tomales Bay is a dank expanse of mud flats.

Canada and the Far North

True North

MARGARET ATWOOD

"Where does the north begin? Every province, every city, has its own road north. . . ." For Canadian writer Margaret Atwood the north of her past becomes more difficult to find.

> *Land of the silver birch,*
> *Home of the beaver,*
> *Where still the mighty moose*
> *Wanders at will,*
> *Blue lake and rocky shore,*
> *I will return once more;*
> *Boom-diddy-boom-boom*
> *Boom-diddy-boom-boom*
> *Boo-OO-oo-oo-oom.*
> *—Archaic Song*

WE sang this once, squatting around the papier-mâché Magic Mushroom in the Brownie pack, while pretending to be wolves in Cub Scouts, or while watching our marshmallows turn to melted Styrofoam on the ends of our sticks at some well-run, fairly safe summer camp in the wilds of Muskoka, Haliburton, or Algonquin Park. Then we grew up and found it corny. By that time we were into Jean-Paul Sartre and the lure of the nauseous. Finally, having reached the age of nostalgia, we rediscovered it on a cassette in The Children's Book Store, in a haunting version that invested it with all the emotional resonance we once thought it possessed, and bought it, under the pretence of giving our children a little ethnic musical background.

It brought tears to our eyes, not for simple reasons. Whales get to us that way too, and whooping cranes, and other things hovering on the verge of extinction but still maintaining a tenuous foothold in the world of the actual. The beavers are doing all right—we know this because they just decimated our poplars—but the mighty moose is having a slimmer time of it. As for the blueness of the lakes, we worry about it: too blue and you've got acid rain.

Will we return once more, or will we go to Portugal instead? It depends, we have to admit, partly on the exchange rate, and this makes us feel disloyal. I am, rather quixotically, in Alabama, teaching, even more quixotically, a course in

Canadian literature. Right now we're considering Marian Engel's novel *Bear*. Since everything in Canada, outside Toronto, begins with geography, I've unfolded a large map of Ontario and traced the heroine's route north; I've located the mythical house of the book somewhere on the actual shore of Georgian Bay, northern edge. I've superimposed a same-scale map of Alabama on this scheme, to give the students an idea of the distances. In the north, space is larger than you think, because the points of reference are farther apart.

"Are there any words you came across that puzzled you?" I ask.

Blackfly comes up. A large black fly is proposed. I explain blackflies, their smallness, their multitude, their evil habits. It gives me a certain kick to do this: I'm competing with the local water moccasins.

Mackinaw. A raincoat? Not quite. *Loon. Tamarack. Reindeer moss. Portage. Moose. Wendigo.*

"Why does she make Lucy the old Indian woman talk so funny?" they ask. Lucy, I point out, is not merely Indian but a *French-speaking* Indian. This, to them, is a weird concept.

The north is another country. It's also another language. Or languages.

Where is the north, exactly? It's not only a place but a direction, and as such its location is relative: to the Mexicans, the United States is the north, to Americans Toronto is, even though it's on roughly the same latitude as Boston.

Wherever it is for us, there's a lot of it. You stand in Windsor and imagine a line going north, all the way to the pole. The same line going south would end up in South America. That's the sort of map we grew up with, at the front of the classroom in Mercator projection, which made it look even bigger than it was, all that pink stretching on forever, with a few cities sprinkled along the bottom edge. It's not only geographical space, it's space related to body image. When we face south, as we often do, our conscious mind may be directed down there, towards crowds, bright lights, some Hollywood version of fame and fortune, but the north is at the back of our minds, always. There's something, not someone, looking over our shoulders; there's a chill at the nape of the neck.

The north focuses our anxieties. Turning to face north, face the north, we enter our own unconscious. Always, in retrospect, the journey north has the quality of dream.

Where does the north begin?

Every province, every city, has its own road north. From Toronto you go up the 400. Where you cross the border, from here to there, is a matter of opinion. Is it the Severn River, where the Shield granite appears suddenly out of the earth?

Is it the sign announcing that you're halfway between the equator and the North Pole? Is it the first gift shop shaped like a wigwam, the first town—there are several—that proclaims itself The Gateway to the North?

As we proceed, the farms become fewer, rockier, more desperate-looking, the trees change their ratios, coniferous moving in on deciduous. More lakes appear, their shorelines scraggier. Our eyes narrow and we look at the clouds: the weather is important again.

One of us used to spend summers in a cottage in Muskoka, before the road went in, when you took the train, when there were big cruise ships there, and matronly motor launches, and tea dances at the hotels, and men in white flannels on the lawns, which there may still be. This was not just a cottage but a Muskoka cottage, with boathouse and maid's quarters. Rich people went north in the summers then, away from cities and crowds; that was before the cure for polio, which has made a difference. In this sort of north, they tried to duplicate the south, or perhaps some dream of country life in England. In the living room there were armchairs, glass-fronted bookcases, family photos in silver frames, stuffed birds under glass bells. The north, as I said, is relative.

For me, the north used to be completely in force by the Trout Creek planing mill. Those stacks of fresh-cut lumber were the true gateway to the north, and north of that was North Bay, which used to be, to be blunt, a bit of an armpit. It was beef-sandwich-on-white-bread-with-gravy-and-canned-peas country. But no more. North Bay now has shopping malls, and baskets of flowers hanging from lampposts above paving-stone sidewalks, downtown. It has a Granite Club. It has the new, swish, carpeted buildings of Laurentian University. It has gourmet restaurants. And in the airport, where southbound DC-9s dock side by side with northbound Twin Otters, there's a book rack in the coffee shop that features Graham Greene and Kierkegaard, hardly standard airport fare.

The south is moving north.

We bypass North Bay, which now has a bypass, creeping southerliness, and do not go, this time, to the Dionne Quints Museum, where five little silhouettes in black play forever beside an old log cabin, complete with the basket where they were packed in cotton wool, the oven where they were warmed, the five prams, the five Communion dresses.

Beyond North Bay there is a brief flurry of eccentricity—lawns populated with whole flocks of wooden-goose windmills—and then we go for miles and miles past nothing but trees, meeting nothing but the occasional truck loaded with lumber. This area didn't used to be called anything. Now it's the Near North Travel Area. You can see signs telling you that. Near what, we wonder uneasily? We don't want to be near. We want to be far.

At last we see the Ottawa River, which is the border. There's a dam across it, two dams, and an island between them. If there were a customs house it would be here. A sign faces us saying *Bienvenue;* out the back window there's one saying *Welcome.* This was my first lesson in points of view.

And there, across the border in Québec, in Témiscaming, is an image straight from my childhood: a huge mountain made of sawdust. I always wanted to slide down this sawdust mountain until I finally did, and discovered it was not like sand, dry and slippery, but damp and sticky and hard to get out of your clothes. This was my first lesson in the nature of illusion.

Continue past the sawdust mountain, past the baseball diamond, up the hill, and you're in the centre of town, which is remarkable for at least three things: a blocks-long public rock garden, still flourishing after more than forty-five years; a pair of statues, one a fountain, that look as if they've come straight from Europe, which I think they did; and the excellent, amazingly low-priced hamburgers you can get at the Boulevard Restaurant, where the décor, featuring last year's cardboard Santa Claus and a stuffed twenty-three-pound pike, is decidedly northern. Ask the owner about the pike and he'll tell you about one twice as big, forty-five pounds in fact, that a fellow showed him strapped to the tailgate of his van, and that long, too.

You can have this conversation in either French or English: Témiscaming is a border town and a northern one, and the distinctions made here are as likely to be north-south as French-English. Up in these parts you'll hear as much grumbling, or more, about Québec City as you will about Ottawa, which is, after all, closer. Spit in the river and it gets to Ottawa, eh?

For the north, Témiscaming is old, settled, tidy, even a little prosperous-looking. But it's had its crises. Témiscaming is the resource economy personified. Not long ago it was a company town, and when the company shut down the mill, which would have shut down the town too, the workers took the unprecedented step of trying to buy it. With some help they succeeded, and the result was Tembec, still going strong. But Témiscaming is still a one-industry town, like many northern towns, and its existence is thus precarious.

Not so long ago, logging was a different sort of business. The men went into the woods in winter, across the ice, using horse-drawn sledges, and set up camp. (You still come across these logging camps now and then in your travels through the lakes, abandoned, already looking as ancient as Roman aqueducts; more ancient, since there's been no upkeep.) They'd cut selectively, tree by tree, using axes and saws and the skills that were necessary to avoid being squashed or hacked. They'd skid the trees to the ice; in the spring, after the ice went out, there would be a run down the nearest fast river to the nearest sawmill.

Now it's done with bulldozers and trucks, and the result is too often a blitzed shambles; cut everything, leave a wreck of dead and, incidentally, easily flammable branches behind. Time is money. Don't touch the shoreline though, we need that for tourists. In some places, the forest is merely a scrim along the water. In behind it's been hollowed out.

Those who look on the positive side say it's good for the blueberries.

Sometimes we went the other way, across to Sudbury, the trees getting smaller and smaller and finally disappearing as you approached. Sudbury was another magic place of my childhood. It was like interplanetary travel, which we liked to imagine, which was still just imagination in those days. With its heaps of slag and its barren shoulders of stone, it looked like the moon. Back then, we tell the children, before there were washer-dryers and you used something called a wringer washer and hung the sheets out on something called a clothesline, when there weren't even coloured sheets but all sheets were white, when Rinso white and its happy little washday song were an item, and Whiter than White was a catch phrase and female status really did have something to do with your laundry, Sudbury was a housewife's nightmare. We knew people there; the windowsills in their houses were always grey.

Now the trees are beginning to come back because they built higher smoke-stacks. But where is all that stuff going now?

The Acid Rain Dinner, in Toronto's Sheraton Centre, in 1985. The first of these fund-raising events was fairly small. But the movement has grown, and this dinner is huge. The leaders of all three provincial parties are here. So is the minister of the environment from the federal government. So are several labour leaders, and several high-ranking capitalists, and representatives of numerous northerly chambers of commerce, summer residents' associations, tourist-camp runners, outfitters. Wishy-washy urban professionals who say "frankly" a lot bend elbows with huntin', shootin', fishin', and cussin' burnt-necks who wouldn't be caught dead saying "frankly." This is not a good place to be overheard saying that actually acid rain isn't such a bad thing because it gets rid of all that brown scum and leeches in the lake, or who cares because you can water-ski anyway. Teddy Kennedy, looking like a bulky sweater, is the guest speaker. Everyone wears a little gold pin in the shape of a rain drop. It looks like a tear.

Why has acid rain become the collective Canadian nightmare? Why is it—as a good cause—bigger than baby-seal bashing? The reasons aren't just economic, although there are lots of those, as the fishing-camp people and foresters will tell you. It's more than that, and cognate with the outrage aroused by the uninvited voyage of the American icebreaker *Polar Sea* through the Northwest Passage, where almost none of us ever goes. It's territorial, partly; partly a felt violation of some area in us that we hardly ever think about unless it's invaded or tampered with. It's the neighbours throwing guck into our yard. It's our childhood dying.

On location, in summer and far from the glass and brass of the Sheraton Centre, we nervously check our lakes. Leeches still in place? Have the crayfish, among the first to go, gone yet? (We think in terms of "yet.") Are the loons reproducing, have you seen any young? Any minnows? How about the lichen on the rocks? These inventories have now become routine, and that is why we're willing to fork out a hundred dollars a plate to support our acid-rain lobbyists in Washington. A summer without loons is unthinkable, but how do you tell that to people who don't know it because they've never had any to begin with?

We're driving through Glencoe, in the Highlands of Scotland. It's imposing, as a landscape: bleak, large, bald, apparently empty. We can see why the Scots took so well to Canada. Yet we know that the glens and crags round about are crawling with at least a thousand campers, rock climbers, and other seekers after nature; we also know that, at one end of this glen, the Campbells butchered the MacDonalds in the seventeenth century, thus propelling both of them into memorable history. Go walking here and you'll find things human: outlines of stone fences now overgrown, shards of abandoned crofts.

In Europe, every scrap of land has been claimed, owned, re-owned, fought over, captured, bled on. The roads are the only no-man's-land. In northern Canada, the roads are civilization, owned by the collective human *we*. Off the road is *other*. Try walking in it, and you'll soon find out why all the early traffic here was by water. "Impenetrable wilderness" is not just verbal.

And suppose you get off the road. Suppose you get lost. Getting lost, elsewhere and closer to town, is not knowing exactly where you are. You can always ask, even in a foreign country. In the north, getting lost is not knowing how to get out.

You can get lost on a lake, of course, but getting lost in the forest is worse. It's tangly in there, and dim, and one tree does begin to look remarkably like another. The leaves and needles blot up sound, and you begin to feel watched: not by anyone, not by an animal even, or anything you can put a name to, just watched. You begin to feel judged. It's as if something is keeping an eye on you just to see what you will do.

What will you do? Which side of the tree does moss grow on, and here, where there are ferns and the earth is damp, or where it's dry as tinder, it seems that moss grows everywhere, or does not grow at all. Snippets of Boy Scout lore or truisms learned at summer camp come back to you, but scrambled. You tell yourself not to panic: you can always live off the land.

Easier said than done, you'd soon find. The Canadian Shield is a relatively foodless area, which is why even the Indians tended to pass through it, did not form large settlements except where there was arable land, and remained limited in numbers. This is not the Mekong delta. If you had a gun you could shoot something, maybe, a red squirrel perhaps; but if you're lost you probably don't have a gun, or a fishing rod either. You could eat blueberries, or cattail stems, or crayfish, or other delicacies dimly remembered from stories about people who got lost in the woods and were found later in good health although somewhat thinner. You could cook some reindeer moss, if you had matches.

Thus you pass on to fantasies about how to start a fire with a magnifying glass—you don't have one—or by rubbing two bits of stick together, a feat at which you suspect you would prove remarkably inept.

The fact is that not very many of us know how to survive in the north. Rumour has it that only one German prisoner of war ever made it out, although many made it out of the actual prisoner-of-war camps. The best piece of northern survival advice is: *Don't get lost.*

One way of looking at a landscape is to consider the typical ways of dying in it. Given the worst, what's the worst it could do? Will it be delirium from drinking salty water on the high seas, shrivelling in the desert, snakebite in the jungle, tidal waves on a Pacific isle, volcanic fumes? In the north, there are several hazards. Although you're probably a lot safer there than you are on the highway at rush hour, given the odds, you still have to be a little wary.

Like most lessons of this sort, those about the north are taught by precept and example, but also, more enjoyably, by cautionary nasty tale. There is death by blackfly, the one about the fellow who didn't have his shirt cuffs tight enough in the spring and undressed at night only to find he was running with blood, the ones about the lost travellers who bloated up from too many bites and who, when found, were twice the size, unrecognizable, and dead. There is death from starvation, death by animal, death by forest fire; there is death from something called "exposure," which used to confuse me when I heard about men who exposed themselves: why would they intentionally do anything that fatal? There's death by thunderstorm, not to be sneered at: on the open lake, in one of the excessive northern midsummer thunderstorms, a canoe or a bush plane is a vulnerable target. The north is full of Struwwelpeter-like stories about people who didn't do as they were told and got struck by lightning. Above all, there are death by freezing and death by drowning. Your body's heat-loss rate in the water is twenty times that in air, and northern lakes are cold. Even in a life jacket, even holding on to the tipped canoe, you're at risk. Every summer the numbers pile up.

Every culture has its exemplary dead people, its hagiography of landscape martyrs, those unfortunates who, by their bad ends, seem to sum up in one grisly episode what may be lurking behind the next rock for all of us, all of us who enter the territory they once claimed as theirs. I'd say that two of the top northern landscape martyrs are Tom Thomson, the painter who was found mysteriously drowned near his overturned canoe with no provable cause in sight, and the Mad Trapper of Rat River, also mysterious, who became so thoroughly bushed that he killed a Mountie and shot two others during an amazing wintertime chase before being finally mowed down. In our retelling of these stories, mystery is a key element. So, strangely enough, is a presumed oneness with the landscape in question. The Mad Trapper knew his landscape so well he survived in it for weeks, living off the land and his own bootlaces, eluding capture. One of the hidden motifs in these stories is a warning: maybe it's not so good to get *too* close to Nature.

I remember a documentary on Tom Thomson that ended, rather ominously, with the statement that the north had taken him to herself. This was, of course, pathetic fallacy gone to seed, but it was also a comment on our distrust of the natural world, a distrust that remains despite our protests, our studies in the ethics of ecology, our elevation of "the environment" to a numinous noun, our save-the-tree campaigns. The question is, would the trees save us, given the chance? Would the water, would the birds, would the rocks? In the north, we have our doubts.

A bunch of us are sitting around the table, at what is now a summer cottage in Georgian Bay. Once it was a house, built by a local man for his family, which finally totalled eleven children, after they'd outgrown this particular house and moved on to another. The original Findlay wood-burning cook stove is still in the house, but so also are some electric lights and a propane cooker, which have come since the end of the old days. In the old days, this man somehow managed to scrape a living from the land: a little of this, a little of that, some fishing here, some lumbering there, some hunting in the fall. That was back when you shot to eat. "Scrape" is an appropriate word: there's not much here between the topsoil and the rock.

We sit around the table and eat, fish among other things, caught by the children. Someone mentions the clams: there are still a lot of them, but who knows what's in them any more? Mercury, lead, things like that. We pick at the fish. Someone tells me not to drink the tap water. I already have. "What will happen?" I ask. "Probably nothing," they reply. "Probably nothing" is a relatively recent phrase around here. In the old days, you ate what looked edible.

We are talking about the old days, as people often do once they're outside the cities. When exactly did the old days end? Because we know they did. The old days ended when the youngest of us was ten, fifteen, or twenty; the old days ended when the oldest of us was five, or twelve, or thirty. Plastic-hulled super-boats are not old days, but ten-horsepower outboard motors, circa 1945, are. There's an icebox in the back porch, unused now, a simple utilitarian model from Eaton's, ice chamber in the top section, metal shelves in the bottom one. We all go and admire it. "I remember iceboxes," I say, and indeed I can dimly remember them, I must have been five. What bits of our daily junk—our toasters, our pocket computers—will soon become obsolete and therefore poignant? Who will stand around, peering at them and admiring their design and the work that went into them, as we do with this icebox? "So this was a *toilet seat*," we think, rehearsing the future. "Ah! A *light bulb*," the ancient syllables thick in our mouths.

The kids have decided some time ago that all this chat is boring, and have asked if they can go swimming off the dock. They can, though they have to watch it, as this is a narrow place and speedboats tend to swoosh through, not always slowing down. Waste of gas, in the old days. Nobody then went anywhere just for pleasure, it was the war and gas was rationed.

"Oh, *that* old days," says someone.

There goes a speedboat now, towing a man strapped in a kneeling position to some kind of board, looking as if he's had a terrible accident, or is about to have one. This must be some newfangled variety of water-skiing.

"Remember Klim?" I say. The children come through, trailing towels. "What's Klim?" one asks, caught by the space-age sound of the word.

"Klim was 'milk' spelled backwards," I say. "It was powdered milk."

"Yuk," they say.

"Not the same as now," I say. "It was whole milk, not skim; it wasn't instant. You had to beat it with an eggbeater." And even then some of it wouldn't dissolve. One of the treats of childhood was the little nodules of pure dry Klim that floated on top of your milk.

"There was also Pream," says someone. How revolutionary it seemed.

The children go down to take their chances in the risky motorized water. Maybe, much later, they will remember us sitting around the table, eating fish they themselves had caught, back when you could still (what? Catch a fish? See a tree? What desolations lie in store, beyond the plasticized hulls and the knee-skiers?). By then we will be the old days, for them. Almost we are already.

A different part of the north. We're sitting around the table, by lamplight—it's still the old days here, no electricity—talking about bad hunters. Bad hunters, bad fishers, everyone has a story. You come upon a campsite, way in the back of beyond, no roads into the lake, they must have come in by float plane, and there it is, garbage all over the place, beer cans, blobs of human poop flagged by melting toilet paper, and twenty-two fine pickerel left rotting on a rock. Business executives who get themselves flown in during hunting season with their high-powered rifles, shoot a buck, cut off the head, fill their quota, see another one with a bigger spread of antlers, drop the first head, cut off the second. The woods are littered with discarded heads, and who cares about the bodies?

New way to shoot polar bear: you have the natives on the ground finding them for you, then they radio the location in to the base camp, the base camp phones New York, fellow gets on the plane, gets himself flown in, they've got the rifle and the clothing all ready for him, fly him to the bear, he pulls the trigger from the plane, doesn't even get out of the g.d. *plane,* they fly him back, cut off the head, skin it, send the lot down to New York.

These are the horror stories of the north, one brand. They've replaced the ones in which you got pounced upon by a wolverine or had your arm chewed off by a she-bear with cubs or got chased into the lake by a moose in rut, or even the ones in which your dog got porcupine quills or rolled in poison ivy and gave it to you. In the new stories, the enemies and the victims of old have done a switch. Nature is no longer implacable, dangerous, ready to jump you; it is on the run, pursued by a number of unfair bullies with the latest technology.

One of the key nouns in these stories is "float plane." These outrages, this banditry, would not be possible without them, for the bad hunters are notoriously weak-muscled and are deemed incapable of portaging a canoe, much less paddling one. Among their other badnesses, they are sissies. Another key motif is money. What money buys these days, among other things, is the privilege of no-risk slaughter.

As for us, the ones telling the stories, tsk-tsking by lamplight, we are the good hunters, or so we think. We've given up saying we only kill to eat; Kraft dinner and freeze-dried food have put paid to that one. Really there's no excuse for us. However, we do have some virtues left. We can still cast a fly. We don't cut off heads and hang them stuffed on the wall. We would never buy an ocelot coat. We paddle our own canoes.

* * *

We're sitting on the dock at night, shivering despite our sweaters, in mid-August, watching the sky. There are a few shooting stars, as there always are at this time in August, as the earth passes through the Perseids. We pride ourselves on knowing a few things like that, about the sky; we find the Dipper, the North Star, Cassiopeia's Chair, and talk about consulting a star chart, which we know we won't actually do. But this is the only place you can really *see* the stars, we tell each other. Cities are hopeless.

Suddenly, an odd light appears, going very fast. It spirals around like a newly dead firecracker, and then bursts, leaving a cloud of luminous dust, caught perhaps in the light from the sun, still up there somewhere. What could this be? Several days later, we hear that it was part of an extinct Soviet satellite, or that's what they say. That's what they would say, wouldn't they? It strikes us that we don't really know very much about the night sky at all any more. There's all kinds of junk up there: spy planes, old satellites, tin cans, man-made matter gone out of control. It also strikes us that we are totally dependent for knowledge of these things on a few people who don't tell us very much.

Once, we thought that if the balloon ever went up we'd head for the bush and hide out up there, living—we naively supposed—off the land. Now we know that if the two superpowers begin hurling things at each other through the sky, they're likely to do it across the Arctic, with big bangs and fallout all over the north. The wind blows everywhere. Survival gear and knowing which moss you can eat is not going to be a large help. The north is no longer a refuge.

Driving back towards Toronto from the Near North, a small reprise runs through my head:

> Land of the septic tank,
> Home of the speedboat,
> Where still the four-wheel-drive
> Wanders at will,
> Blue lake and tacky shore,
> I will return once more:
> Vroom-diddy-vroom-vroom
> Vroom-diddy-vroom-vroom
> Vroo-OO-oo-oom.

Somehow, just as the drive north inspires saga and tragedy, the drive south inspires parody. And here it comes: the gift shops shaped like teepees, the maple-syrup emporiums that get themselves up like olde-tyme sugaring-off huts; and, farther south, the restaurants that pretend to offer wholesome farm fare, the stores that pretend to be general stores, selling quilts, soap shaped like hearts, high-priced fancy conserves done up in frilly cloth caps, the way Grandma (whoever she might be) was fondly supposed to have made them.

And then come the housing developments, acres of prime farmland turning overnight into Quality All-Brick Family Homes; and then come the Industrial Parks; and there, in full anti-bloom, is the city itself, looming like a mirage or a chemical warfare zone on the horizon. A browny-grey scuzz hovers above it, and we think, as we always do when facing re-entry, we're going into *that*? We're going to breathe *that*?

But we go forward, as we always do, into what is now to us the unknown. And once inside, we breathe the air, not much bad happens to us, we hardly notice. It's as if we've never been anywhere else. But that's what we think, too, when we're in the north.

Letters
from America

RUPERT BROOKE

*Before the outbreak of World War I, young
English poet Rupert Brooke traveled extensively
in North America. His descriptions of train
travel to the western grain capital of Winnipeg
in Manitoba and through the Canadian
Rockies reflect the sensitivity and poetic nature
of the writer. Brooke died of blood poisoning
while serving in the Dardanelles in 1915 and
was buried on the island of Skyros. He is best
remembered for his lines:*

*If I should die, think only this of me:
That there's some corner of a foreign field
That is forever England.*

To Winnipeg

*T*HE boats that run from Sarnia the whole length of Lake Huron and Lake
Superior are not comfortable. But no doubt a train for those six hundred miles
would be worse. You start one afternoon, and in the morning of the next day
you have done with the rather colourless, unindividual expanses of Huron, and
are dawdling along a canal that joins the lakes by the little town of Sault Ste.
Marie (pronounced, abruptly, "Soo"). We happened on it one Sunday. The
nearer waters of the river and the lakes were covered with little sailing or rowing
or bathing parties. Everybody seemed cheerful, merry, and mildly raucous.
There is a fine, breezy, enviable healthiness about Canadian life. Except in some
Eastern cities, there are few clerks or working-men but can get away to the
woods and water.

As we drew out into the cold magnificence of Lake Superior, the receding
woody shores were occasionally spotted with picnickers or campers, who
rushed down the beach in various deshabille, waving towels, handkerchiefs, or
garments. We were as friendly. The human race seemed a jolly bunch, and the
world a fine, pleasant, open-air affair—"some world," in fact. A man in a red
shirt and a bronzed girl with flowing hair slid past in a canoe. We whistled, sang,

and cried "Snooky-ookums!" and other words of occult meaning, which imputed love to them, and foolishness. They replied suitably, grinned, and were gone. A little old lady in black, in the chair next mine, kept a small telescope glued to her eye, hour after hour. Whenever she distinguished life on any shore we passed, she waved a tiny handkerchief. Diligently she did this, and with grave face, never visible to the objects of her devotion, I suppose, but certainly very happy; the most persistent lover of humanity I have ever seen. . . .

In the afternoon we were beyond sight of land. The world grew a little chilly; and over the opaque, hueless water came sliding a queer, pale mist. We strained through it for hours, a low bank of cloud, not twenty feet in height, on which one could look down from the higher deck. Its upper surface was quite flat and smooth, save for innumerable tiny molehills or pyramids of mist. We seemed to be ploughing aimlessly through the phantasmal sand-dunes of another world, faintly and by an accident apprehended. So may the shades on a ghostly liner, plunging down Lethe, have an hour's chance glimpse of the lights and lives of Piccadilly, to them uncertain and filmy mirages of the air.

To taste the full deliciousness of travelling in an American train by night through new scenery, you must carefully secure a lower berth. And when you are secret and separate in your little oblong world, safe between sheets, pull up the blinds on the great window a few inches and leave them so. Thus, as you lie, you can view the dark procession of woods and hills, and mingle the broken hours of railway slumber with glimpses of a wild starlit landscape. The country retains individuality, and yet puts on romance, especially the rough, shaggy region between Port Arthur and Winnipeg. For four hundred miles there is hardly a sign that humanity exists on the earth's face, only rocks and endless woods of scrubby pine, and the occasional strange gleam of water, and night and the wind. Night-long, dream and reality mingle. You may wake from sleep to find yourself flying through a region where a forest fire has passed, a place of grey pine-trunks, stripped of foliage, occasionally waving a naked bough. They appear stricken by calamity, intolerably bare and lonely, gaunt, perpetually protesting, amazed and tragic creatures. We saw no actual fire the night I passed. But a little while after dawn we noticed on the horizon, fifteen miles away, an immense column of smoke. There was little wind, and it hung, as if sculptured, against the grey of the morning; nor did we lose sight of it till just before we boomed over a wide, swift, muddy river, into the flat city of Winnipeg.

Winnipeg is the West. It is important and obvious that in Canada there are two or three (some say five) distinct Canadas. Even if you lump the French and English together as one community in the East, there remains the gulf of the Great Lakes. The difference between East and West is possibly no greater than that between North and South England, or Bavaria and Prussia; but in this country, yet unconscious of itself, there is so much less to hold them together.

The character of the land and the people differs; their interests, as it appears to them, are not the same. Winnipeg is a new city. In the archives at Ottawa is a picture of Winnipeg in 1870—Mainstreet, with a few shacks, and the prairie either end. Now her population is a hundred thousand, and she has the biggest this, that, and the other west of Toronto. A new city; a little more American than the other Canadian cities, but not unpleasantly so. The streets are wider, and full of a bustle which keeps clear of hustle. The people have something of the free swing of Americans, without the bumptiousness; a tempered democracy, a mitigated independence of bearing. The manners of Winnipeg, of the West, impress the stranger as better than those of the East, more friendly, more hearty, more certain to achieve graciousness, if not grace. There is, even, in the architecture of Winnipeg, a sort of *gauche* pride visible. It is hideous, of course, even more hideous than Toronto or Montreal; but cheerily and windily so. There is no scheme in the city, and no beauty, but it is at least preferable to Birmingham, less dingy, less directly depressing. It has no real slums, even though there is poverty and destitution.

But there seems to be a trifle more public spirit in the West than the East. Perhaps it is that in the greater eagerness and confidence of this newer country men have a superfluity of energy and interest, even after attending to their own affairs, to give to the community. Perhaps it is that the West is so young that one has a suspicion money-making has still some element of a child's game in it—its only excuse. At any rate, whether because the state of affairs is yet unsettled, or because of the invisible subtle spirit of optimism that blows through the heavily clustering telephone-wires and past the neat little modern villas and down the solidly pretentious streets, one can't help finding a tiny hope that Winnipeg, the city of buildings and the city of human beings, may yet come to something. It is a slender hope, not to be compared to that of the true Winnipeg man, who, gazing on his city, is fired with the proud and secret ambition that it will soon be twice as big, and after that four times, and then ten times . . .

> *"Wider still and wider*
> *Shall thy bounds be set,"*

says that hymn which is the noblest expression of modern ambition. *That* hope is sure to be fulfilled. But the other timid prayer, that something different, something more worth having, may come out of Winnipeg, exists, and not quite unreasonably. That cannot be said of Toronto.

Winnipeg is of the West, new, vigorous in its way, of unknown potentialities. Already the West has been a nuisance to the East, in the fight of 1911 over Reciprocity with the United States. When she gets a larger representation in Parliament, she will be still more of a nuisance. A casual traveller cannot venture to investigate the beliefs and opinions of the inhabitants of a country, but he can record them all the better, perhaps, for his foreign-ness. It is generally believed in the West that the East runs Canada, and runs it for its own advantage. And the East means a very few rich men, who control the big railways, the banks, and the Manufacturers' Association, subscribe to both political parties, and are generally credited with complete control over the Tariff and most other Canadian affairs. Whether or not the Manufacturers' Association does arrange the Tariff and control the commerce of Canada, it is generally believed to do so. The only thing is that its friends say that it acts in the best interests of Canada, its enemies that it acts in the best interests of the Manufacturers' Association. Among its enemies are many in the West. The normal Western life is a lonely and individual one; and a large part of the population has crossed from the United States, or belongs to that great mass of European immigration that Canada is letting so blindly in. So, naturally, the Westerner does not feel the same affection for the Empire or for England as the British Canadians of the East, whose forefathers fought to stay within the Empire. Nor is his affection increased by the suspicion that the Imperial cry has been used for party purposes. He has no use for politics at Ottawa. The naval question is nothing to him. He wants neither to subscribe money nor to build ships. Europe is very far away; and he is too ignorant to realise his close connection with her. He has strong views, however, on a Tariff which only affects him by perpetually raising the cost of living and farming. The ideas of even a Conservative in the West about reducing the Tariff would make an Eastern "Liberal" die of heart-failure. And the Westerner also hates the Banks. The banking system of Canada is peculiar, and throws the control of the banks into the hands of a few people in the East, who were felt, by the ever optimistic West, to have shut down credit too completely during the recent money stringency.

The most interesting expression of the new Western point of view, and in many ways the most hopeful movement in Canada, is the Co-operative movement among the grain-growers of the three prairie provinces. Only started a few years ago, it has grown rapidly in numbers, wealth, power, and extent of operations. So far it has confined itself politically to influencing provincial legislatures. But it has gradually attached itself to an advanced Radical programme of a Chartist description. And it is becoming powerful. Whether the outcome will be a very desirable rejuvenation of the Liberal Party, or the creation of a third—perhaps Radical-Labour—party, it is hard to tell. At any rate, the change will come. And, just to start with, there will very shortly come to the Eastern Powers, who threw out Reciprocity with the States for the sake of the Empire, a demand from the West that the preference to British goods be increased rapidly till they be allowed to come in free, also for the Empire's sake. Then the fun will begin.

Through the Rockies

At Calgary, if you can spare a minute from more important matters, slip beyond the hurrying white city, climb the golf links, and gaze west. A low bank of dark clouds disturbs you by the fixity of its outline. It is the Rockies, seventy miles away. On a good day, it is said, they are visible twice as far, so clear and serene is this air. Five hundred miles west is the coast of British Columbia, a region with a different climate, different country, and different problems. It is cut off from the prairies by vast tracts of wild country and uninhabitable ranges. For nearly two hundred miles the train pants through the homeless grandeur of the Rockies and the Selkirks. Four or five hotels, a few huts or tents, and a rare mining-camp— that is all the habitation in many thousands of square miles. Little even of that is visible from the train. That is one of the chief differences between the effect of the Rockies and that of the Alps. There, you are always in sight of a civilisation which has nestled for ages at the feet of those high places. They stand, enrobed with worship, and grander by contrast with the lives of men. These unmemoried heights are inhuman—or rather, irrelevant to humanity. No recorded Hannibal has struggled across them; their shadow lies on no remembered literature. They acknowledge claims neither of the soul nor of the body of man. He is a stranger, neither Nature's enemy nor her child. She is there alone, scarcely a unity in the heaped confusion of these crags, almost without grandeur among the chaos of earth.

Yet this horrid and solitary wildness is but one aspect. There is beauty here, at length, for the first time in Canada, the real beauty that is always too sudden for mortal eyes, and brings pain with its comfort. The Rockies have a remoter, yet a kindlier, beauty than the Alps. Their rock is of a browner colour, and such rugged peaks and crowns as do not attain snow continually suggest gigantic castellations, or the ramparts of Titans. Eastward, the foothills are few and low, and the mountains stand superbly. The heart lifts to see them. They guard the sunset. Into this rocky wilderness you plunge, and toil through it hour by hour, viewing it from the rear of the Observation-Car. The Observation-Car is a great invention of the new world. At the end of the train is a compartment with large windows, and a little platform behind it, roofed over, but exposed otherwise to the air. On this platform are sixteen little perches, for which you fight with Americans. Victorious, you crouch on one, and watch the ever-receding pan-orama behind the train. It is an admirable way of viewing scenery. But a day of being perpetually drawn backwards at a great pace through some of the grandest mountains in the world has a queer effect. Like life, it leaves you with a dizzy irritation. For, as in life, you never see the glories till they are past, and then they vanish with incredible rapidity. And if you crane to see the dwindling further peaks, you miss the new splendours.

The day I went through most of the Rockies was, by some standards, a bad one for the view. Rain scudded by in forlorn, grey showers, and the upper parts of the mountains were wrapped in cloud, which was but rarely blown aside to reveal the heights. Sublimity, therefore, was left to the imagination; but desolation was most vividly present. In no weather could the impression of loneliness be stronger. The pines drooped and sobbed. Cascades, born somewhere in the dun firmament above, dropped down the mountain sides in ever-growing white threads. The rivers roared and plunged with aimless passion down the ravines. Stray little clouds, left behind when the wrack lifted a little, ran bleating up and down the forlorn hill-sides. More often, the clouds trailed along the valleys, a long procession of shrouded, melancholy figures, seeming to pause, as with an indeterminate, tragic, vain gesture, before passing out of sight up some ravine.

Yet desolation is not the final impression that will remain of the Rockies and the Selkirks. I was advised by various people to "stop off" at Banff and at Lake Louise, in the Rockies. I did so. They are supposed to be equally the beauty-spots of the mountains. How perplexing it is that advisers are always so kindly and willing to help, and always so undiscriminating. It is equally disastrous to be a sceptic and to be credulous. Banff is an ordinary little tourist-resort in mountainous country, with hills and a stream and snow-peaks beyond. Beautiful enough, and invigorating. But Lake Louise—Lake Louise is of another world. Imagine a little round lake 6,000 feet up, a mile across, closed in by great cliffs of brown rock, round the shoulders of which are thrown mantles of close dark pine. At one end the lake is fed by a vast glacier, and its milky tumbling stream; and the glacier climbs to snowfields of one of the highest and loveliest peaks in the Rockies, which keeps perpetual guard over the scene. To this place you go up three or four miles from the railway. There is the hotel at one end of the lake, facing the glacier; else no sign of humanity. From the windows you may watch the water and the peaks all day, and never see the same view twice. In the lake, ever-changing, is Beauty herself, as nearly visible to mortal eyes as she may ever be. The water, beyond the flowers, is green, always a different green. Sometimes it is tranquil, glassy, shot with blue, of a peacock tint. Then a little wind awakes in the distance, and ruffles the surface, yard by yard, covering it with a myriad tiny wrinkles, till half the lake is milky emerald, while the rest still sleeps. And, at length, the whole is astir, and the sun catches it, and Lake Louise is a web of laughter, the opal distillation of all the buds of all the spring. On either side go up the dark processional pines, mounting to the sacred peaks, devout, kneeling, motionless, in an ecstasy of homely adoration, like the donors and their families in a Flemish picture. Among these you may wander for hours by little rambling paths, over white and red and golden flowers, and, continually, you spy little lakes, hidden away, each a shy, soft jewel of a new strange tint of green or blue, mutable and lovely. . . . And beyond all is the glacier and the vast fields and peaks of eternal snow.

If you watch the great white cliff, from the foot of which the glacier flows—seven miles away, but it seems two—you will sometimes see a little puff of silvery smoke go up, thin, and vanish. A few seconds later comes the roar of terrific, distant thunder. The mountains tower and smile unregarding in the sun. It was an avalanche. And if you climb any of the ridges or peaks around, there are discovered other valleys and heights and ranges, wild and desert, stretching endlessly away. As day draws to an end the shadows on the snow turn bluer, the crying of innumerable waters hushes, and the immense, bare ramparts of west-ward-facing rock that guard the great valley win a rich, golden-brown radiance. Long after the sun has set they seem to give forth the splendour of the day, and the tranquillity of their centuries, in undiminished fulness. They have that other-worldly serenity which a perfect old age possesses. And as with a perfect old age, so here, the colour and the light ebb so gradually out of things that you could swear nothing of the radiance and glory gone up to the very moment before the dark.

It was on such a height, and at some such hour as this, that I sat and considered the nature of the country in this continent. There was perceptible, even here, though less urgent than elsewhere, the strangeness I had noticed in woods by the St. Lawrence, and on the banks of the Delaware (where are red-haired girls who sing at dawn), and in British Columbia, and afterwards among the brown hills and colossal trees of California, but especially by that lonely golden beach in Manitoba, where the high-stepping little brown deer run down to drink, and the wild geese through the evening go flying and crying. It is an empty land. To love the country here—mountains are worshipped, not loved—is like embracing a wraith. A European can find nothing to satisfy the hunger of his heart. The air is too thin to breathe. He requires haunted woods, and the friendly presence of ghosts The immaterial soil of England is heavy and fertile with the decaying stuff of past seasons and generations. Here is the floor of a new wood, yet uncumbered by one year's autumn fall. We Europeans find the Orient stale and too luxuriantly fetid by reason of the multitude of bygone lives and thoughts, oppressive with the crowded presence of the dead, both men and gods. So, I imagine, a Canadian would feel our woods and fields heavy with the past and the invisible, and suffer claustrophobia in an English countryside beneath the dreadful pressure of immortals. For his own forests and wild places are windswept and empty. That is their charm, and their terror. You may lie awake all night and never feel the passing of evil presences, nor hear printless feet; neither do you lapse into slumber with the comfortable consciousness of those friendly watchers who sit invisibly by a lonely sleeper under an English sky. Even an Irishman would not see a row of little men with green caps lepping along beneath the fire-weed and the golden daisies; nor have the subtler fairies of England found these wilds. It has never paid a steamship or railway company to arrange for their emigration.

In the bush of certain islands of the South Seas you may hear a crashing on windless noons, and, looking up, see a corpse swinging along head downwards at a great speed from tree to tree, holding by its toes, grimacing, dripping with decay. Americans, so active in this life, rest quiet afterwards. And though every stone of Wall Street have its separate Lar, their kind have not gone out beyond city-lots. The maple and the birch conceal no dryads, and Pan has never been heard amongst these reed-beds. Look as long as you like upon a cataract of the New World, you shall not see a white arm in the foam. A godless place. And the dead do not return. That is why there is nothing lurking in the heart of the shadows, and no human mystery in the colours, and neither the same joy nor the kind of peace in dawn and sunset that older lands know. It is, indeed, a new world. How far away seem those grassy, moonlit places in England that have been Roman camps or roads, where there is always serenity, and the spirit of a purpose at rest, and the sunlight flashes upon more than flint! Here one is perpetually a first-comer. The land is virginal, the wind cleaner than elsewhere, and every lake new-born, and each day is the first day. The flowers are less conscious than English flowers, the breezes have nothing to remember, and everything to promise. There walk, as yet, no ghosts of lovers in Canadian lanes. This is the essence of the grey freshness and brisk melancholy of this land. And for all the charm of those qualities, it is also the secret of a European's discontent. For it is possible, at a pinch, to do without gods. But one misses the dead.

Journey to the Arctic Ocean

SAMUEL HEARNE

*Employed by the Hudson's Bay Company to
search for "Copper Mines and a North West
Passage," Samuel Hearne, in 1770–71,
became the first European to explore the North
American arctic. Hearne journeyed on foot
accompanied by a capable Indian guide,
Matonabbee, reaching the mouth of the
Coppermine River. The expedition ended the
myth of an ocean channel through the
continent and the discovered copper mine
proved a failure. At the Indian settlement of
Clowey, below the Arctic Circle, Hearne
observed the art of canoemaking and learned
about the polygamous society of Matonabbee's
tribe. His account was first published in 1795.*

May 1771

O N our arrival at Clowey on the third of May, we found that the Captain's
brother, and those who were sent a-head with him from Theley-aza River, had
only got there two days before us; and, on account of the weather, had not made
the least progress in building the canoe, the plan of which they had taken with
them. The same day we got to Clowey several other Indians joined us from
different quarters, with intent to build their canoes at the same place. Some of
those Indians had resided within four or five miles, to the South East of Clowey
all the Winter; and had procured a plentiful livelihood by snaring deer, in the
manner which has been already described.

Immediately after our arrival at Clowey, the Indians began to build their
canoes, and embraced every convenient opportunity for that purpose: but as
warm and dry weather only is fit for this business, which was by no means the
case at present, it was the eighteenth of May before the canoes belonging to my
party could be completed. On the nineteenth we agreed to proceed on our
journey; but Matonabbee's canoe meeting with some damage, which took near
a whole day to repair, we were detained till the twentieth.

Those vessels, though made of the same materials with the canoes of the Southern Indians, differ from them both in shape and construction; they are also much smaller and lighter; and though very slight and simple in their construction, are nevertheless the best that could possibly be contrived for the use of those poor people, who are frequently obliged to carry them a hundred, and sometimes a hundred and fifty miles at a time, without having occasion to put them into the water. Indeed, the chief use of these canoes is to ferry over unfordable rivers; though sometimes, and at a few places, it must be acknowledged, that they are of great service in killing deer, as they enable the Indians to cross rivers and the narrow parts of lakes; they are also useful in killing swans, geese, ducks, &c. in the moulting season.

All the tools used by an Indian in building his canoe, as well as in making his snow-shoes, and every other kind of wood-work, consist of a hatchet, a knife, a file, and an awl; in the use of which they are so dextrous, that every thing they make is executed with a neatness not to be excelled by the most expert mechanic, assisted with every tool he could wish.

In shape the Northern Indian canoe bears some resemblance to a weaver's shuttle; being flat-bottomed, with straight upright sides, and sharp at each end; but the stern is by far the widest part, as there the baggage is generally laid, and occasionally a second person, who always lies down at full length in the bottom of the canoe. In this manner they carry one another across rivers and the narrow parts of lakes in those little vessels, which seldom exceed twelve or thirteen feet in length, and are from twenty inches to two feet broad in the widest part. The head, or fore part, is unnecessarily long, and narrow; and is all covered over with birch-bark, which adds considerably to the weight, without contributing to the burthen of the vessel. In general, these Indians make use of the single paddle, though a few have double ones, like the Esquimaux: the latter, however, are seldom used, but by those who lie in wait to kill deer as they cross rivers and narrow lakes.

During our stay at Clowey we were joined by upward of two hundred Indians from different quarters, most of whom built canoes at this place; but as I was under the protection of a principal man, no one offered to molest me, nor can I say they were very clamorous for any thing I had. This was undoubtedly owing to Matonabbee's informing them of my true situation; which was, that I had not, by any means, sufficient necessaries for myself, much less to give away. The few goods which I had with me were intended to be reserved for the Copper and Dogribbed Indians, who never visit the Company's Factories. Tobacco was, however, always given away; for every one of any note, who joined us, expected to be treated with a few pipes, and on some occasions it was scarcely possible to get off without presenting a few inches to them; which, with the constant supplies which I was obliged to furnish my own crew, decreased that article of my stock so fast, that notwithstanding I had yet advanced so small a part of my journey, more than one half of my store was expended. Gun-powder and shot also were articles commonly asked for by most of the Indians we met; and in general these were dealt round to them with a liberal hand by my guide Matonabbee. I must, however, do him the justice to acknowledge, that what he distributed was all his own, which he had purchased at the Factory; to my certain knowledge he bartered one hundred and fifty martins' skins for powder only; besides a great number of beaver, and other furrs, for shot, ball, iron-work, and tobacco, purposely to give away among his countrymen; as he had certainly as many of these articles given to him as were, in his opinion, sufficient for our support during our journey out and home.

Matonabbee's canoe having been repaired, on the twentieth we left Clowey, and proceeded Northward. That morning a small gang of strangers joined us, who informed my guide, that Captain Keelshies was within a day's walk to the Southward. Keelshies was the man by whom I had sent a letter to Prince of Wales's Fort, from Cathawhachaga, in the beginning of July one thousand seven hundred and seventy; but not long after that, having the misfortune to break my quadrant, I was obliged to return to the Fort a second time; and though we saw many smokes, and spoke with several Indians on my return that year, yet he and I missed each other on the barren ground, and I had not seen or heard of him since that time.

As Matonabbee was desirous that I should receive my letters, and also the goods I had written for, he dispatched two of his young men to bring them. We continued our journey to the Northward; and the next day saw several large smokes at a great distance to the Eastward on the barren ground, which were supposed to be made by some parties of Indians bound to Prince of Wales's Fort with furrs and other commodities for trade.

On the twenty-second and twenty-third, we proceeded to the North, at the rate of fourteen or fifteen miles a-day; and in the evening of the latter, got clear of all the woods, and lay on the barren ground. The same evening the two young men who were sent for my letters, &c. returned, and told me that Keelshies had promised to join us in a few days, and deliver the things to me with his own hand.

The twenty-fourth proved bad and rainy weather, so that we only walked about seven miles, when finding a few blasted stumps of trees, we pitched our tents. It was well we did so, for toward night we had excessively bad weather, with loud thunder, strong lightning, and heavy rain, attended with a very hard gale of wind from the South West; toward the next morning, however, the wind veered round to the North West, and the weather became intensely cold and frosty. We walked that day about eight miles to the Northward, when we were obliged to put up, being almost benumbed with cold. There we found a few dry stumps, as we had done the day before, which served us for fewel.

The weather on the twenty-sixth was so bad, with snow and thick drifting sleet, that we did not move; but the next morning proving fine and pleasant, we dried our things, and walked about twelve miles to the Northward; most of the way on the ice of a small river which runs into Peshew Lake. We then saw a smoke to the Southward, which we judged to be made by Keelshies, so we put up for the night by the side of the above-mentioned Lake, where I expected we should have waited for his arrival; but, to my great surprize, on the morrow we again set forward, and walked twenty-two miles to the Northward on Peshew Lake, and in the afternoon pitched our tents on an island, where, by my desire, the Indians made a large smoke, and proposed to stay a day or two for Captain Keelshies.

In the night, one of Matonabbee's wives and another woman eloped: it was supposed they went off to the Eastward, in order to meet their former husbands, from whom they had been sometime before taken by force. This affair made more noise and bustle than I could have supposed; and Matonabbee seemed entirely disconcerted, and quite inconsolable for the loss of his wife. She was certainly by far the handsomest of all his flock, of a moderate size, and had a fair complexion; she apparently possessed a mild temper, and very engaging manners. In fact, she seemed to have every good quality that could be expected in a Northern Indian woman, and that could render her an agreeable companion to an inhabitant of this part of the world. She had not, however, appeared happy in her late situation; and chose rather to be the sole wife of a sprightly young fellow of no note, (though very capable of maintaining her), than to have the seventh or eighth share of the affection of the greatest man in the country. I am sorry to mention an incident which happened while we were building the canoes at Clowey, and which by no means does honour to Matonabbee: it is no less a crime than that of having actually stabbed the husband of the above-mentioned girl in three places; and had it not been for timely assistance, would certainly have murdered him, for no other reason than because the poor man had spoken disrespectfully of him for having taken his wife away by force. The cool deliberation with which Matonabbee committed this bloody action, convinced me it had been a long premeditated design; for he no sooner heard of the man's arrival, than he opened one of his wives' bundles, and, with the greatest composure, took out a new long box-handled knife, went into the man's tent, and, without any preface whatever, took him by the collar, and began to execute his horrid design. The poor man anticipating his danger, fell on his face, and called for assistance; but before any could be had he received three wounds in the back. Fortunately for him, they all happened on the shoulder-blade, so that his life was spared. When Matonabbee returned to his tent, after committing this horrid deed, he sat down as composedly as if nothing had happened, called for water to wash his bloody hands and knife, smoked his pipe as usual, seemed to be perfectly at ease, and asked if I did not think he had done right?

FROM

Notes from the Century Before

EDWARD HOAGLAND

*The interior of British Columbia—along the
Stikine and Spatsizi river basins and the
mountainous Telegraph Trail—was still wild
and mostly silent when Ed Hoagland went to
live among ''the extraordinary old men'' who
had settled there many years ago. The
following are from his diary entries of 1966.*

July 12, Tuesday

*T*HE pleasure of fiddling with fire. A fire is air. Building a fire is based upon
having a feeling for air. A boy named Paul, a sixth-grader next year, has taken a
liking to me. He whistles like a whippoorwill as a signal of greeting and runs
wherever he goes, bursting into a sprint. As a grandson of Dogan Dennis, he is
Bear Lake Billy's great-grandson.

The horses were shod today and Mrs. Walker apportioned supplies for the
hunting caches. Her husband was patching spark holes in the tents and repairing
the generator which powers his radio. He's an extraordinary man, indeed a
visionary, who still stakes himself lovely plots of land wherever he goes. (If it
happens to be on their territory, his rival guides pull the stakes out when they
find them and send a protest to Victoria.) He's a shy, charitable, interested man
close up, more likable than at a distance with his hiring problems and his
jealousy of his competitors, whereas bold Mrs. Walker is more likable at a
distance than at close range. I'm afraid that I'm not doing justice to him. It's a
peculiarity of mine that unless I like somebody considerably, I'm liable to lavish
whatever fairness I have on people who are decidedly different from me, like
Frank Pete or Steele Hyland, whom I have nothing in common with. Besides, as
I mentioned, Walker skips away when he sees me coming, as if the map to a gold
mine were printed across the front of his shirt.

* * *

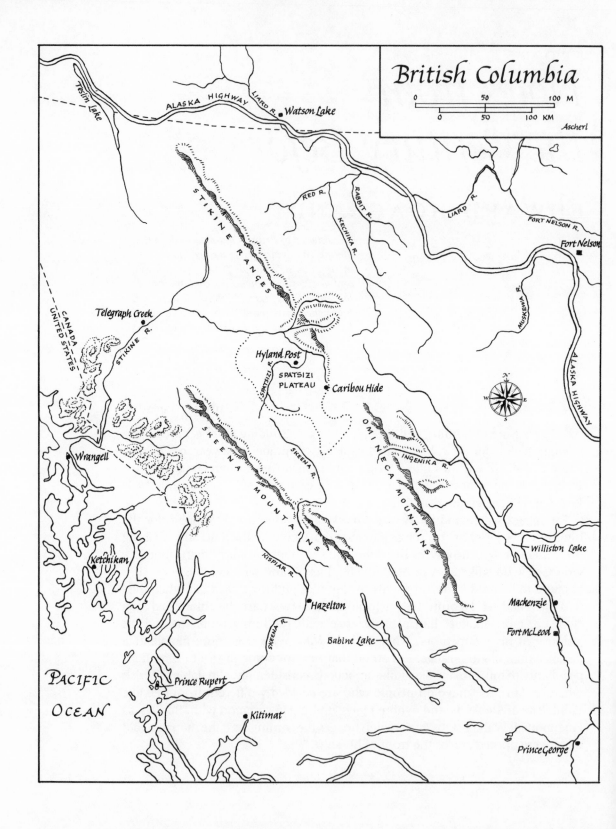

British Columbia

0   50   100 M

0   50   100 KM

Ascherl

Teslin Lake

ALASKA HIGHWAY

LIARD R.

Watson Lake

RED R.

RABBIT R.

KECHIKA R.

LIARD R.

FORT NELSON R.

Fort Nelson

STIKINE RANGES

MUSKEWA R.

ALASKA HIGHWAY

Telegraph Creek

CANADA
UNITED STATES

STIKINE R.

Hyland Post

SPATSIZI R.

SPATSIZI
PLATEAU

Caribou Hide

OMINECA MOUNTAINS

INGENIKA R.

SKEENA MOUNTAINS

SKEENA R.

Wrangell

Williston Lake

Ketchikan

KISPIAR R.

Mackenzie

Hazelton

Fort McLeod

SKEENA R.

Babine Lake

PACIFIC

OCEAN

Prince Rupert

Kitimat

Prince George

The cabins and tents are set in front of a grassy, flattened-off mountain where the caribou gather for love play in the fall, hundreds of them in sight at a time. Across the lake a series of rhythmic high ridges and draws leads into a complex massif called Nation Peak, where the clouds stir about. Everything is immediate and close, timberline being only five hundred feet up. Through the spotting scope we've been watching nine goats browse on a steep slope. Above them are several specks in the snow which are probably goats lying down where the flies will leave them alone. The basins where Walker and Alec Jack explored fifteen years ago lie behind. They'd climb and stumble upon thirty-eight, thirty-three, forty-one Stone sheep rams convocating together in a hammock-shaped cirque and get that quizzical innocents' stare which is only seen once.

I walked up the caribou mountain through an old burn, with the willows and aspen head-high and lupine and yarrow and fireweed growing. A few spruce were left alive on knolls and in hollows which the fire skipped by. From the lake, the line of mountains across the way looked like a row of elephants' backsides, but when I got higher they mounted and took more imposing forms, less rounded and climbing more, linking the valleys hanging between them with the valley under the principal peak. The valley of Cold Fish Lake itself is headless, emptying at one end into the Spatsizi and at the other end into another tributary of the Stikine. The winter trail from Caribou Hide, which the Indians ran with dog sleds, went along the bottom of it on the ice, while the summer trail was up on the high plateau I was climbing toward, where the walking wasn't obstructed by brush.

It was hot. The game was napping. I went down into the forest again, picking out numerous tracks of moose. A moose's two toes are straighter than a caribou's, like two half moons joined. A caribou's foot, in order to aid him in snow, bows out like two quarter moons. In a couple of other places I found bear tracks in the mud, smudged over, and also a short series of wolf tracks, which are bigger than a coyote's and longer in the foot than a cougar's or lynx's.

An enormous added dimension is given a country by its game—to watch for a file of caribou weaving on the skyline (six were seen this morning) and to tremble for grizzly. No combination of stunning scenery can make up for its loss. Of course we pacifists who go into the woods without guns owe our safety to those who don't. It wasn't long ago that an English Indian agent named Harper Reed and one companion encountered what he estimated as 150 wolves on Cold Fish Lake. The wolves, in one of the winter assemblies they hold, were engaged in herding moose, but they curled round in a sickle-shaped line to face him instead and began to press in, like Khartoum. He was terribly pleased.

I sunned for a while on a bluff. A perfect reflection of the opposite mountains was combed into the lake. The moss was so deep that my elbows and knees sank in a foot. Though most of the trees were white spruce, they looked like the gamut of evergreens because the raw soil withers them before they grow very large. The roots grope out of the ground; the needles change. I watched a blue grouse peck about. A caribou swam across the lake, buoyant and tireless all the way. She was a pretty bleached tan with two-pronged antlers in velvet, and she splashed in the shallows like a filly, muzzling the bugs off her rear. The animals all get elated, sleeping, waking irregularly when the days are as lush and long as this. They have more noddling about to do than they can find time for. It must be particularly joyful for a flustery creature like a caribou. Vulnerable animals that they are, they're soon to die. When I lived in Hazelton the last ones there were being killed. The previous winter some Tsimshians, out for a weekend, had discovered a remnant band of sixteen in deep snow and killed them all. Caribou give up the ghost very quickly, as if suddenly coming unstrung. Whether shot or speared, they spill out their blood lavishly, unlike goats and sheep, who bleed and die with great reluctance. When I lived on the Clearwater River, which is further south, they were already remembered as a sort of a vanished prize. Because of the tall flair of their carriage and their superb, airy antlers, they'd been the biggest game. Their herds had defined the wilderness, moving along, eating the drooping black lichen on the low limbs of the trees. As a matter of fact, one settler told me that he had chosen the valley for its caribou. He was hiking through looking for ground to homestead when he climbed a side ridge and caught sight of a band of twenty-two in the meadows on top. Like most such people, he was no youngster then, but watching them, he felt as though he had never been so happy or certain about a decision before. And now he was surrounded by strawberry fields and cream-giving cows. He lived in a cabin floored with halved logs that the whole valley held dances on, and he had a housekeeper caring for him, so the loss of the caribou was small next to that. Because of the logging, even the lichens were gone. He was smiling, not tolling a bell, but he was remembering the talk—how silly and giddy caribou are, how simple to kill, how they mill and fool and join the pack mules, how they won't run away if you raise your arm until they know why you are raising your arm. I've been hearing the same. It's like a bunch of buffalo hunters talking about their staple game, or the malicious gossip about the Indians at Eddontenajon. When it stops the herds will be gone and the Indian settlement will have become a museum piece.

A ring appeared around the sun, meaning rain. When the ring is around the moon, they say you can tell how many days the rain will hold off by counting the stars inside the ring.

About ten, as the sun set, the lake turned to mercury and the mountains acquired stately proportions. The Walkers were working at building their ump-teenth cabin, nailing purlins to the rafters. They intend it to be a "hideout," off by itself on a pretty cove, as opposed to the main camp on the lake and the overnight cabin at the opposite end or the camps that they keep at Hyland Post and Eddontenajon. Goodness knows how many more they built at Bella Coola before they even arrived in the north. And yet as they kibbitz each other they might be putting a wing on a house in Bryn Mawr. It's not the people who are so different here, it's the events, the mode of living, a most ancient mode going back to when the Greeks landed in Sicily or the Danes settled in Iceland. Each mode of living is a choice, and so we have one less choice now.

July 13, Wednesday

Scooted down the Spatsizi to Hyland Post today by plane, the lazy man's way. I flew with Danny Bereza again, the mail-run man who originally took me from Telegraph Creek to Eddontenajon. He's a chattery, prim, preoccupied guy, and he popped through a pass from nowhere, materializing magically over Cold Fish Lake. The noise was stifled in drizzle and fog. The plane seemed to pause in the air, the size of a dragonfly against the mountain, before plumping down. Bereza was stuffed up with a cold and the plane was crammed to the roof with canned goods, fertilizer, horseshoes, lick salt, blasting powder, though this was only one errand of many for him. He expected to work twelve hours by nightfall and to fly something like nine hundred miles. My first feeling when we shook hands was pity. The sky was so soupy that although maybe today he'd be lucky and find enough holes to complete his trips, it was hard to imagine him getting through the rest of the summer. Once we were up in the air, however, the view was different. For every cloud there was a hole, at least at our level, and some of the clouds were no worse than fogged glasses to look through. In such extravagant country a plane's speed seems slow. We jiggled along as if we were sitting in a simulating machine, hitching up, hitching down, when the wind abused us. These headwater valleys tip and slide in a primitive fashion. Down is where they're going, but not very efficiently. They aren't canyons; they're rudimentary scoops between heights of ground. You look across at the rock strata above timberline and at the terraced, sparse forest below, and the ponds, sloughs, myriad streams and river braidings straight below, and part of the world is very wet and part very dry. Being so close to the head of the Spatsizi, we could see upriver to the last curve. The river wound like a willowing, picture-book road climbing to a castle, and it seemed as though all the world's secrets were hoarded just there, just beyond, just out of sight in those mountainous rocks. The impulse was not as much to go right away and see and gloat as it was to delight in being so near. Thus it is that a man who has become a millionaire overnight first balances his checkbook in the morning with his old funds and pays his phone bill.

I had too many sights going by. The valley enlarged; the mountains flattened into broad buttes which were spaced at leisurely intervals. We passed over chains of minute natural meadows in the waterlogged, spraddled-out forest. I was watching, absorbed, when directly ahead a parrot-green oblong presented itself. It was a great surprise, a glorious swank little festival rip in the forest, as green as a banner. It was the green of new timothy hay, fervid and strident and hectic and loud. I could hardly stay in the plane. It was like a piece of green carpet; I thought I could simply step down. The river was the only place to land, so we banked down onto a bumpy slim strip between abrupt bends. The braking action of the current made it possible for us to land there, but we struggled to taxi upriver against it and even to hold our own. Finally we managed to park in a tiny slough that was narrower than the wingspread of the plane, and two people scrambled down to where we were. One was a vacationing high-school boy named Rick Milburn, and the other a wolfer and explorer, fifty-six, bearing the appropriately anonymous name of Jim Morgan, he being the last of a breed. An Indian boy seventeen, Jim Abou, had flown in with me to join them.

I was immediately taken with Morgan. He's a slender, abstracted, slightly built man with nothing to say at all. He's a gazer. He might be watching the woods or he might be watching motes dance in the air. He looks frail and tenacious; he looks like Walter Huston and Gabby Hayes combined and brought real. Or if you could plug a history book into an electrical socket in order to bring the illustrations to life, he would be one.

Danny Bereza roared off for his next rendezvous in a spray of rainbows, barely evading the wall of trees. Since he works with mineral geologists principally, he doesn't say where he flies. We carried the sacks of goods up to the cabins and suppered on moosemeat and strawberry foam, a pudding of Milburn's that failed. During the evening I hurried about, seeing where I was, a horse-kick of happiness going inside. It was another gleeful arrival for me. It seemed like the finest arrival of all, it seemed as if this were the center of things. The chipmunks were climbing the dandelions and eating the seeds in the summer's full frenzy—the sun wouldn't set—chittering, eyeing me appraisingly. The woodpile bulked bigger than the cabins did. The fences were so new that the poles still had more bark on them than some of the trees—the traditional first fence, the snake fence, which squanders the cleared trees in a zigzag course end to end and atop one another like clasped fingers, but standing eight feet high.

The river, which rises or falls according to whether the sun is shining on the snowfields, ran too fast and muddy for the trout to be able to see as they fed, so they swam into our little plane-parking slough. With a stick, a short bit of line on the end of the stick and a tatter of moose at the end of the line, I caught two Dolly Varden and two Arctic grayling. The dollies are delicate, spotted, cannibal fish; the grayling are hefty, long-finned fellows, more bluff and gregarious. Then at eleven o'clock Morgan set fire to the outhouse, since it had gotten chock full in the course of the year. It blazed up impassionedly above the river as if the fire relished its fuel, a regular fanfare announcing our presence to the creatures around. A crow would need to fly for a hundred and fifty miles to reach any other clearing like this.

July 14, Thursday

I went for a walk in the morning along the creek which ascends behind Hyland Post. The path is a modest game trail between tumbled windfalls, both on the ground and overhead in the form of crossed swords that you duck through. The moss everywhere is a triple-mattress bed sprinkled with cones and ground pine. Higher up, I came to some breaks in the forest with dry forageable grass, and also a soaking fern bog full of black and red birds and fed by a spring, the ferns growing over my head. The mountain face was a blunt backdrop. The mosquitoes and biting flies settled on me to stay, being accustomed to animals that can't slap, but they were too numerous to slap anyway. White tufts of caribou hair had snagged on the trees. There were lots of hoof marks cut in the moss and piles of droppings left from the months when the caribou had wintered at close quarters here, accompanied by wolf-family turds. I was forever peering up at meadows I hadn't the energy to reach. The caribou and wolves mostly range high in this midsummer period, but wherever I crossed any mud I saw fresh moose and coyote tracks, or a dead log a bear had smashed open, looking for grubs. It always takes me a while in grizzly country to get over my fear of grizzlies, and this was the real Red Riding Hood forest, the trees topsy-turvy, fighting for sun, the ground rank and murky with primeval plants. The boulders and pines were affected with giantism; the ungainly terrain traveled in heaves; the creek caromed and plummeted too crudely to have carved a bed—it fell through a series of gashes. Each ascent snicked a snip off my heart and left me still looking up at a mountain wall with another meadow showing on top. The deadfalls that were caught on the living trees creaked in the breeze. A cloud that resembled swirling steam swallowed a clump of trees above me.

I saw a deer, of all scarce and unlikely things, bounding to keep me in sight as it fled. It looked like a jackrabbit in the supersized landscape, compared with the animals I was anticipating. But its feminine grace gave it importance. People here have a sheltering feeling for deer; they're so helpless after a snow, like conies before the wolves. They will shoot a moose for meat instead, although standards got rather general for the old-timers who were out in the bush alone. When somebody did shoot a doe, seeing that fawn-skinned, small womanly body stretched on the ground, he must have swarmed over her with his knees and hands and practically made it with her then and there. Maybe not. One of the contrasts I've noticed between the actual wilderness and the wilderness which writers incorporate into their books is the absence of sadism here. Sadistic images seem to abound in wilderness books, and yet all these people whom I've been meeting are quite free of that. With few exceptions, there's hardly a whiff as they talk.

Returning at noon, I had to cross a field of buckbrush which reached to my chest and head. It's so tough it's almost impenetrable, and is sometimes called hardtack by ranchers because of its poor food value. The leaves turn a brilliant red in September and are cup-shaped, so that they hold a rainfall and drench anybody who walks through. I was remembering Cliff Adams' experience in this same field two years ago, when he was chased by a mother grizzly. He was working with a friend who was carrying the rifle they'd brought along, but who wasn't within sight or hearing. He kept yelling, "Shoot the damn bear! Shoot the damn bear!" as he ran for his life, and from the distance he'd hear that Commonwealth query, "Eh? Eh?" He kept turning sharply as though he were trying to escape a bull. The mother broke off the pursuit, however, and went back to her cubs. When she did, conservationist that he is, he started to yell to his friend, "*Don't* shoot the bear! *Don't* shoot the bear!" Just at that moment the man caught sight of her at last. BANG. (Missed.)

I'm the type who in the army wore combat boots with my civilian clothes on weekends, but when I was on duty I had gotten myself the sort of a job for which I wore ordinary business shoes. This was a combat-boot crossing, though.

I finally got to the Spatsizi, which was like home. It swings briskly by the three cabins, bending symmetrically out of view in either direction as soon as it can, as if to say, get your glimpse, this is all you will see. It's already a fuliginous rich yellow-brown, and from forty to sixty yards wide, like a not very miniaturized Stikine. The ducks use it for a flyway, hurtling below the treetops at tremendous speed. A Canada goose flew by, having come up from heaven knows where, Acapulco last spring? And in the midst of his rocketing, he saw me from the corner of his eye. He stopped flying—he nearly collapsed in midair from surprise—and emitted a queer, flabbergasted *awp,* as if he were thinking, *Here?*

F R O M
Arctic Dreams

B A R R Y L O P E Z

On a walk through the tundra along the Yukon Territory–Canadian border, nature writer Barry Lopez considers "the country of the mind" and how maps of the imagination have influenced exploration.

ONE September morning I traveled east (the way I envisioned it) with several friends in a small boat from our scientific base camp at Beaufort Lagoon, near the Canadian border. It was a balmy day, exhilarating weather after a week of cold wind and rain and overcast skies during which we had been working at sea. We were headed for the Yukon border, which had for all of us a romantic allure. We traveled about 25 miles along the coast before we were cut off in the shore lead by ice. Fortuitously, we were within a hundred yards of the border.

We doffed our parkas and wandered about the tundra somewhat aimlessly, in the vicinity of a cluster of weathered driftwood piles that marked the dividing line between the two countries. Caribou trails and the sight of migrating ducks and geese, the absence of immigration officials, and, not least, the sun shining brightly in a cloudless sky made us all take crossing the border less seriously. We found tufts of polar bear fur caught in the dry tundra grasses, and the tracks of a bear in the steep embankment, where it had descended the coastal bluff to the ice and headed out to sea.

In such benign circumstances it was hard to imagine the deadly tension that characterized other national borders on that same day. We were all of us more affected by an exotic childhood idea—reaching the Yukon Territory. We took our bearings from a country in our heads—it was an *idea* that brought us here, to a spot on the tundra we would be hard pressed to distinguish in terms of plant life or animal life or topography from the tundra a mile farther to the east, or back to the west. To come here at all was an act of carefree innocence. We stood around for nearly an hour. We took each other's pictures. We were delighted by the felicitous conjunction of this good weather and our idea of "the Yukon Territory."

Ideas no less real and far more affecting brought European explorers into the Arctic hundreds of years ago. They were searching for lands and straits they knew existed but which they had never seen; and they could not believe they did not exist when they failed to find them. As there was a Strait of Magellan at Cape Horn, they thought, so too should there be a northern strait, a Strait of Anian, just as there were Western and Eastern, Northern and Southern oceans. Did not the most learned references of the day, the sea charts, depict such a passage? And did it not make sense that Frobisher should find gold in the Arctic, just as the Spaniards had in the tropics?

When the early arctic explorers wrote down in official commentaries what they had seen, they were hesitant to criticize the wisdom of the day, what the esteemed maps indicated. They were prone, in fact, to embellish, in order to make themselves seem more credible. They even believed on occasion that they *had* sensed something where there was nothing because it seemed ordained that it should happen—did not the eye glimpse faintly a shore before the fog closed in? Had not the ear recorded a distant surf before darkness and a contrary wind conspired against it? The land, they believed, should corroborate, not contradict, what men knew from sources like Ptolemy about the shape of the world. The accounts of such explorers were read and passed on; the entangled desires and observations of the writers, with a liberal interpretation by cartographers with reputations of their own to protect, perpetuated a geography of hoped-for islands and straits to the west of Europe that could not be substantiated, a geography only of the mind.

The influence of these images, of course, was considerable. Such a mental geography becomes the geography to which society adjusts, and it can be more influential than the real geography. The popular image of a previously unknown region, writes J. Wreford Watson, is "compounded of what men hope to find, what they look to find, how they set about finding, how findings are fitted into their existing framework of thought, and how those findings are then expressed." This, says Watson, is what is actually "found" in a new land.

Another geographer, John L. Allen, pondering the way we set off for a fresh landscape, writes, "When exploration is viewed as a process rather than as a series of distinct events, its major components [are seen to be] clearly related to the imagination. No exploratory adventure begins without objectives based on the imagined nature and content of the lands to be explored." The course of discovery is guided, then, by preconceived notions. Field observations, writes Allen, "are distorted by these images. The results of exploration are modified by reports written and interpreted in the light of persistent illusions and by attempts made to fit new information into partly erroneous systems and frameworks of geographical understanding."

Over the past twenty years, some of the focus of academic geography has shifted away from descriptions of the land and focused instead on landscapes that exist in the human mind. The extent and complexity of these geographical images, called mental maps, are wonderful. An urban resident, for example, sees himself situated in urban space with specific reference to certain stores, parking spaces, and public transportation stations. He assigns one street or building more importance than another as a place for chance meetings with friends. He knows which routes between certain points are safest and how to get to a certain restaurant even though he doesn't know the names of any of the streets on the way. The mental map of an Eskimo might be an overview of the region where he customarily hunts—where caribou are likely to turn up in the spring, where berries are to be found, where consistent runs of char are located, where the ground is too swampy to walk over in June, where good soapstone is to be had, or a regular supply of driftwood.

The mental maps of both urban dweller and Eskimo may correspond poorly in spatial terms with maps of the same areas prepared with survey tools and cartographic instruments. But they are proven, accurate guides of the landscape. They are living conceptions, idiosyncratically created, stripped of the superfluous, instantly adaptable. Their validity is not susceptible of contradiction.

Our overall cultural perception of a region requires another term. Mental maps are too personal; and the term does not convey sufficiently the richness of the invisible landscape, that component of a regional image that aboriginal groups dwell on at least as much as they consider a region's physiographic components. Jahner's term, the spiritual landscape, refers more specifically to relationships inherent in the physical landscape which make us aware of the presence of the forces and relationships that infuse our religious thought. If one can take the phrase "a country of the mind" to mean the landscape evident to the senses, as it is retained in human memory and arises in the oral tradition of a people, as a repository of both mythological and "real-time" history, then perhaps this phrase will suffice.

Amos Rapoport, an Australian architect, and like Tuan and Carpenter curious about the meaning of "place," made a landmark study among Kurna, Arunda, Walbiri, and other Australian aborigines. He mapped their mythological landscapes. He understood that the stories that compose a tribe's mythological background, their origin and their meaning and purpose in the universe, are "unobservable realities" that find their expression in "observable phenomena." The land, in other words, makes the myth real. And it makes the people real.

The stories that unfold against the local landscape, and that give expression to the enduring relationships of life, said Rapoport, are as critical for people as food or water. The mythic landscape is not the natural landscape, Rapoport concluded, but the mythic and natural landscapes overlap at certain visible points in the land. And the limits of the local landscape, he emphasized, are not something that can be politically negotiated; they are fixed in mythology. They are

267

not susceptible of adjustment. Rapoport's study made it eminently clear, as he put it, that Europeans may "completely misunderstand the nature of the landscape because of their point of view."

It is always somewhat risky to extrapolate from one aboriginal culture to another. I know of no work comparable to Rapoport's in the Arctic, however, and his observations come as close to being generically sound as any anthropologist's I know. The journals of the most attentive arctic explorers, those with both a flair for listening and a capacity to record metaphorical impressions without judgment, are filled with references to mythological events that occurred at particular places. Eskimos are not as land-conscious as aborigines; they are more sea-conscious, and the surface of the sea is impermanent, new every year. Still, the evidence for a landscape in the Arctic larger than the one science reports, more extensive than that recorded on the United States Coast and Geodetic Survey quadrangle maps, is undeniable. It is the country the shamans shined their *qaumaneq,* their shaman light, into.

The aspiration of aboriginal people throughout the world has been to achieve a congruent relationship with the land, to fit well in it. To achieve occasionally a state of high harmony or reverberation. The dream of this transcendent congruency included the evolution of a hunting and gathering relationship with the earth, in which a mutual regard was understood to prevail; but it also meant a conservation of the stories that bind the people into the land.

I recall a scene in one of the British discovery expeditions to the Arctic of a group of ship's officers standing about somewhat idly on a beach while three or four Eskimo men drew a map for them in the sand. The young officers found the drawing exotic and engaging, but almost too developed, too theatrical. I can imagine the Eskimos drawing a map they meant not to be taken strictly as a navigational aid, but as a recapitulation of their place in the known universe. Therefore, as they placed a line of stones to represent a mountain range and drew in the trend of the coast, they included also small, seemingly insignificant bays where it was especially good to hunt geese, or tapped a section of a river where the special requirements for sheefish spawning were present. This was the map as mnemonic device, organizing the names of the places and the stories attached to them, three or four men unfolding their meaning and purpose as people before the young officers. They did not know what to leave out for these impatient men. There was no way for them to separate the stories, the indigenous philosophy, from the land. The young officers later remembered only that the maps were fascinating. Had the Eskimos told them that the Pentateuch was merely fascinating, they would have thought them daft.

The place-fixing stories that grew out of the land were of two kinds: The first kind, which was from the myth time and which occurred against the backdrop of a mythological landscape, was usually meticulously conserved. (It was always possible that the storyteller would not himself or herself grasp completely the wisdom inherent in a story that had endured, which had proved its value repeatedly.)

The second kind of story included stories about traveling and what had happened to everyone in the years that could be recalled. It was at this place that my daughter was born; or this is where my brother-in-law killed two caribou the winter a bear killed all my dogs; or this, Titiralik, is the place my snow machine broke down and I had to walk; Seenasaluq, this is a place my family has camped since before I was born.

The undisturbed landscape verifies both sorts of story, and it is the constant recapitulation in sacred and profane contexts of all of these stories that keeps the people alive and the land alive in the people. Language, the stories, holds the vision together.

To those of us who are not hunters, who live in cities with no sharp regret and enjoy ideas few Eskimos would wish to discuss, such sensibilities may seem almost arcane. And we may put no value to them. But we cut ourselves off, I think, from a source of wisdom. We sometimes mistake a rude life for a rude mind; raw meat for barbarism; lack of conversation for lack of imagination. The overriding impression, I think, for the visitor in the Arctic who walks away from the plane, and waits out the bouts of binge drinking, the defensive surliness and self-conscious acting in the village, is that a wisdom is to be found in the people. And once in a great while an *isumataq* becomes apparent, a person who can create the atmosphere in which wisdom shows itself.

This is a timeless wisdom that survives failed human economies. It survives wars. It survives definition. It is a nameless wisdom esteemed by all people. It is understanding how to live a decent life, how to behave properly toward other people and toward the land.

It is, further, a wisdom not owned by anyone, nor about which one culture is more insightful or articulate. I could easily imagine some Thomas Merton–like person, the estimable rather than the famous people of our age, sitting with one or two Eskimo men and women in a coastal village, corroborating the existence of this human wisdom in yet another region of the world, and looking around to the mountains, the ice, the birds to see what makes it possible to put it into words.

One July evening I flew with two paleontologists from Ellef Ringnes Island some 400 miles southwest to their new camp near Castel Bay on Banks Island. In the years before, these two people had elucidated a wonderful bit of arctic history. A collection of fossils they assembled from a thick layer of interbedded coal and friable rock called the Eureka Formation on Ellesmere Island indicated that 40 to 50 million years ago, during the Eocene, the Arctic was a region forested with sequoias and ginkgo trees. It enjoyed a moist and temperate, almost warm climate and a collection of animals that showed a resemblance to the kinds of animals that have been discovered in Eocene deposits in Europe. At the time, the Eurasian and North American crustal plates were just beginning to separate at the northern end of the Atlantic Ocean, and animals had only recently ceased moving back and forth.

Robert West and Mary Dawson and I sat in the jump seats of an aircraft called a Twin Otter, amid their camp gear and fossil collections, for several hours. I listened to them explain their work, and took pleasure in it, in the fulfilled hopes and dashed dreams of a field season, and in some of the scenes they envisioned in the land below us during the Eocene, when three-toed horses, ancestral flying lemurs, and prehistoric crocodiles lived. It was not something they could see clearly, only imagine. They recounted their patient search through frost-riven rubble in the Arctic, looking for bits of mineralized bone, teeth, and shells, for pieces of petrified wood and casts of fallen leaves, the shreds of evidence that suggested a landscape.

It was a long flight. To be heard we had to shout a little over the sound of the engines or draw things on pieces of paper. Somewhere over Melville Island the pilot, Duncan Grant, turned around in his seat to listen. The copilot flew on. Grant began to tell us about the history of arctic exploration, a subject upon which he was keen and knowledgeable. We were approaching Dealy Island on the south coast, where Kellett and his crew wintered in 1852 aboard HMS *Resolute*. He wanted us to see that, and, farther on, the winter quarters of Parry at the bay now called Winter Harbor.

As we crossed from Melville Island to Banks Island we looked down on massive pressure ridges, the jumbled, very heavy ice of M'Clure Strait. As we neared the coast, Grant, shouting, tried to get us to see what Pim had seen as he approached Banks Island, when he made a dash from Dealy Island in the spring of 1853 to rescue M'Clure and the men aboard the *Investigator*. Even though it was July, a different cast of light entirely, you could see what Grant meant and how the event loomed for him as we approached. We all stopped talking. For the last half hour we just looked out the windows.

We flew over herds of muskoxen. The slanting light was so bucolic in its effect on the hillsides that they looked like herds of black angus grazing in English pastures. We crossed the mouth of the Thomsen River and then circled while West and Dawson surveyed the terrain and decided where to camp. Grant landed on a gravel ridge, where only a few plants were growing—a good exposure of the Eureka Formation. We unloaded their gear and then stood there, just looking around. It was a beautiful evening. We were all smiling with an unspoken hope that their work would be successful.

Dawson handed me a packet of letters they had written to their families and asked me to mail them when we got back to Resolute. We waved, a mixture of regret and good wishes at parting. I rode for hours with the letters on the seat beside me. I thought about the great desire among friends and colleagues and travelers who meet on the road, to share what they know, what they have seen and imagined. Not to have a shared understanding, but to share what one has come to understand. In such an atmosphere of mutual regard, in which each can roll out his or her maps with no fear of contradiction, of suspicion, or theft, it is possible to imagine the long, graceful strides of human history.

I thought about it all the way back to Resolute, watching Melville Island and then Bathurst disappear beneath the clouds, as weather moved in from the west.

FROM

Going to Extremes

JOE McGINNIS

To get acquainted with the extremes of modern Alaska, writer Joe McGinnis spent a lonely period in a cabin on Crescent Lake, the Kenai Peninsula.

THE Federal Writers Project book on Alaska, published in 1939, reprinted a diary found next to the body of a man who had lived the last six months of his life alone in a cabin in the Alaskan wilderness.

Oct. 4th,
1917. Getting sick packing, now looking for camping place. Cold in the lungs with a high fever.
6th. Less fever, less pain, but getting weak.
7th. Feeling better but very weak.
9th. Getting a little stronger.
10th. Going to build a house. Will not be able to pull canoe up this fall, got to wait for the ice.
13th. Shot a glacier bear.
14th. Shot a goat.
17th. House finished.
18th. Taking out some traps.
20th. Made a smoke house.
21st. Shot one goat.
25th. Shot one lynx.
27th. Shot a wolf and a bear cub.
28th. Winter has come. Strong wind, two feet of snow.
Nov.
4th. Shot one lynx.
6th. Made one pair of bearskin pants.
8th. Sugar is all gone.
13th. Made two pair of moccasins.
18th. Finished one fur coat of bear, wolf, and lynx.
21st. Finished one sleeping bag of bear, goat, blankets, and canvas. Rain for several days.
22nd. Left eye bothers me. Shot one goat.
26th. Shot one lynx while eating breakfast.

27th.	Made one pair of bearpaw snowshoes.
Dec. 1st.	Getting bad. Cold for several days, river still open.
4th.	River raised six feet in 24 hours.
6th.	Slush stiffening, slowly making ice.
7th.	The wind is so strong that you can't stand upright. River froze except a few riffles. Too much snow and too rough for sleighing. Snow getting deeper now.
15th.	Very cold and strong wind, impossible to be out without skin clothes.
19th.	Snowing but still very cold. Riffles up in the bend still open. Can't travel. Don't believe there will be ice a man can run a sleigh over this winter. Very little grub, snow too deep and soft for hunting goats. Stomach balking at straight meat, especially lynx.
21st.	Shot a goat from the river.
25th.	Very cold. A good Christmas dinner. Snow getting hard. River still open in places above camp.
26th.	Broke through the ice. Skin clothes saved the day.
31st.	Finished new roof on the house. One month of cold weather straight. Last night and today rain. Stomach getting worse.
Jan. 8th, 1918.	River open as far as can be seen. Health very poor.
12th.	Lynx moving down the river one or two a night; no chance to catch them.
15th.	Goats moving out of reach. Using canoe on the river.
16th.	One lynx. Weather getting mild.
20th.	Rain today.
22nd.	One lynx.
28th.	One goat, been cold for a few days, no ice on river.
Feb. 1st.	Cold weather nearly all month of January. Lynx robbed my meat cache up river. Salt and tea but once a day. Gradually getting weaker.
5th.	Colder weather, feeling very bad. Just able to take care of myself.
10th.	Milder, feeling very bad. Heavy fall of snow.
15th.	Good weather continues, feeling some better.
24th.	More snow. Living on dry meat and tallow.
26th.	Shot one goat from the river.
Mch.	
2nd.	Shot one goat.
11th.	Starting for Dry Bay, believing the river open. Out about one hour and struck ice. Can't go either way. Too weak to haul the canoe. Snow soft, no game here.
25th.	Trying to get to the house. River is frozen in places and rising. The sleigh is now only three miles from there, but open river and perpendicular cliffs keep me from getting any farther. At present cannot find anything to eat here. Eyes are getting bad.
28th.	Eyes can't stand the sun at all. Finest kind of weather.

Apr. 1st. Got to the house with what I could carry. Wolverines have been here eating my skins, robes, and moccasins, old meat, and also my goatskin door. They tried to run me last night, came through the stovepipe hole showing fight. Heavy fall of snow. Canoe and some traps down the river about five miles, close to Indian grave mark. Camp about halfway.

3rd. Still snowing. Cooking my last grub, no salt, no tea.

4th. Shot one goat, using all but three of my shells. Can't see the sights at all.

7th. Wolverine working on camp below carrying away my things. Ate part of my bearskin pants. Packed the old .30-.30 out into the brush. Eyes getting worse again, don't even stand the snow.

10th. Wolverines at my bedding and one snowshoe. In the tent, getting shaky in the legs. A five-mile walk a big day's work.

12th. Seen a fox track today. Birds are coming too. Fine weather.

15th. The no-salt diet is hitting me pretty hard. Eyes are getting worse, in the bunk most of the time.

17th. Rain yesterday and today.

20th. Finest weather continues again, cooking the last grub, got to stay in bunk most of the time—my legs won't carry me very far. My eyes are useless for hunting, the rest of my body also useless. I believe my time has come. My belongings, everything I got I give to Joseph Pellerine of Dry Bay; if not alive, to Paul Swartzkoph, Alsek River, April 22, 1918.

V. Swanson.

From the apartment I had just moved into, I walked to the Forest Service office on Fireweed Lane and picked out a cabin at Crescent Lake, on the Kenai Peninsula, about a hundred miles south of Anchorage. I planned to spend three days there alone. It was late February, and although winter still had a long way to run, there was already more light in the sky.

I had moved out of Tom and Marnie's guest room, finally, and into a one-bedroom apartment in a brand-new two-story building called a six-plex. The apartment was near Fifteenth and Gambell, just behind the ball field at Mulcahy Park, where the Anchorage Glacier Pilots baseball team played their home games in the summer. It was about a fifteen-minute walk from Tom and Marnie's and about twenty minutes from downtown. There were three liquor stores within a five-minute walk of the apartment, all of them open from 8 a.m. to 2 a.m., seven days a week. The liquor store was where you went to buy your paper on Sunday morning. To buy a quart of milk, you had to walk more than a mile.

My one-bedroom apartment, unfurnished, rented for $350 a month. I borrowed most of the furniture I needed from Tom and Marnie and bought the rest secondhand. The apartment next to mine was occupied by the night bartender at the Petroleum Club, who snored loudly through most of the day. I was one flight down, below street level, and had no views of Cook Inlet or Mount McKinley, but from my bedroom window, if I stood on tiptoe, I could look out past a vacant lot and see the Chugach Mountains. That would change with the first hint of spring, when a new apartment house would be built on the vacant lot.

Tom loaned me the equipment I would need: sleeping bag, an ax, a Coleman lantern that burned unleaded gas, and snowshoes, because I had never used cross-country skis.

I left on a Sunday afternoon, a clear cold day with bright sunshine. In addition to what I had borrowed from Tom, I brought a box of food and the boots and parka I was wearing. That was all. I brought no books, no magazines, no beer or wine or brandy; no cigarettes. I wasn't even carrying a watch. I wanted three days and three nights of unbroken contact with the winter environment. Total solitude. No escapes of any kind. I would be alone, in a cabin, at the edge of a frozen lake, surrounded by mountains. The cabin had a wood-burning stove. I had my food, but I would have to cut my own firewood to stay warm. After three days, the chartered plane would come back.

In a single-engine Super Cub, it was a fifty-five minute flight to Crescent Lake. Across Turnagain Arm and then over the snow-covered, uninhabited mountains of the Kenai Peninsula. Turnagain Arm was a body of water that branched off from Cook Inlet. In 1780, Captain Cook thought it might be the Northwest Passage for which he was searching. But then, after fifty miles, it narrowed and ended, and he had to turn back, not for the first time, which led him to call it Turnagain.

The pilot banked steeply and flew very close to the side of a mountain. Strong winds were making the plane bounce. I could see the pine trees, then the individual branches of the trees. Where there were no trees, I could see, all too clearly, the rocks of which the mountains were composed. A gust of wind hit the plane and it lurched and dipped even closer. I tried looking in the other direction, but there was a mountain out that window, too.

On the first try, only one of the two landing skis locked into place. The pilot picked up a hammer and smacked something. On the second try, both skis came down.

The lake was five miles long, less than one mile across, and curved like a crescent. There were mountains all around it, and mountains rising steeply, to 5,000 feet, from either side. The cabin was at the west end of the lake. The pilot taxied to it and I climbed out and unloaded my gear. The plane took off. In an hour, it would be back in Anchorage. I was here, alone.

The temperature was only a few degrees above zero, and a wind was blowing hard across the lake. In summer, people came here to canoe and to fish and to hike in the mountains. In winter, there was none of that. In winter, there was firewood to cut.

Actually, that afternoon I cut no wood. There was enough for the first night cut already and stacked near the wood stove in the cabin. Each person who used the cabin was supposed to leave behind at least as much wood as had been there when he arrived. That way, if someone wound up at the cabin in an emergency, there could at least be a fire right away.

I put on my snowshoes and walked to the center of the lake. The mountain on the north side rose like a cresting wave. From half a mile out, the cabin seemed just a black dot in the snow. The only sound was the sound of the wind. The sun and snow were bright against the eyes. It was clumsy going in the snowshoes, which I had never worn before. I kept tripping. With each step, the back of one snowshoe would wind up on top of the front of the other. Eventually, I learned to slide my feet forward, and to shuffle, instead of step.

It was staying light now until almost six o'clock. But the mountains were high enough to block the sun from the lake long before that. I went back to the cabin and built a fire. Tom had explained to me how to light the Coleman lamp, but, alone in the cabin, it seemed risky to fool around with matches and unleaded gas. I heated a can of stew on top of the stove and ate by flashlight. I was afraid the lantern might burn the cabin down. After I ate the stew, I went to bed. Solitude was fine, except there was nothing to do.

The thermometer outside the cabin had said zero. Once the fire in the stove had gone out, the temperature inside the cabin could not have been much higher than that. There were spaces between the logs big enough to serve as windows. And enough holes in the roof so that fresh snow fell in with each gust of wind. I wore long underwear, woolen socks, a woolen shirt, and a woolen hat on my head, and I wrapped myself inside the sleeping bag like a mummy. It was a very good sleeping bag, the best that Eddie Bauer made, and I zipped it up to cover my whole head. Even so, it was by far the coldest night I'd ever spent. I would lie awake shivering in the dark, hearing the noise of little animals rustling on the floor by the stove. Each time I fell asleep I dreamed it was morning, that the sun was shining and I was warm. Then I would wake up in the dark. Having no way to tell time, not knowing how much of the night still remained. It was not only the coldest but the longest night I'd ever spent.

Until I'd come to Alaska, I had never even used a sleeping bag. What was I doing here at Crescent Lake? And why had I decided to stay for three nights? I felt an overwhelming urge to call the flying service in the morning and to tell them to come and get me right away. Except, of course, there was no phone. In Alaska, when you went out of a city, you stuck to the plan you had made. Three days was three days. Which would mean two more nights after this. Then the wind blew harder and I heard a rumbling noise from somewhere and I began to imagine how easy it would be for the cabin to be buried in an avalanche.

I dreamed again it was morning and when I woke up it really was. I was shivering inside the sleeping bag, but I unzipped and dressed quickly and started a fire in the stove. This morning, I would have to cut wood. There was a saw in the cabin, and I had Tom's ax. I had never cut firewood before, but if it stayed this cold I was sure I'd be able to learn.

Outside, the temperature was 10 above and the sky was gray. Sure signs of snow. I walked, on my snowshoes, into the woods. The idea was to find trees already down. Deadwood. I would saw limbs off and drag them back to the cabin through the snow. Then I would saw them into pieces small enough to fit in the stove. Then split them with the ax, so they would be easier to burn.

I spent the whole morning doing this. I became obsessed with firewood. I wanted a stack big enough to go from floor to ceiling, around all four walls. I worked until my arms were so weary that I could no longer raise the ax above my head. I sweated so much, cutting wood, that I had to take off my parka and my wool shirt and work in only my undershirt.

Then the snow began to fall. Lightly at first, small flakes, with no wind. I ate some cheese and a can of sardines for lunch. After lunch, I shuffled back out on the lake. Even in light snow, the tops of the mountains were obscured. Before long, it was hard to see the cabin. I walked back. I could see how easy it would be to get turned around in a storm and to walk for hours searching for your cabin, while being only a quarter mile from it all the time. I had heard many stories through the winter of people found frozen to death after storms, sometimes within fifty yards of their homes.

I spent the rest of the afternoon cutting wood. Not so much because I needed more, but because there was nothing else to do. I was developing a desperate craving for a book.

A pilot had told me about a young woman named Charlotte who had come into a village in interior Alaska, at the beginning of winter, and had asked him to fly her to a cabin about fifty miles up a river tributary. She had met a man in Fairbanks and now she was going there to live with him. The pilot took her. About six weeks later he decided to fly up and see how she was doing. He found out even before he landed his plane. She had laid pine boughs in the snow, to make a big sign, visible to any plane flying low: CHAR WANTS OUT. CAN YOU TAKE?

I was starting to understand how she felt, and I had only been here for a day. The idea of stripping all vicariousness from your life, of immersing yourself totally in where you were and what you did, would not be easily mastered by someone from the urban Northeast, where one grew addicted to vicarious experience, and where one became as dependent upon outside stimulus as upon food and drink every day.

Toward dusk, on the second day, the wind began to blow. The snow, which had been falling lightly but steadily since midmorning, now came down thick and hard. I ate the second half of my stew, surrendered to a surge of self-pity, and crawled into my sleeping bag while the wood fire was still burning hard.

I felt quite small, with much that was big all around me. But on the state of Alaska highway map, Crescent Lake was considered so insignificant as to be not even listed by name. And these mountains above it were so ordinary—by Alaskan standards—that they, too, were without names.

What was it? Tuesday? Light out? Hard to tell. *Jesus Christ*, the wind was blowing. As I woke more fully, I looked around the cabin and saw that everything inside, even my sleeping bag, was covered with snow. The wind had blown so hard overnight that in the corners of the cabin the snow was almost two feet deep.

It was good I had cut so much wood the day before, because now I was stuck in a blizzard. The temperature had risen to the mid-20s, but the wind had risen far more than that. The snow was blowing so hard I could not see past the cabin porch. I opened the door and the snow was waist-high outside. I had to climb a snowdrift in my snowshoes in order to make my way to the outhouse. And when I got there I saw that only the roof was sticking up above the snow.

The wind blew all day. The snow fell. It was as dark gray as in Barrow at noon. There was nothing to do, no place to go, no way to mark the passage of time.

I had brought a section of the Sunday Anchorage *Times,* to use in getting fires started. And so I cheated, even though I had told myself I would not read. It was the real estate section. I studied every house that was for sale, every apartment that was for rent. And imagined what it would be like to be in each. With electricity, running water, and heat. With magazines and books. And a refrigerator full of meat and fish and beer. And a big double bed with clean sheets, and with a lovely woman to share it all. With even radio and television, which I had never before felt dependent upon. Television, in fact, was something to which I had a powerful aversion. But now I craved it. Just for the noise. Just for the sound of human voices. Just for sound other than this wind.

The blizzard lasted for two days. On the second day, I had to go out and cut more wood. At some point during the two days I saw a moose. Moving slowly through the snow near the edge of the lake. I wished that he would not go away. The sight of another living creature proved to be a great boost for my morale. Other than the voles that scrabbled around the cabin floor at night, I'd had no

278

contact with anything animate for seventy-two hours. By far the longest such stretch of my life, and unrelieved by even the temporary distraction of a book.

What the hell time was it? It seemed to take forever to get light, and then it seemed to take forever to get dark. Did this have something to do with relativity? No, it probably just had to do with being alone. In a cabin. In a blizzard. At the edge of a snow-covered lake. In Alaska. At the end of February. Char Wants Out. Can You Take? And at least Char had been living with a friend.

The pilot had been due back on Wednesday, but Wednesday had been a blizzard day, so I'd cut my firewood and eaten my cheese and wished that the moose would return.

On Thursday it was bright and clear and I woke up filled with joy. I could see across the lake again, could see the tops of the mountains, and the sky. The wind had subsided and all was quiet once more. The first noise I would hear would be the noise of the plane. Then I would see it in the sky. I figured the pilot would be there about noon. Whenever noon was. It did not matter. Having endured four days, including two and a half in a blizzard, I could certainly handle an hour or two in the sun. Knowing that so soon I would be out. Climbing into the plane, putting my sleeping bag and food box and snowshoes and unused Coleman lantern in the back, and then bumping along the lake surface through the snow. Then taking off. And rising above the tops of the mountains that had been looming above me for what had come to seem half my life. I would be heading toward Anchorage. Toward people. Toward life. I didn't think I would be able to explain to anyone exactly how it had felt, being here. I didn't think I'd even want to try. I just wanted to go to a movie, and to a place that served pizza, and I wanted to drink beer and play songs on a jukebox and take a hot shower and make love in the bed in my apartment.

But the pilot didn't come. All day, there was nothing in the sky but the sun. All day, not a sound around the lake. I could tell when it was about midday, and then I watched, disbelieving, as the afternoon shadows slowly started to rise up the sides of the mountains and to cover the surface of the lake. I didn't cut wood. I didn't take a walk. I just sat on my fully packed duffel bag, in front of the cabin, and watched the sky.

It got dark. There was no plane. I went to bed, filled with bitterness and rage. In the morning, I said, I would walk out. From the far end of the lake there was supposed to be a trail that led, eventually, to a road at a place called Moose Pass. I would get out that way on my snowshoes, dragging my duffel bag through the snow, carrying the lantern and the ax. And I would find someone, somewhere, maybe in this place called Moose Pass, and I would get myself back to Anchorage. And when I reached Anchorage I would go out to the office of the flying service, and I would start swinging the ax. And I would chop the wings off all their planes. Rotten bastards. Sons of bitches. Suppose I had chopped a toe off cutting firewood? Suppose I'd accidentally sawed through my wrist? I could be lying on the cabin floor bleeding to death and these bastards hadn't even come to pick me up. This was the worst moment I'd had in Alaska, by far. I even began to feel anger toward Tom, for loaning me all this crap that had enabled me to come here in the first place, and toward the U.S. Forest Service, for having even built this goddamned cabin, and toward anyone who had ever lived in a cabin, in the winter, in the woods. Eventually, beneath the sheer weight of so much impotent rage, I fell asleep.

I was awakened by a knock on the cabin door.

"Come on, let's go," the pilot said. "My coffee's already perking in Anchorage."

It was morning. Another clear day. I hadn't even heard the plane come in.

"Hell," the pilot said. "Usually when I'm two days late for someone, they're sitting on top of their duffel bag ready to go. Looks like you might want to stay."

"Oh, no. That's okay. I'm ready to go."

"Well, you know why I didn't get here Wednesday. That was one hell of a storm, turned to freezing rain in Anchorage, ice all over the planes. Then yesterday I climbed up on a wing to try to chip some of the ice off the struts, and I slipped on the goddamn stuff and fell off the wing and busted my ribs. Wound up in the hospital instead of here. Got 'em all taped up now, but they still hurt like hell. I'm just damn glad we ought to have a smooth flight. Doctor told me definitely to take today off. Stay in bed. Which I am gonna do. But I figured I'd better come down here and get you. Figured maybe you'd been here long enough."

And we climbed into the plane, and bumped along the lake surface through the snow, and took off, and rose above the tops of the mountains, and on a gorgeous, sunny, cold morning—the first of March—we flew smoothly back to Anchorage.

FROM

Coming into the Country

JOHN McPHEE

"With a clannish sense of place characteristic of the bush, people in the region of the upper Yukon refer to their part of Alaska as 'the country.' A stranger appearing among them is said to have 'come into the country,' " John McPhee wrote in introducing some of the settlers he got to know during his stay deep in the territory. One of them, who had lived alone in a cabin near the Yukon River, kept a journal of his experience at survival.

RICH CORAZZA came into the country in 1974. In Wyoming and Colorado, he had worked in the open, and the attraction held for him by the upper Yukon was unarguably succinct: "There ain't no barbed wire up here." Trapping in winter, gold-mining in summer—he would try whatever the country might offer, but not to take and go. He did not seek a living so much as a life. He was twenty-three, and he was in love with a woman named Sara, but she was thousands of miles away—outside—and, while he fervently hoped she would join him, she was, for the time being, less appealing than the Yukon. In the fall of 1975, he learned of a cabin where he might spend the approaching winter. It had been built by Sarge Waller, who had used it one winter and decided not to do so again. Waller's cabin is just upstream of where the Kandik River, coming in from Canada, gives itself up to the Yukon. Corazza would be alone there, but he would not be entirely without neighbors. There were three occupied cabins within a quarter of a million surrounding acres.

After hitching a boat ride or two, he finished his journey on foot. Walking upriver, he came to the Kandik on the seventh of October, late in the day. The Kandik surprised him—too big and fast to ford. So he slept where he was, his dog, Molly, beside him. When he woke, his bag was covered with an inch of snow. He built a raft and crossed the river.

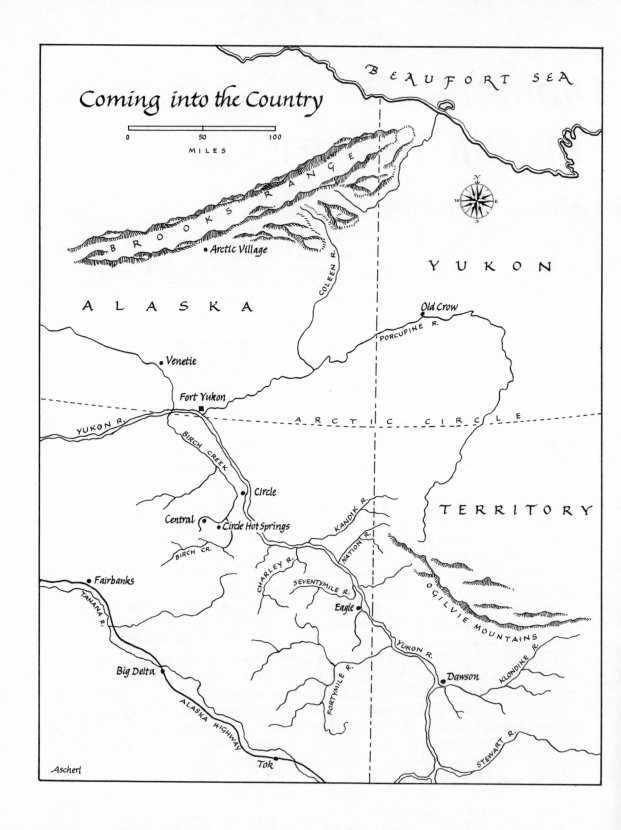

For several months, he kept company with a journal, written on loose sheets of ruled yellow paper.

> Thursday, Oct 9 . . . Seen a white weazel right outside the cabin, his nest is in the dog house. Plan to cut wood tomorrow, seems like Molly and I are just waiting for winter. Things are pretty well straightened up at the cabin and damn it sure feels like home. Wish we had a moose! Good night, Sara.

The writing atrophied when perhaps he felt even more at home. The seasons changed, and he went elsewhere in the country to mine gold. Behind him he left only two signs of his occupancy: beaver castors hanging from a beam, and, up on one wall, the record of his novice days.

> Friday, Oct 10 . . . I have 3 Swede saws here and the biggest works the best, it is a 5 footer. After a hardy breakfast, I will now attempt to secure the winter's wood.

One day in June, I stopped in at the cabin, on my way by canoe downriver. The mouth of the Kandik is roughly halfway between Eagle and Circle, the upper and lower gateways of the country. The mountainous land between them comes to an end with a final bluff near Circle. Beyond that bluff is another world, an almost oceanic peneplain known as the Yukon Flats. Brad Snow had never been near this natural boundary, and was interested in expanding his knowledge of the river. He had the canoe. For my part, I was on my way to a lengthy visit with Ed and Virginia Gelvin, in Central, and with miners of the Birch Creek district, and was only too pleased to be able to make the journey in Snow's nineteen-foot Grumman freighter. We left Eagle in what was locally termed a heat wave—seventy degrees. Steve Casto, standing on the high bank watching us go, said it was too hot a day to drink coffee.

> . . . Sure is nice to come into a warm cabin. As Sally once wrote, "It's never too cold to cut wood when you're out of fire."

> Saturday, Oct 11 . . . Just a skiff of snow on the ground, the Yukon isn't flowing ice yet, but I think maybe she will shortly. Driftwood really burns good and there is a load of it about 100 yards from the cabin. It's rough cutting but I'll get after it today. Good morning, Sara!

> Sunday, Oct 12. Cut wood & hauled it for 5 hours yesterday, good thing too on account that the ground is white this morning and still snowing, good day to set by the stove. 37° and windy on the Yukon.
> Didn't get much accomplished today. It snowed off and on again, dropped to about 30° and is hanging there. I went hunting near a lake about a mile

from here. No sign of anything except squirrel, of which I shot one and boiled it up for Molly, she's looking awful thin. It would be nice to throw her a moose bone (me too).

Just as the country ends with an isolated bluff, it was thought once to begin with one—a high, mansarded prominence that looms above Eagle. When Lieutenant Frederick Schwatka, U.S. Army, was sent to look over the area in 1883, he was instructed to determine, roughly, where the Yukon came into Alaska. Rafting hundreds of miles through Canadian mountains down the giant bending river, he noted shifts in its direction, guessed distances, guessed current velocities, ran the data through his mind, and what is now named Eagle Bluff he called Boundary Butte. It was some guess—like a sailor's fixing his position by the feel of it—for the hundred-and-forty-first (boundary) meridian was scarcely twelve miles upstream, and, by air line, six miles away. William Ogilvie, sent by Ottawa, surveyed the border four years later. Eagle, Alaska, looking east from a bend in the river, has all before it a sweep of boundary ridgelines, and behind them rise the Ogilvie Mountains, Yukon Territory. The international boundary is now absurdly shaved. Trees are levelled and brush kept cut in a thirty-foot swath.

> Monday, Oct 13. 28° and wintery at 8 this morning. My wood supply looks meager for the weeks of cold weather ahead. (So does my meat supply.) Keeps me on the ball.

When Brad Snow's canoe went out past Eagle Bluff, the buildings of the town diminished behind until the white ones looked like dentils against the pale green of birch and aspen that were just coming into their leaves. There were blocks of shelf ice still along the shore. Belle Isle, in the river at Eagle, was a dark loaf of spruce. American Summit, the southern backdrop, and the Ogilvies, to the east, were dusted white. I was wearing a T-shirt in the bright June sun, but I soon put on a sweater. The temperature of the river was forty-six, and the air close above it was cool. Six miles downstream, I had added a down vest, a 60/40 windbreaker, and a rain suit, hood to heel. Brad Snow was in a rain suit, too. We were driving into a head-on squall, and there were whitecaps on the river. Another bend and there was sun again; another bend, more rain.

> . . . Met Harold today, he is Fred's partner. They're pretty much "hippies" it seems to me but real nice fellas. Found out he is the one who came down on the raft with all the supplies for he and his new found gal from Kentucky. Strange world, but I remember the time I resorted to offering a gal life in the woods. How can an adventurous young thing resist?

Some of the people who live together in remote settings along the river refer to themselves not as couples but as units. It happens at times that two half-its will decide to form a new unit. Or one might go out to Fairbanks and come back with someone new. The country is not without its citadels of righteousness, wherein certain burghers seem to look with disdain upon what they refer to as "river people's morals." They have possibly forgotten that this river is not the St. Mary, the Ste. Anne, the St. Croix, and does not flow uphill or in any sense suggest detachment from the functions of the earth. In their disdain, they overlook tradition. Beside the Yukon, a young woman of indisputable appeal once presented herself to a saloonful of miners and auctioned herself to the highest bidder. She offered fair terms. If she were to back out at any time within six months, he would get a complete refund. If he backed out, she would keep the money. All right, now, get up your pokes, boys. Who's the first bidder? There were bidders enough, and she brought down the gavel for a pretty sum. So far as is known, she stayed with the winner forever.

When people seeking gold first came across the high southeastern passes to the headwater lakes of the river, they hewed boats out of the forest and took them down the Yukon in small, inexperienced navies. One young wife fell out of a boat and appeared on her way to drowning. She thrashed and bobbed and went under at least twice, while her husband anxiously watched. At length, another man in another boat saved her. When her husband rowed over to pick her up, she demanded instead her duffel. Then and there, she formed a new unit.

Tuesday, Oct 14. 21° . . . Walked through the spruce and hit the Kandik about 1½ miles up. It's pretty well froze in places. A guy couldn't even line a canoe up for the ice. . . . Still no ice on the Yukon . . . I only been wearing longhandles and a wool shirt and I've been sweating at times.

Wednesday, Oct 15. 28°. Sunny. Prettyful.

Thursday, October 16. Fred came down yesterday, left a dog here overnight, and said that some people on the river will be meeting for the spring equinox at Nation (the old Taylor place).

Sun Oct 19 . . . Beaver is one of the best tasting meats I've ever had—fatty and kinda naturally sweet. I got the castors and am soaking the oil glands in water for scent.

Sun Oct 26. 20°. Windy. Still snowing. About 6-8 inches on the level. This morning big sheets of ice were flowing on the sides of the river, and by now (11:45 A.M.) there is ICE all the way ACROST. BIG sheets 40–50 ft long and they just keep packin' together, fusing to the sides (banks) or just keep flowing downstream, quite a site.

Brad Snow said that if the canoe were to tip over, it would have to be abandoned, because the river, even now, in June, was too cold to allow the usual procedure of staying with the boat and kicking it to shore. "Keep your clothes on in the river. They provide some insulation, and you will need them later on. It's a good idea to have some matches tucked away in a dry container. We would need a drying fire." With luck, and fair probability, the canoe would go into an eddy, he said, and might be recovered there.

Nothing much was going to turn us over, though. Only at one or two points in a hundred and sixty miles did we see anything that remotely suggested rapids, and these were mere drapefolds of white in the otherwise broad, flat river. Sleepers were in the water—big logs flushing down out of Canada and floating beneath the surface—but they were going in our direction and were much less dangerous than they would have been had we been heading upstream. The great power of the Yukon—six and more fathoms of water, sometimes half a mile wide, moving at seven knots—was unostentatiously displayed. The surface was deceptively calm—it was only when you looked to the side that you saw how fast you were flying.

From the hull, meanwhile, came the steady sound of sandpaper, of sliding stones, of rain on a metal roof—the sound of the rock in the river, put there by alpine glaciers. Dip a cupful of water and the powdered rock settled quickly to the bottom. At the height of the melting season, something near two hundred tons of solid material will flow past a given point on the riverbank in one minute. Bubbling boils, like the tops of high fountains, bloomed everywhere on the surface but did not rough it up enough to make any sort of threat to the canoe. They stemmed from the crash of fast water on boulders and ledges far below. Bend to bend, the river presented itself in large segments—two, three, six miles at a stretch, now smooth, now capped white under the nervously changeable sky. We picked our way through flights of wooded islands. We shivered in the deep shadows of bluffs a thousand feet high—Calico Bluff, Montauk Bluff, Biederman Bluff, Takoma Bluff—which day after day intermittently walled the river. Between them—in downpourings of sunshine, as often as not—long vistas reached back across spruce-forested hills to the rough gray faces and freshly whitened summits of mountains. Some of the walls of the bluffs were of dark igneous rock that had cracked into bricks and appeared to have been set there by masons. Calico Bluff—a sedimentary fudge, folded, convoluted in whorls and ampersands—was black and white and yellow-tan. Up close it smelled of oil. It was sombre as we passed it, standing in its own shadow. Peregrine falcons nest there, and—fantastic fliers—will come over the Yukon at ballistic speeds, clench their talons, tuck them in, and strike a flying duck hard enough (in the neck) to kill it in midair. End over end the duck falls, and the falcon catches it before it hits the river. As we passed the mouth of the Tatonduk, fifteen ducks flew directly over us. Brad Snow reached for his shotgun, and quickly fired twice. Fifteen ducks went up the Tatonduk. Above the Nation, steep burgundy mountainsides reached up from the bright-green edges of the river, then fell away before tiers of higher mountains, dark with spruce and pale with aspen, quilted with sunlight and shadow. Ahead, long points of land and descending ridgelines reached toward one another into the immensity of the river, roughed now under a stiff wind. Filmy downspouts dropped from the clouds. Behind the next bend, five miles away, a mountain was partly covered with sliding mist. The scene resembled Lake Maggiore and might have been the Hardanger Fjord, but it was just a fragment of this river, an emphatic implication of all the two thousand miles, and of the dozens of tributaries that in themselves were major rivers—proof and reminder that with its rampart bluffs and circumvallate mountains it was not only a great river of the far northwestern continent but a river of preëminence among the rivers of the world. The ring of its name gave nothing away to the name of any river. Sunlight was bright on the mountains to both sides, and a driving summer rain came up the middle. The wind tore up the waves and flung pieces of them through the air. It was not the wind, though, but the river itself that took the breath away.

> Mon Oct 27. Good morning, Sara! 6° . . . The water froze in the water buckets and I slept good. . . . The river is really flowin' a lot of ice, but it is still moving—ripping and tearing at the shelf ice on the banks.
>
> Wed Oct 29. −20° this morning, clear as a church bell and feels good. Got a ruffed grouse and a squirrel yesterday, also set some rabbit snares.

Rain gone, and in sun again we could hear the consumption of an island. Large pieces of the bank fell thunderously into the water, because the Yukon had decided to yaw. We passed a deep fresh indentation in the shore where a dozen tall spruce had plopped at once. They were sixty-foot trees, and so much of the ground that held them had fallen with them that they now stood almost vertically in thirty feet of river. Ordinarily, as a river works its way into cut-bank soil the trees of the bank gradually lose their balance and become "sweepers"—their trunks slanting downward, their branches spread into the water. The islands of the Yukon have so many sweepers that from a distance they look like triremes. The river roars through the crowns of the trees with a sound of heavy rapids.

> Fri Oct 31. −32° & clear. Thank God for wood!
>
> Sat Nov 1. −33°. It sure got to cracking and buckin' last night. She is really still out this morning. It took 8 days to freeze since the ice started flowing. The Yukon is froze solid.

Often, after the general freeze-up, there is a lead in the left-bank bend beside Eagle—the current keeping open a patch of river long after the rest is ice. It can stay open for more than two months. A cold snap—reaching, say, seventy below zero—will finally close it.

Barney Hansen, who came into the country fifty years ago to mine gold, says he once watched a file of thirteen caribou pick their way down Eagle Bluff to drown in the river lead. The bluff approaches sheer, and its face is rough with crags and ledges and plunging tight ravines. Slowly, surely, the thirteen creatures descended, almost every move a feat of balance and decision. Poised there, each avoiding a fall to destruction, they gave Hansen and whoever else may have been watching plenty of time to wonder why they had chosen that route. They could readily have swung wide of both the town and the bluff. Finally, they reached the ice and started across the river. Everywhere around the lead, the ice was solid to the farther shore. Yet the thirteen caribou one after another jumped into the open water. The current drew them to the downstream end, where it sucked them under the ice.

In May, when big floes begin to move downriver like ships, caribou have been observed upon them. Caught crossing the river when the ice moved, they now stand in huddled helplessness, riding to certain death as the support beneath them crashes, cracks, diminishes in size, and ultimately rolls over.

Sun Nov 2. −35° ... Beautiful, clear day. Still no moose sign. Lots of overflow on the Yukon. I set out some traps and snares tonight, feels good to be runnin through the woods lookin for them little critters.

Mon Nov 3. −38°. Still and clear.

Wed Nov 5. −31°, still clear and I still love Sara a bunch. Today is woodchoppin day, so I et 3 lbs. of taters, a pound of spam, and a gallon of coffee. I'm not full, but it'll have to do.

Thur Nov 6. −30° ... Seen a fresh cat track today where the lynx had bedded down right beside a rabbit run. Twice he had picked himself a good spot to lay in readiness for a meal.

Sun Nov 9. −24°. Reset some traps. Got a lynx comin to one of 'em. Put some squirrels in a couple for marten bait. Did a lot of snowshoeing & breakin trail and am tuckered out.

Mon Nov 10. −12° cloudy and may snow. Today is the anniversary of being in Alaska for exactly one year now. Quite a lot has happened and if I had Sara now it would be the end of a near perfect year. Still, it was the best decision I ever did make, and am very glad things worked out. If I was religious, I might say, "Thank you, Lord." Amen.

Approaching the mouth of the Kandik, Snow and I maneuvered among shoals and heavy driftwood in an attempt to get to shore, going in for an assessive look at our friend Sarge Waller's cabin. We went up the bank. Snow gave the cabin a long, professional sniff—a construction worker's frank inspection. "This," he said finally—and paused a moment to mortise the words—"this is the most poorly built cabin you ever will see." The walls were convex. The foundation was not banked. The roof was virtually without insulation. The corners were mail slots for the wind. The loose sheets of Corazza's journal were held by a metal clip hanging on a wall. I took them down and riffled through them.

The journal was roughly four thousand words. (Only fragments are here.) The author's name was nowhere on it so far as I could see. It had been left in an empty cabin, in near-absolute wilderness, on land that belonged to the people of the United States, of whom I was one. If ever a piece of writing was born in the public domain, surely this was it. Yes—but it seemed private. It wasn't like food in a cache, to take and later replace. I returned it to the wall.

A few weeks later, I was sitting in the roadhouse in Central talking with a man who was down from the mining claims on Porcupine Creek. He was young, dark-haired, strongly built. Like most bush Alaskans, however new to the bush they might be, he had greeting in his face. In the course of a second beer, he mentioned that he had spent the winter in a cabin near the mouth of the Kandik.

I surprised him by telling him I had glanced at his journal, and had wished I could someday read it. He said he had a little time off and had been thinking of going up there anyway; he would see me again in a few days. He went eighty miles up the river and brought back the journal.

> Wed Nov 12. −3° cloudy & snowing. Molly of the North, great Alaskan cat hound, says she likes this turn in the weather. She has put on considerable weight and looks real strong.
>
> Saw a gyrfalcon today. Flew right over my head clippin along at a pace so fast it sounded like a jet. Almost white bird. Could have been a female, it was pretty good size. Also saw a bird killed hare yesterday near the cabin. Bet it's that gyr's meal. This country is neat.

We carried mail with us downriver, and now and again Brad would, in effect, toss it into the woods. There were people in there who would read it. The names on the packages and envelopes were not familiar to me. Snow said, "There are those on the river who are discreet and those who are not. People like Dick Cook and Charlie Edwards need to talk and be chatty in Eagle. Others come into town rarely, say nothing much, and leave."

We stopped one morning in a hidden slough with letters for Jan Waldron. She was slender, lankily built, with long blond hair, a quick and friendly smile. She ran down the bank and fairly jumped into the canoe. "Gosh, it's so good to see you." Her husband, Seymour Abel, had been away many days. Their home was a wall tent on supporting courses of logs, with a door that was more like a window. We crawled in. She and Seymour were just camping in this tent, she explained, and opened some beer she had brewed there. She pointed proudly to a cavity in the earth at her feet. To surprise and please Seymour, she had passed the time removing a stump. I remembered meeting Seymour, briefly, in Eagle, where we had talked about bears, and the pros and cons of carrying a protective gun. "If you're going to get et, you're going to get et," he had said, conclusively, and, repeating himself, "If you're going to get et, you're going to get et, whether you have a rifle or not." Seymour came into the country from Tennessee. Jan is a born Alaskan. "I'm so glad to see you," she said again, and opened another beer. The top of the tent was lined with Styrofoam. In the gable was a shelf of books. There was a plank table, a Singer sewing machine, a banjo, a guitar, a violin. There was a barrel stove. The chimney, where it poked through the tent, was flashed with a two-gallon can. Dark-haired sled dogs were staked outside. A day or so before, they had raised a great clamor. To Jan, it signalled the nearness of a bear. Carrying clothes for washing to a small clear stream, she took along a gun because of the bear. "Are you sure you have to go?" she said as we stood up. "It's so good to see you. Why go?"

Around the turn of the century, when dog teams travelled more frequently on the river, there was an isolated roadhouse not far from where Jan lives now. The woman who ran it would shoot at people who tried to go by without stopping.

Fri Nov 14. −28°. Clear. I have become pretty well used to the cold now and can get a roarin fire going awful quick these days. Caught a hare and one beautiful red fox today. The fox had been caught in a trail-set about a mile from where I crossed his tracks. She had broken the wire I had tied to the trap chain. I followed her to the river and then ran up to within shooting distance. She was moving pretty good with a #3 double spring on her front paw. I shot her right below the eye at 100 ft. with the pistol (Ruger). She sure is pretty and would make Sara a nice hat.

Sun Nov 16. *Full moon,* and the Yukon is in party dress. Everything is lit up just prettiful. . . . I jumped a bunch of grouse (ruffed) roosting. Got 5 with the pistol and about 18 shots. Could have got more but I run plumb out of shells. I sure do love that grouse meat.

The moon cycle is funny up here. It starts waxing in a small arc through the southern sky, then day by day it gets brighter and the arc gets higher and longer till it's full moon almost overhead and stay light all night. Just magnificent!

2 of them grouse I got at 40 yds with that little Ruger (makes a guy proud). Wish Sara would fix em up for us.

We passed fish camps all down the river, for the most part established by Indians and abandoned now—places that once netted as much as thirty tons of salmon a year. At one fish camp stood the biggest cache I have seen in Alaska, virtually a full-size cabin in the air, resting on columnar stilts. All it contained was a beaver's forepaw.

> Tues Nov 18. −22°. The other day when I got them grouse, a funny thing happened. The last grouse was perched in the top of an alder about 30 ft high. I shot at it twice from about 35 yds and thought I'd missed it. But it stayed up there. I snuck up to about 20 yds from it and emptied the pistol. It still sat there. It was gettin dark and I was out of shells. I figured that that grouse wouldn't be a meal for me. Then all of a sudden I got MAD, went over to the tree, shook it, and yelled, "Get outa there you son of a bitch." Well, down comes a blanket of snow on my head—but also Mister Grouse, who is only winged. He scooted along the ground for awhile and then just disappeared! By God, he was gone just like that. Then I flashed to a memory that Dad had told me a story of a grouse he had winged and the dog pointed at a bunch of leaves. Finally he seen a feather stickin out of the leaves, took off his hat and caught him a grouse in it. Well, I seen where he last was and used my mitten (it was 20 below and didn't want to take off my hat) to clamp down on the snow and by Jesus if I didn't come up with another supper in my hands. Made me laugh just a bit to think that my anger had been changed so fast into a memory. Had some grouse gumbo last night. Ummm!
>
> The brilliance of this north country under the full moon is dazzling to say the least. At midnight the sky is still a deep blue with the twinkling of many bright stars. Moon shadows of the tall spruce are everywhere and the Yukon River lays quiet and white. This moon seems to stand guard on this country.

There has long been talk of a tourist road connecting Eagle and Circle. Running for the most part beside the river, it would "open up" what is generally regarded as the handsomest stretch of the Yukon in Alaska. The longest piece of road along the Yukon now runs three miles upriver from Eagle to Eagle Indian Village. On the river near that road, I have paddled more than once in dust that was thicker than smoke.

> Mon Nov 24. −6°. Plan to go upriver.
>
> Tues Nov 25. −4°. On the way up, Bob's lead dog got caught in one of Fred's Conibears. Boy it was a mad scramble for Bob and I to get to the front of 9 dogs and prise the jaws apart on that trap. The dog acted like nothing had

ever happened and went right on again. Could have been tragic but it turned out funny. . . . Found out that Thanksgiving is on the 27th. . . . It was fun to run them 9 dogs all strung out single. Bob and I took turns as it was a rough run over the muskeg and the sled was loaded heavy (probably 500 lbs +). It tipped over 5 or 6 times but things went smooth. Both of us were wore plumb out. . . . I fell through the ice 2 or 3 times yesterday, & ran around with wet pacs. Feels like I frosted the ends of my big toes a bit, but they're far from my heart, so I'll keep on truckin.

We stopped one night at an abandoned cabin, containing so much clutter of junk debris that we decided to sleep outside. Mosquitoes were dense there but tolerable—not yet coming in clouds. In the Yukon Flats, beyond the mountains, were thirty-six thousand lakes and ponds, with geese, canvasbacks, scaup, cranes, swans, teal, and widgeons in millions, and mosquitoes in numbers a physicist would understand. But we were still upriver, and only five or six thousand of them were now close around us. I asked Brad if he would like to share my netted tent. Inside it moments later, he told me how his wife plays what she calls Revenge. In the security of a tent, she places near the netting an example of her flesh until it drives to frenzy the singers in the night. A truly ambitious mosquito will soon thrust its proboscis through the net. She then seizes the proboscis and yanks the bugger inside. For my part, I mentioned that when mosquitoes seek human blood they are fulfilling their sexual cycle, doing what nature is instructing them to do, and therefore an authentic conservationist will never react unfavorably to the attentions of a mosquito. This simple test—a way of telling the phonies from the truly committed—I had first come upon long ago in the Lower Forty-eight. Gradually in Alaska, however, I had come to realize that an Alaska mosquito is not a Lower Forty-eight mosquito that has moved north. Before getting into the tent, I had slapped my leg, turned the palm up, and counted seventeen corpses in my hand.

Sat Dec 13 . . . The weather has been −50° or lower (−60° was the lowest) for 12 days but this morning the wind started blowing and the weather warmed up some 40° to −8. I ran the dogs down across the river to get a load of fish yesterday. Saw fresh moose sign and Errol & I spent all day today hunting. Lots of sign but no luck. I haven't checked my line since the new moon and it's already past half. Tomorrow will be the day. There seems to be more cat around since it got cold.

Sun Dec 21 . . . Errol and I were hunting cause the 2 moose were staying in this area. Errol ran into them and got us both of them, by God! We eatin high nowadays. Moose liver and steak for breakfast. Hmm! We had a real chinook for a few days and the temp went up to 39° above. Couldn't believe it.

Mon Dec 22. Zero. Oboy! Biscuits gravy & moose steak this fine day. Yepper, sure wish Sara were back home where she belongs.

Tues Dec 23. Zero and clear . . . Made a few more cat sets today in the slough. Missed a cat in one of my cubbies.

A "cat" is a lynx. A "lynk" is also a lynx. Nine times out of ten, people who say "lynk" are trying to sound like trappers.

Mon Dec 29. +15° . . . Walked up to 3 Mile today with Molly on a lead rope (she was leading me). We didn't hit a fresh track till after dark on the way back. She struck out on the cat's trail but didn't run it very far, it was in thick alders. She sure wanted to though.

Jan 7. −40°. I've had some bad luck. Molly run off about 3 days ago at 25 below. I could hear her howling bloody murder from the cabin here. I'd just got a fire started after a 6 mile hike down river. Well, I figured, she got herself in a trap, so I went to looking for her. Found her 3 hours later, almost to Errol's cabin with her right front paw in a number 4 doublespring. It was frozen solid. My lantern had run out of fuel and there was no moon. We ran to Errol's cabin where I soaked her paw in lukewarm water for about an hour. It swelled plumb up as big as a cat track, but today it started to blister and I think it may heal. The swelling's gone down a bit. Poor ole Molly Blue!

Jan 8. −40°. Red is the color of my barrel stove when it's 40° below, when it's 40° below! A bit nippy these last few days, but it's nice to set by a roarin stove.

Snow and I lingered at the mouths of tributary streams, and went miles up the Charley, the river of Leon Crane. Logs cruised toward us like alligators, and with the same stately glide. We surprised ravens, geese, a bald eagle, which lumbered into flight. It slowly achieved altitude, its wings barely recovering from flap to awkward flap. Peregrines, which nest on bluffs above the Charley, can pin down one of these eagles and keep it where it is indefinitely—the falcons diving, pecking, strafing, dominating, while the symbol of national grandeur cowers on the ground, a screaming eagle. After nine or ten miles, the Charley, with riffles, increased its gradient rise, and the immense, confining forest began to open to big, long-distance views. Far up the corridor of the river were white-patched mountains, and far behind them more and higher mountains totally covered with newly fallen snow. We tied up in an island slough and climbed the steep face of a bluff—loose, flaky shale; no trees; not much to hang on to—and when we had worked our way upward five hundred vertical feet I looked back at what seemed a straight plunge to the river. It was a bluff of swallows and lupine, blueberries and bears. We saw only sign of the bears. Brad was carrying his rifle. He remarked that his friend David Evans, who has been in the country about as long as he has, apparently rejoices in a nearly perfect state of "anestrophic anticipation." Asked to explain what that is, Snow said, "You have no sense of catastrophe. You walk through the valley of the shadow of death and you fear no evil—not because you are fearless but because you have no awareness of what may happen. David walks miles and miles, unarmed, and doesn't seem to understand that there's a chance of being mauled."

We sat down and ate berries, looking up frequently at many hundreds of square miles of dark broadloom forests curling at the edges into rising tundra fells, which ended in mountain rock. Through the mountains came the clear river, often deep within its peregrine bluffs, which were pinpointed white with visible Dall sheep and darkened by invisible bears. It was landscape uncompromised, under small white cumulus by the tens of dozens evenly spaced to the corners of the sky. I remembered Frank Warren, in Circle, talking about the Park Service's yen for the Charley, and saying, "What can you do to improve an area that is perfect? What possible satisfaction could a hiker ever get walking on a man-made trail?" We descended the bluff and descended the stream, stopping at the cabin built by Al Ames, where the government had posted a sign beside the door forbidding habitation.

We drifted down the Yukon through a windless afternoon. The fast-flowing water was placid and—with its ring boils—resembled antique glass. Down one long straightaway, framed in white mountains, we saw ten full miles to the wall of the coming bend.

> Fri Feb 6. Been traveling this ole Yukon from Sam Creek (at times to Coal Creek) all the way to 20 miles this side of Eagle. Not much cat sign anywhere . . . Molly is healed up pretty good.
>
> Sat Feb 7. −37° before sunrise, now an hour later it's −40° and droppin fast, looks like another snapper! Beautiful light show last night . . . Sara, where are you?

A Journey to the Woods

SUSANNAH MOODIE

Roughing It in the Bush, Susannah Moodie's account of the challenges she faced raising her family in the remoteness of Upper Canada in 1832, has become a classic in emigrant-traveler literature. This passage suggests the immense courage she needed to make a new life deep in the northern forests.

*I*T was a bright frosty morning when I bade adieu to the farm, the birthplace of my little Agnes, who, nestled beneath my cloak, was sweetly sleeping on my knee, unconscious of the long journey before us into the wilderness. The sun had not as yet risen. Anxious to get to our place of destination before dark, we started as early as we could. Our own fine team had been sold the day before for forty pounds; and one of our neighbours, a Mr. D—, was to convey us and our household goods to Douro for the sum of twenty dollars. During the week he had made several journeys, with furniture and stores; and all that now remained was to be conveyed to the woods in two large lumber-sleighs, one driven by himself, the other by a younger brother.

It was not without regret that I left Melsetter, for so my husband had called the place, after his father's estate in Orkney. It was a beautiful, picturesque spot; and, in spite of the evil neighbourhood, I had learned to love it; indeed, it was much against my wish that it was sold. I had a great dislike to removing, which involves a necessary loss, and is apt to give to the emigrant roving and unsettled habits. But all regrets were now useless; and happily unconscious of the life of toil and anxiety that awaited us in those dreadful woods, I tried my best to be cheerful, and to regard the future with a hopeful eye.

Our driver was a shrewd, clever man, for his opportunities. He took charge of the living cargo, which consisted of my husband, our maid-servant, the two little children, and myself—besides a large hamper, full of poultry—a dog, and a cat. The lordly sultan of the imprisoned seraglio thought fit to conduct himself in a very eccentric manner, for at every barn-yard we happened to pass, he clapped his wings, and crowed so long and loud that it afforded great amusement to the whole party, and doubtless was very edifying to the poor hens, who lay huddled together as mute as mice.

"That 'ere rooster thinks he's on the top of the heap," said our driver, laughing. "I guess he's not used to travelling in a close conveyance. Listen! How all the crowers in the neighbourhood give him back a note of defiance! But he knows that he's safe enough at the bottom of the basket."

The day was so bright for the time of year (the first week in February), that we suffered no inconvenience from the cold. Little Katie was enchanted with the jingling of the sleigh-bells, and, nestled among the packages, kept singing or talking to the horses in her baby lingo. Trifling as these little incidents were, before we had proceeded ten miles on our long journey, they revived my drooping spirits, and I began to feel a lively interest in the scenes through which we were passing.

The first twenty miles of the way was over a hilly and well-cleared country; and as in winter the deep snow fills up the inequalities, and makes all roads alike, we glided as swiftly and steadily along as if they had been the best highways in the world. Anon, the clearings began to diminish, and tall woods arose on either side of the path; their solemn aspect, and the deep silence that brooded over their vast solitudes, inspiring the mind with a strange awe. Not a breath of wind stirred the leafless branches, whose huge shadows reflected upon the dazzling white covering of snow, lay so perfectly still, that it seemed as if Nature had suspended her operations, that life and motion had ceased, and that she was sleeping in her winding-sheet, upon the bier of death.

"I guess you will find the woods pretty lonesome," said our driver, whose thoughts had been evidently employed on the same subject as our own. "We were once in the woods, but emigration has stepped a-head of us, and made our'n a cleared part of the country. When I was a boy, all this country, for thirty miles on every side of us, was bush land. As to Peterborough, the place was unknown; not a settler had ever passed through the great swamp, and some of them believed that it was the end of the world."

"What swamp is that?" asked I.

"Oh, the great Cavan swamp. We are just two miles from it; and I tell you that the horses will need a good rest, and ourselves a good dinner, by the time we are through it. Ah! Mrs. Moodie, if ever you travel that way in summer, you will know something about corduroy roads. I was 'most jolted to death last fall; I thought it would have been no bad notion to have insured my teeth before I left C—. I really expected that they would have been shook out of my head before we had done manœuvring over the big logs."

"How will my crockery stand it in the next sleigh?" quoth I. "If the road is such as you describe, I am afraid that I shall not bring a whole plate to Douro."

"Oh! the snow is a great leveller—it makes all rough places smooth. But with regard to this swamp, I have something to tell you. About ten years ago, no one had ever seen the other side of it; and if pigs or cattle strayed away into it, they fell a prey to the wolves and bears, and were seldom recovered.

"An old Scotch emigrant, who had located himself on this side of it, so often lost his beasts that he determined during the summer season to try and explore the place, and see if there were any end to it. So he takes an axe on his shoulder, and a bag of provisions for a week, not forgetting a flask of whiskey, and off he starts all alone, and tells his wife that if he never returned, she and little Jock must try and carry on the farm without him; but he was determined to see the end of the swamp, even if it led to the other world. He fell upon a fresh cattle-track, which he followed all that day; and towards night he found himself in the heart of a tangled wilderness of bushes, and himself half eaten up with mosquitoes and black-flies. He was more than tempted to give in, and return home by the first glimpse of light.

"The Scotch are a tough people; they are not easily daunted—a few difficulties only seem to make them more eager to get on; and he felt ashamed the next moment, as he told me, of giving up. So he finds a large thick cedar-tree for his bed, climbs up, and coiling himself among the branches like a bear, he was soon fast asleep.

"The next morning, by daylight, he continued his journey, not forgetting to blaze with his axe the trees to the right and left as he went along. The ground was so spongy and wet that at every step he plunged up to his knees in water, but he seemed no nearer the end of the swamp than he had been the day before. He saw several deer, a raccoon, and a ground-hog, during his walk, but was unmolested by bears or wolves. Having passed through several creeks, and killed a great many snakes, he felt so weary towards the close of the second day that he determined to go home the next morning. But just as he began to think his search was fruitless he observed that the cedars and tamaracks which had obstructed his path became less numerous, and were succeeded by bass and soft maple. The ground, also, became less moist, and he was soon ascending a rising slope, covered with oak and beech, which shaded land of the very best quality. The old man was now fully convinced that he had cleared the great swamp; and that, instead of leading to the other world, it had conducted him to a country that would yield the very best returns for cultivation. His favourable report led to the formation of the road that we are about to cross, and to the settlement of Peterborough, which is one of the most promising new settlements in this district, and is surrounded by a splendid back country."

We were descending a very steep hill, and encountered an ox-sleigh, which was crawling slowly up it in a contrary direction. Three people were seated at the bottom of the vehicle upon straw, which made a cheap substitute for buffalo robes. Perched, as we were, upon the crown of the height, we looked completely down into the sleigh, and during the whole course of my life I never saw three uglier mortals collected into such a narrow space. The man was blear-eyed, with a hare-lip, through which protruded two dreadful yellow teeth that resembled the tusks of a boar. The woman was long-faced, high cheekboned, red-haired, and freckled all over like a toad. The boy resembled his hideous mother, but with the addition of a villainous obliquity of vision which rendered him the most disgusting object in this singular trio.

As we passed them, our driver gave a knowing nod to my husband, directing, at the same time, the most quizzical glance towards the strangers, as he exclaimed, "We are in luck, sir! I think that 'ere sleigh may be called Beauty's egg-basket!"

We made ourselves very merry at the poor people's expense, and Mr. D—, with his odd stories and Yankeefied expressions, amused the tedium of our progress through the great swamp, which in summer presents for several miles one uniform bridge of rough and unequal logs, all laid loosely across huge sleepers, so that they jump up and down, when pressed by the wheels, like the keys of a piano. The rough motion and jolting occasioned by this collision is so distressing that it never fails to entail upon the traveller sore bones and an aching head for the rest of the day. The path is so narrow over these logs that two waggons cannot pass without great difficulty, which is rendered more dangerous by the deep natural ditches on either side of the bridge, formed by broad creeks that flow out of the swamp, and often terminate in mud-holes of very ominous dimensions. The snow, however, hid from us all the ugly features of the road, and Mr. D— steered us through in perfect safety, and landed us at the door of a little log house which crowned the steep hill on the other side of the swamp, and which he dignified with the name of a tavern.

It was now two o'clock. We had been on the road since seven; and men, women, and children were all ready for the good dinner that Mr. D— had promised us at this splendid house of entertainment, where we were destined to stay for two hours, to refresh ourselves and rest the horses.

"Well, Mrs. J—, what have you got for our dinner?" said our driver, after he had seen to the accommodation of his teams.

"Pritters and pork, sir. Nothing else to be had in the woods. Thank God, we have enough of that!"

D— shrugged up his shoulders, and looked at us.

"We've plenty of that same at home. But hunger's good sauce. Come, be spry, widow, and see about it for I am very hungry."

I inquired for a private room for myself and the children, but there were no private rooms in the house. The apartment we occupied was like the cobbler's stall in the old song, and I was obliged to attend upon them in public.

"You have much to learn, ma'am, if you are going to the woods," said Mrs. J—.

"To unlearn, you mean," said Mr. D—. "To tell you the truth, Mrs. Moodie, ladies and gentlemen have no business in the woods. Eddication spoils man or woman for that location. So, widow (turning to our hostess), you are not tired of living alone yet?"

"No, sir; I have no wish for a second husband. I had enough of the first. I like to have my own way—to lie down mistress, and get up master."

"You don't like to be put out of your *old* way," returned he, with a mischievous glance.

She coloured very red; but it might be the heat of the fire over which she was frying the pork for our dinner.

I was very hungry, but I felt no appetite for the dish she was preparing for us. It proved salt, hard, and unsavoury.

D— pronounced it very bad, and the whiskey still worse, with which he washed it down.

I asked for a cup of tea and a slice of bread. But they were out of tea, and the hop-rising had failed, and there was no bread in the house. For this disgusting meal we paid at the rate of a quarter of a dollar a-head.

I was glad when the horses being again put to, we escaped from the rank odour of the fried pork, and were once more in the fresh air.

"Well, mister; did not you grudge your money for that bad meat?" said D—, when we were once more seated in the sleigh. "But in these parts, the worse the fare the higher the charge."

"I would not have cared," said I, "if I could have got a cup of tea."

"Tea! it's poor trash. I never could drink tea in my life. But I like coffee, when 'tis boiled till it's quite black. But coffee is not good without plenty of trimmings."

"What do you mean by trimmings?"

He laughed. "Good sugar, and sweet cream. Coffee is not worth drinking without trimmings."

Often in after years have I recalled the coffee trimmings, when endeavouring to drink the vile stuff which goes by the name of coffee in the houses of entertainment in the country.

We had now passed through the narrow strip of clearing which surrounded the tavern, and again entered upon the woods. It was near sunset, and we were rapidly descending a steep hill, when one of the traces that held our sleigh suddenly broke. D— pulled up in order to repair the damage. His brother's team was close behind, and our unexpected stand-still brought the horses upon us before J. D— could stop them. I received so violent a blow from the head of one of them, just in the back of the neck, that for a few minutes I was stunned and insensible. When I recovered, I was supported in the arms of my husband, over whose knees I was leaning, and D— was rubbing my hands and temples with snow.

"There, Mr. Moodie, she's coming-to. I thought she was killed. I have seen a man before now killed by a blow from a horse's head in the like manner." As soon as we could, we resumed our places in the sleigh; but all enjoyment of our journey, had it been otherwise possible, was gone.

When we reached Peterborough, Moodie wished us to remain at the inn all night, as we had still eleven miles of our journey to perform, and that through a blazed forest-road, little travelled, and very much impeded by fallen trees and other obstacles; but D— was anxious to get back as soon as possible to his own home, and he urged us very pathetically to proceed.

The moon arose during our stay at the inn, and gleamed upon the straggling frame-houses which then formed the now populous and thriving town of Peterborough. We crossed the wild, rushing, beautiful Otonabee river by a rude bridge, and soon found ourselves journeying over the plains or level heights beyond the village, which were thinly wooded with picturesque groups of oak and pine, and very much resembled a gentleman's park at home.

Far below, to our right (for we were upon the Smith-town side) we heard the rushing of the river, whose rapid waters never receive curb from the iron chain of winter. Even while the rocky banks are coated with ice, and the frost-king suspends from every twig and branch the most beautiful and fantastic crystals, the black waters rush foaming along, a thick steam rising constantly above the rapids, as from a boiling pot. The shores vibrate and tremble beneath the force of the impetuous flood, as it whirls round cedar-crowned islands and opposing rocks, and hurries on to pour its tribute into the Rice Lake, to swell the calm, majestic grandeur of the Trent, till its waters are lost in the beautiful bay of Quinté, and finally merged in the blue ocean of Ontario.

The most renowned of our English rivers dwindle into little muddy rills when compared with the sublimity of the Canadian waters. No language can adequately express the solemn grandeur of her lake and river scenery; the glorious islands that float, like visions from fairy land, upon the bosom of these azure mirrors of her cloudless skies. No dreary breadth of marshes, covered with flags, hide from our gaze the expanse of heaven-tinted waters; no foul mudbanks spread their unwholesome exhalations around. The rocky shores are crowned with the cedar, the birch, the alder, and soft maple, that dip their long tresses in the pure stream; from every crevice in the limestone the harebell and Canadian rose wave their graceful blossoms.

The fiercest droughts of summer may diminish the volume and power of these romantic streams, but it never leaves their rocky channels bare, nor checks the mournful music of their dancing waves.

Through the openings in the forest, we now and then caught the silver gleam of the river tumbling on in moonlight splendour, while the hoarse chiding of the wind in the lofty pines above us gave a fitting response to the melancholy cadence of the waters.

   The children had fallen asleep. A deep silence pervaded the party. Night was above us with her mysterious stars. The ancient forest stretched around us on every side, and a foreboding sadness sunk upon my heart. Memory was busy with the events of many years. I retraced step by step the pilgrimage of my past life, until arriving at that passage in its sombre history, I gazed through tears upon the singularly savage scene around me, and secretly marvelled, "What brought me here?"

   "Providence," was the answer which the soul gave. "Not for your own welfare, perhaps, but for the welfare of your children, the unerring hand of the Great Father has led you here. You form a connecting link in the destinies of many. It is impossible for any human creature to live for himself alone. It may be your lot to suffer, but others will reap a benefit from your trials. Look up with confidence to Heaven, and the sun of hope will yet shed a cheering beam through the forbidding depths of this tangled wilderness."

   The road now became so bad that Mr. D— was obliged to dismount, and lead his horses through the more intricate passages. The animals themselves, weary with their long journey and heavy load, proceeded at foot-fall. The moon, too, had deserted us, and the only light we had to guide us through the dim arches of the forest was from the snow and the stars, which now peered down upon us, through the leafless branches of the trees, with uncommon brilliancy.

Second Prize

JAN MORRIS

*The author visited the Canadian city of
Toronto during its sesquicentennial celebration,
yearning for "the old grandeur of the North,
its size and scale and power." She found that
Toronto is Toronto, with its own considered
reserve.*

Toronto, 1984

*A*S I waited for my bags at the airport carousel I considered the faces of my
fellow arrivals. They mostly looked very, very Canadian. Calm, dispassionate,
patiently they waited there, responding with only the faintest raising of eyebrows or clenching of gloved fingers to the loudspeaker's apology for the late
delivery of baggage owing to a technical fault, edging gently, almost apolo-
getically, inwards when they spotted their possessions emerging from the chute.
They looked in complete command of their emotions. They looked well fed, well
balanced, well behaved, well intentioned, well organized, and well preserved.
Sometimes they spoke to each other in polite monosyllables. Mostly they just
waited.

But like a wayward comet through these distinctly fixed stars there staggered
ever and again a very different figure: a middle-aged woman in a fur hat and a
long coat of faded blue, held together by a leather belt evidently inherited from
some earlier ensemble. She was burdened with many packages elaborately
stringed, wired and brown-papered, she had a sheaf of travel documents generally in her hands, sometimes between her teeth, and she never stopped moving,
talking, and gesticulating. If she was not hurling questions at those expression-
less bystanders in theatrically broken English, she was muttering to herself in
unknown tongues, or breaking into sarcastic laughter. Often she dropped
things; she got into a terrible mess trying to get a baggage cart out of its stack
("You—must—put—money—in—the—slot." "What is slot? How is carriage
coming? Slot? What is slot?"); and when at last she perceived her travelling
accoutrements—awful mounds of canvas and split leather—erupting on to the
conveyor, like a tank she forced a passage through the immobile Canadians,
toppling them left and right or barging them one into another with virtuoso
elbow-work.

No, I have not invented her—touched her up a little, perhaps, as I have
heightened the characteristics of the others, in the interests not so much of art as

of allegory. I don't know where she came from, whether she was in Canada to stay or merely to visit her favourite married nephew from the old country, but she represented for me the archetypal immigrant: and she was arriving at the emblematic immigrant destination of the late twentieth century, Toronto, whose citizens are certainly not all quite so self-restrained as those passengers at the airport, but which is nevertheless one of the most highly disciplined and tightly organized cities of the Western world.

I watched that first confrontation with sympathy for both sides: and though I lost sight of the lady as we passed through customs (I suspect she was involved in some fracas there, or could not undo the knots on her baggage), I often thought of her as we both of us entered Toronto the Good in its sesque—sesqua—sesqui—well, you know, its one hundred and fiftieth year of official existence.

There are moments when Toronto offers, at least in the fancy, the black and terrible excitements of immigration in the heyday of the New World. I woke up the very next morning to such a transient revelation. A lowering mist lay over the downtown city, masking the tops of the great buildings, chopping off the CN Tower like a monstrous tree trunk; and under the cloud the place seemed to be all a-steam with white vapours, spouting, streaming with the wind, or eddying upward to join the darkness above. Lights shone or flickered through the haze, the ground everywhere was white with snow, and the spectacle suggested to me some vast, marvellous, and fearful cauldron, where anything might happen, where villains and geniuses must walk, where immediate fortunes were surely to be made, where horribly exploited Montenegrin seamstresses probably lived in unspeakable slums, and towering manufacturers swaggered in huge fur coats out of gold-plated private railway cars.

The mist cleared, the cloud lifted, even the steam subsided as the first spring weather came, and it was not like that at all. Toronto has come late in life to cosmopolitanism—even when I was first here, in 1954, it seemed to me not much less homogeneous than Edinburgh, say—and as a haven of opportunity it is unassertive. No glorious dowager raises her torch over Lake Ontario, summoning those masses yearning to breathe free, and conversely there are no teeming slums or sweatshop ghettos, still less any passionate convictions about new earths and heavens. I heard no trumpet blast, no angel choirs perform, as I took the streetcar downtown.

The promise of Toronto, I presently realized, was promise of a more diffuse, tentative, not to say bewildering kind. On a modest building near the harbour-front I happened to notice the names of those entitled to parking space outside: D. Iannuzzi, P. Iannuzzi, H. McDonald, R. Metcalfe and F. Muhammad. "What is this place?" I inquired of people passing by. "Multicultural TV," they said, backing away nervously. "Multi-*what* TV?" I said, but they had escaped by then—I had yet to learn that nothing ends a Toronto conversation more quickly than a supplementary question.

Multiculturalism! I had never heard the word before, but I was certainly to hear it again, for it turned out to be the key word, so to speak, to contemporary Toronto. As ooh-la-la is to Paris, and *ciao* to Rome, and *nyet* to Moscow, and hey you're looking *great* to Manhattan, so multiculturalism is to Toronto. Far more than any other of the great migratory cities, Toronto is all things to all ethnicities. The melting-pot conception never was popular here, and sometimes I came to feel that Canadian nationality itself was no more than a minor social perquisite, like a driving licence or a spare pair of glasses. Repeatedly I was invited to try the Malaysian vermicelli at Rasa Sayang, the seafood pierogi at the Ukrainian Caravan, or something Vietnamese in Yorkville, but when I ventured to suggest one day that we might eat Canadian, a kindly anxiety crossed my host's brow. "That might be more difficult," he said.

A whole new civic ambience, it seems, has evolved to give some kind of unity to this determined centrifugalism—I never knew what a heritage language was either, until I came to Toronto—but I soon got used to it all. I hardly noticed the street names in Greek, or the crocodiles of schoolchildren made up half and half, it seemed, of East and West Indians. I was as shocked as the next Torontonian, three days into the city, to hear a judge tell a disgraced lawyer that he had betrayed not only the standards of his profession but also the trust of the Estonian community. I was not in the least surprised to see a picture of the Azores as a permanent backdrop for a Canadian TV newscast, or to find the ladies and gentlemen of the German club swaying across my screen in full authenticity of comic hats and Gemütlichkeit. "My son-in-law is Lithuanian," a very WASPish materfamilias remarked to me, but I did not bat an eyelid. "Only on his father's side, I suppose?" "Right, his mother's from Inverness."

But multiculturalism, I discovered, did not mean that Toronto was all brotherly love and folklore. On the contrary, wherever I went I heard talk of internecine rivalries, cross-ethnical vendettas, angry scenes at the Metro Guyanese political rally, competing varieties of pierogi, differing opinions about the Katyn massacre, heated debates over Estonian legitimacy, the Coptic succession, or the fate of the Armenians. There turned out to be a darkly conspiratorial side to multiculturalism. I have never been able to discover any of those writers' hangouts one is told of across the world, where the poets assemble over their beers; but in Toronto I felt one could easily stumble into cafés in which plotters organized distant coups, or swapped heavy anarchist reminiscences. (It costs only twelve dollars to broadcast a thirty-second announcement in Korean on

CHIN, Toronto's multilingual radio station: how much, I wondered, as a head-strong nationalist myself, for an inflammatory exhortation in Welsh?)

But actually, this is not the sort of fulfilment I myself wanted of Toronto. I am not very multicultural, and what I chiefly yearned for in this metropolis was the old grandeur of the North, its size and scale and power, its sense of wasteland majesty. Fortunately now and then I found it, in between the Afro-Indian takeaway, the Portuguese cultural centre, and the memorial to the eminent Ukrainian poet in High Park. Here are a few of the signs and symbols which, at intermittent moments, made me feel I was in the capital of the Ice Kingdom.

Names such as Etobicoke, Neepawa Avenue, Air Atonabee, or the terrifically evocative Department of the North.

Weekend breaks to go fishing in the frozen lake at Jackson's Point (All Huts Stove-Heated).

The sculpted reliefs on the walls of the Bay Street postal office, thrillingly depicting the state of the postal system from smoke-signals and an Indian-chased stage-coach to an Imperial Airway flying-boat and Locomotive 6400.

High-boned faces in the street, speaking to me of Cree or Ojibawa; "Raw and Dressed Skins" in a furrier's window, taking me to forests of fox and beaver.

The great gaunt shapes of the lake freighters at their quays, with huge trucks crawling here and there, and a tug crunching through the melting ice.

The fierce and stylish skating of young bloods on the Nathan Phillips rink, bolder, burlier, faster, and more arrogant than any other skaters anywhere.

And best of all, early one morning I went down to Union Station to watch the transcontinental train come in out of the darkness from Vancouver. Ah, Canada! I knew exactly what to expect of this experience, but still it stirred me: the hiss and rumble of it, the engineers princely in their high cab, the travel-grimed gleam of the sleeper cars, "Excelsior," "Ennishore"—the grey faces peering out of sleeper windows, the proud exhaustion of it all, and the thick tumble of the disembarking passengers, a blur of boots and lumberjackets and hoods and bundled children, clattering down the steps to breakfast, grandma, and Toronto, out of the limitless and magnificent hinterland.

These varied stimuli left me puzzled. What were the intentions of this city? On a wall of the Stock Exchange, downtown, there is a mural sculpture entitled "Workforce," by Robert Longo: and since it expresses nothing if not resolute purpose, I spent some time contemplating its significance.

Its eight figures, ranging from a stockbroker to what seems to be a female miner, do not look at all happy—the pursuit of happiness, after all, is not written into the Canadian constitution. Nor do they look exactly inspired by some visionary cause: it is true that the armed forces lady in the middle is disturbingly like a Soviet Intourist guide, but no particular ideology seems to be implied. They are marching determinedly, but joylessly, arm-in-arm, upon an undefined objective. Wealth? Fame? Security? The after-life? I could not decide. Just as, so Toronto itself has taught us, the medium can be the message, so it seemed that for the Stock Exchange workforce the movement was the destination.

Well, do cities have to have destinations? Perhaps not, but most of them do, if it is only a destination in the past, or in the ideal. Toronto seems to me, in time as in emotion, a limbo-city. It is not, like London, England, obsessed with its own history. It is not an act of faith, like Moscow or Manhattan. It has none of Rio's exuberant sense of young identity. It is neither brassily capitalist nor rigidly public sector. It looks forward to no millennium, back to no golden age. It is what it is, and the people in its streets, walking with that steady, tireless, infantrylike pace that is particular to this city, seem on the whole resigned, without either bitterness or exhilaration, to being just what they are.

Among the principal cities of the lost British Empire, Toronto has been one of the most casual (rather than the most ruthless) in discarding the physical remnants of its colonial past. In Sydney, in Melbourne, in Wellington, even in Cape Town, not to mention the cities of India, the imperial memorials remain inescapable, sometimes even dominant. In Toronto they are all but over-whelmed: a lumpish parliament, a university, a statue or two, a mock castle, a few dull buildings forlornly preserved, tea with cream cakes at the Windsor Arms, and on the face of things that's about it. Nobody could possibly mistake this for a British city now: it comes as a queer shock (and a degraded one, for a republican like me) to see the royal coat of arms still above the judge's bench in a Toronto court of law.

On the other hand there is no mistaking this for a city of the United States, either. If that lady at the airport thought she was entering, if only by the back door, the land of the free and the home of the brave, she would be taken aback by the temper of Toronto. Not only do Torontonians constantly snipe at all things American, but this is by no means a place of the clean slate, the fresh start. It is riddled with class and family origin. Humble parentage, wealthy back-grounds, lower-class homes and upper-class values are staples of Toronto dia-logue, and the nature of society is meticulously appraised and classified. Think of buying a house in Gore Vale? Don't, it's 27 per cent service industry em-ployees. Deer Park? Nineteen per cent executive—that's better!

For it is not a free-and-easy, damn-Yankee sort of city—anything but. Even its accents, when they have been flattened out from the Scots, the Finnish, or the Estonian, are oddly muted, made for undertones and surmises rather than certainties and swank. There is no raucous equivalent of Brooklynese, no local cockney wryness: nor will any loud-mouthed Torontonian ocker come sprawling into the café, beer can in hand, to put his feet up on the vacant chair and bemuse you with this year's slang—Sydney has invented a living language all its own, but nobody has written, so far as I know, a dictionary of Torontese.

It is as though some unseen instrument of restraint were keeping all things, even the vernacular, within limits. One could hardly call authority in Toronto Orwellian—it seems without malevolence; but at the same time nobody can possibly ignore it, for it seems to have a finger, or at least an announcement, almost everywhere. Where else could it be said of a work of art, as it says on a plaque beside the Flatiron mural in Toronto, that it was initiated by the city of Toronto and Development Department, Urban Design Group, the project being coordinated by an Arts Administrator? Imagine! "Commissioned by the Chapel Improvement Board of the Holy Vatican, supervised by the Sistine Executive Subcommittee . . ."

If authority in Toronto is not admonishing you to save energy it is riding about on motor-bike side-cars looking for layabouts; if it is not hoisting one flag outside city hall it is hoisting another outside the Ontario parliament; in the middle of shopping streets you find its incongruous offices, and no one but it will sell you a bottle of Scotch. I have heard it address criminals as "sir" ("I'm going to send you to prison, sir, for three months, in the hope that it will teach you a lesson") and say "pardon" to traffic offenders (Offender: "Well, hell, how'm I supposed to get the bloody thing unloaded?" Policeman: "Pardon?"). Yet it is treated by most Torontonians with such respect that if the bomb itself were to be fizzing at the fuse on King Street, I suspect, they would wait for the lights to change before running for the subway.

Toronto is the capital of the unabsolute. Nothing is utter here, except the winters I suppose, and the marvellous pale expanse of the lake. Nor is much of it crystal clear. To every Toronto generalization there is an exception, a contradiction, or an obfuscation. A kind of cabalistic device, like a spell, tells the baffled stranger the frequency of services on the Harbourfront courtesy bus, and a fine example of the true Toronto style, I thought, was this announcement at the city hall skating-rink: "Hours of Operation. Monday through Saturday, 9 a.m. until 10 p.m. Sunday, 9 a.m. until 10 p.m."

What's that again? Sometimes I felt I could never quite get to grips with Toronto. For instance in many ways it appears to the stranger, even now, almost preposterously provincial. Appearances count, conventions apply, theatre-goers attend matinées dressed, if not for weddings, at least for gubernatorial luncheon parties. Toronto critics indulge themselves in childish vitriolics, like undergraduates in university magazines. Toronto preoccupations can be loftily local. (Torontonian: "I suppose you're going to meet William Davis." Me: "Who's William Davis?" Torontonian: "My God. Do you know what I mean when I say 'The Dome'?")

Yet it is not really provincial at all. It is a huge, rich and splendid city, metropolitan in power—not only much the biggest city in Canada but a money centre of universal importance. Mighty capitalists reside here! Millions and millions of dollars are stacked! The world's tallest freestanding structure is in this city! The world's largest cinema complex! The world's biggest freshwater yacht club! Mary Pickford was born in Toronto! Insulin was invented! A housewife whose name I forget wrote "I'll Never Smile Again!"

Provincial indeed! No wonder those eight stalwarts of the Stock Exchange mural, clutching their stethoscopes, their briefcases, and their picks, are marching so irresistibly towards—oh, I was going to suggest the dawn, but I see they're facing west. Towards Spadina Avenue, then.

And why not? Toronto is Toronto, and perhaps that is enough. I look out of my window now, on a bright spring afternoon, and what do I see? No Satanic mills, but a city clean, neat, and ordered, built still to a human scale, unhurried and polite. It has all the prerequisites of your modern major city—your revolving restaurants, your Henry Moore statue, your trees with electric lights in them, your gay bars, your outdoor elevators, your atriums, your Sotheby Parke Bernet, your restaurants offering (Glossops on Prince Arthur Avenue) "deep-fried pears stuffed with ripe camembert on a bed of nutmeg-scented spinach." Yet by and large it has escaped the plastic blight of contemporary urbanism, and the squalid dangers too.

Only in Toronto, I think, will a streetcar stop to allow you over a pedestrian crossing—surely one of the most esoteric experiences of travel in the 1980s? Only in Toronto are the subways quite so wholesome, the parks so mugger-less, the children so well behaved (even at the Science Centre, where the temptation to fuse circuits or permanently disorient laser beams must be almost irresistible). Everywhere has its galleria nowadays, Singapore to Houston, but none is quite so satisfying as Toronto's Eaton Centre—just like one of the futuristic cities magazine artists liked to depict in the 1930s, except that instead of autogiros passing beneath the bridges, only lovely sculpted birds float down from the high vaulting . . .

Toronto citizens, who seem to be at once defensively cap-à-pie, as though always expecting you to make fun of them, and relentlessly self-critical, as though afraid you might think them smug, often say that compared with a European city theirs doesn't offer much to *do*. "Oh when I think of Paris," they say, or, "Goodness, when we were in New York we went to a theatre almost every night . . ." They do not, however, often recall evenings of cultural delight in Brest or Indianapolis. Only the greatest of the world's cities can outclass Toronto's theatres, cinemas, art galleries and newspapers, the variety of its restaurants, the number of its TV channels, the calibre of its visiting performers. Poets and artists are innumerable, I am assured, and are to be found in those cafés where writers and painters hang out, while over on the Toronto Islands, though permanently threatened by official improvements, a truly bohemian colony still honourably survives, in a late fragrance of the flower people, tight-knit, higgledy-piggledy, and attended by many cats in its shacks and snug bungalows.

I spent a morning out there, guided by a genial and gifted littérateur, taking sherry with a charming English lady ("Now you won't be *too* hard on Toronto, will you"), watching the pintail ducks bobbing about the ice and the great grey geese pecking for worms in the grass; and seen from that Indianified sort of foreshore—the city's "soul-kingdom," the poet Robert Sward has suggested—the achievement of Toronto, towering in gold and steel across the water, seemed to me rather marvellous: there on the edge of the wilderness, beside that cold, empty lake, to have raised itself in 150 years from colonial township to metropolis, to have absorbed settlers from half the world, yet to have kept its original mores so recognizable still!

For it is in many ways a conservative, indeed a conservationist achievement. What has *not* happened to Toronto is as remarkable as what *has* happened. It ought by all the odds to be a brilliant, brutal city, but it isn't. Its downtown ought to be vulgar and spectacular, but is actually dignified, well proportioned, and indeed noble. Its sex-and-sin quarters, where the young prostitutes loiter and the rock shops scream, are hardly another Reeperbahn, and the punks and Boy Georges to be seen parading Yonge Street on a Saturday night are downright touching in their bravado, so scrupulously are they ignored.

If "multiculturalism" does not key you in to Toronto, try "traditionalism." It is a potent word too. The Toronto weekend, once notorious for its Presbyterian severity, still seems to me more thoroughly weekendish than most—especially as, having whiled away Saturday morning with the huge weekend editions of *The Globe* and the *Star*, you can lie in on Sunday with the mammoth *New York Times*. The Toronto Stock Exchange, at least as seen from the visitors' gallery, is marvellously cool and gentlemanly. It costs up to $8,000 to get into the Royal Canadian Yacht Club; the club's two private launches were built in 1898 and 1910 respectively. And though some of the Toronto rich build themselves houses, on the Bridle Path for instance, of almost unimaginable ostentation, to judge by the realty advertisements most Torontonians aspire to nothing less decorous than mock-Tudor, neo-Georgian, or sham-Château — "Gracious, grand and affordable," with elegant libraries, gourmet kitchens, and "classic fluted columns to punctuate the expansiveness of sunken conservatories . . ."

The real achievement of Toronto is to have remained itself. It says something for the character of this city that even now, 150 years old, with 300,000 Italian residents, and 50,000 Greeks, and heaven knows how many Portuguese, Hungarians, Poles, Latvians, Chileans, Maltese, Chinese, Finns, with skyscrapers dominating it, and American TV beamed into every home—with condominiums rising everywhere, and a gigantic Hilton dominating the waterfront, and those cheese-stuffed pears at Glossops—it says something for Toronto that it can still be defined, by an elderly English lady over a glass of sherry, with a Manx cat purring at her feet and a portrait of her late husband on the sidetable, as "not such a bad old place—don't be too hard on it!"

So this is the New World! Not such a bad old place! Again, for myself it is not what I would want of a Promised Land, were I in need of one, and when I thought of that woman at the airport, and tried to put myself in her shoes, wherever she was across the sprawling city, I felt that if fate really were to make me an immigrant here I might be profoundly unhappy.

Not because Toronto would be unkind to me. It would be far kinder than New York, say, or Sydney down under. It would not leave me to starve in the street, or bankrupt me with medical bills, or refuse me admittance to discos because I was black. No, it would be a subtler oppression than that—the oppression of reticence. Toronto is the most undemonstrative city I know, and the least inquisitive. The Walkman might be made for it. It swarms with clubs, cliques and cultural societies, but seems armour-plated against the individual. There are few cities in the world where one can feel, as one walks the streets or rides the subways, for better or for worse, so all alone.

All around me I see those same faces from the airport carousel, so unflustered, so reserved; I caught the eye once of a subway driver, as he rested at his controls for a few moments in the bright lights of the station, waiting for the guard's signal, and never did I see an eye so fathomlessly subdued—not a flicker could I raise in it, not a glint of interest or irritation, before the whistle blew and he disappeared once more into the dark. It takes time, more time than a subway driver has, for the Toronto face, having passed through several stages of suspicion, nervous apprehension, and anxiety to please, to light up in a simple smile. Compulsory lessons in small talk, I sometimes think, might well be added to those school classes in Heritage Languages, and there might usefully be courses too in How to Respond to Casual Remarks in Elevators.

Sometimes I think it is the flatness of the landscape that causes this flattening of the spirit—those interminable suburbs stretching away, that huge plane of the lake, those long grid roads which deprive the place of surprise or intricacy. Sometimes I think it must be the climate, numbing the nerve ends or even the sheer empty vastness of the Toronto sky, settled so conclusively upon the horizon, wherever you look, unimpeded by hills. Could it be the history of the place, and the deference to authority that restrains the jay-walkers still? Could it be underpopulation; ought there to be a couple of million more people in the city, to give it punch or jostle? Could it be the permanent compromise of Toronto, neither quite this or altogether that, capitalist but compassionate, American but royalist, multicultural but traditionalist?

Or could it be, I occasionally ask myself, me? This is a city conducive to self-doubt and introspection. It is hard to feel that Torontonians by and large, for all the civic propaganda and guidebook hype, share in any grand satisfaction of the spirit, hard to imagine anyone waking up on a spring morning to cry, "Here I am, here in T.O., thank God for my good fortune!" I asked immigrants of many nationalities if they liked Toronto, and though at first, out of diplomacy or good manners they nearly all said yes, a few minutes of probing generally found them less than enthusiastic. Why? "Because the people is cold here." "Because these people just mind their own business and make the dollars." "Because the neighbours don't smile and say hullo, how's things." "Because nobody talks, know what I mean?"

Never I note because the citizenry has been unkind, or because the city is unpleasant: only because, in the course of its 150 years of careful progress, so calculated, so civilized, somewhere along the way Toronto lost, or failed to find, the gift of contact or of merriment. I know of nowhere much less merry than the Liquor Control Board retail stores, clinical and disapproving as Wedding Palaces in Leningrad. And even the most naturally merry of the immigrants, the dancing Greeks, the witty Poles, the lyrical Hungarians, somehow seem to have forfeited their *joie de vivre* when they embraced the liberties of this town.

Among the innumerable conveniences of Toronto, which is an extremely convenient city, one of the most attractive is the system of tunnels which lies beneath the downtown streets, and which, with its wonderful bright-lit sequences of stores, cafés, malls and intersections, is almost a second city in itself. I loved to think of all the warmth and life down there, the passing crowds, the coffee smells, the Muzak, and the clink of cups, when the streets above were half-empty in the rain, or scoured by cold winds; and one of my great pleasures was to wander aimless through those comfortable labyrinths, lulled from one Golden Oldie to the next, surfacing now and then to find myself on an unknown street corner far from home, or all unexpectedly in the lobby of some tremendous bank.

But after a time I came to think of them as escape tunnels. It was not just that they were warm and dry; they had an intimacy to them, a brush of human empathy, absent from the greater city above our heads. Might it be, I wondered, that down there a new kind of Torontonian was evolving after all, brought to life by the glare of the lights, stripped of inhibition by the press of the crowds, and even perhaps induced to burst into song, or dance a few steps down the escalator, by the beat of the canned music?

"What d'you think?" I asked a friend. "Are they changing the character of Toronto?"

"You must be joking," he replied. "You couldn't do that in a sesquicentury."

He's probably right. Toronto is Toronto, below or above the ground. And you, madame, into whatever obscurely ethnic enclave you vanished, when we parted at the airport that day, have they changed *you* yet? Have they taken you up to Bloor Street to rig you out in mix 'n' match? Have they taught you not to push, or talk to yourself, or hurl abuse at officialdom? Are you still refusing to pay that customs charge, or have they persuaded you to fill in the form and be sure to ask for a receipt for tax purposes? Are you happy? Are you homesick? Are you still yourself?

Whatever has happened to you, destiny has not dealt you a bad hand in bringing you to this city by the lake. You are as free as we mortals can reasonably expect, there are dumplings on your dinner plate and a TV in your living-room, if not classic fluted columns in a sunken conservatory. Your heart may not be singing, as you contemplate the presence around you of Toronto the Good, but it should not be sinking either. Cheer up! You have drawn a second prize, I would say, in the Lottario of Life.

People of the Deer

FARLEY MOWAT

*The author's fascination with the arctic plains
began with a train trip he took at the age of
fifteen from Winnipeg to the edge of Hudson
Bay.*

*I*N the spring of 1935, when I was an undersized youth of fifteen, I made my
first journey into arctic lands, under the tutelage of a great-uncle who was an
amateur but fanatical student of birds. My Uncle Frank's consuming interest in
wild things had been perpetuated in me, for from the age of six I too had been
passionately interested in all the animals that haunted the rolling prairies near
my home in Saskatoon. Our house in that western city had for long years been
shared with pet skunks, coyotes, crows, gophers and rattlesnakes of uncertain
disposition. Even my human friends were chosen almost exclusively from the
half-wild and suitably ragged children at the Dundurn Indian Reserve, for I
shared with those sons of nomads a strange devotion to the illusory freedom of
the broad prairie plains. That restless longing to find affinity with primordial
things was a legacy from my father, but it took shape and gained direction under
the influence of Great-uncle Frank. He, at my mother's request, undertook to
take me with him on one of his yearly pilgrimages to the ancient tundras of the
arctic, where we were to spend a summer among the curious Northern birds
whose very names were mystery in my ears, and whose ways of life were old
before ours were begun.

In the first week of May 1935, the meadowlarks brought spring to Saskatoon—and Uncle Frank was close behind. Tall, gaunt and weather-worn, he
was still filled with the indestructible energy which had carried him through
arduous years of struggle with the tough sod of an Alberta wheat farm. He had
acquitted himself well in that long battle against hail and blight, and now in his
late sixties he was able to indulge his lifelong hobby, and so each new spring saw
him voyaging to some distant place to watch birds whose lives he longed to
know and understand.

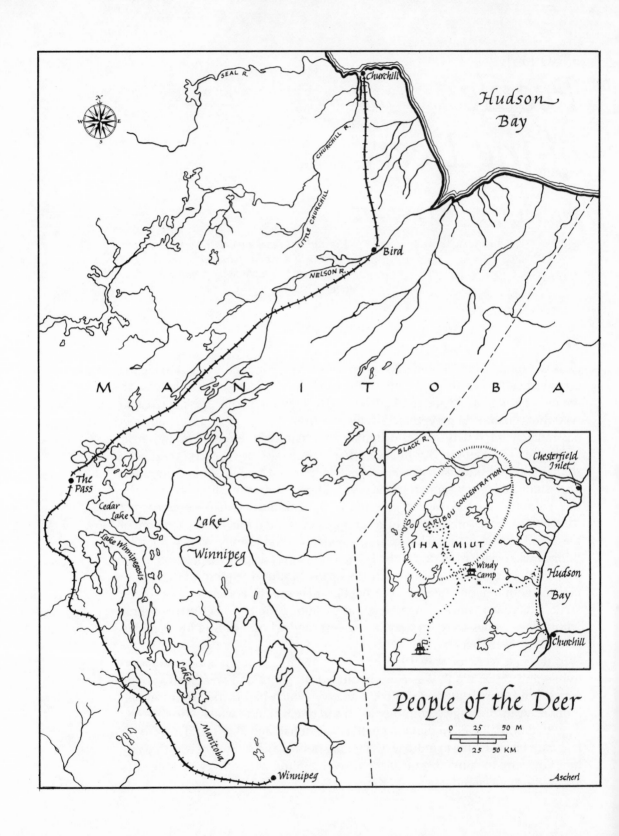

SEAL R.

Churchill

Hudson
Bay

CHURCHILL R.

LITTLE CHURCHILL

Bird

NELSON R.

M A N I T O B A

The
Pass

Cedar
Lake

Lake
Winnipeg

Lake Winnipegosis

Lake Manitoba

Winnipeg

BLACK R.

Chesterfield
Inlet

CARIBOU CONCENTRATION

I H A L M I U T

Windy
Camp

Hudson
Bay

Churchill

People of the Deer

0   25   50 M

0   25   50 KM

Ascherl

To my young eyes, Uncle Frank was a somewhat dusty Olympian and beside him I felt as insignificant as a blade of twitch grass. Yet when he looked down upon me from his great, spare height, he seemed to be vaguely satisfied with what he saw and so, on the day following his arrival at Saskatoon, we two set off together for Winnipeg, the central gateway to the arctic lands. It was the beginning of an Odyssey.

From Winnipeg the railroad sweeps westward in a wild curve over the flat, rich wheatlands which are the bed of ancient Lake Agassiz, a mighty lake that died with the last glacier. Then the steel bends northward and the train passes through the flat farmlands, and little villages go by—each marked by the bulge of an orthodox steeple and the square monument of a grain elevator. Slowly the forests extend their rough fingers into the black soil of the farms, until the fingers close tightly. The prairies are gone, and only the matted disorder of forests remains.

The train runs more cautiously now, for it is entering a land that is hostile to strangers. It makes its way northward through the low forests which are the home of the Cree Indians, and at last it draws up with gusty relief at the frontier town of The Pas. Here, in a decaying cluster of buildings, the Winnipeg train turns gratefully back to the south and hurries to leave behind it the anonymous tangle of forests and muskegs.

But The Pas, that seedy settlement which has been left behind to wither and rot as the frontier has pushed north, is not yet the end of the steel. Instead, it is the southern terminus for a cockeyed political shenanigan that is proudly known in Canada's capital as "the Hudson Bay Railway" but is better known in the land where it lives as "the Muskeg Express." A rebellious and contrary railway that may have an equal in the wilds of Siberia, the Muskeg Express has no relatives on this continent. It stretches northward for five hundred desolate miles to the shore of Hudson Bay. It thinks nothing of running a hundred miles at a time without curves and without bends to relieve the heavy-footed pace it maintains.

For part of the way its roadbed is built on blocks of ancient peat moss, and this moss in turn sits uneasily on the perpetual ice of the muskegs and swamps, whose black depths hold the last dominions of the old, vanished glaciers.

The only passenger accommodation on the train was in the caboose. So Uncle Frank and I lived there for the three days and two nights that the journey consumed. I amused myself by keeping track of the little white-painted signboards which marked off each mile and by counting the number of rail spikes per mile that flew out of the ties and went buzzing off through the air like bullets, as the train passed along. I was grateful to the mile-boards, and to the spikes, for the monotony of that northward journey through the unchanging and somber forests was almost unbroken by anything else.

But at Mile 410 something *did* happen, something that was to lead me into an undreamed-of world in the years which still lay far ahead. Near Mile 400, I had noticed that the maddening succession of stunted and half-drowned spruce trees was beginning to be pierced by long, finger-like openings running down from the northwest. When I pointed them out to my Uncle Frank, he explained that these were the slim tentacles which were being thrust southward by those great arctic plains we call the Barrens, and the presence of these fingers of the plains marked the passing of the dominion of forests.

I climbed up to the high bench of the caboose cupola to have a better look at the new lands which were appearing, and I was there when the marker for Mile 410 came into view, and simultaneously the rusty whistle of the old engine began to give tongue. It was to continue sounding for a full half-hour, with a reckless disregard for steam pressure. But at the first blast I looked forward over the humped backs of the freight cars—and noticed the whistle no more!

A brown, flowing river had appeared and was surging out of the edge of the dying forests and plunging across and over the snow-covered roadbed ahead. A broad, turbulent ribbon of brown ran out of an opening to the southeast and traced its sinuous course northwest over the snows of a land that was still completely gripped by the frosts—for this was no river of water, but a river of life. I had my binoculars to my eyes in the instant, and through the lenses I saw the stream dissolve into its myriad parts and each part of that river was long-legged shape of a deer!

''*C'est la Foule!*'' The French-Canadian brakeman stood beside me, and at the sound of his words I understood what it was that I was beholding. ''It is the Throng!'' Those were the words that the first of the early French explorers wrote in his journal when he beheld what is perhaps the most tremendous living spectacle that our continent knows—the almost incredible mass migration of the numberless herds of caribou—the reindeer of the Canadian North.

The train whistle continued to blow with increasing fury and exasperation but the rolling hordes of the caribou did not deviate from their own right of way, which took precedence over man's. They did not hurry their steady lope and, as we drew up to them, the engine gave up its futile efforts to intimidate the Throng, and with a resigned whiffle of steam we came to a halt. It was a long halt. For the next hour we stayed there, and for an hour the half-mile-wide river of caribou flowed unhurriedly north in a phenomenal procession, so overwhelming in its magnitude that I could hardly credit my senses. Then, abruptly, the river thinned out and in a few moments was gone, leaving behind it a broad highway beaten into the snow. The old train gathered its waning strength; the passengers who had alighted to brew up some tea climbed aboard, and we too continued into the north.

The stunted trees closed in again and the white mile-boards flickered past as if the sight of the Throng had been only an illusion in time and in space. But it was no illusion, for every detail of that sight remains with me now, with a clarity that does not belong to illusions. It was a sight that a boy—or a man—does not forget. And the sight I beheld at Mile 410 was, many years later, to draw me inexorably back to the land of *la Foule*.

In its own good time, the Muskeg Express brought us out of the forests and within sight of the ice-filled waters of Hudson Bay, and to the end of a journey. I spent that summer at Churchill in a fly-haunted search for birds' eggs, under the untiring direction of my uncle. The spectacle of *la Foule* faded to the back of my mind, for on the sodden muskegs there were too many strange birds calling— the Hudsonian curlews with their haunting whistles; the godwits, and the snow buntings and longspurs. There was too much for me to see, there on the south verges of the arctic, and too much to hear.

With the last summer days of 1935 I again climbed back aboard the Muskeg Special and left the tantalizing borders of the Barrens behind me for a decade. I returned home with a large box of birds' eggs, a tin can containing six live lemming-mice, and a crate holding a queer bird called a jaeger (a hunter), which looks like a gull and acts like a hawk.

In addition to these things I brought back many memories, both varied and vivid. Yet, as time passed, it was the memory of the great herd of caribou at Mile 410 that emerged as the strongest of all. And that particular memory was kept alive, and grew more powerful as I grew older because of an intangible longing that the arctic had implanted so deeply in my heart that its fever could not be chilled even by the passing years.

It is, I suppose, a sort of disease—an arctic fever—and yet no microscope can discover its virus and it remains completely unknown to the savants of science. The arctic fever has no effect on the body but lives only in the mind, filling its victim with a consuming urge to wander again, and forever, through those mighty spaces where the caribou herds flow like living rivers over the roll of the tundra. It is a disease of the imagination, and yet it attacks men whom you would not normally accuse of being imaginative. It is this unknown disease that drives taciturn white men back to their crude log shanties year after year, back to the desperate life of the interminable winter night, and back to the wind and the search through the gray snow for the white fox and ermine. The disease is one of great power indeed, for it does not leave such victims as these until life itself leaves them.

The infection lay dormant in me for many years. From 1935 until 1939 my life held so many things that the call of the bleak lands to the north was never strong enough to take command of my will. During those years I went on with my schooling, spending my holidays on the prairies, in the mountains to the west, and in the forests to the east—but never completely forgetting the stark plains to the north. In those years I was particularly engrossed in the study of birds and mammals, for I had decided that I would become a zoologist and spend my life at that study.

But then, when I was nineteen years old, I had to exchange my old shotgun for a Lee-Enfield rifle, for I became a soldier in the Hastings and Prince Edward Regiment. I exchanged the prairies and mountains for the close confines of an infantry regiment, and the world that now lay outside those narrow bounds suddenly became a mad, nightmare creation which I feared and could not understand. 1941 came, and I was part of the phony war in southern England and on my brief leaves I watched without comprehension as the walls of great cities crumbled over the dismembered bodies of men. I began to know a sick and corroding fear that grew from an unreasoned revolt against mankind—the one living thing that could deliberately bring down a world in senseless slaughter. The war drove inexorably on. My regiment moved through Italy, then up through France into Belgium and Holland, and at long last into the Reich. And one day there were no more crashes of shellfire in the air—and it was done.

In the spring of 1946 I returned to my own land—but it was a far cry from my return to my home in 1935. I wished to escape into the quiet sanctuaries where the echoes of war had never been heard. And to this end, I at once arranged to become what is called a "scientific collector" who would go into far places and bring back rare specimens for science to stare at. Desperately seeking for some stable thing rooted deep in reality, I grasped the opportunity to labor in what I thought was the austere pursuit of knowledge for its own sake.

So it was that at the end of 1946 I found myself far up in the forests of northern Saskatchewan at a place called Lac La Ronge. Nominally I was there to collect birds for a museum, but I had put my gun away, for I soon had enough of "scientific" destruction, even as I had had enough of killing in wartime. The search for tranquillity which had led me hopefully into science had failed, for now I could see only a brutal futility in the senseless amassing of little bird mummies which were to be preserved from the ravages of life in dark rows of steel cabinets behind stone walls. So I was simply living, without any particular aim, in a remote settlement of Cree Indian half-breeds; and there, among a people who had been brutalized and who had been degraded and led to decay by all that is evil in civilized life—there I found a man who unwittingly gave me a direction and a new goal.

From old Henry Moberly, a half-breed who had spent most of his years on the borders of the northernmost forests, I once again heard of the caribou that I had seen so many years before. Henry told me living tales of the "deer"—as the caribou are universally called in the land—so that I remembered *la Foule* with startling clarity; and it was then that the quiescent disease of the arctic sprang to new life within me, and began to possess me completely.

With the picture of the deer held firmly in my mind as a spiritual talisman, I returned to the cities for the winter, and my heart was closer to knowing peace than it had been in six years. I went back to the university and took a zoological course which would fit me to become a student of the deer, for in those days the habits and life of the caribou were a great mystery waiting to be solved and I had decided that the pursuit of this mystery was to be my endeavor. Perhaps not completely an honest endeavor, for even then I was dimly aware that the deer were to serve primarily as my excuse for a return to the North, which was calling to me. Nevertheless I worked hard during the winter, and in my spare time I read every book about the arctic that I could lay hands on, until I began to have some conception of what lies behind that unrevealing word.

As I read I came to understand that the arctic is not only a world of frozen rivers and ice-bound lakes but also of living rivers and of lakes whose very blue depths are flanked by summer flowers and by sweeping green meadows. The arctic not only knows the absolute cold of the pole but it also knows days of overpowering heat when a naked man sweats with the simple exertion of walking. And most important of all, I came to understand that the arctic is not only the ice-covered cap of the world but is also nearly two million square miles of rolling plains that, during the heat of midsummer, are thronged with life and brilliant with the colors of countless plants in full bloom. It was these immense plains which drew my special attention, and when I found them on a map of the continent, I saw that they formed a great triangle, with its narrow apex pointing west to the shore of the Arctic Ocean, not far from the mouth of the Mackenzie River and the Alaskan border. The triangle's base lies along the west shore of Hudson Bay, and its two arms extend westward, one along timber line and the other along the coast of the Arctic Sea. And the name of this vast, treeless land is the Barrenlands.

I saw it in my mind's eye as a mighty land and a strange one. As geological time is reckoned, it emerged only yesterday from under the weight of the glaciers, and today it remains almost as it was when the ponderous mountains of ice finished grinding their way over its face. It is a land of undulating plains that have no horizon, of low hills planed to a shapeless uniformity by the great power of the ice. It is a land of gravel, of sand, and of shattered gray rocks, but without soil as we know it. It is also a land that seems to be struggling to emerge from a fresh-water ocean, for it is almost half water, holding countless numbers of lakes

319

and their rivers. And this was the land where I would have to seek out the caribou, for it is their land.

Toward the end of the winter I met an old army friend, who, in peacetime, was a mining engineer, and I told him something of my interest in the arctic. he was a little amused at the idea of anyone's heading out into those lands where he might be reaping the value of five years' war exile from the rich postwar fabric of the boom. But he did me a favor, a much greater one than he knew. He gave me a stack of old government mining reports his father had owned, and he said that he thought some of them might deal with the North I wanted to know. He was right, for in that musty old pile of books I found my lodestone to the land of the deer.

I looked through the pile of pamphlets and books which he had given me. One of the dingiest of the lot bore the prosaic title, *Report on the Dubawnt, Kazan, and Ferguson Rivers and the North West Coast of Hudson Bay*. It had been published in 1896 and on the surface it appeared to be a dry-as-dust compilation of outdated facts, written by some dull-eyed servant of government. But appearances were deceptive. I recognized the author's name—Joseph Burr Tyrrell— and I remembered that in some obscure paper I had read an old account of Tyrrell's fantastic explorations through the central Barrenlands of Keewatin. For Tyrrell had been the first—and the last—man ever to traverse the full breadth of the Barrens from south to north.

I opened his report eagerly. It was not quite like the usual run of official documents, for though Tyrrell had been devoted to his gods, mineralogy and geography, he had written about them with an undertone of enthusiasm and excitement which did not seem to belong between those staid covers and government seals. There was an ephemeral quality about his writings that made even his endless comments on the minerals he had examined seem interesting and fresh. And yet, in the Dubawnt Report there was only room for brief hints about the true nature of the land and about the trials and troubles which had beset Tyrrell.

Here and there I did come across scattered references to the deer and, in one place, Tyrrell spoke succinctly of seeing what may have been the greatest single herd ever to be seen by a white man—a herd so vast that for many miles the surface of the land was obscured beneath the blanket of living beasts! The mental image of this magnificent spectacle strengthened my desire to go to the Barrens, but I found one other thing hidden in Tyrrell's report that finally confirmed my resolve.

For Tyrrell spoke also of a "People of the Deer." Out in those endless spaces, along the river he called Kazan, Tyrrell found a race of men where it was thought that no men could live. And interwoven between his lists of rocks were fragmentary and tantalizing references to these men, who had remained completely cut off from the world's knowledge until the day of Tyrrell's coming. In the Dubawnt Report, a shadow of this forgotten race emerged for the first time before our eyes. And it was clear enough that they were a people who, in Tyrrell's day, had been living the same lives they had led before the Viking longboats first discovered the eastern shores of North America. Tyrrell could spare them only a few terse and niggardly paragraphs, yet he said enough to make the Barrens People seem as fascinating as dwellers in another world. Obviously they were men whose total strength had been devoted to a bitter struggle against the implacable natural forces of the Barrens, and the idea came to me that they might never have found the will or the desire to turn their strength against one another. If this was indeed true, then it was certain they were a people I wanted to know.

But half a century had intervened since Tyrrell discovered this inland race of Eskimos, and it seemed inevitable that during that time great changes must have come to the land and to its inhabitants. I renewed my search of the literature of the arctic in an effort to discover how much was known of the People, and of the land, which Tyrrell had seen, and to my secret satisfaction I found no further word about Tyrrell's people, though there were sufficient rumors and secondhand reports to convince me that those men of the deer still lived in their hidden world. I sent to Ottawa for the most recent maps of the central plains. When they arrived, I spread them out on the floor and studied them with mounting excitement—for they showed little more than the tenuous dotted outlines of those features which Tyrrell had drawn half a century before. For the most part the maps were unsullied white, defaced only by small printed legends, reading "Unmapped."

To the north of this clouded region, the coast of the continent was accurately shown, and it was studded with the settlements of Eskimos who had been in contact with our race for better than a hundred years. To the east, along the shoreline of Hudson Bay, the picture was the same. To the south lay the forests and the old river routes of the *Voyageurs* who had explored the timberlands centuries earlier. And to the distant west lay the rich and busy valley of the Mackenzie. But in the middle of all these lay only emptiness, not only on the maps but in the books as well.

There was a reason for this. When the first white men looked across the borders of this land, they named it "the Barrens" and shuddered at its terrible rawness. And so they turned from it, never knowing that it held rivers of life in its depths.

The existence of this barrier built upon an indefinable fear was made known to me when I sought definite information about ways and means to enter the land. I went to the books, but again they were not much of a help. I found that several men had indeed traveled in the boundary regions of the Barrens, and a few had even penetrated deeply into the narrow western neck of the plains, where they are squeezed between timber line and the seacoast. Yet all who had attempted to write of what they found had evidently been seized by an inarticulate paralysis when they tried to put their deepest impressions into their writings. They seemed to grope futilely for words with which they could express the emotions the Barrens had instilled in their hearts. And they were all baffled by that effort to speak clearly. Most of them gave up the attempt and sought refuge in minute descriptions of the component parts, which only if they are taken in their entirety can give the true measure of the great arctic plains.

It seemed to me to be a great mystery, this impenetrable obscurity that could not even be shattered by men who gave all their senses and their perceptions to the task.

But on a day in the spring of 1947, when I had almost completed my own plans to set out for the North, I received the first real clue to the nature of that mystery.

It was contained in a letter from a former Royal Canadian Mounted Police constable whom I had known during the war. I had written, asking if he had any personal experience with the arctic plains, and his answer told me of a time when he had gone into the western Barrens in pursuit of a suspected murderer. The fugitive escaped—from the police at least—and my friend turned back just in time to save his own life, for he was starved and half-frozen before he reached the shelter of a coastal trading post. Writing to me, he summed up all the Barrens had meant to him in these few, straightforward words:

> I guess it was the emptiness that bothered me most. That damn and bloody space—it just goes on and on until it makes you want to cry, or scream—or cut your own damn throat!

Emptiness and the terrible space! These were the things which had haunted the imaginations of the few white men who had known the Barrens. And yet, somewhere in the hidden depths of that space there lived—if they still lived—not only the great herds of the deer, but also men . . . the People of the Deer.

North of Sixty

MORDECAI RICHLER

Capital of one third of Canada, "wonderful, demented" Yellowknife stands alone—and far removed—from other North American cities. Novelist Mordecai Richler, a veteran visitor, explains why with all its rocky ugliness, spare facilities, and uncertain access, Yellowknife has its personal charm.

*T*HAT indispensable weekly *The Yellowknifer* once ran the following small ad by a new settler:

> *Lawn mower* FOR SALE. LIKE NEW. REASON FOR SELLING. NO GRASS. OR WOULD CONSIDER PURCHASING LAWN.

Yellowknife, out there in the Northwest Territories, some 272 miles south of the Arctic Circle, may be a tacky little town. Functional here, downright sleazy there. With a new aluminum-sided courthouse that looks like the ultimate Greyhound bus station. An ugly main street. Restaurants that serve unspeakable food. Mobile-home settlements here, there, and everywhere. But, for all that, Yellowknife is also absolutely wonderful.

Dug into the oldest rock in the world, the Precambrian Shield, Yellowknife rides a basement 5,000 feet deep that is seamed with gold. It lies on the northern arm of the Great Slave Lake, the gateway to waters that abound in northern pike, Arctic greylings, walleyes, whitefish, and lake trout. Yellowknife, legendary Yellowknife, can also lay claim to the only golf course in the world whose clubhouse once literally flew off to war, as well as a band of Indians who earn their living providing a delicacy for the Jewish Sabbath table.

The Yellowknife Golf Club, a typical act of north-of-sixty defiance, has no grass, but is rooted in sand and rock. Until 1947, it was also without a clubhouse. Then an American DC-3 transport crash-landed on the course, sluing through the jack pines just short of the airport. It was immediately converted into the golf course's first amenity. It filled that social office until 1952, when an American order recalled DC-3s everywhere. Along came some USAF personnel to screw an engine onto the clubhouse and fly it into battle in Korea. *Is it a bird? Is it a plane? No, it's Yellowknife's flying clubhouse.*

There is now a fish plant, run by Dogribs, on the shores of the Great Slave Lake, for which the enterprising Indians net whitefish and pike.

"What do you do with it?" I asked.

"Oh, we ship it to the Jews in Chicago, who use it to make what they call gefilte fish."

Eschewing summer, the blackfly season, I first flew into Yellowknife in the late winter, starting out of Edmonton, traveling with Pacific Western Airlines—PWA—which northerners have dubbed "Pray While Aloft" or "Probably Won't Arrive." I flew into town forearmed with a pocket-size wind-chill chart, which warned me that starting at fifteen below zero, given a wind of twenty-five miles per hour, the flesh may freeze within one minute. I was also toting copies of *Northern Survival* and *Down But Not Out*, the former insisting that "everybody who travels on land in the Arctic or barren lands should be able to build a snow house," and the latter that if our plane went down, "mice and lemmings were edible and should not be overlooked by the survivor." Considerably sobered, I called for the stewardess. "Have you any cognac?"

"Sorry," she said, "but we only serve hard liquor."

Like, I was soon to discover, Hudson's Bay Overproof Rum, which is only available in the NWT and is still traditionally offered as a first drink to unwary visitors, a test of any southerner's fortitude. In Canada's ten provinces, I should point out, liquor is a government monopoly, available from provincial liquor stores. But in Yellowknife the bustling liquor store is privately owned by the good Messrs Eggenberger and Pollack, who also run the local dairy. "Those guys have got us by the short and curlies," I was told. "You know, from the cradle to the grave."

A prominent sign in the liquor store reads:

YOU BREAK IT,
YOU PAY FOR IT.

Lowering into the airport, I immediately noticed the bush pilot operators' sheds. Wardair, Ptarmigan, Gateway, NWT.

Not only was there a last frontier on the continent's frost-encrusted roof, but also the ultimate pony express. Appropriately grizzled, idiosyncratic bush pilots who fly out of Yellowknife, Tuktoyaktuk, Gjoa Haven, Fort Good Hope, and Cambridge Bay, among other places. They fly charters, taking off into the barrens on floats or wheel-skis, but primarily on instinct, an uncanny ability to read the tundra. The first time I took off with one of them out of Yellowknife, driving into the seemingly endless barrens, across Hudson Bay, bouncing over Baffin Island, dipping through the bleak and intimidating mountain passes of the eastern Arctic, finally coming down in Pangirtung, I flew forewarned.

"You taking off with Daryl today?" I was asked.

"Right."

"Well, you needn't worry. He's one of the best around."

I nodded, appreciative.

"How come, you'll want to know. Well, I'll tell you. He's the only bush pilot in Yellowknife who can drink scotch standing on his head."

"And when did he last manage that?"

"Four o'clock this morning."

Actually, before attempting the postage-stamp-size strip in Pang, we had to put down in Frobisher, in deference to a partial whiteout. Daryl strode into the air terminal and returned to report, "Nothing's flying."

The man in charge of our shivering party, big Stuart Hodgson, then commissioner of the Territories, cuffed Daryl on the shoulder. "Yeah, but you'll get us through, you bastard, won't you?"

Flying on memory, a third eye, and a hangover, a grudging Daryl finally landed, bouncing, then skidding to a stop just short of a sheer mountain wall. Only after we had all emerged shakily from the plane did a delighted Hodgson ask me, "Did you know that this flight was against regulations?"

"No. Why?"

"The runway," he said, heaving with laughter, "is four hundred feet too short for the Grumman."

Inhabitants of the Territories, or north of sixty, as many of them prefer, dismiss the rest of Canada (and, indeed, the world) as "the outside." The Territories cover roughly a third of Canada, more than a million and a quarter square miles, and from subzero end to end there are but 40,000 frostbitten, stubborn people: a third Eskimo or Inuit; about a third Indian and métis; a third white. A good many of the whites, and an increasing number of the Inuit, are civil servants, government men more than once removed from the gray proprieties of distant Ottawa. Until 1969, the Territories' Eskimos were known to their Ottawa bookkeepers by no more than an identification disk, a sequence of digits. In 1969, Commissioner Hodgson decided this was undignified. So he dispatched one Abraham Okpik on a two-year mission through the bitterly cold, vast land to offer surnames to his people, any surnames they chose, which accounts for the fact that a celebrated Yellowknife hooker is known as Sophie Football.

If the northern civil servant is a special breed, so was the Territories' scholarly supreme court judge of the Seventies, the late Mr. Justice Morrow of Yellowknife. Morrow, packing his court party and survival kit on board an aging DC-3, regularly carried Her Majesty's justice to even the most remote settlements of the high Arctic. Among the court party, when I traveled with it, was chief federal prosecutor Orville Troy, who used to sport a T-shirt with ASS embossed on it. ASS for Arctic Secret Service. "The Arctic Secret Service is so secret," he confided to me, "that you may be a member and not even know it yet."

Once, after a tire flattened on a strip that was no more than a cleared icefield, the court party's resourceful pilot pumped it full and, in the absence of a proper repair kit, pissed on the puncture, freezing it closed immediately before takeoff. Another time, bound for yet another distant settlement, the pilot informed the judge that the weather was closing in; they would have only an hour on the ground or, conversely, could be stuck there for a week, maybe ten days, before the skies cleared again. The judge, improvising, shed his sealskin parka, hurried into his robes, and announced that court would be convened on board. The business on hand, an Eskimo divorce case, was heard in the cabin of the DC-3 with the engines shut off, the temperature rapidly sinking to thirty degrees below zero. Mr. Justice Morrow had flown 1,500 miles just to hear the divorce petition, but, as a matter of form, first asked the applicant if there was any possibility of a reconciliation.

The Eskimo, eager to please, grinned shyly. "Sure. Why not?"

"In that case," the judge asked, "where is your wife?"

His manner rueful, he explained his wife was in yet another settlement, 1,200 miles away.

Teeth chattering, the judge pronounced, "We'll be back in the spring."

In the old days when the bush pilots still flew planes with open cockpits through the subzero weather, there were C. H. "Punch" Dickins and Max Ward. Dickins holds a number of Arctic records and Ward is now president of Wardair, Canada's largest international charter airline. Whiskey Papa, or Welby Phipps, has also retired. Daddy Ho Ho, or Bob Engle, today runs his own airline, a burgeoning business. And so now there are Dunc, Charlie, Jim, Pete, Gene, and many more who come and go, drifting from settlement to settlement. Some are known for their proficiency in flying the barrens, above the tree line; others for their ability to read the almost equally confusing bush country. At least one, Rocky Parsons, is reputed to be very good on the ground. "If you're going to go down," I've heard it said again and again, "you want a pilot who can live off the land. You want Parsons. He'll keep you alive for weeks." Another, Dunc Matheson, is known as the best damn navigator north of sixty. "Equipment, hell. Give him the sun or stars and a piece of string and he'll find his way anywhere."

The trade, a risky one, makes natural provision for survival of the fittest.

"Whatever you do," I was warned, "never fly with anybody who hasn't been working the country for more than five years. If he's made five and survived, he's got to be safe."

"Or overdue?"

"You believe it."

There is also a certain snobbery attached to the trade, the bush pilots knowing and recognizing each other by the craft they fly. This one can't be trusted in an expensive twin-engine job, that one is too clumsy to be allowed floats. All of them are obliged to land on makeshift airstrips in remote settlements, rough clearings on the ice, the so-called runway lit at night by no more than fires set off in oil drums. The worst that can be said for a pilot is that he has no feeling for his plane. He doesn't merely scan his instrument panel, taking it all in with a knowing glance, but is obliged to contemplate each dial individually. And the worst that can be said for a plane is that it is unforgiving.

The bush pilots, an undoubtedly intrepid bunch, are far from foolish, and what they dread most is a whiteout. To be caught in a whiteout, one of them explained to me, is like flying through a bottle of milk. There is absolutely no horizon. And on occasion, even the most experienced bush pilot, riding into a whiteout, wheeling and turning, his sense of gravity lost, is inclined to doubt his instruments and fly upside down into the ground. Inevitably, it happens two, maybe three, times a winter, and then the army comes in, the whole town is organized, everybody who possibly can taking part in the search-and-rescue mission. Nurses, garage mechanics, clerks, volunteering to fly the tundra, secured by straps, suspended from the open underbelly of a four-engine Hercules, tears freezing on their faces as they scan the glittering snow for signs of a camp or wreckage. Smoke. A flare. The glint of the sun on a snapped wing. "Even if you know where the plane is," a search officer told me, "it is very difficult to spot on the barrens or in the bush." There are further complications. Aside from a survival kit, each pilot carries an ELT, a primitive battery-run radio that is supposed to be set off on impact, emitting a signal that can be readily picked up by a high-flying, radar-equipped RCMP airplane. "The problem is," the search officer said, "once a plane goes down, every bush pilot from here to Frobisher Bay decides to test his own ELT, giving it a hard whack and setting it off. We pick up signals everywhere."

One bush pilot, in the late Fifties, survived for almost sixty days in the barrens before he was rescued. Others, like Jim McAvoy's brother, have yet to be discovered. He went down years ago, but to this day, between jobs, McAvoy takes off into the barrens, still searching. The other pilots shake their heads—it's hopeless, utterly hopeless—but nobody says a word to McAvoy. Besides, the next time it could be you.

Stunted jack pines and mean scrub stands of spruce, sufficiently hardy to take root in the Precambrian Shield, line the approach to feisty Yellowknife, capital city of one-third of Canada, its population roughly 10,000. Once a tent city, no more than a mining camp, Yellowknife is now civilized, which is to say Colonel Sanders has come. There is also a legion hall, an Elks, and even an Odd Fellow's Lodge. There are not only Anglican and Baptist churches, but also a place of worship for those who practice the Baha'i World Faith. There's the Hudson's Bay store, without which no northern settlement would be complete, and of course there are the bars. The Hoist Room, La Gondola, the Snowshoe Lounge, the Trapline. On a Saturday afternoon in Yellowknife, the bush pilots and miners drift between the coffee shop in the seedy Yellowknife Inn and the smoke-filled bar in the squalid Gold Range, where they shoot the breeze over the traditional "two and a juice": two glasses of draft beer and a jug of tomato juice to serve as a mixer. The talk tends to be about jobs available and, naturally, the weather, every northerner's most immediate concern.

On my most recent trip to Yellowknife, a summer fishing expedition, I was glad to see the town's spirit hadn't faltered. The federal government in distant and sometimes utterly daft Ottawa had just awarded the town $40,000 worth of fireworks to be set off on Canada Day, July 1. The locals, instead of rising to cheer, were rolling about with laughter. Reason for laughter: no darkness.

Although the sun shines only tentatively for six hours a day during the punishing winter months, Yellowknife provides twenty exhilarating hours of daylight and four hours of twilight during summer. Late in June, on the week-end of the Midnight Sun, there is the annual Folk on the Rocks Festival out on Long Lake, when fiddlers out of Tuktoyaktuk, Indian drummers out of Fort Rae, and Eskimo throat singers roll into town, all of them more enthusiastic than talented. Then, on June 21, the very Night of the Midnight Sun, the Yellowknife Golf Club, its present clubhouse securely anchored, starts its annual tournament at midnight. Royal Canadian Golf Association rules are followed with one important modification: "No penalty assessed when ball carried off by raven." And there are ravens, ravens everywhere. The big black bold birds are omni-present in Yellowknife. Perched on powerlines in the chill of winter. Diving down on garbage pails, three or maybe four of them rocking the pail until it topples and they are free to scavenge.

Until 1960, there was no road out of Yellowknife. Weeks before the Mack-enzie Highway system, the 947-mile winding link with Edmonton, was com-pleted, a visiting reporter asked an old settler what he would do once the road was ready. Without hesitation, he replied: "Drive the hell out of here." But he is still there, of course.

When its first mile of road was completed in 1944, and two cars were brought in by river barge, they managed a head-on collision within a week. Now there are miles of paved roads and even rows of parking meters on Franklin Avenue. A few years ago, Chief Arrowmaker, a Dogrib, was brought before a magistrate for failing to feed the meter. Outraged, he protested, "I can't read the white man's symbols."

"If you can drive a white man's machine," he was told, "you should be able to read his symbols."

"And not only that," Arrowmaker continued, fulminating, "but this is my land anyway."

Who the land actually belongs to—Indians, métis, Eskimos, or white men— and whether the once contemplated construction of a $7 billion natural-gas pipeline would destroy the environment beyond repair, was debated at the Mackenzie Valley Pipeline Inquiry, conducted in the Northwest Territories from 1974 through 1977 by Mr. Justice Berger.

Fred Andrew, a Slavey trapper, told the inquiry, "I have heard that the pipeline is to go, I can't say anything . . . [but] this is our land, we worry about fires, forest fires, but still the fires keep catching on. Since I recall, I hear that people keep their money in banks. The Indian people don't do that, they go out in the land and kill their meat . . . We make our living off the land. If we don't have any rabbit or moose or fish, we don't have anything. I have nothing . . . We don't write, we use our heads, we use our heads the right way. I have been to the white man's land, and there to go to the bathroom I have to pay ten cents . . . and now, they go all over our land, and they are not paying."

There will be no pipeline, but even so the native way of life seems doomed. Gone, already, are the legendary dog teams, displaced by snowmobiles. Eskimo lads from the Arctic coast, educated by missionaries, or in schools provided by the government, have lost their traditional skills. And now, ironically, it is the RCMP that runs special classes to teach them how to hunt caribou or seal.

Yellowknife took its name from a band of Indians, a branch of the Chipewyans, who used to inhabit the region and were known to early explorers as Yellow-knives or Copperknives, so called for the weapons they fashioned from local copper deposits. For years the ferocious Yellowknives lorded it over the neighboring Dogribs. Then one night, as the Yellowknives lay ravaged by a smallpox epidemic, the Dogribs fell on them, decimating the tribe, survivors fleeing across the Great Slave Lake, south to Snowdrift.

The white man was no more than an occasional interloper until 1934, when gold was discovered, and the Old Town, as it came to be known, began to take shape on the steep sides of the huge central rocks. Those, those were the days of the notorious Rex Café, cat and gaming houses, and log-cabin banks, and then the raw mining camp began to attract those characters who have since become part of the capital city's heritage. Among them, Burial Smith, town drunk and undertaker, who used to barrel through Yellowknife in a van that served as both a taxi and a hearse, a sign prominently displayed in the window: $15 lying down, $2.50 sitting up. Smith, who unfortunately could not abide corpses, took to guzzling embalming fluid as well as other potent brews. As no graves could be dug into the permafrost in the wintertime, he was obliged to estimate the coming season's losses in summer and, anticipating, dig the necessary holes. "There used to be a saying here," an old resident told me, "that if you died during the winter, they would sharpen your head and drive you in with a sledgehammer or, if you were a crooked bastard, they'd simply screw you into the ground."

If Burial Smith is no more, another character, the mysterious Tom Doornbos, lingered well into the Seventies. A septuagenarian when I encountered him, Doornbos could still be seen prowling the streets, his shabby coat ankle-length, a tattered briefcase always to hand. Years ago, before plumbing came to Yellowknife, Doornbos used to wander the same streets wearing a yoke, vending buckets of fresh water. He was rumored to have fled Amsterdam following a stock-market scandal, and as he wandered through town, he also scoured the streets for old bits of linoleum, string, bent nails, anything. Then, shortly after World War II, when there was a temporary shortage of nails, Doornbos shuffled into Walt England's hardware store and sold him a bucket of invaluable nails, all of which had been straightened out. He had, by this time, begun to acquire lots in and around Yellowknife, and is rumored to have died fabulously rich, a large landholder, but nobody ever really knew for sure.

As late as 1960, the population of Yellowknife was no more than 3,000. Then, in 1967, a sea change occurred, after which nothing was the same any more in Yellowknife, not to say the entire NWT. In 1967, big, incomparably ebullient, and plain-spoken Stuart Hodgson, the newly appointed commissioner, lifted the territorial government out of Ottawa, where it was traditionally ensconced, and flew it en masse into Yellowknife. "I'd only just started the job in Ottawa," he said, "when I realized you simply cannot walk into an office here—two thousand miles from where all the action is—take off your southern coat and put on your northern coat . . . Now when the people of the North are cold, I'm cold also; when their basements are flooded, so is mine."

Hodgson, a former West Coast union organizer, was affectionately known as Oomemak, or the musk ox, to the Eskimos. He carried the government to them, flying into even the most remote settlements at least once a year. A hellraiser, a mover, as deeply involved with the North as he was impatient of the traditionally vacillating bureaucrat. Descending into a settlement with his attendants, Hodgson would call a community meeting, demanding that the Eskimos state their grievances. Once, he told me, a disgruntled Eskimo trapper stopped him as he left a meeting hall. "How come," he asked, "my 'rats [muskrats] were only worth a dollar each this year?"

"Well now," Hodgson began, "after you come in from your trapping in the barrens, we ship your 'rats to Montreal. You know Montreal?"

The trapper shook his head no. Drawing a map in the snow, Hodgson explained that it was a big city in Canada.

"I understand," the trapper said.

"Good. Well, from Montreal, they send your 'rats across the big sea to a city called Paris in France." He drew another map in the snow. "You understand that?"

"I understand."

"In Paris, there is a house called Dior and they create fashions for the ladies and, if they feature furs, you are paid lots of money for your 'rats. You understand what I'm saying?"

"Yes. I understand."

"But if they do not use furs, we can't get you much money for your 'rats. Last year they did not include furs. You understand?"

"Yes."

"Good."

"But how come my 'rats were only worth a dollar each this year?"

If furs continue shaky, gold has enjoyed a revival. Yellowknife's Great Consolidated Mining Company, as well as the neighboring Giant Yellowknife, extract something like half an ounce of gold out of a ton of pulverized rock, working either end of a seam that passes directly under the town. Once, however, the seam was much richer. According to the town's first newspaper, the six-page mimeographed weekly *Prospector*, the first gold brick poured in the NWT was cast as the Great Con on Monday, September 5, 1938. "Weight of the history-making brick was 72½ ounces." A later issue of the *Prospector*, December 15, 1938, announced on the first page, FIRST WHITE CHILD BORN IN YELLOWKNIFE. It was a girl, Margaret Karin Lundquist. The same issue of the newspaper proclaimed, IT'S HERE!, *Stella Dallas*, at the Pioneer Theatre, with Barbara Stanwyck. It also revealed RADIO TELEPHONE LINKS NORTH WITH OUTSIDE. "Commercial radio-telephone service between Yellowknife and the outside is now in operation . . . from Yellowknife to any part of the world . . ."

Now, of course, Yellowknife has its own radio station, CBC-TV via satellite, as well as the weekly *Yellowknifer*. Even more important, possibly, are the militant *Native Press*, published by the Indian Brotherhood, and, out of Frobisher Bay for distribution throughout the entire NWT, the Eskimo newspaper, *Inukshuk*. Both native newspapers feature an uncommonly large proportion of stories on alcoholism, the most serious social problem in the Territories. A recent *Inukshuk* headline ran: DRUNKS HAVE FORGOTTEN CHRISTIAN GOD. "A drunkard, according to Anglican Archdeacon Whitebread, will not get into heaven. He was speaking at Alcohol Education Day . . ."

The sales of alcohol in the NWT are prodigious, and no large northern community, including Yellowknife, is without its deintoxication center. And so, ten years ago, two imaginative government officials, Jake Ootes and Art Sorensen, came up with a grabber, *Captain Al Cohol Comics*, which warned unwary northern readers that LIQUOR DOESN'T MAKE HEROES! BOOZE IS FOR BUMS! Captain Al, who enjoyed superhuman powers until he was tempted by booze, which rendered him into a blundering fool, was featured in four stirring comic books, which have since become collectors' items. He was to be followed, Ootes told me, by yet another problem hero, Corporal Clap. Alas, the corporal never surfaced, and even Captain Al was banned. Native groups adjudged him a racist, fair-skinned and fair-haired, although most of the people in the north were native. So, in the end, the delightful captain was killed by bureaucracy, not booze.

But booze remains an enormous problem.

Once when I was visiting Yellowknife, vast herds of caribou were reported in nearby Snowdrift. The Indians were potting them by the hundreds, shipping planeloads to market in Yellowknife, netting as much as $1,200 a flight. But no sooner had the cash been turned over than yet another plane was chartered to fly from Yellowknife and return laden with $1,200 worth of liquor. The hunt would not resume until all the bottles were gone, $1,200 changed hands again, and more liquor was sent for. Then, too, to enter the Yellowknife Inn on any day of the week is to elbow your way past knots of despondent Indians and Eskimos, some of them teenagers, most of them drunk, all of them seemingly waiting for somebody or something never to arrive.

For all that, whatever its problems, wonderful, demented Yellowknife has more spirit than any other town I know of in Canada. Take the referendum, for instance, called some years back to determine whether or not the town wanted home mail delivery. Yellowknifers voted a resounding "No," even though winter temperatures can plunge to forty below zero, if only because during the long dark months many of them get to meet each other only when they pick up their mail at the post office. And then, a miner, stopped outside the post office by an inquiring photographer from the *Yellowknifer* and asked what social facility, presently missing, would most enhance the quality of life in town, promptly replied: "A whorehouse."

Mexico, the Caribbean, South America

FROM
American Journals

ALBERT CAMUS

Camus wrote his journals during lecture tours of North America in 1946 and South America in 1949. In Brazil, where he was received as a literary celebrity, he suffered much physical and mental distress but managed graphic descriptions of his experiences, the land, and the people.

The Trip to Iguape
August 5

WE leave for the religious festivals of Iguape, but at 10 instead of 7 as planned. In fact we were supposed to drive all day inland, on the deplorable Brazilian roads, and it would have been better to arrive before nightfall. But there were delays, the car wasn't ready, etc. We leave São Paulo and begin driving south. The road, whether made of dirt or stone, is covered with red dust, and the vegetation on each side of the road for half a mile is covered with a layer of dried mud. After several miles we too—that is, the driver who looks like Auguste Comte; Andrade and his son, whose head is full of philosophers; Sylvestre, the French cultural attaché; and myself—are covered with the same dust. It gets in through every opening in the large Ford pickup truck and slowly fills up our noses and mouths. On top of it all a ferocious sun that roasts the earth and brings all life to a halt. After thirty miles, a disturbing noise. We stop. A spring in front is broken, visibly sticking out from the cluster of springs and brushing against the rim of the tire. Auguste Comte scratches his head and announces that we can get it fixed ten miles up the road. I advise him to take the broken spring out immediately before it gets wedged against the tire. But he's optimistic about it. We go another three miles and stop—the spring is stuck. Auguste Comte decides to get a tool: from a chest in the back of the truck, he pulls out a thick iron rod which he uses as a hammer, banging it harder and harder against the plate, imagining that he can force it loose.

I explain that there's a nut to take off and the tire itself. But finally I realize that he's set out on these bad roads for a long trip without a monkey wrench. We wait, beneath a sun that could kill, until finally a truck comes along, and the driver, thank goodness, has a monkey wrench. The tire is taken off, the nut unscrewed, and the plate of the spring is finally removed. We set out again between the pale, craggy mountains; from time to time we sight a starving water buffalo with an escort of sad vultures. At 1 o'clock we arrive in Piédade, an unpleasant little village, where we're warmly welcomed by the innkeeper Doña Anesia whom, at one time, Andrade must have courted. Served by Maria, an Indian métis, who ends up offering me artificial flowers. An interminable Brazilian meal which one manages to get down thanks to the *pinga*, which is the name of the local *cachasa*. In the meantime they've repaired the spring, and we leave. We're constantly ascending and the air is becoming very thin. There are immense uninhabited and uncultivated expanses. The terrible solitude of this unlimited wilderness explains certain things about this country. Arrive at Pilar at 3. But there Auguste Comte realizes that he's made a mistake. We're told that we've driven 40 miles too far. Which means, here, two or three hours of traveling. Our bodies aching from the bumpy ride, and covered with dust, we set off to find the right road. In fact, it's not until the end of the day that we begin to descend the other side of the Serra. I have time to see the first miles of virgin forest, the density of this sea of vegetation, to imagine the solitude in the middle of this unexplored world, and night falls as we plunge into the forest. We drive for hours, pitching and rocking along a narrow road that runs between walls of high trees, amid a thick, sugary odor. From time to time through the thickness of the forest, fireflies pass, and birds with red eyes brush against the windshield. Apart from that the immobility and muteness of this dreadful world are absolute, even though from time to time Andrade thinks he's heard an ocelot. The road weaves and winds, continues over bridges of swaying planks that cross little rivers. Then comes the fog and a fine rain that dissolves the light from our headlights. We're not driving, but literally creeping along. It's almost 7 P.M., we've been on the road since 10 A.M., and our fatigue is such that we receive with a certain fatalism Auguste Comte's announcement that we're running out of gas. However, the forest is not quite so thick—and slowly, the landscape is changing. We finally reach the open air and a small village where we're halted by a large river. Light signals on the other side and we see a large ferry boat approaching by means of rods pulled by mulattoes in straw hats, the oldest system there is. We embark and the ferry drifts slowly across the Ribeira river. The river is wide and flows gently towards the sea and the night. On the banks the forest is still dense. Misty stars in the thick sky. On board nobody speaks. The absolute silence of the hour is broken only by the lapping of the river against the flanks of the ferry. In the bow of the ferry, I watch the river descend; the strangeness of this setting, which is nonetheless familiar. Bizarre bird cries and the call of bullfrogs rise from the two banks. At this exact moment it is midnight in Paris.

Disembarkment. Then we continue to creep towards Registro, a true Japanese capital in the middle of Brazil, where I have the time to glimpse houses delicately decorated and even a kimono. We're told that Iguape is only 40 miles farther.

We set off again. A humid breeze, an incessant mist indicate that the sea is not far. The road becomes sand—more difficult and dangerous than it was before. It's midnight when we finally arrive at Iguape. Not counting stops, it took us ten hours to drive the 180 miles that separate us from São Paulo.

Everything is closed at the hotel. A distinguished townsman, whom we meet by chance in the night, takes us to the mayor's house (he's called the prefect here). Through the door the mayor tells us that we're sleeping at the hospital. Set off for the hospital. Despite my fatigue, the city seems to me to be beautiful, with its colonial churches, the nearby forest, its low, naked houses and the thick softness of the damp air. Andrade imagines that we can hear the sea. But it's far. At the Happy Memory Hospital (that's its name), the friendly city father leads us to a renovated ward that smells of fresh paint from thirty yards away. We're told that in fact it's been repainted in our honor. But there's no light: the local power plant shuts down at 11 P.M. In the glow from our lighters we nonetheless see six clean and simple beds. It's our dormitory. We put down our suitcases. And the city father wants us to join him for a sandwich at his club. Exhausted, we go to the club. The club is a kind of second floor bistro where we meet other distinguished persons who shower us with their respects. Once again I notice the exquisite Brazilian politeness, perhaps a bit ceremonious, but still much better than the European tactlessness. Sandwich and beer. But a tall imbecile who can hardly stand on his own feet is struck with the curious idea of demanding to see my passport. I show him my passport, and he tells me that it's invalid. Tired, I send him packing. Indignant, the personages huddle together for a moment, and then come over to tell me that they're going to put this policeman (for that's what he is) in prison, and that I will be able to choose the charges that I want to press against him. I beg of them not to put him in prison. They explain to me that this foul-mouthed imbecile has disregarded the great honor that I have done Iguape, and that his bad manners must be punished. I protest. But they're determined to honor me in this way. The affair lasts until the following evening when I finally find the right approach, asking them, as a personal favor to me, to spare this scatter-brained policeman. They proclaim my chivalry and tell me that it shall be done according to my wishes.

In any case, the night of the drama we leave for the hospital and halfway there meet the mayor, who has gotten up to accompany us to our beds. He has also awakened the power plant personnel, and we have lights. They make sure we're comfortable almost to the point of tucking us in, and finally, at 1 A.M., overwhelmed with fatigue, we try to sleep. I say try because my bed slants a little and my neighbors turn from side to side and Auguste Comte snores ferociously. Finally, very late, I fall into a dreamless sleep.

August 6

Wake up very early. Unfortunately, no water in this hospital. I shave and wash a little using mineral water. Then the personages arrive and take us to the main ward for breakfast. Finally, we go out into Iguape.

In the little garden of the Fountain, soft and mysterious with clusters of flowers between the banana trees and the palms, I regain a little ease and tranquillity. In front of a grotto, some métis, mulattoes and the first gauchos that I've seen wait patiently to obtain some pieces of the "growing stone." In fact Iguape is a city where an effigy of the Good Jesus was found in the water by some fishermen who came to this grotto to wash it. Ever since, a stone grows there ineluctably, and people come to chisel off beneficent pieces of it. The city itself, between the forest and the river, is crowded around the large church of the Good Jesus. Several hundred houses in a single style—low, stuccoed, multi-colored. Beneath the fine rain that soaks its badly paved streets, with the motley crowd—gauchos, Japanese, Indians, métis, elegant, distinguished persons—which is its population, Iguape bears the colonial stamp. The melancholy there is particular; it's the melancholy of places that are at the ends of the earth. Aside from the heroic route that we took, only two weekly flights connect Iguape to the rest of the world. One could find refuge here.

Throughout the day the kindness of our hosts is constant. But we've come for the procession. As soon as the afternoon begins firecrackers are going off everywhere, startling into flight the bald vultures adorning the rooftops. The crowd gets bigger. Some of these pilgrims have been travelling the deplorable inland roads for five days. One of them who looks Assyrian, with a beautiful black beard, tells us that he was saved by the Good Jesus from a shipwreck, after one night and one day stranded in high seas, and that he has vowed to carry a 130-pound stone on his head for the entire procession. The hour approaches. From the church come penitents in surplices: first the blacks, then the whites; then children dressed as angels; then the "children of Mary"; then an effigy of the Good Jesus himself, behind which the bearded man advances, barechested and carrying an enormous slab on his head. Finally an orchestra comes, playing a double-step and, at the end of the procession, the crowd of pilgrims, which is the only really interesting sight, the rest being ordinary and rather sordid. But the crowd that proceeds down a narrow street, filling it almost to bursting, is one of the strangest assemblages that one could imagine. The ages, races, the colors of the clothes, the classes, the infirmities, all are mixed together in a gaudy, oscillating mass, lit up at intervals by bursts of holy candles, above which firecrackers explode incessantly. From time to time an airplane—out of place in this ageless world—also passes overhead. Mobilized for the occasion, it rumbles by at regular intervals above the personages in their elegance and the Good Jesus. We go to wait for the procession at another strategic point, and when it passes in front of us, the bearded man is wincing with fatigue and his legs are trembling. But he makes it to the end nonetheless. The bells ring, stores and houses on the route of the procession which had closed their doors and windows now open them—and we go to dinner.

After dinner, in the square the young gauchos sing, and everyone sits in a circle around them. The firecrackers continue, and a child gets a finger blown off. He cries and screams as they're taking him away. "Why did the Good Jesus do that?" (This cry of the soul is translated for me.)

I go right to bed because we're leaving early the next day. But the firecrackers and the horrendous sneezes of Auguste Comte keep me from falling asleep until very late.

In Patagonia

B R U C E   C H A T W I N

The author described his travels through Patagonia as a ''Quest or Wonder Voyage,'' and they resulted in a narrative of wit and curious detail that bring light to the haunted southern end of South America. His search for Lake Kami, inspired by a childhood reading of The Uttermost Part of the Earth, *led him along a forlorn wilderness track.*

*I*N his autobiography *The Uttermost Part of the Earth,* Lucas Bridges tells how his father's manuscript was filched by Frederick A. Cook, a glib American doctor on the Belgian Antarctic Expedition of 1898–99, who tried to pass it off as his own work. Cook was the mythomane traveller from Rip van Winkle country who began with a milk-round and claimed the first ascent of Mount McKinley and to have beaten Robert Peary to the North Pole. He died at New Rochelle in 1940, after serving a sentence for selling forged oil shares.

The manuscript of the dictionary got lost in Germany during the Second World War, but was recovered by Sir Leonard Woolley, the excavator of Ur, and presented by the family to the British Museum.

Lucas Bridges was the first White to make friends with the Onas. They trusted him alone when men like the Red Pig were butchering their kin. *The Uttermost Part of the Earth* was one of my favourite books as a boy. In it he describes looking down from Mount Spión Kop on the sacred Lake Kami, and how, later, the Indians helped him hack a trail linking Harberton with the family's other farm at Viamonte.

I had always wanted to walk the track.

But Clarita Goodall did not want me to go. The distance to Lake Kami was about twenty-five miles but the rivers were in spate and the bridges had fallen.

"You could break a leg," she said, "or get lost and we'd have to send a search party. We used to ride it in a day, but you can't get a horse through now."

And all because of the beavers. A governor of the island brought the beavers from Canada and now their dams choked the valleys where once the going was clear. But still I wanted to walk the track.

And in the morning early she woke me. I heard her making tea in the kitchen. She gave me slabs of bread and blackcurrant jam. She filled my thermos with coffee. She took sticks soaked in kerosene and put them in a watertight bag: so if I fell in the river I should at least have fire. She said: "Do be careful!" and stood in the doorway, in the half-light, in a long pink housecoat, waving slowly with a calm sad smile.

A film of mist hung over the inlet. A family of red-fronted geese rippled the water, and at the first gate more geese stood by a puddle. I passed along the track that led up into the mountains. Ahead was Harberton Mountain, black with trees, and a hazy sun coming over its shoulder. This side of the river was rolling grass country, burned out of the forest and spiked with charred trees.

The track rose and fell. Platforms of logs were laid in corrugations in the hollows. Beyond the last fence was a black pool ringed with dead trees and from there the path wound uphill in among the first big timber.

I heard the river before I saw it, roaring at the bottom of a gorge. The track snaked down the cliff. In a clearing were Lucas Bridges's old sheep pens now rotting away. The bridge was gone, but a hundred yards upstream the river opened out and slid over slippery brown stones. I cut two saplings and trimmed them. I took off my boots and trousers and eased out into the water, testing each footfall with the left stick, steadying myself with the right. At the deepest point the stream swirled round my buttocks. I dried off in a patch of sunlight on the far bank. My feet were red from cold. A torrent duck flew upstream. I recognized its striped head and thin whirring wings.

The track soon lost itself in the forest. I checked the compass and struck north towards the second river. It was a river no longer, but a swamp of yellow peat moss. Along its edge, young trees had been felled with sharp oblique cuts, as if with the swipe of a machete. This was beaver country. This is what beavers did to a river.

I walked three hours and came up to the shoulder of Mount Spión Kop. On ahead was the valley of the Valdez River, a half-cylinder running north twelve miles to the thin blue line of Lake Kami.

A shadow passed over the sun, a whoosh and the sound of wind ripping through pinions. Two condors had dived on me. I saw the red of their eyes as they swept past, banking below the col and showing the grey of their backs. They glided in an arc to the head of the valley and rose again, circling in the upthrust, where the wind pushed against the cliffs, till they were two specks in a milky sky.

The specks increased in size. They were coming back. They came back heading into the wind, unswerving as raiders on target, the ruff of white feathers ringing their black heads, the wings unflinching and the tails splayed downwards as air-brakes and their talons lowered and spread wide. They dived on me four times and then we both lost interest.

In the afternoon I *did* fall into the river. Crossing a beaver dam I trod on a log that felt firm but was floating. It pitched me head first into black mud and I had a hard time getting out. Now I had to reach the road before night.

The track showed up again, yawning a straight corridor through the dark wood. I followed the fresh spoor of a guanaco. Sometimes I saw him up ahead, bobbing over fallen trunks, and then I came up close. He was a single male, his coat all muddied and his front gashed with scars. He had been in a fight and lost. Now he also was a sterile wanderer.

And then the trees cleared and the river wound sluggishly through cattle pastures. Following their tracks I must have crossed the river twenty times. At one crossing I saw boot-marks and suddenly felt light and happy, thinking I would now reach the road or a peon's hut, and then I lost them and the river sluiced down a schist-sided gorge. I struck out across the forest but the light was failing and it was unsafe to clamber over dead trees in the dark.

I spread my sleeping-bag on a level space. I unwrapped the sticks and piled up one half with moss and twigs. The fire flared up. Even damp branches caught and the flames lit the green curtains of lichen hanging from the trees. Inside the sleeping-bag it was damp and warm. Rainclouds were covering the moon.

And then I heard the sound of an engine and sat up. The glare of headlights showed through the trees. I was ten minutes from the road, but too sleepy to care, so I slept. I even slept through a rainstorm.

Next afternoon, washed and fed, I sat in the parlour Viamonte, too stiff to move. For two days I lay on the sofa reading. The family had gone camping all except Uncle Beatle. We talked about flying saucers. The other day he had seen a presence in the dining-room, hovering round a portrait.

From Viamonte I crossed the Chilean half of the island to Porvenir and took the ferry to Punta Arenas.

Observations after Landfall

CHRISTOPHER COLUMBUS

The landfall controversy about the exact location in the Bahamas where Christopher Columbus arrived in 1492 continues. The available communications he made to the Spanish court following his maiden voyage are abstractions, such as the following.

I, IN order that they might feel great amity towards us, because I knew that they were a people to be delivered and converted to our holy faith rather by love than by force, gave to some among them some red caps and some glass beads, which they hung round their necks, and many other things of little value. At this they were greatly pleased and became so entirely our friends that it was a wonder to see. Afterwards they came swimming to the ships' boats, where we were, and brought us parrots and cotton thread in balls, and spears and many other things, and we exchanged for them other things, such as small glass beads and hawks' bells, which we gave to them. In fact, they took all and gave all, such as they had, with good will, but it seemed to me that they were a people very deficient in everything. They all go naked as their mothers bore them, and the women also, although I saw only one very young girl. And all those whom I did see were youths, so that I did not see one who was over thirty years of age; they were very well built, with very handsome bodies and very good faces. Their hair is coarse almost like the hairs of a horse's tail and short; they wear their hair down over their eyebrows, except for a few strands behind, which they wear long and never cut. Some of them are painted black, and they are the colour of the people of the Canaries, neither black nor white, and some of them are painted white and some red and some in any colour that they find. Some of them paint their faces, some their whole bodies, some only the eyes, and some only the nose. They do not bear arms or know them, for I showed to them swords and they took them by the blade and cut themselves through ignorance. They have no iron. Their spears are certain reeds, without iron, and some of these have a fish tooth at the end, while others are pointed in various ways. They are all generally fairly tall, good looking and well proportioned. I saw some who

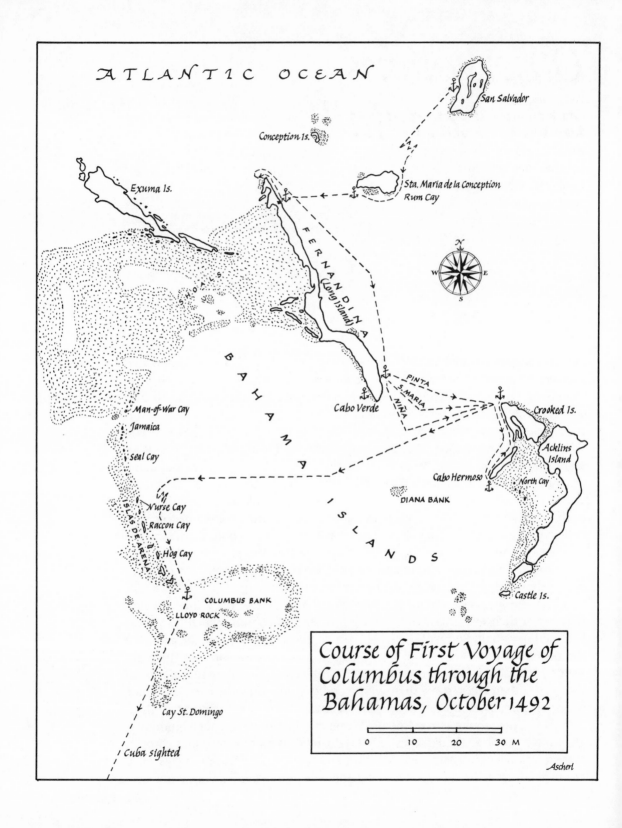

ATLANTIC OCEAN

San Salvador

Conception Is.

Sta. Maria de la Conception
Rum Cay

Exuma Is.

F
E
R
N
A
N
D
I
N
A
(Long Island)

SHOALS

B
A
H
A
M
A

Man-of-War Cay

Jamaica

Seal Cay

ISLAS DE ARENA

Nurse Cay

Raccon Cay

Hog Cay

COLUMBUS BANK

LLOYD ROCK

Cabo Verde

PINTA
S. MARIA
NINA

Crooked Is.

Acklins
Island

Cabo Hermoso

North Cay

DIANA BANK

I
S
L
A
N
D
S

Castle Is.

Cay St. Domingo

Cuba sighted

Course of First Voyage of Columbus through the Bahamas, October 1492

0   10   20   30 M

Ascherl

bore marks of wounds on their bodies, and I made signs to them to ask how this came about, and they indicated to me that people came from other islands, which are near, and wished to capture them, and they defended themselves. And I believed and still believe that they come here from the mainland to take them for slaves. They should be good servants and of quick intelligence, since I see that they very soon say all that is said to them, and I believe that they would easily be made Christians, for it appeared to me that they had no creed. Our Lord willing, at the time of my departure I will bring back six of them to Your Highnesses, that they may learn to talk. I saw no beast of any kind in this island, except parrots.

F R O M

The European Discovery of America

SAMUEL ELIOT MORISON

Historian Samuel Eliot Morison's popular study of the voyages of Columbus, The European Discovery of America: The Southern Voyages, 1492–1616, *includes this synthesized description of the approach to and the reaching of landfall by Columbus in October 1492.*

*O*N the first day of October the wind increased, rain fell in torrents, replenishing the water casks, and in five days (2 to 6 October) the fleet made 710 miles. On the sixth, when they had passed longitude 65° W and actually lay directly north of Puerto Rico, Martín Alonso Pinzón shot his agile *Pinta* under the flagship's stern and shouted, "Alter course, sir, to southwest by west . . . Japan!" Columbus did not understand whether Martín Alonso meant that he thought they had missed Japan and should steer southwest by west for China, or that Japan lay in that direction; but he knew and Pinzón knew that the fleet had sailed more than the 2400 miles which, according to their calculations, lay between the Canaries and Japan. Naturally Columbus was uneasy, but he held to the west course magnetic, which, owing to the variation for which he did not allow, was about west by south, true.

On 7 October, when *Niña* made another false landfall, great flocks of birds passed over the ships, flying west-southwest; this was the autumn migration from eastern North America to the West Indies. Columbus decided that he had better follow Pinzón and the birds rather than his chart, and changed course accordingly that very evening. A very good guess, for this was his shortest route to the nearest land. Every night the men were heartened by seeing against the moon (full on 5 October) flocks of birds flying their way. But mutiny once more reared its ugly head. Even by Columbus's phony reckoning which he gave out, they had sailed much further west than anyone had expected. Enough of this nonsense, sailing west to nowhere; let the Captain General turn back or else—! Columbus, says the record, "cheered them as best he could, holding out good hope of the advantages they might gain; and he added, it was useless to complain, *since he had come to go to the Indies, and so had to continue until he found them, with the help of Our Lord."*

How typical of Columbus's determination! Yet even he, conscious of divine guidance, could not have kept on indefinitely without the support of his captains and officers. According to one account, Martín Alonso Pinzón cheered him by shouting, *Adelante! Adelante!* which the poet Joaquin Miller translated, "Sail on! Sail on!" But, according to Oviedo, one of the earliest historians who talked with the participants, it was Columbus who persuaded the Pinzóns to sail on, with the promise that if land were not found within three days he would turn back. This promise was made on 9 October. Next day the trade wind blew fresher, sending the fleet along at 7 knots, and on the 10th the fleet made a record day's run. On the 11th the wind continued to blow hard, with a heavy following sea. Now signs of land, such as branches of trees with green leaves and even flowers, became so frequent that the people were content with their commander's decision, and the mutinous mutterings died out in keen anticipation of making a landfall in the Indies.

As the sun set under a clear horizon 11 October, the northeast trade breezed up to gale force, and the three ships tore along at 9 knots. Columbus refused to shorten sail, signaled everyone to keep a particularly sharp watch, and offered extra rewards for first landfall in addition to the year's pay promised by the Sovereigns. That night of destiny was clear and beautiful with a late-rising moon, but the sea was the roughest of the entire passage. The men were tense and expectant, the officers testy and anxious, Columbus serene in the confidence that presently God would reveal to him the promised Indies.

At 10:00 P.M., an hour before moonrise, Columbus and a seaman, also simultaneously, thought they saw a light "like a little wax candle rising and falling." Others said they saw it too, but most did not; and after a few minutes it disappeared. Volumes have been written to explain what this light was or might have been. It may well have been a mere illusion created by over-tense watchfulness. But Mrs. Ruth Malvin, a long-time resident of San Salvador, believes it to have been a bonfire lighted by natives living on cliffs or hills on the windward side, to keep sand fleas out of their cabins; and this is the best rational explanation yet made. She had fires lighted on High Cay and other places, and when some 28 miles out to sea could see light "rising and falling" just as Columbus said.

The little light does not cause Columbus to alter his course. His ships rush on, pitching, rolling, and throwing spray, white foam at their bows and wakes reflecting the moon. *Pinta* is perhaps half a mile in the lead, *Santa Maria* on her port quarter, *Niña* on the other side. Now one, now another forges ahead. With the fourth glass of the night watch, the last sands are running out of an era that began with the dawn of history. Not since the birth of Christ has there been a night so full of meaning for the human race.

At 2:00 A.M. 12 October, Rodrigo de Triana, lookout on *Pinta,* sees something like a white cliff shining in the moonlight and sings out, *Tierra! tierra!* "Land! land!" Captain Pinzón verifies the landfall, fires a gun as agreed, and shortens sail to allow the flagship to catch up. As *Santa Maria* approaches, Columbus shouts across the rushing waters, "Señor Martín Alonso, you *did* find land! Five thousand maravedis for you as a bonus!"

Land it was this time; gray clay cliffs, white in the moonlight, on the windward side of a little island of the Bahama group. The fleet would have crashed had it held course, but these men were no fools to pile up on a lee shore. Columbus ordered sail to be shortened and the fleet to jog off and on until daylight. At dawn they made full sail, passed the southern point of the island, and sought an opening on the west coast through the barrier reef. Before noon they found it, sailed into a shallow bay, and anchored in the lee of the land, in five fathoms.

Here on a gleaming beach of white coral occurred the famous first landing of Columbus. The commander (now by general consent called Admiral) went ashore in the flagship's longboat displaying the royal standard of Castile, accompanied by the two Captains Pinzón in their boats, flying the banner of the expedition—a green crowned cross on a white field. "And, all having rendered thanks to Our Lord, kneeling on the ground, embracing it with tears of joy for the immeasurable mercy of having reached it, the Admiral rose and gave this island the name *San Salvador*"—Holy Saviour.

From Africa to the New World

OLAUDAH EQUIANO

The horrors of passage by slave ship were related in 1791 by this African who was taken to Bridgetown, Barbados, in the British West Indies.

*T*HE first object which saluted my eyes when I arrived on the coast was the sea, and a slave ship, which was then riding at anchor, and waiting for its cargo. These filled me with astonishment, which was soon converted into terror; when I was carried on board I was immediately handled, and tossed up, to see if I were sound, by some of the crew; and I was now persuaded that I had got into a world of bad spirits, and that they were going to kill me. Their complexions too differing so much from ours, their long hair, and the language they spoke (which was very different from any I had ever heard) united to confirm me in this belief. Indeed such were the horrors of my views and fears at the moment, that, if ten thousand worlds had been my own, I would have freely parted with them all to have exchanged my conditions with that of the meanest slave in my own country. When I looked round the ship too and saw a large furnace of copper boiling, and a multitude of black people of every description chained together, every one of their countenances expressing dejection and sorrow, I no longer doubted of my fate; and, quite overpowered with horror and anguish, I fell motionless on the deck and fainted. When I recovered a little I found some black people about me, who I believed were some of those who had brought me on board, and had been receiving their pay; they talked to me in order to cheer me, but all in vain. I asked them if we were not to be eaten by those white men with horrible looks, red faces, and long hair. They told me I was not; and one of the crew brought me a small portion of spirituous liquor in a wine-glass; but being afraid of him, I would not take it out of his hand. One of the blacks therefore took it from him and gave it to me, and I took a little down my palate, which, instead of reviving me, as they thought it would, threw me into the greatest consternation at the strange feeling it produced, having never tasted any such liquor before. Soon after this the blacks who brought me on board went off, and left me abandoned to despair. I now saw myself deprived of all chance of returning to my native country, or even the least glimpse of hope of gaining the shore, which I now considered as friendly; and I even wished for my former slavery in preference to my present situation, which was filled with horrors of every kind, still heightened by my ignorance of what I was to undergo. I was not long suffered to indulge my grief; I was soon put down under the decks, and there I received such a salutation in my nostrils as I had never experienced in my life: so that with the loathsomeness of the stench, and crying together, I became so sick and low that I was not able to eat, nor had I the least desire to taste anything. I now wished for the last friend, death, to relieve me; but soon, to my grief, two of the white men offered me eatables; and, on my refusing to eat, one of them held me fast by the hands, and laid me across, I think the windlass, and tied my feet, while the other flogged me severely. I had never experienced any thing of this kind before: and, although not being used to the water, I naturally feared that element the first time I saw it, yet, nevertheless, could I have got over the nettings, I would have jumped over the side, but I could not; and, besides, the crew used to watch us very closely who were not chained down to the decks, lest we should leap into the water: and I have seen some of these poor African prisoners most severely cut for attempting to do so, and hourly whipped for not eating. This indeed was often the case with myself. In a little time after, amongst the poor chained men, I found some of my own nation, which in a small degree gave ease to my mind. I inquired of these what was to be done with us? they gave me to understand we were to be carried to these white people's country to work for them. I then was a little revived, and thought, if it were no worse than working, my situation was not so desperate: but still I feared I should be put to death, the white people looked and acted, as I thought, in so savage a manner; for I had never seen among any people such instances of brutal cruelty; and this not only shown towards us blacks, but also to some of the whites themselves. One white man in particular I saw, when we were permitted to be on deck, flogged so unmercifully with a large rope near the foremast, that he died in consequence of it; and they tossed him over the side as they would have done a brute. This made me fear these people the more; and I expected nothing less than to be treated in the same manner. I could not help expressing my fears and apprehensions to some of my countrymen: I asked them if these people had no country, but lived in this hollow place (the ship)? they told me they did not, but came from a distant one, "Then," said I, "how comes it in all our country we never heard of them!" They told me, because they lived so very far off. I then asked where were their women? had they any like themselves? I was told they had: "And why," said I, "do we not see them?" they answered, because they were left behind. I asked how the vessel could go? they told me they could not tell; but that there were cloth put upon the masts by the help of the ropes I saw, and then the vessel went on; and the white men had some spell or magic they put in the water when they liked in order to stop the vessel. I was exceedingly amazed at this account, and really thought they were spirits. I therefore wished much to be from amongst them, for I expected they would sacrifice me: but my wishes were vain; for we were so quartered that it was impossible for any of us to make our escape. While we stayed on the coast I was mostly on deck; and one day, to my great astonishment, I saw one of these vessels coming in with the sails up. As soon as the whites saw it, they gave a great shout, at which we were amazed: and the more so as the vessel appeared larger by approaching nearer. At last she came to an anchor in my sight, and when the anchor was let go I and my countrymen who saw it were lost in astonishment to observe the vessel stop; and were now convinced it was done by magic. Soon after this the other ship got her boats out, and they came on board of us, and the people of both ships seemed very glad to see each other. Several of the strangers also shook hands with us black people, and made motions with their hands, signifying I suppose, we were to go to their country; but we did not understand them. At last, when the ship we were in had got in all her cargo, they made ready with many fearful noises, and we were all put under deck, so that we could not see how they managed the vessel. But this disappointment was the least of my sorrow. The stench of the hold while we were on the coast was so intolerably loathsome that it was dangerous to remain there for any time, and some of us had been permitted to stay on the deck for the fresh air; but now that the whole ship's cargo were confined together, it became absolutely pestilential. The closeness of the place, and the heat of the climate, added to the number in the ship, which was so crowded that each had scarcely room to turn himself, almost suffocated us. This produced copious perspirations, so that the air soon became unfit for respiration, from a variety of loathsome smells, and brought on a sickness amongst the slaves, of which many died, thus falling victims to the improvident avarice, as I may call it, of their purchasers. This wretched situation was again aggravated by the galling of the chains, now become insupportable; and the filth of the necessary tubs, into which the children often fell, and were almost suffocated. The shrieks of the women, and the groans of the dying, rendered the whole a scene of horror almost inconceivable. Happily perhaps for myself I was soon reduced so low here that it was thought necessary to keep me almost always on deck; and from my extreme youth I was not put in fetters. In this situation I expected every hour to share the fate of my companions, some of whom were almost daily brought upon deck at the point of death, which I began to hope would soon put an end to my miseries. Often did I think many of the inhabitants of the deep much more happy than myself, I envied them the freedom they enjoyed, and as often wished I could change my condition for theirs. Every circumstance I met with served only to render my state more painful, and heightened my apprehensions and my opinion of the cruelty of the whites. One day they had taken a number of fishes; and when they had killed and satisfied themselves with as many as they thought fit, to our astonishment who were on the deck, rather than give any of them to us to eat, as we expected, they tossed the remaining fish into the sea again, although we begged and prayed for some as well as we could, but in vain; and some of my countrymen, being pressed by hunger, took an opportunity, when they thought no one saw them, of trying to get a little privately; but they were discovered, and the attempt procured them some very severe floggings. One day, when we had a smooth sea and moderate wind, two of my wearied countrymen who were chained together (I was near them at the time), preferring death to such a life of misery, somehow made through the nettings and jumped into the sea: immediately another quite dejected fellow, who on account of his illness, was afforded to be out of irons, also followed their example; and I believe many more would very soon have done the same if they had not been prevented by the ship's crew who were instantly alarmed. Those of us that were the most active were in a moment put down under the deck, and there was such a noise and confusion amongst the people of the ship as I never heard before, to stop her, and get the boat out to go after the slaves. However two of the wretches were drowned, but they got the other, and afterwards flogged him unmercifully for thus attempting to prefer death to slavery. In this manner we continued to undergo more hardships than I can now relate, hardships which are inseparable from this accursed trade. Many a time we were near suffocation from the want of fresh air, which we were often without for whole days together. This, and the stench of the necessary tubs, carried off many. During our passage I first saw flying fishes, which surprised me very much: they used frequently to fly across the ship, and many of them fell on the deck. I also now first saw the use of the quadrant; I had often with astonishment seen the mariners make observations with it, and I could not think what it meant. They at last took notice of my surprise: and one of them, willing to increase it, as well as to gratify my curiosity, made me one day look through it. The clouds appeared to me to be land, which disappeared as they passed along. This heightened my wonder; and I was now more persuaded than ever that I was in another world, and that every thing about me was magic. At last we came in sight of the island of Barbados, at which the whites on board gave a great shout, and made many signs of joy to us. We did not know what to think of this; but as the vessel drew nearer, we plainly saw the harbour, and other ships of different kinds and sizes; and we soon anchored amongst them off Bridge-Town. Many merchants and planters now came on board, though it was in the evening. They put us in separate parcels, and examined us attentively. They also made us jump, and pointed to the land, signifying we were to go there. We thought by this we should be eaten by these ugly men, as they appeared to us; and, when soon after we were all put down under the deck again, there was much dread and trembling among us, and nothing but bitter cries to be heard all the night from these apprehensions, insomuch that at last the white people got some old slaves from the land to pacify us. They told us we were not to be eaten, but to work, and were soon to go on land, where we should see many of our country people. This report eased us much; and sure enough, soon after we landed, there came to us Africans of all languages. We were conducted immediately to the merchant's yard, where we were all pent up together like so many sheep in a fold, without regard to sex or age. As every object was new to me, every thing I saw filled me with surprise. What struck me first was that the houses were built with bricks and stories, and in every other respect different from those I had seen in Africa: but I was still more astonished on seeing people on horseback. I did not know what this could mean; and indeed I thought these people were full of nothing but magical arts. While I was in this astonishment one of my fellow prisoners spoke to a countryman of his about the horses, who said they were the same kind they had in their country. I understood them, though they were from a distant part of Africa, and I thought it odd I had not seen any horses there; but afterwards when I came to converse with different Africans, I found they had many horses amongst them, and much larger than those I then saw. We were not many days in the merchant's custody before we were sold after their usual manner, which is this:—On a signal given, (as the beat of a drum) the buyers rush at once into the yard where the slaves are confined, and make choice of that parcel they like best. The noise and clamour with which this is attended, and the eagerness visible in the countenances of the buyers, serve not a little to increase the apprehension of terrified Africans, who may well be supposed to consider them as the ministers of that destruction to which they think themselves devoted. In this manner, without scruple, are relations and friends separated, most of them never to see each other again. I remember in the vessel in which I was brought over, in the men's apartment, there were several brothers, who, in the sale were sold in different lots; and it was very moving on this occasion to see and hear their cries at parting. O, ye nominal Christians! might not an African ask you, learned you this from your God, who says unto you, Do unto all men as you would men should do unto you? Is it not enough that we are torn from our country and friends, to toil for your luxury and lust of gain? Must every tender feeling be likewise sacrificed to your avarice? Are the dearest friends and relations, now rendered more dear by their separation from their kindred, still to be parted from each other, and thus prevented from cheering the gloom of slavery with the small comfort of being together, and mingling their sufferings and sorrows? Why are parents to lose their children, brothers their sisters, or husbands their wives? Surely this is a new refinement in cruelty, which, while it has no advantage to atone for it, thus aggravates distress, and adds fresh horrors even to the wretchedness of slavery.

The Traveller's Tree

PATRICK LEIGH FERMOR

When he was an eighteen-year-old student in London in the 1930s, Patrick Fermor began his career of travel and distinguished travel writing by walking to Constantinople. He was a decorated officer of the Irish Guards in World War II, a resistance organizer during the German occupation of Greece and Crete. His postwar travels took him through the length of the Caribbean archipelago and resulted in these observations on the beauty of Grenada.

W̲E left Trinidad, for some reason, in the small hours of the morning; driving, half asleep, to the aerodrome at Cocorite, through caverns of bamboo that the headlights summoned out of the darkness. There we waited a long time in the empty white halls, nodding among coffee cups until the unearthly voice from the loudspeaker roused us. Sleepy officials loaded us and our luggage into the plane, where we fell into a sleep whose surface was only ruffled now and then by the jolt of an air pocket. The ninety miles of flight into the north, the landing in Grenada and climbing, as dawn broke, into a motor, were incidents that affected us as remotely as though we had been sleep-walkers, and it was only in the middle of some mountains that we really woke up.

Nothing can be more mysterious and, in their sinister fashion, beautiful than these tarns in the craters of dead volcanoes. Here was another, lying high in the windy folds of the watershed; the water, in this early morning light, stagnant and smooth and steel grey. But the Grand Etang was even more unearthly than the bottomless lake of Dominica, because the forest, as it waded into the lake, seemed to have fallen under a curse which had killed it dead. The far bank was an unearthly wood of skeleton mahogany trees as white and exsanguine as though every single one had been separately struck by lightning and frozen in the moment of death into a demonstrative posture of horror. It was a forest in its agony, the pale, cold scaffolding of a wood, and as we watched the reflections of the trees in the lake they vanished. The surface of the water was broken up into millions of pock-marks as the rain began.

Dark green woods glimmered through the tracks of the rain-drops across the window-panes after we left this deserted place. Steep hills rose and fell and rose again in a final eminence before sinking into the sea. Among the trees of the last apex a great Regency building appeared: Government House, the driver told us. Remembering a letter of introduction that Mrs. Napier had given us, we dug it out and left it in the hands of a splendid-looking white uniformed servant who was standing among brass cannon under the portico, and drove downhill towards the sea and the outskirts of St. George's.

The capital of Grenada and the pinnacled belfries under the rain, the steep streets and the wet stone columns and fanlights of Adam houses, the glimpses along the lanes of a grey and turbulent sea—all this resembled a beautiful eighteenth-century Devonshire town in mid-winter. The car drove into the yard of a small hotel that might have been a coaching inn. Dashing indoors through the downpour, we expected to plunge into a world of crops, goloshes, toby-jugs, superannuated advertisements for Apollinaris Water, and copies of Pears' Cyclopaedia; which was, indeed, more or less what we found.

By the time we woke up, the rain had stopped and the little capital wore a different, but no less charming, aspect. How dissimilar everything in Grenada was from the immensity, the trams and the ugliness of Port of Spain! The change in atmosphere, tempo, mood and scenery was complete.

Like Roseau, St. George's is a large village that has evolved easily and slowly into a small country town, but the houses, instead of wood and lattice and shingle, are built of stone: fine, solid dwellings, with graceful balustraded staircases running up to pilastered doorways supporting fanlights and pediments. The burnished knockers and door-knobs and letter-boxes reflect the morning sunlight. So steep is the hillside on which the town clusters that the cobbled lanes and streets twist in many directions, and it was only by climbing to the top of the town that we could get an idea of its economy as a whole.

The coast is a succession of volcanic craters, of which one of the largest, the Carenage, is the harbour of St. George's. The capital itself is built on the steep crater's rim, which is submerged at its outer segment to form a gap over which the ships can sail out and in; the broken circumference, emerging from the water in bluffs, ascends under its load of houses and churches, to unite with the forested slopes inland. Lagoons engrail the coast with pale blue crescents and discs, and from their landward circumferences the island soars in a steep and regular geometry of volcanic peaks. Old fortresses lie along the hilltops commanding the town, and, on the escarpment of the crater's rim that ends and completes St. George's—rising into a final knoll before its steep plunge under water—the old French Fort Royal (later re-baptized Fort George) rears its defences. The road along the waterfront follows a tunnel through the heart of this castellated tufa, and re-emerges under a little bandstand which rests on the sunlit slope like an empty birdcage.

Windward Islands sloops lay at anchor, and a long way below a schooner under full sail was gliding out of the Carenage into the Caribbean. From our point above the town we could see the law courts, the tower of the eighteenth-century parish church, the tropical-Gothic belfry of the Scottish kirk with its high finials and crockets, and the high roofs of the town, whose steep mansard-gables and beautiful rose-coloured and semi-circular tiles all overlapping like fish-scales must be an architectural device which has lingered here from the time of the French. The town was first laid out by the French Governor, M. de Bellair, in 1705, and continued by the English when it was granted them by treaty in 1763. It has remained British ever since, except for the four years after it was attacked by the fleet of Count d'Estaing and captured by a landing force under Count Dillon, the Irish Commander of Dillon's Regiment of the French Army. The French relinquished it again at the Treaty of Versailles in 1783.

But these roofs seemed to derive from an older tradition than the eighteenth century, and the first progenitors of these Grenadian roofs and gables may well be the steep summits of the Marais and the Place des Vosges. Of French origin, too, are the beautiful wrought-iron balconies on many of the older houses. Everywhere among the roofs and towers the tops of trees appeared, and hibiscus and bougainvillea and flamboyant overflowed the walls, as though the little town were built on an effervescent foundation of tropical flora which sprang foaming through every available gap, pillowing the upper storeys on a tide of leaves and flowers.

To the north of our elevation, the land dived down to a large circle of grass, another volcano's mouth, in the middle of which, far below us and over-shadowed by the wooded peaks, a game of football was in progress. The striped jerseys of the players moved about the field in pursuit of the invisible ball with the purposeless motion of insects, and the ragged square of spectators swarmed in bulges, and thinned out and swarmed again with the fluctuations of the game. The rumour of their shouts came faintly to our ears across the green hollow. Our sylvan vantage-point was deserted except for an overgrown cemetery and a young Negro reclining Byronically on a tombstone, under a mango tree, reading *The Prose Works of Oliver Goldsmith*.

Grenada is only twenty-one miles from north to south, and twelve miles at its broadest point from east to west; but owing to the mountainous ridge running along its spine, and the deep valleys that radiate from it on either side, it seems very much larger. Our road along the west coast was overshadowed by the steep mountains of the interior, a towering geometrical organization of green volcanic cones. Valley after valley discharged their rivers under the bridges. They loitered in wide loops for a furlong or two by the waterside and joined the sea through shallow troughs of sand. These junctions of sweet and salt water were the emplacement of villages, each of them built in a little coppice, where Negroes sat weaving lobster-pots in the shade, and the women spread their laundry to dry on the boulders of their little estuaries. A forest of coconut palms stretched in a tenuous belt between the road and the smooth sea, and here and there we passed fishermen hammering away at their half-built sloops, standing under the leaves among their palisades of props. One of them was almost ready for launching, and the shipbuilder and his brother were painting tar on to the clean white timbers of the hull. By her side, all ready for use, lay the freshly cut rollers over which, a week or two later, the sloop would ride into the water. These vessels were the points of departure for the impressively expert colloquies between Rosemary Grimble and the shipbuilders, and we would sit and smoke on one of the bulwarks listening to our beautiful and Brontean companion and these elderly Sinbads as they conversed of tonnages and winds and currents and rigs. Most of these shipbuilders are from Carriacou, the little island half a dozen miles long which lies to the north of Grenada, where the majority of the islanders are engaged in the craft, and their vessels do much of the carrying trade in the archipelago. They are an industrious and thrifty race of Negro, Scotch, English and French descent. Their Scotch ancestry dates from the time when much of the land in Carriacou was in the hands of Scotsmen, and though they seem to have vanished now they have bequeathed to the islanders, along with their other characteristics, a Scots accent. Cattle and poultry raising, with ship-building and farming, form their main industries, and until recently Carriacou ponies were the best bred in the Windward Islands.

So close did the road run to the sea that twice we stopped while the path was momentarily blocked by teams of fishermen hauling in their nets; and waited until the final loop, with its agitated haul of captives, was dragged on to the shore. The fishermen dispatched the larger fish by grasping their tails and striking them against the sand, while the smaller ones were poured into rotund wicker amphoras, which were hoisted on to the fishermen's heads and carried away, still shaking and reverberating with the languishing throes of the fish.

A notice in the small township of Gouyave announced a sweepstake of which the first prize was a free funeral for the ticket holder or for any friend or relation. This, and the fact that the town (so Rosemary told us) was equipped with a lilac-coloured hearse emblazoned with the words *Bon Voyage,* seems to hint that the burghers of Gouyave have an individual attitude to death of which one would be glad to learn the secret. Reach-me-down coffins were advertised in the usual glowing terms.

We settled for our picnic in a grassy clearing above the sea at a north-eastern point of the island, called Sauteurs. An overgrown cliff lay on one side of us, and on the other the village green, and a spinney in the middle of which stood the pretty tropical-Gothic church of St. Patrick. Carriacou was a long blur on the horizon, only just visible through the line of scattered inlets and rocks that lay due north of the bay. Rosemary, drawing on her fund of nautical lore, pointed them out and named them: Sugar Loaf, Green Island, Sandy Island, Mouche Carrée, Ile Ronde, Les Tantes, Isle de Caille, London Bridge, and the jagged spike of Kickem Jenny—a transliteration, it is believed, of *Caye* (reef) *qu'on gêne* or *qui gêne*.

Sauteurs—or Sotairs as it is alternatively pronounced—gained its name in a gruesome way. After the discovery of Grenada, Spain displayed her customary indifference, and when (except for an abortive attempt at settlement by a company of London merchants) the island had been left to the Caribs for well over a century, Richelieu claimed it for Louis XIII in 1626. Next year Charles I granted it, along with nearly all the Caribbees, to the Earl of Carlisle but neither France nor England attempted to enforce their claims. The great buccaneer Longvilliers de Poincy attempted to land a few years later, but was driven off by the Caribs. The formidable Duparquet (whom I have mentioned in connection with Martinique) had better luck. For the sum of 1,660 *livres,* he bought Martinique, St. Lucia and Grenada from the French "Company of the Isles of America," settled in Martinique, and, landing in Grenada with a gang of adventurers in 1650, also succeeded in buying the island from the Caribs for (Father du Tertre records) "some knives and hatchets and a large quantity of glass beads, besides two bottles of brandy for the chief himself." Leaving a relation of his behind as governor, Duparquet sailed back to Martinique. Le Comte had orders to exterminate the Caribs if they should attempt to go back on their bargain, which the poor wretches were not slow to do—they could not stop killing Frenchmen whenever they got the chance. The campaign of annihilation began, and the Caribs, who were powerless against the armour and the muskets of the French, were routed from the leewardside with terrible losses. Père Labat describes their last stand, which took place exactly where we were eating our hard-boiled eggs. The savages withdrew to the summit of a steep *morne* surrounded by terrible precipices, which could only be climbed by a narrow secret pathway. Having at last discovered it, the French attacked them by surprise. A fierce fight took place, and those of the Caribs who survived the battle preferred to hurl themselves to death from the top of this rock rather than surrender. Father du Tertre, who describes the same event, remarks that the victors marched home *bien joyeux.* The Caribs on the leewardside retaliated by killing every isolated

Frenchman they saw, and Le Comte (who, it appears, would have spared them if his orders had been less definite) surprised their headquarters, where the majority of the remaining Caribs in the island were assembled, and, without regard to age or sex, butchered them all. The last evidence of the race was recorded in 1705, when a handful of them still lived in a valley in the north-west of Grenada.

As we rounded the north-eastern corner of the island, the scenery changed instantaneously. The smooth sand and water were replaced by the rough windward waves and a gusty shore from which the more luxuriant trees had retreated inland. The only growth on these bleak dunes was the sea-grape, that stubborn shrub which alone is able to resist the violence of the weather. The Trade Winds had twisted and topiaried it into innumerable fantastic shapes; growing normally on the sheltered side, the part of the bush which was exposed to the east appeared to have been shorn away in flat, slanting planes. These extraordinary contortions infect the whole coastline with a disquietingly harassed and tyrannized air, as though the landscape might all at once be blown away, leaving the traveller locked there knee deep in the wet sand like a scapegoat.

It took me some time to determine, as we travelled inland through the wooded hills, what it was that made the country so pleasant and so distinct from other tropical forests. There was none of that sodden and noxious splendour about these trees which in the past had moved us to admiration and rage, and when they made way for clearings, no monotonous sweep of sugar-cane broke loose. For we were driving through plantations of nutmeg and cacao. The straight stems of the cacao trees and their large, pointed and almond-shaped leaves were gathered in woods and groves which were filled with an unreal and filtered light, an atmosphere resembling that of a medieval tapestry or the mysterious background of a nocturnal hunting scene by Paolo Uccello. The cacao beans hung on the end of short stalks, like red and purple hand-grenades. Weeds, for some reason, refuse to grow under the cacao and the nutmeg, so the trunks are free of the choking tangle of undergrowth and creeper and parasite that muffles the shapes of nearly everything else in these latitudes. The architecture of the forest is unencumbered, and one can gaze among their trunks down glimmering vistas of luminous and variable green. A great luxury after a month or two of the throttling and claustrophobic underwood of the tropics.

It is a pleasure for which one can thank the Emancipation Act. For here, as in Trinidad and most of the islands, the freed Negroes preferred to settle on their own land, or just to squat; or, rather than work as paid labourers on the hated sugar estates, to earn their living as charcoal burners. Labour was imported from Malta and Madeira, but the scheme was a failure. A few of the Maltese became porters or wandering pedlars, but most of them emigrated to Trinidad, and the

Portuguese settled down as shop-keepers or plantation assistants, but seldom as labourers. The cultivation of sugar had to be practically abandoned, and its place was taken by the nutmeg and cacao which have become the chief industries of the country. Their cultivation is many times less laborious than the back-breaking grind of the canefields, and much more suited to the character of the islanders; as it would be to anybody's.

In clearings by the road, we saw little farmhouses where solitary Negroes were superintending barbecues—flat trays that could be slid under cover at the approach of rain—on which nutmeg and cacao beans, and the frail scarlet network that covers the nutmeg, were spread to roast in the sun. This red substance is formed by a juice that oozes through the shell of the nut, which, when it dries, becomes a tight, russet lacy substance: the mace of commerce.

Moving through this beautiful forest, then, we blessed the events that had put down sugar from its high place, and made way for these spices, and for the limes and grapefruit and coconut palms, for coconuts and bananas are also an important cultivation. Palms, though they may be monotonous sometimes or inappropriate, are never ugly; and, among the civilized Grenadian flora, even the banana trees looked acceptable. But above all one must revere the memory of the early Spaniards who brought the cacao tree from the banks of the Amazon and the fastnesses of Ecuador.

Derelict sugar-mills mouldered among the usurping trees. Their chimneys were broken, and the semi-circular tiles were moulting from their roofs; and in the long grass by these surrendered palaces, giant cauldrons lay, in which the cassava-flour for the slaves used to be baked. These vessels are an essential part of the Antillean landscape. They are the exact shape of tin helmets in the British Army, but six or eight feet in diameter, and made out of cast iron. Covered with rust and moss, they are another reminder in the abandoned mills of the Antilles of the recentness of slavery and the ravished omnipotence of sugar.

Villages are scarce in the eastern reaches of Grenada. Now and then Rosemary would point out an old plantation house and occasionally we drove through a group of wooden cabins; but most frequent were the mills. Outside one of them in an alcove of the forest a lonely peasant was sharpening a cutlass on a grindstone; pedalling away, pausing every now and then to examine minutely the edge of the glittering blade, and then applying it once more to the screaming and spark-shedding disc. An oddly disquieting vision.

Sessions in the public libraries and, if they existed, the town museums of the different islands had long ago become a point of routine. They vary—many of the insular capitals have beautiful libraries which they owe to the munificence of the later Mr. Andrew Carnegie—but they are invariably pleasant retreats, equipped with several thousand books, and always with the Encyclopedia Britannica, the ordinary works of reference, and most of the books concerning the island in which they are situated. The British colonies are gratifyingly superior to those of any other Caribbean power in this matter.

Grenada, though it somehow missed the benevolence of Carnegie, is no exception. One of the most rewarding books I found there had an unpromising title and a prosaic official binding: *The Grenada Handbook and Directory, 1946*—nearly four hundred closely printed pages of information about the little island. Much of it is dry, official stuff. But many pages are concerned with the animals, birds, reptiles, fish, insects, trees and flowers of the island, and, best of all, over seventy beautifully written, almost Gibbonian, pages (anonymous, alas) are devoted to the island's history. Wars, earthquakes, hurricanes, religious debates, civil disturbances, reforms, eclipses of the sun, presents of plate to retiring governors, epidemics of whooping cough—nothing has been forgotten. Turning back to the period of which I was in pursuit, I was arrested by the following incident:

> About 8 o'clock P.M. on October 5, 1797, a large ship approached the town of Gouyave, showing no lights, whereupon the detachment of the 2nd West Indian Regiment stationed there . . . fired a gun at her from the battery, which was returned from the ship by two or three broadsides at the battery and the town. Believing the French were landing at Gouyave, the inhabitants of the neighbourhood began to fly to St. George's. The next morning H.M.S. *Favourite* (Captain Lord Camelford) anchored at St. George's, and it was ascertained that this bombardment of a peaceful town had been done at the order of Lord Camelford, who, without thinking of the suspicion his stealthy movements must have excited on the shore, considered himself insulted by the gun fired from the battery in the first instance, and had retaliated in the disgraceful manner described.

"Believing the French were landing . . ."—this was the period I was after.

When Victor Hugues, the emissary of the Convention, had fought and overcome the French Royalists and their British allies, and had erected the guillotine in Guadeloupe, he formed a plan to recapture from the English the islands of Martinique, St. Lucia and Grenada. Owing to tension between the English and French colonists, Grenada was the likeliest starting-point, and it was there that he dispatched his envoys to stir up revolt. A coloured planter called Julien Fédon was chosen as leader of the insurrection.

"At midnight on March 2, 1795, the storm broke; a body of insurgents under Fédon surrounded the town of Grenville and a horrible massacre of the British subjects ensued. Neither age nor sex proved a bar to the ferocity of the rebels, and by morning the town was a reeking shambles, from which the butchers retreated to the mountains, laden with spoil.'' The rebels entrenched themselves on Fédon's estate on Morne Quaqua, near the Grand Etang.

The Lieutenant-Governor, ''instead of being at headquarters at such a time, was spending some days with a party of gentlemen at his estate, Paraclete,'' in the eastern foot-hills near Grenville. The party of fifty-one hastily embarked in a sloop and, sailing round the island, landed at Gouyave, which they did not realize was also in a state of rebellion. They were all promptly captured and marched as prisoners to Fédon's camp and ''subjected to every indignity that malice could suggest, and were further informed by Fédon that, if an attack were made on his camp, they would be slaughtered without mercy.'' Reinforcements were rushed to the island, and siege was laid to Morne Quaqua. But the camp, owing to the incessant rain, the scarcity, to begin with, of troops, the fever, and the suicide, in a fit of delirium, of the English commander, was still untaken a month later. But more troops arrived and ''the assault was characterized by intrepid bravery on both sides. The difficulty had been underestimated of storm-ing the crest of an almost inaccessible mountain protected by strong *abattis* of felled trees in the face of a galling fire and on ground so slippery from continual tropical rains that even a foothold was difficult to obtain.''

Inside the stockade, meanwhile, a terrible tragedy was taking place, a descrip-tion of which I discovered in a narrative by Dr. John Hay, who almost suffered the fate of his companions: ''A voice was heard saying, 'The prisoners are to be shot.' The guard . . . appeared very much agitated, and trembling with impa-tience, and some seemed to have their guns cocked. A few prisoners called out 'Mercy!' No reply was made. Others, who were not in stocks, were on their knees praying. Not a word was exchanged among us . . . The door was opened; two men appeared with hammers to take the prisoners out of the stocks. Those who were not in confinement were ordered to go out . . . Fédon began the bloody massacre in the presence of his wife and daughters, who remained there, unfeeling spectators of his horrid barbarity. He gave the word *'Feu!'* himself to every man as soon as he came out; and of fifty-one prisoners, only Parson McMahon, Mr. Kerr and myself were saved.'' ''With one or two exceptions,'' resumes the anonymous historian of the *Handbook,* ''where protracted suffering had affected their minds, they met their fate as became their race and station. There can be little doubt that the immediate cause of this execrable deed was the death of Fédon's brother, who fell early in the day.''

The rebellion took about three months to subdue. (No help could come from the neighbouring island of St. Vincent, which was in the throes of the black Carib revolt, or from St. Lucia, where Jervis was coping with an insurrection of the Maroons: distant explosions of the French Revolution, touched off on the spot by the agents of Victor Hugues.) But after the arrival of Sir Ralph Abercromby the rebel strong-points were reduced one by one. Morne Quaqua was the last to fall. "No quarter was given to the rebels," as the soldiers were incensed by a last act of wanton barbarity on their part, twenty white prisoners, having just been led out and "brutally murdered before the eyes of the advancing troops." There were many fierce battles in the last phases—bayonet charges by the Buffs under a commander with the familiar name (in such circumstances) of Brigadier-General Campbell, sieges by the 57th Regiment, and assaults by Prince Löwenstein's German Jäger-regiment under Graf von Heillimer, "whose troops were well accustomed to mountain and forest warfare." After the capture of the governor, the Attorney-General sent letters asking for assistance from the neighbouring islands, among others to the Spanish Governor in Trinidad, none other than Don José Maria Chacon, who was the first to respond by sending two brigs, filled with soldiers. One cannot help wondering what must have been the feelings of this Spanish gentleman when, two years later, with his fleet still burning in Port of Spain harbour to save it from capture, he had to surrender the island of Trinidad to the British.

A special Court of Oyer and Terminer was called to deal with the rebels. Forty-seven were condemned without hearing to be hanged, on proof of identity alone. But Lieutenant-Governor Houston pardoned all except fourteen of the ringleaders. His clemency, though warmly applauded by the British Government, was bitterly attacked by the colonists, who so far prevailed that, in the end, thirty-eight were executed. But he succeeded in saving many others who were caught later. These, like the rank and file of the slaves—and like the Black Caribs of St. Vincent—were deported to British Honduras. "It is gratifying to record that the Legislators so far blended justice with mercy as to make a grant to some of the families of those who suffered the extreme penalty of the law in consequence of their treason."

The strangest part of the story is the total disappearance of the villain—or the hero—of the whole affair. After hiding some time in the woods, Fédon was completely lost sight of; and nothing certain is known of his fate, "although it is conjectured that he was drowned while seeking escape to Trinidad in a small canoe." It was as though he had been lifted into the sky as unvestigially as Enoch and Elijah, and borne away to some Negro garden of the Hesperides.

Mount Moritz, an inland valley north of the town, is inhabited by a little colony of whites; transplanted offshoots of the Redlegs of Barbados, and so, most of them, descendants of the Duke of Monmouth's followers. They were shy, simple people, living the same rustic life as the coloured islanders—which in Grenada, and in comparison with the living conditions and the arduous labour of many rural populations in England, is not at all bad—and speaking the same difficult English. Strolling up the path of the scattered village, we again listened in vain for the accents of the West Country. They looked stronger and bigger than the "Poor Whites" of Guadeloupe and the Saints and Barbados, and if their cotton clothes were changed into corduroy and tweed, indistinguishable from English country people. The darker colour of the children—almost nonexistent among the older villagers—indicated that mixed marriages are becoming more frequent. One old woman we met said that her family was Scottish, or so she thought; probably one of the "unruly Scots" deported to the Indies by Cromwell. In the village school I had a look through the list of the children's names. Several of them were Scotch—Alexander, Campbell, Kerr—and the others looked completely English, not at once noticeably deriving, I should have thought, from any specific region—Dowden, Edwards, Greaves, Medford, Searles, Winbush—but as likely to have originated in the south-western counties as anywhere. Two of the boys had the Christian names of Aubrey and Taflin, and a little girl, I noticed with interest, was called Lilith.

The Government House of Grenada is a building suitable to the dignity of the Governor and Commander-in-Chief of the Windward Islands. For Sir Arthur Grimble's hegemony embraced not only Grenada, but Carriacou and the Grenadine islands, St. Vincent and St. Lucia, and, since 1940, it has flung out a long loop to the north to include Dominica, which until then belonged to the administrative unit of the Leeward Islands. The Government Houses of Dominica, St. Lucia and St. Vincent are the bases of three Administrators who, in the absence of the Governor in Grenada, preside over the affairs of the three colonies.

We spent pleasant, unhurried hours there, looking at Rosemary Grimble's beautiful drawings of Caribbean life, or talking with the Governor about Island life and, among other things, I remember, of religion and politics, and books and poetry and sonnet-forms; and listening to our host's accounts of Pacific islands: hours of singular charm that always came to an end too soon. The Governor was about to retire and settle in England after half a lifetime spent in helping to administer and, later, in governing different parts of the Empire. A note of valediction pervaded those large and beautifully proportioned rooms; and we also felt sadder at the prospect of leaving Grenada than we had felt anywhere else.

Half-way down the hill on our last night, we stopped to gaze at the Seventh Day Adventist chapel, a lovely classical building, built entirely of wood, with a pediment sustained by fine Doric columns; as cool and serene among the moonlit trees as though it had been built out of Parian marble on a headland in Attica. There must be something in the atmosphere of Grenada that prevents an architect from going wrong.

All the lights were out in the rectory, and the quayside was silent. The sea here is not relegated to a slum as though it were a magnified drain. It is right in the town, and the houses begin at the quay. The air in some of the back lanes is heavy with the smell of stored spices, and the shops on the waterfront are deep, cool caves of shade reaching back from a colonnade of rounded vaults. Grocers and ships' chandlers mostly.

As we strolled along the quay, hardly a ripple moved the reflections of the sloops and the street lamps and the moon. They hung drowned and immobile in the middle of the sleeping town. The stars shone like blue pendant balls, so close, in appearance, that an outstretched hand might almost pluck them down.

But the capital was not quite asleep, for the sound of singing came floating down the lanes. We pursued it to its source, and, climbing a flight of stairs, looked into a kind of parish hall. About a hundred Grenadians were lustily singing, and a white clergyman, with his mouth also manfully distended in song, played a harmonium. He accentuated the beat by swinging his head, in a semi-jocular fashion, from side to side. They were practising carols—a fact that made us suddenly realize how close we were to Christmas. "Through de rude wind's wild lament," they roared, "and de bitter wedder." The mixture of familiarity and unfamiliarity was pleasing and strange. At first I could not understand why it should seem so odd. ". . . where de snow lay dinted," they went on, "Heat was in de very sod where de Saint had printed . . ." Of course! the snow. We descended again into the hot night. The tops of tropical trees appeared above the roofs. How many conversations I had recently had about snow!

"Yes, but what's it like?"

"Well, it's light, like confetti. It falls out of the sky and blows about in the wind. It's terribly cold, and when it settles it resembles cassava or mashed potatoes. Your feet leave marks on it as though you were treading on sand, and you can make balls of it, or even snowmen. It is so heavy it sometimes breaks the branches of trees. It's deep and crisp and even . . ."

"I'm sorry, I don't get it, maan. I don't get it at all. Not what it's *really* like . . ."

Landscape of the Pampas

W. H. HUDSON

A lifelong devotion to nature began for William Henry Hudson when he lived and worked on the family farm in Argentina. After emigrating to England in 1869 his stylized writings on nature and man earned him critical acclaim and a large audience. He is the author of the romance Green Mansions, A Shepherd's Life, *and* Idle Days in Patagonia. *The following is from* Long Ago and Far Away, *published in 1918.*

*A*S a small boy of six but well able to ride bare-backed at a fast gallop without falling off, I invite the reader, mounted, too, albeit on nothing but an imaginary animal, to follow me a league or so from the gate to some spot where the land rises to a couple or three or four feet above the surrounding level. There, sitting on our horses, we shall command a wider horizon than even the tallest man would have standing on his own legs, and in this way get a better idea of the district in which ten of the most impressionable years of my life, from five to fifteen, were spent.

We see all around us a flat land, its horizon a perfect ring of misty blue colour where the crystal-blue dome of the sky rests on the level green world. Green in late autumn, winter, and spring, or say from April to November, but not all like a green lawn or field: there were smooth areas where sheep had pastured, but the surface varied greatly and was mostly more or less rough. In places the land as far as one could see was covered with a dense growth of cardoon thistles, or wild artichoke, of a bluish or grey-green color, while in other places the giant thistle flourished, a plant with big variegated green and white leaves, and standing when in flower six to ten feet high.

There were other breaks and roughnesses on that flat green expanse caused by the *vizcachas,* a big rodent the size of a hare, a mighty burrower in the earth. *Vizcachas* swarmed in all that district where they have now practically been exterminated, and lived in villages, called *vizcacheras,* composed of thirty or forty huge burrows—about the size of half a dozen badgers' earths grouped together.

The earth thrown out of these diggings formed a mount, and being bare of vegetation it appeared in the landscape as a clay-coloured spot on the green surface. Sitting on a horse one could count a score to fifty or sixty of these mounds or *vizcacheras* on the surrounding plain.

On all this visible earth there were no fences, and no trees excepting those which had been planted at the old estancia houses, and these being far apart the groves and plantations looked like small islands of trees, or mounds, blue in the distance, on the great plain or pampa. They were mostly shade trees, the commonest being the Lombardy poplar, which of all trees is the easiest one to grow in that land. And these trees at the estancias or cattle-ranches were, at the time I am writing about, almost invariably aged and in many instances in an advanced state of decay. It is interesting to know how these old groves and plantations ever came into existence in a land where at the time there was practically no tree-planting.

The first colonists who made their homes in this vast vacant space, called the pampas, came from a land where the people are accustomed to sit in the shade of trees, where corn and wine and oil are supposed to be necessaries, and where there is salad in the garden. Naturally they made gardens and planted trees, both for shade and fruit, wherever they built themselves a house on the pampas, and no doubt for two or three generations they tried to live as people live in Spain, in the rural districts. But now the main business of their lives was cattle-raising, and as the cattle roamed at will over the vast plains and were more like wild than domestic animals, it was a life on horseback. They could no longer dig or plough the earth or protect their crops from insects and birds and their own animals. They gave up their oil and wine and bread and lived on flesh alone. They sat in the shade and ate the fruit of trees planted by their fathers or their great-grandfathers until the trees died of old age, or were blown down or killed by the cattle, and there was no more shade and fruit.

The summer change in the aspect of the plain would begin in November: the dead dry grass would take on a yellowish-brown colour, the giant thistle a dark rust brown, and at this season, from November to February, the grove or plantation at the estancia house, with its deep fresh unchanging verdure and shade, was a veritable refuge from the vast flat yellow earth. It was then, when the water-courses were gradually drying up and the thirsty days coming to flocks and herds, that the mocking illusion of the mirage was constantly about us. Quite early in spring, on any warm cloudless day, this water-mirage was visible, and was like the appearance on a hot summer's day of the atmosphere in England when the air near the surface becomes visible, when one sees it dancing before one's eyes, like thin wavering and ascending tongues of flame—crystal-clear flames mixed with flames of a faint pearly or silver grey. On the level and hotter pampas this appearance is intensified, and the faintly visible wavering flames change to an appearance of lakelets or sheets of water looking as if ruffled by the wind and shining like molten silver in the sun. The resemblance to water is increased when there are groves and buildings on the horizon, which look like dark blue islands or banks in the distance, while the cattle and horses feeding not far from the spectator appear to be wading knee- or belly-deep in the brilliant water.

The aspect of the plain was different in what was called a "thistle year," when the giant thistles, which usually occupied definite areas or grew in isolated patches, suddenly sprang up everywhere, and for a season covered most of the land. In these luxuriant years the plants grew as thick as sedges and bulrushes in their beds, and were taller than usual, attaining a height of about ten feet. The wonder was to see a plant which throws out leaves as large as those of the rhubarb, with its stems so close together as to be almost touching. Standing among the thistles in the growing season one could in a sense *hear* them growing, as the huge leaves freed themselves with a jerk from a cramped position, producing a crackling sound. It was like the crackling sound of the furze seed-vessels which one hears in June in England, only much louder.

To the gaucho who lives half his day on his horse and loves his freedom as much as a wild bird, a thistle year was a hateful period of restraint. His small, low-roofed, mud house was then too like a cage to him, as the tall thistles hemmed it in and shut out the view on all sides. On his horse he was compelled to keep to the narrow cattle track and to draw in or draw up his legs to keep them from the long pricking spines. In those distant primitive days the gaucho if a poor man was usually shod with nothing but a pair of iron spurs.

By the end of November the thistles would be dead, and their huge hollow stalks as dry and light as the shaft of a bird's feather—a feather-shaft twice as big round as a broomstick and six to eight feet long. The roots were not only dead but turned to dust in the ground, so that one could push a stalk from its place with one finger, but it would not fall since it was held up by scores of other sticks all round it, and these by hundreds more, and the hundreds by thousands and millions. The thistle dead was just as great a nuisance as the thistle living, and in this dead dry condition they would sometimes stand all through December and January when the days were hottest and the danger of fire was ever present to people's minds. At any moment a careless spark from a cigarette might kindle a dangerous blaze. At such times the sight of smoke in the distance would cause every man who saw it to mount his horse and fly to the danger-spot, where an attempt would be made to stop the fire by making a broad path in the thistles some fifty to a hundred yards ahead of it. One way to make the path was to lasso and kill a few sheep from the nearest flock and drag them up and down at a gallop through the dense thistles until a broad space was clear where the flames could be stamped and beaten out with horse-rugs. But sheep to be used in this way were not always to be found on the spot, and even when a broad space could be made, if a hot north wind was blowing it would carry showers of sparks and burning sticks to the other side and the fire would travel on.

I remember going to one of these big fires when I was about twelve years old. It broke out a few miles from home and was travelling in our direction; I saw my father mount and dash off, but it took me half an hour or more to catch a horse for myself, so that I arrived late on the scene. A fresh fire had broken out a quarter of a mile in advance of the main one, where most of the men were fighting the flames; and to this spot I went first, and found some half a dozen neighbours who had just arrived on the scene. Before we started operations about twenty men from the main fire came galloping up to us. They had made their path, but seeing this new fire so far ahead, had left it in despair after an hour's hard hot work, and had flown to the new danger-spot. As they came up I looked in wonder at one who rode ahead, a tall black man in his shirt sleeves who was a stranger to me. "Who is this black fellow, I wonder?" said I to myself, and just then he shouted to me in English, "Hullo, my boy, what are you doing here?" It was my father; an hour's fighting with the flames in a cloud of black ashes in that burning sun and wind had made him look like a pure-blooded negro!

During December and January when this desert world of thistles dead and dry as tinder continued standing, a menace and danger, the one desire and hope of everyone was for the *pampero*—the south-west wind, which in hot weather is apt to come with startling suddenness, and to blow with extraordinary violence. And it would come at last, usually in the afternoon of a close hot day, after the north wind had been blowing persistently for days with a breath as from a furnace. At last the hateful wind would drop and a strange gloom that was not from any cloud would cover the sky; and by-and-by a cloud would rise, a dull dark cloud as of a mountain becoming visible on the plain at an enormous distance. In a little while it would cover half the sky, and there would be thunder and lightning and a torrent of rain, and at the same moment the wind would strike and roar in the bent-down trees and shake the house. And in an hour or two it would perhaps be all over, and next morning the detested thistles would be gone, or at all events levelled to the ground.

After such a storm the sense of relief to the horseman, now able to mount and gallop forth in any direction over the wide plain and see the earth once more spread out for miles before him, was like that of a prisoner released from his cell, or of a sick man, when he at length repairs his vigour lost and breathes and walks again.

To this day it gives me a thrill, or perhaps it would be safer to say the ghost of a vanished thrill, when I remember the relief it was in my case, albeit I was never so tied to a horse, so parasitical, as the gaucho, after one of these great thistle-levelling *pampero* winds. It was a rare pleasure to ride out and gallop my horse over wide brown stretches of level land, to hear his hard hoofs crushing the hollow desiccated stalks covering the earth in millions like the bones of a countless host of perished foes. It was a queer kind of joy, a mixed feeling with a dash of gratified revenge to give it a sharp savour.

After all this abuse of the giant thistle, the *cardo asnal* of the natives and *Carduus mariana* of the botanists, it may sound odd to say that a "thistle year" was a blessing in some ways. It was an anxious year on account of the fear of fire, and a season of great apprehension too when reports of robberies and other crimes were abroad in the land, especially for the poor women who were left so much alone in their low-roofed hovels, shut in by the dense prickly growth. But a thistle year was called a fat year, since the animals—cattle, horses, sheep, and even pigs—browsed freely on the huge leaves and soft sweetish-tasting stems, and were in excellent condition. The only drawbacks were that the riding-horses lost strength as they gained in fat, and cow's milk didn't taste nice.

The best and fattest time would come when the hardening plant was no longer fit to eat and the flowers began to shed their seed. Each flower, in size like a small coffee-cup, would open out in a white mass and shed its scores of silvery balls, and these when freed of heavy seed would float aloft in the wind, and the whole air as far as one could see would be filled with millions and myriads of floating balls. The fallen seed was so abundant as to cover the ground under the dead but still standing plants. It is a long, slender seed, about the size of a grain of Carolina rice, of a greenish or bluish-grey colour, spotted with black. The sheep feasted on it, using their mobile and extensible upper lips like a crumb-brush to gather it into their mouths. Horses gathered it in the same way, but the cattle were out of it, either because they could not learn the trick, or because their lips and tongues cannot be used to gather a crumb-like food. Pigs, however, flourished on it, and to birds, domestic and wild, it was even more than to the mammals.

The Cloud Forest

PETER MATTHIESSEN

En route to a solitary exploration of the South American wilderness—from Amazonian rain forest to Tierra del Fuego—the author boarded a small southward-bound freighter, the M.S. Venimos, at a Brooklyn pier. He kept a log of the freighter's meandering voyage through the heavy weathers of the Caribbean until its arrival, forty days out of New York, at Iquitos, on the Amazon in Peru.

December 24

*T*HE forest increases in stature, it seems, as we ascend the river. There are fewer clearings, and the few *caboclos* standing on the bank as we go by, watching dispassionately as the wash from our wake bangs their frail canoes together, look darker to me, more Indian—though even a century ago, in Bates's time, the tribes of the main river banks were already extinct or absorbed by the whites and Negroes. New birds continue to appear, including tropic kingfishers, one of them dark and tiny, with a white nape. In the river the floating debris is increasing, littering great areas of the expanse, but it is the jungle which changes most. A number of trees I have not noticed before, and especially one with a smooth purple-mahogany trunk—I'm told this is the purpleheart. The larger trees have aerial gardens of red-flowered epiphytes, *Bromelia,* and strange silver cylinders—these are hornets' nests—hanging like Christmas ornaments; everywhere, fastened leechlike to the trunks, are the dark masses of white ants' nests. The lowest branches of these trees must be fifty feet from the ground; in the evening light, its pale marble columns mysterious in the greens, the forest is truly beautiful; it is difficult to conceive of a lovelier forest in the world.

Tonight is Christmas Eve.

Christmas Day

Early on Christmas morning two brilliant macaws streamed out across the river in front of the ship, and in the fiery green of the dawn bank I saw an enormous white flower. I have not seen this flower before.

371

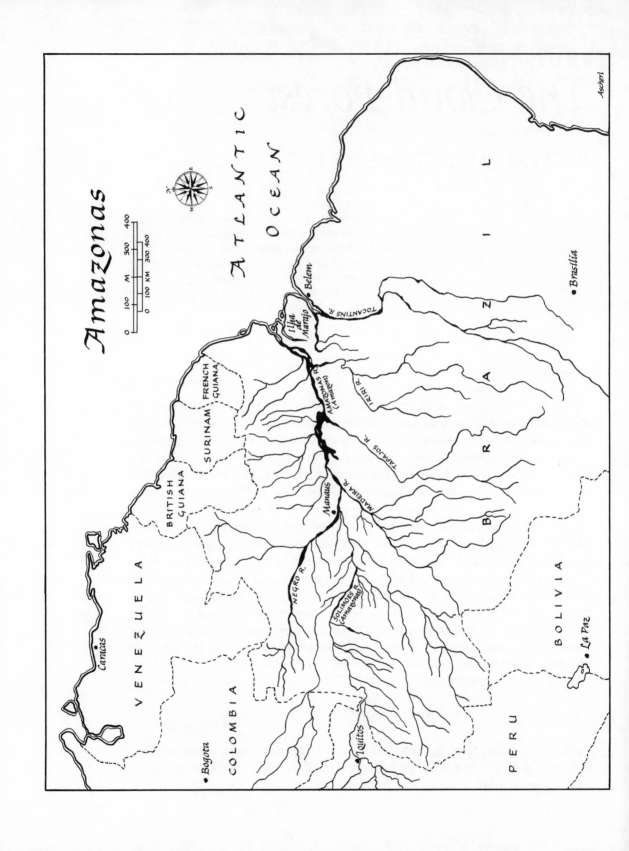

We are not a religious ship, and, the Dutch missionaries having been left behind in Manaus, there was no formal worship. To soothe our savage breasts the captain played us carols on his phonograph, and a great variety of secular music as well, everything from cha-cha-cha to *The Merry Widow*. The music was absorbed attentively by a gathering of *caboclos* who convened on the bank and in their small canoes at the point near the mouth of the Urucu River where, toward noon, the ship dropped anchor in order that all her company might celebrate Christmas dinner together.

The small salon, decorated by the captain himself, was festive in a heartbreaking sort of way, and there was even a small spruce tree, a renegade from the consignment of Christmas trees left at Saint Vincent. The odor of this humble evergreen, so crisp and strange in the damp, redolent atmosphere of the jungle river, brought me as close as I have come to homesickness—I caught myself easing up to it every little while and furtively inhaling. Past the branches of the spruce, through the bright porthole, could be seen the rapt faces of the half-breeds on the steaming bank, and the tumbled mass of the jungle rising like a great engulfing wave behind them.

The captain served rum to his passengers and officers in person (this is the custom, and later the officers would serve Christmas dinner to the stewards). He did his courtly best to make a party of it, and to my faint surprise succeeded, pouring our drinks lavishly and with grace. Emboldened by rum, and carried on at table by wine and port, we were able to don our paper hats and snap our snappers with some gusto. The chief engineer claimed the port bottle was his own, and when this claim was contested pointed at the lettering, crying out, "Me bloody name's Fernandez, isn't it?"; behind his head our young Ortega, the swiftest waiter in the world, produced a mask with red nose, mustache, and owlish glasses, and, crossing himself, clapped it suddenly on his own face.

We feasted on ham and turkey of a kind, and there were grapes and nuts in place of the usual dessert "sweet," a tapioca or semolina decked out, according to the joint daily inspiration of the cook and steward, in a variety of brilliant colors and exotic names, and resembling nothing so much, under the effects of the ship's vibration, as a low marine organism, a community of hydroid animals, shuddering with life. This staple item was suppressed upon the Lord's Day, but I have no doubt that naked masses of it, as yet unadorned, are cached somewhere about the ship, quaking away until tomorrow.

The rest of Christmas remains a little hazy in my mind. The noon euphoria was followed, by those officers not on watch, by a humid afternoon of drinking and an access of somber homesickness. Even the chief, who earlier had appropriated the comic mask and kept popping up at portholes all over the ship, now complained bitterly that the company had not sent the ship a Christmas cable. "First ship I was ever on," he grumped, "where they didn't have the courtesy to send the lads a little message." The third mate was snarling and unhappy, and the Second Engineer subsequently succumbed to the eulogies of Scotland, and the good life in the Far East as a tanker "mon," for which he has become notorious on the *Venimos*. (In Haiti one afternoon, forgetting where he was, he abused the longshoremen in Chinese, and a week later, happening upon one of the only two Chinese in Barbados, he celebrated and "went adrift," as these men say—he failed, that is, to appear aboard ship when his watch came around the following day—and this for the first time in twelve years at sea.) Unlike the Brazilian and Peruvian crewmen, who see their families on every run, the majority of the officers have not been at home in months and, in a few cases, years; though the morale of the ship is ordinarily high, there are two officers disliked cordially by the rest, and these resentments flowered on Christmas Day, in company with each man's longings and eccentricities. Nevertheless, these men are generous and intelligent (the most intelligent are Sparks and the third engineer; at least, they thrash me regularly at chess), and on this long voyage—we are now thirty-five days out—I have made good friends among them.

By nightfall morale had restored itself somewhat. There was a very comic and touching collection of absurd presents which the captain presented to me with a speech at supper, and a fine evening of lusty singing on the afterdeck. "The Londonderry Air" bestirred the lightless jungle, and in the reflective silence afterward the air was tightened by the squeak of bats. Overhead stars livened the whole tropic sky, sparkling outward from the mast silhouettes and crowding down on the black horizons on all sides. Some of these stars, those off to the south, never rise above our night skylines in North America. It came as a start, that realization in the silent evening that these far, endless galaxies I was seeing for the first time in my life.

December 26

The Paraná de Manycão, a narrow channel cutting across a long bend in the river to the east of the Rio Juruá: a heavy rain this morning, and in the rain I saw three ivory-colored herons with black crests and head plumes and extraordinary bright blue bills. There are still new birds each day as we move westward—the hawks seem to change every few miles—and of the birds seen in the first days on the river only the black vulture, large-billed tern, river swallow, egrets, and green parrots are still in evidence. The mammals remain hidden, all but the bats and porpoises, and so do the crocodilians, but there are periodic swirls of some great fish.

A young native, hunting with canoe and light spear in the arrow reeds. The ship starts up the egret he is stalking, and he stares at us impassively over his shoulder as he drifts astern. There are a few more of the large white Christmas flowers, and red flowers of the wild banana trees. And at last, a monkey, a large black one, hurling himself out of a high tree onto the lower canopy, where he scrambles a moment before disappearing among the leaves. With those shaken branches, the whole forest quite suddenly comes alive.

December 27

Sometime tomorrow we shall reach Peru. There are more flowers here—yellow ones, and small red and pink-purple, growing on the vines—and a new yellow-flowered tree, quite large in size. A palm in this country, called the *ubussu*, has enormous fronds, like an outsize fern, which dance violently in the slightest air. Parasites and air plants are everywhere, some flowering and lovely, others grotesque; one tree has spheres, like linked coconuts, hanging down its trunk. I think this is the cannon-ball tree, *Couroupita*. Another tree, unnoticed until today, has bark gray with a greenish tint and very smooth, like the skin of some ancient dinosaur.

Strange whirlpools and eddies increase along the banks; the river has risen markedly. The banks are clogged with snags and floating islands, and spinning logs which, moved slowly upstream in the eddies, look deceptively like animals. Some of the trees are caught on the bottom and yaw viciously in the current, and others sink mysteriously, to rise some distance away; the dull boom which shakes the ship when one of these trees is struck at the wrong angle is now periodic. A heavy bird with the head of a fowl and the flight of a vulture is common on the banks and floating debris—this is the *camungo*, or screamer, a great black and gray relation of the geese, with long spikes or horns on the shoulders of its wings.

The animals come forward as we move upriver. This morning a group of four or five red howler monkeys, rusty in the sunrise light, observed us from the top of a tall tree, and this afternoon I saw a sloth. This unprepossessing mammal, long-armed, with an earless face like a husked coconut, was apparently roused out of its torpor by the ship; it was climbing upward and inward toward the trunk of its bare tree at top speed, which is to say, about as fast as a very old fireman on a ladder. Its dingy coat was green-tinted with algae and lichens, which serve it as a kind of camouflage; by the time it reached a crotch behind the trunk and hunched down, resembling some parasitic growth, the ship was already past; I observed its last precautions through binoculars.

December 28

For the second straight day the river was shrouded in heavy fog in the night and early morning, retarding us. Gray weather, and the morale of the ship is now at a low ebb. All of us are drinking more, and the chief confesses—not entirely without his usual considerable charm—that he is sorry for himself. Probably it would not be far-fetched to say that the climate, abetting fatigue and drink, has brought home his age in a very painful way; he is to retire after this trip, and while he is longing to go home to his garden near Bristol, he is a man who loves life, or loved it once, and he sees in retirement some sort of admission of defeat.

The third mate is also sorry for himself and angry at the world. In the beginning of the trip he was looking forward to Peru—I remember his enthusiasm on one blue day at sea, south of Bermuda—but now he cries out his hatred of the river and of "the stinking nay-tives," the trees, and the humidity—it doesn't matter what. He is a good-looking boy in his early twenties, with a wife in England and a child he has never seen, but there is more violence than love in him, and an unquenchable frustration that his natural assets have brought him nothing but responsibility. He speaks longingly of a trip in a sloop around the world, away from everything.

A solitary red howler in the morning, perched disconsolately on a long limb, and at evening great flights of green and white parakeets, birds by the thousands, their electric screeching clearly audible above the engine even at a distance. They bank and whirl among the trees in bands of four or five hundred, perpetually excited. There are also large black and yellow river orioles, and here and there the trees bear dozens of their hanging fiber nests, some of these three feet in depth.

December 29

Last night the *Venimos* arrived at the Brazilian frontier post of Benjamin Constant (called formerly, I have read, Remate de Males, or "Culmination of Evils"), on the Javarí River; the first sight of Peru was a light across the void of jungle darkness. We then moved on to the military post of Tabatinga, and finally to the border village of Ramón Castillo in Peru; at one point, under flashes of slow lightning which illumined the horizons, the faceless corners of Brazil, Peru, and Colombia could be made out simultaneously (I got up out of my berth to observe this minor marvel, but I can't really say I got much out of it).

This morning Peru lies to port and Colombia to starboard. The Colombian foothold on the Amazon (between Manaus and Tabatinga the river is called the Solimões, and in Peru the Marañón, but it is still Amazonas, "El Río Mar") is small, and the jungle here seems low and scrubby. Colombia is left behind in the middle of the morning, its one distinctive feature a delicate pearl-gray hawk with a black and white barred tail, which circled out across the bow before sliding back over the trees. I have not seen this species before, and because I think of it at this moment as Colombian, I hope unreasonably that I shall not see it again.

December 30

The weather remains overcast and somber and very cool for the equator—72 degrees plus at times. Without sun the jungle assumes a monotone and oppressive aspect; even the bird activity seems diminished. Tonight the ship arrives at Iquitos, forty days out of New York, and though she has been comfortable and pleasant, I can't say I'll be sorry to leave her. But I shall miss my friends; the chief came this morning and gave me his address, asking me to visit him, and I certainly hope I shall.

The Bus Plunge Highway

TOM MILLER

In The Panama Hat Trail *the author writes of some of the steady chances one must take to reach the source of panama-hat making in Ecuador.*

*O*NE of the hatters told me how to reach Victor González, an importer of raw *toquilla* straw from the coast. When I walked into his house, he started to hand me a fifty-*sucre* note. (The *sucre* was worth slightly more than a penny at the time.) I hadn't yet introduced myself. "No, no," I protested, "there must be some mistake. I telephoned this morning and spoke with your daughter Fanny about—" Fanny, entering the front courtyard, interrupted. "He thinks you're from the government," she apologized. "I'll tell him again what you're interested in." As she explained, her father relaxed somewhat, and he led the way to a room filled with large sacks tightly wrapped in light cloth, about three feet by five feet, holding the raw straw.

"These are called *bultos*. They come like this from the coast. If you're going up to the town they come from, take this, will you?" He wrote a note to his suppliers listing the prices he was paying for *bultos* that week. I was closing in on the beginning of the trail.

"You'll be going to Febres Cordero."

I stopped and stared. That was the name of the country's president, elected in 1984. "He's got nothing to do with it," Fanny said. "It was named for his grandfather, a military officer."

"From Guayaquil," her father continued, "take a bus to La Libertad, and from there to Febres Cordero. It's easy. Make sure you give them my price list."

To reach the town of Febres Cordero I took a bus to Guayaquil—at 1.6 million, the country's most populous city. The 150-mile ride started smoothly despite my apprehension. Bus rides through Latin America have always induced fear in me, brought on by years of reading one-paragraph bus-plunge stories used by newspapers in the States as fillers on the foreign-news page. The datelines change, but the headlines always include the words *bus plunge*, as in 12 DIE IN SRI LANKA BUS PLUNGE, or CHILEAN BUS PLUNGE KILLS 31. "We can count on one every couple of days or so," an editor at *The New York Times* once told me. "They're always ready when we need them." Never more than two sentences long, a standard bus-plunge piece will usually include the number feared dead, the identity of any group on board—a soccer team, church choir, or school bus—and the distance of the plunge from the capital city. The words *ravine* and *gorge* pop up often. Most of the stories come from Third World countries, the victims comprising just a fraction of the faceless brown-skinned masses. "A hundred Pakistanis going off a mountain in a bus make less of a story than three Englishmen drowning in the Thames," noted foreign correspondent Mort Rosenblum in *Coups & Earthquakes.* Is there a news service that does nothing but supply daily papers with bus-plunge stories? Peru and India seem to generate the most coverage; perhaps the wire services have more stringers in the Andes and Himalayas than anywhere else.

If an Ecuadorian bus driver survives a plunge fatal to others, according to Moritz Thomsen in *Living Poor,* "he immediately goes into hiding in some distant part of the country so that the bereaved can't even up the score. There are rumors of whole villages down in the far reaches of the Amazon basin populated almost entirely by bus drivers. This is probably apocryphal. . . ."

If you anticipate a bus trip in Latin America, go through the following checklist prior to boarding:

> Look at the tires. If three or more of the six tires (most buses include two rear sets of two each) are totally bald, the probability of bus plunge increases. Visible threads on the tires means a blowout is imminent.

> Does the bus have at least one windshield wiper? Good. If it's on the driver's side, so much the better. Try to avoid buses whose windshields are so crowded with decals, statues, and pictures that the driver has only a post-card-sized hole through which to see the future. Shrines to saints, pious homilies, boastful bumper stickers, and religious trinkets do not reflect the safety of a bus. Jesus Christ and Ché Guevara are often worshiped on the same decal. This should give neither high hopes nor nagging suspicion.

> The driver's sobriety isn't a factor. The presence of his wife or girlfriend is. If she's along, she will usually sit immediately behind him, next to him, or on his lap. He will want to impress her with his daring at the wheel, but he will also go to great lengths not to injure her. If he has no girlfriend or wife, the chances of gorge-dive increase.

> You can't check the bus for brakes. Once I asked a driver in Guatemala about the brakes on his bus. "Look," he said, "the bus is stopped, isn't it? Then the brakes must work."

> On intercity buses, seats are often assigned before boarding. Refuse the seat directly behind the driver or in the front right. If your ride takes place during

the day, you'll be subjected to at least one heart-skip a minute as your bus casually passes a truck on an uphill blind curve or goes head-to-head with an oncoming bus. At night, the constant glare of approaching headlights will shine in your eyes. At any hour, the driver's makeshift radio speaker will dangle closer to your ears than you'd like.

Always have your passport ready. Random military inspections take place when you least expect them. I once delayed a bus full of cross-country travelers for ten minutes a couple of miles outside Esmeraldas, on the Pacific Coast south of Colombia, while frantically searching first for my bag atop the bus, then my passport within the bag.

In defense of Latin-American buses: They go everywhere. *Everywhere*. No road is so dusty, bumpy, unpopulated, narrow, or obscure that a bus doesn't rumble down it at least once every twenty-four hours. The fare is very little—Cuenca to Guayaquil cost less than three dollars—and, barring plunges, they almost always reach their destination. If your window opens, you'll get a view of the countryside unmatched in painting or postcard. Your seatmate may be an aging *campesina* on her way home or a youthful Indian on his first trip to the big city. Dialects of Spanish and Quichua unknown to linguists float past you. Chickens, piglets, and children crowd the aisles or ride on top.

At Cuenca's *terminal terrestre*, the bus station, I had a choice of taking a regular bus or an *aerotaxi* to Guayaquil. The former travels slower, hence theoretically safer. The latter, a small twenty-four-seater, whizzes along far faster, has less leg room, and is more plunge-prone. I resisted the odds and took an *aerotaxi*.

The trip, five and a half hours long, begins at eighty-four hundred feet above sea level, climbs somewhat higher, and descends to a sea level straightaway for the final ninety minutes or so. The advantage of the drive toward Guayaquil is that the precipitous ravine usually falls off on the left side of the two-lane road; the disadvantage is that you're headed downhill most of the way. Guard railings, few and far between, relieved a bit of my fear, except when the downhill section was bent outward or was simply broken off. For the better part of the first hour we followed a cattle truck, which moved only slightly faster than its cargo could have managed on its own.

The cattle turned off at Azogues, and we pushed on deep into the province of Cañar. The temperature dropped. I looked out the left side onto the clouds surrounding peaks nearby and distant. The thin air above the clouds in the Andes gave the sunlight colors unknown below. Only occasionally did our driver attempt a suicide squeeze—overtaking someone around a blind curve—and we settled into a quiet passage. Crude signs advertised local cheeses. Small piles of *toquilla* straw lay on the ground near doorless houses where women sat in the entrances weaving Panama hats. Julio, the driver, knew all the potholes and bumps on that road and managed to hit every one. Pepe, his helper—the driver's assistant is almost always a younger brother, son, or nephew—fidgeted with the radio until he found a distant station whose static muffled a brass band. We passed Cañari Indians heading home; in front the father, directly behind him his wife, behind her a passel of kids, and bringing up the rear a burro and a goat. Each party in the procession was connected to the one behind by a rope tied around the midsection. A dog yipped alongside.

We descended into the thick of the clouds and Julio downshifted. The white line down the center of the curving two-lane road was his only guide; even the hood ornament had disappeared into the clouds. After five minutes he slowed further and then stopped. Pepe walked through the *aerotaxi* collecting money. I nudged Horacio next to me. "What's this for?"

"We're at the shrine," he replied. "Each driver stops at this shrine along the way and leaves some money. It's their way of asking God's blessings for a safe journey." Often the saints are next to a police checkpoint so that the driver can make two payoffs at once. Offering insurance money to some saint required a gargantuan leap of faith, but if it would assure us a trip free of bus plunge, I wanted in. I coughed up a few *sucres*.

Pepe trotted across the road to leave our money at the shrine when suddenly a half-dozen Indian faces appeared out of the clouds pressing against the windows. *"¡Choclos! ¡Choclos! ¡Diez cada uno!"* They were selling sweet corn cooked with onion, cheese, and egg for slightly more than ten cents each. Two barefoot Indian women in felt hats and thick mud-stained ponchos slipped onto the bus and walked up and down the aisle. *"¡Choclos! ¡Choclos! ¡Nueve cada uno!"* The price had gone down some. Another vendor with a glazed look in her eyes and a baby in her arms rapped desperately on a window trying to get a passenger to open it. Her shrill voice seemed as distant as her eyes. Pepe returned, and the Indians withdrew into the Andean mist.

Bus drivers' assistants throughout Latin America display keen skills at hopping on and off moving buses, keeping track of which passenger is due how much change for his fare, pumping gas, climbing through a window to the roof to retrieve some freight before the bus stops, and changing blowouts. Pepe performed all these feats in the course of the run to Guayaquil, and excelled at hopping on the bus when it was already in second gear. Trotting apace of the bus, he first took a short skip on the ground to get the spring in his feet, then a short jump at a forty-five-degree angle calculated to land him on the first step while he grasped a metal bar next to the doorway. His motion appeared so fluid and effortless, he seemed to be simply stepping onto a bus in repose.

The right rear tire blew out on the southern edge of the town of Cañar. Julio pulled into an abandoned service station and Pepe had us back on the road within ten minutes. In more restful moments he sat on a makeshift seat between

Julio and the door. The only job forbidden him was highway driving, and even then he was allowed to maneuver the bus around the terminals.

The ride down the western face of the Andes settled into a relatively peaceful journey once the tire was changed and the saint paid off. We went through long stretches where the only hint of life was an occasional *choza,* a straw thatched hut, set back from the road. Valleys with streams and rivers flowing toward the Pacific held small towns. Our descent to sea level was practically complete and we entered a different climate, province, and culture. Bribing the saint had worked; we had passed the bus-plunge zone safely.

The air hung heavier, more humid, and warmer. Roadside vegetation grew more lush. Thick grass grew right up to roadside. Towns suddenly burst upon the highway—healthy, lively towns, active, jumping, noisy, uncaring. A church was just another building near the plaza, nothing more. Men and boys wore shorts, thongs, and torn T-shirts. Women and girls wore slacks or short, loose cotton dresses. Card tables were surrounded by men who looked like they'd sat there months on end encircled by a floating crowd of onlookers. Shot glasses of *puro* were constantly drained and refilled. Every structure was made of bamboo—split, dry, and aged. There was loud laughter, backslapping, gold-toothed grins, ass-pinching, life with few worries and less money. We had encountered our first *costeños*—people who live in the coastal region. Julio raced to Guayaquil on a road studded with potholes bigger than our *aerotaxi.* The tropics had begun.

Nothing to Declare: Memoirs of a Woman Traveling Alone

MARY MORRIS

*These intimate memoirs reveal much of what
the author discovered about herself as she
made her own way through Mexico and parts
of Central America. On a small island off
Honduras she coped with odd visitors and the
risks of swimming alone.*

I GREW restless again as the weeks went by, and it wasn't long before I found
myself en route back to Honduras to the Bay Islands off the coast, where the
Carib people were black and everyone spoke English. It was the first English I'd
heard spoken in many months and the change amazed me. I spent a day resting
in San Pedro Sula, having traveled from Tegucigalpa by bus, and was setting out
for La Ceiba and the ferryboat to Roatán.

At the bus station a child with a clubfoot dragging behind her came begging,
barefoot, and I was sure her parents had sent her out to beg, but I couldn't refuse.
I gave her money and bought her some cakes and fruit. Everywhere people sold
contraband. Wrist watches, radios, Jockey shorts. A black woman stood with
two children. One was crying, and the black woman kept beating her with her
purse. An enormous black woman with a bandanna around her head walked by
and began beating the woman who was beating the child. A small riot broke out.

Finally the doors of the bus opened and the black women in their red-
checkered turbans pushed and shoved. I managed to get a seat on this bus,
having failed to get one on the seven-thirty bus. I could not bear the thought of
standing up for three hours in this heat which, even in the early morning hours,
was already completely unbearable, and I felt I'd faint if the bus did not move.

At last it pulled out and a breeze blew in. People in the back of the bus were
singing. We drove through miles and miles of banana plantations and fruit

farms, mostly, I am certain, owned by United Fruit. Honduras is a true Banana Republic, and most of its agriculture is owned by American economic interests. I recalled lines from Neruda: "Among the bloodthirsty flies, the Fruit Company lands its ships, taking off the coffee and the fruit." I stared out the window as we drove by. The trees that lined the road were filled with buzzards.

At one o'clock, hot and hungry, we reached La Ceiba, and the bus driver let a few passengers disembark at the dock. With my South American guidebook open to the page that said, "Ferries leave regularly from the dock at La Ceiba to Roatán and the other islands," I walked slowly toward the lapping water along the rotting wood pier, the lifeless wharf, the absence of anything resembling a ferryboat.

A young couple, the same guidebook opened to the same page, stared forlornly at the same deserted dock, where we were the only signs of life. "This doesn't look very promising," the man said. We introduced ourselves. Andrew was a tall, very attractive attorney from San Francisco, and his girlfriend, Becky, was a biologist. "We've come a long way," he said.

"So have I." They were also trying to get to the Bay Islands and said they'd be glad to go with me to Roatán if we could find a way.

It was clear that there had been no regular-service ferry in years, and we were contemplating the prospect of turning around and traveling overland back across Honduras when a little man in a white linen suit, drenched in sweat, seemed to materialize out of nowhere. "Hello, I'm Charlton Jenks." He held out his hand. "Glad to meet you. I'm from Los Angeles. Researching a screenplay." He saw us, fingers pressed into our guidebooks. I had a feeling immediately that he stood at this dock all day, waiting for the misdirected like us. "No boats for the *islas* from here," he said. "Somebody ought to write those guys in England. Tell them there aren't any ferries. Everyone who comes overland and wants to get to the islands has the same problem. Hasn't been a regular ferry in a decade. If you don't mind waiting around until Sunday, you might find a boat to take you." Sunday was three days away and La Ceiba didn't look like the kind of place where you'd want to spend three days.

"Is there any other way to get there?" Andrew asked.

"Oh, there are ways. I know a place we can go for lunch. Why don't we relax and discuss it at our leisure over a nice plate of rice and beans."

Charlton took my bag and we followed him, shrugging at each other, not sure what else to do. Over lunch Charlton Jenks—former band leader, TV and radio director, real estate developer, novelist whose *Mayan Magic* was made into a film by MGM—said that he was working on a screenplay of his last novel, which would be the first movie set in Honduras. He had been doing research in La Ceiba for the past five years. Andrew, Becky, and I glanced at one another with looks that formed our friendship, each of us trying to imagine spending half a decade of our lives in La Ceiba. "I've got a friend," he said. "A pilot. He'll get you to Guanaja. Owns half the island. You should go to the airport. I'll go with you. See if we can't get him to fly us to Guanaja."

We finished our lunch and Charlton dug around in his pockets for money. "Damn it," he said. "I've gotta go to the bank and cash a check." So he suggested we follow him to the bank and he'd cash a check, but when we got to his bank he had left his checkbook on Guanaja. "Must have left it in my hotel room there." He said he'd pay us back if we'd just front him the money to the island. We were beginning to get suspicious of him and we had already gotten out of him the crucial piece of information—the existence of an airport—and so we got into a taxi, leaving Charlton Jenks behind, and headed for the airport.

In the early evening we managed to get a flight, and for thirty dollars we flew to Roatán. As the plane soared over the Caribbean, we felt peaceful and relaxed, as if the worst part of our journey were done. When we got to the island, we checked into a place in downtown Roatán, a rather unappealing town. Andrew and Becky wanted to stay in town, but Walter Weinstein in Panajachel had given me a tip on a place to stay called Roberts' Hill. Walter had said it was a peaceful, small guest house on an isolated tip of the island, run by two island people, Ruby and Robert Roberts, and I wanted to get there as soon as I could.

The town of Roatán is built on stilts for hurricanes and mud. We trudged through and checked into the Corral, a dump near a spot of sea that smelled like a sewer. The Corral had no bath or running water. I got a room near the toilet which stank all night long. Andrew and Becky took a room near mine, also adjacent to the toilets. But for the night it would do.

The Corral was three floors high with a wrap-around porch in rather shabby condition on each floor. Our rooms were off to the side, but three men and a woman sat on the porch out front. The men wore army fatigues, drank beer, and piled the bottles into a kind of fortress. They were completely soused and falling out of their chairs while the woman pranced back and forth.

We sat down on the porch near them. "So," one of the men said to me, "where you from?"

When I said we were North Americans, they all smiled. They said they were Somocistas, Nicaraguans from Somoza's National Guard. Andrew rolled his eyes and Becky looked dismayed.

That night as we were asleep someone came in my room and suddenly turned on the light. I screamed and shot out of bed. It was the woman who had been with the Nicaraguans, and she was bumbling around in my room. "I'm lost," she muttered, "I'm lost," and she staggered out again. I got up to go to the toilet.

When I stepped outside, I tripped over the body of one of the drunk Nicaraguans who had collapsed earlier that evening and had been rolling around on the porch all night. I screamed, but no one came.

In the morning on our way back from breakfast, the Nicaraguans stopped us and offered to show us their boat. It was down by the water and we walked that way. The boat was small, with an outboard. One of them pulled back a tarp and revealed a pile of guns. When we returned to the Corral, the other Nicaraguans were displaying rifles. They were very drunk and very macho as they held up their pieces. "Good U.S. rifles," one of them said. He offered to let me hold it, but I declined.

Roberts' Hill sat on a small hill, about fifty yards up from the beach, on an island paradise of white beaches, coconut palms, turquoise water. It had eight rooms. The rooms had no walls, only screened-in porches with wooden louvers to shut out the wind and the rain; otherwise we were exposed to the outside. For twelve dollars a day we got a room and three very square meals.

"Well," Andrew said when we arrived, "this was a good tip." As I had been packing my bags to head to the outskirts of the island, Andrew and Becky had come to my room. They'd been planning to stay in town but were having second thoughts. "Where did you say that place was where you're going to stay?" And so they had come along.

We got settled and at noon we sat down to a family-style lunch of fresh fish fried in coconut oil, fried potatoes, some kind of greens, warm bread, and custard for dessert. When Andrew saw the platters of food, he seemed to get nervous. "How much do you plan to eat?" he asked me.

"How much do I plan to eat?" I repeated.

"I mean, do you plan to eat a lot?"

I looked at this six-foot-four, hulking man. "Not much," I replied.

Becky was laughing. "Oh, Andrew," she said, "just tell her your problem."

Andrew explained that he had a kind of anxiety attack when he had to eat family style. He came from a family of ten children and there were always thirteen people for dinner. His mother cooked enough food for seventeen and the family was served youngest to oldest. You got seconds when you finished your firsts, which meant that the oldest had to eat the fastest to get more. To this day, Andrew said, he panics when food is served family style.

I asked Andrew what it was like growing up in a family of so many children. He said it wasn't easy. Even his father had difficulty keeping everyone straight. "Once I came back from three months in Costa Rica, and my father greeted me at the airport with 'Welcome home, Jeffrey.' But Jeffrey told me not to worry,"

Andrew went on. "He said that Dad had been calling him Pinky on and off." Pinky, Andrew explained, was a family dog who'd died several years before.

It wasn't until evening settled in and we sat on the porch, sipping beers and watching the ocean, that we noticed Ted. Ted had been at lunch but he was at another table, and we had managed to miss him somehow. He was one of the strangest-looking people I'd ever seen. Ted had been on the island almost two months now, and one of the first things he told us was that he'd come to Roberts' Hill to recover. It occurred to us later that he'd come to recover from a sex-change operation. The problem was that we could not determine which way the operation had gone. Ted was half man, half woman. He had a woman's voice, beardless features, a man's body type and musculature, no breasts, and what appeared to be a bulge in the crotch of his shorts.

He reminded me of Truman Capote, and he knew everything about anything. He came out on the porch during cocktail hour and, once he realized Becky was a biologist, began telling us about the snakes and ticks that inhabit the island. He described Robert's encounter with a boa, which he said was eighteen to twenty feet long, thick as a coconut palm, with a red comb in its hair. Becky looked bewildered and I could see she was trying to think through her knowledge of snakes to see if such a creature was plausible.

He said he was a medical doctor with an innate sense for the stock market. During our brief cocktail hour he managed to explain how the DC-3 is a World War II plane, to direct us to the best swimming, to tell us about barracuda biting off a man's calf. He talked about head-hunters and cannibals and altered states of consciousness. He went on with Sufi legends and talk of transformation, political intrigue, and the decline of America. In this remote and peaceful place, we would never be able to get away from him/her. No matter what hour of the day or what book sat in our laps, Ted would appear, droning on and on about whatever entered his mind. And that evening as we waited for dinner, listening to the barking of a dog, Ted said the dog had found a boa. And the boas would become mythological creatures to me, like unicorns or baobab trees.

Ted told us about a canyon he liked to swim to. As he was leaving for this spot in the morning, he asked if we wanted to swim along. Though we didn't want to go with him, he knew the way, so we agreed. Andrew noticed that Ted wore a T-shirt and Bermuda shorts to go scuba diving, instead of trunks. In the week I spent on the island, Ted never took off his T-shirt and never swam in trunks, deepening our suspicions that he'd had some kind of surgery.

We swam in shallow water over thick, waving sea grass that continued almost to the reefs. We reached the canyon which was, in fact, like a canyon, and swam through it. At the bottom of the canyon a giant sea turtle was resting, and Andrew dove down and made the turtle swim. The giant turtle, sluggish, resisted at first, but Andrew dove and dove and finally the lazy turtle stretched and tediously swam away.

After several days of eating Ruby's lunches and dinners cooked in coconut oil and swimming on the reefs, Andrew and Becky decided they had to go. They asked if I wanted to come with them. They were going to Huehuetenango, but I had planned a different route for myself and also did not feel ready to leave. I accompanied them to Sandy Bay, where the rich people vacationed. Planes came down from Miami to Roatán and the Americans stayed at resorts on Sandy Bay.

We rented a boat and took it over to the bay, because Charlie, the driver provided by Roberts' Hill, was on a binge, and there was no telling how long he would stay that way. The driver we hired sold shells and he tried to do business with us. He had conchs and shark jaws. He held up a hammerhead with seven rows of teeth—all of which rise up when the animal is ready to kill. The man, a black Carib, said that every fish out there that you ate would eat you. "You have it for dinner. It have you for lunch." Snapper, he said, was bad. "She's go to a thousand pounds and eat a cow." But what they feared, he told us, was barracuda. "Cuda can rip you apart with one bite."

We waited for the transport to take Andrew and Becky to town, and the transport was very slow, but at last it came. While we waited, we sat under a palapa sipping Cokes. On the beach two boys were having a knife fight. Vultures sat like spectators in the trees, watching them.

"Be careful in Huehue," I told them. "You know there's trouble there."

"And you be careful where you're going," they said.

The minute they left, I wished I'd gone with them. I thought perhaps I'd made a mistake by staying. I felt sad and empty to see them leave and I wondered how I would fare on the rest of this trip.

A new couple arrived, Lawrence and Felicity. They referred to each other as soul partners and said they were bonded in a spiritual way. Ted and Lawrence and Felicity seemed to have a great deal in common and over lunch all they talked about was spiritual bonding. I missed Andrew and Becky already.

In the evening Ted sat on the porch, talking to me about civil rights. "I've been punched in the face because of the way I look," he admitted. "I know I look strange. I've been refused hotel rooms." Ted was bitter about America and he said he had no intention of going home. He told me he was on a spiritual quest and was in the process of becoming a Sufi. He said that Omar Khayyám was a Sufi, and he believed that Dag Hammarskjöld was as well. He talked on about dervishes and dreams and memory and the meanings of stories. He told me a strange tale about a man and a donkey with ginger in his anus, but I didn't get the meaning, and he told me to meditate on the story and the meaning would come to me. But I've forgotten the story, and the meaning never came.

I felt troubled and restless all night long and I couldn't sleep. I was besieged as if by ghosts. A tremendous sense of loneliness came over me and I wondered if I wouldn't always be alone. If I'd spend my entire life alone, without a true traveling companion. This thought terrified me and kept me awake. It wasn't yet dawn when I got up and went outside. I sat on the porch, watching for a redheaded woodpecker with a white feathery crown, indigenous only to the Bay Islands, which Becky used to sit and watch for, and now I sat, waiting for the sunrise and for the woodpeckers to reveal themselves to me.

I had thought to myself the whole time I had been away that there would be a moment when everything would become clear, when I would understand what I had not understood before. I had been waiting for a clear moment when I would know that I'd traded cruelty for kindness, passion for companionship, anger for love. But now I knew that it would not happen this way.

As I sat out on that porch, I understood that growth comes over time. Change happens step by step. All along things had been changing inside of me, bit by bit, in small, imperceptible ways. It had been subtle, not sudden. It had been happening over time.

Before breakfast I put on my gear and went out alone in the ocean to swim to the reef, something I knew I shouldn't do, but the water out to the reefs was only about four feet deep and there was no danger of drowning. I swam for about a quarter of a mile in the warm, clear water until I realized that I was quite far from shore. In the distance I saw the now shrunken palmettos, the tiny guest house.

As I swam back, a school of blue jacks came toward me. And behind the blue jacks was a barracuda, thick waisted, several feet long. Its well-toothed jaws opened and closed as it fed in their school. The barracuda passed me and I kept swimming. I thought of Ted's tales of cuda and what the Carib man had said. I swam steadily until I noticed that now I was surrounded by the school of blue jacks—thousands of them, all around me, little blue fish, hurrying away. Turning my head slowly, I found the barracuda, its eyes set, its mouth opening and closing at my heels.

I have been told that if an animal confronts you, often the best thing to do is surrender. You cannot outrun or outswim it. It will probably maul you, but you will live. But reason left me and my stubbornness prevailed. I ripped a gold chain from my wrist, in case the glitter was attracting the barracuda, and let the bracelet, a keepsake, float out to sea. Then I took a deep breath and I swam. I swam in fast, steady strokes, at every moment expecting the cuda to rip through the muscle of my calf or tear off my heel. I swam and swam, breathing, hoping, believing, and when I reached the shore, I pulled myself up and collapsed in the sand, breathless, safe.

FROM
The Middle Passage

V. S. NAIPAUL

*The author was born in Trinidad, a
descendant of immigrants from India, and
lived in England after being educated at
Oxford. His novels and travel writing reflect a
sense of displacement, a difficulty in accepting
a cultural identity. The title of his first travel
book, published in 1962, refers to ''the middle
passage'' of the slave ships from Africa to the
Caribbean colonies. In this excerpt Naipaul
confronts his fear on a return to Trinidad.*

*A*S soon as the *Francisco Bobadilla* had touched the quay, ship's side against
rubber bumpers, I began to feel all my old fear of Trinidad. I did not want to stay.
I had left the security of the ship and had no assurance that I would ever leave
the island again. I had forgotten nothing: the wooden houses, jalousied half-
way down, with fretwork along gables and eaves, fashionable before the concrete era; the concrete houses with L-shaped verandas and projecting front
bedrooms, fashionable in the thirties; the two-storeyed Syrian houses in pat-
terned concrete blocks, the top floor repeating the lower, fashionable in the
forties. There were more neon lights. Ambition—a moving hand, drink being
poured into a glass—was not matched with skill, and the effect was Trinidadian:
vigorous, with a slightly flawed modernity. There were more cars. From the
number plates I saw that there were now nearly fifty thousand vehicles on the
road; when I had left there were less than twenty thousand. And the city
throbbed with steel bands. A good opening line for a novelist or a travel-writer;
but the steel band used to be regarded as a high manifestation of West Indian
Culture, and it was a sound I detested.

When one arrives for the first time at a city, and especially if one arrives at
night, the people in the streets have, just for that moment, a special quality: they
are adepts in a ritual the traveller doesn't know; they are moving from one
mystery to another. But driving now through Port of Spain, seeing the groups
lounging at corners, around flambeau-lit stalls and coconut carts, I missed this
thrill, and was distressed, not so much by the familiarity, as by the feeling of
continuation. The years I had spent abroad fell away and I could not be sure
which was the reality in my life: the first eighteen years in Trinidad or the later

391

years in England. I had never wanted to stay in Trinidad. When I was in the fourth form I wrote a vow on the endpaper of my Kennedy's *Revised Latin Primer* to leave within five years. I left after six; and for many years afterwards in England, falling asleep in bedsitters with the electric fire on, I had been awakened by the nightmare that I was back in tropical Trinidad.

I had never examined this fear of Trinidad. I had never wished to. In my novels I had only expressed this fear; and it is only now, at the moment of writing, that I am able to attempt to examine it. I knew Trinidad to be unimportant, uncreative, cynical. The only professions were those of law and medicine, because there was no need for any other; and the most successful people were commission agents, bank managers and members of the distributive trades. Power was recognized, but dignity was allowed to no one. Every person of eminence was held to be crooked and contemptible. We lived in a society which denied itself heroes.

It was a place where the stories were never stories of success but of failure: brilliant men, scholarship winners, who had died young, gone mad, or taken to drink; cricketers of promise whose careers had been ruined by disagreements with the authorities.

It was also a place where a recurring word of abuse was "conceited," an expression of the resentment felt of anyone who possessed unusual skills. Such skills were not required by a society which produced nothing, never had to prove its worth, and was never called upon to be efficient. And such people had to be cut down to size or, to use the Trinidad expression, be made to "boil down." Generosity—the admiration of equal for equal—was therefore unknown; it was a quality I knew only from books and found only in England.

For talent, a futility, the Trinidadian substituted intrigue; and in the exercise of this, in small things as well as large, he became a master. Admiration he did have: for boys who did well at school, such academic success, separate from everyday life, giving self-respect to the community as a whole without threatening it in any way; for scholarship winners until they became conceited; for racehorses. And for cricketers.

Cricket has always been more than a game in Trinidad. In a society which demanded no skills and offered no rewards to merit, cricket was the only activity which permitted a man to grow to his full stature and to be measured against international standards. Alone on a field, beyond obscuring intrigue, the cricketer's true worth could be seen by all. His race, education, wealth did not matter. We had no scientists, engineers, explorers, soldiers or poets. The cricketer was our only hero-figure. And that is why cricket is played in the West Indies with such panache; that is why, for a long time to come, the West Indians will not be able to play as a team. The individual performance was what mattered. That was what we went to applaud; and unless the cricketer had heroic qualities we did not want to see him, however valuable he might be. And that was why, of those stories of failure, that of the ruined cricketer was the most terrible. In Trinidad lore he was a recurring figure; he appears in the Trinidad play, *Moon on a Rainbow Shawl,* by Errol John.

Though we knew that something was wrong with our society, we made no attempt to assess it. Trinidad was too unimportant and we could never be convinced of the value of reading the history of a place which was, as everyone said, only a dot on the map of the world. Our interest was all in the world outside, the remoter the better; Australia was more important than Venezuela, which we could see on a clear day. Our own past was buried and no one cared to dig it up. This gave us a strange time-sense. The England of 1914 was the England of yesterday; the Trinidad of 1914 belonged to the dark ages.

There was an occasional racial protest, but that aroused no deep feelings, for it represented only a small part of the truth. Everyone was an individual, fighting for his place in the community. Yet there was no community. We were of various races, religions, sets and cliques; and we had somehow found ourselves on the same small island. Nothing bound us together except this common residence. There was no nationalist feeling; there could be none. There was no profound anti-imperialist feeling; indeed, it was only our Britishness, our belonging to the British Empire, which gave us any identity. So protests could only be individual, isolated, unheeded.

It was only towards the end of the war that stories of limited success began to be known, stories of men who had served with distinction in the RAF, of men who had become lecturers in English and American universities, of singers who had won recognition abroad. These people had all escaped. "Conceited" at home, they had won distinction abroad; and as theirs was not the despised local eminence Trinidad accepted them with a ready generosity and exaggerated their worth.

The threat of failure, the need to escape: this was the prompting of the society I knew.

Port of Spain is the noisiest city in the world. Yet it is forbidden to talk. "Let the talkies do the talking," the signs used to say in the old London Theatre of my childhood. And now the radios and the rediffusion sets do the talking, the singing, the jingling; the steel bands do the booming and the banging; and the bands, live or tape-recorded, and the gramophones and record-players. In restaurants the bands are there to free people of the need to talk. Stunned, temples throbbing, you champ and chew, concentrating on the working of your jaw muscles. In a private home as soon as anyone starts to talk the radio is turned on. It must be loud, loud. If there are more than three, dancing will begin. Sweat-

sweat-dance-dance-sweat. Loud, loud, louder. If the radio isn't powerful enough, a passing steel band will be invited in. Jump-jump-sweat-sweat-jump. In every house a radio or rediffusion set is on. In the street people conduct conversations at a range of twenty yards or more; and even when they are close to you their voices have a vibrating tuning-fork edge. You will realize this only after you have left Trinidad: the voices in British Guiana will sound unnaturally low, and for the first day or so whenever anyone talks to you you will lean forward conspiratorially, for what is being whispered is, you feel, very secret. In the meantime dance, dance, shout above the shuffle. If you are silent the noise will rise to a roar about you. You cannot shout loud enough. Your words seem to be issuing from behind you. You have been here only an hour, but you feel as exhausted as though you had spent a day in some Italian scooter-hell. Your head is bursting. It is only eleven; the party is just warming up. You are being rude, but you must go.

You drive up the new Lady Young Road, and the diminishing noise makes it seem cooler. You get to the top and look out at the city glittering below you, amber and exploding blue on black, the ships in the harbour in the background, the orange flames issuing from the oil derricks far out in the Gulf of Paria. For a moment it is silent. Then, above the crickets, whose stridulation you hadn't noticed, you begin to hear the city: the dogs, the steel bands. You wait until the radio stations have closed down for the night—but rediffusion sets, for which there is a flat rental, are never turned off: they remain open, to await the funnelling of the morning noise—and then you wind down into the city again, drowning in the din. All through the night the dogs will go on, in a thousand inextricably snarled barking relays, rising and falling, from street to street and back again, from one end of the city to another. And you will wonder how you stood it for eighteen years, and whether it was always like this.

When I was a boy the people of Port of Spain used to dress up and walk around the Savannah on a Sunday afternoon. Those who had cars drove around in them slowly. It was a ritual parade which established the positions of the participants. It was also a pleasant walk. To the south lay the fine buildings of the wealthy and the Queen's Park Hotel, to us the last word in luxury and modernity. To the north were the botanical gardens and the grounds of Government House. And to the west lay Maraval Road.

Maraval Road is one of the architectural wonders of the world. It is a long road with few houses: it used to be the street of the very wealthy. At the north it begins with a Scottish baronial castle. Then comes Whitehall, an odd Moorish-Corsican building; before it was turned into government offices—the name Whitehall, however, came first—it was hung with tapestries depicting shepherds and shepherdesses, and had papier mâché logs in dummy fireplaces. Beyond Whitehall there is a palace with much wrought-iron decoration; it has a strong oriental flavour but is said to be copied from a French chateau. Then there is a monumental ochre-and-rust Spanish Colonial mansion. And the street ends with the blue-and-red PWD Italianate of Queen's Royal College, whose clock has Big Ben chimes.

This was the taste of the old Trinidad: individual, anarchic, not arising out of the place—in spite of the fireplaces every office in Whitehall needs two or three fans—but created out of memories. There were no local standards. In the refinements of behaviour, as in architecture, everything was left to the caprices of the individual. In the immigrant society, memories growing dim, there was no guiding taste. As you rose you evolved your own standards, and they were usually those of modernity.

There was no guiding taste because there was no taste. In Trinidad education was not one of the things money could buy; it was something money freed you from. Education was strictly for the poor. The white boy left school at an early age, "counting on his fingers," as the Trinidadian likes to say; but this was a measure of his privilege. He went to work in a bank, in Cable and Wireless or in a large business firm; and for many Trinidadians to be a bank clerk or a salesman was therefore the peak of ambition. Those of the white community who eccentrically desired an education nearly always left the island. The white community was never an upper class in the sense that it possessed a superior speech or taste or attainments; it was envied only for its money and its access to pleasure. Kingsley, in spite of all his affection for his white hosts in Trinidad, observed: "French civilization signifies, practically, certainly in the New World, little save ballet-girls, billiard-tables, and thin boots: English civilization, little save horse-racing and cricket." Seventy years later James Pope-Hennessy repeated and extended the observation. "Educated people of African origin would speak to him of subjects about which he was accustomed to talk in his own country: about books, music or religion. English persons on the other hand spoke mainly of tennis-scores, the country-club, whisky or precedence or oil." Education was strictly for the poor; and the poor were invariably black.

With the opening up of the colonial society the white community finds itself at a disadvantage, and the attitude to education has changed. It is now seen as not discreditable, possibly even useful, and the white community has decided to expose itself to it. A new boarding-school, which appears to be whitish in intention, has been opened. While I was there the principal, brought down from England to direct this Custer's last stand, was issuing unrealistic statements about building character. Unrealistic because too late: the taste of the society has hardened.

The cultures represented by the buildings in Maraval Road and the figures in the Kingsley engraving have not coalesced to form this taste. They have all been abandoned under the pressure of every persuasive method: second-rate newspapers, radio services and films.

It might have been expected that journalism would provide an outlet for the talent that could not find expression elsewhere. But local talent, like the local eminence, was automatically condemned. Experts were continually imported, the English Hattons and Morrows; and journalism in Trinidad remained undervalued and underpaid, never ranking as high as motor-car-selling. The newspapers relied to a great extent on space-filling syndicated American and English columns, comic strips, the film gossip of Louella Parsons and beauty hints about the preservation of peaches-and-cream complexions.

Again and again one comes back to the main, degrading fact of the colonial society; it never required efficiency, it never required quality, and these things, because unrequired, became undesirable.

The radio came later, and it was worse. America sent Hatton and Morrow. Britain sent Rediffusion. A generation has now been brought up to believe that radio, modern radio, means a song followed by a jingle, soap-operas five and fifteen minutes long, continually broken for commercials, so that in a five-minute morning serial like *The Shadow . . . of . . . Delilah!,* to which I found all Trinidad thrilling, two minutes, by my reckoning, were given over to advertising. This type of commercial radio, with its huckstering geniality, has imposed its values so successfully that there was widespread enthusiasm when Trinidad, not content with one such radio service, acquired two.

Newspapers and radio were, however, only the ancillaries of the cinema, whose influence is incalculable. The Trinidad audience actively participates in the action on the screen. "Where do you come from?" Lauren Bacall is asked in *To Have and Have Not.* "Port of Spain, Trinidad," she replies, and the audience shouts delightedly, "You lie! You lie!" So the audience continually shouts advice and comments; it grunts at every blow in a fight; it roars with delight when the once-spurned hero returns wealthy and impeccably dressed (this is important) to revenge himself on his past tormentor; it grows derisive when the hero finally rejects and perhaps slaps the Hollywood "bad" woman (of the *Leave Her to Heaven* type). It responds, in short, to every stock situation of the American cinema.

Nearly all the films shown, apart from those in the first-run cinemas, are American and old. Favourites are shown again and again: *Casablanca,* with Humphrey Bogart; *Till the Clouds Roll By;* the Errol Flynn, John Wayne, James Cagney, Edward G. Robinson and Richard Widmark films; vintage Westerns like *Dodge City* and *Jesse James;* and every film Bogart made. Films are reputed for their fights. *The Spoilers* is advertised as having the longest fight ever (Randolph Scott and John Wayne, I believe). *The Brothers* was one of the few British films to win favour; it had a good fight and was helped not a little by the scene in which Maxwell Reed prepares to beat Patricia Roc with a length of rope ("You must be beaten"): the humiliation of women being important to the Trinidad audience. And there are serials—*Daredevils of the Red Circle, Batman, Spycatcher*—which are shown in children's programmes in the countries of their origin but in Trinidad are one of the staples of adult entertainment. They are never shown serially but all at once; they are advertised for their length, the number of reels being often stated; and the latecomer asks, "How much reels gone?" When I was there *The Shadow,* a serial of the forties, was revived; the new generation was being urged to "thrill to it like your old man did."

In its stars the Trinidad audience looks for a special quality of style. John Garfield had this style; so did Bogart. When Bogart, without turning, coolly rebuked a pawing Lauren Bacall, "You're breathin' down mah neck," Trinidad adopted him as its own. "That is man!" the audience cried. Admiring shrieks of "Aye-aye-*aye!*" greeted Garfield's statement in *Dust Be My Destiny:* "What am I gonna do? What I always do. Run." "From now on I am like John Garfield in *Dust Be My Destiny,*" a prisoner once said in court, and made the front page of the evening paper. Dan Duryea became a favourite after his role in *Scarlet Street.* Richard Widmark, eating an apple and shooting people down in *The Street With No Name,* had style; his chilling dry laugh was another endearing asset. For the Trinidadian an actor has style when he is seen to fulfil certain aspirations of the audience: the virility of Bogart, the man-on-the-run romanticism of Garfield, the pimpishness and menace of Duryea, the ice-cold sadism of Widmark.

After thirty years of active participation in this sort of cinema, the Trinidadian, whether he sits in the pit or the house or the balcony, can respond only to the Hollywood formula. Nothing beyond the formula is understood, even when it comes from America; and nothing from outside America is worth considering. British films, until they took on an American gloss, played to empty houses. It was my French master who urged me to go to see *Brief Encounter;* and there were two of us in the cinema, he in the balcony, I in the pit. As Trinidad was British, cinemas were compelled to show a certain footage of British film; and they complied with the regulations by showing four British films in one day, *Brief Encounter* and *I Know Where I'm Going* in the afternoon, say, and *The Overlanders* and *Henry V* in the evening.

This attitude to British films is understandable. I had enjoyed *Our Man in Havana* in London. Seeing it again in Trinidad, I was less enchanted. I saw how English and narcissistic it was, how provincial, and how meaningless to the audience were the English jokes about Englishness. The audience was silent through all the comedy and came to life only during the drama. There were even approving shouts during the game of draughts played with miniature bottles of liquor, each piece being drunk when taken: this, for the Trinidadian, was style.

A Board of Censors, which knows about the French, bans French films. Italian, Russian, Swedish and Japanese films are unknown. Indian films of Hollywood badness can be seen; but Satyajit Ray's Bengali trilogy cannot find an exhibitor. Nigerians, I believe, are addicted to Indian films as well as to those from Hollywood. The West Indian, revealingly, is less catholic; and in Trinidad the large and enthusiastic audiences for Indian films are, barring an occasional eccentric, entirely Indian.

If curiosity is a characteristic of the cosmopolitan, the cosmopolitanism on which Trinidad prides itself is fraudulent. In the immigrant colonial society, with no standards of its own, subjected for years to the second-rate in newspapers, radio and cinema, minds are rigidly closed; and Trinidadians of all races and classes are remaking themselves in the image of the Hollywood B-man. This is the full meaning of modernity in Trinidad. . . .

I had never liked the sugarcane fields. Flat, treeless and hot, they stood for everything I had hated about the tropics and the West Indies. "Cane Is Bitter" is the title of a story by Samuel Selvon and might well be the epigraph of a history of the Caribbean. It is a brutal plant, tall and grass-like, with rough, razor-edged blades. I knew it was the basis of the economy, but I preferred trees and shade. Now, in the uneven land of Central and South Trinidad, I saw that even sugarcane could be beautiful. On the plains just before crop-time, you drive through it, walls of grass on either side; but in rolling country you can look down on a hillside covered with tall sugarcane in arrow: steel-blue plumes dancing above a grey-green carpet, grey-green because each long blade curves back on itself, revealing its paler underside.

The cocoa woods were another thing. They were like the woods of fairy tales, dark and shadowed and cool. The cocoa-pods, hanging by thick short stems, were like wax fruit in brilliant green and yellow and red and crimson and purple. Once, on a late afternoon drive to Tamana, I found the fields flooded. Out of the flat yellow water, which gurgled in the darkness, the black trunks of the stunted trees rose.

After every journey I returned to Port of Spain past Shanty Town, the mangrove swamp, the orange mist of the burning rubbish dump, the goats, the expectant corbeaux, all against a sunset that reddened the glassy water of the Gulf.

Everyone has to learn to see the West Indies tropics for himself. The landscape has never been recorded, and to go to the Trinidad Art Society Exhibition is to see how little local painters help. The expatriates contribute a few watercolours, the Trinidadians a lot of local colour. "Tropical Fruit" is the title of one painting, a title which would have had some meaning in the Temperate Zone. Another, startlingly, is "Native Hut." There are the usual picturesque native characters and native customs, the vision that of the tourist, at whom most of these native paintings seem to be aimed. The beach scenes are done with colours straight out of the tube, with no effort to capture the depth of sky, the brilliancy of light, the insubstantiality of colour in the tropics. The more gifted painters have ceased to record the landscape: the patterns of the leaves are too beguiling. In art, as in almost everything else, Trinidad has in one step moved from primitivism to modernism.

St. Lucia

JEAN RHYS

Memories of childhood dominate the brief,
unfinished autobiography Smile Please, *by*
Jean Rhys. The author of After Leaving Mr.
Mackenzie, The Wide Sargasso Sea, *and*
Good Morning, Midnight *was born and*
brought up on Dominica in the West Indies.
Before she died in her late eighties in 1979, she
recalled her first trip away from Dominica and
her first voyage on a large ship.

W HEN I was about twelve years old, I went with Auntie B to St. Lucia. I was
to be bridesmaid at my uncle's wedding in Castries. Castries, an exciting place. A
regiment was stationed there, horse racing and a lot of French people who gave
parties and dances.

Passing Martinique, the Trois Pitons, Castries early in the morning. Unlike
Roseau Bay, Castries was a coaling station and harbour where the ships came
right up to the land. Little boys diving for money that the tourists threw overboard.

The bride-to-be, Evelina, was pretty with a thick fringe and large brown eyes.

We stayed in St. Lucia for about three months and it was a very happy time for
me. My aunt's warnings about fer-de-lances, a very poisonous snake, and
tarantula spiders, both supposed to be plentiful in St. Lucia, didn't worry me.
She had talked of my fear of the dark and every night Evelina would come to my
room and whistle to me until I slept. She had a clear whistle, like a boy's. Of
course I imitated her, and began whistling myself. One morning Auntie B said:
"A whistling woman and a crowing hen is fit for neither God nor men." She
spoke to me but she looked at Evelina. Instantly I knew they didn't like each
other and they'd have to live in the same house. Auntie B had always ruled
supreme at Geneva. Breakers ahead, as my father would say.

Staying in Castries for the wedding was a young man called Mr. Kennaway.
When he watches me I can see that he doesn't think I am pretty. O God, let me
be pretty when I grow up. Let me be, let me be. That's what is in his eyes: "Not a
pretty little girl." He is English.

The night before the wedding my aunt plaited my hair into many tight little
plaits, so it should be wavy next morning. And it was. With my bridesmaid's

dress, my wavy hair, and holding my bouquet, I looked at Mr. Kennaway when we met. But his eyes were just the same: "Not a pretty little girl."

My uncle was very much in love with Evelina. When he looked at her he had a rather silly expression, I thought.

After the wedding, when Evelina and her husband left for their honeymoon in Trinidad, we stayed on. Evelina's brother was like her but with red hair. He took me for long walks, showed me Castries, and one day asked if I would like to see a fight between a tarantula and a scorpion. "We put them in a bottle and watch," he said.

I asked who won.

"Neither wins. The spider bites, the scorpion stings, and they both die."

But I didn't want to see the fight.

Cocks crowing, fine weather. The sea is so blue, I like this place, I wish I could stay here forever.

Then I was back home again but remembering the blue weather, the cocks crowing and Evelina whistling.

This stay in Castries was a definite stage in my life. It was the first time I had ever left Dominica or been on a big ship. If Evelina troubled to whistle to me every night because she knew the dark frightened me, she must have liked me. If her red-haired brother offered to arrange a fight between a tarantula spider and a scorpion, he too must have liked me. As for Mr. Kennaway, well, I needn't think about him. Some people were kind. By the time I left Castries Auntie B had made me some dresses I liked, a liberty bodice had been ordered for me from England, my stockings no longer drooped and I no longer thought of myself as an outcast.

The memory from St. Lucia of a long line of women carrying coals to the ship. Some of them looked very strained up and tired, carrying those huge baskets. I didn't like to think of them, but I hadn't asked any questions. I knew someone would say, "They're very well paid," and another, "Yes, but women are cheaper."

Soon after our visit to St. Lucia there was a big fire in Castries, and as all the houses were wood, it did a lot of damage. But as far as I knew it was built up again. I was very shocked when I heard someone recently, after they had made a trip to the West Indies, talk of Castries as a shanty town. I suppose they call Roseau a shanty town too, now.

I didn't know whether to answer "It isn't true!" or "We didn't do that!"

So, as usual, I said nothing.

As I had foreseen, Auntie B and the new bride didn't like each other at all. The time came when they quarrelled openly, though we were never told why. Was it perhaps the pepper pot (meat preserved in red peppers)? The Geneva pepper pot was supposed to be one hundred years old. Perhaps the bride thought it time to throw it out. Or more likely it was the garden, which she may have found melancholy and decided to change.

In any case Auntie B left and came to live in Roseau. Left behind the silk-cotton mattress, the cool dressing room, packed, left and never went back. My father was very fond of her and thought she had been treated disgracefully, so we were never allowed to go back to Geneva. I never saw Aunt Jane again. What happened at Geneva I never knew.

After Auntie B left Geneva for good and for keeps she went to England, and I think Edinburgh, for a long time. When she came back she seemed a stranger. She never stopped talking about the theatre. She ceaselessly talked about the actors, the actresses and above all the scenery, which transported her.

She also bought a big hat with feathers on it. I remember it was pinned to the top of her trunk in such a way that the feathers weren't disturbed. She must have looked magnificent in it but I never saw her wear it.

I think Auntie B must have been rather accident prone, for after all this, when she came back she broke her leg. I went to see her, very nervous, and she said, "Now then, don't look like dying Dick and solemn Davy, I'm not dead yet!"

But I was always a little nervous of Auntie B and couldn't muster up anything else than a rather forced smile. I think Auntie B was very brave, not like people are now. My mother was a quieter copy of her.

Incidents of Travel in Yucatán

JOHN L. STEPHENS

*The result of a pioneer expedition to Yucatán
in the 1840s by writer John Stephens,
accompanied by artist Frederick Catherwood,
was a memorable book of archaeological
discovery and dramatic travel writing.
Stephens's work remains an absorbing guide
today for visitors to Maya Indian sites in
Yucatán.*

*E*ARLY the next morning we set out for the rancho of Nohcacab, three
leagues distant. The proprietor had gone before daylight, to receive us on the
ground. We had not gone far when Mr. C. complained of a slight headache, and
wishing to ride moderately, Doctor Cabot and myself went on, leaving him to
follow with the luggage. The morning air was fresh and invigorating, and the
country rolling, hilly, and picturesque. At the distance of two leagues we
reached what was called a hebe, or fountain. It was a large rocky basin, about
ninety feet in circumference and ten feet deep, which served as a receptacle for
rain-water. In that dry country it was a grateful spectacle, and beside it was a
large seybo tree, that seemed inviting the traveller to repose under its branches.
We watered our horses from the same waccal, or drinking cup, that we used
ourselves, and felt strongly tempted to take a bath, but, with our experience of
fever and ague, were afraid to run the risk. This fountain was a league from the
rancho to which we were going, and was the only watering-place for its inhabitants.

At nine o'clock we reached the rancho, which showed the truth of the
Spanish proverb, "La vista del amo engorda el caballo;" "The sight of the master
fattens the horse." The first huts were enclosed by a well-built stone wall, along
which appeared, in various places, sculptured fragments from the ruins. Beyond
was another wall, enclosing the hut occupied by the master on his visits to the
rancho, the entrance to which was by a gateway formed of two sculptured

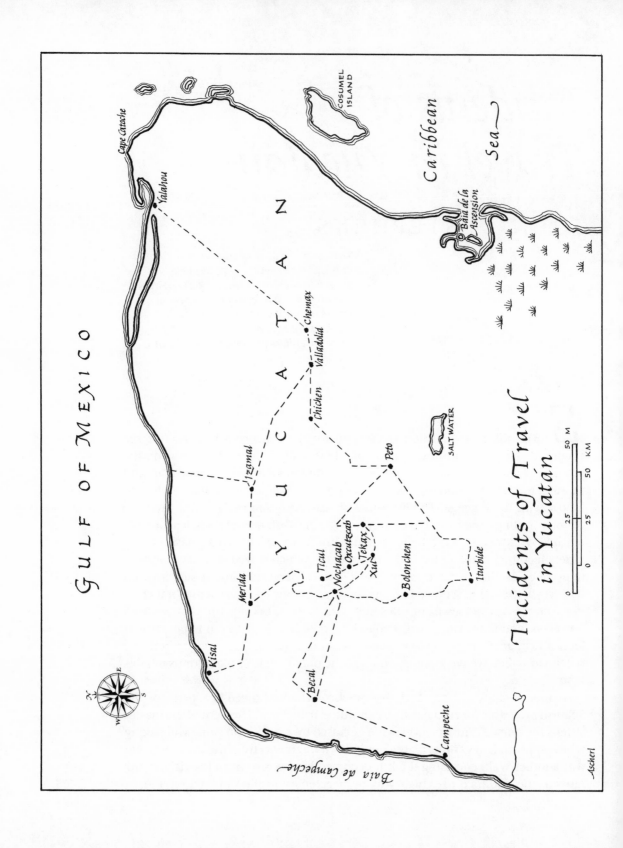

GULF OF MEXICO

Caribbean Sea

COSUMEL ISLAND

Cape Cattache

Yalahou

YUCATAN

Chemax

Valladolid

Chichen

Bahia de la Ascension

Izamal

Peto

SALT WATER

Ticul

Nochacab

Oxcutzcab

Tekax

Xul

Bolonchen

Iturbide

Merida

Kisal

Becal

Campeche

Bahia de Campeche

Incidents of Travel in Yucatán

50 M

KM

50

25 · 25

0 · 0

Ascherl

monuments of curious design and excellent workmanship, raising high our expectations in regard to the ruins on this rancho, and sustaining the accounts we had heard of them.

The proprietor was waiting to receive us, and, having taken possession of an empty hut, and disposed of our horses, we accompanied him to look over the rancho. What he regarded as most worth showing was his tobacco crop, lying in some empty huts to dry, which he contemplated with great satisfaction, and the well, which he looked at with as much sorrow. It was three hundred and fifty-four feet deep, and even at this great depth it was dry.

While we were thus engaged, our baggage carriers arrived with intelligence that Mr. Catherwood was taken ill, and they had left him lying in the road. I immediately applied to the proprietor for a coché and Indians, and he, with great alacrity, undertook to get them ready; in the mean time I saddled my horse and hastened back to Mr. Catherwood, whom I found lying on the ground, with Albino by his side, under the shade of the tree by the fountain, with an ague upon him, wrapped up in all the coverings he could muster, even to the saddlecloths of the horses. While he was in this state, two men came along, bestriding the same horse, and bringing sheets and ponchas to make a covering for the coché; then came a straggling line of Indians, each with a long pole, and withes to lash them together; and it was more than an hour before the coché was ready. The path was narrow, and lined on each side with thorn bushes, the spikes of which stuck in the naked flesh of the Indians as they carried the coché, and they were obliged to stop frequently and disentangle themselves. On reaching the rancho I found Doctor Cabot down with a fever. From the excitement and anxiety of following Mr. Catherwood under the hot sun, and now finding Doctor Cabot down, a cold shivering crept over me, and in a few minutes we were all three in our hammocks. A few hours had made a great change in our condition; and we came near bringing our host down with us. He had been employed in preparing breakfast upon a large scale, and seemed mortified that there was no one to do it justice. Out of pure good feeling toward him, I had it brought to the side of my hammock. My effort made him happy, and I began to think my prostration was merely the reaction from over-excitement; and by degrees what I began to please our host I continued for my own satisfaction. The troubles of my companions no longer disturbed me. My equanimity was perfectly restored, and, breakfast over, I set out to look at the ruins.

Ever since our arrival in Yucatán we had received courtesies and civilities, but none more thorough than those bestowed by our host of Nohcacab. He had come out with the intention of passing a week with us, and the Indians and the whole rancho were at our service as long as we chose to remain.

Passing through one of the huts, we soon came to a hill covered with trees and very steep, up which the proprietor had cut, not a mere Indian path, but a road two or three yards wide, leading to a building standing upon a terrace on the brow of the hill. The façade above the cornice had fallen, and below it was of plain stone. The interior was entire, but without any distinguishing features. Following the brow of this hill, we came to three other buildings, all standing on the same range, and without any important variations in the details, except that in one the arch had no overlapping stone, but the two sides of the ceiling ran up to a point, and formed a complete angle. These, the Indians told us, were the only buildings that remained. That from which the pillars in the church at Xul were taken was a mere mass of ruins. I was extremely disappointed. From the accounts which had induced us to visit this place, we had made larger calculations. It was the first time I had been thoroughly disappointed. There were no subjects for the pencil, and, except the deep and abiding impression of moving among the deserted structures of another ruined and desolate city, there was nothing to carry away. The proprietor seemed mortified that he had not better ruins to show us, but I gave him to understand that it was not his fault, and that he was in nowise to blame. Nevertheless, it was really vexatious, with such good-will on his part, and such a troop of Indians at command, that there was nothing for us to do. The Indians sympathized in the mortification of their master, and, to indemnify me, told me of two other ruined cities, one of which was but two leagues from the village of Xul.

I returned and made my report, and Mr. Catherwood immediately proposed a return to the village. Albino had given him an alarming account of the unhealthiness of the rancho, and he considered it advisable to avoid sleeping there a single night. Doctor Cabot was sitting up in his hammock, dissecting a bird. A recurrence of fever might detain us some time, and we determined on returning immediately to Xul. Our decision was carried into execution as promptly as it was made, and, leaving our luggage to the care of Albino, in half an hour, to the astonishment of the Indians and the mortification of the proprietor, we were on our way to the village.

It was late in the evening when we arrived, but the cura received us as kindly as before. During the evening I made inquiries for the place of which the Indians at the rancho had told me. It was but two leagues distant, but of all who happened to drop in, not one was aware of its existence. The cura, however, sent for a young man who had a rancho in that direction, and who promised to accompany me.

At six o'clock the next morning we started, neither Mr. Catherwood nor Doctor Cabot being able to accompany me. At the distance of about two leagues we reached an Indian rancho, where we learned from an old woman that we had passed the path leading to the ruins. We could not prevail on her to go back and show us the way, but she gave us a direction to another rancho, where she said we could procure a guide. This rancho was situated in a small clearing in the midst of the woods, enclosed by a bush fence, and before the door was an arbour covered with palm leaves, with little hammocks swinging under it, and all together the picture of Indian comfort.

My companion went in, and I dismounted, thinking that this promised a good stopping-place, when, looking down, I saw my pantaloons brown with garrapatas. I laid hold of a twig, intending to switch them off, and hundreds fell upon my hand and arm. Getting rid of those in sight as well as I could, and mounting immediately, I rode off, hoping most earnestly not to find any ruins, nor any necessity of taking up our abode in this comfortable-seeming rancho.

We were fortunate in finding at this place an Indian, who, for reasons known to himself and the wife of the master, was making a visit during the absence of the latter at his milpa; but for which we should not have been able to procure a guide. Retracing our steps, and crossing the camino real, we entered the woods on the other side, and tying our horses, the Indian cut a path up the side of a hill, on the top of which were the ruins of a building. The outer wall had fallen, leaving exposed to view the inner half of the arch, by which, as we approached it, my attention was strongly attracted. This arch was plastered and covered with painted figures in profile, much mutilated, but in one place a row of legs remained, which seemed to have belonged to a procession, and at the first glance brought to my mind the funeral processions on the walls of the tombs at Thebes. In the triangular wall forming the end of the room were three compartments, in which were figures, some having their heads adorned with plumes, others with a sort of steeple cap, and carrying on their heads something like a basket; and two were standing on their hands with their heels in the air. These figures were about a foot high, and painted red. The drawing was good, the attitudes were spirited and life-like, and altogether, even in their mutilated state, they were by far the most interesting paintings we had seen in the country.

Another apartment had been plastered and covered with paintings, the colours of which were in some places still bright and vivid. In this apartment we cornered and killed a snake five feet long, and as I threw it out at the door a strong picture rose up before me of the terrific scenes which must have been enacted in this region; the cries of woe that must have ascended to Heaven when these sculptured and painted edifices were abandoned, to become the dwelling-place of vultures and serpents.

There was one other building, and these two, my guide said, were all, but probably others lie buried in the woods. Returning to our horses, he led me to another extraordinary subterraneous well, which probably furnished water to the ancient inhabitants. I looked into the mouth, and saw that the first descent was by a steep ladder, but had no disposition to explore it.

In a few minutes we mounted to return to the village. Ruins were increasing upon us, to explore which thoroughly would be the work of years; we had but months, and were again arrested by illness. For some days, at least, Mr. Cather-wood would not be able to resume work. I was really distressed by the magni-tude of what was before us, but, for the present, we could do nothing, and I determined at once to change the scene. The festival of Ticul was at hand, and that night it was to open with el báyle de las Mestizas, or the Mestiza ball. Ticul lay in our return route, nine leagues from the village of Xul, but I determined to reach it that evening. My companion did not sympathize in my humour; his vaquero saddle hurt him, and he could not ride faster than a walk. I had need to economize all my strength; but I took his hard-trotting horse and uneasy saddle, and gave him mine. Pushing on, at eleven o'clock we reached Xul, where I had my horse unsaddled and washed, ordered him a good mess of corn, and two boiled eggs for myself. In the mean time, Mr. Catherwood had a recurrence of fever and ague, and my horse was led away; but the attack proved slight, and I had him brought out again. At two o'clock I resumed my journey, with a sheet, a hammock, and Albino. The heat was scorching, and Albino would have grumbled at setting out at this hour, but he, too, was ripe for the fiesta of Ticul.

In an hour we saw in the woods on our right large mounds, indicating that here, too, had once stood an ancient city. I rode in to look at them, but the buildings which had crowned them were all fallen and ruined, and I only gained an addition to the stock of garrapatas already on hand. We had not heard of these ruins at the village, and, on inquiring afterward, I could find no name for them.

At the distance of three leagues we commenced ascending the sierra, and for two hours the road lay over an immense ledge of solid rock. Next to the Mico Mountain, it was the worst range I ever crossed, but of entirely different charac-ter; instead of gullies, and holes, and walls of mud, it consisted of naked, broken rock, the reflection of the sun upon which was intense and extremely painful to the eyes. In some places it was slippery as glass. I had crossed the sierra in two different places before, but they were comparatively like the passage of the Simplon with that of San Bernard or San Gothard across the Alps. My horse's hoofs clattered and rang at every step, and, though strong and sure-footed, he stumbled and slid in a way that was painful and dangerous to both horse and rider; indeed, it would have been an agreeable change to be occasionally stuck in the mud. It was impossible to go faster than a walk, and, afraid that night would overtake us, in which case, as there was no moon, we might lose our way, I dismounted and hurried on, leading my horse.

It was nearly dark when we reached the top of the last range. The view was the grandest I had seen in the country. On the very brink stood the church of La Hermita, below the village of Oxcutzcab, and beyond a boundless wooded plain, dotted in three places with villages. We descended by a steep and stony path, and, winding along the front of La Hermita, came upon a broad pavement of stones from the ruined buildings of an aboriginal town. We passed under an imposing gateway, and, entering the village, stopped at the first house for a draught of water, where, looking back, we saw the shades of night gathering over the sierra, a token of our narrow escape. There were ruined mounds in the neighbourhood, which I intended to look at in passing, but we had still four leagues to make, and pushed on. The road was straight and level, but stony, and very soon it became so dark that we could see nothing. My horse had done a hard day's work, and stumbled so that I could scarcely keep him from falling. We roused the barking dogs of two villages, of which, however, I could distinguish nothing but the outline of their gigantic churches, and at nine o'clock rode into the plaza of Ticul. It was crowded with Indians, blazing with lights, and occupied by a great circular scaffold for a bull-ring, and a long, enclosed arbour, from the latter of which strains of music gave notice that the báyle de las Mestizas had already begun.

Once more I received a cordial welcome from the cura Carillo; but the music from the arbour reminded me that the moments of pleasure were fleeting. Our trunks had been ordered over from Nohcacab, and, making a hurried toilet, I hastened to the ball-room, accompanied by the padre Brizeña; the crowd outside opened a way, Don Philippe Peon beckoned to me as I entered, and in a moment more I was seated in one of the best places at the báyle de las Mestizas. After a month in Indian ranchos, that day toiling among ruins, almost driven to distraction by garrapatas, clambering over a frightful sierra, and making a journey worse than any sixty miles in our country, all at once I settled down at a fancy ball, amid music, lights, and pretty women, in the full enjoyment of an armchair and a cigar. For a moment a shade of regret came over me as I thought of my invalid friends, but I soon forgot them.

The enramada, or enclosure for the ball-room, was an arbour about one hundred and fifty feet long and fifty feet wide, surrounded by a railing of rude lattice-work, covered with costal, or hemp bagging, as a protection against the night air and sun, and lighted by lamps with large glass shades. The floor was of hard cement; along the railing was a row of chairs, all occupied by ladies; gentlemen, boys, and girls, children and nurses, were sitting promiscuously on the floor, and Don Philippe Peon, when he gave me his chair, took a place among them. El báyle de las Mestizas was what might be called a fancy ball, in which the señoritas of the village appeared as las Mestizas, or in the costume of Mestiza women: loose white frock, with red worked border round the neck and skirt, a man's black hat, a blue scarf over the shoulder, gold necklace and bracelets. The young men figured as vaqueros, or major domos, in shirt and pantaloons of pink striped muslin, yellow buckskin shoes, and low, round-crowned, hard-platted straw hat, with narrow brim rolled up at the sides, and trimmed with gold cord and tassels. Both costumes were fanciful and pretty, but at first the black hat was repulsive. I had heard of the sombreros negros as part of the Mestiza costume, and had imagined some neat and graceful fabric of straw; but the faces of the girls were so soft and mild that even a man's hat could not divest them of their feminine charm. Altogether the scene was somewhat different from what I expected, more refined, fanciful, and picturesque.

To sustain the fancy character, the only dance was that of the toros. A vaquero stood up, and each Mestiza was called out in order. This dance, as we had seen it among the Indians, was extremely uninteresting, and required a movement of the body, a fling of the arms, and a snapping of the fingers, which were at least inelegant; but with las Mestizas of Ticul it was all graceful and pleasing, and there was something particularly winning in the snapping of the fingers. There were no dashing beauties, and not one who seemed to have any idea of being a belle; but all exhibited a mildness, softness, and amiability of expression that created a feeling of promiscuous tenderness. Sitting at ease in an arm-chair, after my sojourn in Indian ranchos, I was particularly alive to these influences. And there was such a charm about that Mestiza dress. It was so clean, simple, and loose, leaving "Every beauty free / To sink or swell as Nature pleases."

The ball broke up too soon, when I was but beginning to reap the fruit of my hard day's work. There was an irruption of servants to carry home the chairs, and in half an hour, except along a line of tables in front of the audiencia, the village was still. For a little while, in my quiet chamber at the convent, the gentle figures of las Mestizas still haunted me, but, worn down by the fatigues of the day, I very soon forgot them.

At daylight the next morning the ringing of bells and firing of rockets announced the continuance of the fiesta; high mass was performed in the church, and at eight o'clock there was a grand exhibition of lassoing cattle in the plaza by amateur vaqueros. These were now mounted, had large vaquero saddles, spurs to match, and each was provided with a coil of rope in hand; bulls of two years old were let loose in the plaza, with the bull-ring to double round, and every street in the village open to them. The amateurs rode after them like mad, to the great peril of old people, women, and children, who scampered out of the way as well as they could, but all as much pleased with the sport as the bull or the vaqueros. One horse fell and hurt his rider, but there were no necks broken.

This over, all dispersed to prepare for the báyle de dia, or ball by daylight. I sat for an hour in the corridor of the convent, looking out upon the plaza. The sun was beaming with intense heat, and the village was as still as if some great calamity had suddenly overtaken it. At length a group was seen crossing the plaza: a vaquero escorting a Mestiza to the ball, holding over her head a red silk umbrella to protect her from the scorching rays of the sun; then an old lady and gentleman, children, and servants, a complete family group, the females all in white, with bright-coloured scarfs and shawls. Other groups appeared crossing in other directions, forming picturesque and pleasing spectacles in the plaza. I walked over to the arbour. Although in broad daylight, under the glare of a midday sun, and shaded only on one side by hemp bagging, as the Mestizas took their seats they seemed prettier than the night before. No adjustment of curtain light was necessary for the morning after the ball, for the ladies had retired at an early hour. The black hat had lost its repugnant character, and on some it seemed most becoming. The costumes of the vaqueros, too, bore well the light of day. The place was open to all who chose to enter, and the floor was covered with Indian women and children, and real Mestizoes in cotton shirts, drawers, and sandals; the barrier, too, was lined with a dense mass of Indians and Mestizoes, looking on good-humouredly at this personification of themselves and their ways. The whole gathering was more informal and gayer, and seemed more what it was intended to be, a fiesta of the village.

The báyle de dia was intended to give a picture of life at a hacienda, and there were two prominent personages, who did not appear the evening before, called fiscales, being the officers attendant upon the ancient caciques, and representing them in their authority over the Indians. These wore long, loose, dirty camisas hanging off one shoulder, and with the sleeves below the hands; calzoncillos, or drawers, to match, held up by a long cotton sash, the ends of which dangled below the knees; sandals, slouching straw hats, with brims ten or twelve inches wide, and long locks of horse hair hanging behind their ears. One of them wore awry over his shoulder a mantle of faded blue cotton cloth, said to be an heirloom descended from an ancient cacique, and each flourished a leather whip with eight or ten lashes. These were the managers and masters of ceremonies, with absolute and unlimited authority over the whole company, and, as they boasted, they had a right to whip the Mestizas if they pleased.

As each Mestiza arrived they quietly put aside the gentleman escorting her, and conducted the lady to her seat. If the gentleman did not give way readily, they took him by the shoulders, and walked him to the other end of the floor. A crowd followed wherever they moved, and all the time the company was assembling they threw everything into laughter and confusion by their whimsical efforts to preserve order.

At length they undertook to clear a space for dancing, backing the company in a summary way as far as they could go, and then taking the men and boys by the shoulder, and jamming them down upon the floor. While they were thus engaged, a stout gentleman, of respectable appearance, holding some high office in the village, appeared in the doorway, quietly lighting another straw cigar, and as soon as they saw him they desisted from the work they had in hand, and, in the capricious and wanton exercise of their arbitrary power, rushed across, seized him, dragged him to the centre of the floor, hoisted him upon the shoulders of a vaquero, and, pulling apart the skirts of his coat, belaboured him

411

with a mock vigour and earnestness that convulsed the whole company with laughter. The sides of the elevated dignitary shook, the vaquero shook under him, and they were near coming down together.

This over, the rogues came directly upon me. El Ingles had not long escaped their eye. I had with difficulty avoided a scene, and my time seemed now to have come. The one with the cacique's mantle led the way with long strides, lash raised in the air, a loud voice, and his eyes, sparkling with frolic and mischief, fastened upon mine. The crowd followed, and I was a little afraid of an attempt to hoist me too on the shoulders of a vaquero; but all at once he stopped short, and, unexpectedly changing his language, opened upon me with a loud harangue in Maya. All knew that I did not understand a word he said, and the laugh was strong against me. I was a little annoyed at being made such a mark, but, recollecting the achievement of our vernacular at Nohcacab, I answered him with an English oration. The effect was instantaneous. He had never before heard a language that he could not understand, bent his ear earnestly, as if by close attention he could catch the meaning, and looked up with an air of real perplexity that turned the laugh completely against him. He began again, and I answered with a stanza of Greek poetry, which had hung by me in some unaccountable way; this, again, completely silenced him, and he dropped the title Ingles, put his arms around my neck, called me "amigo," and made a covenant not to speak in any language but Castilian.

This over, he ordered the music to commence, planted a vaquero on the floor, and led out a Mestiza to dance, again threw all the bystanders into confusion, and sat down quietly on the floor at my feet. All the Mestizas were again called out in order, presenting the same pretty spectacle I had seen the evening before. And there was one whom I had noticed then, not more than fifteen, delicate and fragile, with eyes so soft and dovelike that it was impossible to look upon them without a feeling of tenderness. She seemed sent into the world to be cherished and cared for, and closeted like the finest china, the very emblem of purity, innocence, and loveliness; and, as I had learned, she was the child of shame, being the crianza, or natural daughter, of a gentleman of the village; perhaps it was that she seemed so ill fitted to buffet with contumely and reproach that gave such an indescribable interest to her appearance; but, fortunately, brought up in her father's house, she may go through life without meeting an averted face, or feeling that a stain rests upon her name.

As may be supposed, the presence of this señorita on the floor did not escape the keen eyes of the mercurial fiscal. All at once he became excited and restless, and, starting to his feet, gazed at her for a moment as if entranced by a vision, and then, as if carried away by his excitement, and utterly unconscious of what he was about, he pushed aside the vaquero who was dancing with her, and, flinging his sombrero on the ground, cried out in a tone of ecstasy, "Voy baylár con vd, mi corazon!'' ''I am going to dance with you, my heart!'' As he danced, his excitement seemed to increase; forgetting everything around him, the expression of his face became rapt, fixed, intense; he tore off his cacique's mantle, and, dancing toward her, spread it at the lady's feet. This seemed only to excite him more; and, as if forgetful of everything else, he seized the collar of his camisa, and, dancing violently all the time, with a nervous grasp, tugged as if he meant to pull it over his head, and throw all that he was worth at her feet. Failing in this, for a moment he seemed to give up in despair, but all at once he thrust his hands under the long garment, seized the sash around his waist, and, still dancing with all his might, unwound it, and, moving up to her with mingled grace, gallantry, and desperation, dropped it at her feet, and danced back to his place. By this time his calzoncillos, kept up by the sash, were giving way. Grasping them furiously, and holding them up with both hands, as if by a great effort, he went on dancing with a desperate expression of face that was irresistibly ludicrous.

During all this time the company was convulsed with laughter, and I could not help remarking the extreme modesty and propriety of the young lady, who never even smiled or looked at him, but, when the dance was ended, bowed and returned to her seat. The poor fiscal stood gazing at the vacant place where she had stood, as if the sun of his existence had set. At length he turned his head and called out ''amigo,'' asked if there were any such Mestizas in my country; if I would like to take her home with me; then said that he could not spare this one, but I might take my choice of the others; insisting loudly upon my making a selection, and promising to deliver any one I liked to me at the convent.

At first I supposed that these fiscales were, like the vaqueros, the principal young men of the village, who, for that day, gave themselves up to frolic and fun, but I learned that these were not willing to assume such a character, but employed others known to them for wit and humour, and, at the same time, for propriety and respectability of behaviour. This was a *matador de cochinos,* or pig butcher, of excellent character, and *muy vivo,* by which may be understood ''a fellow of infinite wit and humour.'' The people of the village seemed to think that the power given him to whip the Mestizas was the extremity of license, but they did consider that, even for the day, they put him on equal terms with those who, in his daily walks, were to him as beings of another sphere; for the time he might pour out his tribute of feeling to beauty and attraction, but it was all to be regarded as a piece of extravagance, to be forgotten by all who heard it, and particularly by her to whom it was addressed. Alas, poor matador de cochinos!

According to the rules, the mantle and sash which he had thrown at the feet of the lady belonged to her, and he was obliged to appeal to the charity of the spectators for money to redeem them. In the mean time the dance continued. The fiscales, having once taken ground as dancers, were continually ordering the vaqueros to step aside, and taking their places. At times, too, under the direction of the fiscales, the idle vaqueros seated themselves on the ground at the head of the arbour, and all joined in the hacienda song of the vaqueria, in alternate lines of Maya and Castilian. The chorus was led by the fiscales, with a noise that drowned every other sound; and while this boisterous merriment was going on, the light figures of the Mestizas were moving in the dance.

At twelve o'clock preparations were made for a déjeuner à la fourchette, dispensing, however, with knives and forks. The centre of the floor was cleared, and an enormous earthen jar, equal in capacity to a barrel, was brought in, containing frigoles, or black beans fried. Another vessel of the same size had a preparation of eggs and meat, and near them was a small mountain of tortillas, with all which it was the business of the Mestizas to serve the company. The fiscal did not neglect his amigo, but led to me one of whom I had expressed my opinion to him in confidence, and who brought in the palm of her hand a layer of tortillas, with frigoles in the centre, and turned up at the sides by means of the fingers, so as to prevent the frigoles from escaping. An attempt to acknowledge the civility was repressed by the fiscal, who crowded my hat over my eyes, saying that they passed no compliments on the haciendas, and we were all Indians together. The tortillas, with the frigoles in them, were not easy to hold without endangering my only pair of white pantaloons. I relieved myself by passing them over the railing, where any number of Indians stood ready to receive them; but I had hardly got rid of this when another Mestiza brought another portion, and while this engaged my one hand a third placed tortillas with eggs in the other, and left me afraid to move; but I contrived to pass both handfuls over the railing. Breakfast over, the dancing was resumed with new spirit. The fiscales were more amusing than ever; all agreed that the ball was muy alegre, or very gay, and I could not but notice that, amid all this motley company and extraordinary license, there was less noise than in a private drawing-room at home. At two o'clock, to my great regret, the ball of las Mestizas broke up. It was something entirely new, and remains engraven on my mind as the best of village balls.

The Sea and the Jungle

H. M. TOMLINSON

In 1909 the tramp steamer Capella *carried the author, then a London journalist, to Brazil and two thousand miles along the forest paths of the Amazon and Madeira rivers.*

*T*HE forest of the Amazons is not merely trees and shrubs. It is not land. It is another element. Its inhabitants are arborean; they have been fashioned for life in that medium as fishes to the sea and birds to the air. Its green apparition is persistent, as the sky is and the ocean. In months of travel it is the horizon which the traveller cannot reach, and its unchanging surface, merged through distance into a mere reflector of the day, a brightness or a gloom, in his immediate vicinity breaks into a complexity of green surges; then one day the voyager sees land at last and is released from it. But we have not seen land since Serpa. There are men whose lives are spent in the chasms of light where the rivers are sunk in the dominant element, but who never venture within its green surface, just as one would not go beneath the waves to walk in the twilight of the sea bottom.

Now I have been watching it for so long I see the outer aspect of the jungle does vary. When I saw it first on the Pará River it appeared to my wondering eyes but featureless green cliffs. Then in the Narrows beyond Pará I remember an impression of elegance and placidity, for there, the waters still being tidal and saline, the palms were conspicuous and in profuse abundance. The great palms are the chief feature of that forest elevation, with their graceful columns, and their generous and symmetrical fronds which sometimes are like gigantic green feathers, and again are like fans. A tall palm, whatever its species, being a definite expression of life—not an agglomeration of leaves, but body and crown, a real personality—the forest of the Narrows, populous with such exquisite beings, had marges of straight ascending lines and flourishing and geometrical crests.

Beyond the river Xingu, on the main stream, the forest, persistent as a presence, again changed its aspect. It was ragged and shapeless, an impenetrable

415

tangle, its front strewn with fallen trees, the vision of outer desolation. By Obidos it was more aerial and shapely again, but not of that light and soaring grace of the Narrows. It was contained, yet mounted not in straight lines, as in the country of the palms, but in convex masses. Here on the lower Madeira the forest seems of a nature intermediate between the rolling structure of the growth by Obidos, and the grace of the palm groves in the estuarine region of the Narrows. It is barbaric and splendid, easily prodigal with illimitable riches, sinking the river beneath a wealth of forms.

On the Madeira, as elsewhere in the world of the Amazon, some of the forest is on *terra firma,* as that land is called which is not flooded when the waters rise. There the trees reach their greatest altitude and diameter; it is the region of the *caá-apoam,* the "great woods" of the Indians. A stretch of *terra firma* shows as a low, vertical bank of clay, a narrow ribbon of yellow earth dividing the water from the jungle. More rarely the river cuts a section through some undulating heights of red conglomerate—heights I call these cliffs, as heights they are in this flat country, though at home they would attract no more attention than would the side of a gravel-pit—and again the bank may be of that cherry and saffron clay which gives a name to Itacoatiara. On such land the forest of the Madeira is immense, three or four species among the greater trees lording it in the green tumult expansively, always conspicuous where they stand, their huge boles showing in the verdant façade of the jungle as grey and brown pilasters, their crowns rising above the level roof of the forest in definite cupolas. There is one, having a neat and compact dome and a grey, smooth, and rounded trunk, and dense foliage as dark as that of the holm oak; and another, resembling it, but with a flattened and somewhat disrupted dome. I guessed these two giants to be silk-cottons. Another, which I supposed to be of the leguminous order, had a silvery bole, and a texture of pale green leafage open and light, which at a distance resembled that of the birch. These three trees, when assembled and well grown, made most stately river-side groups. The trunks were smooth and bare till somewhere near ninety feet from the ground. Palms were intermediate, filling the spaces between them, but the palms stood under the exogens, growing in alcoves of the mass, rising no higher than the beginning of the branches and foliage of their lords. The whole overhanging superstructure of the forest— not a window, an inlet, anywhere there—was rolling clouds of leaves from the lower rims of which vines were catenary, looping from one green cloud to another, or pendent, like the sundered cordage of a ship's rigging. Two other trees were frequent, the pao mulatto, with limbs so dark as to look black, and the castanheiro, the Brazil nut tree.

The roof of the woods lowered when we were steaming past the igapo. The igapo, or aqueous jungle, through which the waters go deeply for some months of the year, is of a different character, and perhaps of a lesser height—it seems less; but then it grows on lower ground. I was told to note that its foliage is of a lighter green, but I cannot say I saw that. It is in the igapo that the Hevea Braziliensis flourishes, its pale bole, suggestive of the white poplar, deep in water for much of the year, and its crown sheltered by its greater neighbours, so that it grows in a still, heated, and humid twilight. This low ground is always marked by growths of small cecropia trees. These, with their white stems, their habit of free and regular branching, and their long leaves, digital in the manner of the horse-chestnut, have the appearance of great candelabra. Sometimes the igapo is prefaced by an area of cane. The numberless islands, being of recent formation, have a forest of a different nature, and they seldom carry the larger trees. The upper ends of many of the islands terminate in sandy pits, where dwarf willows grow. So foreign was the rest of the vegetation, that notwithstanding its volume and intricacy, I detected those humble little willows at once, as one would start surprised at an English word heard in the meaningless uproar of an alien multitude.

The forest absorbed us; as one's attention would be challenged and drawn by the casual regard, never noticeably direct, but never withdrawn, of a being superior and mysterious, so I was drawn to watch the still and intent stature of the jungle, waiting for it to become vocal, for some relaxing of its static form. Nothing ever happened. I never discovered it. Rigid, watchful, enigmatic, its presence was constant, but without so much as one blossom in all its green vacuity to show the least friendly familiarity to one who had found flowers and woodlands kind. It had nothing that I knew. It remained securely aloof and indifferent, till I thought hostility was implied, as the sea implies its impartial hostility, in a constant presence which experience could not fathom, nor interest soften, nor courage intimidate. We sank gradually deeper inwards towards its central fastnesses.

By noon on our first day on the Madeira we reached the village of Rozarinho, which is on the left bank, with the tributary of the same name a little more up stream, but entering from the other side. Here, as we followed a loop of the stream, the Madeira seemed circumscribed, a tranquil lake. The yellow water, though swift, had so polished a surface that the reflections of the forest were hardly disturbed, sinking below the tops of the inverted trees to the ultimate clouds, giving an illusion of profundity to the apparent lake. The village was but a handful of leaf huts grouped about the nucleus of one or two larger buildings with white walls. There was the usual jetty of a few planks to which some canoes were tied. The forest was a high background to those diminished huts; the latter, as we came upon them, suddenly increased the height of the trees.

In another place the shelter of a family of Indians was at the top of a bank, secretive within the base of the woods. A row of chocolate babies stood outside that nest, with four jabiru storks among them. Each bird, so much taller than the

417

babies, stood resting meditatively on one leg, as though waiting the order to take up an infant and deliver it somewhere. None of them, storks or infants, took the least notice of us. Perhaps the time had not yet come for them to be aware of mundane things. Certainly I had a feeling myself, so strange was the place, and quiet and tranquil the day, that we had passed world's end, and that what we saw beyond our steamer was the coloured stuff of dreams which, if a wind blew, would wreathe and clear; vanish, and leave a shining void. The sunset deepened this apprehension. There came a wonderful sky of orange and mauve. It was over us and came down and under the ship. We moved with glowing clouds beneath our keel. There was no river; the forest girdled the radiant interior of a hollow sphere.

The pilots could not proceed at night. Shortly after sundown we anchored, in nine fathoms. The trees were not many yards from the steamer. When the ship was at rest a canoe with two Indians came alongside, with a basket of guavas. They were shy fellows, and each carried in his right hand a bright machete, for they did not seem quite sure of our company. After tea we sat about the poop, trying to smoke, and, in the case of the [ship's] Doctor and the Purser, wearing at the same time veils of butterfly nets, as protection from the mosquito swarms. The netting was put over the helmet, and tucked into the neck of the tunic. Yet, when I poked the stem of the pipe, which carried the gauze with it, into my mouth, the veil was drawn tight on the face. A mosquito jumped to the opportunity, and arrived. Alongside, the frogs were making the deafening clangour of an iron foundry, and through that sound shrilled the cicadas. I listened for the first time to the din of a tropical night in the forest. There is no word strong enough to convey this uproar to ears which have not listened to it.

January 24

A bright still sunrise, promising heat; and before breakfast the ship's ironwork was too hot to touch. The novelty of this Madeira is already beginning to merge into the yellow of the river, the blue of the sky, and the green of the jungle, with but the occasional variation of low roseous cliffs. The average width of the river may be less than a quarter of a mile. It is loaded with floating timber, launched upon it by "terras-cahidas," landslides, caused by the rains, which carry away sections of the forest each large enough to furnish an English park with trees. Sometimes we see a bight in the bank where such a collapse has only recently occurred, the wreckage of trees being still fresh. Many of the trees which charge down on the current are of great bulk, with half their table-like base high out of the water. Occasionally rafts of them appear, locked with creepers, and bearing flourishing gardens of weeds. This characteristic gives the river its Portuguese name, "river of wood." The Indians know the Madeira as the Cayary, "white river."

Its course to-day serpentines so freely that at times we steer almost east, and then again go west. Our general direction is south-west. At eight this morning, after some anxious moments when the river was dangerous with reefs, we passed the village of Borba, 140 miles from Serpa. Here there is a considerable clearing, with kine browsing over a hummocky sward that is well above the river on an occurrence of the red clay. This release of the eyes was a smooth and grateful experience after the enclosing walls. Some steps dug in the face of the low cliff led to the white houses, all roofed with red tiles. The village faced the river. From each house ascended the leisurely smoke of early morning. The church was in the midst of the houses, its bell conspicuous with verdigris. Two men stood to watch us pass. It was a pleasant assurance to have, those roofs and the steeple rising actually into the light of the sky. The dominant forest, in which we were sunk, was here definitely put down by our fellow-men.

We were beyond Borba, and its parana and island just above it, before the pilot had finished telling us, where we watched from the "Capella's" bridge, that Borba was a settlement which had suffered much from attacks of the Araras Indians. The river took a sharp turn to the east, and again went west. Islands were numerous. These islands are lancet-shaped, and lie along the banks, separated by side channels, their paranas, from the land. The smaller river craft often take a parana instead of the main stream, to avoid the rush of the current. The whole region seems lifeless. There is never a flower to be seen, and rarely a bird. Sometimes, though, we disturb the snowy heron. On one sandy island, passed during the afternoon, and called appropriately, Ilho do Jacaré, we saw two alligators. Otherwise we have the silent river to ourselves; though I am forgetting the butterflies, and the constant arrival aboard of new winged shapes which are sometimes so large and grotesque that one is uncertain about their aggressive qualities. As we idle on the poop we keep by us two insect nets, and a killing-bottle. The Doctor is making a collection, and I am supposed to assist.

When I came on deck on the morning of our arrival in the Brazils it was not the orange sunrise behind a forest which was topped by a black design of palm fronds, nor the warm odour of the place, nor the height and intensity of the vegetation, which was most remarkable to me, a new-comer from the restricted north. It was a butterfly which flickered across our steamer like a coloured flame. No other experience put England so remote.

A superb butterfly, too bright and quick to be anything but an escape from Paradise, will stay its dancing flight, as though with intelligent surprise at our presence, hover as if puzzled, and swoop to inspect us, alighting on some such incongruous piece of our furniture as a coil of rope, or the cook's refuse pail, pulsing its wings there, plainly nothing to do with us, the prismatic image of joy. Out always rush some of our men at it, as though the sight of it had maddened them, as would a revelation of accessible riches. It moves only at the last moment, abruptly and insolently. They are left to gape at its mocking retreat. It goes in erratic flashes to the wall of trees and then soars over the parapet, hope at large.

Then there are the other things which, so far as most of us know, have no names, though a sailor, wringing his hands in anguish, is usually ready with a name. To-day we had such a visitor. He looked a fellow the Doctor might require, so I marked him down when he settled near a hatch on the afterdeck. He was a bee the size of a walnut, and habited in dark blue velvet. In this land it is wise to assume that everything bites or stings, and that when a creature looks dead it is only carefully watching you. I clapped the net over that fellow and instantly he appeared most dead. Knowing he was but shamming, and that he would give me no assistance, I stood wondering what I could do next; then the cook came along. The cook saw the situation, laughed at my timidity with tropical forms, went down on his knees, and caught my prisoner. The cook raised a piercing cry.

On the bridge I saw them levelling their glasses at us; and some engineers came to their cabin doors to see us where we stood on the lonely deck, the cook and the Purser, in a tableau of poignant tragedy. The cook walked round and round, nursing his suffering member, and I did not catch all he said, for I know very little Dutch; but the spirit of it was familiar, and his thumb was bleeding badly. The bee had resumed death again. The state of the cook's thumb was a surprise till the surgeon exhibited the bee's weapons, when it became clear that thumbs, especially when Dutch and rosy, like our cook's, afforded the right medium for an artist who worked with such mandibles, and a tail that was a stiletto.

In England the forms of insect life soon become familiar. There is the housefly, the lesser cabbage white butterfly, and one or two other little things. In the Brazils, though the great host of forms is surprising enough, it is the variety in that host which is more surprising still. Any bright day on the "Capella" you may walk the length of the ship, carrying a net and a collecting-bottle, and fill the bottle (butterflies, cockroaches, and bugs not admitted), and perhaps have not three of a species. The men frequently bring us something buzzing in a hat; though accidents do happen half-way to where the Doctor is sitting, and the specimen is mangled in a frenzy. A hornet came to us that way. He was in violet armour, as hard as a crab, was still stabbing the air with his long needle, and working on a fragment of hat he held in his jaws. But such knights in mail are really harmless, for after all they need not be interfered with. It is the insignificant little fellows whose object in life it is to interfere with us which really make the difference.

So far on the river we have not met the famous pium fly. But the motuca fly is a nuisance during the afternoon sleep. It is nearly of the size and appearance of a "blue-bottle" fly, but its wings, having black tips, look as though their ends were cut off. The motucas, while we slept, would alight on the wrists and ankles, and where each had fed there would be a wound from which the blood steadily trickled.

The mosquitoes do not trouble us till sundown. But one morning in my cabin I was interested in the hovering of what I thought was a small, leggy spider which, because of its colouration of black and grey bands, was evasive to the sight as it drifted about on its invisible thread. At last I caught it, and found it was a new mosquito. In pursuing it I found a number of them in the cabin. When I exhibited the insect to the surgeon he did not well disguise his concern. "Say nothing about it," he said, "but this is the yellow-fever brute." So our interest in our new life is kept alert and bright. The solid teak doors of our cabins are now permanently fixed back. Shutting them would mean suffocation; but as the cabins must be closed before sundown to keep out the clouds of gnats, the carpenter has made wooden frames, covered with copper gauze, to fit the door openings at night, and rounds of gauze to cap the open ports; and with a damp cloth, and some careful hunting each morning, one is able to keep down the mosquitoes which have managed to find entry during the night and have retired at sunrise to rest in dark corners. For, our care notwithstanding, the insects do find their way in to assault our lighted lamps. The Chief, partly because as an old sailor he is a fatalist, and partly because he thinks his massive body must be invulnerable, and partly because he has a contempt, anyway, for protecting himself, each morning has a new collection of curios, alive and dead, littered about his room. (I do not wonder Bates remained in this land so long; it is Elysium for the entomologist.) One of the live creatures found in his room the Chief retains and cherishes, and hopes to tame, though the object does not yet answer to his name of Edwin. This creature is a green mantis or praying insect, about four inches long, which the Chief came upon where it rested on the copper gauze of his door-cover, holding a fly in its hands, and eating it as one would an apple. This mantis is an entertaining freak, and can easily keep an audience watching it for an hour, if the day is dull. Edwin, in colour and form, is as fresh, fragile, and translucent as a leaf in spring. He has a long thin neck—the stalk to his wings, as it were—which is quite a third of his length. He has a calm, human face with a pointed chin at the end of his neck; he turns his face to gaze at you without moving his body, just as a man looks backwards over his shoulder. This uncanny mimicry makes the Chief shake with mirth. Then, if you alarm

Edwin, he springs round to face you, frilling his wings abroad, standing up and sparring with his long arms, which have hooks at their ends. At other times he will remain still, with his hands clasped up before his face, as though in earnest devotion, for a trying period. If a fly alights near him he turns his face that way and regards it attentively. Then sluggishly he approaches it for closer scrutiny. Having satisfied himself it is a good fly, without warning his arms shoot out and that fly is hopelessly caught in the hooked hands. He eats it, I repeat, as you do apples, and the authentic mouthfuls of fly can be seen passing down his glassy neck. Edwin is fragile as a new leaf in form, has the same delicate colour, and has fascinating ways; but somehow he gives an observer the uncomfortable thought that the means to existence on this earth, though intricately and wonderfully devised, might have been managed differently. Edwin, who seems but a pretty fragment of vegetation, is what we call a lie. His very existence rests on the fact that he is a diabolical lie.

Gossamers in the rigging to-day led the captain to prophesy a storm before night. Clouds of an indigo darkness, of immense bulk, and motionless, reduced the sunset to mere runnels of opaline light about the bases of dark mountains inverted in the heavens. There was a rapid fall of temperature, but no rain. Our world, and we in its centre on the "Capella," waited for the storm in an expectant hush. Night fell while we waited. The smooth river again deepened into the nadir of the last of day, and the forest about us changed to material ramparts of cobalt. The pilot made preparations to anchor. The engine bell rang to stand-by, a summons of familiar urgency, but with a new and alarming note when heard in a place like that. The forest made no response. A little later the bell clanged rapidly again, and the pulse of our steamer slowed, ceased. We could hear the water uncoiling along our plates. The forest itself approached us, came perilously near. The Skipper's voice cried abruptly, "Let go!" and at once the virgin silence was demolished by the uproar of our cable. The "Capella" throbbed violently; she literally undulated in the drag of the current. We still drifted slowly down stream. The second anchor was dropped, and held us. The silence closed in on us instantly. Far in the forest somewhere, while we were whispering to each other in the quiet, a tree fell with a deep, significant boom.

A Journey to Brazil in 1932

EVELYN WAUGH

"One does not travel, any more than one falls in love, to collect material. It is simply part of one's life. For myself and many better than me, there is fascination in distant and barbarous places, and particularly in the borderlands of conflicting cultures. . . ."
Waugh's fascination by travel to unlikely corners of the world was put to test along the frontier of Brazil and British Guiana.

THE life of the Brazilian frontier must, I should think, be unique in the British Empire. In its whole length from Mount Roraima to the Courantyne—a distance of about five hundred miles—Bon Success is the only British government station, and that is under the admirable management of Mr. Melville, who is half Indian by birth and married to a Brazilian. On the other side there is no representative of law nearer than Boa Vista. There are no flags, no military, no customs, no passport examinations, no immigration forms. The Indians have probably very little idea of whether they are on British or Brazilian territory; they wander to and fro across the border exactly as they did before the days of Raleigh.

Throughout the whole district, too, there is only one shop and that is in two parts, half in Brazil and half in British Guiana. The proprietor is a Portuguese named Mr. Figuiredo. On his own side of the river he sells things of Brazilian origin, hardware, ammunition, alcohol in various unpalatable forms, sugar and *farine*, a few decayed-looking tins of fruit and sweets, tobacco, horses, saddlery and second-hand odds and ends extorted from bankrupt ranchers; on the British side he sells things brought up from Georgetown, mostly male and female clothing, soaps and hair oils, for which the more sophisticated Indians have a quite unsophisticated relish, and brands of patent medicines with engraved, pictorial labels and unfamiliar names—"Radways Rapid Relief," "Canadian Healing Oil," "Lydia Pynkham's Vegetable Product." If a Brazilian wants anything from the British side he and Mr. Figuiredo paddle across the river and he buys it there; and vice versa. Any guilt of smuggling attaches to the customer.

Father Mather and I went to breakfast with Mr. Figuiredo one day. He gave us course after course of food—stewed *tasso* with rice, minced *tasso* with *farine*, fresh beef with sweet potatoes, fresh pork, fried eggs, bananas, tinned peaches and crème de cacao of local distillation. His women folk were made to stand outside while we ate, with the exception of one handsome daughter who waited. After breakfast we went into the shop and Mr. Figuiredo made an effortless and unembarrassing transition from host to shopkeeper, climbing behind the counter and arguing genially about the price of coffee. He has no competition within two hundred miles and his prices are enormous; but he lives in a very simple fashion, dressing always in an old suit of pyjamas and employing his family to do the work of the house.

After a week David returned from the round-up—suave, spectacled, faultlessly efficient—and took over the arrangements for my journey to Boa Vista.

David's Brazilian brother-in-law Francisco joined us; the luggage was divided—unequally, for I took only hammock, blanket and change of clothes—between our three horses. Then after breakfast on 1st February, we set off for the border. The sun was obscured and a light drizzle of rain was falling.

The ford was about three miles upstream from St. Ignatius. Our horses waded through the shallow water, stretching forward to drink; half way over we were in Brazil. A lurch and scramble up the opposite bank; we forced our way through the fringe of bush, leaning low in the saddle to guard our faces from the thorn branches; then we were out into open country again, flat and desolate as the savannah we had left; more desolate, for here there was no vestige of life; no cattle track, no stray animals; simply the empty plain; sparse, colourless grass; ant-hills; sandpaper trees; an occasional clump of ragged palm; grey sky, gusts of wind, and a dull sweep of rain.

On the fourth day we reached the bank of the Rio Branco at an empty hut immediately opposite Boa Vista.

Since the evening at Kurupukari when Mr. Bain had first mentioned its name, Boa Vista had come to assume greater and greater importance to me. Father Mather had been there only once, and then in the worst stage of malignant malaria, so that he had been able to tell me little about it except that some German nuns had proved deft and devoted nurses. Everybody else, however, and particularly David, had spoken of it as a town of dazzling attraction. Whatever I had looked for in vain at Figuiredo's store was, he told me, procurable at "Boa Vist' "; Mr. Daguar had extolled its modernity and luxury—electric light, cafés, fine buildings, women, politics, murders. Mr. Bain had told of the fast motor launches, plying constantly between there and Manaos. In the discomfort of the journey there, I had looked forward to the soft living of Boa Vista, feeling that these asperities were, in fact, a suitable contrast, preparing my sense for a fuller appreciation of the good things in store. So confident was I that when we first came in sight of the ramshackle huddle of buildings on the further bank, I was quite uncritical and conscious of no emotion except delight and expectation.

The river was enormously broad and very low; so low that as we gazed at the town across sand dunes and channels and a fair-sized island it seemed to be perched on a citadel, instead of being, as was actually the case, at the same dead level as the rest of the plain. Two *vaqueiros* were lying in hammocks by the bank, and from these David elicited the information that a boat was expected some time in the next few hours to ferry them across. The *vaqueiros* studied us with an air that I came to recognize as characteristic of Boa Vista; it was utterly unlike the open geniality of the ranches; conveying, as it did, in equal degrees, contempt, suspicion and the suggestion that only listlessness kept them from active insult.

With David's assistance, I began some enquiries about accommodation. There was none, they said.

"But I understood there were two excellent hotels."

"Ah, that was in the days of the Company. There was all kinds of foolishness in the days of the Company. There is nowhere now. There has not been an hotel for two years."

"Then where do strangers stay?"

"Strangers do not come to Boa Vist'. If they come on business, the people they have business with put them up."

I explained that I was on the way to Manaos and had to wait for a boat. They showed complete indifference, only remarking that they did not know of any boat to Manaos. Then one of them added that possibly the foreign priests would do something for me—unless they had left; last time he was in Boa Vist' the foreign priests were all sick; most people were sick in Boa Vist'. Then the two men started talking to each other.

My enthusiasm had already cooled considerably by the time we saw a boat put out from the opposite shore and make slowly towards us. We all got in, David, Francisco, I, the two surly *vaqueiros*, the saddles and the baggage, so that the gunwales were only an inch clear of the water. Then partly paddling, partly wading and pushing, we made our way across. There were women squatting on the further shore, pounding dirty linen on the rocks at the water's edge. We hauled our possessions up the steep bank and found ourselves in the main street of the town. It was very broad, composed of hard, uneven mud, cracked into wide fissures in all directions and scored by several dry gulleys. On either side was a row of single-storeyed, whitewashed mud houses with tiled roofs; at each doorstep sat one or more of the citizens staring at us with eyes that were insolent, hostile and apathetic; a few naked children rolled about at their feet. The remains of an overhead electric cable hung loose from a row of crazy posts, or lay in coils and loops about the gutter.

The street rose to a slight hill and half-way up we came to the Benedictine Mission. This at any rate presented a more imposing aspect than anything I had seen since leaving Georgetown. It was built of concrete with a modestly orna-mented façade, a row of unbroken glass windows, a carved front door with an electric bell, a balustraded verandah with concrete urns at either end; in front of it lay a strip of garden marked out into symmetrical beds with brick borders.

We approached rather diffidently, for we were shabby and stained with travelling and lately unaccustomed to carved front doors and electric bells. But the bell need have caused us no misgiving, for it was out of order. We pressed and waited and pressed again. Then a head appeared from a window and told us, in Portuguese, to knock. We knocked several times until the head reap-peared; it was Teutonic in character, blond and slightly bald, wrinkled, with a prominent jaw and innocent eyes.

"The gentleman is a stranger too. He speaks Portuguese in a way I do not understand," said David. "He says there is a priest but that he is probably out."

I was used to waiting by now, so we sat on the doorstep among our luggage until presently an emaciated young monk in white habit appeared up the garden path. He seemed to accept our arrival with resignation, opened the door and led us into one of those rooms found only in religious houses, shuttered, stuffy and geometrically regular in arrangement; four stiff chairs ranged round four walls; devotional oleographs symmetrically balanced; a table in the exact centre with an embroidered cloth and a pot of artificial flowers; everything showing by its high polish of cleanliness that nuns had been at work there.

The monk was a German-Swiss. We spoke in halting French and I explained my situation. He nodded gloomily and said that it was impossible to predict when another boat would leave for Manaos; on the other hand a new Prior was expected some time soon and that boat must presumably return one day. Meanwhile I was at liberty to stay in the house if I chose.

"Will it be a question of days or weeks?"

"A question of weeks or months."

David thought the Boundary Commission had a boat going down in a few days; he would go into the town and enquire. With rather lugubrious courtesy the monk, who was named Father Alcuin, showed me a room and a shower bath; explained that he and the other guest had already breakfasted; sent across to the convent for food for me. I ate the first palatable meal since I had left St. Ignatius, changed and slept. Presently David returned with reassuring informa-tion. The Commission boat was passing through in four or five days; a week after that there would be a trade launch. He smiled proudly both at bringing good news and because he had bought a startling new belt out of his wages. Then he and Francisco bade me good-bye and went to rest with the horses on the other bank of the river.

Already, in the few hours of my sojourn there, the Boa Vista of my imagination had come to grief. Gone; engulfed in an earthquake, uprooted by a tornado and tossed sky-high like chaff in the wind, scorched up with brimstone like Gomorrah, toppled over with trumpets like Jericho, ploughed like Carthage, bought, demolished and transported brick by brick to another continent as though it had taken the fancy of Mr. Hearst; tall Troy was down. When I set out on a stroll of exploration, I no longer expected the city I had had in mind during the thirsty days of approach; the shady boulevards; kiosks for flowers and cigars and illustrated papers; the hotel terrace and the cafés; the baroque church built by seventeenth-century missionaries; the bastions of the old fort; the bandstand in the square, standing amidst fountains and flowering shrubs; the soft, slightly swaggering citizens, some uniformed and spurred, others with Southern elegance twirling little canes, bowing from the waist and raising boater hats, flicking with white gloves indiscernible particles of dust from their white linen spats; dark beauties languorous on balconies, or glancing over fans at the café tables. All that extravagant and highly improbable expectation had been obliterated like a sand castle beneath the encroaching tide.

Closer investigation did nothing to restore it. There was the broad main street up which we had come; two parallel, less important streets and four or five more laid at right angles to them. At a quarter of a mile in every direction they petered out into straggling footpaths. They were all called Avenidas and labelled with names of politicians of local significance. The town had been planned on an ambitious scale, spacious, rectangular, but most of the building lots were still unoccupied. There was one fair-sized store, a little larger and a little better stocked than Figuiredo's, half a dozen seedy little shops; an open booth advertising the services of a barber-surgeon who claimed to wave women's hair, extract teeth and cure venereal disease; a tumbledown house inhabited by the nuns, an open schoolhouse where a fever-stricken teacher could be observed monotonously haranguing a huge class of listless little boys; a wireless office, and a cottage where they accepted letters for the post; there were two cafés; one on the main street was a little shed, selling *farine*, bananas and fish, there were three tables in front of it, under a tree, where a few people collected in the evening to drink coffee in the light of a single lantern; the second, in a side street, was more attractive. It had a concrete floor and a counter where one could buy cigarettes and nuts, there were dominoes for the use of habitués and, besides coffee, one could drink warm and expensive beer.

The only place, besides the Benedictine Priory, which had any pretensions to magnificence was the church, a modern building painted in yellow and orange horizontal stripes, with ornate concrete mouldings; there were old bells outside, and inside three sumptuous altars, with embroidered frontals and veils, carved reredoses, large, highly coloured statues, artificial flowers and polished candle-sticks, decorated wooden pews, a marble font bearing in enormous letters the name of the chief merchant of the town, a harmonium; everything very new, and clean as a hospital—not a hen or a pig in the building. I was curious to know by what benefaction this expensive church had come into being and was told that, like most things, it had started "in the days of the Company."

I discovered one English-speaking person in the town; a singularly charmless youth, the illegitimate son of a prominent Georgetown citizen whom I had met there at Christmas time. This served as a fragile link between us, for the young man told me that he hated his father and had thought of shooting him on more than one occasion. "Now I have been married and have written five times for money and had no answer."

He was completely fleshless like all the inhabitants of Boa Vista, with dank, black hair hanging over his eyes, which were of slightly lighter yellow than the rest of his face. He spoke in a melancholy drawl. He was almost the only person I saw doing any work in the whole town. He owned a small blacksmith's shop where he made branding irons and mended guns. Most of the other inhabitants seemed to have no occupation of any kind, being caught up in the vicious circle of semi-starvation. Perhaps they picked up a few casual wages during the flood season when boats ran from Manaos fairly frequently and the ranchers came in for stores and needed labour for shipping their cattle. All the time that I was there I scarcely saw anyone except the school teacher earn anything—or spend any-thing. Even in the café the majority of customers came to gossip and play domi-noes and went away without ordering a cup of coffee. At some miles distance was a settlement of soldiers who brought a few shillings into the town; they were reservists bedded out with wives on small allotments. An aged town clerk pre-sumably received some sort of wages; so no doubt did the itinerant government vet who appeared from time to time; so did the wireless operator and an official of villainous aspect called the "Collector." But the other thousand odd inhabitants spent the day lying indoors in their hammocks and the evenings squatting on their doorsteps gossiping. Land was free, and, as the nuns proved, could produce excellent vegetables, but the diet of the town was *farine, tasso* and a little fish, all of which were of negligible cost. But it was far from being a care-free, idyllic improvidence. Everyone looked ill and discontented. There was not a fat man or woman anywhere. The women, in fact, led an even drearier life than the men. They had no household possessions to care for, no cooking to do, they left their children to sprawl about the streets naked or in rags. They were pretty—very small and thin, small-boned and with delicate features; a few of them took trouble with their appearance and put in an appearance at Mass on Sundays in light dresses, stockings and shoes, and cheap, gay combs in their hair.

From fragmentary and not altogether reliable sources I picked up a little history of Boa Vista. It was a melancholy record. The most patriotic Brazilian can find little to say in favour of the inhabitants of Amazonas; they are mostly descended from convicts, loosed there after their term of imprisonment as the French loose their criminals in Cayenne, to make whatever sort of living they can in an inhospitable country. Practically all of them are of mixed Indian and Portuguese blood. There is no accurate census, but a recent medical survey in the *Geographical Magazine* reports that they are dying out, families usually becoming sterile in three generations; alien immigrants, mostly German and Japanese, are gradually pushing what is left of them up country; Boa Vista is their final halting place before extinction. The best of them go out into the ranches; the worst remain in the town.

They are naturally homicidal by inclination, and every man, however poor, carries arms; only the universal apathy keeps them from frequent bloodshed. There were no shootings while I was there; in fact there had not been one for several months, but I lived all the time in an atmosphere that was novel to me, where murder was always in the air. The German at the Priory constantly slept with a loaded gun at his bedside and expressed surprise at seeing me going shopping without a revolver; the blacksmith, partly no doubt owing to his avocation, spoke of little else; one of his main preoccupations was altering trigger springs so that they could be fired quick on the draw.

There was rarely a conviction for murder. The two most sensational trials of late years had both resulted in acquittals. One was the case of a young Britisher who had come across from Guiana, panning gold. He had no right there and one evening in the café tipsily expressed his willingness to shoot anyone who interfered with him. The boast was accepted as constituting provocation when, a few nights later, he was shot in the back and robbed, while entering his house.

The other case was more remarkable. Two respected citizens, a Dr. Zany and a Mr. Homero Cruz, were sitting on a verandah talking, when a political opponent rode up and shot Dr. Zany. His plea of innocence, when brought to trial, was that the whole thing had been a mistake; he had meant to kill Mr. Cruz. The judges accepted the defence and brought in a verdict of death from misadventure.

From time to time attempts have been made to raise the condition of the town. A little before the War a German appeared with ample capital and began buying cattle. He offered and paid a bigger price than the ranchers had ever before received; he fitted out a fleet of large motor launches to take the beasts down to market at Manaos. The project was perfectly sound financially and would have brought considerable advantage to the district, but it was destined to failure. Before the first convoy had reached the market, he had been shot and killed by an official whom he had neglected to bribe. The defence was that he had been shot while evading arrest on a charge of collecting turtles' eggs out of season. The murderer was exonerated and the boats never reappeared at Boa Vista.

A more recent enterprise had been that of "the Company," so frequently referred to. I never learned the full story of this fiasco, for the Benedictines were deeply involved in it and I did not like to press the question at the Priory. The blacksmith gravely assured me that the scandal had been so great that the Archbishop had been taken to Rome and imprisoned by the Pope. There certainly seemed to have been more than ordinary mismanagement of the affair. Father Alcuin never mentioned it except to say that things had not gone as well as they had hoped. So far as I could gather the facts are these:

A year or two ago, inflamed by charitable zeal, the wealthy Benedictines at Rio conceived the old plan of bringing prosperity and self-respect to Boa Vista. Geographically and politically the town held the key position to the whole, immense territory of the Northern Amazon tributaries. The monks saw that instead of its present position as a squalid camp of ramshackle cut-throats, it might be a thriving city, a beacon of culture illuminating the dark lands about it, a centre from which they could educate and evangelize the Indians. They imagined it, even, as a miniature ecclesiastical state where industry, commerce, and government should be in the benevolent hands of the Church; a happy dream, glowing with possibilities of success to those imperfectly acquainted with the real character of Boa Vista.

Accordingly "the Company" was launched, under the highest ecclesiastical patronage, financed by Benedictine money and managed by the brother of one of the hierarchy. The method by which the town was to be raised to prosperity was, again, sensible enough to anyone who expected normal working conditions. Instead of the cattle being transported to the slaughter-houses at Manaos, they were to be butchered on the spot and tinned. Cheap corned beef, it was assumed, would rapidly take the place of the unnourishing *tasso* and would provide a more valuable and more manageable export than live cattle. The factory would provide regular and remunerative employment to all in the district and, following the best tradition of big business, "the Company" would also provide the necessaries and amusements on which their wages should be spent; the profits, rapidly circulating, would be used in public services. No one had any ulterior motive; the whole scheme was for the glory of God and the comfort of the people of the place. In Rio, on paper, it all seemed faultless. Operations were begun on a large scale.

The canning factory was built and installed with the best modern machinery, an electric plant was set up, providing the streets and the houses with light; a fine Church, a hospital and a small school were built; there was soon to be a larger school, a Priory and a convent; liberal wages were paid out, two hotels and a cinema opened; a refrigerator provided Boa Vista with the first ice it had ever seen. Everything seemed to be going admirably.

But the monks at Rio had reckoned without the deep-rooted, local antagonism to anything godly or decent; a prejudice which at the moment was particularly inflamed by the unforeseen arrival of an irresponsible American with a rival scheme for improvement. His more ambitious proposal was to run a motor road and railway through the impassable bush that separated the town from Manaos, a project more or less equivalent in magnitude to the making of the Panama Canal. Finding that concessions had already been granted to the Benedictines which made his already impracticable railway legally impossible, he fell back on explaining to the inhabitants the great advantages of which they had been deprived, the higher wages he would have paid, the greater prosperity which he would have initiated. The citizens, naturally disposed to see a sinister purpose in any activity, however small, had already become suspicious of the great changes that were taking place. The American emphasized the foreign birth of most of the Order and the relationship between the manager of the company and the high ecclesiastic in Rio, with the result that by the time the monks and nuns reached their new home, they found everyone fairly convinced that a swindle was being perpetrated at their expense. It was only with difficulty and some danger that they succeeded in landing, being attacked with hostile demonstrations and showers of stones.

From then onwards everything went against the Benedictines, who were insulted and boycotted. The canning factory proved a failure; no one would use the ice—an unnatural, impermanent substance, typical of everything foreign; dishonest stuff that had lost half its weight even before you got it home—they didn't want the hospital, much preferring to sicken and die in their hammocks in the decent manner traditional to the place; no one paid his electric light bill and the plant had to be stopped. The priests went down with fever and, one by one, had to be sent back to Manaos. "The Company" became bankrupt and all further work was stopped. No Priory was built, no big school, no convent. At the time of my arrival things were at their lowest ebb. Father Alcuin was the last priest left and he was so ill that only supernatural heroism kept him at his work. Often he was only able to totter to the Church to say his Mass and then retire to bed in high fever for the remainder of the day. The palatial house in which he was living was the building originally intended for the hospital. Its two big wards were now occupied by a carpenter engaged in making benches for the Church, and a government vet who fitted up a laboratory there, which he used from time to time between his rounds of the ranches; he was investigating a prevalent form of paralysis in horses which he attributed to worms. Whatever minute flicker of good still survived in the town was preserved by the nuns, silent, devoted, indefatigable, who lived in appalling quarters near the river-bank, kept a school for the handful of bourgeois daughters, and nursed a Negro and an aged diamond prospector who had arrived separately in a dying condition from up country and were in no mood to respect the prejudices of the town. It was, as I have said, the lowest point; a new Prior was expected daily to reorganize things and set them to right. . . .

I found very little to occupy my time. There was an edition of Bossuet's sermons and a few lives of the Saints in French for me to read; I could walk to the wireless office and learn that no news had been heard of the Boundary Commissioner's boat; I could visit the English-speaking blacksmith and watch him tinkering with antiquated automatic pistols. This young man would not come with me to the café on account of his having recently beaten the proprietor—an act of which he was inordinately proud, though it can have required no great courage since he was a very old man and slightly crippled. I could give bananas to the captive monkey and I could study the bottled worms in the laboratory; I could watch the carpenter in his rare moments of industry, sawing up lengths of plank. There was really quite a number of things for me to do, but, in spite of them all, the days seemed to pass slowly.

The blacksmith, who knew all that was going on in the town, promised to tell me as soon as the Commissioner's boat was sighted, but it so happened that he forgot to do so, and I only learned from Mr. Steingler, one morning after I had been six days in the Priory, that it had arrived the previous evening and was due to leave in an hour; the Commissioner was at that moment at the wireless station. I hurried off to interview him. Things might have been less difficult if Father Alcuin had been able to accompany me, but it was one of the days when he was down with fever. Alone I was able to make no impression. The Commissioner was an amicable little man, in high good humour at the prospect of a few days' leave in Manaos, but he flatly refused to have me in his boat. I cannot hold it against him. Everyone in that district is a potential fugitive from justice and he knew nothing of me except my dishevelled appearance and my suspicious anxiety to get away from Boa Vista. I showed my passport and letters of credit, but he was not impressed. I besought him to cable to Georgetown for my credentials, but he pointed out that it might take a week to get an answer. I offered him large wads of greasy notes. But he was not having any. He knew too much about foreigners who appeared alone and unexplained in the middle of Amazonas; the fact of my having money made me the more sinister. He smiled, patted my shoulder, gave me a cigarette, and sharp on time left without me.

I cannot hold it against him. I do not think that the British Commissioners would have done any more for a stray Brazilian. But it was in a despondent and rather desperate mood that I heard his boat chugging away out of sight down the Rio Branco.

Acknowledgments

THE UNITED STATES

"Peter Rugg: An American Folktale," from THE LIFE TREASURY OF AMERICAN FOLKLORE by the Editors of *Life*. Copyright © 1961 by Time-Life Books, Inc.

"Memories of a Day's Walk," from SPRING JAUNTS by Anthony Bailey. Copyright © 1977 by Anthony Bailey. Originally appeared in *The New Yorker*. Reprinted by permission of Farrar, Straus and Giroux, Inc.

"The Lonely Road to Mora," from DEATH COMES FOR THE ARCHBISHOP by Willa Cather. Copyright 1927 by Willa Cather and renewed 1955 by the Executors of the Estate of Willa Cather. Reprinted by permission of Alfred A. Knopf, Inc.

Excerpt from THE PROVINCIAL LADY IN AMERICA by E. M. Delafield reprinted by permission of Academy Chicago Publishers and Peters Fraser & Dunlop Group Ltd.

"Notes from a Native Daughter," from SLOUCHING TOWARDS BETHLEHEM by Joan Didion. Copyright © 1965, 1968 by Joan Didion. Reprinted by permission of Farrar, Straus and Giroux, Inc., and William Morris Agency, Inc., on behalf of the author.

From OUT WEST by Dayton Duncan. Copyright © 1987 by Dayton Duncan. All rights reserved. Reprinted by permission of Viking Penguin, a division of Penguin Books U.S.A., Inc.

From ON THE ROAD by Jack Kerouac. Copyright © 1955, 1957 by Jack Kerouac. Copyright renewed © 1983, 1985 by the Estate of Jack Kerouac. All rights reserved. Reprinted by permission of Viking Penguin, a division of Penguin Books U.S.A., Inc.

From THE WONDERFUL COUNTRY by Tom Lea; Texas A & M University Press, 1984. Reprinted by permission of the publisher.

From THE WINTER BEACH by Charlton Ogburn, Jr. Copyright © 1966 by Charlton Ogburn, Jr. Reprinted by permission of William Morrow and Company, Inc., and McIntosh and Otis, Inc.

"Nevada Old and New," from HOME COUNTRY by Ernie Pyle. Copyright 1935, 1936, 1937, 1938, 1939, 1940 by Scripps Howard Newspaper Alliance. Reprinted with permission of the Scripps Howard Foundation.

From OLD GLORY by Jonathan Raban. Copyright © 1981 by Jonathan Raban. Reprinted by permission of Simon & Schuster Inc.

"Other People's Houses," from WHEREABOUTS by Alastair Reid. Copyright © 1987 by Alastair Reid. Reprinted by permission of North Point Press.

From NIGHT FREIGHT by Clyde H. Rice, Sr. Copyright © 1987 by Clyde H. Rice, Sr. Reprinted by permission of Breitenbush Books.

From CHEYENNE AUTUMN by Mari Sandoz. Copyright 1953 by Mari Sandoz. Copyright © renewed 1981 by Caroline Pifer. Reprinted by permission of McIntosh and Otis, Inc.

From TRAVELS WITH CHARLEY by John Steinbeck. Copyright © 1961, 1962 by The Curtis Publishing Co., Inc. Copyright © 1962 by John Steinbeck. All rights reserved. Reprinted by permission of Viking Penguin, a division of Penguin Books U.S.A., Inc., and William Heinemann Limited.

"Last Run," from ALL ABOARD WITH E. M. FRIMBO by Rogers E. M. Whitaker and Anthony Hiss (Viking Penguin). Originally in *The New Yorker*. Copyright © 1967 The New Yorker Magazine, Inc. Reprinted by permission.

Excerpt from "The Railroad," by E. B. White, copyright © 1960 by E. B. White, from ESSAYS OF E. B. WHITE by E. B. White. Reprinted by permission of Harper & Row, Publishers, Inc.

CANADA AND THE FAR NORTH

"True North," by Margaret Atwood. Copyright Margaret Atwood. First appeared in January 1987 *Saturday Night* magazine. Reprinted by permission of the author.

Excerpt from NOTES FROM THE CENTURY BEFORE by Edward Hoagland. Copyright © 1969, 1982 by Edward Hoagland. Reprinted by permission of North Point Press.

From ARCTIC DREAMS by Barry Lopez. Copyright © 1986 Barry Holstun Lopez. Reprinted with the permission of Charles Scribner's Sons, an imprint of Macmillan Publishing Company.

From GOING TO EXTREMES by Joe McGinnis. Copyright © 1975 by Joe McGinnis. Reprinted by permission of Sterling Lord Literistic, Inc.

Excerpt from COMING INTO THE COUNTRY by John McPhee. Copyright © 1976, 1977 by John McPhee. Reprinted by permission of Farrar, Straus and Giroux, Inc.

"Second Prize: Toronto, 1984," from AMONG THE CITIES by Jan Morris. Copyright © 1985 by Jan Morris. Reprinted by permission of Oxford University Press, Inc.

From PEOPLE OF THE DEER by Farley Mowat. Copyright © 1975 by Farley Mowat. Reprinted by permission of the author.

"North of Sixty," from HOME SWEET HOME: MY CANADIAN ALBUM by Mordecai Richler. Copyright © 1984 by Mordecai Richler. Reprinted by permission of Alfred A. Knopf, Inc., and Chatto & Windus/The Hogarth Press.

MEXICO, THE CARIBBEAN, SOUTH AMERICA

From AMERICAN JOURNALS by Albert Camus. Copyright © 1987 by Paragon House Publishers. Copyright © 1978 by Editions Gallimard. Published by Paragon House and Hamish Hamilton Ltd.

From IN PATAGONIA by Bruce Chatwin. Copyright © 1977 by Bruce Chatwin. Reprinted by permission of Summit Books, a division of Simon & Schuster Inc.

"Observations After Landfall," from THE JOURNAL OF CHRISTOPHER COLUMBUS, translated by Cecil Jane. Copyright © 1960 by Clarkson N. Potter, Inc. Used by permission of Clarkson N. Potter, Inc.

From THE GREAT EXPLORERS: EUROPEAN DISCOVERY OF AMERICA [a compilation of previously published works] by Samuel Eliot Morison. Copyright © 1978 by Oxford University Press. Reprinted by permission of Oxford University Press.

From THE TRAVELLER'S TREE by Patrick Leigh Fermor. Copyright 1950 by Patrick Leigh Fermor. Reprinted by permission of Anthony Sheil Associates and John Murray (Publishers) Ltd.

"Landscape of the Pampas," from FAR AWAY AND LONG AGO by W. H. Hudson. Published by Eland Books, London, and Hippocrene Books, Inc., New York.

From THE CLOUD FOREST by Peter Matthiessen. Copyright © 1961 by Peter Matthiessen. All rights reserved. Reprinted by permission of Viking Penguin, a division of Penguin Books U.S.A., Inc.

From "The Bus Plunge Highway," from THE PANAMA HAT TRAIL by Tom Miller. Copyright © 1986 by Tom Miller. Reprinted by permission of William Morrow and Company, Inc.

From NOTHING TO DECLARE by Mary Morris. Copyright © 1988 by Mary Morris. Reprinted by permission of Houghton Mifflin Company.

From THE MIDDLE PASSAGE by V. S. Naipaul. Copyright © 1962 by V. S. Naipaul. Reprinted by permission of V. S. Naipaul.

"St. Lucia," from SMILE, PLEASE by Jean Rhys. Copyright © 1979 by the Estate of Jean Rhys. Foreword copyright © 1979 by Diana Athill. Reprinted by permission of Harper & Row, Publishers, Inc.

"A Journey to Brazil in 1932," from WHEN THE GOING WAS GOOD by Evelyn Waugh. Copyright 1934, 1946, copyright © 1962 by Evelyn Waugh. Reprinted by permission of Little, Brown and Company and Peters Fraser & Dunlop Group Ltd.